Discovering Philosophy

Discovering Philosophy

Second Edition

Thomas I. White
Loyola Marymount University

PEARSON
Prentice
Hall

Upper Saddle River, NJ 07458

Library of Congress Cataloging-in-Publication Data

White, Thomas I.
  Discovering philosophy / Thomas I. White.— Brief ed., 2nd ed.
    p. cm.
  Includes bibliographical references and index.
  ISBN 0-13-230212-8
  ISBN 978-0-13-230212-8
  1. Philosophy—Introductions. I. Title.
  BD21.W47 2008
  100—dc22   2006032310

Editor-in-Chief: Sarah Touborg
Senior Acquisitions Editor: Mical Moser
Editorial Assistant: Carla Worner
Senior Media Editor: Anita Castro
**Vice President/Director of Production
  and Manufacturing:** Barbara Kittle
Senior Managing Editor: Joanne Riker
Production Liaison: Louise Rothman
Prepress and Manufacturing Manager: Nick Sklitsis
Prepress and Manufacturing Buyer: Christina Amato

Director of Marketing: Brandy Dawson
Assistant Marketing Manager: Andrea Messineo
Director, Image Resource Center: Melinda Reo
Manager, Visual Research: Beth Brenzel
Cover Image Specialist: Karen Sanatar
**Composition and Full Service Project
  Management:** Vijay Kataria/Techbooks
Printer/Binder: RR Donnelley/Harrisonburg
Cover Printer: RR Donnelley/Harrisonburg

Credits and acknowledgments borrowed from other sources and reproduced, with permission, in this textbook appear on appropriate page within text (or on page 445).

Pearson Education LTD
Pearson Education Singapore, Pte. Ltd
Pearson Education Canada, Ltd
Pearson Education—Japan

Pearson Education Australia PTY, Limited
Pearson Education North Asia Ltd
Pearson Educación de Mexico, S.A. de C.V.
Pearson Education Malaysia, Pte. Ltd

10 9 8 7 6 5 4 3 2 1
ISBN–10: 0-13-230212-8
ISBN–13: 978-0-13-230212-8

To Lisa

Contents

Part Three   Fundamental Theoretical Issues

Chapter 8   The Nature of Reality   217

Chapter 9   What Is Knowledge?   249

Chapter 10   Does God Exist?   283

Chapter 11   The Purpose of Life:
                     Marx and Buddha   311

Note: Every effort has been made to provide accurate and current Internet information in this book. However, the Internet and information posted in it are constantly changing, so it is inevitable that some of the Internet addresses listed in this textbook will change.

Preface

This book aims to be a comprehensive and challenging introduction to philosophy for the student who is more comfortable with secondary than with primary sources. Although philosophers do speak in their own words in this text when appropriate, this book consists primarily of summary, explication, and discussion of the major arguments on the issues involved. The writing style is relatively informal.

The text is organized in a fairly conventional and straightforward way. It begins with an overview of philosophy (Chapter 1) and an introduction to philosophical thinking and logic (Chapter 2). It then explores a series of basic issues related to human action and our dealings with each other: freedom and determinism (Chapters 3 and 4), ethics and its ultimate justification (Chapters 5 and 6), the legitimacy of democracy (Chapter 7). Next, it proceeds to more theoretical issues: the nature of reality (Chapter 8), knowledge (Chapter 9), the existence of God (Chapter 10), and the meaning of life (Chapter 11). The book then concludes with three chapters on the philosophical implications of some emerging, contemporary issues: scientific explanations of reality (Chapter 12), the issue of whether gender affects how we think (Chapter 13), and the question of whether a dolphin is a "person" (Chapter 14).

Spirit of the Book

My first goal in writing this book was to produce a text that students would actually read. Thus, the style, tone, and content aim to make the text easy-to-read, unintimidating, and intellectually engaging. In the same spirit, I have also included a fair amount of material from other disciplines. One of the most difficult aspects of teaching introductory philosophy is students' limited prior exposure to it. They usually know something about the natural and social sciences, however, so certain chapters may help some students feel more comfortable. The treatment of freedom and determinism in Chapters 3 and 4 employs arguments from psychologists B. F. Skinner, Sigmund Freud, and Albert Ellis. Chapter 12, "Scientific Explanations of Reality," is built around the physics of Newton and Einstein. Chapter 13, "Does Gender Affect How We Think?," returns to psychological research in discussing whether gender affects the way we think about knowledge and ethics. And Chapter 14, "Is a Dolphin a Person?," draws on marine biology.

More than anything else, however, I have tried to write a book that helps students become adept and comfortable with doing philosophy—and doing it at an intellectually respectable level. Central to this book, therefore, is the activity of argumentation and thorough consideration of the intricacies of the arguments we explore. The aim here is to teach students not so much about what philosophers think as about how to think philosophically themselves. Accordingly, I usually choose depth over breadth in each chapter, relying on the sheer bulk of the book to ensure a reasonable representation of major figures and philosophical traditions.

In the exploration of an argument, you will find that I sometimes hazard my own opinion about the strengths or weaknesses of certain positions. (Whenever I do this, however, I try to make it plain that my opinion is just that—my opinion, not the "correct answer," and not something with which you or your students will necessarily agree.) I do this primarily to demonstrate that after understanding a philosopher's position we are supposed to react to it, not memorize it. I also do this to stimulate students' thinking and to help generate class discussion. My opinion is usually offered simply in passing comments, but I have also included one extended interpretation of some of the philosophical literature discussed. In Chapter 6, I offer a speculative reading of Socrates' idea that vice harms the doer. Chapter 14 reflects my own research on the question of dolphins and personhood.

I hope that this book achieves these aims, helps you in working with your students, and helps them reach the goals you set for them in your course. I will be grateful for any reactions, positive or negative, that you or your students have to this text and particularly for any suggestions for improving it.

This edition aims to follow the helpful suggestions from a variety of individuals. In particular, I would like to thank Helen L. Dwyer, University of Wisconsin-Baraboo, Donald E. LeBlanc, University of Massachusetts at Lowell, and Ronald C. Pine, Honolulu Community College. The main changes are as follows:

- *Chapter 2.* The use of Venn diagrams and the discussion of validity and soundness have been dropped in favor of a logical puzzle from the first *Harry Potter* novel. I also introduce some very basic elements of symbolic logic. Two informal fallacies (begging the question and straw man) have been added.

- *Chapter 3.* The connection between determinism and materialism has been made more explicit.

- *Chapter 4.* The fact that the Boston Red Sox finally won the World Series in 2004 necessitated a change in the opening scenario. I have also tried to improve the description of the pragmatic criterion of truth by simplifying it.

- *Chapter 5.* A short discussion of ethical relativism is now included. The discussion of Mill's idea that there are qualitative differences in pleasures and pains now includes a questionnaire that should make it easier for students to understand what Mill has in mind. Kant's "maxim/universal law of nature" formulation of the categorical imperative has been moved from a footnote to the main body of the discussion.

- *Chapter 6.* This chapter has been renamed "Why Be Ethical?" The discussion has also been modified slightly to keep the focus on "acting ethically" rather than "virtue" in general.

- *Chapter 7.* A short discussion of the discomfort some students might feel at questioning democracy has been included. The questionnaire connected with Plato's idea that different parts of the soul predominate in different individuals has been shortened and improved. I have also added a section on B. F. Skinner's nondemocratic government for his utopian community Walden Two.

- *Chapter 8.* The problem of appearance versus reality is now introduced with issues from *The Matrix* movies. References to "myth" and "mythic thinking" have been deleted in favor of keeping the focus on "anthropomorphism." Discussion of the pre-Socratics has been shortened and streamlined. Plato's "line" explanation now precedes the allegory of the cave. And a discussion of Berkeley has been added.

- *Chapter 9.* A new scenario introduces this chapter. Statements that suggest that absolute certainty is required for knowledge have been omitted or revised. The discussion of Hume has been extended to lead to inclusion of Gilbert Ryle's notion of the "category mistake" and consideration of the value of induction. I've strengthened the explanation of Kant's idea that the mind orders sense data with the categories to give us our everyday experience of reality.

- *Chapter 10.* The discussion of arguments for God's existence now includes Bertrand Russell's position.

- *Chapter 12.* The treatment of quantum mechanics has been improved, and a short discussion of string theory has been added.

- *Chapter 14.* The discussion of whether dolphins are nonhuman persons has been revised in light of my ongoing research in this area.

I would also like to thank: Jeff Herman (my agent); Ross Miller, Mical Moser, Carla Worner, Andrea Messineo, and Louise Rothman (from Prentice Hall); Donna Mulder; and Vijay Kataria and the staff of Techbooks.

Thomas I. White
Redondo Beach, California

To the Student

Western philosophy emerged centuries ago on the shores of the Aegean and in the dusty streets of Athens. To the thinkers of ancient Greece, doing philosophy was a natural part of being human. "What is the nature of the world around us?" they asked. "How do our minds work?" "What is the path to happiness?"

The spirit of philosophy has not changed in the two thousand years that have followed. Philosophy is still devoted to understanding the world around us and within us. It requires that we use our minds to explore reality in general and the human experience in particular. Despite the stereotyped image of the philosopher as someone out of touch with everyday experience, philosophy has the most practical of aims—to understand the basic issues of life. This book is written with the original spirit of philosophy in mind. Its first aim is to show you how natural a part of life philosophy is and that, without knowing it, you have already wrestled with many philosophical problems.

The methodology of philosophy does not come as naturally, however. Accordingly, this book also hopes to introduce you to philosophical argumentation and to skills of analytical and critical thought needed for practicing philosophy. Its second aim, then, is to get you comfortable doing philosophy.

Ultimately, I hope that this book will help you experience firsthand the value, the pleasure, and the adventure of philosophy. Philosophy enriches our lives in ways that nothing else does. It expands our sense of the nature of our world and of ourselves. It gives us a new universe to explore. It helps us clarify our life's goals and choose the means by which we hope to achieve them. Philosophy strengthens our control over our own lives and thus helps us remain the "captain of our souls." As you experience this for yourself, I hope you will make philosophy an integral part of your life.

What Is Philosophy?

- *What Is Philosophy About?*
- *The Basic Issues*
- *Why Studying Philosophy Is Valuable*
- *Previews of Coming Chapters*

Most of us have either the wrong idea or no idea at all of what studying philosophy is all about. If you're feeling uncomfortable about the prospect of taking a philosophy course, perhaps the following will help ease your mind.

First off, you're probably feeling uncertain because you don't know what to expect from a philosophy course. You've already studied subjects like mathematics, history, english, foreign languages, biology, and chemistry. You may have also done a little anthropology, sociology, or political science. You have worked with computers. You know what art and music are, whether you studied them or not. Your previous experience, then, gives you some idea of what's coming in college courses on these subjects.

But philosophy? That's different. You haven't encountered anything like philosophy. So it's natural that you would be uneasy about a subject so new and different.

There is also something about philosophy and philosophers that's alien to the way average people see themselves. After you graduate, you probably expect to be a lawyer, computer programmer, sales manager, teacher, or corporate executive. You may even be able to imagine yourself as a rock-and-roll singer, or a movie star, or the president of the United States. But who wants to be a philosopher? You know the image most of us have—someone impractical, unrealistic, and absentminded, some character with hair flying in every direction, lost in thought while pondering "great ideas."[1]

This image of the philosopher being "out of touch" is even suggested by the very word "philosophy." Literally, the word means "love of wisdom." (It derives from two ancient Greek words: *philia,* "love," and *sophia,* "wisdom.") And who's going

---

[1]One of the first caricatures we have of a philosopher is that of the Greek thinker Socrates. In the comedy entitled *The Clouds,* Aristophanes portrays the philosopher as someone absolutely useless and ridiculous. When we first meet Socrates in the play, he's sitting in a basket suspended in midair and staring at the sky.

to go around saying that they "love wisdom" except somebody who's a little strange? Would anyone want to be like that?

Besides these concerns, you may also be feeling a little afraid. You don't know what to expect, and most people are afraid of the unknown. You don't know if you'll be able to do whatever it is when you've never done anything like it before, especially something so theoretical. You will find, however, that philosophy is a natural activity. In one way or another most people either already think like philosophers or can do so with just a little help. That's because when it comes down to it, as you're about to see, philosophy is a way of thinking that comes naturally. So you really have nothing to be anxious about.

What Is Philosophy About?

What is **philosophy** about?[2] And how is philosophy such a natural thing to do that you're probably already doing it without knowing it?

More than anything else, philosophy is *thinking*. The main instrument that philosophers use in conducting their investigations is the human mind. They don't try to solve philosophical problems by conducting scientific, empirical research. They think. And so do you. You think just because you're human.

Of course, philosophers don't just think about whatever crosses their minds. They think about *life's most basic questions*:

- What is the purpose of life?
- Is there a God?
- How do we know the difference between right and wrong?
- Are our actions free or determined?

But who doesn't think about some very basic questions every now and then? You may not make a career out of it, but you have done it. You can't be human without doing it sometimes.

Philosophers also try to come up with answers to these questions, to explain them to other people, and to defend them against criticism and opposing answers. And you have surely also done some of that.

Philosophy even tries to get something positive out of uncertainty, confusion, and argument. If disagreeing philosophers can't prove which answer is right, they believe that discussion can still produce a greater understanding of the issues at stake. And you have probably had that experience as well.

> **philosophy** Philosophy is an active, intellectual enterprise dedicated to exploring the most fundamental questions of life.

---

[2]The first time a word listed in the glossary appears, it will be in boldface.

"Doing" Philosophy in Real Life

Imagine, for example, that your friend Sam asks you to help him cheat on an assignment. You're torn between loyalty to a friend and uneasiness about doing something dishonest. You tell Sam you would rather not help him cheat. Sam tries to get you to change your mind, explaining that he doesn't see anything wrong with what he's asking. But you don't see it that way. The two of you get into a long discussion of cheating—why you think it is wrong, why he doesn't, why he thinks friendship is more important, and why you do not. It may surprise you to hear that this fairly typical event in the life of a college student contains all the basic elements of doing philosophy.

How you determine the difference between right and wrong is certainly a basic issue. We base all our actions on our sense of right and wrong. So the subject of your disagreement with Sam is philosophical. In your discussion with him you're forced to explain your decision, so you have to think seriously about your assumptions. In order to handle his objections, you have to think further about the issues and defend your position against his arguments. Let's say that ultimately neither one of you convinces the other. Has the discussion produced anything? Sure—a better understanding of the issue and of each other.

This is what philosophers do too. They think about basic questions and come up with answers, explain why they think that way, and defend their positions against people who disagree. Philosophers do this in the hope of either settling the matter or at least producing a greater understanding of the issues involved.

Now consider all the times you think about fundamental questions. You wonder whether God exists and if there is any way of proving it. Your best friend discovers she's pregnant and the two of you talk about whether she should have an abortion. You consider taking drugs, even though you know it's illegal. In all these cases, you're thinking about standard philosophical questions, coming to some personal answers, and growing in your understanding. The only difference between you and a professional philosopher is that he or she thinks about the same questions in a more technical, disciplined, and informed way.

So, you see, doing philosophy is one of the most common activities of life, something natural, normal, and, best of all, familiar.

Philosophy—Activity, Not Content

Note in particular that philosophy is an activity. Philosophy is active, not passive. It's a way of thinking, something you do, a skill you get better at as you practice, not a body of facts that you memorize. And there is a good and bad side to that.

The good news is that once you get the hang of it, philosophical thinking expands your ability to see things. It also encourages you to think independently. You can entertain all kinds of ideas or theories about an issue, then make up your own mind. No philosophy teacher will ever say to you, "I don't care what you think, just give me the correct answer to my question." How you think about the questions and about other philosophers' answers and how you explain and defend what you think are what it's all about.

Moreover, philosophers are not "authorities." They are only as good as their arguments. If their arguments are not convincing, forget it. The ancient Greek thinker Socrates may have been a great philosopher, but that doesn't mean that what he says is true. He still must convince you.

The bad news, however, is that since you probably haven't studied anything like this before, you're going to have to learn new ways of handling things. In a philosophy course, you can't fall back on memorizing the theories of great philosophers like Plato and Aristotle. You have to know what different thinkers say, but you also have to genuinely understand their ideas. And that's not all. After you think about it, you have to come up with your own reaction.

For example, do you agree or disagree with Immanuel Kant's ideas about what makes an action morally wrong? Totally? Partially? What are the strengths and weaknesses of his ideas? What would you change? Why? How would you convince Kant to change his mind? Suppose the person sitting next to you disagrees with you. How would you try to change her mind?

Philosophy is a dynamic process. That is one of the things that makes it so interesting—and hard to get used to. It isn't just learning the answers that earlier philosophers have come up with. It's also coming up with your own answers. So get used to the idea that you are about to embark on an active enterprise.

The Basic Issues

Because the subject of philosophy is the "basic issues" of life, it's not surprising that we encounter a wide range of issues when we study philosophy. Fortunately, philosophers are very logical, so philosophy has been divided into several branches, each devoted to different, but still basic, questions. What are these issues and what are the parts of philosophy?

The Most Fundamental Issues

Every philosophical question is basic. But some questions are more basic than others, and philosophy starts with those.

Reality

What's the most elementary thing you can say about yourself? That you're tall? Short? White? Black? No. That you are male or female? Simpler than that. That you are human? Still simpler. Just that you are. What's the most fundamental characteristic of any object you can describe? Distinguishing characteristics? No. Simply that it is real. It exists. Now we've hit bedrock, because the nature of reality, or of existence, is the most basic issue we can talk about. The most fundamental philosophical question, then, is: What is the nature of *reality*?

What do we mean when we say something is "real"? What's the difference between "real" and "not real" or "imaginary"? Does something have to exist physically to be real? Or is it enough that it exists in our minds? Which are more real? Chairs and tables that present themselves to our eyes but that will eventually wear out, break up, and be thrown out precisely because they're material objects? Or the circles and triangles that we see only with our mind's eye, which are "perfect" and haven't changed or decayed a bit since humans discovered the abstract world of mathematics thousands of years ago?

Personhood

Think again about yourself and the other things and people in your life. We've already seen that they have existence in common. They're alike in that they're real. But what makes each of these entities different from all the others? One way to account for these differences is through some distinguishing set of properties or characteristics. How are you different from this book in your hand, for example? For openers, you're alive and the book isn't. So now we're talking about the defining characteristics that make something be what it is. We're referring to what we call the "nature" or "essence" of a thing.

To narrow this down, let's focus just on human nature. What is a very basic characteristic of human beings? We're alive, but then so are all nonhuman animals, so we need something more specific. What in our life sets us apart from other living beings? Probably that each of us is a "person." This brings us to a point where we can frame another basic philosophical question: What is the essence of the special property *personhood*?

What does it mean to be a "person"? To answer this question, use yourself as an example and contrast your kind of life with that of plants and animals. Notice that you have a particular kind of self-awareness and high intellectual abilities. You can communicate with other people. And you can control your own actions.

But are all humans "persons"? Fetuses don't have any of these characteristics, so some thinkers argue that they are not "persons" in their own right. But, then, infants cannot do most of these things either, and most of us recognize them as "persons." Furthermore, must a "person" be "human"? How about other animals? Some chimpanzees have learned sign language. Some people think that dolphins may be as intelligent as humans. And many individuals claim they've had encounters with intelligent beings from another planet. None of these entities is human, but they seem to have many characteristics and abilities that humans do. Should we think of them as "persons"?

Free Will

Consider another basic aspect of life. Think again about the most fundamental things you can say about yourself. You exist. You're alive. You're a person. Part of being a person means that you can control your actions; that is, your deeds are not merely automatic products of instinct. You have what philosophers call *free will*.

But now think about it. Sure, we all *feel* free. Yet aren't our choices influenced by our upbringing, the values we're taught, the norms provided by our culture? Perhaps some of our behavior is determined by our genetic makeup. What about the impact of our worst, irrational fears? What about the power of the unconscious mind? Perhaps you believe that God has people's lives all planned out; perhaps you believe in fate. And if the future is somehow already determined, what room is left for choice? These problems lead us to yet another basic philosophical question: How "free" are we?

Knowledge

Think back for a moment to our discussion of what makes a person. Surely one of the most important characteristics a person has is intelligence. A person can think and know things. Intellectual activity is such a basic part of human life that our species is named for this ability—*Homo sapiens* ("thinking man"). This brings us to another philosophical issue: What is involved in *knowing* something?

At first this might look like a simple question. We say we know something when we have acceptable reasons or proof for what we claim. I can say that I know that my computer is sitting in front of me because I can see it. I also know that the great English humanist Sir Thomas More died in 1535 because I've done research on More for years, and that is what the historical records show. I even know that the sum of the interior angles of every triangle that ever has or ever will exist is 180 degrees. Have I measured them all? Not very likely. How do I know it? Because this is, in fact, the definition of a triangle.

Each of these three examples involves knowledge, but each example is different. I claim to know something in each case, but the reasons I give keep changing. My first claim is based on direct sense experience. The second involves secondhand evidence, or hearsay, ultimately based on someone else's firsthand experience. And the third doesn't rely on sense experience at all. If they're all so different, do all these examples involve knowledge? The same kind of knowledge? As you see, questions about knowledge can be quite complicated.

So far our questions have focused mainly inward, on what it means to be a living person from the inside. When we turn our attention outward, however, we encounter different kinds of philosophical questions.

God, Life After Death, and the Purpose of Life

What do we see when we look outside ourselves? We, and others of our kind, exist, but we're not alone. Plants and other animals also exist. So does the enormous universe that surrounds us. And if we reflect on its complexity and majesty, we've got to ask ourselves, "Where did it all come from?"

We didn't create our universe, so how did it get here? Is it the result of natural processes operating over billions or trillions of years? Or did someone create it? Are we alone in this universe, or is there a *God* as well? Not surprisingly, proofs for the existence of God have been debated by philosophers for thousands of years.

The question of God's existence raises other fundamental questions. For example, if there is a spiritual dimension to reality, does that mean that we have "souls" or "spirits" that continue to exist after our bodies wear out? Is there life after death? For that matter, have we lived other lives before this one? More people on this planet believe in reincarnation than reject the idea. Who is right?

And the idea of an afterlife, or of other lives, leads us to wonder, What is the *purpose of life*? Is it a test of some sort? If so, what counts as "passing"? Making a lot of money and becoming rich and famous? Doing some kind of important work? Devoting our lives to helping people less fortunate than ourselves? Growing personally or spiritually as much as possible? Questions of the ultimate purpose of life, then, are also common grist for the philosopher's mill.

So far we've identified the most basic questions of philosophy.

- What is the nature of "reality"?
- What is a "person"?
- How free are we?
- What can we "know" and how can we "know" it?
- Is there a God?
- What is the purpose of life?

These, then, are the most fundamental, theoretical questions we ask in philosophy. But we also take up more practical issues.

Practical Issues

We've been looking at the issues raised by the simple fact that we exist (reality, personhood), that we do things (free will), and that we know (knowledge). What else is characteristic of human beings but a little less abstract?

Standards of Conduct: Right and Wrong

When we choose what to do, we use certain standards or values to guide us. We also use these values to evaluate what other people do. Our society, like all societies, suggests some standards for our behavior, the most important of which are laws and customs. Organizations we belong to, schools we go to, religious groups we belong to, and companies we work for also have their rules, regulations, and policies.

But sometimes those are not enough, or they may conflict with each other. For example, even though it is illegal, many underage students use false IDs to buy liquor. Do you think they're doing something wrong? The traffic laws say you should stop at red lights and stop signs. But what should you do if you are rushing a sick friend to the hospital? Your religion tells you that sex before marriage is wrong, but you are deeply in love with someone and you don't feel that anything you do would be wrong. These ethical dilemmas lead us to yet another philosophical question: How do we separate *right* from *wrong*?

Questions about right and wrong can get as complicated as those about reality or knowledge. We need an ultimate standard of conduct. But where do we find something like that? How do you choose between two actions, both of which seem wrong to you? How would you explain the basis of your standard of right and wrong to someone who disagrees with you? Maybe your standard is influenced by your personal religious beliefs. Yet how could you convince an atheist that you were right? Even if you do have some standard for separating right from wrong, why should you act on it? Why should you do right and not do wrong? What if you can't afford to fix your car and you can steal a few hundred dollars from somebody who's rich? Is there any good reason not to steal, especially if you can get away with it?

So you see, many questions come up when we look at the everyday problem of evaluating human actions against some fundamental standard. And, it will come as no surprise, these are philosophical questions.

How Do We Organize Our Communities?

Questions of right and wrong come up because we live with other people and we need some standard for judging their conduct as well as our own. But the fact that we live with other people in communities also creates some issues on a larger scale—and still more philosophical questions. How should decisions be made that affect the common good? Does everybody vote about every little thing? Or do you assign some of these decisions to others—that is, do you create a government? What kind of government do you want? Who gets to make the rules that everybody in the group must live by? What if the group's rules force some people to do things that they find wrong according to their personal standards? Are they entitled to disobey those rules? How do you decide if a law is "just" or not?

Other Concerns of Philosophy

We exist. We choose our actions. We know things. We evaluate what we do and what others do. We live among other people. Trying to understand and explain these most basic facts of life is what philosophy mainly does.

Yet philosophy also studies the conceptual foundations of some of the more complicated dimensions of human life—art, science, religion, law, education, artificial intelligence, genetic engineering, ethical issues in business and medicine and the other professions. In fact, the most abstract ideas of virtually every human endeavor are the domain of philosophy.

The Subject Matter of Philosophy

This quick survey of a few basic questions should give you a decent idea of what philosophy is all about. It is not some arcane study that has nothing to do with real life. It is an intellectual activity devoted to understanding the most basic dimensions of what it means to exist as a human being alone and in community with others. As such, it has everything to do with real life.

Philosophical Questions

The questions that philosophers ask are obviously varied. One thing they have in common is that all these questions arise from thinking about the fundamental aspects of life. But they also share something else that is distinctive of a philosophical question—their conceptual nature.

If I ask you if it's raining, how do you find out the answer? You look outside. And if I ask you how many students are in a particular classroom at noon on Monday? You go and count the people. In each case, you get the facts. Many questions are like this. They're answered by doing some empirical investigation. Scientific questions are empirical questions: they can be answered by "getting the facts." Questions that have factual answers are not philosophical questions.

Or what if you want to know if you can leave your car somewhere overnight without getting a ticket? You call the police. Or if you want to know what the Catholic church says about the morality of birth control? Ask a priest. In these cases, you're still getting facts, but they're facts of a different kind. There are specific answers that will settle your questions, but you must find the right person, book, or body of law that tells you what they are. You must seek the judgment of an authority. Questions like these are not philosophical questions either.

Instead, philosophical questions involve conceptual issues. Think about the account of the philosophical topics you just read. All those philosophical questions boil down to basic concepts or principles. And that is the defining feature of a philosophical question. Reality, knowledge, right, wrong, justice, and the like are all concepts. The challenge of a philosophical investigation is exploring the principles and concepts at issue and applying the results to situations that involve those ideas.

Philosophical "Answers"

Similarly, the "answers" to these questions share an important property that also characterizes philosophy. Because of the conceptual nature of the fundamental issues philosophy considers, philosophers can never give absolute proof that they are right.

Philosophical questions do not get "solved," as empirical questions do. The empirical question "How many pages are in this book?" has a single, correct answer; all others are wrong. But a philosophical question like "Is abortion wrong?" has more than one plausible answer. Depending on the positions taken on such debatable issues as "life," "personhood," and "rights," we can find even completely opposing arguments that are reasonable and believable. Similarly, we can make a plausible case for saying that we're free to choose anything we want whenever we want to. On the other hand, we can also make an intelligent case for saying that our sense of freedom is an illusion—that we fool ourselves into thinking we're free when our behavior is actually determined. It is simply a characteristic of philosophical issues that we fall short of absolute certainty. And this means that philosophical thinking generally deals more in probability and plausibility than absolute truth and falsehood.

The Parts of Philosophy

You now have an understanding of the subjects that philosophy discusses and something of the nature of philosophy. However, without realizing it, you also have acquired a sense of the primary branches of philosophy.

Very fundamental and abstract issues relating to existence in general (like the nature of reality and the existence of God) and human existence in particular (such as free will) are taken up in the part of philosophy called **metaphysics.** The ancient Greek philosopher Aristotle called this branch of philosophy "first philosophy," and that's a good way to think about it. Metaphysics concentrates on the first or most fundamental questions we encounter when we begin studying the most basic issues of life.[3]

Another fundamental part of philosophy is theory of knowledge, or **epistemology,** which takes up the questions we saw earlier related to the nature of knowledge. "Epistemology" combines two Greek words, *epistéme* and *logos,* and literally means "the study of knowledge." *Epistéme* means "knowledge." *Logos* has many meanings, but in this context it means "the study of." The suffix "-logy" can be found at the end of many English words: "biology" (the study of life), "geology" (the study of the earth), and so on.

When we encounter the practical issues of philosophy, we move into **ethics,** or *moral philosophy,* and **political philosophy.** "Ethics" is the part of philosophy that discusses right and wrong, and the word is derived from the Greek word for "custom, habit, or character," *ethikos.* ("Moral" comes from the Latin word for "character," *mores.*) "Political philosophy" takes up the wider issues that arise from our living together, such as legitimate authority, justice, and speculation about the ideal society. Its root is *polis,* another Greek word, which means "city."

Metaphysics, epistemology, ethics, and political philosophy are the main divisions of philosophy. But given the wide range of topics that philosophers study, it should come as no surprise that there are also many important but more narrowly focused branches of philosophy, like philosophy of art, philosophy of science, and

---

metaphysics Metaphysics is the part of philosophy concerned with the most basic issues, for example, reality, existence, personhood, and freedom versus determinism. Metaphysics was originally referred to by Aristotle as "first philosophy."

epistemology Epistemology, also called "theory of knowledge," is the part of philosophy concerned with "knowledge" and related concepts.

ethics Ethics, also called "moral philosophy," is the part of philosophy concerned with right, wrong, and other issues related to evaluating human conduct.

political philosophy Political philosophy is the part of philosophy that addresses the philosophical issues that arise from the fact that we live together in communities. These issues include the nature of political authority, justice, and the problem of harmonizing freedom and obligation.

---

[3]"Metaphysics" comes from two ancient Greek words, *meta* "after," and *physika* "physics." In light of contemporary usage, where "metaphysical" usually means "abstract" or "abstruse," you might think that "metaphysics" takes its name from the fact that it studies highly abstract issues "beyond the physical realm." While such questions are "metaphysical," the word is actually a historical accident. The Greek philosopher Aristotle gave a series of lectures dealing with the most basic questions in philosophy; as I mentioned, he called this "first philosophy." The treatise containing these lectures was never given a title, but after Aristotle's death his students traditionally filed it after Aristotle's lectures on nature, which the philosopher called "the physics." Thus, *METAPHYSICS* meant something more like "the scroll filed after The Physics" than "lectures on transcendental questions." That is why the best way to understand metaphysics is to remember that Aristotle called it "first philosophy." That is, think of it as the part of philosophy that asks the "first" or most basic questions.

philosophy of language. Finally, in a class by itself, there is **logic,** the part of philosophy devoted to studying reason itself and the structure of arguments. Logic is the foundation on which any philosophical investigation is built, and modern philosophy of logic explores some highly technical philosophical questions.

Why Studying Philosophy Is Valuable

So far you have seen that philosophy stems quite naturally from thinking about life's basic questions. And you have been introduced to some of those questions and to the different branches of philosophy. You should now be ready for what we're going to study in the chapters ahead.

Before we move on, however, we should address one more issue—why studying philosophy is worthwhile. Whatever you imagine you will get out of a philosophy course, let me assure you that if you work hard through this course, you will develop skills, abilities, and insights that will help you for the rest of your life.

Analytical Abilities

The skills you will pick up are easy to describe. You will develop better analytical abilities. You will handle abstract problems better. You will learn how to argue more effectively. And you will have a stronger imagination. Philosophy helps to shape in a positive way what we might call the "general cut of your mind." This is invaluable in whatever career you choose to follow. The most successful people use analysis and argument all the time. Successful people make their mark by solving difficult problems and convincing other people they're right.

In preparing this book, I asked several successful executives to tell me what they thought students should study if they wanted to succeed in business. They listed only a few technical subjects—accounting and finance, for example. (The technical end of business, they said, you learn mainly on the job.) Otherwise they suggested courses that help develop your ability to think about problems analytically and to communicate your analysis and recommendations to other people. Time and again, these executives identified philosophy as one of the most important areas you can study for learning how to think in a disciplined, analytical, and imaginative way.

Vision and Insight

The way that philosophy helps you see the world is no less real than its practical benefits to your career. Studying philosophy exposes you to a wide range of problems that you wouldn't meet otherwise. It simply lets you see more of the world. It stretches your imagination. It challenges you to come up with your own answers to tough issues that do not have ready-made solutions. If you take it seriously, philosophy teaches you different ways of looking at the world.

---

logic Logic is the part of philosophy devoted to studying reason itself and the structure of arguments.

Studying philosophy helps you to develop insight into some of life's great puzzles and to fashion your own vision of what life is all about. As you go through life, you will be challenged all along the way to make decisions about who you are and what's important to you. What will you do with your life? What career will you pursue? Will you marry? And if so, what kind of person? Will you have children? How will you rear them? What will you tell them is important? What are you willing to do for money and success? How will you cope with the crises you will encounter in your own life or in the lives of those you love—illness, accidents, problems on the job or at home, death? Philosophy helps you develop a sense of what life is all about and where you're going.

In fact, Socrates, one of the first great philosophers, thought that philosophy is the single most important element in making our lives worthwhile. "The unexamined life," he said, "is not worth living." The habit of thinking philosophically lets us scrutinize our values, our goals, and the means we've chosen to achieve them, and it helps us keep our lives on course. In Socrates' mind, at least, philosophy makes it possible for us to control our own destiny. And that's no small matter.

As you now know, philosophy is simply thinking systematically about life's most basic issues. When it comes down to it, there is no way that thinking about these questions cannot make you better prepared to live your life.

Previews of Coming Chapters

Now that you have a sense of what philosophy is, you're ready to plunge in yourself. What's coming up in the rest of this book? We cannot cover every important aspect of such a large subject in an introductory text. We will, however, talk about most of philosophy's basic topics and a few specialized ones.

We'll start preparing ourselves by "tuning the instrument," that is, the mind. Since we do philosophy by thinking, the best place to begin is by studying some of the "rules of reason" alluded to earlier. Chapter 2, "Philosophical Thinking," will introduce you to the ground rules regarding logic and critical thinking.

In the next section, "Exploring the Basics of Who We Are and Dealing with Others," we look at some of the most fundamental characteristics of our existence. We start with two chapters that consider opposing points of view about the issue of human freedom. In "The Case for Determinism" (Chapter 3), we look at the arguments in favor of determinism, and we explore the case for free will in Chapter 4 ("The Case for Freedom"). Then we examine basic issues related to our living with other people. We look at how philosophers talk about "right" and "wrong" in Chapter 5, "Right and Wrong." In Chapter 6, "Why Be Ethical?", we ask why we should bother doing what's right. And Chapter 7, "Democracy," inquires into the underpinnings of our political system.

In the chapters that make up "Fundamental Theoretical Issues," we explore basic philosophical problems of a more abstract nature. We start with absolute bedrock—"The Nature of Reality"—in Chapter 8. Chapter 9, "What Is Knowledge?", looks at the basic ways philosophers have looked at knowledge. In Chapter 10, "Does God Exist?", we examine the main "proofs" for the existence of God. In Chapter 11, "The Purpose of Life: Marx and Buddha," we tackle one of life's most perplexing questions as seen through the eyes of two very different philosophers. We conclude with three specialized topics in "Contemporary Challenges." Chapter 12, "Scientific Explanations of Reality," looks at philosophical issues raised by the ideas of theoretical physicists about the nature of the world. Then we consider some philosophical questions raised by some fascinating psychological theories that women and men have unique ways of thinking about knowledge and of engaging ethical problems (Chapter 13, "Does Gender Affect How We Think?"). And in Chapter 14 ("Is a Dolphin a Person?"), we examine the philosophical implications of the remarkable discoveries that scientists have made about dolphins.

This book, then, will give you a basic but solid understanding of what philosophy is all about. It will serve as a road map for what many of us feel is one of life's most exciting, enriching, and engaging adventures—discovering philosophy. You will see new sights, explore new worlds, expand your horizons, and, most importantly, learn much about yourself. As with any journey, what you get out of it is mainly up to you. But if you give philosophy half a chance, it just might take you to a place you never want to leave.

Main Points of Chapter 1

1. Philosophy is a conceptual discipline that focuses on life's most basic questions. It is the activity of thinking about these issues yourself, not simply understanding what philosophers from the past have said about these questions.

2. The most fundamental issues that philosophy investigates are highly abstract: the nature of reality, free will, knowledge, the existence of God, and the purpose of life. Philosophy also addresses more practical issues: right and wrong, and the organization of societies.

3. The main branches of philosophy include logic, metaphysics, epistemology, ethics, and political philosophy.

4. Studying philosophy will strengthen your analytical abilities, your capacity for abstract thought, and your ability to argue.

Discussion Questions

1. Have you already thought about any of the philosophical questions identified in this chapter? What spurred this? Another course? A debate about a controversial issue? An experience in your life? Your own proclivity to think about life?

2. Later chapters of this book will explore in depth the main philosophical issues identified previously. But try your hand at taking a position and fashioning an argument on any of the following questions: How free are our actions? What makes an action morally wrong? Does God exist?

3. What do you expect to get out of studying philosophy? What will make it worth all the time and effort you will put in? Will just a good grade do it? If philosophy doesn't help you become more successful in your career, does that mean it has no value?

Selected Readings

A superb source for detailed information about almost every philosopher and philosophical issue is *The Encyclopedia of Philosophy*, edited by Paul Edwards, 8 volumes (New York: Macmillan and the Free Press, 1967). For an excellent history of philosophy, see F. C. Copleston, *History of Philosophy*, 8 volumes (Garden City, NY: Doubleday, 1965). For a popular account of the development of philosophy, consult Will Durant, *The Story of Philosophy* (New York: Pocket Books, 1953).

2

Philosophical Thinking

- *Analytical Thinking: Necessary and Sufficient Conditions*
- *Critical Thinking*
- *One Last Word About Logic*
- *Appendix: An Overview of the Fallacies*

The preceding chapter described philosophy as thinking about the basic issues of life. But philosophy is not just any kind of thinking. Scientists and religious or political authorities, for example, think in the process of their inquiries, but they direct their attention to empirical data, sacred texts, or legal records. The grist for the philosopher's mill, however, is neither scientific facts nor the conclusions of authorities. Rather, it is *ideas*—"reality," "free will," "determinism," "knowledge," "right," "wrong," and the like. Philosophers direct their attention to concepts, and they try to sort out the abstract issues using a special kind of thinking that is **analytical** and **critical**.[1] Thus, the building blocks of philosophical thinking are *concepts* and *arguments*.

> **analytical thinking** Analytical thinking is one of the basic tools of philosophy. It aims to define the concept under investigation by uncovering its defining characteristics, that is, its necessary and sufficient conditions.
>
> **critical thinking** To think critically is to judge whether some claim is believable and convincing, that is, whether it is based on solid facts or good reasons. All intellectual disciplines that deal with evidence and proof are based on critical thinking.

---

[1]The fact that philosophy is so conceptual, that the results of philosophical thinking are ultimately judged by rules of reason, and that arguments are evaluated for how "reasonable," "convincing," or "plausible" they are reveals another and perhaps the most general hallmark of philosophy. This is difficult to put simply, but we might say that unlike enterprises like science, law, or religion, the ultimate point of reference in philosophy is the mind itself. Scientific thinking, for example, can be critical, analytical, conceptual, and lead to arguments that are no more than probable; but in the end its final focus is on the physical world. Not so with philosophy. In philosophy we do think about issues related to the world of science, religion, law, medicine, and so on, but philosophical thinking focuses on the theoretical and conceptual dimensions of these disciplines. Simply put, philosophical thinking is a product of the ideas we find in or create with our minds: We think about simple ideas (concepts), put our conclusions into larger ideas (arguments), and evaluate those arguments by still other ideas (the rules of reason). Philosophy is ultimately and essentially a mental enterprise.

15

Analytical Thinking: Necessary and Sufficient Conditions

The word "analysis" comes from the Greek word meaning to "break up." Analytical procedures of all stripes aim to reveal the nature of something by breaking up the matter in question into its constituent parts. For instance, when a chemist is confronted with an unknown substance, the first thing she does is to analyze it; that is, she uses different chemicals to break the material down into its basic elements. The first stage of philosophical thinking is also analytical. A philosopher tries to clarify an issue by using certain mental tools to break the general concepts under inquiry into smaller ideas that are easier to work with. In practice, this amounts to searching for specific definitions of the ideas or concepts involved in the philosophical issue under investigation.

For example, a significant issue in the abortion debate is whether a fetus is a person. A philosophical approach, then, would begin with an intellectual analysis of the concept "person." At the outset of a philosophical investigation, photographs of embryonic development at particular stages or biological analyses of tissue samples are irrelevant. Scientific facts will be important, but only after the basic concept—"person"—has been analyzed and defined. What are the constituent "parts" of personhood? What conditions must be met for us to label something a "person": A particular biological form? Self-awareness? Intellectual abilities? Must these characteristics be present now or is it enough that they will develop eventually? Only by exploring questions like these, that is, only if we engage in analytical thinking, will we understand exactly what we mean when we ask, "Is a fetus a person?"

To define the concepts we're investigating, we must first identify what are called the *necessary and sufficient conditions* for a concept. We start with clear-cut examples, or *model cases,* of the concept. After we determine the defining characteristics of our model cases, we test them against *counterexamples,* that is, cases that share the characteristics of the concept but are not examples of it. This then forces us to refine our original list. Ultimately, we arrive at the precise characteristics that define the concept.

A familiar example from a field outside philosophy should help to clarify this. Let's use the concept of a "square."

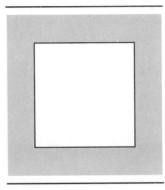

A square

Necessary conditions are the properties that "absolutely, positively" must be present for something to count as an example of the concept in question.

In the case of our "square," "having four sides" is a good candidate for a necessary condition. It agrees with our drawing, and we all know that something cannot be a square if it doesn't have four sides. But this condition isn't all that is necessary, because we can think of *counterexamples* that have four sides, but nonetheless are not squares. For example,

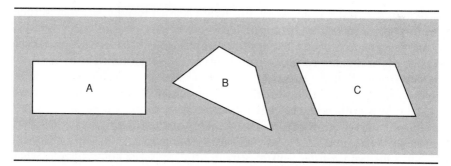

Thus, we must specify that in addition to having four sides, the two pairs of sides must also be "parallel." This condition eliminates the quadrilateral (B) but leaves the other two as counterexamples. Saying "the sides have to be equal" takes care of the rectangle (A). And "having four internal angles of 90 degrees" removes the parallelogram (C).

Each one of these conditions, then, is necessary: four sides, equal and parallel sides, 90-degree internal angles. But, as we've seen, just because a characteristic is necessary, having it doesn't make some object a square. Each one may be necessary, but each alone is not enough—or sufficient—to make something a square. For that we've got to put all the necessary conditions together. That gives us the **sufficient conditions** for a "square."

Philosophers often refer to the list of necessary and sufficient conditions for a given concept as the set of criteria for that concept. "Criteria" (the singular is "criterion") is the term used to describe those characteristics that must be present for something to qualify for a particular category.

Take another example. In the following list, which conditions are *necessary* and which are *sufficient* to hear music from your Walkman?

a. The Walkman is in good working order

b. The batteries are good

---

necessary conditions Necessary conditions are those properties that must be present for something to be an example of the concept in question.

sufficient conditions The sufficient conditions of a concept are the set of necessary conditions that, if met, qualify something as an example of a particular concept.

c. The Walkman is yellow

d. It's raining out

e. The earphones are plugged in

f. The tape has music on it and is in good condition

g. You must operate the controls correctly

Each of a, b, e, f, and g is necessary. But only taken all together are they sufficient. The other two, c and d, are irrelevant.

Defining a concept works like this most of the time. You'll generate several conditions or characteristics, each of which is necessary but insufficient by itself. Only the combination of all the necessary conditions gives us the sufficient conditions.

Once in a great while, however, you'll encounter another kind of case where one condition is both necessary and sufficient. For example, to get a grade in this course you have only to register. That's it. That single condition is necessary and sufficient at the same time. Of course, we're talking just about getting a grade—any grade. Once you register, you're guaranteed to get some kind of grade, whether it be A, B, C, D, F, I, or W. The necessary and sufficient conditions for getting a good grade are more than that. But that's not what we're talking about. This is one case where necessity and sufficiency turn out to be the same thing. And keep in mind that there are other such cases.

Once you determine the necessary and sufficient conditions of the concepts involved in your philosophical inquiry, you have defined the terms of your investigation and you can now tackle the question at hand. At this point, philosophical thinking becomes more critical than analytical.

A Short Example: Personhood

Defining concepts might look to you only like some abstract academic exercise. But don't underestimate its philosophical importance. Take the concept of a "person," for example, which regularly comes up in debates about abortion, euthanasia, and animal rights. If we took the time to analyze the concept and develop a list of necessary and sufficient conditions, we'd end up with something like this:

A "person"

1. is alive

2. is aware

3. feels positive and negative sensations

4. has a sense of self (self-consciousness) with emotions

5. controls its own behavior (can be held responsible)

6. recognizes other persons and treats them appropriately

7. is capable of analytical, conceptual thought

8. is able to learn; can retain and recall information

9. can solve complicated problems with analytical thought

10. has the capacity for communication that suggests thought

If this analysis is correct, it has a number of important implications. For example, it explains why many people object to calling it "murder" when someone terminates life support for a patient who is "brain dead." (There may still be other reasons that we're morally obligated to continue life support, but this analysis rules out "not murdering someone.") Similarly, this list suggests that members of other intelligent species—dolphins and chimps, for example—who demonstrate all of these abilities are also persons.[2] And this calls into question whether the use of non-human persons for profit, food, research, or entertainment is ethically justifiable. In other words, something as basic as a precise analysis of concepts can help clarify serious ethical dilemmas and even reveal important philosophical problems that we may have been blind to before.

Critical Thinking

The idea that philosophical thinking is critical may at first suggest to you that it aims to find fault or criticize. "Critical," however, is derived from the ancient Greek word *kritikos*, which means "skilled in judging." To think critically, then, simply means to judge whether or not some claim is believable and convincing, that is, whether it's based on solid facts or good reasons. All intellectual disciplines that deal with evidence and proof are based on critical thinking, so to this extent philosophy is similar to other areas.

Critical thinking combines healthy skepticism and analytical skills in a way that lets you determine for yourself the truth or legitimacy of the claims someone is making. Accepting without question the statements of someone in authority is not thinking critically. For example, if you said "abortion is morally acceptable because it is legal" or "abortion is wrong because the Pope says so," you would not be thinking critically. You want to get behind the positions of these authorities (law, on the one hand, and a religious official, on the other) and judge whether they have good reasons for their conclusions.

Considering how often someone tries to persuade you of something, critical thinking should be a constant feature of your life. Your parents try to convince you to aspire to medical school, to take a particular major, or to study harder. Your friends might challenge some of your parents' arguments, encouraging you to major in music and trying to persuade you that studying too hard will ruin your social life. Advertisements try to induce you to buy a new product; political speeches, to vote for a particular candidate. We are barraged by other people's explanations for why we should act or think in a particular way. Furthermore, we just as often attempt to convince other people of things. You try to get a co-worker to trade hours with you so that you can go on a special date. You attempt to talk your

---

[2]On the question of whether a dolphin is a person, see Chapter 14 ("Is a Dolphin a 'Person'?").

teacher into excusing you from the final exam because you have a straight A average. You design the publicity for a campus event with an eye to getting as many people as possible to attend. Our lives—what we do, what we experience from others—sometimes seem like endless rounds of persuasion.

What Is Argumentation?

Philosophical thinking is essentially *critical* thinking. Philosophers are not "authorities" making pronouncements that you are simply supposed to accept. Philosophers make claims backed up by *reasons* and *arguments,* and they offer them for public scrutiny. Philosophers judge other thinkers' arguments, and they expect their own words to be treated the same way. As a type of critical thinking, then, philosophy is an active, intellectual process that sifts and sorts through whatever facts, concepts, theories, and speculations can be used to argue in support of competing positions in a philosophical controversy. Philosophical thinking is critical thinking in that its primary focus is on arguments.

The term *argument* does not mean the emotional fights you have with your friends, roommate, parents, siblings, spouse, or significant loved one. Instead, an **argument** is a rational attempt to prove a point by offering reasons or evidence and drawing some conclusion from it. Unlike the angry, one-sided, emotional blowout, a good philosophical argument is reasoned, orderly, logical, and convincing—or, at least, plausible. And it's not as dull as it sounds. People develop a lot of feeling about positions they hold, and discussions often get spirited. But if you start an evening talking calmly about an important issue and later find yourself looking around for something to throw at your opponent, you've probably stopped arguing and started fighting. Just keep the difference between the two clear.

In the same vein, remember that critical, philosophical thinking appeals to the intellect. A philosophical argument does not use language the way advertisers, courtroom attorneys, and politicians do—as a device to sway people's emotions. If it does, it is no longer properly philosophy. What, then, is the hallmark of good critical thinking? What are the characteristics of strong and weak arguments?

What Is Logic?

In much the same way that we have building codes to ensure that a house is built well, there is also a "thinking code," that is, guidelines and rules for what makes an argument pass "philosophical inspection." We find this code in that part of philosophy called *logic.*

Logic is the branch of philosophy devoted to determining what counts as solid, disciplined, reasoned thinking. In fact, the ancient Greek philosopher

---

argument An argument is a series of statements that you make either orally or in writing, one of which is a claim of some sort, and the rest of which are your reasons for making this claim.

Aristotle sees it as so basic that he calls it not so much a part of philosophy as the "instrument" we use to do philosophy. Logic is both a process of reasoning and the rules that govern the process, and we use those rules to distinguish between correct and incorrect conclusions when we engage in an intellectual investigation of a question.

It's difficult to learn much about logic in just one chapter of a textbook because it usually takes at least a full semester to start getting comfortable with this part of philosophy. So we're going to look at just some basic issues related to good, logical thinking (on the one hand) and poor, illogical thinking (on the other).

Logic and wizards

We're going to start our study of logic where you'd probably least expect it—talking not about some philosopher but about some wizards-in-training. In J. K. Rowling's book *Harry Potter and the Philosopher's Stone*, Harry Potter, Ron Weasley, and Hermione Granger discover that hidden somewhere in Hogwart's castle is the "Philosopher's Stone," a magical object that can guarantee immortality. Fearing that it might be used to bring the dark wizard Lord Voldemort back to power, the young wizards decide to find it before one of Voldemort's supporters does. The three friends get past a variety of enchantments designed to protect the stone, but then Harry and Hermione find themselves trapped by walls of fire. In front of them, however, is a table with seven bottles and a piece of paper containing a poem that gives clues for getting through the fire. After reading the poem, Hermione points out that it's actually a riddle. It gets solved by logic, not magic.

Since logic is no more than careful thinking, it's something that you already use—for example, when you make an important decision or simply try to solve some murder mystery that you're reading. So you already have some experience with this kind of thinking—although you may not call it "logic." To show you what I mean, why don't you see how far you can get with Hermione's puzzle?

Here are the seven bottles on the table.[3]

1   2   3   4   5   6   7

[3]I owe this bottle arrangement to Marc Kummel. See his discussion of this problem at www.rain.org/~mkummel/stumpers/17mar00.html.

The poem says that one of the seven bottles lets you go through the room, one takes you back where you came from, two contain wine, and three hold poison. Poison is always to the left of wine but isn't in either the biggest or smallest bottle, the bottles on either end are different but don't contain the potion to go forward, and the bottles that are second from the left and second from the right contain the same thing.

Which of the bottles will let you go through the fire and thwart Voldemort? Take some time and see if you can figure it out before continuing to read.

How did you do? If you think the answer is bottle 3, you get 500 points, and you ensure that your house will win the Hogwarts' "House Cup." If you came up with the right answer like Hermione, you did so just by thinking logically. Seeing exactly how you and Hermione figured this out, then, will teach us something about logic. So let's go through this problem step by step and see how to solve it by just thinking logically.

Step One

The first part of the poem tells us that of the seven bottles, three contain poison, two have nettle wine, one contains a potion that will let us move through the fire in front of us, and one has a potion that will let us get through the fire behind us.

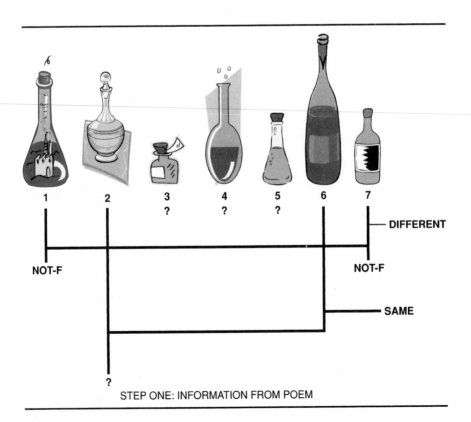

STEP ONE: INFORMATION FROM POEM

As a shorthand, let's label the different contents **P** (poison), **W** (wine), **B** (the potion that will let us go back), and **F** (the potion that we want, that is, the one that will let us go forward). Then the rest of the poem gives us four clues:

> *Clue 1*: Poison will always be on the left side of the nettle wine.

> *Clue 2*: Bottles 1 and 7 contain different substances but not the potion that will let us go forward.

> *Clue 3*: The bottles are different sizes, and neither the "dwarf" nor the "giant" bottle contains poison.

> *Clue 4*: Bottles 2 and 6 contain the same substance.

Step Two

So, how should we proceed? Because we're told there are three bottles of poison on the table, it's probably a good idea to start by seeing if we can figure out which bottles to avoid. Fortunately, Clue 3 gives us some helpful information—neither the "dwarf" nor the "giant" contains poison. If we examine the size of the bottles, we

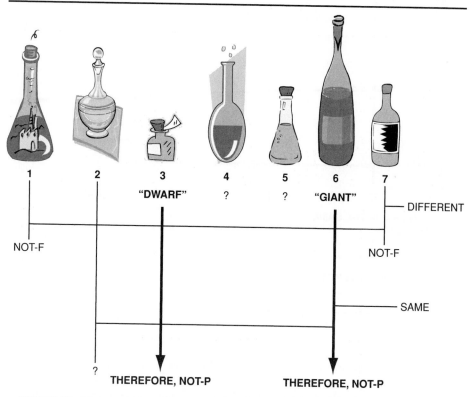

STEP TWO: COMPARING THE SIZE OF THE BOTTLES AND USING CLUE 3

can see that bottle 3 is the smallest and bottle 6 is the largest. So, we can conclude that neither bottle 3 nor bottle 6 has poison.

Step Three

What can we figure out next? If we put together what we just learned (that bottle 6 isn't poison) with Clue 4 (that bottles 2 and 6 contain the same substance), we can conclude that bottle 2 isn't poison either.

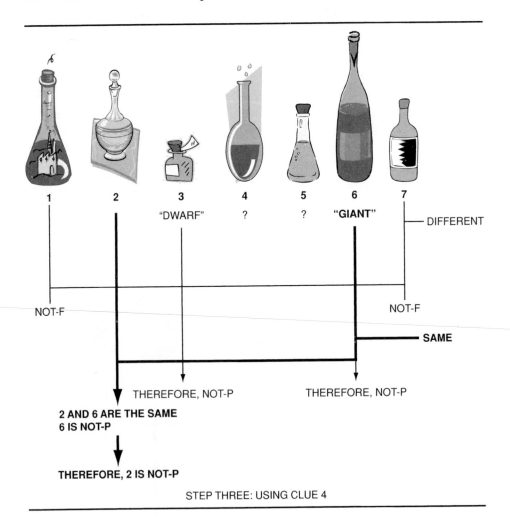

STEP THREE: USING CLUE 4

Step Four

Let's keep our focus on avoiding the poison. We now know that the poison isn't in bottles 2, 3, and 6. That leaves four bottles to worry about because we've been told that there are three bottles of poison. Clue 2 tells us that bottles 1 and 7 are different. Since bottles 1 and 7, then, can't both be poison, that means that the poison is in

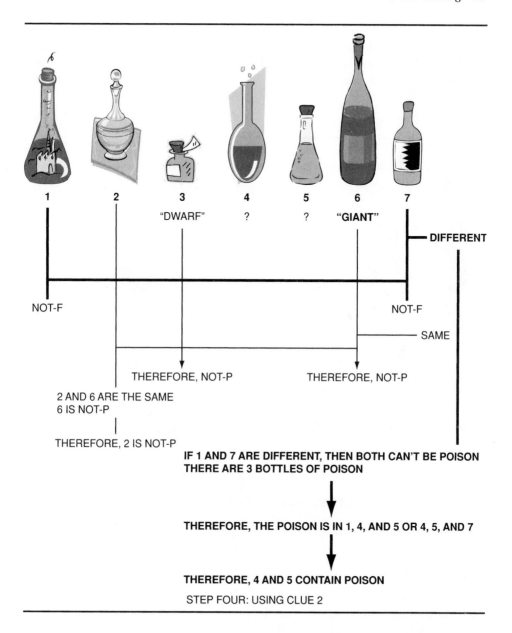

1	2	3	4	5	6	7
		"DWARF"	?	?	"GIANT"	

DIFFERENT

NOT-F   NOT-F

SAME

THEREFORE, NOT-P   THEREFORE, NOT-P

2 AND 6 ARE THE SAME
6 IS NOT-P

THEREFORE, 2 IS NOT-P

**IF 1 AND 7 ARE DIFFERENT, THEN BOTH CAN'T BE POISON
THERE ARE 3 BOTTLES OF POISON**

↓

THEREFORE, THE POISON IS IN 1, 4, AND 5 OR 4, 5, AND 7

↓

THEREFORE, 4 AND 5 CONTAIN POISON

STEP FOUR: USING CLUE 2

either bottles 1, 4, and 5 or 4, 5, and 7. And because bottles 4 and 5 are there under both possible combinations, we know that both bottles 4 and 5 are definitely poison.

Step Five

Let's take stock for a minute. We know that bottles 4 and 5 are poison. That leaves the third bottle of poison unaccounted for. We're also still looking for the two bottles of wine, the potion that will let us go forward, and the potion that will let us go back. It may not look like we've gotten very far, but remember that Clue 4 tells us that bottles 2 and 6 contain the same substance. And that means that bottles 2 and 6 must be wine. Only *one* bottle of poison, *one* forward potion, and *one* backward potion are left to locate. *Wine* is the only thing that's in *two* of the bottles.

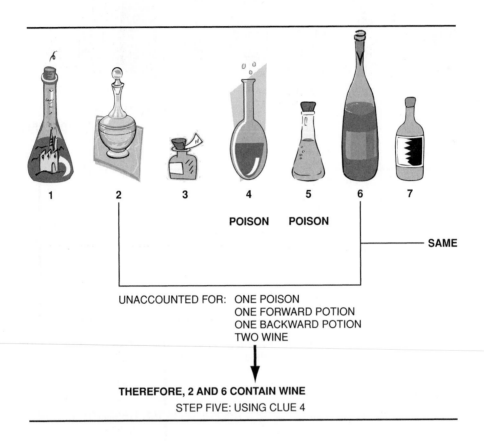

UNACCOUNTED FOR: ONE POISON
ONE FORWARD POTION
ONE BACKWARD POTION
TWO WINE

THEREFORE, 2 AND 6 CONTAIN WINE
STEP FIVE: USING CLUE 4

Step Six

Now that we know where the two bottles of wine are, we can locate the missing bottle of poison. Clue 1 tells us that the poison will always be on the left side of the nettle wine. We already know that bottles 4 and 5 are poison, and they're to the left of the nettle wine in bottle 6. Because we now know that bottle 2 is nettle wine, this means that bottle 1 is the third bottle of poison.

Step Seven

We're down to the final two bottles: 3 and 7. One has the magic potion that will let us go through the flames in front of us; the other has the potion that gets us through the flames behind us. Because Clue 2 tells us that bottle 7 won't let us go forward, that one must have the potion that will let us go back.

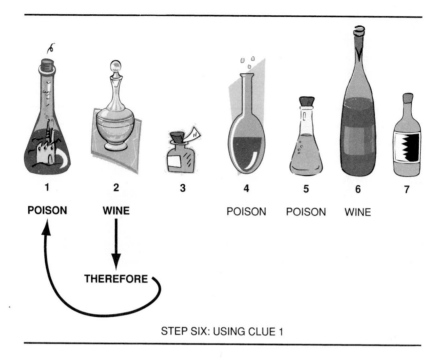

STEP SIX: USING CLUE 1

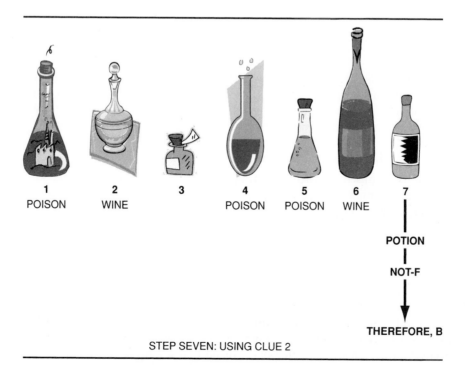

STEP SEVEN: USING CLUE 2

Step Eight

Since we've accounted for six bottles, that just leaves bottle 3. So that must be the potion we've been looking for the whole time—the one that will let us go through the fire ahead of us.

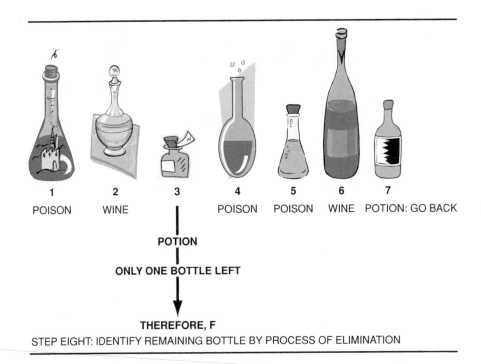

| 1 | 2 | 3 | 4 | 5 | 6 | 7 |

POISON   WINE   POISON   POISON   WINE   POTION: GO BACK

POTION

ONLY ONE BOTTLE LEFT

THEREFORE, F

STEP EIGHT: IDENTIFY REMAINING BOTTLE BY PROCESS OF ELIMINATION

You should be able to see that we figured out which bottle contained the correct magic potion simply by applying the information from the poem to the facts at hand in a careful and methodical way. Now let's examine the steps we took and see how they demonstrate good, logical thinking.

Hermione's solution and logic: constructing *arguments*

While in commonsense terms we can say that we have a *puzzle* here that we want to *solve*, from a philosophical perspective, we'd say that we're faced with constructing an **argument** that shows us what we want to know. An **argument** is simply a series of statements that gives us good *reasons* to think that the argument's **conclusion** is true (or at least very likely to be true). In our case, we're looking to construct an argument that reveals which bottle we should drink. That is, we're looking to be able to say: "On the basis of clues and facts A, B, C, D, and so forth, bottle X will get us through the fire ahead of us." Think of it this way. As much as you might trust Hermione, wouldn't you feel more comfortable drinking the bottle she hands you if she explained the *reasons* she's so sure it's the right bottle? Her explanation to you would be an **argument.** As a general rule in philosophy, we're expected to offer good arguments that explain why we think as we do. Arguments have two parts: the **conclusion** (the ultimate claim that we're making) and the **premises** (the reasons for accepting our conclusion). In ordinary conversation, people in effect "signal" that they're giving you the premises of an argument when they use words or phrases like "because," "since," "in light of the fact that," and "the reason being that." Words or phrases that signal a conclusion include "therefore," "so," "as a result," "it must be the case that," and the like.

Notice what our process of uncovering the correct bottle looks like when we think of it in terms of constructing an **argument.** In *Step One*, we took the first step in building a good argument by identifying what we could be sure about—the initial premises of our argument. In this case, our premises are the information and clues that come from the poem and from the way the bottles are placed on the table.

Our initial premise—the information we're given—is:

1. There are seven bottles standing in the following order. (We know this because we can see it.)

2. Three contain poison, two wine, one a potion for going forward, and one a potion for going back. (The first few lines of the poem tell us this.)

3. Poison will always be on the left side of the nettle wine. (Clue 1)

4. Bottles 1 and 7 contain different substances but not the potion that will let us go forward. (Clue 2)

5. The bottles are different sizes, and neither the "dwarf" nor the "giant" bottle contains poison. (Clue 3)

6. Bottles 2 and 6 contain the same substance. (Clue 4)

---

conclusion The technical label for the argument's claim, point, or result is the conclusion.

premises The reasons that allegedly lead to the conclusion of an argument are called premises.

Once we knew what information to start with, we could get rolling. In *Step Two*, we combined Clue 3 (neither the "dwarf" nor the "giant" contains poison) with what we could see—that bottle 3 is the smallest and bottle 6 is the largest—to conclude that neither bottle 3 nor 6 contained poison.

Notice that while it's absolutely common sense to conclude that bottles 3 and 6 don't have the poison if we're told that neither the smallest nor the largest has the poison, from the perspective of logic, we actually have two short arguments. Notice how the conclusion follows from the premises in each argument.

A. 1. Neither the "dwarf" nor the "giant" contains poison. (Clue 3) **[Initial Premise]**

2. Bottle 3 is the "dwarf." (Looking at the bottles) **[Initial Premise]**

3. Therefore, bottle 3 doesn't contain poison. **[Conclusion]**

B. 1. Neither the "dwarf" nor the "giant" contains poison. (Clue 3) **[New Premise]**

2. Bottle 6 is the "giant." (Looking at the bottles) **[Initial Premise]**

3. Therefore, bottle 6 doesn't contain poison. **[Conclusion]**

In *Step Three*, we put together another short argument. And notice how both conclusions that we just arrived at now serve as new facts or reasons (that is, premises) that we can use to draw new conclusions.

1. Bottles 2 and 6 contain the same substance. (Clue 4) **[Initial Premise]**

2. Bottle 6 doesn't contain poison. (What we just concluded from the arguments in Step One) **[New Premise]**

3. Therefore, bottle 2 doesn't contain poison. **[Conclusion]**

With *Step Four*, we came up with another argument. But this one is a little more involved because it's like a chain of small arguments with conclusions that we immediately use to keep going.

1. Of the seven bottles, bottles 2, 3, and 6 don't contain poison. (What we concluded in our arguments from Steps Two and Three) **[New Premise]**

2. Therefore, there could still be poison in bottles 1, 4, 5, and 7. **[Preliminary Conclusion]**

3. However, of the seven bottles, only three contain poison. (Information from the first part of the poem) **[Initial Premise]**

4. Therefore, the poison is in:

   a. 1, 4, 5

   b. 1, 4, 7

   c. 1, 5, 7 or

   d. 4, 5, 7   **[Preliminary Conclusion]**

5. But bottles 1 and 7 are different; that is, they can't both be poison. (Clue 2) **[Initial Premise]**

6. Therefore, there are only two possibilities for where the poison is:

   a. 1, 4, 5 or

   b. 4, 5, 7   **[Preliminary Conclusion]**

7. And since bottles 4 and 5 are part of both possibilities, we know that bottles 4 and 5 contain poison. **[Conclusion]**

Step Five

Step Five shows the benefit of simply stopping and thinking. Instead of continuing to ask, "Where's the poison?" we took a different tack and ended up finding the two bottles of nettle wine.

1. Bottles 2 and 6 contain the same substance. (Clue 4) **[Initial Premise]**

2. Because bottles 4 and 5 contain poison and because there are three bottles of poison, only *one* more bottle of poison needs to be accounted for. (Conclusion from Step Four argument, combined with information from the poem) **[New Premise]**

3. Similarly, only *one* of the remaining bottles contains the potion that will let us go forward and only *one* contains the potion that will let us go back. (Information from the poem) **[Initial Premise]**

4. There are *two* bottles of wine to be identified. (Information from the poem) **[Initial Premise]**

5. Therefore, bottles 2 and 6 must be wine. **[Conclusion]**

Step Six

Once we determined the location of the wine, we were on our way to our final conclusion. *Step Six* identified the last bottle of poison.

1. Bottle 2 is wine. (Conclusion from argument in Step Five) **[New Premise]**

2. Poison is always on the left side of the nettle wine. (Clue 1) **[Initial Premise]**

3. Therefore, bottle 1 contains poison. **[Conclusion]**

Step Seven

Once we knew the contents of five of the seven bottles, *Step Seven* gave us the location of one magic potion—the one that will let us go back.

1. Bottles 3 and 7 contain the two magic potions. (Information from the poem combined with the conclusions of the arguments from Steps Four, Five, and Six) **[New Premise]**

2. Bottle 7 doesn't contain the potion for going forward. (Clue 2) **[Initial Premise]**

3. Therefore, bottle 7 contains the potion for going back. **[Conclusion]**

Step Eight

Once we can identify six of the bottles, that leaves just the one we're looking for.

1. The contents of six of the seven bottles are as follows: 1—poison, 2—wine, 4—poison, 5—poison, 6—wine, 7—potion for going back. (Conclusions from arguments in Steps Four through Seven) [**New Premise**]

2. The only substance unaccounted for is the potion for going forward. (Information from the poem) [**Initial Premise**]

3. Therefore, bottle 3 contains the potion for going forward. [**Conclusion**]

So the first thing that the process of using logic to find the correct magic potion shows us about logic is primarily about putting together good *arguments*—where the conclusions follow from the premises.

Hermione and logic: allowable and forbidden "moves"

The second thing that we can learn about logic from Hermione's solution is the *structure* of good arguments. Despite the variety of facts that we took into account in solving our problem, each of the small arguments we constructed along the way had a similar structure. For clarity, we're going to rephrase the arguments a little. But they're still the same as what we did previously. For example,

Step Two. IF a particular bottle is the "dwarf," THEN it doesn't contain poison. Bottle 3 is the "dwarf."

THEREFORE, bottle 3 doesn't contain poison.

Step Two. IF a particular bottle is the "giant," THEN it doesn't contain poison. Bottle 6 is the "giant."

THEREFORE, bottle 6 doesn't contain poison.

Step Three. IF a particular substance is in bottle 6, THEN that same substance is in bottle 2.

The substance in bottle 6 is something other than poison.

THEREFORE, the substance in bottle 2 is something other than poison.

Step Five. IF we can identify which substance can be in two bottles, THEN we know what's in bottles 2 and 6.

The only substance that can be in two bottles is wine.

THEREFORE, bottles 2 and 6 contain wine.

All four of these arguments have the same structure:

1. *We know that IF (one particular thing) were true, THEN (a second particular thing) would also be true.*

2. *We know that (the first particular thing) is in fact true.*

3. *THEREFORE, we know that (the second particular thing) is also true.*

In fact, this (IF A, THEN B; A; THEREFORE, B) structure for an argument reflects one of the most basic rules of logic. And if we took the time, we could reconstruct every argument in our solution so that it had a similar step-by-step, premise(s)–conclusion structure.

Good, Logical Thinking and Rules

This reference to "rules" of logic, by the way, suggests a somewhat different way that we can talk about arguments that might help keep things clear. If you know the story in *Philosopher's Stone,* you recall that one of the challenges that came before Harry and Hermione encountered the seven bottles was a chess game. Harry, Ron, and Hermione found themselves on a huge chessboard, and the only way they could continue their search was to play their way across. So the three take their places as chess pieces and Ron masterminds a victory. Chess, like every game, has particular rules. There are two players and each has 16 pieces: 8 pawns, 2 rooks, 2 knights, 2 bishops, 1 queen, and 1 king. Each piece is allowed to move only in specific ways. For example,

Rook—as many spaces as you want (without jumping another piece), straight ahead, straight back, left or right

Bishop—as many spaces as you want (without jumping another piece) but only diagonally

Queen—what applies to both a rook and bishop combined

Knight—something of an "L-shaped" move in which you can jump over other pieces

Every time it was Ron's turn, he had to make sure that the move he had in mind was *allowed by the rule* that governs what each piece can do. In essence, he had to be able to say, "I can move this piece diagonally because it's a bishop, and the rule that describes how a bishop can move allows it."

Logic is the same. That is, there are *rules* that govern good, logical thinking. And the only way we can, as it were, make "moves" that take us through an argument and to a conclusion is if they're allowed by those rules.

As just mentioned previously, our (IF A, THEN B; A; THEREFORE, B) structure is one of the most basic rules of logic. *If we have an "IF . . . , THEN . . ." statement, and if we can say that the IF part is true, then we're entitled to conclude that what's in the THEN part is also true.* For example,

IF someone is a student at Hogwart's, THEN he or she is studying witchcraft and wizardry. Neville Longbottom is a student at Hogwart's. THEREFORE, Neville Longbottom is studying witchcraft and wizardry.

Logicians have a Latin name for this rule: *modus ponens.* Loosely translated, we can simply call it the *Asserting Rule*—which says something like, "If you have an

IF A, THEN B statement that you know to be true; and if you can *assert* that A is true; then you can conclude that B is true." (IF A, THEN B; A; THEREFORE, B.) It doesn't matter what the subject matter of our argument is. Any argument that follows that rule gives us a conclusion that we can believe.

> If someone was born in London, then he was born in England. Neville was born in London. Therefore, he was born in England.

> If today is Tuesday, then tomorrow is Wednesday. Today is Tuesday. Therefore, tomorrow is Wednesday.

> If a bottle contains poison, then it stands to the left of nettle wine. Bottle 5 contains poison. Therefore, bottle 5 stands to the left of nettle wine.

Or, if you want to keep thinking about the parallel with chess, we can "move" through the premises of an argument to the conclusion, as long as we meet the conditions laid down in this rule.

But what about this argument?

> IF someone is a student at Hogwart's, THEN he or she is studying witchcraft and wizardry. Dudley Dursley is NOT studying witchcraft and wizardry. THEREFORE, Dudley Dursley is NOT a student at Hogwart's.

From a commonsense viewpoint, the conclusion seems right. We're told that Dudley isn't studying witchcraft and wizardry, and that if you're a student at Hogwart's, that's exactly what you're studying. So Dudley can't be at Hogwart's. But this conclusion isn't covered by our *Asserting Rule* (IF A, THEN B; A; THEREFORE, B), so what do we do? Fortunately, this "move" is covered by another rule for precisely such circumstances. Logicians call it *modus tollens,* and we can call it the *Denying Rule.* That is, "If you have an IF A, THEN B statement that you know to be true; and if you can *deny* that B is true; then you can also *deny* that A is true." (IF A, THEN B; NOT-B; *THEREFORE,* NOT-A.) As with our Asserting Rule, it doesn't matter what the subject matter of our argument is. Any argument that follows this rule gives us a legitimate conclusion—only, strictly speaking, it's about what *isn't* the case, not what *is* the case.

> If someone was born in Paris, then he was born in France. Kevin was *not* born in France. Therefore, Kevin was *not* born in Paris.

> If today is Tuesday, then tomorrow is Wednesday. Tomorrow is *not* Wednesday. Therefore, today is *not* Tuesday.

> If a bottle contains poison, then it stands to the left of nettle wine. Bottle 7 does *not* stand to the left of nettle wine. Therefore, bottle 7 does *not* contain poison.

We've discovered two rules so far—our *Asserting Rule* (IF A, THEN B; A; THEREFORE, B) and our *Denying Rule* (IF A, THEN B; NOT-B; THEREFORE, NOT-A). Can we uncover a third one from another argument with a NOT in it—only in a different part of the argument?

> IF someone is a student at Hogwart's, THEN he or she is studying witchcraft and wizardry. Dudley Dursley is NOT a student at Hogwart's. THEREFORE, Dudley Dursley is NOT studying witchcraft and wizardry.

At first, you might think that the conclusion follows from the premises and that this points to another kind of Denying Rule—one in which we deny that the IF part of the first premise is true (IF A, THEN B; NOT-A; THEREFORE, NOT-B). But before you draw that conclusion, look at this version of the argument—only this time applied to Fleur Delacour, a student at Beauxbatons Academy of Magic, the French school for witchcraft and wizardry.

> IF someone is a student at Hogwart's, THEN he or she is studying witchcraft and wizardry. Fleur Delacour is NOT a student at Hogwart's. THEREFORE, Fleur Delacour is NOT studying witchcraft and wizardry.

Since we know that Fleur Delacour is studying witchcraft and wizardry—only at a different school—the conclusion to this argument can't be true. And yet, the argument seemed logical when we applied it to Dudley Dursley a moment ago. What's going on?

Poor, Illogical Thinking: Structural (or Formal) Fallacies

The problem with our arguments about Dudley and Fleur is that we've now gone from good, logical thinking to poor, illogical thinking. How do we identify bad thinking? Fortunately, we do so in a way that's similar to how we recognize good thinking. That is, in the same way that following specific rules guarantees that we'll have a *logical* argument, there are standard ways of *breaking* the rules that guarantee that we'll end up with an *illogical* argument. No matter how much it *looks like* the conclusion follows from the premises, it doesn't.

Offering illogical arguments of this sort is like *cheating* in a game. Imagine that you're playing chess with a friend, and you decide to move your bishop a few squares—but you jump over other pieces to do it. And if your friend challenges the move, you say: "The rules say that bishops can move diagonally. I moved my bishop diagonally. So, the move's OK." Unless your friend truly knows the rules of chess, she may go along with your explanation. But the fact is that you cheated. The rule describing what a bishop can do doesn't really authorize the move you just made.

It's the same in the case of the Dudley and Fleur arguments that we've just been looking at. To "move" from the premises in those two arguments to the conclusions may seem logical, but it actually *breaks* a rule of logic. It's like cheating. Any argument with this form (IF A, THEN B; NOT-A; THEREFORE, NOT-B) is actually illogical. In fact, this classic bit of rule breaking has a specific name in logic: *Denying the Antecedent.* (Logicians call the IF part of a sentence the "antecedent," and the THEN part the "consequent"—hence, "denying the antecedent.") The poor logic here is obvious in these examples.

> IF someone was born in Paris, THEN he or she was born in France. Henri was NOT born in Paris. (Henri was born in Tours.) THEREFORE, Henri was NOT born in France. (The error revealed: If Henri was born in Tours, then he obviously *was* born in France.)

IF it's July, THEN it must be after June. It is NOT July. (It is September.) THEREFORE, it is NOT after June. (The error revealed: September is NOT July but obviously *is* after June.)

In the hands of clever manipulators, it is surprisingly easy to be taken in by bad logic. So it's important to be on guard against this sort of trickery and deception. For example, imagine that a political candidate says, "For the entire time that Senator Smith has been in office, the crime rate in our state has been increasing. And you can count on that continuing as long as he's in Washington because Senator Smith is soft on crime. But if you elect me, my tough, anticrime plan will make that crime rate plummet." It's possible, of course, that this candidate has a good plan for combating crime. However, what he's offered us at this point is nothing more than the following bad argument:

IF Senator Smith remains in office, THEN the crime rate will continue to increase. Elect me and Senator Smith will NOT be in office. THEREFORE, elect me and the crime rate will NOT continue to increase.

So unless this candidate gives us a more convincing argument for why his approach to crime is better than Senator Smith's, not only does he not deserve our vote, he also deserves to be exposed as a manipulator.

Logicians call logical mistakes **fallacies.** The fallacy we've just been looking at (Denying the Antecedent) is considered to be a *structural* or *formal* fallacy because the mistake is in the *structure* or the *form* of the argument. If you take a logic course at some point, you'll learn more structural fallacies. But for the purposes of this textbook, it makes more sense for us to move on to fallacies that we're more likely to run into in everyday life. These are called *informal* fallacies, and they're logical mistakes that appear in the language used or the kind of claims that are made in an argument rather than the formal structure of the argument.

More Poor, Illogical Thinking: Informal Fallacies

Let's approach poor thinking the same way we approached logic in general by means of Hermione's potions dilemma; that is, with an example. Only your challenge now isn't to use logical thinking to solve a puzzle but rather to use it to uncover bad thinking.

Therefore, we'll spend the rest of this chapter looking at badly flawed thinking. The topic of the following dialogue—the relative superiority of the sexes—comes up occasionally among college students. As you read the dialogue, try to spot the problems and—even more important—try to explain what makes the thinking illogical. Most of the fallacies are "informal," but there are a couple of structural fallacies for you to see how they might come up in a real-life discussion.

> **fallacies** Fallacies are weaknesses or mistakes in argumentation. Fallacies concerned with an argument's "form" or logical structure are formal fallacies. Subject-matter fallacies are called informal fallacies.

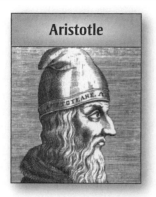

Aristotle

Aristotle (384–322 B.C.) was born in the small town of Stagira in Macedonia, just to the north of Greece proper, into a family with a strong medical tradition. His father was the court physician to the king of Macedonia, and this medical heritage strongly influenced Aristotle's intellectual development. Aristotle's philosophical investigations covered an extraordinary range of topics and were characterized by a largely empirical approach, but he also did work in such natural sciences as biology and astronomy.

Aristotle arrived in Athens at the age of eighteen and studied at Plato's Academy until the death of his teacher some twenty years later. Leaving Athens, Aristotle traveled to Asia Minor, where he seems to have spent a few years studying marine biology. He was then recalled to the Macedonian court in order to tutor the son of King Phillip. The boy was Alexander, whose military conquests subsequently left him remembered as "Alexander the Great." Aristotle returned to Athens in 334 B.C. and established his own school, the Lyceum, where he taught for the next eleven years. The death of Alexander in 323 B.C., however, unleashed a wave of anti-Macedonian sentiment in Athens, and a charge of impiety, a capital offense, was leveled against Aristotle. Rather than allow Athens to "sin twice against philosophy," as Aristotle put it (the philosopher Socrates had been executed on the same charge in 399 B.C.), Aristotle left Athens for an island north of the city, where he died the following year.

The Dialogue

FRANK: Hey, Heather, I've been thinking a lot about this male/female equality thing. I gotta tell you, I just can't see it. All the evidence says that men are superior.

HEATHER: *Men* superior? Are you kidding? The sexes are unequal, all right. But *women* are superior.

FRANK: Come on. Who holds all the athletic records? Who runs the fastest and jumps the highest? Men.

HEATHER: That's just what I'd expect to hear from a man.

FRANK: And you're objective, I suppose?

HEATHER: That's right. Look at the facts. Who lives longer? Women. Who has more heart attacks? Men. Women tolerate pain better than men. What's more, women have always taken care of other people. Men don't do that. They kill each other. These things, not sports, prove natural superiority.

FRANK: But nearly all the world's leaders are men. Same thing in business and politics. And men have always been in charge of their families. That's the way nature meant it to be.

HEATHER: And look at the results—war, famine, and poverty. If women ran the world, it would've been different.

FRANK: What makes you so sure?

HEATHER: It's obvious. Men were in charge, so they were responsible for all the bad stuff we're stuck with. *Women* leaders would have made a better world—like with less war. How many times do you see women getting into a fistfight?

FRANK: See, that's exactly my point. Girls don't duke it out because they have less upper body strength than men. That makes them less able to handle heavy weapons as well as men can. So women aren't as well equipped as men to protect other people. Do you really think that a battalion of babes who cry every time they break a nail could repel an assault by a few companies of seasoned male warriors?

HEATHER: Frank, weren't you listening to me? I said that women don't fight because we're *feminine.* We're talking about the nature of *femininity,* not the size of someone's biceps.

FRANK: But men have traditionally been the protectors and the leaders. Even in a family, the man is the head and the woman is the heart. And what about centuries of economic, political, and technological progress? That came from men being in charge. And you want to throw that away?

HEATHER: You're forgetting that men were tyrants and dictators, too. What about all the poor people who suffered under those men? How would you feel if someone in your family died because of some terrible dictator? Don't you have any compassion?

FRANK: Fine, men aren't perfect, but you're still not looking at the most important fact. *God* put men in charge. The Bible makes it clear in a couple of places. Are you going to tell me that God doesn't know what *He's* talking about?

HEATHER: God? How do you know there even is a God?

FRANK: Heather! You're impossible. Ignore God if you want, but since you're a woman, you can't ignore what would happen to families if men weren't in charge. If women ran things, they'd stop acting like women, divorce would increase, the family would disintegrate, and women would stop having children. Female superiority? Ha! You girls are talking about the end of the human race.

HEATHER: Frank, are all you macho jocks so dim-witted? But I should have expected this from you. You hang out in bars drinking beer and listening to country music with that guy named Hugh. How can I expect good sense from you when you've got such a stupid, male chauvinist friend?

FRANK: Hey! There's no reason to insult my friends. And Hugh knows what he's talking about. In fact, just last week he did a survey on exactly this question for his psychology class, and 80 percent of the people he asked agreed that men are superior.

HEATHER: And I don't suppose that a lot of the people he asked were his beer-guzzling buddies, were they?

FRANK: So what if they were? Everybody knows that women are too emotional about this subject to be objective.

HEATHER: Frank, I don't know what I'm going to do with you. But you haven't proved that men are superior. So I guess that makes me right.

A Thicket of Faulty Thinking

The relative strengths and weaknesses of the two sexes is a perennial subject of conversation. Yet neither Frank nor Heather argues very well when we measure their words against standards of critical thinking. Both make many logical errors; that is, they use unallowed "shortcuts" to try to convince each other. In fact, they make mistakes that are so common that there are even standard labels for them.

People don't usually make so many mistakes in so short a space. But most of the mistakes that these two make involve subject matter rather than logical structure, and this is the kind of weakness we find most often in everyday conversations, in journalism, in speeches, and in advertisements. This dialogue, then, is a fair place to practice judging how convincing the arguments we encounter are.

In addition to paying attention to the specific logical mistakes that infest this conversation, you should also give some thought to *why* the thinking is so faulty. The reasons behind weak thinking are harder to identify than the fallacies themselves, because they are usually subjective and emotional. Fear, loyalty, greed, prejudice, and self-interest are common barriers to clear, effective thinking. We often let such feelings influence our thoughts; we know what conclusion will make us feel better, and we twist our arguments so that they arrive at the predetermined outcome. It may be impossible for us to know what lies behind someone's allegiance to arguments that are objectively unconvincing. However, if you want to develop as a critical thinker, you must at least search your own thoughts and feelings for similar barriers to thinking effectively. Keep this in mind as we work through the dialogue.

1. FRANK: Hey, Heather, I've been thinking a lot about this male/female equality thing. I gotta tell you, I just can't see it. All the evidence says that men are superior.

   HEATHER: *Men* superior? Are you kidding? The sexes are unequal, all right. But *women* are superior.

For all the weak thinking to come, this isn't a bad start. Frank and Heather each begin by stating the conclusions they hope their arguments will prove: "men are superior"/"women are superior." It's in their premises, or reasons for their claims, that they make their logical mistakes.[4]

Ambiguity. There is one problem with the way the discussion opens, however. What kind of "superiority" are they talking about? Physical? Mental? Moral? The term "superiority" can have more than one meaning and this looseness of meaning is bound to make trouble later in the argument. When we use a term that has more than one meaning in an argument, we commit the fallacy called *ambiguity.* Notice how ambiguity comes to play in the next exchange.

2. FRANK: Come on. Who holds all the athletic records? Who runs the fastest and jumps the highest? Men.

   HEATHER: That's just what I'd expect to hear from a man.

---

[4]As mentioned earlier, most of the mistakes Frank and Heather make relate to the subject matter of their statements, not the logical structure. Unless an error is labeled "formal," it is an "informal" fallacy.

FRANK: And you're objective, I suppose?

HEATHER: That's right. Look at the facts. Who lives longer? Women. Who has more heart attacks? Men. Women tolerate pain better than men. What's more, women have always taken care of other people. Men don't do that. They kill each other. These things, not sports, prove natural superiority.

Ambiguity Again. Now you can see how ambiguous the idea "superiority" is. Both disputants start out using the term to mean "physical superiority." But when Heather says that women are caregivers and men are killers, she changes the concept to "moral superiority." The argument is too young for much to ride on this shift of meaning, but at this point, both parties should define their terms and agree on precisely what they're arguing about. If they don't, the entire debate will probably be ill-defined and fuzzy.

In everyday life, we use general terms all the time: "fair," "equal," "moral," "patriotic," and so on. Whenever such a concept comes up in one of your discussions, insist that it be defined specifically. If you don't do that, your argument won't go anywhere.

Hasty Conclusion, Incomplete Evidence. A second mistake that both parties make in this exchange is a combination of *hasty conclusion* and *incomplete evidence*. A hasty conclusion is what you arrive at when you try to prove too much from the evidence you cite. Your evidence may be relevant—it just isn't strong enough to support the conclusion you jump to. The error of *incomplete evidence* occurs when you don't incorporate into your argument all the relevant evidence. Either you ignore contrary evidence or you stop short of examining evidence that is available. In other words, you do not look deeply enough into a question before arriving at an opinion. Hasty conclusion and incomplete evidence often occur together.

Neither speaker gives enough evidence to support his or her claims, even if we limit the debate to physical superiority. Athletic records do not prove Frank's case. World-class athletes are not a representative group. Even if the winner of a marathon race, for example, is always a man, the top women still beat most men in the field. And Frank cites only speed and strength. Heather counters with longevity and endurance.

Heather's points don't settle things either. On average, women do live longer than men. But this need not be due to biological superiority. Women have had fewer heart attacks, but as more women enter high-stress occupations, heart disease among them is on the rise. On that score, their bodies endure no better than men's. Both Frank and Heather, then, draw hasty conclusions from relevant but incomplete evidence.

Ad Hominem. Heather's first comeback contains another weakness. The retort "that's just what I'd expect to hear from a man" is irrelevant because she doesn't address the issue—she attacks Frank. This is called arguing *ad hominem*, a Latin phrase for "against the person." By implying that Frank is biased because he's male, Heather tries to undermine his credibility. She implies that anything he says is wrong because of who he is—a wrongheaded male.

Attacking the source rather than the position is also called a *genetic fallacy* (*genesis* is Greek for "origin") or, more informally, *poisoning the well.* Whatever you call it, the idea is the same. If the source cannot be trusted, anything he says is biased or polluted. This, of course, denies the obvious truth that even bad people can say true and relevant things.

When we argue, we all like to dismiss what the other person says without looking at it carefully. It's very easy just to say that our opponent is "stupid," "a chauvinist," "a radical feminist," "a conservative," "a communist," "a fundamentalist," "an atheist," "a homosexual," or whatever. But logic and the standards of critical thinking don't entitle us to do that. As much as we want to discount people who come up with ideas we dislike, their personal qualities are irrelevant. We must deal with the facts of the argument, not the person doing the arguing.

Contradiction: A Structural Fallacy. Frank's suggestion that Heather is biased as well is quite logical. If he's too prejudiced to argue convincingly for male superiority because he is male, Heather must also be too prejudiced to argue for her side of the question because she is female. Heather dismisses this out of hand. But, in doing so, she contradicts herself.

A *contradiction* is one of the simplest mistakes in arguing. Heather's statements that gender implies bias when it comes to Frank but that gender does not imply bias when it comes to her are in direct opposition to each other. The fact that Heather's assumption that "gender implies bias" is false has nothing to do with it. The reasoning error lies in the contradiction itself.

The weakness of a contradiction lies in the very structure of the statement. So here we come upon a structural fallacy that is different from what we saw previously. If I symbolize the idea that "gender implies bias" with the letter G, I can symbolize the opposite idea, "gender does not imply bias" with *not-G*. So we can represent Heather's contradiction as G and *not-G*.

The essence of a contradiction is that it doesn't matter what G stands for. If you put together one statement with another that denies it, each cancels the other out and you end up saying nothing. It is the verbal equivalent of trying to add -5 to $+5$. All you end up with is 0.

3. FRANK: But nearly all the world's leaders are men. Same thing in business and politics. And men have always been in charge of their families. That's the way nature meant it to be.

HEATHER: And look at the results—war, famine, and poverty. If women ran the world, it would've been different.

FRANK: What makes you so sure?

HEATHER: It's obvious. Men were in charge, so they were responsible for all the bad stuff we're stuck with. *Women* leaders would have made a better world—like with less war. How many times do you see women getting into a fistfight?

Questionable Cause. Granting the ambiguity of the term "superior" and assuming that being "in charge" is relevant to being "superior" in some way, what about the rest of Frank's statement? It is true that most of the world's leaders are men, but

Frank attributes this to the "nature" of things. Apparently, Frank thinks that men are in charge because they are by nature superior.

Here is a clear example of the error called *questionable cause.* This mistake in thinking involves an unwarranted conclusion drawn about the cause of something. Is it possible that most leaders are men because nature has endowed them with a superior ability to assume authority? It's possible, but not very likely. Are other causes of this phenomenon more plausible? Of course—everything from the way boys are socialized to outright discrimination against women. But to miss the obvious causes and insist on a less likely one is to commit the fallacy of *questionable cause.*

Questionable Cause: Post Hoc Ergo Propter Hoc. A special version of questionable cause is worth noting here. It's called *post hoc ergo propter hoc* (Latin for "after this, therefore because of this"). For short, it's just *post hoc.* We make this mistake when we claim that because one event preceded another, the first event must have caused the second. This fallacy is at work when, for example, elected officials claim that every good thing that happened while they were in office happened *because* they were in office. (Of course, their opponents claim that the incumbents caused every *bad* thing that took place.) Heather makes the same mistake when she blames "war, famine, and poverty" on the male leadership that preceded this terrible situation. Causes do precede their effects, of course. But the mere fact that one thing precedes another is not enough to establish it as the cause.

Questionable cause and *post hoc* thinking is faulty because it takes a complicated situation and oversimplifies it. Anyone who makes this mistake overlooks relevant facts or alternative explanations. Look what Heather does. There are many complex reasons for famine, poverty, and war, but the sex of a country's leaders is not one of them.

Denying the Antecedent: A Structural Fallacy. Heather's second statement in this segment may strike you as plausible. Yet her very first line, "men were in charge, so they were responsible" involves a *post hoc* fallacy. Then she gets to her conclusion, "women leaders would have made a better world," by claiming that if men are *not* in charge (and women *are*), then there will not be war and misery. This may sound logical, but it's not because this is an example of the first structural fallacy we identified earlier, *denying the antecedent.*

If we reconstruct Heather's argument, the fallacy is more apparent:

IF men are in charge, THEN we have war, famine, and poverty.

IF men are NOT in charge (that is, if women are in charge), THEN we do NOT have war, famine, and poverty.

This is the same kind of illogical argument that we saw previously in the example:

IF someone is a student at Hogwart's, THEN he or she is studying witchcraft and wizardry.

Fleur Delacour is NOT a student at Hogwart's.

THEREFORE, Fleur Delacour is NOT studying witchcraft and wizardry.

Heather's argument here is just as weak.

Contrary-to-Fact Conditional. Still another content fallacy crops up here. It's closely related to what Heather is trying to conclude by denying the antecedent, so look closely at how it differs from what we were just looking at.

If Heather's claim that "*women* leaders would have made a better world" is right, it would blunt Frank's assertion that nature has made men superior leaders. But Heather speaks as though it's a fact that things would be different if women had been in charge. How can she know something like this? Perhaps the point can be argued plausibly, but that's not what she does here.

What she does do is give us what's called a *contrary-to-fact conditional.* (The technical name for this is *hypothetical, contrafactual.*) A *conditional* is any "if-then" statement. Heather uses a conditional, or hypothetical, statement ("if women led the world") that is contrary to the facts (most leaders are men). The problem, however, lies in the conclusion Heather draws (world history would have been dramatically different, and we wouldn't have had all this tragedy). There is no way to know that things would be different if women had been world leaders. The factors that bring about peace and prosperity are too complicated for anybody to be sure what would have happened if women had been in charge.

Not all contrary-to-fact conditionals are illogical. You could say with a fair degree of confidence, for example, that if you had unplugged your refrigerator yesterday, then all the ice cubes would have melted. We can be confident of simple, well-established statements of cause and effect. But most matters that we argue about are far more complicated, and you must guard against contrary-to-fact conditionals in your own arguments.

Hasty Conclusion and Incomplete Evidence, Again. One final problem in this exchange occurs with the reappearance of *hasty conclusion* and *incomplete evidence.* (In an argument, of course, the same mistakes can appear over and over again in different guises.) This time, Heather tries to prove the point that women are less warlike than men by asking, "How many times do you see women getting into a fistfight?" Clearly, she expects an answer of "not many."

If this answer established that women were less hostile than men, she would have a point. But it doesn't. Most psychologists believe that men and women are equally hostile and aggressive, they just express those feelings differently. Men express their hostility more directly and more physically. Some women do slug it out, but most women respond less overtly.

Even if women in general were less hostile, that would not mean that individual women who rise to power are any less likely than men to wage war. After all, those women—and men—who are gentle, compassionate, and peace loving do not usually seek military or political power. So far, female political leaders haven't acted any differently than men. Look at women like Elizabeth I and Catherine the Great. And twentieth-century leaders like Golda Meir, Indira Gandhi, and Margaret Thatcher have certainly held their own with any man when it came to waging war.

Once again, Heather's argument rests on *hasty conclusion* and *incomplete evidence*. On that basis, her conclusion is unwarranted.

> **4. FRANK:** See, that's exactly my point. Girls don't duke it out because they have less upper body strength than men. That makes them less able to handle heavy weapons as well as men can. So women aren't as well equipped as men to protect other people. Do you really think that a battalion of babes who cry every time they break a nail could repel an assault by a few companies of seasoned male warriors?
>
> **HEATHER:** Frank, weren't you listening to me? I said that women don't fight because we're *feminine*. We're talking about the nature of *femininity*, not the size of someone's biceps.

Irrelevant Reason, Questionable Conclusion, and Straw Man. Frank combines a few fallacies here, which isn't unusual. Bad thinking is easy and seductive—once people get rolling, they often just pick up speed and compound the problem by making one illogical claim after another.

Frank starts by suggesting that Heather's point about female fistfights can be explained by differences in upper body strength between men and women. However, while a smaller woman may avoid picking a fight with a man because he has a huge chest, shoulder, and arm muscles, differences between men and women are *irrelevant* here. Two women who get angry with each other don't think to themselves, "If only I had arms like a man, I'd slug that witch." Comparative anatomical differences are irrelevant.

Frank next draws the *questionable conclusion* that less upper body strength means that women can't handle heavy weapons. He seems to imagine that all weapons are like massive, medieval broadswords—which they aren't. He also ignores the fact that the proper use of leverage can often compensate for a lack of brute strength. He then draws a second *questionable conclusion* when he claims on the basis of this that women are less able to protect other people. Many weapons are light and easy to use, and military strategy isn't the province of men only. So there's no plausible connection between body strength and the ability to protect other people.

Once we get to Frank's comment about "a battalion of babes who cry every time they break a nail," however, the point of his first couple of comments is clear. He's giving us a picture of women's abilities (or, rather, lack of abilities) that is supposed to make his position seem too obvious to challenge. In reality, he's greatly misrepresenting women's abilities. The fallacy here is called *straw man*. The very label suggests that when we commit this fallacy, we're trying to characterize someone else's position in such a way that it's easy to knock down.

Begging the Question. We have to give Heather credit for her initial response because she tries to draw Frank back to the point she wanted to make. However, she goes on to commit a new fallacy—*begging the question* or *circular reasoning*.

The mistake is very apparent when we take what Heather says and reconstruct it into argument form.

1. Women are "feminine"; that is, they aren't physically aggressive. [**Premise**]

2. Therefore, women aren't physically aggressive; that is, they don't fight. [**Conclusion**]

As you see, the premise and the conclusion make the same point. Heather's simply gone in a circle—hence, the label *circular reasoning.* The heart of this fallacy is that we take the point that we're trying to *prove,* and we simply *assume* that it's true. Heather hasn't given us any reason to believe her point about women not fighting. She simply restates the same claim twice. She uses different words, but it amounts to saying the same thing. Instances of this fallacy can sometimes be very elaborate and may seem appropriately technical and sophisticated. But it doesn't change the fact that—as far as the argument goes—we've never left the starting gate.

By doing this, Heather is refusing to answer the question: "Why is the claim about women and fistfights relevant to the issue we're discussing?" or "How does the point about women and fistfights support the general claim that women are su-perior to men?" That is, Heather is "begging off" answering the question—hence, the label *begging the question.*[5]

> **5. FRANK:**   But men have traditionally been the protectors and the leaders. Even in a fam-ily, the man is the head and the woman is the heart. And what about centuries of economic, political, and technological progress? That came from men being in charge. And you want to throw that away?
>
> **HEATHER:**   You're forgetting that men were tyrants and dictators, too. What about all the poor people who suffered under those men? How would you feel if someone in your family died because of some terrible dictator? Don't you have any compassion?

Appeal to Authority. Here Frank suggests that persistent traditions must have good reasons behind them. Without any analysis of those reasons, however, this is just another fallacy, *appeal to authority* or *appeal to traditional wisdom.* Many traditions work well and endure for good reason, but not all. So what if men have tradition-ally been in charge of families? The mere fact that something is done doesn't es-tablish it as a good thing. That something is a tradition means nothing more than that. Frank's argument is a barefaced appeal to authority, not logic.

Appeal to authority and genetic fallacies like *ad hominem* are two sides of the same coin. *Ad hominem* tries to discredit an argument by disparaging its source. Appeal to authority tries to prove a point by overvaluing its source. In both cases, the arguer tries to short-circuit the argument by sidestepping the requirement to stick to relevant evidence.

Appeals to authority come in many varieties. Sometimes the authority is amor-phous, like traditional wisdom. But sometimes it's specific, like the testimony of a single person. If you argue with a friend about economics and she says, "You're wrong because Milton Friedman thinks differently," she's appealing to Friedman as an authority. The Nobel-winning economist may very well be right, but you don't hear Friedman's reasons, only his conclusion, as if that settled the matter. When ex-perts themselves make pronouncements without spelling out their reasons, it's the same thing. However you cut it, their opinions alone do not prove anything.

---

[5]In everyday parlance, the term "beg the question" is regularly misused to mean "suggests another related question." For example: "Your point about the harm that comes from athletes using performance-enhancing drugs *begs the ques-tion* of why athletes would even consider using drugs in the first place." So don't be confused when you run into this usage.

We also very commonly appeal to the authority of this or that group of people. Yet this is the fallacy of *popularity, democracy,* or *numbers.* You should know by now that the number of people who agree with an idea says absolutely nothing about whether it is true or false. At different times, millions of people thought that the earth was flat, the sun moved around the earth, the atom could not be split, and people other than white males were inferior. These majority opinions, however, were all wrong. The legitimacy of an idea stands or falls on knowledge, proof, and logic, not popularity.

False Analogy. "Even in a family, the man is the head and the woman is the heart," Frank says. This figure of speech in which you talk about one thing as if it were something else is called an analogy. In an analogy you establish a similarity between things and, thus, a comparison. Analogies can illustrate a point in a short, colorful fashion, but they must be accurate. Unfortunately, Frank's analogy isn't. Thus, he bases his position on yet another mistake, *false analogy.*

The suggestion that the family is like a human body means that it can have only one head that controls all the other functions of the body. But a family is not a body, and it doesn't resemble one in any way. At the very least, a family has as many "heads" as there are family members. At best, the analogy is too weak to bear Frank's conclusion. And on this basis, Frank's argument doesn't get off the ground.

Questionable Cause or Irrelevant Reason. Next Frank attributes "centuries of progress" to male leadership. As we have noted already, the reasons behind social, political, economic, and technological progress are extremely complex. Indeed, male leadership could easily be irrelevant to the issue, and basing a case on an irrelevant reason is obviously faulty thinking. Here it's difficult to tell whether the fallacy is *questionable cause* or *irrelevant reason.*

False Dilemma. So far, Frank and Heather have usually drawn unwarranted conclusions from relevant premises. But now Frank posits a faulty premise by creating a *false dilemma.* In this fallacy a speaker distorts the situation in which a decision must be made, giving you fewer options to pick from than is actually the case. All but one of the alternatives is then described as unthinkable, ruling out every possibility except, not surprisingly, the choice the speaker favors.

Frank's rhetorical question to Heather ("And you want to throw that away?") implies "It comes down to male leadership and prosperity or female rulers and poverty." Since poverty is unacceptable, the only choice is the governance of men. But Frank is deliberately stacking the deck in his favor. Female leaders can bring about prosperity. So can men and women working together. So when someone tells you that your choice is between wonderful option A or terrible option B, assume you're being handed a *false dilemma* and look for the truth.

Appeal to Emotions. Heather is right to challenge Frank's reliance on the past, but she now launches into a new fallacy of her own, an *appeal to emotion.* An appeal to emotion is similar to irrelevant reason. It's an attempt by a speaker to sway or persuade you by appealing to your feelings, not your mind, and this is always inappropriate in a philosophical argument.

Note that "swaying" and "persuading" are very different from "convincing." When you try to convince someone of something, you offer the most rational, objective facts and arguments you can find in order to present the truth of a matter. But when you want to sway or persuade somebody, you're not so worried about objectivity and truth as about how to get someone to go along with what you want. If you can bypass their rational, critical faculties, so much the better. If you ask for some special treatment from your professor—an extension on your paper or a chance to retake an exam—you don't worry that it isn't fair to everyone else in the class. You don't feel badly that your professor goes along with you because you made her feel sorry for you—that's what you wanted. When you try to sway or persuade somebody, then, you appeal to her heart instead of her head.

Heather tries to stir Frank's sympathy for those who have suffered at the hands of tyrants. She asks him to imagine how he would feel if someone close to him met such a fate. This attempt to shift attention from objective facts to subjective feelings clouds rather than clarifies the issue.

> **6.** FRANK: Fine, men aren't perfect, but you're still not looking at the most important fact. *God* put men in charge. The Bible makes it clear in a couple of places. Are you going to tell me that God doesn't know what *He's* talking about?
>
> HEATHER: God? How do you know there even is a God?

Appeal to Religious Authority. Frank now tries an appeal to a different, higher authority, God. Alluding to texts from the Bible, he assumes it proves his case. But this is not convincing in a philosophical argument. Philosophy is a rational enterprise that investigates matters using the mind. Rejecting an appeal to the authority of the Bible, then, does not mean we reject religion. It's just playing by the rules of critical thinking and logic.

It doesn't matter whether it's a line from the Bible or from Socrates. What is important are the reasons behind the authority's position, not the position itself. The reasoning, not the assertions, tells us whether or not an opinion is logical and persuasive. The authority may have a good argument, but maybe not.

If you're a religious person, however, you may feel uneasy with this. The teachings of your religion's prophets, teachers, priests, mullahs, ministers, rabbis, or elders are important to you. You'd have a hard time saying to yourself that your opinion counts just as much as that of Abraham, Jesus, Mohammed, Confucius, or the Buddha. This natural and understandable tension, the problem of faith versus reason, has been present throughout history and is a philosophical issue in its own right.

For now, we are limiting ourselves to the rules of philosophy wherein we come to conclusions via reason and evidence. We do not assert something as true simply because somebody else says it is true, no matter who says it. The reasons behind some authoritative pronouncement may be important, but concluding something because of the pronouncement alone is bound to be a mistake.

Accent, Unknowable Fact. Frank continues to push his appeal to authority subtly as well. A combination of fallacies lies behind his question, "Are you going to tell me that God doesn't know what *HE's* talking about?" Obviously, he tries to cash in on the perfection of divine wisdom. That is a blatant *appeal to authority.* Notice also that he does this simply by emphasizing one word, "*He.*" What meaning does this emphasis convey? Something like "if God is divine, perfect, and male, being male must be superior to being female." That is a lot to pack into one word. And Frank does it without having to spell it out.

This emphasis illustrates the *fallacy of accent.* Here, a speaker tries to convince you of something just by the way she or he says it. This may be done by emphasis that distorts the meaning of something. Or it may be done by quoting somebody out of context. The fallacy of accent is rampant in political speeches in which one candidate distorts the meaning of an opponent's words. You also find it in advertisements for books, movies, and plays. A critic may write, "This flick is unbelievable! How could anything be this bad?" But a subsequent ad for the film may simply quote "This flick is unbelievable!" implying that the critic liked it.

In the argument we're examining here, Frank uses the fallacy of accent to slip something by without arguing his point. Moreover, his point is probably irrelevant. Even if God were male, the debate is over the relative superiority of male versus female *humans,* not gods.

Furthermore, billions of people on this planet believe in multiple gods, female gods, or no gods at all. Given this variety of beliefs, is it even possible for anyone to know what Frank claims to know? If not, as Heather is aware, we have another error, the fallacy of *unknowable fact.* This occurs when somebody tries to pass off something as established fact that cannot possibly be known.

> **7.** FRANK: Heather! You're impossible. Ignore God if you want, but since you're a woman, you can't ignore what would happen to families if men weren't in charge. If women ran things, they'd stop acting like women, divorce would increase, the family would disintegrate, and women would stop having children. Female superiority? Ha! You girls are talking about the end of the human race.
>
> Heather: Frank, are all you macho jocks so dim-witted? But I should have expected this from you. You hang out in bars drinking beer and listening to country music with that guy named Hugh. How can I expect good sense from you when you've got such a stupid, male chauvinist friend?

Unwarranted Generalization (Stereotypical Thinking). Frank's shock at Heather's questioning his appeal to divine authority does not keep him from making new errors. First, he automatically assumes that because Heather is female, she is oriented toward family issues: marriage, divorce, and children. The traditional roles of our society have encouraged many women to think this way, but that does not allow Frank to conclude anything here. His attempt to do just this is called the fallacy of *unwarranted,* or *sweeping, generalization.* We cannot generalize accurately about all women, or all members of any group, from the characteristics of some of them. Moreover, Frank appeals to a *stereotype* of what women are or "should" be like, and stereotypes are usually wrong.

Unwarranted generalization closely resembles hasty conclusion. Both errors involve drawing conclusions without enough evidence. The critical difference between the two is that unwarranted generalization concludes something about all members of a group.

Slippery Slope. Frank's other new error comes in his response to Heather's earlier claim that female leadership would mean a better world. Frank contends that the actual result would be "the end of the human race." But his reasoning is faulty, an example of slippery slope thinking.

Slippery slope is a special version of *hasty conclusion.* As the name implies, it is the mental version of tripping on a rock and tumbling down a hill so fast that you cannot stop. In logic, once you fall, it's an express trip to the unwarranted conclusions at the bottom. For example, Frank describes the chain of events from female leadership to the end of humanity as if it were a row of dominoes—once the first one falls, the rest follow. But if you look at the real situation, such dire events are by no means inevitable.

This is an extreme example, but the fallacy is common. People often assert that some particular event will lead to disaster as surely as this book will hit the floor if you drop it. So if you find someone suggesting a chain-like string of events, look to see if you're going down a slippery slope.

Emotional Language: Sexism and Name-Calling. *Emotional language* constitutes another fallacy because it is used to make a point without arguing for it logically. Some words are emotionally neutral; others are highly charged, positively and negatively. Thus, word choice dramatically affects the picture of reality presented to the listener. For example, are people who fight against their own government "an opposing faction," "revolutionary fanatics," or "freedom fighters"? All these phrases describe the same people, but the slanted language prejudges the issue of whether this "opposing faction" is good or bad.

At this point in the discussion, both Frank and Heather resort to emotional language. Frank calls women "girls"; Heather calls him a "macho jock." Heather also says Frank is "dim-witted," and labels his friend "sexist" and "a stupid, male chauvinist." None of this is appropriate to respectable argument, of course.

In fact, these two are not arguing any more, they are *name-calling.* Both disputants also specifically choose sexist epithets. Insults do not prove anything. *Sexist language* and *name-calling* are irrelevant to whatever issue you discuss, and you should always avoid them.

When a discussion turns in this direction, do not respond in kind. If your opponent is so frustrated that he or she attacks you, all rational discussion is over and it is pointless to go on. Your opponent may claim victory, but don't fall for it. People who resort to insults do so because they know they have failed to convince you. It may be small consolation, but being the target of personal insults is a sign that your opponent has lost control.

Guilt by Association. Heather also fires her insults at Frank's friend Hugh. Even if it were generally agreed that Hugh is "a stupid, male chauvinist" who likes beer and country music, does that in any way support Heather's argument or undermine Frank's? Not at all. Frank and Hugh's taste in drinks and music is irrelevant to the argument. And Heather also makes a new kind of fallacious argument, *guilt by association.*

Like *ad hominem* and irrelevant reason, guilt by association takes our attention off the merits of an argument and focuses it on some aspect of the argument's source. It is like *ad hominem* in that it attacks someone's credibility. But it does this by linking one's opponent with undesirable associates and then insisting that they all share the same bad qualities. It's like saying that if, for example, a politician can be connected with someone said to be an organized crime figure, then everything the politician says is suspect because he is really "just a puppet of the Mob."

Frank is entitled to have his arguments judged on their own merits. He may hang out in bars and have a sexist friend, but that doesn't mean that everything he says is wrong. Even if he is wrong, Heather must refute his arguments logically. She cannot just dismiss them.

> 8. FRANK: Hey! There's no reason to insult my friends. And Hugh knows what he's talking about. In fact, just last week he did a survey on exactly this question for his psychology class, and 80 percent of the people he asked agreed that men are superior.
>
> HEATHER: And I don't suppose that a lot of the people he asked were his beer-guzzling buddies, were they?
>
> FRANK: So what if they were? Everybody knows that women are too emotional about this subject to be objective.
>
> HEATHER: Frank, I don't know what I'm going to do with you. But you haven't proved that men are superior. So I guess that makes me right.

Statistical Fallacy, Popularity. These two continue to make bad arguments right up to the end. Here Frank gives us a *statistical fallacy* based on an *unrepresentative sample.* Hugh may well have found that 80 percent of the people he surveyed said that men are superior. But his sample came mostly from the male patrons of one particular bar. Heather, of course, calls Frank on this, but inappropriately. When she characterizes the sample as Hugh's "beer-guzzling buddies," she's back to attacking the source. Stated more objectively, the problem is that this group hardly represents the entire population. And even if it were representative, it wouldn't contribute anything to the discussion. It would just be another example of the fallacy of *popularity.* That most people think something is no guarantee that they are right. Frank makes an unwarranted appeal to the authority of the crowd.

British statesman Benjamin Disraeli once said, "There are lies, damn lies, and statistics." This is a good line to remember. Hugh's results are obviously unreliable, but many statistics that look better than Hugh's are just as shaky. When you encounter statistics in somebody's argument, look behind the numbers to see where they came from.

Unwarranted, Sweeping Generalization (Stereotypical Thinking), Again. Frank counters with a challenge to women's objectivity, but he falls back into a mistake he made earlier. He has accepted a stereotype of what women are like and he wants to use it in the argument. He makes the *unwarranted* and *sweeping generalization* that all women are alike. And he tries to pass this off as fact with the expression you have no doubt heard too often, "everybody knows. . . ."

Appeal to Ignorance. Both parties to this argument remain unconvinced and rightly so. But Heather now claims that Frank's failure to prove his case means that she's right. That is fallacious too. In fact, it's a variation on *hasty conclusion* called *appeal to ignorance.*

We regularly see this fallacy at work in the arguments of traditional medical practitioners against various alternative, untraditional therapies. "There's no scientific evidence about how any of these approaches work," some physician might assert, "so it's all quackery." The absence of evidence, however, doesn't prove quite that much. Evidence that supports these approaches is relevant to the question. But it might be that the evidence has not yet been accumulated. The only place where not proving your case counts for anything is in a court of law, and that's because we presume innocence. In an ordinary argument, you cannot build your own case on the fact that other people cannot prove theirs. All that may mean is that your opponents are poor at arguing.

Barriers to Effective Thinking

You have now been exposed to a daunting variety of common errors in thinking. Whenever you encounter any of them, know that the speaker's conclusion rests on shaky ground.

Why do people argue this way? These fallacies are not difficult to understand, so why is there so much uncritical thinking going on?

The easiest explanation is probably that loose, ineffective thinking results from the force of habit, inertia, or laziness. We simply do not want to change, and critical thinking requires hard work, energy, and discipline. The ideas we're familiar with make us feel secure, and we see no reason to change things.

Negative emotions like fear probably have more to do with it, however. The topic discussed between Frank and Heather, for example, is not only controversial but also threatening to both participants. The "loser" in the dispute is put in a vulnerable position and feels fear, anxiety, apprehension, and worry about the consequences of "inferiority." With all that on the line, it's no wonder that Frank and Heather argue as they do. When you're worried about safety and security, it feels more important to win the argument than to worry about being logical. At times like that, we seek victory, not truth.

Take politics, for example. What's at stake? Power. What's the risk? Watching someone else put through laws and policies that may be to your disadvantage. How does that make you feel? Probably threatened and a little afraid. Again, with those feelings inside you, the desire to win by any means, say, by attacking the character of the other candidate, can easily be stronger than wanting to argue logically.

Emotions like worry and fear also underlie the ordinary selfishness that seems to drive our use of fallacies. We want what *we* want, and we don't care about other people. So we use our persuasive powers to get our way. Yet whether we realize it or not, we are treating other people as competitors or out-and-out enemies, and we probably feel that we can't trust them. They may keep us from getting what we need. They are a threat, a force to be feared.

Or consider prejudice. Prejudiced people may be angry and hateful to those they discriminate against, but they may also be afraid of them. People whose skin color, gender, sexual orientation, or ethnic background differs from ours usually make us uncomfortable. We commonly feel uneasy about people unlike ourselves. We don't know what they'll do or how they'll treat us. At best, we keep our distance until we find out what they're like. When we learn they're no different from us, we're no longer afraid of them. But until we know that, we try to keep them from getting enough power to threaten us, and part of that is indulging in biased, faulty thinking. In other words, we give in to our fear and let it cloud our minds.

One of the strongest barriers to good thinking, then, is fear. Fear may show itself as anger, envy, selfishness, or hatred, but these are just expressions of our fear. And don't underrate the power of such emotions. History has shown what devastation fear and hatred among nations can wreak. Our personal fears can be just as damaging to our inner world, blinding our critical faculties with their dark energies. When we argue, then, we must be aware of what we feel as well as what we think. A good critical thinker may have to scrutinize not only the intellectual character of an argument but its emotional temperature as well.

One Last Word About Logic

By now you should have a good idea of the analytical and critical nature of philosophical thinking. You should be able to analyze a concept by identifying its necessary and sufficient conditions. You should be able to recognize an argument, identify its premises and conclusions, understand in general what is convincing and unconvincing, and catch the most common logical fallacies.

And you should also be more sensitive to faulty thinking in everyday life. As you look around, you will find fallacious arguments everywhere—at work, in newspaper articles and editorials, in discussions with family and friends, even, yes, in classrooms. Some people argue this way on purpose; others do it out of ignorance. But no matter what the intention, the result is still the same. Faulty thinking can compromise our freedom and our ability to control our own lives.

Main Points of Chapter 2

1. Philosophers use a special kind of thinking that is analytical and critical.

2. Analytical thinking breaks the general concepts under inquiry into smaller ideas. In practice, this amounts to searching for a specific definition of the ideas or concepts under investigation.

3. The definition of a concept involves identifying the conditions that are individually necessary and jointly sufficient in order for something to be an example of that concept. This is done by using model cases, examples, and counterexamples.

4. Critical thinking involves judging whether or not some claim or contention is believable and convincing, that is, whether it is based on solid facts and good reasons. Philosophical thinking is critical thinking in that its primary focus is on arguments.

5. An argument is a series of statements, one of which is a claim (conclusion), and the rest of which are the reasons (premises) for making this claim.

6. Logic is the part of philosophy that establishes guidelines for arguments.

7. The logical errors that we encounter in ordinary discussion generally involve the subject matter, rather than the logical structure of an argument, and are called "informal fallacies."

Discussion Questions

1. Identify the necessary and sufficient conditions for doing well in this course.

2. Take a newspaper editorial and identify the argument: the premises and the conclusion. How good an argument is it?

3. Is it fair to label *ad hominem* a fallacy? Why should we treat everyone's arguments alike? If someone is a manipulator, or in some other way dishonest or disreputable, isn't he or she probably up to no good? Why shouldn't we be able to discount his or her arguments because of that? By the same token, aren't there some authorities whom we should simply believe?

4. What is your reaction to the fallacious thinking and appeals to emotion used in advertising? Does it really convince people? Is there anything wrong with it?

5. Considering how much the public good is determined by the outcome of our elections, would you support a law requiring that no candidate may make unwarranted, illogical claims in his or her speeches, advertisements, and campaign literature? Is there any reasonable way that anyone could not support such a law? Wouldn't opposing such a law amount to supporting intellectual dishonesty and trickery? How could that be consistent with democracy?

6. What does the pervasiveness of weak thinking say about our society? Is good thinking too tough? Are we simply too selfish to be intellectually honest?

7. Look at your own attempts to convince other people. When are you most likely to "finesse" things with faulty thinking? What lies behind it?

Selected Readings

For a more detailed account of the process involved in analyzing a concept see John Wilson, *Thinking With Concepts* (Cambridge: Cambridge University Press, 1963). The following are good guides for critical thinking and logic: Vincent E. Barry and Joel Rudinow, *Invitation to Critical Thinking* (Fort Worth, TX: Holt, Rinehart, Winston, 1990); Connie A. Missimer, *Good Arguments: An Introduction to Critical Thinking* (Englewood Cliffs, NJ: Prentice Hall, 1990); and Vincent Ryan Ruggiero, *Beyond Feelings: A Guide to Critical Thinking* (Mountain View, CA: Mayfield Publishing, 1990). For two interesting and comprehensive treatments of informal fallacies, see S. Morris Engel, *With Good Reason: An Introduction to Informal Fallacies* (New York: St. Martin's Press, 1986) and Howard Kahane, *Logic and Contemporary Rhetoric: The Use of Reason in Everyday Life* (Belmont, CA: Wadsworth Publishing, 1980). For an introduction to symbolic logic, see, for example, Irving M. Copi, *Introduction to Logic* (New York: Macmillan, 1982).

Appendix: An Overview of the Fallacies

Subject Matter ("Informal") Fallacies

Accent: Implying something (rather than arguing for it) by the way a speaker states a point. This can be done by emphasizing words in certain ways or by quoting someone out of context.

Ad hominem: Latin for arguing "against the person." Trying to undermine an argument by attacking the arguer rather than the reasons he or she cites. This is a special version of *irrelevant reason* because *who* quotes facts is irrelevant to whether they are true and relevant to an alleged conclusion. (Any attack of an argument's source rather than the argument itself is called a *genetic fallacy.*)

Ambiguity: When a term can have more than one meaning in an argument.

Appeal to authority: The flip side of *ad hominem*—trying to prove a point by relying on the authority of its source. The authority can be of an individual, the majority, traditional wisdom, a religion, or the like.

Appeal to emotions: Trying to sway or persuade people by appealing to their feelings, not their minds.

Appeal to ignorance: Claiming that something is true because it cannot be shown to be false.

Begging the question (circular reasoning): *Assuming* to be true what the argument is supposed to *prove* as true.

Contrary to fact conditional: Claiming with absolute certainty that if past events had been different, the outcome would also have been different.

Emotional and sexist language, name-calling: Closely related to appeal to emotions. Describing a situation with emotionally loaded words that slant and distort the account. Hurling personal insults.

False analogy: Using a comparison that does not fit the case at hand.

False dilemma: Misrepresenting a situation by claiming there are fewer options than is actually the case.

Guilt by association: A genetic fallacy in which an argument's source is attacked less directly than in *ad hominem.* Trying to undermine someone by linking him or her with unsavory friends or associates.

Hasty conclusion: Trying to prove too much from your evidence. The evidence is relevant; it just is not strong enough to let you draw the conclusion you want.

Incomplete evidence: Not incorporating relevant evidence into an argument.

Irrelevant reason: Just what it suggests. Facts or theories that do not bear on the matter under discussion.

Questionable cause: Drawing an unwarranted conclusion about the cause of something.

Questionable cause: *post hoc: Post hoc ergo propter hoc* is Latin for "After this, therefore because of this." Assumption that just because one event preceded another, it must have caused it.

Slippery slope: A special version of hasty conclusion, claims that one event will trigger a devastating chain reaction.

Statistical fallacies: Using questionable statistics to reach unwarranted conclusions. Mistakes can involve everything from research design to the method of collecting data, to the sample polled, to the conclusions drawn from the data.

Straw man: Exaggerating or distorting a position to make it easier to refute.

Unknowable fact: Citing a fact that cannot possibly be known and objectively confirmed.

Unwarranted or sweeping generalization: Having insufficient grounds to generalize, arguing from stereotypes, or assuming that what is true of some members of a group is true of all members.

Structural ("Formal") Fallacies

Affirming the consequent: Claiming that if the consequent (then-part) of a particular if-then statement is true, then so is the antecedent (if-part).

Contradiction: Asserting or implying directly opposite statements "A" and "not-A."

Denying the antecedent: Claiming that if the antecedent (if-part) of a particular if-then statement is not true, then neither is the consequent (then-part).

The Case for Determinism

As you're walking along the street one day, you pick up a wallet lying on the sidewalk. You're stunned to find that it's stuffed with $100 bills. A driver's license tells you that the owner lives in a very expensive part of town; a business card identifies her as the president of a major corporation; a receipt from a bank machine gives the hefty balance in a savings account. The wallet clearly belongs to someone very well off.

Now you face a choice. Are you going to return the wallet? Will you keep the cash or leave it there? Will you return the wallet anonymously or identify yourself in the hope of receiving a reward? Or will you just take the cash and throw the wallet into the next trash can you see?

This scenario describes a common human experience—you must now make a *choice,* and it's totally *your* choice. No one is there forcing a particular alternative on you. You are *free* to do what you want.

Suppose you decide to give the wallet back—cash and all—and I ask you to explain yourself.

ME: Why return it? You could use the money.

You: It's the right thing to do. It doesn't belong to me.

ME: You mean you'd feel guilty if you kept it?

You: Yeah . . . I really want the money but I keep thinking that my parents would be disappointed and furious if they knew I didn't give it all back. I can't keep it.

ME: But your folks would never find out.

You: It doesn't matter. I'll still feel too guilty. I can't do it.

Or let's say you keep the money.

> Me: How come?
>
> You: Look, I need it more than she does. Besides, rich people really make me mad. It serves her right to lose the money.
>
> Me: But the money doesn't belong to you.
>
> You: That's life. You know, "finders keepers." It's the law of the street.

In each scenario, you've freely chosen one option over another—on the surface. But is your choice totally free? You mention guilt as a motive for giving the money back. Then we see anger, even vengeance, mixed in with your decision to keep it. Doesn't the presence of these feelings suggest that your decision may be less than totally free? You would probably *feel* free, no matter what you did. But does that prove you *are* free? In fact, are we actually free in anything we do? Or, at least, are we as free as we feel we are?

It seems so obvious that we're free that it may seem ridiculous to question it. But many reputable thinkers unconditionally deny it. They argue that what you do with the wallet is entirely out of your hands, that forces beyond your control determine your actions.

The issue here is one of the most fundamental philosophical questions connected with being human. Do we have the freedom to choose, or control, our actions? And if we believe that we do, is that freedom real or an illusion? The dilemma is usually referred to as the issue of *free will versus determinism.*

The theory of **free will** expresses our everyday experience of feeling free. Those who argue for free will maintain that we have the capacity to size up a situation, think about our options, and choose how we will act. What we do, then, is the result of our own, deliberate free choice. **Determinism** maintains exactly the opposite. Determinists claim that everything in nature happens as a result of *cause and effect,* and this includes human behavior. If every effect already has a cause, then our actions and our choices are simply the result of some preexisting causes that produce them, and they cannot be freely arrived at.

This issue is complex enough to deserve two chapters of explanation, one for each side. You have probably always assumed that you have free will, so let's start with the best arguments for the other side, *determinism.*

---

free will Free will claims that we have control over our actions. Our deeds are seen as the product of reflection and choice, not internal or external causal forces.

determinism Determinists deny "free will" and maintain that everything in nature, including human behavior, happens as a result of cause and effect. If every effect already has a cause, then our actions and our choices are simply the result of some preexisting causes that produce them, and they cannot be freely arrived at.

What Do We Mean by Freedom?

All of us ordinarily *feel* free to do what we like. At this moment you feel free to put this book down and do something else. Whatever you do—get something to eat, jog, go to sleep, or continue reading—seems to be your choice. In the case of the found wallet, you seem to be free to return the money, keep it, split the windfall with your best friend, or give it to charity. We *feel* free. But *are* we free?

Let's examine the wallet example using a commonsense definition of freedom, such as that "free" means that you aren't being forced to do something and that you can choose your actions. In other words, we are free if there are no constraints on our actions.

Constrained by Force

If we apply this definition to the wallet scenario, it does appear that you are free. The choice about what to do with the wallet is entirely yours. The only way you would not be free is if the decision were taken away from you—if the owner of the wallet returned, for example, saw you looking through it, threw you to the ground, and grabbed the wallet out of your hands. She used force to make you hand it over, so your action wasn't freely chosen.

Constrained by Pressure

But what about pressure? Pressure isn't force, but doesn't it too limit our freedom? You're standing on the sidewalk looking in the wallet when someone sticks a gun in your ribs and says, "Hand it over!" You aren't being forced, but you are being threatened. You're still free to resist the mugger. You do have that option—although if you exercise it you may get hurt. But, to be realistic about it, you certainly don't *feel* free in this circumstance. You're being intimidated and coerced in a way that would make *99* out of 100 people feel they had no choice and give in.

Or, to be less dramatic, suppose that you're with your boyfriend or girlfriend when you find the wallet and he or she is shocked when you say you're keeping the money. As the two of you walk along, your friend says, "It's stealing, and I'm not going to be involved with somebody who's dishonest. You can do what you like, but forget about me forever." If you're in love with this person, this can feel like very strong pressure. You're still free to choose, but you surely don't feel as free as if you had been alone when you found the wallet.

Constrained by Feelings

Here is a variation on the pressure theme. Remember when you said, "I really want the money, but I keep thinking that my parents would be disappointed and furious if they knew I didn't give it all back. I can't keep it."

"*Can't* keep it." Notice how you put it. We all get into situations in which as much as we want to do something, when it comes down to it, we feel that we just can't. Nothing physically bars us from taking that action, but we literally cannot go ahead with it. Not that we've decided we don't want to do it—we do. But we don't feel able to.

The very structure of our personalities—the fact that our inner, emotional reactions to certain things influence our behavior so profoundly—seems to set limits to our freedom. Take fear, for example. Most of us have enough fear of high places, falling off ladders, and the like, that hang gliding is about the last thing that appeals to us. Imagine that a friend invites you to go hang gliding with her. Are you *free* to join her, strap yourself into the harness, and throw yourself off the side of a mountain with only a sheet of nylon between you and eternity? Yes and no. No one is stopping you, so you are free. But you would probably be so afraid that you *could not* do it. Not just "preferred not to," but *could not* under any normal circumstances.

Guilt is another feeling that limits our freedom. If you know that guilt will plague you if you take something that belongs to someone else, the anticipation of those feelings can be so strong that you cannot steal. Maybe you were severely punished as a child for stealing. The memories are so vivid that you know that guilt will torment you if you take the money out of the wallet. You know your feelings are irrational, but you feel them anyway. In any event, you don't feel totally free. As with the previous example, in one way we are free, but in another way we're not.

In light of this, then, we have to expand our definition of *freedom* to include more than merely being free from *force*. A truly free act is one we take without being subject to any forces that can determine what we do.

The Contradiction: Freedom and Determinism

The more we look at the issue of how free we are, the more complex, confusing, and full of contradictions it becomes.

On the one hand, if I ask you, "Are you free and in control of your actions?" you would say, "Absolutely!" And you probably believe that other people are just as free as you are. If your friend Lori is doing badly in class because she's not studying, you don't feel much sympathy when she complains that her low grades will hurt her future. You figure that all she has to do is sit down and work. It's her choice. If someone steals a car, we want the thief punished. "He knows what he's doing," we say, "and he deserves the full penalty of the law. Give him something to think about the next time he considers taking somebody's car." We assume the car thief is free and in control of his actions. Therefore, he is the cause of the theft, and he is responsible for it.

Yet as often as we talk about how free people are, we're just as ready to act as though they're puppets. If you learned that the car thief's friends and family were also criminals, and that crime was all he was ever taught, you'd probably concede that his environment had much to do with his current behavior. His upbringing led him to crime. You might then think that the criminal does not need punishment as much as rehabilitation in a better, more law-abiding environment. That is, most of us seem to think that in one way or another, the actions people take are *determined* by something other than their own dispassionate assessment of a situation and their free choice among possible options.

What Do We Mean by Determinism?

Even the staunchest believer in freedom must concede that people can be manipulated and controlled. This means that determinism must be taken seriously.

Determinism, Science, and Materialism

Although deterministic theories may differ in their details, they all contain a common thread—the idea that free choice is impossible because anything that exists is physical and material—and physical, material objects are subject to laws of nature like cause and effect.

One good way to understand determinism is to think about how scientists look at the world. In science, everything that happens is the result of identifiable causes. Think of a chemist who is experimenting with mercury gas and notices the element acting in a new and unusual way. It flares up for no apparent reason. What would you think if she said, "After studying this phenomenon carefully, I've concluded there is absolutely no cause for the mercury to behave like this. It must decide to act that way by itself"? No cause? Deciding on its own? You'd think she was crazy. In the scientific way of looking at things, it cannot be that something has no cause. The whole point of scientific research is to discover what makes things happen the way they do. If the chemist said, "I can't discover a cause," that would make sense. She would then be assuming that there is a cause but she hasn't found it yet. But her saying "there is no cause—it just decides to act that way" is not acceptable. The material world of nature, as scientists—and most of the rest of us—see it, isn't organized that way.

Modern science, however, wasn't the first intellectual perspective to see things this way. The much older philosophical outlook known as *materialism* argues basically the same thing.

Materialism is a theory about the nature of reality that claims that if something exists, it must be physical. Materialism has a long history in philosophy. For example, the ancient Greek philosophers Leucippus (c. 450 B.C.) and Democritus (460–371 B.C.) argued that the building blocks of absolutely everything that existed were tiny material particles too small for us to see. Foreshadowing the modern atomic theory of matter you're surely familiar with, Democritus called these particles "atoms." (*Atomoi* in Greek means "uncuttable.") The great early modern English philosopher Thomas Hobbes (1588–1679) echoes the Greeks with his belief that all that exists are atoms in motion.

According to materialist thinkers, nothing immaterial exists—not souls, spirits, minds, or the like. We may *think* that our "minds" are qualitatively different from our bodies and that our immaterial minds decide what we want to do and then make our material bodies act accordingly. But the materialist says that we're wrong. Anything that we attribute to an immaterial "mind" is a function of something physical—most likely the brain.

Moreover, anything material and physical is subject to natural laws like cause and effect. That is, materialism logically implies determinism. As Leucippus puts it, everything happens "by necessity." If everything that exists is material and physical, how could our actions be anything other than the end result of some chain of cause and effect? "Free choice," then, is an illusion. Our actions are simply the result of

---

materialism Materialism is a theory about the nature of reality claims that if something exists, it must be physical and subject to natural laws like cause and effect. Materialism logically implies determinism.

some combination of material events or forces. Even when we *feel* free, a material-ist thinker would argue that our actions are dictated by something physical. A materialist explanation of human behavior might even argue that the chain of causes that makes us act in a certain way also produces an electrochemical state in the brain that causes us to feel as though we're choosing an action. In fact, Thomas Hobbes argues that actions that we think are "voluntary" are anything but. He explains that when we see something that we like or dislike and then act accordingly (trying to get it or avoiding it), what actually happens is that the impact of the atoms from the object first creates a desire (or aversion) and then produces our action. In other words, our subjective experience that we're "choosing" what to do is a product of material forces.

Given the fact that we don't understand how the brain works well enough to identify all of the precise steps that inevitably determine our actions, isn't it possible that something of this sort is going on when we "choose" our actions? After all, not being able to identify a material cause doesn't mean it's not there. When the plague swept through medieval and Renaissance Europe, medicine wasn't advanced enough to identify the precise cause. Some people even thought it was a punishment from God. However, scientists eventually discovered that the illness was caused by being bitten by a flea carrying the plague bacterium or by handling an animal that was infected. Why couldn't the same sort of thing apply to human behavior in general? That is, even though we can't currently identify all the details of the process that determines our actions, maybe research on the brain will ultimately demonstrate that our actions are simply the last step of a material, biological causal chain.

Determinists, then, see human behavior as simply part of the bigger natural system. Everything that happens in the material, natural world has a cause. Humans and their actions are part of that world. Therefore, our behavior must also be the effect of causes. It makes as little sense to say that we decide what to do on a whim, or at random, as it does to say that the world of nature does. It may be hard to see how all our actions could be only the effects of causes that lead up to them. But the hard-line determinist thinks that if our actions had no prior cause, it would break a fundamental law of nature.

One popular example of determinist thinking is astrology, which maintains that our actions and our fates are caused by the magnetic forces produced by the position of our sun, its planets, and the constellations in our universe. These influences shape our basic personality and they continue to sculpt our lives all our days. Like all deterministic theories, astrology is based on a belief in cause and effect. If you were born at the end of January, the sun's position at your birth makes you an Aquarius. This, in turn, causes you to have a particular set of character traits. If you were born between May 22 and June 21, the sun was in Gemini and supposedly produces different personality traits.

Certain psychological explanations of human behavior express a more intellectually accepted form of determinism. We look at two of these—behaviorism and Freudianism—later in this chapter. These two theories differ greatly in their details, but they share the basic belief that our actions result not from free choice but from other forces.

Determinism, Predestination, and Fate

Be sure to realize, however, that determinism is not the same thing as predestination or fatalism.

Predestination is a not-especially-comforting religious belief that maintains that God has decided from the beginning of time who will be "saved." This is already set. No matter what we do, no matter how hard we try, the outcome will not be changed. Our final destination—heaven or hell—is already logged into the heavenly computer. The argument for this is not philosophical but theological, and this idea raises the question of how a good God could predestine apparently decent people to eternal punishment. Christians who believe in predestination generally cite the argument of Saint Augustine (354–430) that the "original sin" of Adam and Eve, that is, their disobedience to God, was so terrible that God could justly condemn them and their descendants to hell. The central question then becomes why God chooses to save anyone, but that is another problem.

Fatalism is similar, in a way. If you believe that certain things are fated to happen, or that whatever happens to you is simply your destiny, or karma, you think these things take place no matter what you do—they're just "meant to be." Some people believe that there is someone out there that they're meant to meet, fall in love with, and marry. Somehow destiny will bring them together. Some people believe that they're fated to die on a certain day. Whether they're on a plane, in a car, or washing dishes in the kitchen, something fatal will happen.

The ancient Greek tragedy *Oedipus the King* is an excellent example of fate. An oracle warns Laius, King of Thebes, that his throne and his life will be in danger if his newborn son is allowed to grow up. To prevent this, Laius hands the child over to a herdsman with orders to kill him. Taking pity on the boy, the herdsman simply abandons him in the countryside. A peasant comes along, takes the infant home, and he and his wife raise the child as their own. Years later, Laius argues with a stranger on the road. In an exchange of blows, the stranger kills Laius. The stranger, of course, is Laius' son—Oedipus. Thus, despite every precaution, fate prevails and the prophecy is fulfilled.

By now you should begin to see how predestination and fatalism differ from determinism. They share with determinism the belief that what we do is caused by forces other than our free will. But predestination and fate refer to supernatural powers. Determinism refers to knowable natural forces.[1]

---

predestination Predestination is the religious belief that God has decided from the beginning of time who will be saved and who will be damned. This cannot be changed by what we do in this life.

fatalism Fatalism argues that the universe is governed by forces beyond our control that determine everything that happens to us and everything that we do.

---

[1]An idea often confused with determinism is the Christian belief that God knows everything. How can humans have free will if God knows the future? How can we be genuinely free if God already knows what we will do next Tuesday? Doesn't God's foreknowledge mean that all our future choices are already carved in stone?

Thinkers like Augustine try to resolve this problem by claiming that God's knowledge does not cause anything. In fact, our actions determine what God knows. If we acted differently, God would know something different. The key is that Augustine argues that the rules governing the dimension that God inhabits are very different from what we experience. In particular, Augustine says that time is different for God—past, present, and future are known all at once by God because He exists outside of time. The argument for an all-knowing God thus treats the heavenly and earthly realms as operating under quite different natural (or supernatural) laws. This makes it a different issue than the philosophical question we're considering here.

Determinism in Practice

You may have doubts about determinism. Most people do. They just do not believe that it applies to them. The interesting thing, however, is that most of us believe that determinism makes sense when it comes to others. We are free, but the behavior of other people can be shaped. In fact, you are probably much more familiar with a deterministic approach to life than you may at first think.

Take the way students often deal with their instructors. You're working on a term paper, the deadline is tomorrow morning, and there is no way you can finish it on time. What do you do? You ask around about the right approach to take with your professor in order to get an extension. Do you say you need more time to do a really good job? Or that you had to work so many hours at your job that you couldn't finish the paper? Or that you were sick? Or that you have "personal problems" that you would rather not talk about? You believe that saying the right thing will be like pushing a button that will make your teacher say, "No problem, take all the time you want." At times like these, you proceed as though human actions are determined. If you can identify the right cause, you will produce the desired effect.

We also see signs that determinism is taken seriously in the various ways people try to influence our choices by playing to forces assumed to be beyond our control. Advertising is a familiar example. Most ads try to engage our unconscious needs and desires, those psychological forces that make us want to buy a particular product. Ads get their power by appealing to our basic desires—sex, acceptance by our friends, success, self-respect, and the like. Billions of dollars are spent on advertising every year, so there must be something to it.

Freedom, Determinism, and Responsibility

You should be starting to realize that the debate over free will and determinism is not just some academic exercise. There is hardly a more important question than who or what controls our thoughts, feelings, hopes, desires, and actions. However, another reason this debate is so critical is that it leads us directly to the crucial concept of *responsibility.*

Responsibility is at the heart of all our traditions of reward and punishment. When we praise or blame people we assume they *deserve* it. That is, we presume they're free and in control of their actions. Grades, jobs, salaries, promotions, jail terms, elections, marriages, divorces—these and many other positive and negative experiences in life are based on the idea that each of us is the author of his or her actions and can be held responsible for them. Thus, responsibility makes sense only if we are free. But if determinism is correct, doesn't the notion of responsibility evaporate? And if that happens, what kind of world are we left with—personally, socially, politically?

Take the case of Phillip, a student in your chemistry class who is caught red-handed sabotaging your final experiment and those of four other top students. Phillip desperately wanted an A in the class, so he sabotaged the lab work of his chief competitors. Should Phillip be punished?

If everyone is free and in control of his or her actions, of course Phillip should be punished. He knew what he was doing, planned his actions, tried to advance himself by hurting others, and broke time-honored rules of academic honesty. There is no reason to let him off the hook. The only issue is how severe the penalty should be.

But what if we ask, "What *caused* Phillip to do what he did?" Suppose Phillip's domineering parents try to run all their children's lives. They want Phillip to be a physician like his father, so they chose his college (which they pay for), his major, and even the courses he takes. They insist that he get straight A's. But Phillip is poor in science and hates medicine—he would rather go into music. When he told his parents this, they said that if he couldn't get into a top medical school, he could go sweep floors. Furthermore, they said, his failure would kill his father. Phillip was working hard to manage a B+ in the chemistry course, and he figured that his only hope was to sabotage the work of the A students. That way, he would throw off the curve and hope to squeak by.

Years of parental intimidation have made Phillip a weak and frightened young man. He needs his parents' approval and support. He feels guilty at the prospect of letting them down. He also believes that his father's weak heart might not stand the disappointment if he cannot get into a good medical school. He is working as hard as he can—but it's just not enough. As he surveys his situation, he feels hopeless and depressed. One night he's alone in the lab, and in a moment of desperation, he tampers with his competitors' experiments. When the opportunity to cheat arose, Phillip was no more able to resist it than a hungry dog can resist a piece of meat.

What do you think now? Given Phillip's relationship with his parents and their demands, Phillip's action was the predictable result of their pressure and threats. He was desperate to please them, and his cheating was his ultimate response to their insensitivity and domination. Under the circumstances, how much control does Phillip have over what he did? Doesn't he now seem more like a victim?

If you're at all sympathetic, you can feel for Phillip. You may not like what he did, but you can understand it. If you were in his shoes, you might even do what he did. Should he be punished? If so, you probably wouldn't suggest as strong a penalty as you did when we assumed that he was totally free. When you know what caused him to act the way he did, you probably feel sorry for him.

The significance of this example, however, is that if you are willing to let Phillip off the hook, you're saying that he is not fully *responsible* for what he did. He is a victim of his circumstances. His upbringing made him weak, but that isn't his fault either. You can't punish people for that. And that's very different from our first assessment of this case. In other words, as long as we believe in free will, we have no trouble holding people fully responsible for what they do. As soon as we say that other factors determine our actions, the concept of responsibility is the first casualty. Sometimes it's just diluted. Other times, it's washed away altogether.

From a practical standpoint, this is why the free will/determinism dispute is so important. If behavior is determined, what grounds do we have for holding people responsible for what they do? How can we reward or punish, praise or blame, if our accomplishments and mistakes are the result of causes beyond our immediate control? Yet how can we as individuals or as a society function without some concept of responsibility?

Determinism: The Argument from Psychology

Now that you understand the main lines of the free will/determinism debate, we can get down to the main subject of this chapter—the arguments for determinism. (We'll take up the other side—arguments for freedom—in the next chapter.) Rather than considering what traditional philosophers have to say, however, we are going to look at some psychologists' views of the matter. There are four good reasons for this approach.

First, one aim of this book is to show you that philosophical issues are not limited to philosophy books or classes. Rather, they arise because we're human. They're very much a part of any serious investigation of fundamental features of reality and, in particular, the experience of being human.

Second, philosophy and psychology are closely related. Psychology developed out of philosophy, and both disciplines continue to study fundamental dimensions of the human experience although their methods differ greatly. Not surprisingly, the debate about freedom versus determinism goes on among psychologists as well as among philosophers.

Third, what makes most of us think that we are free is the *inner feeling of freedom* we experience when we make our choices. Because psychology specializes in studying the mechanics of our inner world, it should be especially revealing to see how psychologists grapple with the question of whether this feeling of freedom is authentic or an illusion.

Finally, and perhaps most important, two psychologists—B. F. Skinner and Sigmund Freud—present very convincing arguments in favor of determinism. Each claims to have discovered forces and processes that make human freedom virtually impossible. And each man has amassed a large body of data to support his claims. Rather than idle speculators, each believes he is scientifically describing the way things are. This combination of clinical data and interpretation presents a powerful challenge to anyone who wants to argue for freedom.

Determinism: B. F. Skinner and Behaviorism

If you have ever heard of "stimulus–response," "operant conditioning," "positive and negative reinforcement," or "programmed learning," then you have already met B. F. Skinner. All these terms are associated with **behaviorism,** the psychological school that Skinner represents. As you can guess from their name, "behaviorists" focus solely on observable behavior. They also assume that humans act in *predictable* ways in line with natural laws of *cause* and *effect*. Skinner's outlook is captured well in his statement from *Beyond Freedom and Dignity* that "man is a machine in the sense that he is a complex system behaving in lawful ways." Skinner does not deny that

---

behaviorism Behaviorism is the school of psychology that focuses exclusively on observable behavior and denies free will. Behavior is seen as an organism's "response" to a "stimulus"; the likelihood of a behavior recurring is increased by "positive reinforcement," and it is decreased by "negative reinforcement."

B. F. Skinner

Burrus Frederick Skinner (1904–1990) was born in Susquehanna, Pennsylvania, to strict parents. As Skinner put it in his autobiography, "I was taught to fear God, the police, and what people will think." A talented child, Skinner began writing stories while very young, and he published his first poem when only ten. He was interested in gadgets, designing and constructing numerous machines throughout his youth. And he also was strongly interested in music, starting with the piano, moving to the saxophone, and even playing in a jazz band during high school. Skinner graduated from Hamilton College as an English major and, having resolved to be a writer, set up a study in the attic of his parents' home in Scranton. Subsequently moving to New York's Greenwich Village, and then touring Europe for a summer, Skinner gave up on a literary career because he thought he had "nothing important to say." Intensely curious about human behavior, however, Skinner turned from a literary to a scientific approach and he enrolled in graduate school at Harvard University in 1928 to study psychology. After receiving his doctorate, Skinner remained at Harvard conducting his classic experiments on the conditioning of rats. He then went to the University of Minnesota and the University of Indiana before returning to Harvard in 1948. Skinner was a prolific writer, having authored not only scientific works but also popular accounts and defenses of behaviorism, a utopian novel, and his autobiography.

we have inner emotional experiences. But because they cannot be observed and measured, he considers them irrelevant. In this, behaviorism differs from other schools of psychology that make what happens inside us paramount.

Behaviorism looks at human behavior in terms of cause and effect or, in the language of psychology, *stimulus* (cause) and *response* (effect). Our actions do not result from free choice; rather, they are predictable responses to stimuli. Our experience of external events trains, or *conditions,* us so that a specific stimulus always evokes the same response. Skinner maintains that our actions—that is, our responses—are controlled primarily by the consequences that follow what we do. If the consequences are positive, the odds go up that we will act that way again. If the results are negative, the odds go down. Skinner refers to these rewards and punishments as *positive* and *negative reinforcements.*

For example, if you say "Hi" to Mario and he responds with a warm, friendly smile, what will you do the next time you see him? You will repeat your greeting and hope for the smile again. Why? In Skinner's terms, you got "positively reinforced" in the first exchange because Mario's smile made you feel good, and people are highly motivated to feel good. Thus, the next time you encounter Mario (the *stimulus*), the odds are better than even that you will say "Hi, Mario" (the *response*). And if he smiles again (*positive reinforcement*), the odds of your repeating your response and acting that way the next time you run into Mario will be even higher. By contrast, if you say "Good morning" to Bill and he spits on your shoes (*negative reinforcement*), you will be sure to leave him alone tomorrow.

Positive reinforcement increases the odds of a behavior being repeated, while negative reinforcement decreases them.

Skinner's explanation of human behavior is clear, simple, and deterministic. "A scientific analysis of behavior must assume," he explains in *About Behaviorism,* "that a person's behavior is controlled by his genetic and environmental histories rather than by the person himself as an initiating, creative agent. . . . There is no place in the scientific position for a self as a true originator or initiator of action." As far as Skinner is concerned, once we begin studying human behavior scientifically, "freedom" as it is traditionally understood bites the dust.[2]

Whatever Happened to Freedom?

Note that Skinner is not some kind of fascist or dictator. He does not argue, as the Renaissance political theorist Machiavelli does, that clever manipulation is the best strategy. That would be saying simply that people can be controlled. Skinner's theory holds that it is impossible for us *not* to be controlled. It's just the nature of things. The world is constructed in such a way that there is no freedom or genuine choice. Everything we do is the inevitable result of prior causes, and what we imagine to be "freedom" is just that—imaginary.

Perhaps Skinner's best exposition of his position on freedom can be found in his utopian novel *Walden Two.* Skinner explains his ideas in an interesting bit of dialogue between a behavioral scientist (Frazier) and a philosopher (Castle).

> "My answer [to the question of freedom] is simple enough," said Frazier. "I deny that freedom exists at all. I must deny it—or my [science of human behavior] would be absurd. You can't have a science about a subject matter which hops capriciously about. Perhaps we can never prove that man isn't free; it's an assumption. But the increasing success of a science of behavior makes it more and more plausible."
>
> "On the contrary, a simple personal experience makes it untenable," said Castle. "The experience of freedom. I know that I'm free. . . . At least you will grant that you feel free."
>
> "The 'feeling of freedom' should deceive no one," said Frazier. "Give me a concrete case."
>
> "Well, right now," Castle said. He picked up a book of matches. "I'm free to hold or drop these matches."
>
> "You will, of course, do one or the other," said Frazier. "Linguistically or logically there seem to be two possibilities, but I submit that there's only one in fact. The determining forces may be subtle but they are inexorable. I suggest that as an orderly person you will probably hold—ah! you drop them! Well, you see, that's all

---

[2]Not only is human freedom unnecessary to Skinner's theory, but also humans themselves are not needed. Most of Skinner's early work did not even involve humans. He developed his main ideas by working with rats and pigeons; then he applied the same theories to humans.

part of your behavior with respect to me. You couldn't resist the temptation to prove me wrong. It was all lawful. You had no choice. The deciding factor entered rather late, and naturally you couldn't foresee the result when you first held them up. There was no strong likelihood that you would act in either direction, and so you said you were free."

"That's entirely too glib," said Castle. "It's easy to argue lawfulness after the fact. But let's see you predict what I will do in advance. Then I'll agree there's law."

"I didn't say that behavior is always predictable, any more than the weather is always predictable. There are often too many factors to be taken into account. We can't measure them all accurately, and we couldn't perform the mathematical operations needed to make a prediction if we had the measurements."

Castle's Conditioning. This exchange between Frazier and Castle is worth dwelling on for a minute. Castle wants to refute Frazier's claim that we are not free. Castle knows that he *feels* free and assumes that the simple example of holding or dropping a matchbook according to his preference proves Frazier wrong. Castle does not feel that anything compels him to drop the matches. Frazier, of course, sees it differently. First, he believes that everything must have a cause. Here he is convinced that his remark that Castle would hold them caused the philosopher to do just the opposite.

Second, Frazier warns that the feeling of freedom is misleading and that forces can act on us without our noticing it. Their power is considerable even though invisible. That Castle does not *feel* that his action was determined by outside forces does not mean that it *wasn't*.[3]

If Frazier is right, we can assume that over the years Castle has received positive reinforcement when he proved people wrong. Like many professional academics, when Castle exposed the weaknesses in other philosophers' arguments, his colleagues probably praised his sharp, analytical mind. Castle is thus conditioned to expect pleasure from proving people wrong, so he automatically does it again. It is virtually a reflex at this point, and Frazier knows this. However, if Castle had been reinforced differently in the past, he would have acted differently. If he had been positively reinforced for showing people that they were right instead of wrong, he would have held the matches.

Human Freedom and the Weather. Skinner's analogy between predicting behavior and predicting the weather is also instructive.

What are the odds that the forecast you hear today for a couple of days from now will be right? About one in three. Many hurricanes that meteorologists say will slam into Florida veer off at the last moment. Why is the weather so hard to predict? Are meteorologists just a bunch of quacks? Of course not. Unfortunately, the factors that influence the weather are simply too numerous and their interrelationships are too complicated for our scientists to master. We do not know enough yet. But does our difficulty with predicting the weather mean that a storm system with

---

[3]This idea of our vulnerability to strong forces outside of our consciousness is an important aspect of Skinner's thought; when we examine the thinking of Sigmund Freud, we will see an even stronger version of this—our vulnerability to forces beneath our conscious awareness.

a mind of its own exercised its free will and decided to arrive over your picnic on Saturday? Hardly. Even though we do not do terribly well predicting it, we do know that the weather is the result of natural forces behaving in accordance with natural laws, whatever they may be.

What is true for the weather is true for human events, thinks Skinner. Just because we miss a lot in predicting how people will act does not mean that our actions are not determined by outside forces over which we have no control. Like the weather, our behavior is produced by too many factors to be readily understood. Certainly the sources of human behavior are too complex to be understood in every detail by a science very much in its infancy. Nonetheless, Frazier believes, Castle has no more power over his decision to hold or drop the matchbook than a hurricane does over whether it will sock Key West, Boca Raton, or Jacksonville.

Conditioning and Happiness

Even though Skinner says that all our behavior is the result of conditioning, this does not mean that he thinks we're easy marks for some behaviorist dictator. Skinner's ideas do not imply that we can ever fit into some miserable Orwellian world where we are conditioned into thinking we're having the time of our life.

Even though Skinner believes we are not free, he does not think that our behavior can be shaped in just any way that strikes someone's fancy. Human tolerance has limits, he says. Negative reinforcement may work on us to a certain degree, but human beings basically seek pleasure, a motivation that overrides other pressures. That's why positive reinforcement is so much more effective than negative reinforcement. When people are conditioned in a way that they find painful, Skinner says, they respond by engaging in a kind of countercontrol. As he explains it in *About Behaviorism,*

> Organized agencies or institutions, such as governments, religions, and economic systems, and to a lesser extent educators and psychotherapists, exert a powerful and often troublesome control. It is exerted in ways which most effectively reinforce those who exert it, and unfortunately this usually means in ways which either are immediately aversive to those controlled or exploit them in the long run.
>
> Those who are so controlled then take action. They escape from the controller—moving out of range if he is an individual, or defecting from a government, becoming an apostate from a religion, resigning, or playing truant—or they may attack in order to weaken or destroy the controlling power, as in a revolution, a reformation, a strike, or a student protest. In other words, they oppose control with countercontrol.

Skinner suggests here that when the environment is negative enough, the automatic response of the human organism is to seek out more pleasurable conditions. But in so doing, people do not make free, conscious decisions to revolt; they simply react to intensely negative reinforcement. And it is the nature of the human organism that determines what is perceived as positive and negative reinforcement. If a tyrant tried to condition people to enjoy servitude and life at hard labor, it simply would not work because humans do not take pleasure in this.

Skinner actually thinks that "feeling free" is a sign that we're being controlled in ways that do not provoke us to escape, rebel, or countercontrol. At such times, we can say that the basic conditions that make humans happy have been achieved.[4] In other words, Skinner thinks that people can be both controlled and genuinely happy at the same time. And if they're not happy, they will eventually react in a way that will improve things.

Conditioning: An Experiment. You may be getting annoyed at how Skinner could deny something that is so obvious to you—that you are free and in control of your actions. But before you make up your mind, try this experiment in conditioning. Your teacher is your subject.

According to Skinner's theory, our behavior is determined by what is in our environment and whether that makes us feel pleasure. Our behavior is further shaped by the consequences that follow our actions. If we perform an action and then something we like happens (positive reinforcement), we will repeat what we've done. If we perform an action and then something we do not like happens (negative reinforcement), we won't repeat what we've done.

To see how this works, you might try to condition one of your instructors to act in a certain way, without him or her knowing it. Here's what you do. First, explain what you're doing to as many people in the class as you can. Second, pick the behavior that you want to reinforce—walking back and forth, standing in a particular spot, gesturing to the class with a piece of chalk, or whatever. The object of the game is to administer positive reinforcement every time your instructor performs the behavior you have chosen. Look interested, nod your head, ask questions, take notes. When he or she stops the behavior, go to negative reinforcement. Look bored, act confused, shuffle your feet, look at your watch, stare out the window. When your teacher goes back to the chosen behavior, respond positively again. After a while, you should find your teacher doing the behavior you selected most of the time. (One class took "being near the radiator" as the behavior they wanted to reinforce. By the end of the semester, their instructor was so well conditioned that he simply sat on the radiator throughout each class.)

If you do this right, and have not been too obvious about it, you will see that you have controlled someone's behavior without that person's knowledge. You will have conditioned your instructor to act in a certain way because she or he wants the positive feeling that comes with the interest you show.

One of the most disturbing things about Skinner's ideas is that we can usually find similar examples of conditioning in our own lives. Maybe we've been conditioned to please other people, to take care of them, to be aggressive, or to be dependable. Finding conditioning in our own lives is a much more powerful challenge than some abstract theory. So look for some ways that you've already been conditioned, and *when*—not *if*—you find them, ask yourself what you think of Skinner's position on freedom.

Determinism: Freud and Control by the Unconscious

Skinner's brand of determinism may seem extreme, especially if you have never doubted the freedom of your own choices. But at least Skinner limits himself to

---

[4]In *Walden Two,* Skinner claims that human beings need only five things to be happy: health, a minimum of unpleasant labor, a chance to exercise their talents and abilities, intimate and satisfying personal contacts, and relaxation and rest.

Sigmund Freud

Sigmund Freud (1856–1939) was born in what is today Czechoslovakia, but he spent most of his life in Vienna, where his family moved when he was four years old. Freud's forty-year-old, wool merchant father was strict, but his twenty-year-old mother (Freud's father's second wife) was loving and protective. Freud was a brilliant youth. He had been reading Shakespeare since he was eight years old, he entered high school early, and he mastered Hebrew, German, Latin, Greek, French, English, Italian, and Spanish. Hoping for a career in scientific research, Freud studied medicine at the University of Vienna. Freud took three years longer than normal to graduate, however, and studied enough philosophy to make him consider taking a philosophy degree after finishing medical school. Personal and financial pressures led him to go into the practice of medicine, eventually specializing in nervous disorders. Freud studied hypnosis in Paris with the famous French psychiatrist Jean Charcot and then the new "talking cure" of the Viennese physician Josef Breuer. This method, encouraging patients to talk about their symptoms and feelings, was the basis of Freud's landmark work on the unconscious, the structure of the personality, and his creation of psychoanalysis. Freud reached the peak of his career in the early decades of the twentieth century, but at the same time he began suffering from cancer of the mouth (probably induced by his smoking about twenty cigars each day). He underwent many operations and suffered constant pain. After the Nazis occupied Vienna in 1938, Freud was harassed until he left for London. He died there the following year.

observable actions that result from an observable reinforcement process. He doesn't propose anything hidden or mysterious. But what if everything you did was determined by forces located in the depths of your psyche and beyond the reach of your conscious mind? Just such a powerful and intimidating form of determinism has been proposed by Sigmund Freud.

Not merely a giant in the history of psychology, Sigmund Freud is one of the most important figures in the history of Western thought. Freud's theories about the structure of the personality and the power of the unconscious have had as dramatic an effect on our thinking as Galileo's claim that the earth moves around the sun. Freud is one of a handful of thinkers whose ideas have fundamentally changed how we understand ourselves. In the last 200 years, only Darwin and Marx have had as great an impact.

An immensely talented youth, Freud initially pursued physiological research. But he gradually turned to medicine, specializing in what we today call "psychosomatic disorders," those cases in which patients have genuine symptoms without any medical cause.

Freud came to see that the causes of his patients' problems were feelings of anxiety. Moreover, these anxieties had two special properties. First, Freud's patients weren't even aware of these emotions before they began treatment. Second, their anxieties were usually related to events in childhood. In trying to help his patients,

Freud was deeply impressed by the usefulness of hypnosis. He also found that if patients simply talked about troubling experiences from their past, in an unstructured process Freud called *free association,* they could uncover and resolve the feelings causing their illness.

All this convinced Freud that the human mind has more than a *conscious* component. There is also, he proposed, an extremely powerful *unconscious* element—drives and memories and motives of which we are completely unaware. This insight became the foundation on which Freud built a theory of human personality and behavior that has profoundly influenced Western thinking on the subject.[5]

The Conscious, the Preconscious, and the Unconscious

Freudianism proposes three aspects to our personality. The *conscious* part is what we are aware of from moment to moment in our ordinary, everyday experience. You are conscious of the words on this page. When you look around the room you are in, you're conscious of everything you see, hear, and feel. When you're with a group of people, you like and dislike different individuals to different degrees. Your conscious mind is aware of your feelings and the reasons behind them. The conscious part of the mind is the most obvious and readily available dimension.

Then there is the *preconscious.* What did you have for dinner last night? Before you read this question you weren't thinking about that particular experience. It wasn't a part of your conscious mind. But you could remember the experience without much trouble. You got the answer from your preconscious—a kind of data bank where you store memories, thoughts, and feelings that you can easily retrieve and make conscious. (Some people also call this level the *subconscious.*)

The heart of Freud's thought, however, is his formulation of the *unconscious,* that part of our personalities of which we are *not* aware (hence, "*un*conscious") but which nonetheless profoundly influences our thoughts and actions. This is by far the biggest and most important part of the personality. Freud uses the image of an iceberg to express this idea. The *conscious,* he says, is like the visible tip of the iceberg. The *unconscious* is all the rest that is under the surface, the larger and, we might also say, the more dangerous part. If you are sailing among icebergs and steering only according to what you can see, you'll find yourself sinking before long. Similarly, if you ignore the unconscious part of the personality, you may find yourself in deep trouble.

> **Freudianism** Freudianism is the largely deterministic, psychological theory developed by Sigmund Freud that claims that the human personality has both conscious and unconscious dimensions. Behavior is ultimately determined by unconscious primal drives, early childhood experience, and the interplay of the three parts of the personality—the id, ego, and superego.

---

[5]Freud's theory is both complicated and sophisticated, certainly much more complicated than behaviorism. Rather than attempting a full treatment of Freud in these few pages, we will deal with only a few of his major ideas. If you find Freud's ideas interesting, either as a challenge to the concept of free will or as a way to interpret the human personality, the bibliography at the end of this chapter suggests some places to start reading on your own.

Expressions of the Unconscious. Freud believes that the unconscious has a pervasive influence in our lives and surfaces in many ways. The most obvious is in our dreams where the unconscious says things about our lives through a special language of pictures and symbols.

Another common example directly related to the theme of this chapter is what are called "Freudian slips," when our unconscious controls what we say. Sometimes, for example, when you intend to be polite, you may say what you really mean. "What do you think of my new dress?" asks your best friend. You think it's ugly, but you don't want to hurt her feelings, so you try to say "It's gorgeous!" What comes out of your mouth instead is, "It's grotesque!" What you said to your friend, then, was not the product of a free, conscious will. In fact, your unconscious made you say something you consciously did not want to say.

The Unconscious and Determinism. Dreams and "Freudian slips" are just a couple of cases where the unconscious controls what we do. These examples are trivial, however, in comparison to the larger workings of the unconscious.

Just think about how we're bombarded by appeals to our unconscious in everyday life. Advertising uses subliminal messages that are imperceptible to the conscious mind. Status and sex are used so that you'll associate them with particular products—and then buy them. If you ever used a subliminal or self-hypnotic tape to help you stop smoking or relax, you were appealing to the unconscious. Restaurants, stores, hotels, and hospitals carefully select the colors they use because of their unconscious effect on our appetite or sense of well-being. The surgical team in the operating room wears blue or green gowns because these colors make them—and us—feel more relaxed. These are all appeals to unconscious processes.

Freud does not think that the unconscious is merely "important," however. In Freudian thought, the unconscious controls virtually everything we do, usually in ways that we are completely unaware of. Once you grant the existence of the unconscious as Freud defines it, you can begin to see just how deterministic Freudian thought is. Once you understand the structure of the personality as Freud sees it, and how the unconscious works within it, you can make fairly accurate inferences about the forces at work in someone's personality. You can then explain and even predict human behavior. And you do so without reference to "free will."

The Structure of the Personality

A quick sketch of Freud's view of the personality will show you how powerful Freud's case for determinism is.

Even the most superficial treatment of Freud's theory cannot fail to mention the three components of the personality that he posits: the *id,* the *ego,* and the *superego.*

The id. The *id* is the most deeply buried, unconscious part of the personality, and it is the source of our basic drives and all our psychological energy. Primitive and untamed, the id has only two basic drives—sex and aggression—that are instinctual and biologically determined. The id operates according to what Freud calls the "pleasure principle." It is always seeking pleasure through the immediate satisfaction of its needs.

The id is also unrestrained, irrational, and unrealistic—almost "unhuman" in a way. Indeed, Freud suggested the distance between the id and the essence of a healthy, mature human in the very name he chose for it. "Id," after all, is Latin for "it." If the id had its way, it would try to satisfy its every impulse whenever and wherever it felt like it, no matter what the circumstances. It knows no limits—it always wants the impossible. The human race would not survive for long if we lived according to its uncontrolled dictates.

The ego. The *ego* is the second component of the personality. The word "ego" means "I," and the concept conveys something close to our ordinary sense of self. The ego operates according to what Freud calls the "reality principle." It is aware of what's possible and impossible and is able to accept limits and to act in a practical way. The ego's job is to figure out appropriate ways to satisfy the id's desires, and that means determining an acceptable time, place, and fashion for such satisfactions. According to Freud, the relationship between the ego and id is like that of a rider to a spirited horse. The horse provides the power, but the rider, that is, the ego, controls it.

The superego. But the rider isn't alone on the horse. Your riding instructor, so to speak, is on the horse with you, holding onto you telling you how to ride and what you should and shouldn't do. This is Freud's third part of the personality, the *superego*. "Superego" is a Latin word that literally means "over" or "above" the "I." In English, the concept that comes closest to the superego is the "conscience," that part of us that stands over us, looking down at what we do and judging whether our actions are right or wrong. The superego, as Freud uses the term, is that, and then some.

Like the id, the superego is an unconscious mechanism. Generally in place by age 5 or 6, it consists of the internalized prohibitions communicated to us by our parents and our culture. The superego can be a useful guide, but more often it's a pain in the neck. To return to the horse-and-rider image, you can think of the superego as a terribly strict riding master yelling criticism at you all the time. Hardly ever happy with what we do, the superego is as irrational, demanding, and uncompromising as the id. But while the id hungers for immediate gratification, the superego wants moral perfection. Nothing less will do.

Whenever we fall short of perfection, the superego punishes us by making us feel bad. Have you ever felt very guilty about doing something that wasn't really so bad? Have you ever beat yourself up inside for being like everybody else—given to making mistakes, maybe a little selfish now and then? If you ever felt deep shame for being less than a saint, that was your superego at work.

Personality Structure and Determinism

Now that you know something about Freud's idea of how the personality is structured, you can better understand why his theory of human behavior is deterministic. Obviously, the ego is in a no-win situation. It's caught between two insatiable and contradictory desires, one for wanton pleasure, the other for moral perfection. The ego is always under pressure, but sometimes the conflict is unbearable. When this happens, the result is anxiety. The ego that experiences anxiety feels threatened and is compelled to reduce the tension. It looks for the quickest way to restore some sense of equilibrium. As a result, we act in particular ways, or feel specific emotions, or even distort our perception of reality. (We will look at some of these "defense mechanisms" shortly.)

Two aspects of this process bear on the free will/determinism debate. First, the ego's move to reduce anxiety is like a *reflex* action. When the ego feels anxiety, it *automatically* reacts to reduce it much as we automatically pull our hand off a hot stove. Both anxiety and extreme heat are experienced as threats, and we have built-in mechanisms that come into play to defend ourselves. Freud sees this as a natural process.

Second, all this goes on *without our realizing it*. In Freud's theory, the process of reducing anxiety is unconscious and governed by the interplay of the id, ego, and superego. In effect, our unconscious makes a decision and hands it to our conscious mind with orders to carry it out. Our conscious mind, however, experiences all this as coming up with an idea of our own and freely choosing what we do. In reality, the choice was already made, and it wasn't even close to being free.

For example, have you ever wanted to do something that you honestly believed was all right to do but didn't do it because you felt too guilty? Perhaps it was something as simple as wanting to go to a movie but staying home because you felt you should work on a term paper. You might feel as though you freely chose peace of mind over the guilt. But Freud would say that your ego resolved an anxiety-producing situation by caving into the demands of your superego and making you feel so bad that you *couldn't* do what you wanted to do.

This sometimes happens with lying. Some people literally *cannot* lie. Trying to say on the phone that someone is out when that person is there and doesn't want to take the call can make some people so upset they cannot do it. Afterwards, however, they congratulate themselves on having such a commitment to honesty that they place it above everything else.

Anxiety caused by a dominant superego can even bring on physical symptoms. Most of us know someone like Ann, who always gets a sore throat the morning she's supposed to give an oral report in class. Or someone like Jeff, who lies to his boss ("I've got a doctor's appointment next Friday") so that he can go to a ball game—but who, when the day comes, wakes up sick and cannot go. Did Jeff choose to get a 24-hour bug? No. His anxiety is so high, and his superego is so strong, that it cuts him down. But at least now that he did nothing wrong, he doesn't feel guilty.

Defense Mechanisms and Determinism

These limits to our freedom are pretty obvious. A more subtle way that the ego tries to reduce anxiety is through what Freud calls "defense mechanisms."[6] There are numerous defense mechanisms, but they all have two things in common: They relieve anxiety by distorting reality; and they are unconscious processes. Because

---

[6]"Defense mechanisms" are so called because they are psychological strategies that defend the ego against anxiety. Freud's defense mechanisms are repression, reaction formation, projection, regression, rationalization, displacement, and sublimation. For an example of rationalization by one of the characters in one of Plato's philosophical dialogues, see pages 158–165 in Chapter 6, "Why Virtue?" Be Ethical.

we're unaware that we are using them, we accept the distorted picture of reality that they give us as accurate.[7]

Actions produced by the workings of our defense mechanisms are surely the result of something other than rational, free choice. How can we act freely when we deceive ourselves about the facts of a situation? If someone put a hallucinatory drug in your coffee, would you say that everything you did under the influence of the drug was the result of your free choice? Of course not. So why should it be any different if our faulty perception is caused by something psychological rather than chemical? Obviously, the unconscious workings of defense mechanisms are an important part of Freud's determinism.

We don't need to analyze all the defense mechanisms here. We should look quickly at two of them, however, because their existence reinforces the Freudian idea that the unconscious and not the conscious mind controls what we do. And, if that is so, it presents a major obstacle to human freedom.

Projection is the defense we use when we attribute our own feelings—feelings that are unconsciously troubling—to somebody else. Suppose that you're doing poorly in a course and you think it's because your teacher dislikes you. (Actually, you're not studying very hard and the course is tough.) Let's start with the fact that you're unconsciously feeling angry at your teacher for not being easier. Aggression is one of the id's main impulses, and the id is now pressuring your ego to let your teacher really have it. Your superego, however, won't stand for this, and it threatens your ego with what will happen if you give in to the id. Harassed by real conditions in the outside world, as well as by your id and superego, your ego experiences growing anxiety. In projection, the anxiety is relieved by giving in to the superego, but satisfying the id by taking its hostility and attributing it to the person you're angry at. So instead of consciously feeling that *you hate your teacher,* you unconsciously reverse the roles and believe that *your teacher hates you.* In other words, you *project* your feelings onto the object of your feelings and assign them to him or her.

This relieves your anxiety in lots of ways. You keep your own image of being a "nice" person. You avoid the risks involved in getting angry at someone who might penalize you for it. And by blaming someone else for your problems, you can continue to be lazy. So the projection lets you distort reality without knowing you're doing it. And you feel perfectly justified in not working hard. After all, what's the use?

Reaction formation is another way the ego defends itself against anxiety. The essence of this mechanism is that the ego takes a disturbing impulse and unconsciously converts it into its opposite. Some people, for example, find aggressive impulses deeply disturbing. For any number of reasons, they neither understand their angry feelings nor know what to do with them. Furthermore, being aggressive does not conform to their image of a good person. Again, the ego is caught between the id's primal drives and the superego's moral standard, and anxiety develops. In a case of reaction formation, the ego gives in so much to the superego that it now labels as evil everything to do with aggression. The person in the grip of this mechanism

---

[7]This lack of awareness is essential to Freud's definition. The minute we become aware of using these mechanisms, they are no longer working.

may become incredibly sweet, passive, and accommodating, filled with love for everybody he meets. He may go around preaching to everyone else how bad competition and war are. His anger has been converted to its opposite—love. The superego is satisfied, and the person's unconscious tension is reduced.[8]

Freud's defense mechanisms are especially pertinent to our investigation of free will versus determinism because their basic effect is to *distort reality*. If our unconscious gives us a false picture of reality, how can we ever act freely? Rather, we're being manipulated *by ourselves*. In *projection* we attribute our own feelings to someone else. In *denial* we unconsciously refuse to see what is right before our eyes and obvious to everyone else. *Repression* totally erases painful memories and feelings, and it can even affect our bodies. It's not unusual to find cases of impotence, frigidity, and even paralysis caused by unconscious reactions to anxiety.

The Unconscious and the Power of the Past

One other part of Freud's thought bears upon his determinism, and that is his belief in the effect of early childhood experiences on our adult personality. Freud claims that who we are as adults is the direct result of what happened to us in our childhood. We *do not choose* to be the way we are, we are made this way by the interplay between our inner psychological world and people and events outside us.

Our personalities, whom we fall in love with, what kind of careers we choose, what motivates us, even our hobbies, everything about us is supposedly the product of our past. All this significant fashioning is accomplished by the time we are 5 or 6, before we're even aware of what's going on. No wonder, then, that proponents of free choice see this as Freud's biggest assault on their position.

We will not describe Freud's "psychosexual stages of development" here. One example, however, will illustrate Freud's basic claim that the core of our being is shaped by our past.

Your friend Dianah is always getting involved with the wrong man. She is a sensitive, emotional person who finds rich, emotionally distant men irresistible. (The men are also usually married.) And yet it never works out. The pattern is always the same—attraction, love, disappointment. Outsiders can easily see what's wrong. Dianah keeps picking the wrong kind of man. She wants a deep emotional connection with lots of intimacy and expression of feeling. But the men she picks are neither emotional nor communicative.

What advice would you give Dianah? Probably to choose someone more like herself. She seems to be in control of her life in every other way, and it looks like she freely chooses to be involved with such men. "So," you say, "it's easy. Choose somebody different."

Freud, however, would see Dianah's unhappiness as the inevitable and predictable result of her emotional history, which has put into place powerful unconscious forces that compel her to choose whom she does. Even if she dated someone

---

[8]Be sure you realize that defense mechanisms this extreme are not a part of everybody's life. In other words, you might be right that your teacher dislikes you. And many proponents of nonviolence are healthy and sincere in their convictions.

who's "more her type," it wouldn't work. She wouldn't find him interesting. She is locked into a pattern of poor choices and unhappy relationships.

In Freud's scheme of human development, we cannot progress from one stage to the next until particular needs appropriate to each stage are met. For example, at a particular time it is critical for a child to form a satisfying relationship with the parent of the opposite sex. If that parent satisfied our craving for affection and attention in an adequate and supportive way, we unconsciously internalize a picture of the world as a place in which we can be happy with people of the opposite sex and can get what we need from them. We can move on to the next stage without any problems, believing in a reality where healthy, satisfying love relationships are possible.

But if this critical need isn't met, we have a mess. First, the need persists. But because it wasn't met at the right time and in the right way, it moves from being felt consciously to our unconscious, where it remains buried—but very much alive and influential in our lives. Second, we internalize a picture of the world in which we *do not* get what we want from people of the opposite sex, and this is the image we live by. Once all of this is in place, a mechanism forms in the unconscious that compels us to repeat this same unhappy situation time and again, always with the same unsuccessful outcome.

What does this mean in Dianah's case? A Freudian would probably say that Dianah never developed a secure sense of her father's love or experienced him as someone who responded to her needs. Her unmet need went underground, pushed into the unconscious, but it surfaced later in life in her attraction to the kind of man who will, like her father, let her down. She gravitates to rich men because of the promise of being taken care of, but in reality her childhood needs in her unconscious ensure that she falls for only rich, emotionally unresponsive men (like her father).

Once again, the same theme emerges. Actions that feel free are not free. Unconscious forces pull our strings, but because we cannot see the strings, we think that we choose what we do.

You can see how important the unconscious is as a concept and how important that concept is in the argument for determinism. Nonetheless, even though Freud thought that we could never totally escape from the power of the unconscious, he did uncover a way of at least mitigating its painful tyranny.

Psychoanalysis and Happiness

Recall that Freud was a physician who made his discoveries about the personality in his search for ways to heal patients who could not be cured by conventional medical means. Identifying the structure and workings of the personality was only the first step for Freud. He also believed that he had discovered a new form of treatment—*psychoanalysis*—that could neutralize unconscious forces that troubled people. Free of these shackles, they could repair the damage done to their emotional growth by early, traumatic experiences.

Psychoanalysis is a process in which the patient talks freely and seemingly at random, in a process called *free association,* about his or her thoughts and feelings under the guidance of a therapist who understands the workings of the unconscious. It is a slow and painful process, for the patient essentially goes back in time, from a psychological standpoint, confronts the original pain, disappointment, or trauma, resolves the problem, and thereby weakens the power of these unconscious forces. This helps patients reorganize their inner world in ways that are more to their advantage. For example, Dianah might come to see what originally happened with her father, understand and accept that situation, and give up what she was looking for from him. If all this can be brought up into Dianah's conscious mind, she can reevaluate the experience as an adult. This defuses the childhood problem and enables Dianah to live a more satisfying life in the present. Gradually she will stop recreating her unsatisfying relationship with her father and be drawn to different kinds of men with whom she can have more complete and fulfilling relationships.

So, as was the case with Skinner's determinism, Freud's deterministic theory does not preclude human happiness. Unconscious forces can, with difficulty, be rechanneled in a better direction. Indeed, perhaps we can even see a certain amount of freedom in a patient's choice to seek help and engage in a healing process. To that, however, a good Freudian would reply that what actually happens is that someone becomes so unhappy that he or she is virtually *compelled* to get help.

This meager survey of Freud's work has at least introduced you to one of the major schools of deterministic thought in the twentieth century. Now you must ask yourself whether you think any of this holds water in terms of your own experience. Consider very seriously Freud's claim that unconscious forces direct not only our *actions* but also our *feelings* and *the very way we perceive reality.* Not only do they do all this, but also they do it *without any awareness on our part* that they are at work. If Freud is right, then, is there any room for freedom?

Determinism and Responsibility

Freud and Skinner make a very strong case for determinism. Skinner says our actions are the result of external rewards and punishments, that they are products of how we've been reinforced over time. Freud sees our behavior as dictated by personality structure, primitive drives, the need to reduce anxiety, and early childhood experiences.

You should not be surprised, then, that neither thinker puts much weight on notions of blame or moral responsibility. After all, it makes no sense to punish someone for an action that was determined by forces beyond that person's control. Skinner, for example, maintains that "a moral or ethical lapse . . . needs treatment, not punishment." Skinner sees basically no difference between physical and moral illness. "Compare two people," he writes,

> one of whom has been crippled by an accident, the other by an early environmental history which makes him lazy and, when criticized, mean. Both cause great inconvenience to others, but one dies a martyr, the other a scoundrel. Or compare two children—one crippled by polio, the other by a rejecting family. Both contribute little to others and cause trouble, but only one is blamed. The main difference is that only one kind of disability is correctable by punishment, and even then only occasionally. It is tempting to say that only one person in each case could do something about his condition, but should we not say that we could do something besides blaming him?

—About Behaviorism

Skinner rejects punishment as both an inappropriate and inefficient way to change behavior. But punishment at least has a place in behaviorism. It serves as negative reinforcement, and that might change someone's behavior. In Freud's world, however, blame and punishment have no place at all, especially when we talk about people who are psychotic.

For example, insanity is accepted as a legal defense. Even "temporary insanity," that is to say, a transitory mental aberration, is often a legitimate defense. Freud labeled these extreme conditions *psychoses*. Psychotic individuals are totally out of touch with reality; thus, they can neither control what they do nor be held responsible for it. In fact, Freud's description of the causes of psychoses suggests that the psychotic person is as little responsible for his or her condition as someone who is physically ill. "In psychoses," Freud writes in his *New Introductory Lectures on Psychoanalysis,* "the turning-away from reality is brought about in two kinds of ways: either by the unconscious repressed becoming excessively strong so that it overwhelms the conscious, which is attached to reality, or because reality has become so intolerably distressing that the threatened ego throws itself into the arms of the unconscious instinctual forces in a desperate revolt." The process is unconscious—it just happens.

Where does this leave us? At least this much seems clear. The power of the unconscious, to which we are all subject, seems to make personal accountability virtually impossible. If our actions are not under our conscious control, how can we fairly be held responsible for them?

Determinism: A Final Word

The theories of Skinner and Freud may be unsettling, especially if you have never before questioned the existence of free will. Behaviorists and Freudians have produced a substantial body of data that supports their theories. Indeed, they can answer every objection we raise. We can even support their theories with examples from our own lives. Determinism is certainly plausible.

Determinism's strongest argument is probably that it is scientific. And since we live in an age dominated by science, it is hard to resist a no-nonsense approach that explains everything in terms of natural principles backed up by empirical evidence. It makes us feel secure to see everything existing in the world today as having an almost infinite chain of causes, which includes effects of previous causes, which stretch back in time to the creation of the universe, and which are responsible for each thing being the way it is. A universe like this is a rational, logical, ordered place.

The tree outside my window is what it is, stands where it does, reaches 20 feet in the air, and grows well because millions of very specific causes brought about all these effects. The seedling grew from a seed produced by another tree, which in turn was the offspring of another tree, and so on. The climate and the soil conditions supporting this particular species of tree are the result of thousands of years of meteorological and geological events that produce conditions hospitable for such a tree. Everything about the tree is the effect of some cause, which is, in turn, the effect of some prior cause. Even the forces that determined the shape, color, and the exact number of leaves on the tree were already in play hundreds of years ago. The tree did not exist then, but it was "in the pipeline."

But while this is all well and good for natural objects like trees and natural events like the weather, it's not so comforting when we apply it to our own actions. Try telling yourself that you are *not* free, that none of your actions is the result of free choice, but, like everything else in the world, causally determined—the end product of a chain of causes stretching back into infinity. Most of us will admit that we struggle against internal and external forces when we take action. Sometimes they win, sometimes we do. But hardly anyone thinks we *never* win. All of us have experiences that make us absolutely certain that we are free and can control at least some aspects of our own lives. There are times when we make up our minds to do something and doggedly, sometimes heroically, persist against tough opposition and long odds until we succeed. At such moments we are positive that our own strength of will, not conditioning or unconscious forces, let us prevail.

In spite of the arguments of Skinner, Freud, and others, it still seems as if having control over our destiny is a hallmark of being human. Our sense of this power feels too real to most of us to dismiss it as an illusion, the product of prior reinforcement or a defense mechanism. There must be more to it than what we've seen so far. And that is what the next chapter is about.

Main Points of Chapter 3

1. One of the most fundamental philosophical questions connected with being human involves whether or not we freely choose, or control, our actions. This dilemma is referred to as the issue of free will versus determinism.

2. The theory of free will maintains that our actions result from our own deliberate free choice. Determinists hold that our actions and our choices are simply the result of some preexisting causes that produce them and cannot be freely arrived at.

3. Determinists see human behavior as simply part of the bigger natural system. Everything that happens in the material, natural world has a cause. Humans and their actions are part of that world. Therefore, what we do must also have causes.

4. Determinism differs from predestination and fatalism. All three outlooks share the idea that what we do is caused by forces other than our free will. But predestination and fate refer to supernatural powers. Determinism relies on natural forces.

5. One of the most important consequences of determinism is that it raises the question of how much we can hold one another responsible for our actions.

6. Two of the strongest arguments in favor of determinism come from the psychological theories of B. F. Skinner and Sigmund Freud.

7. Skinner's theory of behaviorism looks at human behavior in terms of cause and effect—stimulus and response. The actions we take are not the result of free choices but are responses to stimuli. Our experience of external events trains, or conditions, us so that a specific stimulus always evokes the same response. Skinner maintains that our actions—that is, our responses—are controlled primarily by the consequences that follow what we do. If the consequences are positive, the odds go up that we'll act that way again. If the results are negative, the odds go down.

Skinner refers to these rewards and punishments as positive and negative reinforcements.

8. Freud's version of determinism is based on a division of the personality into conscious and unconscious dimensions, the latter of which is the biggest and most important part of the personality. Indeed, in Freudian thought, the unconscious is responsible for virtually everything we do.

9. The determinism of Freudianism is grounded in the three parts of the personality: id, ego, and superego. The ego's attempt to reduce anxiety caused by the pressure of the other two, irrational parts can be like a reflex action—one that we do not even realize consciously. Freud also claims that unconscious forces determine our actions by a variety of defense mechanisms, psychological mechanisms that distort reality.

10. Of special importance to Freud is the effect of early childhood experience on the adult personality. Freud claims that who we are as adults is the direct result of what happened to us in our childhood. We don't choose to be the way we are; we are made this way by the interplay between our inner psychological world and people and events outside us.

Discussion Questions

1. Reflect on your own life. To what extent do you find your actions free or determined?

2. "Conditioning" is similar to the process by which we develop habits. How many habits do you have? Are there any that you feel you simply could not break—or at least that you would have a great deal of trouble breaking? If so, are these examples of your actions being determined?

3. Do you accept the existence of the unconscious? Do you ever feel that you don't know why you act as you do in certain situations? Is it possible that your actions are being dictated by unconscious forces? If you reject the unconscious, how do you explain dreams?

4. What do you think about the "insanity defense"? What about "temporary insanity"? What about someone who commits a "crime of passion"? Do you think you could ever get so angry that you would lose control of yourself? If you hurt someone as a result, would it be fair to punish you? Do you believe you should be held "responsible" for what you do in such a state?

5. Which of these "deterministic" factors do you think limit the amount of responsibility we have for our actions: conditioning, unconscious forces, childhood trauma, being raised by dishonest parents, social and economic class?

6. What is your astrological "sign"? Do you fit your astrological profile? If so, is this evidence for determinism?

7. Christianity claims that God knows everything—past, present, and future. God knows right now, then, everything you will do tomorrow. In that case, do you really have any choice in the matter? Does God's foreknowledge support determinism?

Selected Readings

General discussions of the problem of freedom versus determinism can be found in: Bernard Berofsky, ed., *Free Will and Determinism* (New York: Harper and Row, 1966); Gerald Dworkin, ed., *Determinism, Free Will, and Moral Responsibility* (Englewood Cliffs, NJ: Prentice Hall, 1970); and Sidney Hook, ed., *Determinism and Freedom in the Age of Modern Science* (New York: Macmillan, 1961).

For B. F. Skinner's main ideas, see *Walden Two* (New York: Macmillan, 1948); *Science and Human Behavior* (New York: Macmillan, 1953); "The Machine That Is Man," *Psychology Today* (April 1969), 20–25, 60–63; *Beyond Freedom and Dignity* (New York: Knopf, 1974); and *About Behaviorism* (New York: Knopf, 1974). For Skinner's life, see the two volumes of his autobiography, *Particulars of My Life* (New York: Knopf, 1976) and *The Shaping of a Behaviorist* (New York: Knopf, 1979), and also Skinner's contribution to *A History of Psychology in Autobiography,* edited by E. G. Boring and G. Lindzey, volume 5 (New York: Appleton-Century-Crofts, 1967), pp. 385–413. The primary source for Freud's writings are the 24 volumes of *The Standard Edition of the Complete Psychological Works of Sigmund Freud,* edited and translated by J. Strachey (London: Hogarth Press, 1953–1974). Individual works are published by W. W. Norton and Company. See in particular *New Introductory Lectures on Psychoanalysis, On Dreams, Civilization and Its Discontents,* and *The Future of an Illusion.* Also see the sections on Skinner and Freud in Leslie Stevenson, *Seven Theories of Human Nature,* second edition (Oxford: Oxford University Press, 1987).

4

The Case for Freedom

- *Aristotle: The Commonsense Philosopher*
- *William James: The Pragmatic Philosopher*
- *Jean-Paul Sartre: The Existentialist Philosopher*
- *Albert Ellis: Freedom Through Right Thinking*
- *Freedom Versus Determinism: A Closing Word*

It's late September and the pennant race in the East is really tight. The Red Sox and the Yankees are neck and neck, and the season's final game between these two teams will settle the matter. Richard, an avid Yankee fan, decides to drive up to Boston with some of his buddies. On the way to Fenway Park, they stop off at a bar for a few beers. During the game, Richard, as usual, has a few too many. Feelings run high, Boston wins, and on the way out of the game, Richard bumps into a jubilant Red Sox fan. The guy looks at Richard's Yankee cap, pushes him and says, "Outta my way, loser!" Richard explodes—he has a hair-trigger temper—slugs the guy and is arrested. When he sobers up the next morning, he says to the judge, "I'm really sorry. I just lost control. The beer, losing the game, the put-down, and my temper—it was too much for me to handle. That guy just pushed my buttons and I lost it."

Did some invisible force beyond Richard's control make him do it? Was the punch simply a conditioned response to a specific stimulus? Or did Richard's ego, weakened by alcohol, lose hold of his id's aggression? Richard himself admits that he "lost control"—he didn't even *feel* he had any choice in the matter. With the alcohol, the excitement, and his temper, we don't need a Skinnerian or Freudian explanation to see his behavior as determined.

But is that all there is?

It's tempting to let Richard off the hook. Between the beer, the game, and the insult, how could he not react as he did? You could have bet on it. Yet, if you were on the wrong end of Richard's fist, would you say, "Hey, no problem—behavior's all determined. We're both victims"? Would you think that Richard had absolutely *no* responsibility for his actions? Not very likely.

Our dilemma, then, remains. Considering the strong cases Skinner and Freud make for determinism, where is there any room for freedom? Can we have it both ways—understanding that human behavior fits into a causal universe but allowing for choice and responsibility?

We must also account for our feelings of freedom. It's normal to believe we are free. We feel as if we choose our actions, and we cannot believe that our choices are just the end products of a long chain of causes that stretches back millions of years. But do our feelings of freedom prove anything about reality? Or do they represent some kind of illusion?

In this chapter, we explore the other side of the free will/determinism question. Thinkers who argue for free will approach the issue in various ways, but they share the conviction that we as human beings are free and in control of what we do. We'll look at the ideas of the Greek philosopher Aristotle, the American philosopher and psychologist William James, the French thinker Jean-Paul Sartre, and an American psychologist, Albert Ellis, who was inspired by Greek philosophy to develop a new school of psychology.

Aristotle: The Commonsense Philosopher

One of the three greatest ancient Greek philosophers, Aristotle emphasized commonsense and empirical observation. He is one of the West's most important philosophers.

Voluntary and Involuntary Acts

The ancient Greeks did not refer to the problem of free will versus determinism in the same terms we use. Aristotle talks instead about **voluntary** versus **involuntary** action. And, like many philosophers who argue for free will, Aristotle does not discuss the question in a vacuum. He comes to it through the question of responsibility. Determinists don't talk much about responsibility, as you saw in the last chapter. But free will philosophers make much of it because freedom and responsibility are inseparable: each implies the other. Thus, in the *Nichomachean Ethics,* Aristotle raises the question of voluntary versus involuntary action in the process of discussing moral responsibility and how human character is formed.

Aristotle is very much a commonsense philosopher, and commonsense tells us that people should be held responsible for what they do. The central question, however, is when to hold people accountable and when to excuse them. Aristotle starts from what he takes as a self-evident fact that we can deliberate about our actions and make choices. Basically, he believes that we are responsible for those actions we

---

voluntary Aristotle labels as "voluntary" actions that are under our control. This includes habits or dispositions that seem to be out of our control but nonetheless result from earlier choices made when the matter was in our power. This also includes actions done from culpable ignorance or negligence. Aristotle thinks we are responsible for all voluntary actions.

involuntary Aristotle labels as "involuntary" actions that result from constraint or ignorance. He does not think we are responsible for involuntary actions.

choose and we are not responsible for those we don't choose. If an action results from constraint or ignorance, it is *involuntary*. If we are free from force or pressure and know everything we should know about what we're doing, the action is *voluntary*.

Richard the Yankee fan might think that Aristotle is on his side. "Because I was drunk and all worked up," he says, "I didn't really know what I was doing. I was *ignorant*, see? I didn't really choose what I did or act *voluntarily*."

Culpable Ignorance and Negligence

But Aristotle is no pushover. In his opinion, if we are responsible for not knowing what we are doing, we are accountable for whatever we do. Showing that this principle is recognized even in the laws of ancient Athens, Aristotle explains that the penalties are twice as high if an offender does something wrong while drunk. A person had the power not to get drunk and is, therefore, responsible for putting himself in a condition in which he doesn't know what he is doing. Obviously, Richard cannot escape on this score.

Aristotle also gets tough with people who simply should have known better. Again referring to the Athenian legal system, he notes that people who are ignorant of the law are punished because they should have known the law, they could easily have known the law, or they were just plain negligent in not knowing it. In contemporary society this is called *culpable ignorance* or *culpable negligence* because the lapse is so serious that we're willing to find someone at fault for it. (*Culpa* is Latin for "fault" or "blame.")

To this, Richard grumbles, "That doesn't make any sense. *What* should I have known? That the Yankees were going to lose? That some jerk was going to ask for trouble? Get real." But aren't there some things about this situation that Richard should have known better about? Couldn't anyone who knew him have predicted what might happen? Wasn't Richard negligent or careless in giving no thought to what he'd probably do at the game?

Notice that after the dust settles, Richard can explain what happened pretty well. He's not saying, "I can't understand it. I've never done anything like that before." He isn't ignorant of what he's apt to do. In fact, it sounds as if Richard often drinks, loses his temper, and punches people out. Maybe once Richard is drunk and wrapped up in the game, he loses control over what he does. But what about beforehand when he's sober and calm? He can think about the situation, realize the risks, and decide not to go to the game. Or if he does go, he doesn't have to drink before or during the game. He can *voluntarily* choose at some point not to put himself in circumstances (a highly emotional game) or a condition (drunk) in which he will probably do something stupid. If he doesn't, can't we say that he is culpably negligent or careless?

Actions or Character: Which Comes First?

Richard still wants to push his case, however. "That might work for somebody with a different character," he explains, "but not with me. I can't control my temper. It's just the way I am. The least little thing and—bam!—I explode and take a swing at somebody. That's my personality. How can you hold me responsible for something like that?"

This is Richard's best defense. He is negligent or careless because of his personality. His actions stem from his character, and who would hold us responsible for the shape of our personalities? Freud wouldn't, as you saw in the last chapter.

Aristotle would, however. He thinks that what we do shapes and defines who we are. Thus, our actions determine our character. Aristotle has met the likes of Richard before:

> It might be objected that carelessness may be part of a man's character. We counter, however, by asserting that a man is himself responsible for becoming careless, because he lives in a loose and carefree manner, he is likewise responsible for being unjust or self-indulgent, if he keeps on doing mischief or spending his time in drinking and the like. *For a given kind of activity produces a corresponding character.* This is shown by the way in which people train themselves for any kind of contest or performance: they keep on practicing for it. Thus, only a man who is utterly insensitive can be ignorant of the fact that *moral characteristics are formed by actively engaging in particular actions.* [Emphasis added.]
>
> —Nichomachean Ethics

As Aristotle sees it, over the years Richard has developed the habit of giving in to his temper, and that is why his temper has become a part of his personality.

The actions we perform while our characters are being shaped, then, determine how we turn out. Aristotle sees the process of character formation as being exactly like that of learning any skill. If you want to be a gymnast, you must start off doing things right from the beginning. You want to develop the right habits so that the proper movements will be second nature to you. If you let yourself do things the wrong way, you will still end up with a set of movements that are second nature, but they will be the *wrong* movements. The same holds for any physical or intellectual skill. Whether we are any good at it in the end depends on what habits we develop while learning it.

Aristotle views the development of our personalities in the same way. The traits we end up with result from how we behave and what inner dispositions we develop. He explains:

> In our transactions with other men it is by action that some become just and others unjust, and it is by acting in the face of danger and by developing the habit of feeling fear or confidence that some become brave men and others cowards. The same applies to the appetites and feelings of anger: by reacting in one way or in another to given circumstances some people become self-controlled and gentle, and others self-indulgent and short-tempered. In a word, characteristics develop from corresponding activities.
>
> —Nichomachean Ethics

So where did Richard's personality traits come from? From what he did in the past, from the bad habits that he allowed himself to develop and for which he is totally responsible. Although Richard's personality and behavior are pretty well set now, had he behaved differently earlier, he would have different personality traits now.

Could Richard have behaved differently? Presumably, he wasn't born like this, and he didn't get like this overnight. Aristotle would argue that at some earlier time in Richard's life it was possible for him to control himself. If he cannot control himself at age 20, it is because he gave in to his anger all along. And even if it has always been hard for him to control his temper, he should have seen this as a problem and found some better ways to express his anger.

Aristotle supports his theory about character development by citing the case of a sick man.

> Let us assume the case of a man who becomes ill voluntarily through living a dissolute life and disobeying doctors' orders. In the beginning, before he let his health slip away, he could have avoided becoming ill: but once you have thrown a stone and let it go, you can no longer recall it, even though the power to throw it was yours. For the initiative was within you. Similarly, since an unjust or a self-indulgent man initially had the possibility not to become unjust or self-indulgent, he has acquired these traits voluntarily; but once he has acquired them it is no longer possible for him not to be what he is.

—Nichomachean Ethics

Richard's Last Try: The Perception of Good

Richard has one argument left. And it's a good last shot.

"Look," he snarls, "your argument is totally irrational! Nobody would freely pick the character I have or any other bad trait. Why would I choose to get in trouble. People are self-interested—we choose what we think will make us happy. Maybe my perception of what's good for me is a little off. I can accept that. I don't like waking up in jail any more than the next guy. But how I see things when they're happening isn't a matter of *choice*. So how can you blame me as if I were cold sober when I clobbered that guy? You call that fair?"

Richard seems to have two good points. For one thing, he suggests people naturally choose what they perceive will lead to their own happiness. For another, he claims that it's not his fault if his perception is off. He may be responsible for his character traits, but how could he be responsible for his very perception of reality?

Actually, Aristotle agrees with Richard that we all choose what we perceive to be in our own interest. Even if some action is ultimately to our disadvantage, at the moment we choose, we do what we think will make us happy. If we give up our life to save somebody else, for example, what we want at that moment is to preserve the other person's life. We can even apply this principle to Aristotle's example of the sick man. Perhaps the person decided he'd feel better by ignoring his physician's orders. Perhaps he foolishly preferred some short-term pleasure instead of long-term health. Such choices still fit the idea that every choice is made in line with our perception of what will bring happiness.

It sounds like Richard is suggesting another variety of determinism in which we all automatically select what we *perceive* will make us happy. If people have no control over their perception of what is good, then is it fair to blame them if they do the wrong thing?

Aristotle gives no ground, however. "If," the philosopher argues back, "the individual is somehow responsible for his own characteristics, he is similarly responsible for what appears to him [to be good]." Aristotle thinks that as we choose the actions that eventually define our personalities, we affect the entire inner mechanism that processes data from the outside world. Thus, we create our own understanding of reality, just as we create our own character. Aristotle might grant that Richard hit the other fellow because, although he was wrong about it, he perceived that that action would make him happy. But he had that perception only because he had given in to his anger for years. The cumulative effect of all of his past actions includes everything that contributed to his latest action—his perception of the situation, his feelings, his inclinations, and so on. In other words, if Richard had acted differently ten years ago when it was in his power to do so, his perception of reality would have been different today.

Aristotle ultimately concedes nothing to Richard. Although Aristotle admits that some actions are the product of bad habits or ignorance, he does not call these acts involuntary. He still holds us accountable for them. In his opinion, we fashion ourselves with every small deed we do when we have the power to make choices. Therefore, we are responsible not only for how our actions turn out but also for what kind of person we become.

Aristotle and Freedom

Aristotle gives us a solid, commonsense defense of freedom. He thinks most of our actions are voluntary, hence, free choices. Moreover, he suggests that, directly or indirectly, we choose our character, habits, and the very way we perceive reality. Thus, we are responsible for any action that flows from any of those factors. Even when forces overwhelm us, unless it's a case of coercion or ignorance, we cannot escape the responsibility that our freedom brings with it.

Aristotle's ideas are dramatically different from those of Skinner and Freud. So if you've been leaning toward determinism, you've certainly got something to contend with now. To Aristotle, it's obvious that we are free. Only the clearest examples of being forced to do something count as "involuntary" for him. He rejects subtle processes of conditioning and invisible forces in the personality. Aristotle *is* aware that at certain moments we may *feel* compelled to do something by habits we have developed. But he firmly believes that the factors that shape our personality were in our power in the past. Therefore, we are responsible today for the consequences of our habits or dispositions that we allowed to take root years ago. On this matter, Aristotle is uncompromising. Unless we have irrefutable evidence to the contrary—like a gun to our head—our actions result from our free choice.

William James: The Pragmatic Philosopher

The American thinker William James was a psychologist as well as a philosopher, and his arguments in favor of free will over determinism put a good deal of weight on inner, subjective states. Like Aristotle, James is a thinker with a practical tilt. He is the most important representative of the school of thought known as **pragmatism**.

> **pragmatism** Pragmatism is a school of thought that takes a practical and inclusive approach to solving philosophical problems. In connection with the debate between free will and determinism, William James defends free will with the argument that, when we take everything into account, "indeterminism" is an explanation that simply "works better."

William James

William James (1842–1910) was born into an accomplished New York family. He was the son of the religious thinker Henry James, Sr., and the brother of the famous novelist Henry James, Jr. Trained as a physician at the Harvard Medical School, James was nonetheless widely educated and interested in a variety of fields. At one point in his life he considered a career as a painter, and he spent a year on a scientific field expedition in Brazil. But he ultimately taught philosophy and psychology at Harvard, where he became prominent in both fields. James is best known in philosophy as an exponent of the pragmatic conception of truth and a defender of free will. He also explored the phenomenon of religion in *The Varieties of Religious Experience.* As one of the founders of American psychology, he established one of the world's first experimental psychology laboratories at Harvard and he wrote *Principles of Psychology.*

Pragmatism and Freedom

Pragmatism is often misunderstood. We use "pragmatic" in everyday speech to mean "practical," "cynical," even "amoral" and Machiavellian. ("You've got to be pragmatic about things," the campaign manager says to the aspiring mayor. "You'll never win if you don't promise to lower taxes. Lie now. Once you're elected you can do what you want. But for now, lie if you have to.") This does not describe the philosophical school of pragmatism, however. Pragmatism is practical, but not *that* practical.

William James's conception of "pragmatism" recognizes that important questions like "Are our actions determined?" aren't simply interesting intellectual puzzles. They are directly connected with the experience of everyday living and, therefore, the best answers to these questions should "work" for us in a very practical way. They should let us understand the world better. They should fit with our general understanding of life that combines both objective and subjective elements. As James explains in "The Dilemma of Determinism,"

> When we make theories about the world and discuss them with one another, we do so in order to attain a conception of things which shall give us subjective satisfaction; and if there be two conceptions, and the one seems to us, on the whole, more rational than the other, we are entitled to suppose that the more rational one is truer.

Echoing this approach in "What Pragmatism Means," James remarks that

> [Pragmatism's] only test of probable truth is what works best in the way of leading us, what fits every part of life best and combines with the collectivity of experience's demands, nothing being omitted.

On the issue of free will versus determinism, then, James's pragmatic outlook makes him favor freedom because he thinks that the presumption that we are free simply "works" better than determinism does. That is, the idea that there is some element of choice in our actions gives us a more rational and satisfying account of experience than the idea that everything is determined.

Be careful that you don't think that because James is both a scientist and a "pragmatic" philosopher, who talks about whether explanations "work" in a practical way, all he's interested in is hard facts. Objectivity and scientific ideas of empirical proof are important to James. But in assessing ideas and explanations, he also looks to see whether they have what he calls "moral rationality." That is, does an explanation fit with our inner, subjective experiences? In the case of the debate between free will and determinism, James would allow us to use our "feeling of freedom" in evaluating arguments for the opposing sides. Thus, James's "pragmatic" approach to the question of freedom versus determinism lets us reflect on our everyday, subjective experience of life.

Rational and Satisfying Explanations

Before we get into the details of James's argument, you should note just how much his approach differs from that of most hard-nosed scientists, for example, B. F. Skinner. For most scientists, the only thing that counts is observable, measurable data. Anything else is subjective, unscientific, and unacceptable. To such a scientist, a rational and satisfying explanation is one that obeys the canons of logic and the demands of scientific proof. A meaningful assertion can be made only on the basis of observable fact. This lets us say only things like "George's sweater is red," "Kathy has brown hair," and "Dolphins have no vocal cords." You can make complicated statements of this sort, but the "bottom line" is always the same. Someone can say, "Prove it," and you must be able to come up with hard evidence.

James's approach is looser and more inclusive. He uses a fairly broad definition of "rational," one that includes logic and science, of course, but adds some of the more subjective human responses. This is particularly clear in situations involving ethics. Suppose, for example, that someone got out of a date with you by telling a lie. You find out about it and confront the culprit. The liar, however, replies, "There's nothing wrong with what I did. There's no law against it. People do it all the time, and nobody really gets hurt." Can you prove that person wrong? Are there empirical facts to summon in support of your view? No. But does the liar's explanation satisfy you? Probably not. Something about it rubs most of us the wrong way. Maybe it's just your feeling that lying shouldn't be excused so readily. Nonetheless, James would consider your disappointment or disapproval rational and relevant evidence in assessing this situation. Thus, you can see that James accepts a wider range of evidence than Skinner would in discussing freedom versus determinism.

Indeterminism

William James's argument for freedom appears in a famous address called "The Dilemma of Determinism." James's basic strategy is to show that determinism is simply not a very satisfying explanation for human actions. Although he doesn't think that anyone can ultimately prove the issue one way or the other, he thinks that free will, which he calls **indeterminism**, explains human behavior better.

James sets up the two positions in stark opposition:

> [*Determinism*] professes that those parts of the universe already laid down absolutely appoint and decree what the other parts shall be. The future has no ambiguous possibilities hidden in its womb. . . . *Indeterminism,* on the contrary, says that the parts have a certain amount of loose play on one another, so that the laying down of one of them does not necessarily determine what the others shall be. . . . Of two alternative futures which we conceive, both may now be really possible.

Indeterminism and Possibilities

James's first argument for indeterminism is more abstract than anything we have looked at so far in this debate. But it homes in on determinism's central claim that when we have choices to make, we aren't really choosing among genuine options or possibilities. It may look as if there are options, the determinists say, but that is our mistake.

Let's say that you're walking from the Student Union to the library and come to a fork in the road. Both paths lead to the library, and they are equally direct, scenic, and flat. You've gone both ways at different times with no pattern of preferring one over the other or of alternating routes. There is no apparent reason for you to choose one or the other now. This time you take the path on the left.

What were the odds of your taking the left fork? One in two. And the right fork? Again, one in two. You would say that, and James would say that. But the determinist says that you're fooling yourself, and that it wasn't even *possible* for you to take the right fork. The odds weren't one in two, but zero. The odds for the left fork, on the other hand, were one in one. A situation may look as if it presents more than one possibility. But the determinist says that, in reality, only one thing can happen.

This, of course, does not square with how we feel about the situation. When presented with a choice of two routes, we feel as though we have two genuine possibilities. Even if we have a strong preference for one, it still feels *possible* for us to select the other. James's first argument for indeterminism, then, is built on this very basic human experience—the feeling that when we make a choice about something, we believe that we have different *possibilities* to pick from. It's no illusion—the choice is real and the outcome genuinely unknown.

Can we prove that these options or possibilities exist? No. But how does it feel to you? Didn't you choose which college to go to? For some people this is a very

---

indeterminism Indeterminism is William James's position that in any circumstance we genuinely have more than one option from which to choose. Accordingly, he argues, our actions are not determined.

difficult decision. Especially early in the process, you probably felt that several schools were real possibilities. And what about your future? Don't you think there are different paths your life might take? Isn't it your choice? Different careers, different people to fall in love with, different places to live? In every area of life, in fact, you probably sense many different possibilities.

As James points out, the determinist says that an apparent option is either necessary or impossible. According to determinism, then, it was necessary and unavoidable that you attend this school. Despite what you went through in trying to make up your mind, deciding to go to a different school was absolutely impossible. The causes of your action were already in place. James, on the other hand, thinks that it was possible for you to have chosen differently.

This idea of possibilities is so important to James because he thinks that it makes his case. To prove that determinism is wrong, James doesn't try to show that a hundred possible options are equally likely every time we're faced with a choice. All it takes, says James, is one other genuine possibility:

> "Free-will" does not say that everything that is physically conceivable is also morally possible. It merely says that of alternatives that really tempt our will, more than one is really possible. Of course, the alternatives that do thus tempt us are vastly fewer than the physical possibilities we can coldly fancy.

So William James's first argument in favor of free will, or indeterminism, is that if it is at least possible for you to select more than one of the apparent choices, then determinism is flat out wrong. If more than one option is genuinely possible, neither the universe nor our actions are fixed and necessary as determinists claim they are.

Pragmatism and Possibilities

But James does not dismiss determinism just because we feel that possibilities exist. As a pragmatist, he needs to show that indeterminism gives us a more rational and more workable explanation of reality than determinism does.

James goes at this by pointing out that he could take two streets to go home after his lecture—Divinity Avenue or Oxford Street. Imagine that he takes Divinity. Now, let's turn back the clock to the point where he makes his choice. This time imagine that he takes Oxford. "Now if you are determinists," James contends,

> you believe one of these universes to have been from eternity impossible. . . . But looking outwardly at these universes, can you say which is the impossible and accidental one, and which the rational and necessary one? I doubt if the most iron-clad determinist among you could have the slightest glimmer of light on this point. In other words, either universe after the fact and once there would to our means of observation and understanding, appear just as rational as the other. There would be absolutely no criterion by which we might judge one necessary.

We can rationally conceive of James taking either road. If determinism is correct, however, one of these choices is impossible. But why? Nothing suggests that one road should be impossible. That idea simply makes no sense. Seen this way, determinism does not give us a rational and satisfying account of the world. Indeterminism, on the other hand, seems to match our experience and our expectations very well. As an explanation, it is more satisfying and "works" better.

James's criticism of determinism is made particularly effective by his comment that when we look at his choice between Divinity and Oxford "after the fact," we fail to discover a causal chain that made it inevitable that he would take the street he did. But that's not always the case with even complicated instances of cause and effect. Take the weather, for example. The behavior of storms and air currents can be very difficult to forecast. Meteorologists, however, can do an excellent job of explaining after the fact why a typhoon veered away from the mainland at the last minute. Once all of the facts are in, a close analysis will show how it was all a matter of cause and effect. James's argument is that his selection of street can't be explained as necessary even looking back at it; therefore, it must have been a function of free choice among more than one genuine possibilities.

Feelings of "Regret"

James's other major argument against determinism is, like his first one, based on ordinary human experience. The first assumes that we're right to think that whenever we make a choice, it's possible for us to have chosen differently. His second position builds on our everyday sense of justice and fairness.

James begins with the basic observation that we regularly feel dissatisfied with life. He says that we live in "a world in which we constantly have to make what I shall, with your permission, call judgments of regret. Hardly an hour passes in which we do not wish that something might be otherwise." Some of these regrets are trivial—it is raining, you have a quiz today, you weigh too much—and you can put them behind you fairly easily. Other dissatisfactions stick with us, however, and they often involve our sense of right and wrong. James writes,

> Some regrets are pretty obstinate and hard to stifle, regrets for acts of wanton cruelty or treachery, for example, whether performed by others or by ourselves. Hardly anyone can remain entirely optimistic after reading the confession of the murderer at Brockton the other day: how, to get rid of the wife whose continued existence bored him, he inveigled her into a desert spot, shot her four times, and then, as she lay on the ground and said to him, "You didn't do it on purpose, did you, dear?" replied, "No, I didn't do it on purpose," as he raised a rock and smashed her skull. Such an occurrence, with the mild sentence and self-satisfaction of the prisoner, is a field for a crop of regrets, which one need not take up in detail. We feel that, although a perfect mechanical fit to the rest of the universe, it is a bad moral fit, and that something else would really have been better in its place.

Once again, whose explanation of such a terrible event works better and is more satisfying, the determinist's or the indeterminist's? Determinism obviously must maintain that the murder was destined from eternity. "For the deterministic philosophy," explains James, "nothing else for a moment had a ghost of a chance of being put into their place. To admit such a chance, the determinists tell us, would be to make a suicide of reason."

This doesn't set right with James—or with most of us. James asks, "If this Brockton murder was called for by the rest of the universe, if it had to come at its preappointed hour, and if nothing else would have been consistent with the sense of the whole, what are we to think of the universe?" Determinism, then, gives us a world in which it is irrational to think that such terrible crimes do not have to happen. Isn't there something basically wrong about such a universe? Seen this way, determinism doesn't strike us as either rational or satisfying.

Determinism may be able to account for all the causal forces that impelled this man to murder his wife. That's what James means when he says that this tragedy has "a perfect *mechanical* fit to the rest of the universe." But James thinks that our analysis cannot stop there. The murder, he says, has "a bad moral fit." To understand the event more fully, we have to consider more than cause and effect. A crime such as this has another dimension that we all respond to on a deeper, more personal level. No ordinary person can contemplate what the husband did without a deep sense of horror and revulsion. Yet determinism argues that such a feeling is both inappropriate and irrelevant to any discussion of the husband's deed.

The way William James expresses this is to say that determinism "violates my sense of moral reality through and through." There is more to understanding and evaluating an action than looking impersonally at cause and effect, he suggests. We must also use what James calls our "moral rationality" and see what our basic sense of ethics tells us about the situation. Our moral outrage over this murder tells us something important that cannot be ignored. Normal people consistently react to cruelty, unfairness, and injustice in a host of ways: shock, dismay, blame, anger, and so on. That is a fact of human experience. *But we wouldn't react this way unless we believed that people could act differently.* It would clearly be irrational to do so.

In effect, James says that when we pay attention to what our ordinary sense of right and wrong (our "moral rationality") tells us about a situation, we have more reasons to reject determinism. Indeterminism gives us a more rational and satisfying explanation because it maintains that the husband who murders his wife because he was bored with her was in control of his actions, did something very wrong, and deserves to be punished.

James and Freedom

As we saw earlier, William James doesn't think it's possible to prove beyond any doubt whether determinism or indeterminism is right. He does, however, make two very important points that lead him to believe that indeterminism is more rational, more satisfying, and simply "works better" as an account of human action.

First, the human mind is more satisfied with the idea that genuine choices, options, or possibilities are real, not imaginary. It simply makes more sense to us. When you go to a theater showing seven different movies, all of which you would like to see, you feel that you have seven genuine alternatives. What if someone walked up to you and said, "No, it's already determined. You have no choice. It is necessary that you see the one you pick and impossible for you to choose any other"? You'd think that this person was more than a little strange. The idea simply does not square with what we take to be an almost self-evident dimension of human life.

Similarly, if someone is cruel to you, it seems perfectly sensible and rational for you to feel that the act was wrong, that it never should have happened, and that the person doing it should be punished. Imagine that you and a friend are walking along and someone jumps out of the shadows, flashes a knife, and takes your money. If after the robber runs off, your friend turns to you and calmly says, "My, that poor devil's id is simply overwhelming his superego," you'd wonder what planet your friend came from. The normal reaction in this circumstance is anger and the certainty that the thief had chosen to do something wrong. And James takes this normal, moral sense as further reason for thinking that our actions are not determined.

There's no great mystery to James's arguments for "indeterminism." Like Aristotle, James relies very much on our everyday sensibilities that people are free and that, from a commonsense standpoint, free will is easier to accept than determinism. Notice that, as was the case with Aristotle's arguments, the idea of responsibility plays a major role here. To accept determinism means that we have to give up a very strong belief—one that feels virtually self-evident—that it is rational and fair to hold each other responsible for what we do. Determinists like Skinner and Freud may argue on scientific grounds. But, like virtually every philosopher who argues for freedom of the will, James and Aristotle build much of their case on moral grounds.

In citing the murder case, James in particular implies that one of the most important things at stake in the free will/determinism debate isn't a philosophical issue at all, but a civic, social, or political one. If determinism is correct, we have no rational basis on which to punish even the most heinous crimes because it is wrong to penalize people for actions they did not choose. Yet if we go in that direction, what kind of a society are we left with?

Jean-Paul Sartre: The Existentialist Philosopher

Both Aristotle and William James make commonsense arguments for free will. We generally feel as if we make real choices. Our conventional moral sense tells us that other people can control their actions and are responsible for them. Not all arguments for free choice rely on our everyday experience, however. Indeed, one of the most extreme defenses of freedom grants us so much freedom that the argument seems to defy commonsense.

Think again about the seven-theater movie house, and imagine that it's on your way home from school. As you drive past it one day, your car, which has been stalling a lot, coughs and dies. The only telephone for miles around doesn't work, so you're stuck there. You were rushing home to study for a big test tomorrow, but now you decide to wait in the lobby to see if you can get a ride from someone. As you stand there, a stranger walks up to you and says, "I've got a gun. Do as I say, and I won't hurt you. You and I are going to see a movie." You go to the ticket window and find that the only show not sold out is a re-release of *Alice in Wonderland,* a movie that gave you nightmares when you saw it as a kid. But you have no choice. The two of you see the movie, and your captor disappears into the night.

Jean-Paul Sartre

The main proponent of existentialism, Jean-Paul Sartre (1905–1980) was a famous novelist and playwright as well as a major philosopher. Educated in Paris, Sartre began his career teaching in France and Germany. He was involved in the resistance during World War II and was politically active throughout his life. His major philosophical opus is *Being and Nothingness.* Some of his literary works include *Nausea, No Exit,* and *Saint Genet.*

Did you have any freedom in this situation? It doesn't look like it. You were stuck someplace you didn't want to be, kidnapped at gunpoint, and forced to watch a movie you didn't want to see. But what if someone told you that you were *totally free* in that situation and that your commonsense perception that you weren't free is a serious mistake on your part?

Before you dismiss this suggestion completely, let's consider the movie scenario again. As background, however, we should look at the "big picture." You *chose* to go to college. You *chose* the college you are in. You *chose* to drive your car in bad shape. You *chose* the course you now have an exam in. You *chose* to study for the exam on the last possible night. The same pattern holds for your immediate predicament. You *chose* to wait at the theater rather than walk home or try to hitch a ride on the road. You *chose* to go along with your kidnapper and not resist. You did that because you *chose* to protect your life.

You've even made choices that determine your emotions. On the one hand, you can *choose* to believe the promise that you will not be hurt; you can *choose* to make the most of the situation and try to enjoy the movie by watching it this time through an adult's eyes. All of this will keep you calm. Or you *choose* to *doubt* your kidnapper's word, focus on your bad fortune, and remind yourself how the movie scared you years ago—which will make you miserable and terrified. Clearly, you make choice upon choice in that situation.

You may think that it is unrealistic to say that you made choices here. But let's face it—you didn't really *have* to do any of the things you did, did you? You don't even *have* to protect your life. Of course, it is nicer to be alive and healthy than dead, but that is your choice. You are free to endanger your life if you want to.

Just look at all the choices you've made with complete freedom. When we look at the story this way, you become the sole architect of almost everything about the situation you find yourself in.

Extreme Freedom and Existentialism

The case for absolute freedom is put most persuasively by the twentieth-century school of philosophy called existentialism. The existentialists argue for a position directly opposed to the determinism of Skinner and Freud who claim that every-thing about us—all our actions and all our feelings—is determined. On the con-trary, existentialism argues that we are totally free and that absolutely everything about us is a product of our own choices. We are completely free at every moment, the existentialists insist, and we are responsible for each and every detail of our lives.

The existentialist position on freedom is so extreme that it may seem unbeliev-able—just as unbelievable, perhaps, as extreme determinism. But give it a chance. **Existentialism** is built on the belief that we humans are free and that shaping our lives according to our own plans is the central project of our lives. And this out-look has made existentialism one of the twentieth century's most important contri-butions to philosophy.

Sartre and Existentialism

One of the best representatives of existentialism is the French philosopher Jean-Paul Sartre. Sartre's basic ideas on freedom are clear and straightforward—hard to accept, perhaps, but nonetheless clear and straightforward.

Sartre's position on human freedom is intimately connected with his overall view of the nature of reality. First, Sartre does not believe God exists. (Not all existen-tialists are atheists, but Sartre is.) Thus, there is no supreme being who dictates the meaning of life or determines the nature of things and the rules of the game. Sartre also rejects the idea that either natural evolutionary forces or inner psychological ones set any direction for human life. Without such forces, absolute freedom is all that is left. To Sartre, freedom is simply a basic fact of human existence—as basic as conditioning is in a Skinnerian world.

Essence Precedes Existence

When Sartre renounces God and all natural forces, he also rejects what he calls the long-standing philosophical belief that **essence precedes existence**. This is the idea that the basic nature of something—its *essence*—determines the shape, activity, and possibilities of its everyday life—its *existence*. Something's essence "precedes" its ex-istence in that it is logically prior to it. That is, it sets the ground rules or bound-aries of what that object or being can do.

For example, the essence, or nature, of the computer I'm using to write this book is to be a device designed to generate, retain, and manipulate electrical im-pulses so that it can store data, perform certain operations, and create images on a screen. What it actually does in the course of a day—its existence—is set by the

---

existentialism Existentialism is a school of thought based on the idea that "ex-istence precedes essence," that is, that our nature is determined by the ac-tions we choose to do. Existentialism argues that freedom is such an un-avoidable, and sometimes uncomfortable, characteristic of life that we are "condemned to be free." We are completely free at every moment, absolutely everything about us is a product of our own choices, and we are responsi-ble for each and every detail of our lives.

computer's capacities and limits—its essence. Within the specifications and possibilities determined by the computer's components installed at the factory, it will run computer programs. And at any given time, its range of activities is determined by whatever program I am running. That's all it can do. It can't fly, make breakfast for me, or engage in interesting conversation. These things, and many others, are beyond its essence, and thus its existence will never include them.

To apply the idea that essence determines existence to humans, let's look back at Freud's thinking. There we find that the essence of being human—our nature, what we are—is to be a biological creature with an inner mental and emotional life characterized by two basic drives (sex and aggression) and a three-part personality structure (id, ego, and superego), which develops through various psychosexual stages and which uses various defense mechanisms. Our existence—what we do in our lives—then, is completely determined by our essence. Our conscious self primarily tries to arbitrate the insatiable and contradictory demands of our id and superego. Within this frame of reference, it would be ridiculous to say, "I choose to live with no instinct for aggression." It is simply beyond our essence.

Existence Precedes Essence

Sartre sees the situation as completely reversed when it comes to humans. He turns the "essence precedes existence" formula around and says that **existence precedes essence**. (This emphasis on "existence" obviously shows up in the name "existentialism.")

Sartre denies that there is such a thing as a "human nature," or a human "essence," that determines or limits our choices. He claims that what we choose to do (our existence) determines our nature (our essence). The first principle of existentialism, then, is, "Man is nothing else but what he makes of himself." If this is so, then people are absolutely free. As he explains in the essay "Existentialism," "If existence really does precede essence, there is no explaining things away by reference to a fixed and given human nature. In other words, there is no determinism, man is free, man is freedom."

The most important thing is what we do with our freedom. Thinking, wanting, or hoping may be important parts of our freedom, but Sartre believes that what is absolutely critical is what we *do*. Sartre claims, "There is no reality except in action. . . . Man is nothing else than his plan; he exists only to the extent that he fulfills himself; he is therefore nothing else than the ensemble of his acts, nothing else than his life."

Life gets its meaning and purpose, then, from what we do with it. It is as if each one of us were given a huge mound of clay. We are sculptors who will give the clay life and shape. Each choice we make in our lives is like the movement of

---

essence precedes existence Philosophers have traditionally held that the "nature" of something determines what it is able to do, its limitations, defining characteristics, and the like, that is, its "existence." This position is rejected by the existential belief that our choices determine our nature ("existence precedes essence").

our hands as we fashion the clay into a definite form. And if we pause, step back, and decide we don't like how the sculpture is turning out, we can start all over and try to make something different. Seen this way, life is a totally open enterprise.

Human Imagination and Creativity

When Sartre argues in favor of freedom by denying a fixed human nature, he's not simply being naive. He does recognize that human beings have certain biological needs and limitations. Who could deny that a human being is a land-based, featherless biped who needs food and water to stay alive? But Sartre sees that choices about even these things are somehow within our power. We are, after all, free to choose whether or not to eat and remain alive. And because of our special abilities, we can search for ways to do things that lie beyond our limits. Take flying, for example. Birds can fly, humans cannot. But we found a way to do the impossible and fly, didn't we? So, in a way, we can transcend our biological limitations.

Obviously, what makes all this possible is human imagination, intellect, will, desire, and the capacity to choose. This is what Sartre means when he says, "Man is freedom." Even if the evidence of your own life leads you to feel that our possibilities are not endless, look at the life of our species. Humans have found ways to do all kinds of "impossible" things: underwater travel, space flight, building roads through mountains, splitting the atom, defeating "incurable" diseases, breaking the 4-minute mile, and becoming fast friends with sworn enemies. The list goes on and on. To say that "**existence precedes essence**," then, is to attest to our enormous creative powers as human beings.

Condemned to Be Free

When you think about it, the tremendous possibilities that come from being as free as Sartre envisions us to be are truly thrilling. Think of that "I-can-accomplish-anything-I-put-my-mind-to" feeling. But Sartre sees freedom as so fundamental and so pervasive that the prospect is not all upbeat. A full awareness of our responsibility for each and every facet of our lives can be troubling. This much freedom ultimately makes us anxious. As Sartre puts it, we are "condemned to be free."

This phrase—"condemned to be free"—suggests a variety of difficulties. First, we have no choice in the matter. We never asked to be born. Yet here we are, thrown into a situation that requires endless, often terrifying decisions about everything in our lives.

The phrase also conveys the idea that we are trapped—sentenced to a situation we can never break out of. Even if we want to avoid freely fashioning our life, we can't. "I bear the whole responsibility without being able, whatever I do, to tear myself away from this responsibility for an instant," Sartre explains in *Being and*

---

existence precedes essence "Existence precedes essence" is the existentialist rejection of the traditional idea that something's nature determines its abilities and limitations in how it lives. Existentialism maintains instead that our choices ("existence") determine our nature ("essence").

Nothingness. "For I am responsible," he continues, "for my very desire of fleeing responsibilities. To make myself passive in the world, to refuse to act upon things and upon Others is still to choose myself." Whether we go our own way, go along with what everyone else does, or try to do nothing, we choose that course of action. We must accept the responsibility for absolutely everything we do, including ducking out on our responsibilities. We always have the choice. We always have an option. We always have control. We can never escape it.

"Man is condemned to be free," writes Sartre,

> because he did not create himself, yet, in other respects is free; because, once thrown into the world, he is responsible for everything he does. The existentialist does not believe in the power of passion. He will never agree that a sweeping passion is a ravaging torrent which fatally leads a man to certain acts and is therefore an excuse. He thinks that man is responsible for his passion.
>
> The existentialist does not think that man is going to help himself by finding in the world some omen by which to orient himself. Because he thinks that man will interpret the omen to suit himself. Therefore, he thinks that man, with no support and no aid, is condemned every moment to invent man.

—"Existentialism"

Responsibility and "Bad Faith"

Freedom, of course, automatically carries with it the fact of responsibility. If you freely choose to do something, you are responsible for your action and its consequences. In Sartre's scheme, we must feel responsible all the time.

That can be quite a punishment, especially when most of us regularly try to avoid taking full responsibility for our lives. Being responsible for making solid, authentic choices at every juncture is hard to handle. Yet when we choose not to do it, Sartre accuses us of acting in "bad faith"—lying to ourselves about our responsibility.

Sartre illustrates bad faith in *Being and Nothingness* with a story about a woman out on a date. The man wants to begin an affair; the woman does not know what she wants to do. She knows she must eventually make a decision, but she tries to put it off. Then the man takes her hand and caresses it. This calls for a decision. The woman now should either take her hand away, indicating her lack of interest, or respond in a way that encourages the man. What happens, however, is that "the young woman leaves her hand there, but she *does not notice* that she's leaving it." She goes on talking about something intellectual, while her hand "rests inert between the warm hands of her companion—neither consenting nor resisting—a thing." Instead of making a decision, she denies that one is called for. She refuses to accept the responsibility for making a choice. For Sartre this is a superb image of how we try to avoid our freedom. This woman acts as though she doesn't even notice that the man has taken her hand.

We all find ways of acting in "bad faith." You don't return a telephone call from someone you want to break up with because you don't want to deliver the bad news. When your friend calls back later you say, "I'm sorry. I was so busy I forgot you called." You try out for the soccer team—but only half-heartedly. When you don't make it, you tell yourself, "I didn't really want to play soccer anyway." In both cases, you deny reality and avoid a real decision.

Of course, "not to decide is to decide." The woman in Sartre's story decided to do nothing now. You have decided to let your friend think the romance is still on. You decided not to do your best at the tryouts. But Sartre thinks that acting in "bad faith" like this is dishonest. The only good way to live is to accept head-on the responsibility that comes with our freedom, make decisions, and face the consequences.

The Extent of Our Responsibility

Sartre is merciless when it comes to our accepting responsibility. No matter what happens in our life, we can never blame anybody else: Our own responsibility is total. "Man being condemned to be free," says Sartre, "carries the weight of the whole world on his shoulders; he is responsible for the world and for himself as a way of being." Responsible for the whole world? "Sartre can't mean it," you say. "Responsible for my small corner? Fine. But more than that's crazy."

Does Sartre actually mean what he says? Absolutely. The most dramatic proof of this lies in a passage from his book, *Being and Nothingness,* where he talks about the responsibility of an individual person for a war. Sartre fought with the French underground in World War II, and you'd think he wouldn't hold the citizens of an invaded country in any way responsible for such a misfortune. Yet in Sartre's view:

> Thus there are no accidents in a life; a community event which suddenly bursts forth and involved me in it does not come from the outside. If I am mobilized in a war, this war is my war; it is in my image and I deserve it. I deserve it first because I could always get out of it by suicide or by desertion; these ultimate possibles are those which must always be present for us when there is a question of envisaging a situation. For lack of getting out of it, I have chosen it. This can be due to inertia, to cowardice in the face of public opinion, or because I prefer certain other values to the value of the refusal to join in the war (the good opinion of my relatives, the honor of my family, etc.). Anyway you look at it, it is a matter of a choice. This choice will be repeated later on again and again without a break until the end of the war. Therefore we must agree with the statement by J. Romains, "In war there are no innocent victims." If therefore I have preferred war to death or to dishonor, everything takes place as if I bore the entire responsibility for this war. Of course others have declared it, and one might be tempted perhaps to consider me as a simple accomplice. But this notion of complicity has only a juridical sense, and it does not hold here. For it depended on me that for me and by me this war should not exist, and I have decided that it does exist. There was no compulsion here, for the compulsion could have got no hold on a freedom. I did not have any excuse; for as we have repeatedly said in this book, the peculiar character of human-reality is that it is without excuse. Therefore it remains for me only to lay claim to this war.
>
> —Being and Nothingness

This is certainly one of Sartre's most troubling ideas. Yet it does dramatize just how much freedom and power Sartre thinks we really have. Believing that you are genuinely responsible for everything around you might overwhelm you. But if you could cope with that responsibility, you would also feel extremely powerful. After all, if you really are responsible for something, you must also have the power to change it.

The Extent of Our Power

Most of us feel uneasy about Sartre's extreme claims because we feel relatively powerless in life. Sartre's war example is perfect. We feel that we have about as much control over a war as we do over an earthquake or the eruption of a volcano. And if we have no power over something, how can we have any responsibility for it?

We do, however, have more power over things than we think we do. Take the simple example of how other people treat you. By and large, people treat you exactly the way you tell them to. It is almost entirely under your control.

"Not so," you say. "I'm shy, withdrawn, and—if I have to admit it—kind of uninteresting. Nobody ever likes to talk to me. I can't help it. It's just the way I am." But how do people know you're "shy, withdrawn, and uninteresting"? Do you wear a sign? Can they read minds? No, you tell them with your actions. You don't mingle with them. You don't smile. You don't say you're glad to see them. You stay quiet and invisible in a conversation. This is how you choose to act around others, and these are cues that say, "Leave me alone."

But try this experiment sometime. When you're with a group of people who don't know you, consciously decide to be different from how you usually are. If you're shy, act outgoing. If you're usually serious, act fun loving. If you usually play dumb, be serious and intellectual. Don't be phony. Say to yourself, "Tonight I choose to be different. I don't have anything to lose, and I don't have to stay like this for the rest of my life. But tonight I'm someone who's genuinely _____." Do you know what will happen? People will respond as though this is exactly how you've been all your life. That's because you're telling them who you are and how to treat you. And who you choose to be inside is the single most important influence on how people treat you.

Now try a bigger exercise in freedom and power. Think of some important issue on your campus or in your community, something that bothers you and that should be changed—some example of unfairness, discrimination, dishonesty, harm to the environment. If someone said to you, "So go change it," you would probably reply, "You're crazy. One person can't change things like that. It's up to the _____ (fill in the blank: "the Student Senate," "Administration," "City Council," etc.). I'm just me."

Now recall Sartre's conviction that each of us is responsible for everything that goes on in the world and *feel* the weight of that responsibility. Think again about what you want changed and feel responsible for it. Suddenly, "I'm just me" becomes "I'm the person responsible for this." You are as important as anyone else connected with it. If this is so, there must be something you can do to make things better.

Suppose it's a college policy you want changed. People made it and people can change it. So get advice about how to proceed. Talk to your professors, counselors, administrators. Find out who else thinks the way you do. When someone says, "We simply cannot change things," find a new path to take. Feel complete responsibility for the situation. If you can't convince the right people, it's because you didn't find the right argument. So try again—there's always somebody else to talk to.

But don't complain and don't blame anybody else. Sartre says, "The peculiar character of human-reality is that it is without excuse." Existentialism does not let you shift responsibility. If you blame somebody else, you abdicate your responsibility.

If you truly accept responsibility for the cause you champion, don't give up, and do everything you can, you will get somewhere. You may not get everything you want, and you may not get it when you want it. But eventually you will change something for the better. Even if that policy stays in place, you will have changed the way some people think. And you may at least have stopped other similar policies from being enacted.

Existentialism maintains that we regularly underestimate how much power we have. If you doubt it, try it.

Sartre and Freedom

Sartre writes about many other philosophical issues, but this is his basic view of freedom. Sartre rejects determinism so completely that he believes that "man is freedom." We choose everything about our lives—even our very essence. Indeed, humans are so free that we are "condemned" to constant choices. Sartre believes that we must feel totally responsible for every facet of our own lives—and even those of others. If we fail to do so, we are acting in "bad faith." As you can see, then, existentialism is the antithesis of determinism.

Albert Ellis: Freedom Through Right Thinking

Despite the arguments of Aristotle, James, and Sartre in favor of free will, the scientific bases of Freudianism and behaviorism may have you leaning toward determinism. After all, Freud and Skinner did not just think up their theories. They tested them against facts—in Freud's case, his clinical experience; in Skinner's case, his experiments. Skinner, in particular, talks about having discovered a "*science* of human nature." It may seem, then, that unless some proponent of free will can validate his ideas by experimental testing, determinism has the edge.

Freud and Skinner have a colleague, however, whose work comes remarkably close to a practical "proof" of free will. The contemporary psychologist Albert Ellis has developed a practical methodology that helps us make significant changes in our lives—the kinds of changes we can make only if we are free. Ellis called this approach **rational-emotive therapy**.

---

rational-emotive therapy Rational-emotive therapy is a psychological school of thought developed by Albert Ellis under the influence of Stoic philosophy. Ellis maintains that the greatest barrier to our freedom is irrational beliefs, and he proposes a method for defusing them.

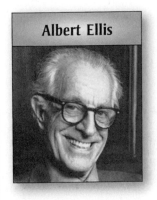

Albert Ellis

Albert Ellis (born 1913) is the founder of the school of psychology known as rational-emotive therapy. Ellis decided as a youth that he wanted a career as a writer but realized he would need a profession to support himself. Accordingly, he studied accounting at New York's High School of Commerce and Baruch College. Graduating during the Depression, he eventually found work at a gift novelty company. He worked at the company for ten years and in his spare time wrote numerous manuscripts, none of which was published. He subsequently began graduate school and received his doctorate in clinical psychology from Teachers College, Columbia University. After working as a psychologist for the state of New Jersey, Ellis trained as a psychoanalyst and established his own counseling practice, becoming one of the first psychologists to specialize in sexual and marital problems. By 1955, he began to develop a therapeutic approach that differed radically from classical Freudian therapy, and in 1959, he established the Institute for Rational-Emotive Therapy. Ellis has written more than 50 books and 600 articles, and he has been widely recognized as one of the most influential practitioners in his field.

Ellis's Thought

Albert Ellis believes as strongly in the individual's power over his or her own life as Skinner, Freud, or any other hard-core determinist denies it. A renegade in American psychology, Ellis was trained in traditional psychoanalysis. In the course of his work, however, he came to believe that the conscious mind has tremendous power over our emotions, and he left the Freudian fold. Ellis became a "cognitive" psychologist; that is, he believes that what we *think* is the most important factor in determining what we feel and how we shape our lives.[1]

According to Ellis, the barriers that block our way to happiness lie inside our minds. (As the comic character Pogo puts it, "We have met the enemy and he is us.") He agrees with other psychologists that we are often held back by foolish fears. But he thinks that these fears stem from "wrong thinking," not from traumatic experiences in childhood or from prior reinforcement. Ellis's approach, however, is based on the notion that these wrong ideas—irrational beliefs about the world— can be changed. Ellis says that if we identify and correct our irrational beliefs, we can make major changes in our lives. With fewer irrational fears, we have more power and control over what we do. We have more options. We have more freedom. If we change the thinking, we change the feeling and free the individual.

---

[1]By contrast, Freud's work is characterized as "psychodynamic" because he concentrates on the ebb and flow of energies stemming from our basic psychological drives. Skinner's work is characterized as "behavioral" because, of course, he focuses exclusively on observable behavior.

Thus, Ellis speaks on the side of freedom and against determinism. We are as free in life as we choose to be. The fears that prevent us from flourishing are chains of our own making. The key to unlock the chains lies in discovering the faulty ideas we have about life. And since thinking is under our conscious control, we can freely choose to think—and thus live—differently.

Emotions and Reason

Although Ellis is not an existentialist, he would agree with Sartre's claim that each of us is largely responsible for his or her own predicament. In particular, Ellis would agree that there is a large element of free choice and, thus, control in how we respond emotionally to situations.

You may have your doubts about this. Thoughts and actions may be controllable, but our feelings? Do we say, "My dog just died. Now I choose to cry"? Or "Hmmm, a pair of rattlesnakes. I guess fear is in order"? Of course not. Our emotions feel like automatic reactions beyond our control. If you walk up to your brand new car in a parking lot and find a big dent in it, how much good does it do for a friend to say, "Come on, it's ridiculous to be upset. It won't fix the dent"? You feel angry for good reason. You can't just turn your feelings off and on like a light switch.

If our feelings just happen, how can Ellis be right? But if he's right, then we would have control over what feel like spontaneous reactions, and that would give us a tremendous amount of freedom.

Ellis believes that our minds do indeed govern our emotions. He explains, "Human emotions do *not* magically exist in their own right, and do not mysteriously flow from unconscious needs and desires. Rather, they almost always directly stem from ideas, thoughts, attitudes, or beliefs."

Ellis's ABCs of human psychology are that an *activating experience* or event (A) produces a certain emotional *consequence* (C) because of what's in our *belief system* (B). For example, your parents surprise you with a new jacket you wanted but couldn't afford (A), and you feel happy that they love you (C). This is because, consciously or unconsciously, you have a belief in your mind (B): "If someone does something nice for me, it shows they care."

$$A \rightarrow B \rightarrow C$$

On the other hand, your friend Darryl receives the same present from his parents and gets upset. Why does the same event (A) produce such a different emotion (C)? Because the relevant part of his belief system (B) tells him: "Whenever my parents send me a surprise like this, it means they're going to force me to do something they know I don't want to do. They're just trying to soften me up." In other words, the present is a warning and a threat.

Thus, you can see how Ellis thinks that emotions are the direct result of our beliefs.

Irrational Beliefs

Ellis thinks that many of the ideas in our belief system are irrational. It's easy to see how we can get the wrong ideas about things. We may be told something by our parents, teachers, or other people in authority. ("People like us don't have a chance to make it to the top.") We may pick them up through the messages we get from advertisements. ("If I drive a dull or banged up car, no one will find me attractive.") We may generalize on insufficient data. ("I didn't do well in math in high school, so I guess I'll always be bad with numbers.") We may be prejudiced about something and have never thought about it. ("Whites and blacks are too different to be friends with each other.") Or we may draw the wrong conclusions from our fears. ("People will laugh at me if I fail.") Accordingly, these erroneous ideas give rise to the emotions that make us unhappy and keep us unfree.

For instance, how would you feel if your teacher told you that next week you would be expected to do a 20-minute oral presentation on freedom and determinism? You are supposed to explain your position, handle questions from your classmates, and defend yourself against attack. Some of you might enjoy doing this, but most of you wouldn't. And for some of you the thought of speaking in front of a group sends you into a genuine panic.

If you find the idea of the class presentation upsetting, Ellis would say it's because of an irrational idea in your belief system that might go something like this:

> If I speak in public, I'll do badly. I'll hem and haw and sound stupid. I may even go blank. Everybody will think that I'm a fool and laugh to themselves about me. They'll never respect me again or even want to be seen with me. Every time they see me again they'll say to one another, "There goes that jerk who did that lousy report. Boy, I'm glad I'm not an idiot like that." It will be horrible. I'll never feel good about myself again. Everyone will reject me, abandon me. I'll be all alone. It'll be so bad I'll just want to die. In fact, it'll be so bad, I will die.

Whew! No wonder you don't like to speak in front of groups.[2]

Furthermore, if that is your belief, it's actually logical for you to avoid public speaking. Given your premises, your conclusion follows. The argument is valid. But how rational is it to think this way? How true are your premises? How sound is your argument?

First of all, if these were the actual consequences of doing a bad presentation, no one would ever speak in public. Do you think any of your teachers would risk stepping in front of a class or an audience of scholars if that's what would happen if they bombed? They'd have to be crazy. In reality, of course, speaking in front of other people can be quite enjoyable. Classes and audiences are usually sympathetic and supportive. Teachers aren't thrilled to have a bad day, but the world doesn't shun them forever. The audience doesn't get up *en masse* and walk out on them in disgust. The president of the college doesn't come up to them and say, "I hear you taught a lousy class today. I'm sorry about this, but we're going to have to take you out back and shoot you."

So, are you positive a class presentation will go badly? No. Even if you do a bad job, will people think you're incompetent? No. Will they talk about it for days

---

[2]You may balk at this description of the source of your fears. "All I know is that I'm scared," you say, "I don't see any "irrational beliefs." The trouble is that most of us don't even know what's in our belief systems. But if you push the examination of your fears far enough, deep down you will inevitably find irrational beliefs.

afterward? No. Will your friends desert you? No. Will doing badly mean that you're a worthless human being who should jump off the nearest cliff so as not to trouble the rest of us with your existence? Hardly.

Your initial belief was simply not rational. A more reasonable one might go something like this:

> If I do a good job in front of the class, I'll feel terrific. But even if I don't do a great job, as long as I prepare adequately, I won't look like an idiot.
>
> After all, I can read my notes. I may feel nervous, but everybody else would feel nervous, too. So they're going to be sitting there saying, "Boy, I'm glad I'm not up there." Afterwards my friends will tell me I did well, even if I didn't. The absolute worst case is that I do poorly. That won't feel good. In fact, I may feel pretty crummy for a while. But the world won't come to an end and I'll get over it. I'll have other chances to pull up my grade and impress people.

If you adopt something like this as your belief (B), what emotions (C) will you connect with the event (A)? Obviously, ones that are a whole lot easier to live with. As Ellis says, once we stop "horribilizing" and "awfulizing" ourselves, we get a lot more latitude. Irrational beliefs make us feel that if something goes wrong, the result will be miserable and catastrophic. Rational beliefs make us feel that failure will simply be unpleasant or inconvenient. This is a lot easier to cope with. So it's through our beliefs that we tell ourselves what our feelings will be.

Irrational Beliefs and a Lack of Freedom

As interesting as Ellis's ideas are on their own, don't forget that this is all leading to a practical "proof" of freedom. The point here is that having irrational beliefs limits our freedom.

Suppose that you are so afraid of public speaking that you avoid talking to groups whenever you can. You feel that you absolutely cannot do it. This has two practical results: You never learn to speak in public and this prevents you from taking advantage of many opportunities in the future. In fact, one study shows that liking to speak to groups is the single most important factor in predicting success in business. Your inability to do this may, thus, severely limit your career later.

Or perhaps you come from a rural area and are afraid of cities. Your irrational belief is something like: "If I move to the city, I'll be miserable. The streets are filthy. People are rude and unfriendly. Crime is everywhere. I'll get insulted, cheated, mugged, and I'll never meet anyone nice to go out with." These beliefs will limit your options about a lot of things: where you live, what kind of job you have, whom you marry, what you do with your leisure time. And surely, the more options, opportunities, and latitude you have, the more freedom you have. That should be obvious by now.

So if we want maximum freedom, we have to rid ourselves of the irrational beliefs that hold us back. The more we can change such beliefs, the freer we will be. Thus, good thinking becomes the key to freedom.

Challenging Irrational Beliefs

To show that we are actually free, however, it's critical to see if Ellis's ideas work in practice. How do we change irrational beliefs? Like most of his ideas, Ellis's method for getting rid of irrational beliefs is straightforward. In a nutshell, he directs us to recognize things in life that trouble us, to identify the irrational beliefs that underlie our distress, and then prove to ourselves that these beliefs are wrong.

This sounds much simpler than it is. It's actually quite difficult because Ellis thinks that the only way to convince yourself of an idea's irrationality is to get empirical proof that your belief is wrong. That means you must put yourself in the very situation you fear, see what happens, and show yourself how wrong you've been. You will feel embarrassment and shame at first—in fact, Ellis calls these experiences "shame-attacking" exercises—so you shouldn't get in too deep too soon. The point of the exercise is, of course, that you gather real data about what happens in that situation and examine it rationally.

Here is how you might work on a fear of public speaking, for example. Start by giving a short speech to an audience of one—your best friend, perhaps. Then expand the group to include other friends. Force yourself to speak at the meetings of clubs and student groups you belong to. You don't have to say much—just enough to show yourself that your fears are unfounded. Gradually work up to something like a class presentation. The important thing is that at every step along the way you examine your data and tell yourself, "I guess this isn't so bad. Sometimes it even feels good. Maybe I'm still uncomfortable and sometimes I feel foolish. But it isn't horrible and terrible when I don't do as well as I'd like. My earlier belief was in fact inaccurate, exaggerated, and irrational. The facts prove it." In short, you gather evidence that the experience is not as bad as you feared.

Ellis tells an interesting story about trying to overcome his own irrational fear of women when he was young. Obviously, he had to gather evidence about what would actually happen if he spoke to a woman. He explains:

> I was always violently interested in women. I would see them and flirt and exchange glances, but I always made excuses not to talk to them and was terrified of being rejected.
>
> Since I lived near The New York Botanical Garden in the Bronx, I decided to attack my fear and shame with an exercise in the park. I vowed that whenever I saw a reasonably attractive woman up to the age of 35, rather than sitting a bench away as I normally would, I would sit next to her with the specific goal of opening a conversation within one minute. I sat next to 130 consecutive women who fit my criteria. Thirty of the women got up and walked away, but about 100 spoke to me—about their knitting, the birds, a book, whatever. I made only one date out of all these contacts—and she stood me up.
>
> According to learning theory and strict behavior therapy, my lack of rewards should have extinguished my efforts to meet women. But I realized that throughout this exercise no one vomited, no one called a cop, and I didn't die. The process of trying new behaviors and understanding what happened in the real world instead of in my imagination led me to overcome my fear of speaking to women.

This is as clear a demonstration of the method as you will find: Ellis identifies the irrational belief, gathers data, and proves the belief false. And what is especially important, as Ellis points out, is that his experience runs directly counter to the precepts of behaviorism. He got much negative reinforcement during this process, *but he didn't take it that way.* Instead, he used his mind to interpret the reactions of the women positively, to see his experience in perspective, and ultimately to acquire a more rational belief about what would happen when he spoke to women.

Ellis shows us, then, a practical way to use our reason to expand the range of activities that we can do comfortably in life. In practice, we see free choice exercised in our decision to examine our beliefs, our willingness to experience uncomfortable situations, and our choice of new, rational beliefs about the world. Ellis does not deny the power of the forces Skinner and Freud point to. In fact, he says that fears we think we've gotten rid of may return when we least expect them. When that happens, we go back to attacking their irrationality. But Ellis's ideas still suggest that in the end we are free to overcome our fears and thereby to live a more expansive and fulfilling life that is the product of our own choices.

Ellis's Debt to Stoicism

This may seem too neat and easy: Wrong thinking is bad; right thinking is good; change your mind and all of your problems will vanish. When you recall how complicated Freud's theory of the human personality is, Ellis's ideas might seem so simple as to be simpleminded. But that would be a mistake because Ellis bases his ideas on a very reputable school of thought—the ancient philosophy of Stoicism.

During the first three centuries of its history, Western philosophy dealt largely with abstract issues—the nature of reality, logic, knowledge, moral virtue, and the like. The discussions of Plato and Aristotle that appear throughout this book testify to this. In the later, Hellenistic period of Greek civilization and throughout the days of the Roman empire, however, many people felt a deep need for a basic guide to living. Various Eastern religions that dealt with such personal matters became very popular, Christianity being the most famous. New schools of philosophy that combined elements of philosophy, religion, and what we now call psychology also sprang up. Instead of exploring logical or theoretical questions exclusively, the thinkers who founded these schools offered people advice on how to achieve happiness and contentment in their lives.

Stoicism is one of the most famous of these philosophical schools. It was founded in Athens by the philosopher Zeno in the third century B.C., and it continued to flourish through the period of the Roman Empire. Two of the most famous Stoics are Epictetus (A.D. 50–138), who began life as a slave, and Marcus Aurelius (A.D. 121–180), one of Rome's emperors. The school gets its name from the Greek word *stoa* for the "porch" of the building where its founder Zeno taught.

Stoicism Stoicism is the late ancient school of philosophy that believes that the world is governed by Fate. The only thing in our power is our attitudes; happiness is achieved by cultivating a disposition of accepting what is inevitable.

We still have the word "stoic" in modern English. To be stoic is to be dignified, unemotional, and unflinching in the face of pain and trouble. This isn't the exact lesson of Stoicism, but it does contain the basic Stoic idea that we have the power to make life's difficulties bearable by controlling our reactions to them.

The Stoics take the somewhat extreme position that the happy soul is the untroubled soul—undisturbed by passion, emotion, and affection, and indifferent to things like money, power, and even health. The goal of the true Stoic was to be unaffected by things beyond human control. They recommend this strategy because they believe that the universe is controlled by the iron hand of Fate or Divine Reason. (The Stoics are "fatalists," then, not "determinists." They believe that we have the freedom to make choices. However, in the end, our actions aren't powerful enough to oppose the overwhelming might of Fate.) In an unchangeable world, our only option is to control our feelings. The only way to be happy is to accept the inevitable, resign ourselves, and calmly accept whatever Fate has in store for us.

The Stoic parable of a dog tied to a wagon illustrates this quite well. As the wagon rolls along, the dog has two choices: either he can cooperate and cheerfully run beside the wagon, or he can be dragged along kicking and howling. Either way, the outcome is the same—he goes where the wagon goes. But at least he can decide whether the trip will be painless. The meaning of the parable is, then, that if we can't control external events, we can at least exercise power over our inner world. To do so, however, we must work on our attitudes toward what happens. "Ask not that events should happen as you will," suggests Epictetus, "but let your will be that events should happen as they do, and you shall have peace."

The key lies in what we think about things. As Epictetus explains,

> What disturbs men's minds is not events but their judgments of events. For instance, death is nothing dreadful, or else Socrates would have thought it so. No, the only dreadful thing about it is men's judgment that it is dreadful. And so when we are hindered, or disturbed, or distressed, let us never lay the blame on others, but on ourselves, that is, on our own judgments. To accuse others for one's own misfortunes is a sign of want of education; to accuse oneself shows that one's education has begun; to accuse neither oneself nor others shows that one's education is complete.
>
> —Enchiridion

We know that our judgment is right when we have made sure that our ideas are rational. In the words of Epictetus, "Man is pained by nothing so much as by that which is irrational; and on the contrary, attracted to nothing so much as to that which is rational."

The Stoics' formula for happiness, then, is to concentrate on right thinking and not to torture yourself with irrational beliefs about the world. This advice sounds very much like that of Albert Ellis, and that's no accident. When Ellis was a college freshman, he encountered the writings of Epictetus in an informal study group. Ellis rejected Stoicism's belief in Fate, but the Greek philosopher's insights about our power to choose how we interpret what happens to us became the basis for this American psychologist's subsequent development of rational-emotive therapy.

Freedom Versus Determinism: A Closing Word

We can make strong cases for both determinism and freedom. We do live in a world of cause and effect, and so far science has given us no reason to doubt that humans are subject to the laws of causality that govern the entire universe. Behaviorism and Freudianism have revealed powerful forces—some internal, some external—that seem to shape virtually everything we do. Yet many philosophers— Aristotle, James, and Sartre among them—refuse to dismiss the sense of freedom that is one of the most distinctive and precious dimensions of human life. Each side presents convincing arguments.

We also seem to give credence to both outlooks in different circumstances without even thinking about the contradiction. As friends get to know one another better—as we learn about each other's personal histories, families, personal quirks—we tend to forgive or overlook things that otherwise might bother us. We act as though much is out of our friends' conscious control. Yet if someone hurts us, we usually are not inclined to dismiss the injury as the unfortunate workings of a deterministic world. We believe that people can choose what they do and we hold them responsible for their actions. We deal with one another and we raise generation after generation on the premise that they can learn how to behave with intelligence, consideration, and responsibility.

Much hangs in the balance. If determinism is true, we cannot reasonably hold people responsible for their actions. How can we blame them for what is beyond their control? Instead, unethical and criminal behavior should be "treated" as if it were an illness. Yet if free will is true, don't we have to give up empathy, understanding, and compassion when we evaluate one another's actions? Why should we take into account extenuating circumstances, the impact of someone's background, or the effects of traumatic experiences in childhood if all of us freely control what we do? Wouldn't those ideas just be excuses for irresponsible behavior?

The debate over free will and determinism, then, is not simply a theoretical issue. It bears directly on the day-to-day realities of life—personal and social responsibility, praise, blame, reward, punishment, mercy, and understanding.

But both sides can't be right. We cannot have it all. So now comes the hard part. You settle the issue.

Main Points of Chapter 4

1. Free will is defended by philosophers in a variety of ways. Aristotle discusses voluntary versus involuntary action in the process of talking about moral responsibility and how human character is formed. He believes that as long as an action is voluntary, we are responsible for it. Aristotle labels as voluntary even actions that result from something like the influence of alcohol or a bad temper. In Aristotle's opinion, not only do we choose our actions, but also the actions we choose determine our personality and what appears to us to be good.

2. William James's "pragmatic" defense maintains that the idea of freedom ("indeterminism") gives us a more satisfying and rational account of experience than determinism does. James argues that when we are presented with a choice, more

than one alternative is genuinely possible. He also asserts that our ordinary feelings of regret and justice suggest that determinism is inadequate as an account of human actions.

3. The existentialist Jean-Paul Sartre offers one of the most extreme defenses possible by arguing that we are totally free and that absolutely everything about us is a product of our own choices. This is the implication of Sartre's metaphysical doctrine that "existence precedes essence." Sartre believes that freedom and choice are so inescapable that we are "condemned to be free" and that we must feel responsible for every aspect of our lives, even those that seem out of our control. To fail to live up to that responsibility is to act in "bad faith."

4. A practical, psychological defense of freedom is offered by the cognitive psychologist Albert Ellis, whose rational-emotive school of thought is almost as extreme as existentialism. Taking his lead from Stoicism, Ellis maintains that the only barrier to our freedom is how we think. Ellis believes that by challenging our irrational beliefs about the world, we can correct faulty thinking and increase the range of our actions.

Discussion Questions

1. Think about the example of Richard the Yankee fan that opened this chapter. Imagine that he's someone about your age. How severely should he be punished? It's not unusual for there to be a lot of drinking at parties on college campuses and for some fights or destruction of property to result. How should the people involved be treated? Should their level of intoxication be taken into account? How? Should it lighten their punishment or make it worse?

2. Do you agree with Aristotle's idea that our actions form our character? If it were true, much of our personalities would be under our control. Think of some of your character traits or habits—particularly ones you are not proud of. Did they develop because you *chose* to act certain ways when you were younger? How much responsibility do your parents have for how you turned out? Is there any part of your personality or character that you think is completely beyond our control?

3. If you are sympathetic to determinism, how do you counter William James's claim that as long as it's *possible* for us to do at least *one* thing other than what we chose in a particular situation, then determinism must be wrong? Maybe we don't have an infinite number of genuine options when we make choices, but don't we generally have at least two?

4. If you think determinism is correct, how do you account for the presence of the ordinary feelings that we have associated with regret, praise, blame, guilt, and responsibility? These have been part of human beings for thousands, if not millions, of years. Why would these feelings—feelings that presume freedom on the part of ourselves and others—persist if they were fictions? Particularly if you think of yourself as a hard-nosed scientist who believes in the evolutionary workings of nature and natural selection, how can you account for their persistence? Wouldn't they have disappeared long ago if they weren't connected to something real—that is, our free will?

5. Sartre claims that "existence precedes essence." Do you agree? How much under your control are fundamental properties of your being? If Sartre is right, changing our "existence" alters our "essence." How much power do you have to make dramatic changes in yourself? Have you ever done so? Most of us don't feel that we have that kind of power, but what about the many stories of people who have absolutely turned their lives around by sheer force of will? Does Sartre exaggerate our control and freedom or do we underestimate them?

6. Have you ever acted in "bad faith"? Do you agree with Sartre that it is a dishonest and inauthentic way to behave? Did you thereby weaken your "essence"?

7. What do you think of Sartre's idea that we are "condemned to be free" and the extent to which he takes the idea of responsibility? You probably cannot relate to Sartre's example of being involved in a war, but think about something that happened to you that was unpleasant, disturbing, and was none of your doing. Is there any value in acting according to Sartre's recommendations: to lay claim to the event, believe that we deserve it, have choice in the situation, bear responsibility for what happens, and so on?

8. Test Ellis's ideas. Identify a fear that you have. Look for an underlying "irrational belief." Construct a safe situation in which you can see that your fears are unrealistic. If this works, does this prove that determinism is wrong?

9. Reflect on Epictetus's thought that "What disturbs men's minds is not events but their judgments of events." Is he right?

Selected Readings

Aristotle's main discussion of voluntary and involuntary action can be found in Book Three of his *Nichomachean Ethics*. William James's argument for "indeterminism" is spelled out in "The Dilemma of Determinism," an address that he delivered to students at the Harvard Divinity School in 1884. For the fundamental tenets of existentialism, see Sartre's *Existentialism and Human Emotions*, translated by Bernard Frechtman (New York: Philosophical Library, 1957) and *Being and Nothingness*, translated by Hazel E. Barnes (New York: Philosophical Library, 1953). *A New Guide to Rational Living* by Albert Ellis and Robert A. Harper (Hollywood, CA: Wilshire Book Co., 1975) presents a concise statement of Albert Ellis's views. Epictetus's views are expressed in the *Enchiridion*. See *Greek and Roman Philosophy after Aristotle*, edited by Jason Saunders (New York: Free Press, 1966) for a good collection of Stoic and Epicurean writings.

5

Right and Wrong

Professor Shih, your philosophy teacher, walks into class one day and schedules a major exam for one week later. On the first day of class, however, she said she would give you two weeks' warning for important tests. When someone in the class complains, Shih says, "Well, I shouldn't have promised that. The exam is still next Wednesday."

You go to the college store with your friend Sharon to pick up the semester's books. After you leave the store, Sharon pulls an expensive anatomy text out of a huge pocket inside of her raincoat. When you express your surprise, Sharon explains, "College costs too much as it is. Tuition is sky high and textbooks are overpriced. When was the last time you spent that much money for one book in a regular bookstore? Lifting stuff from the bookstore every now and then is just my way of making things even."

Ruth and her boyfriend John are both pre-med. They desperately want to go to medical school, get married, and live happily ever after. To make sure that their averages are high, they cheat. They regularly buy term papers, and they copy each other's assignments and exams when they're in the same class. They even steal library books that other students in the class might use in the hope of lowering their grades.

Ron works at a clothing store and goes to school at night. He is married and has one child. He and Tony, another salesman, who happens to be single, are competing for a promotion to store manager that will bring a sizable raise. Ron feels he needs the money more than Tony does, so he hints to the store's owner that Tony used to sell drugs to school kids, figuring the lie will boost his chances.

Bill is a solid student and a member of the cross-country team. He makes friends with a few guys on the team, discovers that they all belong to the same fraternity, and so he expresses an interest in becoming a member himself. Bill is black, however, and he would be the first nonwhite member of the fraternity. Bill's admission is virtually a sure thing, but Jeff, one of the fraternity brothers, is a racist and cannot stand the idea of Bill's being accepted. Jeff decides to make Bill withdraw his name, so he sends Bill anonymous letters full of racial slurs and threats. For example, one letter says that if Bill doesn't withdraw, he'll have an "accident" and find himself with a broken leg at the start of the running season. Bill ignores the threats until he finds the tires on his car slashed one day as a "warning." He changes his mind and pulls out.

Here we have breaking a promise, stealing, cheating, lying, intimidation, abuse, and discrimination. What is your reaction? Most people condemn actions like this. And how would you feel if you were on the receiving end of any of them? Hurt and angry, of course. Asked to explain your reaction, you'd probably say that what these people did was "unfair," "hurtful," "wrong," "uncaring," "lousy," "cruel," or some such thing. In any case, your evaluation of such behavior would surely be negative.

Evaluating behavior is something we do all the time. The evaluation of behavior is also an important area of philosophy. We call it *ethics,* or *moral philosophy.*

In this chapter, we begin looking at one of the branches of philosophy concerned with how we deal with each other. Ethics involves establishing reasonable standards for "acceptable" human conduct and applying those standards to particular cases. The terms "ethics" and "moral" come from Greek and Latin words, respectively, which mean "character."[1] We might say, then, that ethics helps us figure out how someone with a good character would act.

We'll start by examining what an ethical standard looks like. Then we'll explore the two major approaches philosophers have come up with for evaluating the moral character of actions.

Right, Wrong, and Philosophy

What does right and wrong have to do with philosophy anyway, you may be asking. Doesn't religion determine moral standards? Don't laws define right and wrong? Furthermore, aren't right and wrong relative to where you live, and when? We all know that various cultures have different conceptions of morality. And, finally, isn't the individual the only legitimate judge of ethics?

These are good questions, and they reveal two common misconceptions about ethics. People either tend to be too rigid, citing laws or religious teachings as the final word on a moral question. Or they are too loose, throwing out all objectivity and reducing ethics to a cultural or personal question. In fact, right and wrong lie somewhere between those extremes.

Philosophical Ethics

Recall that philosophy studies the most basic features of life using the instruments of reason and logic. Philosophy looks at facts and theories and asks if they form

---

[1]Some people distinguish between the terms "moral" and "ethical," using one term to mean "high standards" and the other to mean "common practice." Others use them to distinguish between "practical" and "theoretical" issues. Because there is no consensus on this matter, however, we use these two terms synonymously in this discussion.

intellectually coherent explanations or rationally convincing arguments. In Chapter 2 you saw that appeals to authority or the emotions result in logical mistakes. Arguments and explanations must stand or fall on their intrinsic merits. Nothing else counts.

Obviously, we evaluate each other's and our own actions all the time. The branch of philosophy that tries to understand this process—philosophical ethics—like the rest of philosophy, uses reason and logic to talk about right and wrong. It measures claims that actions are right and wrong against a philosophical standard. This means that, strictly speaking, religion, law, cultural customs, and your private emotions are largely irrelevant to philosophical ethics.

These nonphilosophical approaches to right and wrong are valuable in their own way, of course. They're just different from a philosophical approach.

Religious and Legal Approaches

You have probably encountered ideas about right and wrong most frequently in the rules and teachings of your religion and the laws of your nation, state, and city or town. Religions and laws give us a standard against which to evaluate our actions. They tell us what we may and may not do. And they back up their judgments with an appeal to some sort of authority. From the standpoint of philosophy, however, determining right and wrong by appealing to religious authority or laws is too rigid an approach.

Religions offer explicit moral evaluations of human conduct. They give us their particular views of good and evil, virtue and sin. They draw these conclusions from sacred texts or the spoken wisdom of their founders, prophets, and current leaders. Ultimately, of course, they attribute their ideas about how we should behave to God.

Philosophy and religion, then, go at questions differently. Philosophers traditionally are skeptical and demand proofs; devout believers must finally give up on proofs, operate on faith, and accept some religious authority. The two just don't speak the same language or operate by the same rules. Thus, we can say that what is acceptable in a religious investigation is generally inappropriate in a philosophical exploration, and vice versa, without implying anything negative about either religion or philosophy.

Note, however, the qualifying phrase "generally inappropriate." To the extent that religious positions raise issues that we can investigate rationally, they are relevant to philosophy. For example, some religious objections to abortion include the assumption that a fetus is so much a "human life" that preventing its birth is equivalent to murder. This assumption is something we can gather data on, discuss, and argue about rationally. We can ask if a fetus is an actual person, and if so, how. If not, we can ask if killing a nonperson or a potential person is the same thing as murder. And so on. Similarly, everything from the Ten Commandments to the teaching of Jesus to the Buddhist Eightfold Path raises ethical issues about how we should treat ourselves and others, which we can talk about philosophically. So although religious arguments don't settle philosophical questions, they do suggest important topics that otherwise might not get enough attention.

The same can be said about laws. Laws are very precise standards for evaluating human conduct, but they arise out of politics, which is quite different from philosophy. Laws are either handed down by despots and ruling councils or enacted through democratic, representative legislatures. We all certainly hope that lawmakers think about philosophical concepts like justice, fairness, and equity when they draw up new statutes or revise old ones. But to be legitimate, a law does not have to be just and fair. It has only to go through whatever process is required for its enactment. A statement of basic principles that laws are supposed to conform to, like our Constitution, makes it more likely that laws will be just, but that is still no guarantee. In the United States, laws that allowed slavery and discrimination were repeatedly judged to be constitutional, even though they are not understood this way now.

This is the same situation we had with religion. The bases for legal judgments and ethical ones are simply different. A statute denying a black person the rights of a "person" may be legal in some political systems, but it is surely unethical in that it violates his or her basic human rights. On the other hand, if you run a string of red lights rushing a critically ill friend to the emergency room at 3 A.M., you may be doing something illegal. But most of us would agree that in that situation it would be wrong for you to scrupulously observe the traffic laws. We all may want our laws to be ethical, but we've got to be realistic. Some unethical actions are illegal (rape, murder), but some are legal (selfishly manipulating and deceiving your best friend). Some illegal actions are probably morally neutral (not putting money into a parking meter), and some illegal actions can even be morally positive (civil disobedience for the sake of correcting an injustice). Thus, in trying to determine the ethical character of an action, its legal status is, strictly speaking, irrelevant.

Again, as with religious positions, whether or not an action is legal may tell us something about its moral character. Or it may at least suggest something to consider in a philosophical discussion. But to claim that right and wrong are determined by the law, just as to claim that they are determined by God, is to make an unwarranted appeal to authority.

Nor is one kind of authority for a law better than another. A dictator's laws produce an appeal to personal authority, relying on precedent gives us traditional wisdom, and democratic laws involve majority opinion. But from a philosophical point of view, these are all equally unacceptable bases for resolving ethical dilemmas.

Both religion and law hold that questions of right and wrong are answerable in terms of some final, objective standard handed down by some sacred or legal authority. But however binding or persuasive this approach may be to devout believers and legalists, others see things quite differently. They are quick to point out that when we survey all the religions on earth, we find considerable disagreement over right and wrong. And there is just as much variety among what is allowed and what is prohibited by the laws of different societies. Consequently, we have to view both religion and law as ultimately undependable in their answers to moral questions.

Differences Among Cultures, Individuals, and Circumstances

Does this mean, then, that ethics is either a completely meaningless enterprise or simply "relative" to societies or individuals? Some people who argue that it is point to contradictory moral norms in different cultures. Others claim that ethics is strictly a personal matter. Although a philosophical approach to ethics generally sees religious and legal approaches as being too rigid, cultural and personal approaches can be much more flexible. Different cultures have different norms. Individuals in the same society vehemently disagree about what's right and wrong. Does this mean that ethics isn't absolute, but "relative" to cultures, individuals, or circumstances?

The great variety of ethical judgments that we find among individuals and societies presents us with some important challenges. We need to think carefully about what we conclude. Consider the following examples:

- Racial and sexual discrimination is the norm in many societies. However, it is usually the case that the privileged groups historically had the greatest amount of raw power and were able to impose their will on the groups now labeled "inferior." It is not unusual for such discrimination to be renounced and to give way to equality—whether through slow change, internal turmoil, or external pressure.

- Throughout human history, it is not unusual to find examples of poor societies practicing infanticide—particularly of ill, deformed, or very weak infants who would never be able to care for themselves as adults. This might be defended as a way to spare the individual from a difficult life and to benefit the community, because it has so few resources.

- At a bar, a friend of yours realizes that he can't find his wallet. He's had a lot to drink, and he imagines that the guy sitting beside him at the bar stole it. He wants to chase after the stranger to beat him up, and your friend asks you if you saw where the guy went. You're sure that your friend has simply misplaced his wallet, but he's too drunk to reason with. So you lie and tell him that the guy just left (he's actually at the far end of the room) and send your friend on a wild goose chase. You feel good about lying like this because you hope it will let your friend sober up and cool down before he does something stupid.

- While out of town on a business trip, you meet someone very attractive. You're married, but you use a phony name and swear that you're unattached so that you can trick this person into having sex with you. You sincerely believe that if you're more than 1,000 miles away from home, there's nothing wrong with what you're doing because your spouse will never find out.

Do these examples help us at all with the idea that ethics is *relative* to one thing or another?

- The example of the racist and sexist society tells us that just because a practice exists in a culture doesn't make it right. This is particularly clear when a society ultimately renounces its own practices, declaring that what went on in the past was wrong.

- The example of infanticide—which is roundly condemned in most modern societies—shows something else. Defenders and critics may take opposite positions, but they actually might appeal to the same general principle. Both might agree that societies have a duty to protect the welfare of their members. However, in this case, aren't they simply disagreeing about how to apply that principle in a situation where a community has serious limitations about how much it can do for its members?

- Your two lies show that there is good reason to think that the same action might be right in some circumstances but wrong in others. Your first lie protects one or two people from being hurt. Your second lie is different and contains a variety of problematic elements—promise breaking, manipulation, using someone as an object for your own pleasure, and self-serving rationalization.

Seen in this light, **ethical relativism** isn't quite as appealing as it first seems.

Even so, you still might want to claim that ethics is a totally subjective matter.[2] However, if we want to end up with any sort of standard that will let us evaluate our own or other people's actions, ethical relativism has serious problems. After all, if we claim that "ethics is all relative to the individual," we would have no basis for criticizing Adolph Hitler, for example, or a terrorist who tortures and then kills innocent children to advance a political cause that he or she sincerely believes in. Sincerity is a wonderful virtue, but most of us know in our hearts that it's not an infallible touchstone for moral truth. And the absolute impossibility of objective ethical standards means that when serious disagreements reach a certain point, our only option is to start using force against one another.

Most of us recognize the importance of respecting other cultures, and we want to be able to accept customs different from our own. We recognize that honoring freedom and individuality means that we need to tolerate ideas or behaviors with which we disagree. And, particularly on personal moral issues, we want the autonomy to make decisions according to our most sincere beliefs, and we want other people to respect our judgments about what is right and wrong for us. However, although many of us may want to conclude on the basis of these desires that "ethics is relative," what we probably mean is something like "ethics is too complicated for simple, objective solutions." The fact that there can be such difference in ethical judgments among cultures and individuals, then, doesn't automatically mean that it's impossible to find some general moral principles that we might all agree on.

Studying cultural and individual variety may help us turn up information that is relevant to a philosophical inquiry. Why are varying practices accepted or condemned in this or that society? If you and I differ, what are our respective arguments? By looking into these things, perhaps we can find something relevant to a rational, philosophical approach to understanding and evaluating human conduct. In fact, many people argue that "ethics is relative" because they see dangerous implications to the belief that there are objective ethical standards. They fear that this can be used as a defense for forcing cultures that are doing things "wrong" to change their ways,

---

> **ethical relativism** Ethical relativism denies the existence of universal, objective ethical principles and asserts that ethical judgments are simply an expression of the limited perspective of individuals or societies.

---

[2]Various important philosophers have defended the idea that ethics is subjective and doesn't really deal in "truth." The eighteenth-century British thinker David Hume, for example, claims that moral judgments are a function of feelings, not reason or facts. The twentieth-century British philosopher A. J. Ayer reduces a statement like, "Stealing money is wrong," to "Stealing money—boo!!!" Discussions of theories of this sort take us into the domain philosophers call "meta-ethics," the analysis of the meaning and validity of the concepts we use when we do "normative ethics," that is, when we make ethical judgments about actions. Because this chapter focuses on normative ethics, we don't have the space to pursue this line of inquiry.

punishing people simply because they don't follow a society's norms, or stigmatizing otherwise good and decent individuals just because they think for themselves. Notice, however, how much this position is based on a belief in the fundamental importance of things like freedom, autonomy, and personal choice. If defenders of ethical relativism say that it's wrong for me to punish someone for his or her beliefs, they're actually—without realizing it—making a case for objective ethical principles.

The Philosophical Approach: Basic Needs and Well-Being

If ethics is not a matter of religious rules, secular laws, cultural traditions, or personal feeling, what does it involve? Is there really a rational, secular, and philosophical standard we can use to evaluate human actions? Can such a standard of right and wrong be firm enough to provide dependability and consistency, yet flexible enough to accommodate differences in individual circumstances?

There is such an ethical standard, and it is surprisingly simple. Philosophers have used it over the centuries to determine the ethical character of actions. It is simply *well-being*. As a rule, when philosophers claim that one action is morally better than another, they are saying that it makes life better in some very fundamental and important way. Ethical actions—keeping promises and treating others fairly—make life more satisfying. Unethical actions—lying, cheating, stealing, and manipulating—make it worse. That's all there is to it.

From a philosophical perspective, then, right and wrong are not related to God's commandments, Mohammed's teachings, the laws of the land, majority opinion, or what makes you personally feel guilty. The ultimate standard philosophers use in evaluating human conduct is simply the welfare, well-being, or happiness of those involved. Right actions increase it; wrong ones decrease it.[3]

Well-Being

Considering how most of us agonize when we face an ethical dilemma, tying ethics to "well-being" may seem off the mark to you. You may be thinking, "You mean that when I'm torn between cheating to get an A and getting stuck with an honest C, I'm debating about my 'well-being'? No way. I *know* what's better for me—a higher grade. That's why I'm tempted to cheat in the first place. And did you say lying makes life *worse*? Are you kidding? Lying may not always be right, but when I lie my way out of a jam, it makes my life *better*, not worse. Why else would I do it?"

---

[3]Philosophers have traditionally referred to the ultimate standard for ethics as "happiness." However, "well-being," or "human welfare" is better because it lacks the emotional connotations present in the contemporary English use of "happiness." These connotations are not there in the original Greek, *eudaimonia*. For the Greeks, being happy did not mean feeling cheerful or joyful but having a quiet, ongoing sense of satisfaction or fulfillment that comes from our basic needs being met and, most importantly, from living a morally good life. Eudaimonia also refers not to how we feel at one time, but how we handle our entire life and whether we have the capacity to handle bad luck with equanimity. Aristotle writes in the *Nichomachean Ethics* that when we talk about happiness, "we must add 'in a complete life,' for one swallow does not make a spring, nor does one sunny day; similarly, one day or a short time does not make a man blessed and happy. . . . The happy man . . . will remain happy throughout his life. For he will always or to the highest degree both do and contemplate what is in conformity with virtue; he will bear the vicissitudes of fortune most nobly and with perfect decorum under all circumstances, inasmuch as he is truly good." So when we use "happiness" in our discussion of ethics in this chapter, keep this meaning in mind, not the modern one.

The problem here, of course, is with what "well-being," "happiness," and "making life better" mean. When philosophers use these ideas in talking about ethics, they mean the state of general contentment that comes from having our most fundamental and important needs met. A "basic sense of satisfaction with our lives" is probably the best way to put this idea.

What does such a "basic sense of satisfaction" feel like? Imagine a life in which you are in good shape physically and emotionally. You are satisfied with your work life and your home life. You and your family feel safe in your community and connected to friends and relatives. You feel that the people in power are responsive to the needs of ordinary citizens. Perhaps you can participate in the political process directly. You are free to hold and express whatever social, political, or religious beliefs you choose. Your dignity as a human being is respected by your neighbors and by your society's institutions. Life has its ups and downs—sickness, difficulties on the job, occasional financial problems, loss of people close to you, plain bad luck—but you can handle them. Life is not perfect, but on balance you feel that it is basically good. This is the sort of state philosophers have in mind when they talk about "well-being" or "happiness."

Can unethical actions such as cheating on a test increase your sense of well-being? Maybe in the short run—if you get away with it. But you may also feel guilty about getting an unfair advantage over honest students, you may drop in the esteem of other students who know about it, and, over the long haul, a habit of cheating will eventually give you problems—on the job, with friends, or with the IRS.

And don't forget that you're hurting other people. When we look at unethical behavior closely and take everyone's interests into account, we can always find ways that it compromises someone's fundamental rights or interests. That's why, from a philosophical point of view, it makes sense to ground ethics in concepts of well-being and happiness.

Human Needs

This understanding of well-being rests on the assumption that all human beings have a set of basic *needs* that must be met for us to feel good about life. This includes survival needs like food, shelter, and clothing. But it also takes in less tangible requirements—freedom from tyranny, for example, justice, fairness, and respect for one's individuality.

Don't confuse casual *wants* with these basic *needs*, however. We all want many things that we don't really need. Wanting a new car but having to buy a used car or to rely on public transportation won't have the same effect on you as going without food. Being dumped by the current love of your life or losing out on that "perfect job" won't kill you, either. It will hurt, but you can eventually find other ways to get these needs met.

Basic human needs, on the other hand, are much more powerful and important than wants. If our survival needs go unmet, we die. If certain emotional needs are unsatisfied when we're young, we suffer lifelong psychological damage. Enslavement and tyranny go so much against the grain of the human spirit that they inevitably ignite violent resistance. It's human needs of this sort that are relevant to ethics. Most ethical issues are less intense and dramatic than slavery, but they still involve some very fundamental human need that virtually all of us would agree is critical to a sense of well-being or happiness in life.[4]

Individual Differences and Adaptability

You may have doubts about this approach and be thinking, "What makes people feel satisfied is an individual matter. People go after different things—some want money, others love; some like business, others like politics, or medicine, or education, or athletics. You just can't say everybody needs the same things." This is both right and wrong. On the surface, people do want very different things in life. But underneath all that they have similar needs. People may pursue widely different careers, but they're all doing much the same thing—looking for ways to support themselves by doing work they like. Just because they take different roads doesn't mean that they aren't trying to reach the same destination.

And don't be fooled by how adaptable the human animal is. There are entire societies today in which large groups of people are not free. Their dignity is ignored and insulted every day. Yet they seem content with life—at least they aren't in a constant state of uproar and revolution. "See," you might say, "people can be happy without things like freedom—especially if their society doesn't value it highly." Yet we cannot assume that these people are really satisfied with life, or at least that their lives would not be much happier under different conditions. All their apparent calm means is that human beings can put up with a lot in order to survive.

We find something similar with physical states. Many people with high blood pressure, for example, are unaware that anything is wrong with them. They *feel* healthy, but they *aren't* healthy. Cardiovascular disease comes on some people so slowly that they don't notice it. They just gradually adjust to not being able to do as much as they used to, and they write it off as something else. The first time they realize that they have a life-threatening disease is when they receive treatment for a symptom and discover that they feel better.

Thus, you can see how people might *feel* satisfied without having their basic needs met. Someone who has been discriminated against all her life may have made her peace with the situation. But once she experiences what she's been missing, she quickly dismisses her earlier satisfactions as a bad counterfeit of the real thing.

Exactly What Do We Need?

A philosophical approach to ethics, then, is based on the idea that we all have roughly the same needs. The more of these needs that are met, the more we experience the

---

[4]Throughout this chapter, remember that when philosophers link notions of right and wrong with basic human needs, they are thinking of things that affect us in some very fundamental and important way. A good way to illustrate this is to think of how you react when someone does something unethical to you. How do you feel if someone steals something from you, lies, spreads false rumors about you, breaks a solemn promise, or manipulates you? Usually you feel deeply troubled. Even if we can repair the damage—replace what was taken, clear up the falsehoods, make someone keep her word—it doesn't make the pain go away. We generally get over physical pain more easily than the pain we feel when we have been treated unethically. That's because we are dealing with issues that are very fundamental to our sense of well-being. And these are the matters that are central to a philosophical approach to ethics.

kind of satisfaction with life possible for humans. Actions that promote such satisfaction are morally better. Those that block it are morally worse.[5]

What are these basic needs that ethics is built on? There is no "official list," and you can probably make a pretty good one of your own just by thinking about it for a while. However, we can infer one standard list of human needs from the United Nations' *Universal Declaration of Human Rights*. Particularly over the last two centuries, many countries have drawn up lists of "human rights," and the U.N.'s listing captures most of the issues on which these different statements agree.

This document refers to "rights," but it may just as well say "needs." In essence, it claims that we have a *right* to something because we have a very basic *need* for it. The United Nations proclaims that these requirements constitute "a common standard of achievement for all peoples and nations." In other words, this is what everyone must have, simply by virtue of being human, in order to find life satisfactory.

Although the actual document is heavy on detail, it lists only the following fundamental rights/needs:

life itself

freedom

equality

personal security

protection by a just legal system

political rights

a private life

the ability to choose marriage and family

freedom of thought and action

access to the benefits of a society (government, culture, education, protection against illness)

work

rest

---

[5]For the sake of simplicity, we've referred so far only to *human* well-being and *human* needs as a basic standard in ethics. But don't mistake this as meaning that ethics doesn't apply to nonhumans. The question of the rights of nonhuman animals is a matter of considerable debate and inquiry among philosophers. Strong arguments have been advanced for the intrinsic value of all nonhumans (see, for example, Tom Regan, *The Case for Animal Rights* [Berkeley, CA: University of California Press, 1983]). In addition, as we discover that some nonhumans have quite sophisticated cognitive and affective abilities, it's apparent that humans are not the only beings on the planet who have self-awareness, personalities, the ability to think abstractly, and the like. (See, for example, Chapter 14: "Is a Dolphin a 'Person'?") And that means that it's very likely that some nonhumans are entitled to rights equivalent to humans. Most humans have never taken seriously the issue of managing a conflict of rights between species. So this matter clearly poses major challenges. For example, all mammals may share a fundamental need for life and safety, but different species probably have different needs (liberty and autonomy may be more important to land mammals, and close relationships may be more important to marine mammals). It is beyond the scope of this chapter to explore these issues any further. However, there's no reason that the basic principle that applies to interactions among humans wouldn't apply in interactions between species—that is, actions that promote the satisfaction of basic needs are morally better, whereas those that block having those needs met are morally worse.

In essence, the *Declaration* claims that these conditions are as necessary for a satisfying human life as food, water, and exercise are for physical health. No matter how adaptable people are, no human being could experience a genuine sense of well-being if deprived of them.[6] Our world is not perfect, of course, so we're talking about the degree to which these needs are fulfilled. People with more of these requirements met will be happier than those with fewer of them met. Still, this document provides a fair statement of what most philosophers mean when they talk about what we need in order to have a sense of "well-being" or "happiness."

Two Categories of Needs

Actually, we can simplify this document—and, therefore, our ethical standard—even more. We can take the needs identified by the *Declaration* and divide them into two types: *material conditions* and *ways of being treated.*

On the one hand, the document says we need things like food, clothing, housing, medical care, property, work, rest, and help in the event of unemployment, sickness, or old age. It also identifies physical conditions that we need protection against: slavery, torture, and degrading treatment. These are all actual, material conditions of life.

The *Declaration* also identifies acceptable versus unacceptable ways of treating people. We are told that we need equality before the law, fairness, a presumption of innocence, impartial tribunals, marriages based only on consent, and equal pay for equal work. Arbitrary and unfair treatment is flatly rejected, no matter what good it produces. In essence, what is at stake here are principles—equality, justice, fairness, individual liberty, and respect for human dignity. In other words, this and virtually every other description of human rights or needs imply that a fundamental sense of happiness or satisfaction with life depends on two things: having certain material needs met and being treated in particular ways.

Something for the Skeptics

You may still have some major reservations about this approach to ethics. Maybe you resist the idea that all humans have roughly the same needs, or that, even if they do, people cannot be happy unless these needs are met. Perhaps you think that individual differences and the human capacity to adapt to difficult circumstances are more important in determining any sense of well-being than the extent to which basic human needs are met. You may even dismiss the *Declaration of Human Rights* as propaganda or an attempt by one group of people to impose their values on everyone else.

---

[6]This idea, which underlies all declarations of human rights, is expressed by many philosophers, often quite succinctly. For example, Phillips Foot has written, "Granted that it is wrong to assume identity of aim between peoples of different cultures; nevertheless there is a great deal that all men have in common. All need affection, the cooperation of others, a place in a community, and help in trouble. It isn't true to suppose that human beings can flourish without these things—being isolated, despised or embattled, or without courage or hope. We are not, therefore, simply expressing values that we happen to have if we think of some moral systems as good moral systems and others as bad. Communities as well as individuals can live wisely or unwisely, and this is largely the result of their values and the codes of behavior that they teach. Looking at these societies, and critically also at our own, we surely have some idea of how things work out and why they work out as they do. We do not have to suppose it is just as good to promote pride of place and the desire to get an advantage over other men as it is to have an ideal of affection and respect. These things have different harvests, and unmistakably different connections with human good."

How can we answer such objections and show that lists like the *Declaration* are rooted in human nature? Consider Article 3, "Everyone has the right to life, liberty, and security of person." Imagine what it would be like if these three things were constantly at risk. You'd always fear being killed, enslaved, or attacked. You couldn't trust anyone because you wouldn't know who was a friend and who was a foe. Your life would be filled with dread, and you would probably plot against the people you thought were most dangerous to you. Such a life is hardly satisfying. Because human beings are adaptable, of course, most of us could adjust to such a life in one way or another. But could you imagine any normal person feeling genuinely satisfied about life under these conditions? Could any normal individual ever feel calm and untroubled—never mind feeling good? Normal, emotionally healthy human beings—no matter what the traditions or norms of their culture—do not find intense fear about losing their lives or liberty satisfying. If you injected such fear into the average day of ordinary people, you would dramatically diminish how much they enjoyed life.

The specific provisions of the United Nations' *Declaration* may be debatable, but the assumption it is built on—that we can specify the basic conditions that must be met for any normal woman or man to live a fundamentally satisfying life—seems solid.

Two Approaches to Ethics

The distinction implicit in the *Declaration's* two categories of human needs points to two different approaches that philosophers have taken to evaluating human actions. Some philosophers ask: Does a given action make the material conditions of life more satisfying or less so? Others ask: Does a given action treat all of the people involved appropriately, that is, equally, impartially, and so on? These questions represent two distinctly different approaches that philosophers have taken to answering questions about right and wrong.

One school of thought, which we can call *results-oriented,* claims that the ethical character of an action depends on whether its *consequences* are positive or negative. This approach focuses on the actual, material conditions of life. Those actions that give us more of the specific "stuff of life" that we need to be happy are judged *morally good.* Actions that result in less satisfying material conditions are labeled in some way *morally wrong.*

This results-oriented approach is also called **teleological**. The term "teleological" comes from the Greek *telos,* which means "end," or "goal." Thus, teleological theories evaluate the ethical character of an action by looking at the actual end or goal that that deed achieves. The most important school of thought that uses the teleological approach to ethics is called **utilitarianism**.

---

teleological A teleological, or results-oriented, approach to ethics claims that the ethical character of an action depends on whether its consequences are positive or negative.

utilitarianism Utilitarianism is a teleological ethical theory advanced by Jeremy Bentham and John Stuart Mill. It uses pleasure and notions like "the greatest good of the greatest number" as standards for judging the morality of actions.

Another school of thought holds that the consequences of an action are less important than the nature of *the action itself.* We call this approach *act-oriented.* Thinkers of this school focus on how people are being treated, not the results of an action. In other words, they claim that some actions "fit" with the fact that they're being done to people, while others fall short and treat us as objects. Act-oriented philosophers judge whether actions are ethical strictly according to whether they are appropriate for people to do or to experience. Actions that respect human needs to be treated with dignity, honesty, equality, and fairness are morally right. Those that deceive, manipulate, and discriminate are morally wrong.

Act-oriented ethics is more formally called **deontological** ethics. *Deontos* is the Greek word meaning "duty." So deontological thinkers believe that when faced with an ethical dilemma, we should ask, "What is my duty or obligation in this situation to the people involved? How should I treat them? Should I act or refrain from acting in particular ways?" The most important proponent of this approach is the German philosopher Immanuel Kant.

Another way to understand these two approaches is to see them as the front and back sides of what we might call an "ethical yardstick," a standard we can use to measure the moral character of an action. With the results-oriented, or teleological, side we measure an action's consequences and find out how much actual good or harm results from them. The act-oriented, or deontological, side sizes up the deed itself and tells us how acceptable that action is to do to somebody else or to experience at the hands of another.

Results-Oriented, or Teleological, Ethics: Utilitarianism

A results-oriented, or teleological, approach is both simple and practical. It says, "Something is right or wrong depending on whether it produces tangible good or harm for the people involved." The only principle involved is that human well-being (or happiness) is a good thing. Actions that advance it are morally better than those that do not.

The school of thought called *utilitarianism* provides us with the clearest explanation of results-oriented ethics. Devised by Jeremy Bentham and elaborated by John Stuart Mill, utilitarianism argues that the ethical character of an action depends on how much pleasure or pain results from it.

Jeremy Bentham

A number of eighteenth-century thinkers advanced the idea that the best actions are those that promote the greatest happiness of the greatest number of people. The British thinker Jeremy Bentham, however, was the first person to develop the idea into a formal theory, which he called "utilitarianism."

---

deontological A deontological, or act-oriented, theory of ethics argues that actions have a moral character apart from their consequences.

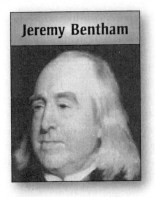

Jeremy Bentham

Jeremy Bentham (1748–1832) attended Queen's College, Oxford, and studied law at Lincoln's Inn in London, but he was more a practical reformer than a lawyer or philosopher. A champion of legal and prison reform in the England of his day, Bentham became the leader of a political movement that ultimately did achieve some important reforms. Bentham was also the founding thinker of utilitarianism, and his most famous work is *An Introduction to the Principles of Morals and Legislation*. Friend of James Mill, Bentham was godfather to another powerful utilitarian thinker, John Stuart Mill. Bentham bequeathed his entire estate to the newly founded University College in London on the condition that his remains be present at all board meetings. Bentham's embalmed body is still displayed in a movable glass case in the main hall of the college.

Bentham was a practical man who was deeply impressed by **empiricism,** the philosophical outlook that stresses the importance of basing knowledge on objective, observable facts and physical evidence. Strongly interested in social reform, Bentham argued that a commonsense, empirical approach was the best way to improve society. Thus, Bentham thought that actions and policies should be evaluated according to how much tangible good they produce. All that counts is demonstrable human good or harm. Bentham called this way of thinking "utilitarianism" because he believed that what is important is how useful something is in producing benefits, that is, how much "utility" it has for making people's lives happier.[7]

Bentham also insisted that actions and their effects be evaluated in a fair, reasonable, and objective manner. He had no use for the "tradition" and "aristocratic privilege" relied on by the upper class. He also rejected religious faith in an all-knowing but invisible god and the wisdom of sacred texts, as well as the belief that suffering and sacrifice are the hallmarks of ethical behavior. Bentham thought all such notions too subjective. And he feared that they could too easily be used to serve the special interests of the ruling classes or the most powerful churches. Bentham's goal was to make the determination of right and wrong as impartial and objective a process as weighing objects on a public scale.

empiricism   Empiricism is the philosophical outlook that stresses the importance of basing knowledge on objective, observable facts and physical evidence.

---

[7]If you have studied economics, you may already have heard about utilitarianism because in modern economics the "utility" of a good or service lies in the benefit, or satisfaction, it brings to the consumer.

"Utility" and Pleasure

Like "well-being" and "happiness," "utility" can be a soft concept upon which to build an objective process of evaluation. Bentham thus has to provide us with a precise and practical idea of what makes something useful. He does this with the ordinary concept of pleasure. In his *Introduction to the Principles of Morals and Legislation,* he writes,

> By utility is meant that property in any object whereby it tends to produce benefit, advantage, pleasure, good, or happiness (all this in the present case comes to the same thing) or (what comes again to the same thing) to prevent the happening of mischief, pain, evil, or unhappiness to the party whose interest is considered; if that party be the community in general, then the happiness of the community; if a particular individual, then the happiness of that individual.

Bentham takes it as self-evident that pleasure makes human life happier and pain makes it worse. Thus, he thinks that the most sensible way to evaluate actions is according to how much pleasure they produce.

Stating this explicitly in terms of ethical judgments, Bentham claims, "Nature has placed mankind under the governance of two sovereign masters, *pain* and *pleasure*. It is for them alone to point out what we ought to do. . . . [T]he standard of right and wrong . . . [is] fastened to their throne." As far as utilitarianism is concerned, an act is morally good to the extent that it produces a greater balance of pleasure over pain for the largest number of people involved. In Bentham's eyes, this is the ultimate, objective standard of morality: "the greatest happiness of all those whose interest is in question [is] the right and proper, and only right and proper and universally desirable, end of human action." Therefore, Bentham's "ethical yardstick" is marked off in units of *pleasure* and held against the *consequences* of actions.

What makes Bentham's theory "teleological," then, is that the morality of an action depends solely on how much pleasure or pain results from it. Bentham believes that an action is not in and of itself right or wrong. Bentham thinks that if we are going to be objective and empirical about things, we have to say that an action is wrong only if it produces harm. If a lie or some "forbidden" pleasure truly did not hurt anyone, it would make no sense to Bentham to say either act was "wrong." To resolve a moral dilemma, Bentham would say something like: "Determine which of your options produces the greatest balance of pleasure over pain in the lives of people involved. That is the 'right thing to do.'" For a teleological theory like utilitarianism, ethics depends totally on the real-life consequences of actions.

Measuring Pleasure: Bentham's "Hedonistic Calculus"

But Bentham does not leave it at simply a general theoretical level. To ensure that the evaluation of actions should be fair, reasonable, and objective, he devised a method of measuring how much pleasure or pain an action produces. He calls this the hedonistic calculus. ("Hedonism" comes from the Greek word meaning "pleasure.")

The **hedonistic calculus** identifies seven different characteristics of the pleasure or pain that results from a particular action:

1. The *intensity* of the feeling

2. How long it lasts—its *duration*

3. The odds that the action will actually produce this feeling—its *certainty* or *uncertainty*

4. How soon the feelings will be experienced—its *propinquity* or *remoteness*

5. The likelihood that this experience will produce even more pleasure in the future—its *fecundity*

6. The chance it will produce pain or unhappiness—its *purity*

7. The number of people affected—its *extent*

Bentham did not provide explicit directions about how to use the calculus. But if we assign an arbitrary numerical value to each of these seven categories for every option we are considering, we can calculate the totals for each action and get an idea of what Bentham has in mind. Whichever action has the higher total, then, is morally better according to Bentham's scheme.

Applying the Calculus: A Case of Racism. Let's take a case from the beginning of this chapter—the case of Bill and the fraternity—as a simple example to see how the hedonistic calculus works. Remember that Bill, a black student, wants to get into a fraternity that some friends belong to. Jeff, a racist, threatens Bill with a broken leg if he doesn't pull out of consideration, and even damages Bill's car. Under this pressure, Bill ultimately withdraws his name.

All decent people would think that what happened to Bill was wrong, and they might explain their judgment in different ways. Bentham, however, would say that the threats and abuse were morally wrong only if they produced a greater balance of pain over pleasure than if Jeff had treated Bill with the same respect he accords people of his own race. If Bentham's ideas are right, then, this should be revealed when we apply the hedonistic calculus to the situation.

Let's use a scale of −10 to +10, with negative numbers standing for pain and positive ones for pleasure. To make the scores that we choose seem to have some logic, let's say that 10 will indicate "high," 5 "moderate," and 1 "low." Let's compare two options: Jeff harasses Bill; Jeff does not harass Bill. We will do separate totals for Bill and Jeff.

---

hedonistic calculus The hedonistic calculus is Jeremy Bentham's system for measuring the amount of pleasure and pain that results from an action. It takes into account seven dimensions of a pleasure or pain: intensity, duration, certainty or uncertainty, propinquity or remoteness, fecundity, purity, and extent.

Jeff harasses Bill.

1. Intensity

How intense is the experience for each of them? Very. The big difference, however, is that it is intensely bad for Bill, who could hardly feel worse. Jeff, however, would be delighted. We can't say that his pleasure is healthy, but it is real.

Bill	*Jeff*
−10	+10

2. Duration

How long will the pleasure or pain last? Bill's unhappiness will probably last a long time. None of us would quickly get over being the object of such hatred and threats. Jeff's pleasure, on the other hand, will likely fade much sooner.

Bill	*Jeff*
−10	+5

3. Certainty

How likely is it that Bill and Jeff will feel pain and pleasure, respectively? It is virtually certain in each case.

Bill	*Jeff*
−10	+10

4. Propinquity

When will the pain and pleasure start? Immediately for Bill. Jeff has to wait until Bill withdraws his application to see if his plan succeeds. But, racist that he is, Jeff will probably enjoy harassing Bill as soon as he starts.

Bill	*Jeff*
−10	+10

5. Fecundity

Will the incident produce any subsequent pleasure in the life of either of them? Bill may get some sympathy from friends, but that's about it. Jeff will probably feel a moderate amount of long-term pleasure. (Scores on fecundity can be only positive since they measure future pleasures. Scores for purity, the next category, take care of the other side of the coin and can be only negative.)

Bill	*Jeff*
+1	+5

6. Purity

Will the incident lead to future unhappiness for either man? The experience will add considerable pain to Bill's life. The episode will probably also make him more suspicious of white people, which will certainly be unpleasant. The memory of the event will always evoke unhappiness. Will Jeff feel anything negative? Probably, but it will be substantially less than Bill's long-term pain. Jeff knows that what's he done is illegal. He will surely worry about whether anyone saw him damage Bill's car, for example. And if he comes to his senses when he is older, and realizes what he did to Bill, he will feel deep regret and shame.

Bill   *Jeff*
−10   −5

7. **Extent**

Do any other people feel pain or pleasure because of this event? Bill will surely tell friends and family about the harassment, and all of them will feel unhappy because of it. Most people on campus who hear about the incident will feel sympathy for Bill and will also be unhappy and angry about it. Jeff will have to be careful about whom he tells, but presumably he will boast about it to a couple of like-minded friends. On balance, however, the pain produced will most likely outweigh the pleasure. Scores for extent pose a special problem. After all, they refer to other people's feelings of pleasure and pain that have their own intensity, duration, certainty, propinquity, fecundity, and purity. So we cannot just add in the score as though it is only one-seventh of the total. Strictly speaking, to determine the extent of pleasure or pain precisely, we should come up with scores for each individual involved. If ten people will be affected by what Jeff did to Bill, we should do a separate calculation for each person and then total them all up. But this is usually impractical.

Bentham does not tell us what to do here, but the best thing is probably to leave the score for extent out of the addition and think of it as some kind of multiplier. You can figure out how to work it in if you want to quantify this altogether. For our purposes, we will consider it informally after looking at the other totals. Our first pass at this problem, then, reveals that if Jeff harasses Bill, we get a greater balance of pain over pleasure. (The scores turn out: Bill −49, Jeff +35.) This isn't promising for Jeff's point of view. But let's consider the other possibility (Jeff does not harass Bill) and see how it compares.

Jeff does not harass Bill.

1. **Intensity**

If Jeff does not harass Bill, Bill has every reason to enjoy looking forward to good times with his friends. Bill's pleasure probably won't be as intense as the pain he'd feel as the victim of racial hatred. But at least he'll feel pleasure. Jeff won't be happy about passing up an opportunity to harass Bill, and he won't take any pleasure at Bill's acceptance into the fraternity. And since Jeff obviously does not belong to the fraternity in question, Bill's admission will have more of a direct effect on Bill's life than on Jeff's. Jeff's unhappiness, then, is probably less than Bill's happiness.

Bill   *Jeff*
+5   −1

2. Duration

How long will this pleasure and pain last for Bill and Jeff, respectively? In the grand scale of things, we aren't talking about something that goes on for very long, in either case. Bill will enjoy the process, his acceptance, and any social events immediately following being admitted. But he will then turn his attention to more pressing matters, such as studying for his courses, so we're probably talking only about a moderate amount of pleasure. (The longer-term pleasures connected with fraternity living and good times with Bill's friends will be covered under fecundity.) Jeff will be annoyed. But he'll doubtless fixate on something else pretty quickly.

Bill	Jeff
+5	−1

3. Certainty

How likely is it that Bill and Jeff will actually feel happiness and annoyance, respectively, as a result of Bill's not being harassed? It's a sure thing in each case.

Bill	Jeff
+10	−10

4. Propinquity

How soon will these positive and negative feelings start? Virtually immediately, in each case.

Bill	Jeff
+10	−10

5. Fecundity

Will Bill's admission lead to any longer-term pleasures for either man? Not for Jeff. But definitely for Bill. That's the whole point of his wanting to join the house: friendships, parties, a comfortable place to live, and the like. Some of these friendships may even last his whole life. Contacts he makes at the house may also benefit him professionally.

Bill	Jeff
+10	0

6. Purity

What about the other side of the coin? Will Bill's not being harassed produce any longer-term unhappiness for Bill or Jeff? Probably not in Bill's case. If Jeff is a hard-core racist, he may occasionally think back to Bill's case and feel annoyed about it. But it's unlikely to amount to any significant amount of unhappiness.

Bill	Jeff
0	−1

7. Extent

And finally, what's the impact of all of this on other people? Bill's presence in the fraternity house will presumably make his friends happy. Jeff's unhappiness at this will probably have no effect on his friends and associates.

The Results. So what is the ethical "bottom line"? Leaving out the scores for extent, the totals are: −49/+35 (Jeff harasses Bill) and +40/−23 (Jeff does not harass Bill). This means that Jeff's racist harassment of Bill produces more pain in his life than pleasure in Jeff's, while leaving Bill alone produces more pleasure for Bill than pain for Jeff. Adding extent only magnifies the difference between harassing and not-harassing because, as we saw, more people would be upset than made happy by Jeff's actions. According to Bentham's system, there is no question that Jeff's harassment is morally wrong.

That, then, is how the "hedonistic calculus" works. In Bentham's mind, it gives us an impartial, quantitative evaluation of a situation. It clearly shows the amounts of pleasure and pain that are produced. And this lets us make an objective judgment about whether an action is right or wrong. In this case, the results of the calculus match our automatic sense of how wrong Jeff's conduct was.

The Strengths of the Hedonistic Calculus.

The Strengths of the Hedonistic Calculus. Bentham's hedonistic calculus seems to work in this case, and it would work in many other cases as well. After all, there is something reasonable about the idea that what determines whether an action is right or wrong is how much good or harm comes from it. The hedonistic calculus seems to measure that fairly well.

The calculus is quantitative, objective, and reasonably inclusive. By requiring scores for seven different categories, it forces us to look at aspects of an action that we otherwise might ignore. If we use it correctly, we consider longer-term effects (fecundity and purity) as well as immediate consequences. It is also democratic. No one person's pleasure or pain counts for more than any other person's.

The utilitarian approach also has the advantage of not prejudging the issue. It has only one ground rule—pleasure is good and pain is bad. Whether an action is morally right or wrong depends exclusively on the circumstances, not on some predetermined judgment of what is right and wrong. In Bentham's mind, actions cannot be "evil" if they produce more benefits than harm, and they cannot be "good" if they result in more pain than pleasure. Every calculation is clean, open, and objective. The facts are all that count.

Bentham seems to have given us precisely what he wanted to—an objective, impartial, and practical way to identify which actions produce the greatest balance of pleasure over pain. And that, for Bentham, is all that right and wrong amount to.

Problems with the Calculus: A Case of Slander.

Problems with the Calculus: A Case of Slander. But surely the anguish we have with our own ethical dilemmas tells us that when debating right and wrong, we have to do more than grab a calculator and figure out the totals. Bentham's approach is appealing, but ethical problems are not always so easily solved. In fact, Bentham's thinking has an important defect.

Consider the case in which Ron lied about Tony in order to get a promotion and a raise. When you read that story, you surely thought that Ron was wrong. Not only will his lie cost Tony the promotion, it also ruins Tony's reputation with the store owner and with anyone else the owner mentions it to.

If the hedonistic calculus were as flawless as it previously seemed, it should reveal that more harm than good comes from lying than from not lying. But it doesn't. What if Ron uses the money to make life much better for himself and his family?

He stays in school and gets his degree. He and his wife can now afford day care so that his wife is able to resume her career. In a few years they are doing well and can provide for their child the way they want to. Perhaps they can now afford to have other children to whom they also give a good start in life. If this turns out to be Ron's "big break," his act dramatically improves the lives of three or more people. The costs, on the other hand, are at best minimal—Tony does not get this promotion. At worst, his future is jeopardized. But he is single, so we are talking about the unhappiness of only one person. What is one person's pain versus the solid pleasure of the three (or more) people in Ron's family? On the other hand, if Ron refuses to lie and the promotion goes to Tony, Tony would have to do a considerable amount of good for himself and for other people to offset the benefits that Ron and his family will now probably never see. From a utilitarian perspective, then, it seems that in this scenario, the lie could be morally good.

If you work through Bentham's hedonistic calculus on this question, the lie will probably come out a clear winner. At least it will be a "close call." So either our first opinion that Ron is wrong to lie was off target, or something is wrong with Bentham's system.

Which is it? Most of us would think that Ron's lie couldn't possibly be "good." No matter how much it benefits Ron and his family, it cannot offset the damage to Tony's reputation. Thus, Bentham's calculus must be overlooking something.

The problem is that all the hedonistic calculus measures is the *amount,* or *quantity,* of pleasure or pain that results from an action. As a result, the pleasure of at least three people outweighs the pain of one, no matter how intense the unhappiness that one person feels. By the same logic, we could say that slavery is morally justifiable as long as it produces more pleasure in the lives of slave owners and their fellow citizens than unhappiness in the lives of comparatively fewer slaves.

Bentham ignores the *kind* or *quality* of pleasure and pain involved. Maybe Ron's family will have a better life because of the lie. But will their satisfactions be of the same kind and degree as the terrible damage done to Tony's reputation? Aren't we comparing apples and oranges? Surely, Tony's right to have his reputation protected from slander is more important than whatever Ron's increased salary will buy. And yet the hedonistic calculus takes no account of this difference.

Bentham did consider the issue of kinds of pleasure—but he rejected it. As he put it, "pushpin [a child's game] is as good as poetry." He apparently thought that differentiating among types of pleasures and ranking them would give the aristocracy an argument that their pleasures were far superior to those of ordinary people. And because Bentham was more concerned with social reform than personal ethical dilemmas, his "agenda" got in his way, and he refused to distinguish between types of pleasures.

One of Bentham's younger British contemporaries noted this and disagreed. He developed a revised version of utilitarianism to take the notion of the quality of pleasures into account. This philosopher was Bentham's godson, John Stuart Mill.

John Stuart Mill

The Quality of Pleasure

John Stuart Mill is, like Bentham, a teleological thinker. Mill accepted Bentham's basic idea that the appropriate standard for evaluating the ethical character of

John Stuart Mill

John Stuart Mill (1806–1873) was the most important British philosopher during the nineteenth century and remains one of the most persuasive representatives of liberalism. Mill was educated by his father, James Mill, to be a defender of utilitarianism. After a serious bout with depression when he was 20, Mill rebelled against the narrow, unemotional, and analytical way he had been trained, and he significantly broadened his philosophical outlook. He became an important administrator of the East India Company and served in Parliament toward the end of his life. Mill was one of only a few philosophers to address the subjugation of women, a concern which no doubt was sparked by his long relationship with Harriet Taylor. Mill and Mrs. Taylor met when Mill was 25 and the two remained close Platonic friends for nearly twenty years. Three years after the death of Mrs. Taylor's husband, the two married. Harriet died only six years later, however. Mill was convinced that Harriet would have been recognized as one of the time's leading thinkers had she been a man, and he claimed that she was a major influence on his thinking.

actions is the pleasure, or happiness, that results from an action. He writes in *Utilitarianism*:

> The creed which accepts as the foundation of morals "utility" or the "greatest happiness principle" holds that actions are right in proportion as they tend to promote happiness; wrong as they tend to produce the reverse of happiness. By happiness is intended pleasure and the absence of pain; by unhappiness, pain and the privation of pleasure.

Mill, however, rejects Bentham's belief that all pleasures are equal. He insists that there exists a whole range of pleasures—some lower, some higher. He explains,

> It is quite compatible with the principle of utility to recognize the fact that some kinds of pleasure are more desirable and more valuable than others. It would be absurd that, while in estimating all other things quality is considered as well as quantity, the estimation of pleasure should be supposed to depend on quantity alone.

> —Utilitarianism

Once pleasures are separated into high and low quality, Mill claims that the better pleasures are so much better that a small amount of high-quality pleasure outweighs a much larger amount of low-quality pleasure. Thus, Mill's "ethical yardstick" is similar to Bentham's in that it measures the consequences of an action. But it also identifies better versus worse kinds of pleasure. It measures quality as well as quantity.

Mill's revision of Bentham's schema makes sense. Even our ordinary intuition tells us that some actions are better than others, and some pleasures are better than others.

What if you promise a friend to help her study for an exam and then break your word at the last minute and go to a great party? You will get more pleasure out of the party than out of helping your friend, but that's not preferable to keeping your word and helping her. In the same way, respecting someone's dignity is superior to making money. Being honest is more important than getting drunk. And so forth.

In the case of Ron and Tony, then, Mill would say that Ron's pleasures do not outweigh Tony's pains. Ron deprives Tony of the pleasure of having a good name and inflicts intense pain on him by ruining his reputation. The pleasures Ron and his family get from his lie are not high enough in quality to offset the damage to Tony. And going back to the case of Bill and Jeff, the pleasures of feeling safe from threats and discrimination are of a much higher quality than whatever pleasure is associated with racially harassing someone.

Identifying Higher and Lower Pleasures

The danger of class bias or special interest that led Bentham to reject a systematic ranking of pleasures is, however, quite real. Can we differentiate between low-quality and high-quality pleasures in a way that is not just a function of our own personal preferences or prejudices? This sort of judgment seems much more subjective and arbitrary than the quantification of the hedonistic calculus.

Mill came up with a simple solution to this problem. He thought we should rely on the judgment of people who already have experienced the range of pleasures involved. He writes:

> If I am asked what I mean by difference of quality of pleasures, or what makes one pleasure more valuable than another, . . . there is but one possible answer. Of two pleasures, if there be one to which all or almost all who have experience of both give a decided preference, . . . that is the more desirable pleasure.
>
> —Utilitarianism

This too seems to make sense. Who is the best person to separate higher- from lower-quality anything? The one who has the greatest amount of experience with both. If you want a good sound system, you don't think much of the opinion of someone who's idea of "great sound" is an AM car radio. If you want to buy good-quality clothing, you look for someone who has style and wears nice clothes.

Why not approach pleasure and a sense of well-being the same way? The opinion of someone who has always been a lying, manipulative troublemaker is poorly informed and one-sided. So is the opinion of some sheltered innocent who knows nothing of the pleasures associated with greed, lust, and selfishness. We want someone who knows all sides of an issue and can make a truly informed judgment. If such a person, having experienced all the pleasures, claims that some are indeed better than others, shouldn't we listen?

What does Mill say these experienced individuals can tell us? He explains,

> Now it is an unquestionable fact that those who are equally acquainted with and equally capable of appreciating and enjoying both do give a most marked preference to the manner of existence which employs their higher faculties. Few human

creatures would consent to be changed into any of the lower animals for a promise of the fullest allowance of a beast's pleasures; no intelligent human being would consent to be a fool, no instructed person would be an ignoramus, no person of feeling and conscience would be selfish and base, even though they should be persuaded that the fool, the dunce, or the rascal is better satisfied with his lot than they are with theirs. . . . Whoever supposes that this preference takes place at a sacrifice of happiness—that the superior being, in anything like equal circumstances, is not happier than the inferior—confounds the two very different ideas of happiness and content. It is indisputable that the being whose capacities of enjoyment are low has the greatest chance of having them fully satisfied; and a highly endowed being will always feel that any happiness which he can look for, as the world is constituted, is imperfect. But he can learn to bear its imperfections, if they are at all bearable; and they will not make him envy the being who is indeed unconscious of the imperfections, but only because he feels not at all the good which those imperfections qualify. It is better to be a human being dissatisfied than a pig satisfied; better to be Socrates dissatisfied than a fool satisfied. And if the fool, or the pig, are of a different opinion, it is because they only know their own side of the question. The other party to the comparison knows both sides.[8]

—Utilitarianism

Mill also suggests a consensus among people who have experienced the full range of pleasures. Such people would say that the "higher" pleasures include intelligence, mental pleasures, education, sensitivity to others, a sense of morality, and health. Among the "lower" pleasures they would place stupidity, ignorance, selfishness, indolence, and physical pleasure—especially sensual indulgence.

You can test Mill's idea for yourself by taking a few minutes to fill out this questionnaire. For each of the following items, indicate how important or serious you think the pleasures and pains are. Use a scale of: LOW, MEDIUM, HIGH. (LOW pleasures still feel good, but, in some way, you feel that they aren't quite as good as MEDIUM and HIGH ones.)

I. PLEASURES

1. getting an A in a difficult course

2. getting an A in an easy course in which everyone else gets an A

3. getting an A in a course by cheating

4. getting your ideal job because you were the best candidate

5. getting your ideal job because your parents knew your boss (better-qualified people were passed over)

---

[8]Be sure you realize that Mill is not making an illegitimate appeal to authority here—whether it be the authority of experience or the authority of Socrates. Whether it involves determining quality in sound equipment, clothes, or pleasure, people with the experience that you lack should be able to show you, on the basis of that experience, how to tell the difference between low and high quality. It is not a matter of taking someone's word. If you let yourself be guided by them, you too could have experiences that would let you develop your judgment.

6. sexual activity with someone with whom you have no special feelings (you're both unattached)

7. sexual activity with someone you're deeply in love with

8. sexual activity with someone you have no special feelings for while you're in love and committed to someone else

II. PAINS/ UNHAPPINESS/ FEELINGS THAT ARE IN SOME OTHER WAY UN-COMFORTABLE OR UNDESIRABLE

(LOW pains are more bearable or less important pains; HIGH are more serious or "worse" pains than LOW or MEDIUM ones)

9. the fear you feel at a "haunted house" at an amusement park

10. the fear you feel as a tire blows out and your car spins out of control on the highway

11. being punished for something that you knew was wrong when you did it

12. being punished for something that you didn't do

13. missing a party so that you can keep your promise to help a friend study

14. the work and sacrifice involved in taking care of someone close to you who is very sick

15. being physically abused by a boyfriend, girlfriend, or spouse

16. discovering that someone stole something out of your car

I have given this questionnaire to hundreds of students in my ethics classes over the years, and their answers have been remarkably consistent. It would be surprising if your answers were very different. Virtually without exception, my students have answered:

Pleasures

1. HIGH

2. MEDIUM

3. LOW

4. HIGH

5. MEDIUM

6. MEDIUM

7. HIGH

8. LOW

Pains

9. LOW

10. HIGH

11. MEDIUM

12. HIGH

13. LOW

14. LOW

15. HIGH

16. HIGH

This questionnaire does two things. First, it provides a simple illustration of Mill's idea that there are qualitative differences among various pleasures and pains—differences that Bentham rejects. Second, it puts to the test Mill's claim that people with roughly the same experience of various pleasures and pains will agree as to which are better and which are worse. The results suggest that he is correct on both counts.

Look at the three pleasures in questions 1–8: getting an A, getting a job, and sexual pleasure. If we discount qualitative differences, the answers to 1–3, 4 and 5, and 6–8 should be the same. Aren't the practical consequences of getting an A, for example, the same—no matter how you get the grade? In fact, considering that the "cost" of getting an A by doing little work or by cheating is dramatically lower than what it takes to do well in a difficult course, shouldn't 2 and 3 be seen as better pleasures than 1? And yet, my students invariably argue just the opposite—the hard work is what makes the grade more satisfying. They offer equivalent arguments about why 4 is better than 5 (there's greater sense of accomplishment from getting a job you've earned) and about why 7 is better than 6 and why 8 is worse than both (deep feelings of love trump physical pleasure, and both leave guilty pleasures in the dust).

We see a similar picture with the pains in questions 9–16. My students explain that real-life fear feels worse than manufactured fear, that how bad a punishment feels depends on whether it is deserved, and that the sacrifices connected with helping someone else (even if they're long term and substantial, as can be the case in looking after someone very ill) simply don't register as especially significant. Interestingly, despite the dramatic differences in the pain connected with 15 and 16—being physically abused versus having an object stolen—both are always ranked as very serious harms. Although the object lost in the car break-in can be replaced, there's a strong sense that one's personal space, privacy, and dignity have been violated.

Mill uses the idea that there are qualitative differences among pleasures and pains to argue that people who have experienced "higher" and "lower" pleasures are willing to tolerate a good deal of low-quality unhappiness for a smaller amount of more satisfying, high-quality pleasure. Put the "Socrates/fool" question to yourself. To get a life of constant but low-grade contentment, would you give up the higher abilities, experiences, and satisfactions of being an intelligent, discerning, and sensitive person? Ask your friends the same thing. If most of you say no, this adds credence to Mill's assertion.

Identifying Long-Term Consequences

The second way that Mill improves on Bentham's utilitarianism lies in his more explicit and astute treatment of the long-term consequences of actions. Mill uses the act of lying as his example. Most of us probably feel that unless we lie so often that people stop believing us, there really are no long-term disadvantages to lying. To this Mill would respond that we simply are not identifying all the long-term consequences of a lie. In the very long view, Mill says, truth telling is one of the most essential conditions for human well-being, or happiness. Consequently, he claims,

> Any, even unintentional, deviation from truth . . . [weakens] the trustworthiness of human assertion, which is not only the principal support of all present social well-being, but the insufficiency of which does more than any one thing that can be named to keep back civilization, virtue, everything on which human happiness on the largest scale depends.
>
> —*Utilitarianism*

It may seem to you that Mill exaggerates here. His point, however, is that to identify all the consequences that result from an action, we have to see just how far the ripples caused by our actions reach. In this case, Mill says, *any* instance of lying makes all of us a little less likely to believe each other, and you can probably see how this might be so. That, of course, tends to make life worse rather than better.

For example, suppose you lie about your qualifications for a job because you really want it. You tell a prospective employer, "I know I don't have experience, but I've learned enough about computers in school to do the job." If you get caught, your boss is going to be a whole lot less sympathetic to the next struggling college student who comes by looking for a chance. He will say to himself, "What's-his-name lied to me. So why should I take this kid's word for it?" Thus, the end result of your lie is that one or more deserving people might not get a job that they need. Even if you get away with your lie, what will happen when you're in a position to hire people yourself? Because you lied, you'll be suspicious of the people you interview and think they are lying to you. Whichever way you cut it, your lie increases distrust in the world and makes life unhappier for people. It's clear, then, that actions, wrong or right, have indirect, long-term consequences as well as direct, short-term ones. And a teleological approach to ethics requires us to look at all consequences, not just immediate ones.

Mill's point here is somewhat unsettling. Everything we do can have far-ranging consequences not only for our own lives but for other people's as well. Our deeds probably have more impact on other people's happiness and unhappiness than we ever realize. A thorough assessment of the consequences of an action, then, requires that we examine the full picture.

Problems with Mill's Theory: A Case of Cheating

Mill accepts most of Bentham's ideas, and his thinking has the same strengths. Evaluating right and wrong is an open, objective process. Pleasure is the good, and actions that increase it are better than those that decrease it. By distinguishing higher from lower pleasures, Mill corrects a major weakness in Bentham's system. And Mill's discussion of long-term consequences reminds us that our actions have large and largely unseen consequences.

Yet there are still some problems. Recall the story about Ruth and John, who cheated in order to get into medical school. Their actions certainly seem wrong, and when we consider the harm they do to other students, they seem even worse. But what if both of them are extremely talented people, much brighter than their grades indicate? And what if they are also highly committed to helping sick people? In short, despite the poor way the two are acting now, we have every reason to believe that they will both be outstanding physicians and give real help to thousands. Imagine that if they decide not to cheat, their places in medical school will go to two people who will be much less altruistic as physicians. When we apply Mill's ideas, however, we encounter a significant problem. The pleasures associated with health and helping people rank high in Mill's scheme, and Ruth and John will undoubtedly produce more high-quality pleasure than their counterparts would throughout their respective careers—careers Ruth and John can get into only by cheating. Taking quality and quantity into account, it looks as if Ruth and John will produce enough pleasure to offset the unhappiness they are currently responsible for.

Whether this scenario is likely or not isn't the question. As long as such a story is possible, it means big problems for Mill's scheme. If the cheating Ruth and John do now makes it possible for them to do a great deal of high-quality good for many people in the long run, are we mistaken to say that cheating is wrong?

If we say that under these conditions Ruth and John's activities are ethically tolerable, we are actually saying that "the ends justify the means." If this is true, then, given the right conditions, absolutely anything can be ethically justified—murder, child abuse, rape, theft, tyranny, slavery, genocide, and so on. Any of these actions could be morally justifiable as long as it ultimately produces enough high-quality good. Clearly, however, something must be wrong with any system that justifies such evils.

There is yet another problem with Mill's utilitarian ethics. The fact that results-oriented, or teleological, ethics refuses to label actions as intrinsically right or wrong seems to be a benefit at first. Such a system permits no prejudgment of issues, and that is probably good. This means, however, that the same action can be right today and wrong tomorrow. If the circumstances permit it today, I may ethically break a promise to you. But if the circumstances change tomorrow, breaking that promise may be ethically quite wrong.

From a practical standpoint, this relativity of right and wrong to a complex set of circumstances may or may not concern you. From an intellectual standpoint, it is much more troublesome. Remember that philosophy is a rational, logical enterprise. And how can we consider a utilitarian approach to ethics rational or logical when it is plagued by such an apparent inconsistency?

The Limits of Results-Oriented Ethics

Many of Bentham's and Mill's ideas seem to make good, common sense. Pleasure and pain are standards that we can all understand. The consequences of an action are certainly a critical part of whether an action is right or wrong. Bentham's "hedonistic calculus" is an honest attempt to quantify in an objective and impartial way the tangible good and harm that results from an action. Mill's addition of the "quality" of pleasure corrects a major flaw in Bentham's system.

However, despite all of these strengths, there also seem to be some weaknesses endemic to results-oriented ethics. First, a teleological approach to ethics theoretically allows any action to be morally right as long as the happiness it produces outweighs the unhappiness it causes. Second, because the ethical character of an action can vary with the circumstances in which it is made, the same deed can be right today and wrong tomorrow. Teleological ethics thus goes beyond the point of being reasonably adaptable. Ultimately, it is too flexible to be a secure ethical standard. Accordingly, in determining whether an action is right or wrong, we also need to take into account the ethical character of the actions themselves.

Act-Oriented, or Deontological, Ethics

As you have seen, Bentham's and Mill's teleological systems can be used to defend some otherwise questionable actions. We saw that under a certain set of conditions, a results-oriented philosopher would have no ethical objection to Ron's lying about Tony or to Ruth and John's cheating. Or, to take another example, what if your parents kept you from making some stupid mistake by cleverly manipulating you on the basis of information they got by eavesdropping on your private conversations and opening your mail? From a teleological standpoint, these questionable actions would probably be morally justifiable.

Yet there is something about actions like lying, cheating, manipulation, invasion of privacy, and promise breaking that still bothers us. They may produce good results, but there must be more to it than that. No matter what, don't you feel that you have a right to expect people to keep their word, compete fairly, and let you make your own decisions? Could you be satisfied in life or have a genuine sense of well-being without these things?

If you found out that your parents read your mail, would you thank them for their initiative and willingness to help you? More likely, you'd feel some conflict about what they did. In some small way you might be glad they cared, but you'd also feel that they violated your privacy. Probably you would simply be furious because you believe you have a right to run your life, including the right to privacy and the right to make your own mistakes.

In short, you *need* to be treated with respect in order to feel good about your life. Think about it for a minute. Can you feel happy and satisfied if you are being manipulated—by parents, by teachers, by politicians, by anybody—even if it is "for your own good"? Most people say "no." It may be irrational, but it is the way we are. Human beings seem to have a basic need to take charge of their own lives and to be treated as free, autonomous entities. The host of behaviors that interfere with this—lying, cheating, manipulation, coercion, promise breaking, deception, and the like—significantly reduce our satisfaction with life. By their very nature these actions block our happiness.

Bentham's and Mill's results-oriented approaches to ethics do not handle this problem. In order to do so, another group of philosophers, which rejects teleological ethics, says that in order to determine right and wrong we must examine precisely *what people do,* not the consequences of their actions. This is the *act-oriented* or *deontological* approach to ethics.

The "Principle of the Thing"

Act-oriented ethics is in many ways easier to understand and apply than results-oriented ethics. The intensity, duration, certainty, purity, and so on of the consequences of an action are no longer relevant. Neither are their short-term versus long-term results. We do not need to calculate the amount of pleasure and pain produced throughout a group of hundreds or even thousands of people. In act-oriented ethics, we focus totally on the action itself and ask ourselves, "Is this an appropriate action for one person to take toward another?"

Act-oriented ethics assumes that human beings need to be treated in certain ways in order to be happy. It assumes that we are constituted in such a way that experiencing unfairness, manipulation, and deceit will significantly diminish our sense of well-being, while being treated with honesty and justice will increase it—no matter what the consequences of such actions. A deontological approach to ethics evaluates an action's *intrinsic* strengths and weaknesses, not, as a teleological approach does, the positive and negative results that are *extrinsic* to the deed. An act-oriented, or deontological, "ethical yardstick," then, is held up against *the action itself* and is marked off in units labeled *fairness, dignity, equality,* and the like.

All of us commonly use an act-oriented approach to ethics when we say we don't care about the consequences of an act we're considering and decide instead on a course of action based strictly on "the principle of the thing." For example, your teacher might never discover that you handed in a term paper from your fraternity's files, but you know it's dishonest, so you do the work. You might get away with cheating on your boyfriend, but it would mean breaking your promise to him, so you just say "no." You may lose your job by reporting to the authorities that the company you work for pollutes the local river, but to stand by and do nothing is to be an accomplice.

We may use anything from sophisticated philosophical arguments to simple religious precepts to a vague sense of personal conscience to explain our choices. But basically the process boils down to drawing a line and saying, "Past this point I will not go, no matter what the rewards or penalties." At times like this, our beliefs or our sense of who we are is what's important. We believe we simply have a *duty* to act in a particular way, whatever the outcome. (Remember that *deontos* is the Greek word for "duty," hence the name *deontological* ethics.)

Immanuel Kant

As Bentham and Mill are the classic representatives of results-oriented ethics, so the great German thinker Immanuel Kant created the model for act-oriented ethics.

Like the Greek thinkers Plato and Aristotle and the medieval saints Augustine and Thomas Aquinas, Immanuel Kant created an elaborate account of virtually every facet of human experience, covering the nature of reality, knowledge, ethics, art, and politics. The slice of Kant's work that we touch on here, although small, is one of the concepts for which his work is best known. Although Kant's entire ethical system is well beyond our scope at this point, his basic standard of right and wrong will serve us well.

Immanuel Kant

Immanuel Kant (1724–1804) spent his entire life in the Prussian city of Konigsberg. After years as a tutor and lecturer, Kant was appointed a professor at the University. Supposedly, Kant's life was so regular that his neighbors would set their clocks by his daily walk, yet he also had a reputation as a witty and entertaining host at frequent dinner parties that he gave. Kant's initial intellectual reputation came from his writings on physics, astronomy, and metaphysics. But beginning in 1781, when Kant was 57, the philosopher issued a series of books that transformed the shape of philosophy and established Kant as one of philosophy's greatest thinkers. Kant first wrote *The Critique of Pure Reason*, then during the next nine years he published the *Prolegomena to any Future Metaphysics*, *The Groundwork of the Metaphysic of Morals*, *Metaphysical Foundations of Natural Science*, *The Critique of Practical Reason*, and *The Critique of Judgment*.

Duty and Dignity

Kant begins his ethics with the concept of *duty*. What makes an action ethically worthwhile is that we do it *just because it is the right thing to do*. Ethical behavior results from the awareness that we simply have a duty to act a certain way, not, as results-oriented ethics contends, because it will produce positive consequences. Kant's emphasis on duty and on disregarding the results of our actions makes him a classic example of the deontological thinker.

But how do we know what we have a duty to do or to avoid? The key here is to recall that act-oriented ethics requires us to focus simply on the action itself. That means that the action we choose must be valuable in itself, not valuable for what it will produce. In other words, it must have *intrinsic* worth. And Kant says that we have a duty to perform such actions. According to Kant, the only actions with intrinsic worth are ethical ones; he cites, for example, keeping promises and being kind to someone. Think about this for a minute. Consider a time when you acted ethically simply because it was the right thing to do. Maybe it made you lose out on something, cost you money, or even got you punished. Despite this, don't you believe that what you did was somehow worthwhile in itself? Don't you feel proud about performing such an action? If so, Kant would say that you are recognizing the "intrinsic worth" of ethical actions.

What makes ethical actions intrinsically worthwhile is that they are actions that fit the essential nature of those who perform them and those who experience them. That is, Kant ultimately links the concept of duty to our nature as "moral agents"— rational beings who are free, who understand concepts of morality, who can deliberate over our actions, and who can be held responsible for our deeds—because we are also beings with "intrinsic worth." In particular, Kant stresses the idea that human beings have intrinsic worth by virtue of being unique creatures—free and autonomous beings—who have *dignity*.

Dignity is a special concept for Kant. He separates the world into things with a "price" and things with "dignity." Things with a price are objects that can be bought and sold. If we lose them, they can be replaced. But as individuals we have no price. Kant says that we are beyond that. Because we "admit of no equivalent" and "have intrinsic worth" we have a dignity, not a price. Accordingly, Kant believes that we simply have a duty to treat people in a particular way. We and everyone else like us are entitled to respect for our dignity, freedom, and desire to control our lives. Anything that compromises these special qualities goes against the grain of our deepest nature; it violates a fundamental sense of who we are as persons. It fails to respect our dignity.

Kant's notion of our duty, then, is to perform only those actions that have intrinsic worth, that is, those actions that respect the special needs and nature of a moral agent with dignity.

Kant's Ethical Standard: The Categorical Imperative

On the basis of Kant's ideas about duty, intrinsic worth, dignity, and our nature as rational beings, Kant formulated a basic moral rule or command by which everyone could live ethically. Kant called this moral rule the **categorical imperative**. By this he meant a command we must follow ("an imperative") that holds in every case without exception ("categorically"). Actions that followed this command would, he thought, be right actions; those that did not would be wrong. Kant states the categorical imperative in a few different ways in his classic work *Groundwork of the Metaphysic of Morals*. We will look at the two most famous versions.

Universal Law of Nature

The first statement of the categorical imperative we're going to consider proceeds from our nature as rational beings and reflects Kant's belief that ethical principles should be as valid as mathematical principles. Proposing a test whereby we can determine whether the principle underlying our action, which Kant calls a "maxim," has universal validity, he writes, "Act as though the maxim of your action were by your will to become a universal law of nature." If we discover that our maxim cannot serve as a universal law of nature, then the action in question is morally unacceptable.

The False Promise

One example Kant uses to illustrate the categorical imperative is the false promise. He writes:

> [A] man in need finds himself forced to borrow money. He knows well that he won't be able to repay it, but he sees also that he will not get any loan unless he firmly promises to repay it within a fixed time. He wants to make such a promise, but he still has conscience enough to ask himself whether it is not permissible and is

---

categorical imperative The categorical imperative is Immanuel Kant's conception of a universal moral law. Two formulations of this principle are: "Act as though the maxim of your action were by your will to become universal law of nature" and "Act in such a way that you treat humanity, whether in your own person or in the person of any other, always at the same time as an end and never simply as a means."

contrary to duty to get out of difficulty in this way. Suppose, however, that he decides to do so. The maxim of his action would then be expressed as follows: when I believe myself to be in need of money, I will borrow money and promise to pay it back, although I know that I can never do so. Now this principle of self-love or personal advantage may perhaps be quite compatible with one's entire future welfare, but the question is now whether it is right. I then transform the requirement of self-love into a universal law and put the question thus: how would things stand if my maxim were to become a universal law? He then sees at once that such a maxim could never hold as a universal law of nature and be consistent with itself, but must necessarily be self-contradictory. For the universality of a law which says that anyone believing himself to be in difficulty could promise whatever he pleases with the intention of not keeping it would make promising itself and the end to be attained thereby quite impossible, inasmuch as no one would believe what was promised him but would merely laugh at all such utterances as being vain pretenses.

Imagine a world in which it is a "law of nature" that people say one thing and do another. What would happen there if you said to someone, "Lend me $5,000 today, and I'll repay you in six months"? He certainly wouldn't believe you. Most likely he'd think you were joking. In such a world, the very concept of a "promise" would not exist. And without the notion of a promise, it's impossible to have a false promise. In other words, it is logically impossible for the maxim of your action to become a universal law of nature. So, according to Kant, the false promise is wrong.

Means and Ends

The second formulation of the categorical imperative focuses on a different dimension of our actions—precisely how we treat others. Kant wrote: "Act in such a way that you treat humanity, whether in your own person or in the person of any other, always at the same time as an end and never simply as a means."

The key here is the idea of treating people as "ends" rather than "means." What does this mean?

What Kant seems to have in mind is that to treat someone as an "end" is to treat him or her with all of the respect due to a human being. Treating people as "ends" particularly means that we respect their freedom and autonomy, that is, their right to be in control of their own lives and not to be involved in something they have not agreed to.

When I treat people as "means," on the other hand, I use them for my ends, not theirs. I don't care about what they want. I give them no more regard than I do an inanimate object. I see them primarily as a tool I can use to get what I want. I try to impose my choice, my decision on them, whether they like it or not. I do not respect their freedom and dignity.

The False Promise Again

Kant also considers the example of the false promise when discussing this formulation of the categorical imperative, and he reaches a similar conclusion:

The man who intends to make a false promise will immediately see that he intends to make use of another man merely as a means to an end which the latter does not likewise hold. For the man whom I want to use for my own purposes by such a promise cannot possibly concur with my way of action toward him.

That is, the person making the false promise is using someone else simply as a means to his or her own end. Because the action fails to respect the freedom, choice, dignity, and autonomy of the person being deceived, Kant believes it to be wrong.

The Uses of Act-Oriented Ethics

Kant's approach to ethics has some important advantages. First, it cancels the two main problems we saw with results-oriented ethics. Kant's "categorical imperative" gives us fairly consistent boundaries between right and wrong. Ethical judgments do not vary so widely as they do when we use results-oriented ethics. A false promise is a false promise—yesterday, today, and tomorrow—and it always violates the same principle. It is still manipulating someone so that they do something they would not otherwise do, and it does not matter if or how circumstances change. From Kant's point of view, that will always be morally unacceptable. Thus, Kant's ethical thought has a core stability that we find lacking in teleological ethics.

Kant also adds something to ethics that thinkers like Bentham and Mill miss—an awareness that no matter how much good some actions produce, they do not really "fit" with very basic features of what it is to be human. Kant focuses on what he takes as the two most important characteristics of our nature—that we are *rational* and that we are *free*.[9] Unlike most other creatures on this planet, we can think about life in a highly sophisticated fashion and then choose our actions on the basis of our thoughts. Kant's ideas imply, then, that short-circuiting this process, for example, by manipulating people so that they cannot freely decide on their own actions, is in a very fundamental way rejecting their humanity. When we do this, strictly speaking, we treat people in an "unhuman" way.

Accordingly, Kant's approach lets us develop an ethical standard from a realistic and practical understanding of who we are as humans. We are free, and something about our nature makes us believe that we, and all other beings like us, deserve to be treated in a particular way. We then label actions that clash with this nature, that is, actions that are manipulative and deceitful, as morally wrong. Those that respect our dignity, on the other hand, are morally right.

The Limits of Act-Oriented Ethics

As much as an act-oriented approach adds to ethics, it also has limitations, of course. It may appeal to our desire for consistency and stability to say it is always wrong to make false promises, to lie, to steal, to coerce people into doing what they despise. But such stability easily slides into a rigid and inflexible standard that virtually all of us would find morally offensive. We all can imagine cases where saying that a particular action is always wrong just doesn't seem realistic. If a gun-waving maniac bursts into your philosophy class and demands that your teacher tell him

---

[9]The two formulations of the categorical imperative may seem very different but recognize that each simply tests how an action measures up against different aspects of our nature. The "maxim/universal law" version is derived from our nature as logical, rational beings. The "means/ends" version refers to our nature as free and autonomous beings.

where you are so that he can kill you, surely it would be all right—even good—for your professor to lie. Stealing food from someone who has plenty in order to save your starving infant may not be the best way to handle a situation, but surely it is ethically superior to letting your child die.

Life is often more complicated than act-oriented systems acknowledge. The ethical dilemmas in the two examples just mentioned are not simply "lie" versus "tell the truth" or "steal" versus "respect someone's property rights." They are more like "lie and protect someone's life" versus "tell the truth and endanger someone's life" and "steal and save an infant" versus "do not steal and allow a child to die." In real life, there might be many more conditions and qualifications to consider. Unfortunately, unlike Mill's version of utilitarianism, act-oriented, or deontological, ethics ordinarily does not help us differentiate or rank actions. Applying Kant's categorical imperative in these situations would probably tell us that all our options were in some way "wrong." Yet surely a good ethical standard should help us make our way through the gray area where, for example, we may feel that our only choice is between the lesser of two evils.

Combining the Two Approaches

Our discussion of Bentham's and Mill's teleological ethics revealed critical weaknesses in their systems. Kant's deontological system seemed to correct these problems, yet it has its own flaws. Thus, it should be apparent that while each approach has much to offer, neither has the last word. Philosophers who construct pure moral theories usually choose one of the major approaches—teleological or deontological, or some other approach—and then try to work out the kinks. For the more practical personal task of deciding what to do when faced with an ethical dilemma, however, it makes sense to pull from both of the approaches we've studied here and get the best of both worlds.

In deciding whether a particular action is right or wrong, you can start by examining its consequences—the amount and type of good or harm it produces, the number of people it affects, its long-term and short-term results. You can also look at the act itself and see how it stands up against Kant's idea of the categorical imperative or against our own basic notions of freedom, dignity, honesty, equality, and the like. Ultimately, you have to make the best judgment you can according to the circumstances of each case. Examining both should give you a good picture of the situation. The more information you have, the better your decision will be.

To see how this might work, let's use this combined approach on the case of Sharon who steals books from the college store. Remember that the two of you go to buy your textbooks for the semester, and after you leave the store, Sharon pulls an expensive anatomy text out from inside of her raincoat. Her excuse is that everything at college is overpriced and this is her way of balancing things out.

Stealing a Textbook: The Consequences

What are the *consequences* of this act? The short-run consequences are obvious—the owner of the bookstore loses the price of the book (pain) and Sharon saves the price of the book (pleasure). A bookstore makes thousands of dollars each year, so the amount involved here less seems like very little. What about over the long term? Sharon says that she steals regularly. But even if she steals thousands of dollars worth of books over the course of her years in college, it still seems that her pleasure from stealing will outweigh any unhappiness felt by the owner of the bookstore.

In the long run, however, Sharon's success might encourage other students to steal books too. That might amount to hundreds or thousands of dollars' worth of stolen goods that could be attributed to Sharon's act. Of course, the bookstore will have to increase its prices to cover its losses. But even a few thousand dollars spread across the whole student population probably would not have painful effects on anyone. So far, it hardly seems to make much difference whether Sharon steals the book or not. By the same token, Sharon's paying for the book wouldn't make a major financial impact on anyone's life. Sharon won't be out that much money. And any profits or savings passed along to others would be inconsequential.

Now let's pursue some other consequences. Bentham's criterion of "certainty" raises the question of the risk Sharon runs. This seems more important than the money lost. If Sharon is caught, the university might expel her. If there's a rash of shoplifting, the bookstore might even hand her over to the police. This is also true of anyone encouraged to steal by Sharon's example. An episode like this could have a dramatically negative effect on someone's life. Indeed, the long-term pain attached to getting caught seems to far outweigh any pleasure that any of the bookstore thieves could get out of the relatively small amount of money each might save. From this standpoint, the risk seems foolish.

In the still longer term, the negative consequences continue to pile up. When someone gets away with a theft, it usually increases the odds that that person will steal again. This may mean a lifetime pattern of thievery for Sharon, everyone who steals because of her example, and everyone who steals because of their example. They may never get in trouble with the police. But they may cheat on their taxes, take office supplies from the company stockroom, or skip out on their debts. Over the long haul, we could be talking about a substantial loss of money that, even if indirectly, could be related to Sharon's stealing.

Another long-term issue relates to what we might call a disposition to respect other people's rights and to refrain from being self-interested. Book-stealing may not lead to the decline of human civilization—to think that would be to commit the fallacy of "slippery slope." But does the spread of dishonesty and selfishness in a society produce more pleasure or pain? Probably the latter. An atmosphere of honesty and trust is more enjoyable for everyone than one in which people are guarded and suspicious. If Sharon's theft represents a general pattern of selfishness on her part, and if this encourages others either to act the same way or to trust people less, then her action lowers the "quality of life" for the people she touches. This suggests that matters of trust and honesty are more important than whatever material pleasures come from selfishness. To use one of Mill's ideas, they seem to be of a higher quality.

Although this issue is hard to pin down, the long-term, wide-ranging, negative consequences of habitual selfishness and dishonesty are real enough and important enough to become a significant factor in this case. Similarly, if Sharon refrains from stealing, it's reasonable to expect more long-term, high-quality benefit than harm. A disposition toward honesty will keep Sharon from preying on other people. And, in its own small way, Sharon's honesty will encourage an atmosphere of mutual trust and respect among people.

Looking at a variety of possible results from Sharon's theft, then, we get a mixed picture. In the short run, the money probably is not an issue either way. But the risk Sharon runs does not appear to be worth it. The long-term, negative consequences of her act are probably substantial. And the high-quality benefits that should come from honesty would doubtless outweigh the relatively small amount of low-quality annoyance that Sharon might feel from paying for her purchases.

Stealing a Textbook: The Act

Now let's look at Sharon's act itself. First, when any of us enters a store, we make an unspoken promise that we will pay for what we take with us. So Sharon gives us another example of a false promise. If we try to imagine a world with the maxim of her action as a universal law ("whenever I want something, I will promise to pay for it, but then simply take the object"), we end up with a place in which there certainly wouldn't be stores of the sort that Sharon is in. There probably wouldn't even be "buying" and "selling" at all—only theft. In addition, Sharon conceals her deed, because no one whose interests are compromised by her act would consent to what she does. She is being selfish and unfair to the students who pay for their books. She takes advantage of the fact that other students are honest and that the bookstore does not search people as they leave. Sharon thus uses any number of people as means to her own ends.

Asked to defend herself, Sharon would probably say that her action was motivated by a sense of equity. She believes she's being overcharged for books in particular and her education in general, so she's trying to even the score. She might also say that she is preventing others from taking advantage of her. However, no one forced Sharon to go to college. Her choosing to go, therefore, commits her to a number of unspoken agreements, ranging from refraining from cheating in classes, to obeying the university rules, to paying for things at the prices charged in the bookstore, and a lot more. Most other people have no problem accepting these terms, and someone assessing Sharon's situation objectively would hardly conclude that she is being taken advantage of in any way. And even if she had a case, her action still is more wrong than right.

Thus, Sharon's action fails to measure up either from a results-oriented point of view or an act-oriented one. Combining elements of the two makes the difficulty of justifying her theft ethically even clearer.

Ethics in Summary

The primary object of this chapter has been to introduce you to thinking about ethics from a philosophical point of view. A philosophical approach aims to develop a standard of right and wrong that is rooted in conceptions of human well-being, not religion, law, emotions, or our own idiosyncratic ideas. Given the consistency of human nature, such a standard strives to be objective and universal. As you have seen, the principles involved in a philosophical approach to ethics are general, and they do not immediately tell us what is right and wrong in specific situations.

Nonetheless, they are more useful, practical, and realistic for solving ethical dilemmas than either a detailed, unchangeable code of rules or the general notion that right and wrong are arbitrary and relative to cultures and individuals.

With its division into teleological and deontological outlooks, a philosophical approach also gives us more than one way to make up our minds. Jeremy Bentham and John Stuart Mill direct our attention to the consequences of our actions, specifically to pleasure and pain. And they encourage us to produce a complete picture of every result of our acts both in the short and long term. Bentham summarizes his outlook in the "hedonistic calculus," which Mill adds to with his ideas about lower versus higher "quality" of pleasure. Yet both say that something is good to the extent that it produces the greatest happiness of the greatest number of people. Immanuel Kant's act-oriented ethics, on the other hand, argues that we should attend simply to the intrinsic ethical character of our actions. His guideline is the "categorical imperative." The issue for Kant is not deciding which actions produce pleasure (or pain), but which we have a duty to perform (or avoid).

Facing ethical dilemmas is always difficult. You are torn between two or more desires, and you are awash in conflict and confusion. Even though it's hard to think straight when you feel like this, this is one of those times when a philosophical approach to life's problems is eminently practical. Try to force yourself to take a rational, objective look both at the consequences of your different options and at the actions themselves. Philosophy often leaves us more confused about problems than when we started, but a philosophical approach is generally very helpful in deciding what is the right thing to do.

Of course, *why* you should do what's right is another matter. And that is what we talk about in the next chapter.

Main Points of Chapter 5

1. Ethics is the branch of philosophy concerned with establishing standards of conduct. A philosophical approach to ethics differs from a religious, legal, cultural, or completely personal approach in basing itself on the concept of human well-being. The ultimate standard philosophers use in evaluating human conduct is human welfare, well-being, or happiness.

2. A philosophical understanding of human well-being assumes that all humans have roughly the same basic needs. The more of these needs that are met, the more we achieve the level of satisfaction that human beings can find in life. Actions that promote such satisfaction are morally better. Those that block it are morally worse. These needs can be broken into two types: material conditions and ways of being treated.

3. There are two major philosophical outlooks about ethics. A results-oriented, or teleological, approach claims that the ethical character of an action depends on whether its consequences are positive or negative. The most important school of thought that uses the teleological approach to ethics is utilitarianism.

4. Utilitarianism was devised by Jeremy Bentham and elaborated on by John Stuart Mill. Utilitarianism argues that the ethical character of an action depends on how much pleasure or pain results from it. Through his hedonistic calculus, Bentham

attempted to quantify the amount of pleasure and pain resulting from actions. Mill argued that the quality of pleasures should also be taken into account so that pleasures can be graded from lower to higher. And he stressed the importance of looking at long-term as well as short-term consequences.

5. An act-oriented, or deontological, approach holds that the consequences of an action are less important than the nature of the action itself. Actions that respect human needs to be treated with dignity, honesty, equality, and fairness are right. Those that deceive, manipulate, and discriminate are wrong. Duty is an important concept for a deontological thinker. The most important proponent of this approach is the German philosopher Immanuel Kant.

6. Kant maintains that we have a moral duty to perform actions with intrinsic worth, actions such as keeping promises and being kind to someone. Kant formalized what he took to be the central rule of morality as the categorical imperative. Two versions of Kant's principle are "Act as though the maxim of your action were by your will to become a universal law of nature" and "Act in such a way that you treat humanity, whether in your own person or in the person of any other, always at the same time as an end and never simply as a means."

7. Each of these two approaches has advantages and disadvantages. A practical strategy for decision making in your life is to try to combine both.

Discussion Questions

1. What is your reaction to the idea that notions of right and wrong should ultimately *not* be based on religious beliefs or laws? What do you say to the idea that if religious and legal judgments about the ethical character of actions cannot be justified philosophically, they should be abandoned as irrational and illegitimate?

2. Do you find the notion of "human well-being" or "happiness" a reasonable and practical standard for determining right and wrong?

3. The Equal Pay Act of 1963 put the notion of "equal pay for equal work" into U.S. law. Does that mean that before 1963 American companies that paid men and women different salaries for the same job were doing something unethical even though it was legal?

4. Results-oriented, or teleological, ethics has a commonsense feel to it. We might say that it is a philosophical version of the maxim in sports, "No harm, no foul." What is your reaction to the fact that such a theory, even with Mill's addition of the concept of "quality," could justify slavery, racism, even terrorism? Should the theory in general be rejected on this basis?

5. Mill writes, "Few human creatures would consent to be changed into any of the lower animals for a promise of the fullest allowance of a beast's pleasures; no intelligent human being would consent to be a fool, no instructed person would be an ignoramus, no person of feeling and conscience would be selfish and base, even though they should be persuaded that the fool, the dunce, or the rascal is better satisfied with his lot than they are with theirs. . . . . It is better to be a human being dissatisfied than a pig satisfied; better to be Socrates dissatisfied than a fool satisfied."

Is he right? If someone offered you the chance of being transformed into Mill's "fool" who was actually more content with his or her life than you are with yours, would you do so, even if it meant giving up most of your intellectual abilities?

6. Kant's act-oriented or deontological outlook suggests that certain actions are *always* either right or wrong. Do you agree?

7. Kant's theory holds that using others as a means to your end in a way that they would not agree with is *always* morally wrong. What is your reaction to that?

8. Does a philosophical approach to ethics offer you any practical help in making decisions about right and wrong in your personal life?

Selected Readings

For a fuller treatment of the themes of this chapter, see Thomas I. White, *Right and Wrong: A Brief Guide to Understanding Ethics* (Englewood Cliffs, NJ: Prentice Hall, 1988) or William K. Frankena, *Ethics* (Englewood Cliffs, NJ: Prentice Hall, 1973). A good sampler of philosophers writing about ethics is A. I. Melden, *Ethical Theory* (Englewood Cliffs, NJ: Prentice Hall, 1967). Bentham's ideas can be found in his *Introduction to the Principles of Morals and Legislation.* For Mill, see *Utilitarianism.* Kant's primary ethical work is *The Groundwork of the Metaphysic of Morals.*

6

Why Be Ethical?

- *Why Act Ethically? Plato and Socrates*
- *Moral Virtue, Vice, and the Soul*
- *Plato: Moral Virtue as the Health of the Soul*
- *Socrates: Vice Harms the Doer*
- *Why Be Ethical?*

You now know something about the nature of philosophical ethics and what it means to examine questions of right and wrong from a rational, nonreligious point of view. You have also been introduced to the two main approaches to ethical questions, one that examines the results of an action, the other that scrutinizes the action itself. With this "conceptual machinery," you can analyze the main features of any ethical dilemma you face.

But simply knowing what is "right" isn't enough. Lots of times we say to ourselves, "I know I shouldn't do this, but I'm going to do it anyway."

Take this case. You're dating someone and have an explicit understanding that you won't see anyone else. One day, however, you meet someone whom you find very attractive. You'd really like to start seeing this person, but you don't want to jeopardize your original relationship in case this new one doesn't work out. You feel that the person you've been seeing trusts you, so you think you could get away with a few lies. But would this be justifiable?

There really shouldn't be any question that lying in this situation is wrong. The action itself is unethical; you're breaking your promise and being deceptive. And the consequences won't be good either. As you spend less time with the first person you were dating, he or she will probably be unhappy; if you feel guilty, you'll be less fun to be with even when you are together; both of the people you're involved with will be hurt if they find out what's going on; and so on. Nonetheless, many people lie in a case like this, simply because they want the pleasure of dating someone else. Deceiving someone may be wrong, but if it'll make you happier, why not go ahead and do it?

Situations like this present us with more than a simple question of right or wrong. We all want to add to our happiness, whether that is some pleasure of the moment, success in a job, or whatever it takes. If what is right and what is in our

157

own interest coincide, we have no problem doing the right thing. Or maybe we're willing to do the right thing (and avoid some guilt) if it's only a little inconvenient. But when what is right and what makes us happy are 180 degrees from each other, we've got real problems.

When strong desires pull us in opposite directions, it's hard to do the ethical thing. When we do resist the pull of temptation, we usually want to feel that somehow we're going to get something for it. That may not be high-minded, but most of us, when confronted with moral dilemmas, ask: If I do what's right, what's in it for me? It doesn't have to be fame and fortune—it may just be a good feeling about who we are. But most of us want a good reason to be good.

Why should we do the right thing? The question is simple; but answering it is probably the most difficult task in ethics. Legal systems and religious traditions have an easy time giving us answers, of course. We should do what is right in order to avoid punishment for doing wrong—either in this life or the next. But philosophy does not approach it this way. It must give a rational, secular account of why living the moral life is valuable in its own right, here and now. This is very hard to do.

Think about it for a minute. What reasons would you give someone for why he or she should do what is right? Most of you will be parents; some of you already are. How will you explain to your children, particularly as they get older and can argue with you, why they should act according to the values you hold? Perhaps you will invoke the Golden Rule and tell your children that since they don't want to be hurt, they shouldn't hurt other people. Or perhaps you will say that other people won't like them if they do this or that. But what if your children say they don't care about these things? What do you say then?

Why Act Ethically? Plato and Socrates
The Case of Gyges' Ring

Few philosophers take up the problem of why we should act ethically. Two who do—the ancient Greek philosopher Socrates and his pupil Plato—address it head on. We begin with Plato because he sets the question up in the toughest form imaginable. He does this in a fictional dialogue called the *Republic,* a work in which he covers a wide range of philosophical topics—justice, the ideal society, knowledge, the nature of reality, and ethics.[1]

The portion of the dialogue that is relevant here concentrates on the question of how we ought to live. A character named Glaucon claims that people are not good willingly and that the only reason any of us does what is right is that we get something from it. If we develop a reputation for being honest, telling the truth, and keeping our commitments, then people will do business with us, elect us to office,

---

[1]The *Republic,* like all of Plato's writings, is a fictional dialogue in which Plato explains his ideas through imaginary conversations that involve a number of different people. Plato generally uses Socrates as his main character, however, and this produces problems about separating Plato from Socrates. Plato's early dialogues probably include primarily "Socratic" ideas, but in works like the *Republic* Plato expresses his own philosophical outlook. At that point he simply uses the character of Socrates as a mouthpiece for his own ideas.

Scholars have arrived at a rough consensus about which of Plato's dialogues are "Socratic" and which are "Platonic," and you will become more aware of this difference if you do any further study in philosophy.

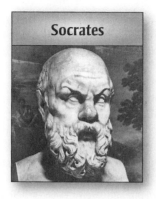

Socrates

One of the most famous ancient philosophers, Socrates (469–399 B.C.) was born, lived, and died in Athens. He came from an honorable but undistinguished middle-class family; his father was a sculptor and his mother a midwife.

Socrates never wrote anything nor did he found a school, but it is impossible to exaggerate his importance to philosophy. While his philosophical predecessors concentrated on issues concerned with the nature of reality, Socrates was the first philosopher to focus on questions of ordinary living. He spent his day in philosophical dialogue challenging his fellow Athenians to scrutinize their lives and to make virtue and caring for their souls their chief concern. Socrates came to believe that he had something like a religious duty to do this after a friend returned from the oracle at Delphi with the message that no one was wiser than Socrates. Because Socrates believed that he was genuinely ignorant, he concluded that the oracle's words must mean that his task was to help others give up their false convictions, among them that money, pleasure, and power were the keys to happiness. If he could help his discussants become as "ignorant" as he was, Socrates believed, then they would see the value of moral virtue. Socrates also shaped the history of philosophy by being the teacher of another philosophical giant, Plato.

Socrates was a devoted son of Athens, fighting in her defense in the army and fulfilling his political obligations as a citizen. He also saw himself as a "gadfly" whose persistent questioning, even if annoying, truly benefited Athens. Not everyone shared this point of view, however, and not long after Athens was defeated by Sparta, Socrates was indicted on the capital charges of impiety and corrupting the young. Socrates' accusers apparently thought that philosophical questioning contributed to Athens' defeat by somehow weakening the city and lessening the respect the young should have for Athens' institutions and its leading citizens. Found guilty by a narrow margin (281 to 220), Socrates was sentenced to death. He died, according to Athenian custom, by drinking a cup of hemlock. His fate remains a sad reminder of the danger that ignorance and fear pose to the honest champion of truth and virtue.

and be our friends. But Glaucon thinks the task is too hard. Living ethically is difficult, unpleasant, and, when it comes right down to it, worse than living unethically, he says. Thus, according to Glaucon, most of us do what is right only because we don't have the power to do what we really want to do and get away with it.

To illustrate his point, Glaucon tells the story of a man named Gyges.

The story is that Gyges was a shepherd in the service of the ruler of Lydia. There was a violent rainstorm and an earthquake which broke open the ground and created a chasm at the place where he was tending sheep. Seeing this and marvelling, he went down into it. He saw, besides many other wonders of which we are told, a hollow bronze horse. There were window-like openings in it; he climbed through them and caught sight of a corpse which seemed of more than human stature, wearing nothing

Plato

Plato's lineage was as stellar as Socrates' was conventional. His father was descended from the last king of Athens, his mother from a great Athenian lawgiver, and his relatives were prominent citizens in the city. Plato (428–348 B.C.) received a privileged upbringing, distinguishing himself in everything from poetry to wrestling, and he was probably being groomed for a political career.

Meeting Socrates changed Plato's life forever, however. He committed himself to philosophy, followed Socrates around, and observed his numerous dialogues. The death of his teacher led Plato to leave Athens and to travel throughout the Mediterranean area for twelve years. When he returned to Athens, he established the first formal school of philosophy, the Academy, where he worked for the rest of his days.

Plato retained an interest in public life, however, and made a series of unsuccessful attempts to educate the rulers of the city of Syracuse on the island of Sicily along the lines of his ideas of the philosopher–king. He lectured widely at the Academy, and, like Socrates, not only was he one of philosophy's greatest lights, but he also was the teacher of another major thinker, Aristotle.

---

but a ring of gold on its finger. This ring the shepherd put on and came out. He arrived at the usual monthly meeting which reported to the king on the state of the flocks, wearing the ring. As he was sitting among the others he happened to twist the hoop of the ring towards himself, to the inside of his hand, and as he did this he became invisible to those sitting near him and they went on talking as if he had gone. He marvelled at this and, fingering the ring, he turned the hoop outward again and became visible. Perceiving this he tested whether the ring had this power and so it happened: if he turned the hoop inwards he became invisible, but was visible when he turned it outwards. When he realized this, he at once arranged to become one of the messengers to the king. He went, committed adultery with the king's wife, attacked the king with her help, killed him, and took over the kingdom.

—Republic

The moral of the story, says Glaucon, is that given the opportunity, everyone would act just the way Gyges acts.

Now if there were two such rings, . . . no one . . . would be so incorruptible that he would stay on the path of justice or bring himself to keep away from other people's property and not touch it, when he could with impunity take whatever he wanted from the market, go into houses and have sexual relations with anyone he wanted, kill anyone, free all those he wished from prison, and do the other things which would make him like a god among men.

—Republic

Plato raises a very interesting question here. If you knew you could get away with absolutely anything you wanted to do, however unethical, how ethical would your behavior be? Plato's character Glaucon thinks that it would not be ethical at all. What would you do if you had a ring like Gyges'?

Plato uses Glaucon to say what he thinks most people believe, and he is probably right. Life today is not all that different from life in Athens in the fifth century B.C. We don't have to look very far to see that dishonest, unscrupulous, selfish people get most of what they want while the rest of us settle for much less. Many of these people never get caught, and, if they do, they aren't punished very severely. If we knew that we could get away with anything we wanted to, most of us would be sorely tempted to cut a few moral corners—or worse.

An Extreme Case

Plato sees the foolishness of arguing that we should do what is right in the hope of receiving a tangible reward. Instead, he comes at the question of whether the moral life has any value by making the starkest possible comparison between the lives of a just person and an unjust one. He writes,

> Let us grant to the unjust the fullest degree of injustice and to the just the fullest justice, each being perfect in his own pursuit. First, the unjust man will act as clever craftsmen do—a top navigator, for example, or physician distinguishes what his craft can do and what it cannot; the former he will undertake, the latter he will pass by, and when he slips he can put things right. So the unjust man's correct attempts at wrongdoing must remain secret; the one who is caught must be considered a poor performer, for the extreme of injustice is to have a reputation for justice; if he makes a slip he must be able to put it right; he must be a sufficiently persuasive speaker if some wrongdoing of his is made public; he must be able to use force, where force is needed, with the help of his courage, strength, and the friends and wealth with which he has provided himself.
>
> Having described such a man, let us now in our argument put beside him the just man, simple as he is and noble, who, as Aeschylus put it, does not wish to appear just but to be so. We must take away his reputation, for a reputation for justice would bring him honour and rewards, and it would then not be clear whether he is what he is for justice's sake or for the sake of rewards and honour. We must strip him of everything except justice and make him the complete opposite of the other. Though he does no wrong, he must have the greatest reputation for wrongdoing so that he may be tested for justice by not weakening under ill repute and its consequences. Let him go his incorruptible way until death with a reputation for injustice throughout his life, just though he is, so that our two men may reach the extremes, one of justice, the other of injustice, and let them be judged as to which of the two is the happier.

—Republic

Here Plato sets the toughest ground rules imaginable. He forces us to compare the life of an unethical person with a reputation for goodness with the life of a good person with a reputation for vice. Now any reason for being virtuous must depend on the value of moral virtue itself, not anything that reputation brings.

This, of course, is the question. Is the moral life intrinsically valuable? Is it worthwhile in and of itself for us to live a moral life instead of getting what we want by lying, cheating, stealing, and manipulating others? Is there any reason to be ethical, especially if we are as clever at vice as Plato's unjust person is, not only getting away with all sorts of wrongdoing but having a reputation for being good to boot?

Think about this for a minute. Which would you rather be, the unethical person with a good reputation or the ethical person with a reputation for injustice? Be honest with yourself. Is there any solid, rational argument for choosing the latter?

Moral Virtue, Vice, and the Soul

It should come as no surprise, of course, that Plato and Socrates think that moral virtue is valuable. Essentially, they believe that virtue is its own reward, and the key to their ideas on the subject lies in the interesting notion that moral virtue is "the health of the soul."

People use the term "soul" in many different ways. We need not go into a long discussion of what the Greeks meant by "soul." For our purposes, it is enough to know that "soul" means the most important part of who we are—our moral and intellectual essence, our "real" self, our "character," the source of our consciousness, the core of our personality.

Whether the soul lives on after death in one form or another is also irrelevant. Here we are interested in the *intrinsic* value of moral virtue, that is, the good it does in this life. (Any good that virtue might do for the soul after death would be an extrinsic benefit.) To keep the issues clear in your mind, then, assume that the soul does not survive death (whether it does or not) and that Plato and Socrates are talking about the importance of acting ethically in the here and now.

In trying to understand what these philosophers mean by the idea that moral virtue is "the health of the soul," we must explore two critical ideas. First, whatever part of us Socrates and Plato mean when they refer to the "soul," they believe that, like the body, it can be healthy and unhealthy. And health is something that most of us would agree is intrinsically worthwhile. We all know what healthy and unhealthy bodies are like, but what is the difference between healthy and diseased souls?

The other important idea is Socrates' belief that the soul's health is determined by what we do—that is, it is affected by the moral character of our actions. Socrates even describes the soul as "that part of ourselves that is improved by just actions and harmed by unjust actions." In particular, Socrates believes that unethical actions harm the person who does them more than the person at whom they are aimed. If someone steals something from you, Socrates thinks that the thief is hurt more than you are by the deed.

Admittedly, the ideas these two men have about the value of moral virtue may seem strange to you. How is being good like being healthy? If you lie about denting someone's new car so that you don't have to pay the repair bill, how do you hurt yourself more than someone else? These are not the easiest notions to swallow when you first hear them. Yet Plato and Socrates have developed them into a substantial answer to the question "Why bother about ethics?" Understanding and exploring that answer is our task in this chapter.

Plato: Moral Virtue as the Health of the Soul

Plato thinks that moral virtue is to the soul what health is to the body. What might a "healthy soul" be like? And what is the difference between healthy and unhealthy souls?

Healthy Bodies, Healthy Souls

Everybody understands the difference between healthy and unhealthy bodies, so let's start there before we extend the comparison to souls.

A healthy body is free of disease and in relatively good shape. When you are healthy, you may not feel euphoric, but you probably feel calm and contented. When you are healthy, you hardly notice any physical discomfort. Your body has its full range of capabilities and you can do what you want to. When you are sick, on the other hand, all you can think about is how rotten you feel. You are too weak to do things. Your discomfort keeps pushing itself into your awareness, and everything seems worse than it is.

In other words, as long as we stay healthy, we can do what we choose and we can choose what we want. The effects of illness and neglect—clouded minds and weak, damaged bodies—limit our activities. With health comes freedom and control over our lives. Health is intrinsically enjoyable and it enables us to get more of what we want. Thus, we are more likely to live happier lives.

What can we say, now, about the healthy "soul" (or "character," or "personality")? Much the same thing that we said for the healthy body. The absence of disease in your "soul" means that your mind is clear and you can see things as they really are. Your view of the world is not distorted by fears, insecurities, irrational anxieties, or overpowering desires. Your judgment is not blinded by greed or self-interest. Thus, your assessment of whether something is right or wrong can be objective. We might say that a healthy soul has a fairly clear *moral vision*. Like the healthy body, the healthy soul has its own kind of freedom and control. Once you decide about something, you have the capacity to carry it out. We might call this *strength of will.*

Say that a friend asks you to help him cheat in his history course. He wants to take a paper you wrote last term and change it just enough so that it won't be recognized as yours. "Come on," he says, "everybody does it. There's nothing wrong. Besides, I'd do it for you." You feel uneasy, but clearly he expects you to do it, and you don't want him to get angry. To see this situation for what it is and to do what you know you should do takes clarity of mind and courage—that is, the strength of a "healthy soul." If your fear of your friend's anger controls you, you won't have the nerve to stand up to him. With a weak and "unhealthy soul," you compromise your own beliefs and allow your fears to take control. With a healthy soul, on the other hand, you have the freedom to live according to your own moral insights. Once you decide what the right thing to do is, you can do it. You have the power to live according to your sense of right and wrong.

Think back to the story about cheating on someone with whom you have a relationship. What would someone with a strong character do when confronted with that dilemma? First, that person could see the ethical issues of the situation without being blinded by selfish desires. Such a person could also act on his or her decision. That is, the strong soul would not immediately reach for a cheap rationalization ("Everybody does something like this now and then—besides, no one will get hurt"). If that person wanted to pursue the new relationship, he or she would probably find the courage to discuss it honestly with the other person.

Plato's Idea of the Healthy Soul: Balance and Control

In the *Republic,* Plato uses this simple parallel between bodies and souls to distinguish between healthy and unhealthy souls. Each of us, he says, is made up of three parts: the *physical,* the *spirited,* and the *intellectual.* (The "spirited" part is our emotions.) In the healthy soul, these three are properly balanced. As we make decisions about how to live, our minds give due regard to our emotional and physical needs, and each of the three parts performs its proper role. The mind is in control, and our emotions help us follow the mind's judgment, particularly when it goes against the inclination of our physical desires. In an unhealthy soul, the balance is lost. Our actions flow not from our good judgment, but from either our emotions or our physical appetites.

For example, think of people who are obsessed with their bodies or their physical appearance. You may know some people who expend huge amounts of energy playing sports, working out, worrying about their diet, or spending time shopping for the right clothes or getting their hair or makeup just right. Virtually everything in their lives—what they do, what they don't do, whom they hang out with— revolves around the physical side of their beings. They may even be addicted to, say, their daily five-mile run, or to buying new clothes. Such people are so driven by their bodies that they cut classes, miss work, or neglect a relationship because of their obsession. Clearly, the physical part of their nature dominates their lives.

Others are driven by their emotions. They need to be in love, to be popular, to be admired by others, or to be famous. Think of people who will do anything to be liked by someone they are involved with. They may even do things that hurt others— or themselves—to hold onto their latest love. And when that relationship ends, they immediately hunt for someone new. These people may also seem to be addicted to whatever they are driven by. Clearly, their lives are dominated by their emotions.

Plato thinks that the unhealthy soul is out of balance and controlled by the wrong aspect of our being. The mind yields to the body or the emotions.

The healthy soul, however, is balanced. It gives due weight to bodily and emotional needs, but the head remains in control and keeps things from going overboard. In Plato's opinion, the person with a healthy soul has a clear mind, freedom, and self-control. As Plato explains in the *Republic* (442 a–d), the healthy soul possesses the classic four cardinal virtues of antiquity: wisdom, courage, moderation, and justice. It is wise in knowing what benefits each of the three parts of the soul. It is courageous in holding fast to the knowledge of what it should and shouldn't fear when confronted with pain or temptation. And it is just and moderate in that it has great self-control, with the mind ruling the emotions and body, but with all three parts getting appropriate attention and working together in harmony.

The Soul's Health and Acting Ethically

Plato believes that physical and emotional desires, particularly when they are out of balance, are the primary factors that cloud our judgment about right and wrong. Unethical people, he thinks, generally act wrongly to serve some physical desire (sex, alcohol, the physical pleasures that money can buy) or some emotion (jealousy, ambition, anger, fear, greed). People with unbalanced, unhealthy souls are so driven by physical or emotional wants that they do not think straight about right and wrong. Their mental power is put to use in servicing their wants, not in examining the morality of their actions. Their minds follow their bodies or their feelings. When we allow this to happen, Plato thinks that there is a strong chance that we will behave unethically in order to get what we want. Having a soul that is out of balance, "unhealthy" in Plato's terms, goes hand in hand with wrongdoing.

By contrast, the freedom, control, and balanced perspective that come with the soul's health result in ethical behavior, Plato believes. Good decisions come only when you are not dominated by your physical or emotional wants. Thus, acting ethically is an expression of the strong, healthy soul—the soul in which a clear mind is in charge.

At this point, you, like Glaucon, may still be skeptical. If a little larceny helps us get what we want, why is that so bad?

And what about Plato's claim that acting unethically hurts us? At this point, we must turn from Plato's thought to that of his teacher, Socrates, who had more to say about the unhealthy soul. In particular, it was Socrates who formulated the idea that vice harms the doer more than those who are its victims.

Socrates: Vice Harms the Doer

The philosopher who could be said to have "invented" ethics is Socrates. During the two centuries before Socrates, Greek philosophers had speculated about the nature of reality. They were interested in "natural philosophy," what we would today call "science," speculating on questions such as: What is the world made of? Is there a basic element out of which everything else is composed? How does the cosmos work? In the words of the Roman philosopher Cicero, "Socrates was the first one to call philosophy down from the heavens and put it into the cities with people and make it ask questions about life and about right and wrong." He was the first philosopher to take how we should live as his main concern.

Socrates is an interesting figure for a number of reasons. For one thing, he represents the rare case of a major philosopher who never wrote down a word. We know about his ideas primarily through the writings of his pupil Plato, who makes Socrates the main figure in most of his dialogues. For another, Socrates was an eccentric character in ancient Athens, having come to believe that he had a mission from the god Apollo to go around encouraging people to live a moral life.

Socrates did not do what most religious teachers do, however. He did not try to change people by preaching to them about the need for virtue. Instead, he approached his fellow Athenians individually, engaging them in philosophical dialogues that tested the validity of their deepest beliefs. For example, Socrates would ask someone what was most important in life. If the person answered "money," for example, or "fame," Socrates would ask for an explanation. When the person responded, Socrates would ask for more, pursuing every point of the answer, trying to show the problems with the other person's thinking. Back and forth it went like that until Socrates had convinced his partner. This "Socratic method" of question/answer, question/answer is still used by many teachers, and especially those in law schools.

An Overview of Socrates' Ethical Beliefs

For someone who is universally considered one of philosophy's brightest lights, Socrates advanced some unusual ideas about why we should act ethically. In terms of everyday life and the dominant values of Western culture from Athens to the present day, Socrates' moral beliefs seem at best peculiar.

For example, Socrates claims:

> When we treat someone unethically and escape unpunished, we hurt ourselves more than we hurt our victim.

> Our greatest protection is moral virtue. Even though someone may kill us, our virtue makes it impossible for anyone to harm us.

> Using the image that virtue is the soul's health and vice its disease, an idea that Plato later developed further, Socrates talks about immorality in a way that suggests that moral compromise makes as little sense as deliberately infecting ourselves with a terminal illness.

> If we do something wrong, Socrates believes that we should seek someone to punish us with the same speed and care that we use when we look for someone to cure us when we are sick.

Citing divine revelation, religious teachers preach ideas every bit as peculiar as those of Socrates. But Socrates does not attribute his beliefs to special advice from Apollo. Rather, he believes that the truth of these propositions can be made evident through intellectual examination and rational argument. In fact, Socrates takes these ideas to be absolutely certain, observable *facts* of human nature, no more "opinions" or "beliefs" than the idea that drinking contaminated water makes us sick.

If we look at typical human behavior from the Athenian agora to Wall Street, however, we seem to find little support for Socrates' ideas. Nonetheless, the fact that most people disagree with him would not convince Socrates that he was wrong. He would simply find it irrelevant. Socrates takes it as an empirical fact that when we do something wrong, we are hurt by it. This is a truism of human nature, he believes. And when he talks about virtue as the health of the soul, this is not some figure of speech. Socrates means it literally. No one can be fully healthy without moral virtue. In that unethical people lack certain capacities and strengths, they are genuinely unhealthy. And they are made that way by their wrongdoing.

How did Socrates try to argue for such an odd idea as that *unethical actions actually harm those who perform them?*

Philosophical Interpretation

The fact is that Socrates did not provide us with a fully developed explanation and conclusive proof of his ideas. Socrates wrote down nothing himself, and even Plato's account of Socrates' ideas is incomplete. Getting less than we want in explanation of a philosopher's ideas is not, however, an unusual problem when we study the history of philosophy, particularly when we talk about thinkers who lived hundreds or thousands of years ago. Many writings have been lost forever over the years, and for some thinkers, we have only a small portion of what they wrote or even simply a few fragments.

So what do we do about this? Speculate and interpret. We look at the writings we do have, and we try to fill in the gaps as best we can. We try to imagine what Socrates, for example, might have meant by certain ideas or how he might have answered our questions. We take what we know for certain as our point of reference and see what other ideas are consistent with this. Thus, when we do philosophy, not only do we speculate about life's basic issues, but we often also speculate about the missing pieces of a philosopher's thought. When we do this, we must keep in mind that our speculations might not be correct, and we have to remain open to opposing interpretations. Nonetheless, sometimes speculation and interpretation are our only choice.

In working out Socrates' claim that vice harms the doer, then, we are forced to speculate. We begin with teachings that Socrates unquestionably held, but in short order we enter the world of philosophical interpretation.

How Vice Changes Us: An Ordinary Example

The idea that doing wrong harms the doer is a prominent Socratic idea, yet it is puzzling. Socrates says, "Wrongdoing is in every way harmful and shameful to the wrongdoer." It is so harmful, counsels Socrates in the Platonic dialogue *Crito,* that even if somebody else hurts us first, "we should never do wrong in return, nor injure any man, whatever injury we have suffered at his hands."[2] But precisely how are we hurt if we do something wrong? How are *we* harmed if we hurt somebody else, especially if they have already wronged us? And what is it that we have to lose?

At stake here is what Socrates calls "that part of ourselves that is improved by just actions and destroyed by unjust actions." Today we call this our character, or our personality, or our self. As you saw earlier, the Greeks called it the soul. Whatever we call it, it is that essence which we feel is most uniquely who we really are, and Socrates takes it to be far more important than our bodies.

Because Socrates believes that "care of the soul" is our most important task, the only thing that counts as harm is something that makes us less able to be virtuous. Unethical actions corrupt us and break down our ability to act virtuously. Thus, each unethical act makes it more likely that we will act unethically in the future by weakening those capacities and faculties we need in order to act more morally.

---

[2]Plato wrote his dialogues using Socrates as the main character. This, of course, produces problems of philosophical interpretation because the Socrates in the dialogue ultimately becomes a mouthpiece for Plato's ideas. However, scholars generally agree that the *Crito* is one of the "Socratic" dialogues in which we can take the Socrates of the dialogue to be speaking ideas held by Socrates himself.

At first, Socrates' belief that doing wrong hurts the wrongdoer may strike you as odd. Hurting other people—that seems obvious. But hurting ourselves—that seems unlikely.

Yet take a simple example. Most people think there is something wrong with telling lies. (Virtually all of us do it at one time or another, but we still believe something is not quite right about it.) Think back to your first lie. It was probably after you had disobeyed your parents and knew you'd be in trouble if they found out. That first lie was probably hard to tell, and you most likely felt guilty afterwards. But if your parents believed you, you found out that lying can get you out of some tough spots. Now think of your second lie, your third lie, and on down the line. Odds are that it got easier and you felt less guilty the more you did it. At this point in your life, you probably feel that lying is not as wrong as you once thought it was, and you probably feel less guilty when you do it.

The question here is, what has happened to you? Socrates would say that you've been corrupted by this gradual process. You haven't turned into Jack the Ripper, but you are less likely now to tell the truth than you were before. You've lost some ground. Getting away with lying lowers our resistance to it in the future. It makes it easier to do and increases the odds that we will do it again in tight spots. It also changes our thinking about how wrong it is. Most people come to feel that there is some good in any act that gets you out of trouble.

How did this happen to you? Did someone force this on you? No, you chose it each time, little by little, by doing what you did. Your allegiance to the truth lessened, even if only to a small degree, with each falsehood. Socrates would argue that you harmed, or weakened, yourself each time by acting unethically. He would claim that it's now less likely and more difficult for you to do the right thing and tell the truth in a tight spot.

Whether or not you agree that you've been harmed or weakened in this process, you have been changed by it. What you do and what you think about what you do have been changed by actions that were initially at odds with your original values. So Socrates' argument has a commonsense validity. We haven't seen enough specifics about precisely how you were harmed for you to judge whether you completely accept this notion, but you can probably agree that the process actually exists.

How Vice Harms Us: An Example from the *Gorgias*

If the process that Socrates is talking about is plausible, is his claim that it leads to serious harm equally plausible? If we are to have good reason to be ethical, we should also have good reason not to be unethical. So far, however, we are still missing a description of exactly how Socrates sees such vice harming us.

An excellent place to find such a description is in the ideas attributed to Socrates in the philosophical dialogue entitled *Gorgias*.[3] This dialogue begins with a discussion of the value of rhetoric (the art of public speaking). Soon, however, the question of how we should live our lives and the value of moral virtue comes up, and it takes over the discussion.

---

[3]Like the *Crito*, mentioned *reword*, the *Gorgias* is considered to be one of Plato's "Socratic" dialogues in which we can take the Socrates of the dialogue to be speaking ideas held by Socrates himself.

Four characters speak in the dialogue. There is Socrates, of course. Then there is Gorgias, a well-known and highly respected teacher of public speaking, for whom the dialogue is named. Gorgias travels from city to city teaching the skills of rhetoric, and, at the beginning of the dialogue, he has just arrived in Athens. Such teachers were common in ancient Greece and they were particularly popular in Athens where speaking eloquently was essential to success. Athens was a democracy in which any citizen could speak at the city's democratic Assembly, and politics was at the heart of the city's life. The key to success in Athens was a reputation as an intelligent and effective speaker.[4] The third character, Polus, is Gorgias' rambunctious young student and follower. And then there is Callicles.

Callicles is a bright, ambitious young Athenian who is hungry for wealth and power. He is talented, educated, refined—but also quite immoral. He believes that people who are bright and cunning should rule the city because they are superior to the rest of the citizenry. He also thinks the strong should take whatever they want as long as they can get away with it, and indulge themselves in all kinds of pleasures as well. He rejects fairness, equality, and moderation as conventional ideas of morality which he dismisses as ways that inferior people make virtues out of their own weaknesses and hold superior people in check. It is in Socrates' discussion with Callicles that we get a clear picture of the harm vice does. After all, considering how unethical—and dangerous—Callicles is, he ought to be a prime example of the damage wrongdoing can do.

Setting Up the Issue

The dialogue starts as a conversation between Socrates and Gorgias about the nature of rhetoric. Gorgias sings the praises of the art he teaches, but Socrates points out its weaknesses—especially that it can be used for unjust ends.

At this point Polus speaks up. Unlike Gorgias, who is a man of great integrity, Polus is not really bothered by the abuse of rhetoric. The discussion slides from the nature of rhetoric to how we ought to live, and Polus holds up the example of Archelaus, the king of Macedonia, who acquired his throne through injustice and brutality. To be a tyrant and to have your evil go unpunished, claims Polus, is a life that everyone envies. Disagreeing, Socrates argues that doing wrong, particularly if you go unpunished, is the greatest of evils. It is always better, argues Socrates, to be the victim of injustice rather than the person who does it. Polus laughs at Socrates, but eventually he is shamed into silence. In the presence of his teacher, the virtuous Gorgias, he is obviously embarrassed to press his point with Socrates.

Callicles, however, has no such shame. Taking up the dialogue at this point, Callicles too ridicules Socrates' idea that the key to happiness lies in moral virtue. Then he launches into a passionate defense of the unbridled pursuit of pleasure and

---

[4]Teachers like Gorgias were commonly called "sophists." Originally the term "sophist," which means "expert in wisdom," or just "wise man," was a title of respect. Gradually, however, a group of sophists arose who were less concerned with teaching how to argue honestly than with teaching rhetorical tricks that would help you in court or in the Assembly even if your case were bad and your reasoning weak. At this point, "sophist" came to mean something akin to "shyster." You can see a residue of this idea in modern English. To engage in "sophistry" or to argue "sophistically" today is to use linguistic trickery. If someone calls you a sophist, you may safely take it as an insult.

of the strong dominating the weak. "A man who is going to live a full life," proclaims Callicles,

> must allow his desires to become as mighty as may be and never repress them. When his passions have come to full maturity, he must be able to serve them through his courage and intelligence and gratify every fleeting desire as it comes into his heart. This, I fancy, is impossible for the mob.
>
> That is why they censure the rest of us, because they are ashamed of themselves and want to conceal their own incapacity. And, of course, they maintain that licentiousness is disgraceful, as I said before, since they are trying to enslave men of a better nature. Because they cannot accomplish the fulfillment of their own desires, they sing the praises of temperance and justice out of the depths of their own cowardice. But take men who have come of princely stock, men whose nature can attain some commanding position, a tyranny, absolute power; what could be lower and baser than temperance and justice for such men who, when they might enjoy the good things of life without hindrance, of their own accord drag in a master to subdue them: the law, the language, and the censure of the vulgar? How could such men fail to be wretched under the sway of your "beauty of justice and temperance" when they can award nothing more to their friends than to their enemies? And that, too, when they are the rulers of the state! The truth, which you claim to pursue, Socrates, is really this: luxury, license, and liberty, when they have the upper hand, are really virtue, and happiness as well; everything else is a set of fine terms, manmade conventions, warped against nature, a pack of stuff and nonsense!
>
> —Gorgias

This speech sets the terms of a long debate between Socrates and Callicles that dominates the rest of the dialogue. The philosopher champions virtue and self-control—a life of being "one's own ruler." The aspiring politician endorses the uncontrolled and self-interested pursuit of pleasure by whatever means you can get away with.

In the ensuing discussion, Socrates goes on to identify two distinct ways we harm ourselves when we do something wrong. Our ability to control ourselves is weakened, and so is our intellect. Although Socrates did not put it in these words, we might interpret him as saying that when we do wrong we weaken our *strength of will* and our *moral vision*. In other words, Socrates suggests that vice destroys precisely those qualities that, as we saw above, characterize the healthy soul.

The Wine Jar Metaphor: Desires and Strength of Will

Socrates would surely see Callicles as an example of someone who's been badly damaged by vice. And the first thing Socrates would point to is that Callicles' remarks show that he has lost control over his desires. What Callicles takes as a strength, Socrates regards as a weakness.

Trying to show Callicles the error of his ways, Socrates contrasts the uncontrolled life his opponent praises with that of a self-controlled and ethical person. To illustrate his point, he draws an analogy to wine jars—some intact, others leaky. "See if you do not say," proposes Socrates,

> that, in a fashion, this metaphor expresses the difference between the two lives: the self-controlled and the unrestrained. There are two men, both of whom have many jars; those of the first are sound and full, one of wine, another of honey, a third of milk, and many others have a multitude of various commodities, yet the source of supply is meager and hard to obtain and only procurable with a good deal of exertion. Now the first man, when he has filled his jars, troubles no more about procuring supplies, but, so far as they are concerned, rests content; but the other man, though his source of supply is difficult also, yet still possible, and his vessels are perforated and rotten, is forced to keep on trying to fill them both night and day on pain of suffering the utmost agony.
>
> —Gorgias

The healthy, self-controlled individual is like a solid wine jar, while someone like Callicles, an unethical person who gives in to his desires, is like the leaking wine jar. If you are like a leaky wine jar, Socrates suggests, you inevitably feel the growing hunger of desire, no matter what you do. And the longer you wait to "fill up," the worse you feel. Thus, your desires run your life. You must constantly satisfy them or feel pain. By contrast, if you are like the solid wine jar, you are content and untroubled. You do not feel the growing craving of unsatisfied desire and you can do with your life what you want, not what your desires compel you to do.

Thus, the unethical person's ability to experience a stable sense of *contentment* or *satisfaction* has been harmed. Someone like Callicles cannot be satisfied because his desires are unchecked and any satisfaction is only temporary. If an unethical person is like a leaky wine jar, then he or she is ultimately unsatisfiable. As soon as she feels a comfortable contentment or fulfillment, the feeling starts slipping away. She is then unsatisfied again and looking around for her next thrill. And this pattern simply repeats itself over and over.

Not surprisingly, Callicles is unpersuaded. He rejects Socrates' ideas, saying that the life of someone like the intact wine jar is dull and boring, "For the man who is full has no longer the slightest taste for pleasure; his life is the life of a stone. Once he is sated, he no longer feels pleasure or pain. But in the other life is the true pleasure of living, with the greatest possible intake." Callicles constantly needs new gratifications of his desires in order to feel pleasure. He finds no stimulation in a temperate and ethical life which includes only what he has rightfully earned.

Most of us would not succeed if we tried to live as Callicles recommends. Constantly finding new sources of pleasure—more money, more power, new jobs, new successes, different lovers, new drugs, exotic places to travel to—is a tall order. Of course, Callicles believes that a truly superior man, a man such as he is, will be able to do this. Surely, he thinks, this refutes the idea that he has been damaged in any way. Socrates, of course, disagrees.

The key to this dispute is who is in control. Callicles himself describes the situation as one in which he ministers to his desires. He does not see, however, that this makes him weaker than his own desires—in fact, the servant of those desires.

It is not whether someone can satisfy his or her desires that matters to Socrates, but whether a person is his or her "own ruler." An ethical person like Socrates can decide which of his desires he'll satisfy. Callicles does not have this choice—his only decision is *how* to satisfy them. His desires control his life. Furthermore, if Socrates is correct and the desires of someone like Callicles (a leaky wine jar) are ultimately unsatisfiable, the whole project is doomed to fail.

In other words, someone like Callicles does not have the *strength of will* to resist his own desires. In Socrates' opinion, when a man goes from virtue to vice, his "wine jar" goes from being solid to leaky, and that individual has lost some power over his own life.

Noncognitive Harm: Insatiable Desires and Loss of Control

The first kind of harm that comes from vice, then, is that the person who indulges in it is uncontrolled and intemperate. Socrates' wine jar analogy implies that the intemperate person lives a life that is out of her or his own control. Driven by the need to satisfy the gnawing hunger of unfulfilled want, unethical individuals experience only fleeting satisfactions because such people are essentially unsatisfiable. This literally compels them to seek more and different pleasures.

There are three important points here. First, the fact that a vice-ridden person's desires become insatiable means that at least part of the harm vice does affects the *noncognitive* dimension of the human personality. That is, the first kind of harm that Socrates points out involves not the mind, but the will and our feelings of desire and satisfaction. The point at which we are satisfied by food, money, sex, power, or whatever is largely a psychological, not an intellectual matter. For example, people with eating disorders "know" perfectly well that their behavior makes no sense. Some psychological difficulty beyond their conscious control, however, makes them unable to control themselves. If we become "leaky wine jars," the psychological mechanism that produces our sense that our wants have been satisfied has been disabled. In this case, instead of feeling a stable sense of contentment with what we have and how we get it, we feel unsatisfied.[5]

Second, it does seem as if genuine harm has been done. To go from master to servant in one's own life is a significant reversal. It is much like the dynamic of addiction in which most of the addict's life becomes geared to gratifying the desire for whatever he or she craves. Although Socrates did not have the concept of "addiction" that we have today, he describes it well where he claims that the "leaky-jar"

---

[5]By using modern, psychological concepts at this point, our interpretation moves beyond notions available to the ancient Greeks. It does appear, however, that much of the harm that Socrates describes is connected to what we today call the "unconscious." Feelings of contentment are generally not under our conscious control.

One obvious example of this is eating. Many people overeat, and many are anorexic or bulimic—despite what their minds tell them about how much food their bodies need in order to be healthy, and despite any signals their bodies send them. Even though such people know and, perhaps, want to act differently, something makes them so discontent with normal eating that they cannot stop themselves.

Or think about some of the quirks you or your friends have. Some people never feel that they have enough money. Others aren't satisfied to have just one of anything—even boyfriends or girlfriends. Some can do things only one way—theirs. Some people are not happy unless everything is neat; others are just the opposite.

Where do these extreme differences in what people want come from? It is largely a function of unconscious forces in our personalities.

person "suffers extreme distress" if he does not satisfy his desires. With desires this compelling, the victim will not spend much time worrying about the ethical character of what has to be done to satisfy them. Such a person is in a downward spiral, becoming even more damaged, out of control, and corrupt the more he tries to satisfy his desires.

Third, Socrates describes a behavior that seems real enough. Think about what happens to people once they give themselves over to self-interest and start acting unethically. Nothing is ever enough for them. Think about the number of times you've heard about someone rich and powerful—an executive, a politician, a minister—who gets caught doing something crooked to get a little more. Haven't you said to yourself, "I don't get it. This guy already has it all, and now he risks losing everything." There is an ongoing stream of such people, many of them otherwise bright, talented people who are caught taking stupid chances for what amounts to small change. The only explanation that makes sense is that these people somehow lost control. Their *strength of will* has all but evaporated. On this evidence, at least, we can say that Socrates has a real point in suggesting that once we cross the line from ethical to unethical behavior to get what we want, our "wine jar" starts to erode, and we lose some control over what we want and what we do.

This loss of control that vice causes, then, is serious. To use an analogy of our own, we might say that vice turns the unethical person into someone trying to navigate a rudderless sailboat, at the mercy of the winds of his or her own desires. If virtue and happiness are analogous to reaching a safe harbor, this person hasn't a chance of getting there.

Cognitive Harm: Weakened Intellect and Damaged Moral Vision

It may surprise you that the first kind of harm that Socrates sees as coming from vice is not intellectual. After all, Socrates is a philosopher. If vice harms the doer, you would think he would find the mind affected. And indeed he does. We just have to dig for it.

Socrates sometimes refers to unscrupulous people who make mistakes in judging what is actually in their own interest. Vice, he implies, has somehow clouded their view of situations and altered their perception of what advances their own ends.[6]

This is nothing new, of course. Take the financier, already a multimillionaire, who gets caught cheating his way to a little more money. To an outside observer, this man cannot be thinking straight. In terms of what he gets by breaking the law, the risks of losing what he already has are extremely high. A little more money, bending the rules, outwitting a few more people—none of this adds anything significant to his life. Yet the cost is astronomically high—public disgrace, divorce, a ruined career, dreams shattered, jail.

---

[6]For example, Socrates proposes the paradox that the tyrant with the reputation for absolute power in reality neither has great power nor even the power to do what he wants. The tyrant wants what is in his interest, but Socrates believes that it is likely that such a person will do only what seems best to him and that his actions will in reality often be to his disadvantage. Since the tyrant never wants what is to his disadvantage, Socrates argues that he often ends up doing what he does not really want to do. If he were as powerful as he seemed, he would not make such mistakes. Hence, the "powerful" tyrant is not powerful.

What was he—and everyone like him—thinking when he took the first step over the line and then got himself in deeper and deeper? He must have thought something—he is a bright, accomplished, highly rational person. But somehow he just didn't think *straight*. Socrates would probably say that he didn't think straight because he *couldn't* think straight. His earlier unethical behavior had dramatically eroded that ability.

Part of that erosion occurs in what we can call someone's *conscience,* or their *moral vision*—their basic sense of right and wrong. Like Callicles, people who have suffered this damage come to believe that ordinary ideas of right and wrong do not apply to them. There also seems to be additional damage to one's practical ability to identify and carry out what is truly in one's own interest. Wrongdoers end up misreading the odds, misjudging the likelihood of getting away with their deeds, and taking chances so foolish that they are sure to be caught.

Commonsense shows you how Socrates might be right when he implies that vice harms its doer by causing us to lose some control over our desires. Now you can see as well the validity of the idea that vice also causes the rational faculties to deteriorate.

Callicles as the Embodiment of Vice

Because Callicles embodies so clearly what Socrates regards as vice, he should also display the full range of the harm Socrates alleges that vice does. Callicles certainly endorses the unordered, intemperate, and licentious life as the path to happiness. We might expect, then, that he lives that way himself, that is, out of control. If so, then we can also expect to see signs of a weakened intellect. In fact, the way that Socrates responds to Callicles' entry into the conversation suggests just such a possibility.

Callicles begins by asking Socrates if he really means what he has been saying to Polus—that it is worse to be the doer than to be the victim of injustice. Instead of answering directly, however, Socrates starts by pointing out how out of control Callicles is. Socrates describes Callicles as someone enslaved by the idea of pleasing the two current loves of his life—one, a beautiful young man, the other, the Athenian public.[7] Socrates remarks,

> Now I have noticed that in each instance, whatever your favorite says, however his opinions may go, for all your cleverness you are unable to contradict him, but constantly shift back and forth at his whim. If you are making a speech in the Assembly and the Athenian public disagrees, you change and say what it desires; and in the presence of the beautiful young son of Pyrilampes your experience is precisely similar. You are unable to resist the plans or the assertions of your favorite; and the result of this is that if anyone were to express surprise at what you say on various occasions under the influence of your loves, you would tell him, if you wanted to speak true, that unless your favorites can be prevented from speaking as they do, neither can you.
>
> —Gorgias

---

[7]It may or may not surprise you that homosexuality and bisexuality were quite acceptable among upper-class men in ancient Greece. Socrates is implying no criticism of Callicles on this score, at least.

Socrates' unflattering remarks reinforce our picture of Callicles as someone who can control neither his desires nor the behavior those desires dictate. In the hope of getting their approval, and probably something more than that, Callicles cannot resist agreeing with either of his two loves—the boy or the people in the Assembly. And because each is fickle, Callicles is also constantly changing. Of course, this is in keeping with Socrates' idea that the person analogous to the "leaky wine jar" is going to be always seeking "refilling," that is, gratification. Callicles desperately wants the adulation of the Athenian public and their support for his rise to power in the democracy. He is also looking for admiration and sexual pleasure from the boy. Socrates' point is that Callicles has no strength of will. He cannot control himself in either his professional or personal life.

Note that Socrates makes a point of saying that what Callicles *says* is influenced by his desires. That Callicles' very words are now aligned with his search for pleasure and not with his reason and the search for truth is a major sign that his *intellect* has been affected by the way he is living—a life Socrates no doubt considers far from virtue.

However, Callicles' unwillingness to change his position during his conversation with Socrates is the most powerful sign that vice has harmed his ability to think rationally. Callicles is Socrates' strongest opponent in the dialogue—far stronger than Gorgias or Polus. Despite all the damage that Callicles has presumably suffered by being unethical, his mental faculties seem undiminished. Callicles hangs in there against Socrates; he does not allow Socrates to refute him on trivial grounds, and he even toys with the philosopher a couple of times in the argument to show his mastery of the issue. Socrates gets Gorgias and Polus to back off and change their minds, but he makes no headway with Callicles. Even though Socrates tries to point out a number of contradictions in Callicles' position, Callicles is convinced that he is right and that Socrates hasn't been able to show otherwise.

Callicles no doubt thinks that he is holding his own against Socrates, that his selfish and relentless pursuit of power and pleasure has in no way diminished his intellectual prowess. Socrates would say, however, that the fact that Callicles does not budge an inch in their discussion is proof enough of the harm done to him. It is because Callicles' intellect is in such *bad* shape that he believes he has held his own against Socrates.

The damage to Callicles' intellect shows up in two main ways. First, in the course of the discussion, Socrates tries to show Callicles that as long as he believes as he does about pleasure and power, right and wrong, his thinking will be riddled with confusion and contradictions. Callicles simply cannot see it. His mind has been so clouded that either he doesn't know or he doesn't care whether he contradicts himself or not. And since tolerating contradictions is an obvious sign of weak thinking, to disregard them in such a cavalier fashion is a serious matter.

Second, and more important, is *why* contradictions don't matter to Callicles. It's not that Callicles' unethical behavior has disabled some neurons in his brain. Rather, we can speculate that it's because most of his mental energy is spent on keeping himself convinced that what he thinks is right.

No doubt you have met people who are so intent on being right that they won't listen to anybody with facts to the contrary. Or if they do listen, they're only waiting to shoot back an answer that proves they're right. Such people may even try to convince you that they're right about something you don't even care about. You wonder why they're wasting their time with you—you don't care, so whom are they trying to convince? And that question is the key to understanding what's going on here. People like this—and like Callicles—are really trying to convince themselves that they're right. It may look as if they're trying to convince other people, but other people have nothing to do with it. They're talking mainly to themselves.

When this happens, some part of us other than our conscious mind is controlling our life. As we have already seen, in Callicles' case it's his physical and emotional desires. And when our desires become obsessive, the mind is pulled in to help the cause and keep everything in place. It has to come up with reasons for why the course we're following is the right way to go. An outside observer, of course, does not see these as good reasons. They're just excuses we give to people so that we don't have to consider the possibility that we're wrong.

Psychologists call this process *rationalizing*. When confronted with something negative about ourselves, we often feel internal pressure to make ourselves feel better, and so we sometimes reinterpret our behavior to make it seem more rational and acceptable. For example, if you do poorly on an exam, instead of feeling regret for spending so much time in fraternity activities and not studying very hard, you may convince yourself that academic success is less important than being involved in campus organizations. You change something wrong into something right. In a genuine case of rationalization, we don't even realize that we are just making excuses. At such times, unconscious forces rule our lives.[8]

If we interpret Callicles' behavior this way, we can say that his arguments are nothing more than a sophisticated set of rationalizations that keep him from seeing his condition. Because Callicles' intellect now serves his desires, he is forced to reinterpret how he lives justifying it to himself as rational, sensible, and defensible. He has been completely fooled by his own greed, lust, and ambition.[9]

A Commonsense Assessment

Socrates sees virtue as necessary for the health of our "souls" and vice as unhealthy. Vice, he suggests, harms the doer in two specific ways.

First, when we get caught up in the selfish pursuit of our own ends at others' expense, we damage a basic mechanism within ourselves that gives us emotional stability and a sense of satisfaction, or contentment, with our lives. This means that

---

[8]If you're sceptical about all this and tempted to downplay the power of the unconscious, bear in mind that unconscious forces can dramatically alter our perception of reality, block facts or memories from our awareness, and even impel us to act in self-destructive ways. Predisposing us to believe arguments that are objectively irrational is a relatively small matter by comparison.

[9]Be sure to realize that all this talk about rationalization and unconscious mechanisms is part of our *speculation about* and *interpretation of* Socrates' ideas. The ancient Greeks, after all, did not have a modern concept of the unconscious, and we certainly cannot say that Socrates did or necessarily would put things this way.

However, the human psyche hasn't significantly changed in the last two thousand years, and the unconscious was as much a part of the actions of ancient Athenians as of anyone today. The force of the unconscious is at times painfully apparent, and Socrates must have noticed it, even if he did not have a convenient way of referring to it. In essence, this interpretation of Socrates' ideas suggests that using a contemporary concept may let us better understand this ancient thinker's claims. This kind of interpretation is allowable in philosophy as long as we acknowledge what we are doing and accept the limitations of such speculation.

we lose some control over ourselves. We don't remain content once our desires are satisfied, and we're driven to find and gratify more needs. Ultimately, our desires become insatiable. We're never really happy, we just want, want, want.

Second, when we becomes slaves to our desires, our minds are pulled into their service too. Our intellects become dulled, we may become less sensitive to important contradictions in our thoughts or behavior, and internal pressures cause us to devise rationalizations that keep us on the path we've chosen. We may explain to others—but primarily to ourselves—that such behavior is reasonable, good, and fulfilling. But we're only kidding ourselves, and we don't even know it.

Such a claim about the harm done by vice seems to make sense. Most of us already know that as we do unethical things, they often get easier to do and harder to resist. Ultimately, we may lose our sense that anything is really wrong with them. If you've ever cheated on a test, for example, you know that it's easier to do the next time and easier to live with. Or look at someone you know who manipulates people all the time. He doesn't hurt others on purpose. He believes he's only doing what is best for himself, his company, or some cause he believes in, and he doesn't see the suffering he causes. Or take a millionaire who gets caught cheating to avoid paying the sales tax on her jewelry purchases. Somehow these people could not see how foolish they are.

This is what corruption is all about. It involves a deterioration of strengths and abilities accompanied by blindness to what is happening. Do you think that corrupt people think they are corrupt? Hardly. They think they've finally gotten smart, or courageous, or realistic. They think they have now found the guts to do what ordinary people dare not do. And when they're caught, do they think that punishment is justified? No, they feel that they were trapped unfairly and that they are being held to unreasonable standards while the real crooks get away with murder.

People are not born corrupt. And in most cases no one coerces them into corruption. How, then, does it happen? Unethical behavior starts with a free choice. But once made, people are drawn in deeper and deeper until their "souls" have sustained serious harm.

Our speculation that this damage takes place on an unconscious level also makes Socrates' claim that vice harms the doer more plausible. The fact that self-interest, greed, jealousy, and hatred lead people into self-destructive behavior, the risks of which they cannot assess rationally, is explained more effectively by an unconscious process than a conscious one. Even though Socrates himself does not put it this way, his ideas are supported by a contemporary psychological understanding of the human personality.

Is Socrates right that vice harms the doer? Without a doubt.

Moral Virtue and Happiness

Ultimately, the reason that the idea "vice harms the doer" is so important is that Socrates thinks that we need to live virtuous lives in order to be happy. If acting unethically affects both our ability to be satisfied and our ability to see things clearly, no matter how much money, beauty, power, or success we have, we will never be content. We will constantly want more. And our vision will be so distorted that we will see things incorrectly, make mistakes, and probably get caught. This is not the path to happiness.

Socrates thinks of happiness as a state of stable contentment produced by satisfying desires that are reasonable and within our power. For this we need to have a realistic view of what is within our reach, enough self-control to keep our desires within bounds, and the good sense not to take foolish, self-destructive risks. And, as we have seen, Socrates claims that we retain these capacities only if we are virtuous. Not that we must live like saints to be happy. But living a decent life is the only way to get the inner contentment, freedom, and self-control that we need to feel good about life. As Socrates expresses it to Polus, "I call a good and honorable man or woman happy, and one who is unjust and evil wretched. . . . You believe it is possible for a happy man to be wrong and be unjust, . . . and I say this is impossible."

What About a Moderate Callicles?

Despite the commonsense validity of Socrates' ideas, you may have some doubts about all of this. "This talk about self-control, rationality, virtue, and happiness seems all well and good," you might say, "but isn't it possible to be a really successful *unethical* individual? The trick is to let your desires grow, but not let them get out of hand, to be prudent in your larceny, to assess the odds of success and failure realistically. In short, if you can be a moderate and more restrained Callicles, you'll have the happiest life imaginable. You'll get most of what you want, you'll be satisfied with it, and you won't get caught."

This brings us full circle to the unprincipled person with the reputation for integrity that we saw Plato describe and reject at the start of this chapter. The problem is, however, that a "moderate Callicles" may simply be impossible. There are too many highly intelligent, successful, talented people who run foolish risks, make mistakes, and get caught to suggest that everyone who gets mired in scandal is second rate. It does seem that objective judgment is one of the first casualties of moral corruption. And if the harm done by vice does take place on an unconscious level, it's no surprise that these people couldn't control how corrupt they were becoming.

Socrates' "wine jar" analogy becomes useful again here. Unethical behavior erodes the "wine jar" of our "soul," and as the jar's contents leak out, the bottom becomes more and more porous. Aware of the empty feeling, we are gradually overwhelmed by our desire to fill up again. We can neither control our desires nor maintain our rational perspective. We become like the addict who believes that his next fix is worth any risks to get the money to pay for it.

You still may not be convinced by this. Perhaps you think that we don't know about truly capable wrongdoers because they never get caught. However, the point here is not to settle the issue unequivocally. Rather, when we confront a philosophical position without as much detail as we need to answer it, we can only try to understand what these ideas might mean and to consider the plausibility of our interpretation. At this point, we can say that our interpretation fits well enough with what we know of the human psyche that it deserves serious consideration.

Repairing the Damage Vice Does

The two main consequences of vice that we speculated about occur largely in the unconscious. The essence of Socrates' claim that vice harms the doer, then, is that it affects that part of the personality that lies beneath our conscious awareness. Thus, the overwhelming danger of vice is that it hurts us in ways that we cannot see, and also builds a psychological mechanism that keeps it in place even after we have noticed a problem. Does the fact that we cannot see the damage as it is being done mean that it cannot be repaired? It's not easy, but it can be done.

Sometimes people do not get the point until they have suffered severe consequences as a result of their own vice. Confronting hard, cold reality—getting caught, fired, jailed, having those you love leave you—can shock some people into realizing they were deceiving themselves, and only themselves. The world did not work the way they thought it did. Seeing the ruin they brought on themselves, they are then willing to approach life differently.

It doesn't always have to be so painful, however. Socrates thought that a "diseased" soul could be healed by getting the afflicted person to see that he can never be happy the way he is living. Psychologists and psychiatrists today also think that unconscious mechanisms can be neutralized and dismantled if they are brought up into conscious awareness. We might say, then, that in his dialogues Socrates aims to bring these self-defeating unconscious mechanisms to the surface. He engages people in exhaustive conversations trying to get them to see the truth about their behavior. He attempts to convince them that as long as they believe that moral virtue is not the most important thing in their life, they cannot be happy. And if the conversation concentrated on an interlocutor's most deeply held beliefs about what is important in life, an encounter with Socrates could be a very powerful emotional experience—the kind that can get you to doubt some of your most basic values and loosen the grip of unconscious forces.

But you don't need a Socrates to do this. Socrates often told people that "the unexamined life is not worth living." In other words, if you don't scrutinize your own life, you may not realize that you're making some fairly significant moral compromises while thinking that there's no problem. The unexamined soul may very well be an unhealthy soul, and the unhealthy soul lacks the freedom, control, and perspective that Socrates thinks is necessary for true human happiness.

One of the most useful things that philosophy can do for you is to train your mind so that you can examine your own life. If you're truthful with yourself, you will notice when you start to give in to excessive desires, to let your wants control you, and to rationalize indefensible behavior. And if you're thinking right, you can correct yourself before you go too far.

Why Be Ethical?

Plato and Socrates give straightforward answers to this question. An unethical person is weak, even unhealthy. Such a person lacks the freedom, self-control, and intellectual clarity that are necessary to live happily.

Plato describes this in terms of the proper balance between our intellect, on the one hand, and our physical and emotional desires, on the other. In the unbalanced, unhealthy soul, he says, people are so driven by physical or emotional wants that they cannot think straight about right and wrong. When their minds service their wants, they cannot examine the morality of their actions. Only the freedom, control, and balanced perspective that come with the soul's health result in ethical behavior. If you aren't dominated by your physical or emotional wants, you can make good decisions. Thus, acting ethically is an expression of the strong, healthy soul, one in which a clear mind is the dominant force in someone's life.

According to Socrates, wrongdoing harms the doer by unleashing our desires, disabling the inner mechanism that makes contentment possible, and diminishing our intellectual power. We speculated here that the harm which comes from vice occurs primarily in the unconscious part of our personality.

So now that you've heard from these two philosophers, ponder this yourself. Examine the effects of virtue and vice in your own life. Look at the lives of people you know and people you read about. Who are the healthier, stronger, and happier people, those who are ethical or those who are unethical? Now look at those people who are clearly unethical. Have they sustained any of the harms Socrates describes? Finally, is there anything in it for you if you live your life trying to do the right thing?

Main Points of Chapter 6

1. One of the most difficult questions in ethics is: Why should we do the right thing?

2. Both Plato and Socrates argue that virtue is its own reward by claiming that "virtue is the health of the soul." They believe that there is a part of us that is improved by acting ethically and harmed by acting unethically. The healthy soul, or personality, is characterized by the freedom, will, and power to live according to one's moral insights.

3. Plato bases his concept of the healthy soul on his idea that we are made up of three parts: the physical, the spirited, and the intellectual. In the healthy soul, the three are properly balanced. The mind is in control and our emotions help us follow the mind's judgment. The unhealthy soul, by contrast, is driven by physical or emotional desires, and its judgment about right and wrong is clouded.

4. Socrates thinks that unethical actions actually harm the person who performs them, that is, that they weaken both the intellect and the ability to control one's desires. We might interpret him as saying that when we do wrong we weaken our strength of will and our moral vision. Vice makes the people who indulge in it uncontrolled, intemperate, and never satisfied. It also seems to make them believe that ordinary ideas of right and wrong don't apply to them, and to damage their practical ability to identify and carry out what is genuinely in their own interest.

Discussion Questions

1. What would your response be to the issue raised by the story of "Gyges' ring"? If you knew you could get away with absolutely anything you wanted to do, however unethical, how ethical would your behavior be? How would you decide what to do?

2. What about Plato's case of the unethical person with a reputation for virtue? As long as everyone around you believed that you were virtuous, would vice really have any negative consequences?

3. Does the idea that virtue is "the health of the soul" make sense to you? How would you describe that notion to someone in contemporary terms?

4. Do you agree with Plato that in the "healthy soul," the proper relationship is for the mind to be making the decisions and for our physical and emotional dimensions to be subservient? Would you agree that giving in to physical or emotional desires against our better judgment is "unhealthy"?

5. What do you make of Socrates' idea that when we do something wrong, we hurt *ourselves*? In particular, what about the two distinct kinds of harm: (a) that we begin to lose control over our wants, and (b) that even our minds are weakened?

6. Have you found it true in your own life that once you started doing something you believed was wrong, it became easier and you did it more often?

7. What is your reaction to the "wine jar" analogy? Is it accurate or deceptive?

8. To some extent, what Socrates and Plato claim about morality and the healthy soul does not fit with some accepted truths in contemporary society. We are told that competing aggressively and advancing our own interests at all costs is a sign of strength. Many people consider that limiting our wants and being good are not only barriers to success but weaknesses. Many people agree with Callicles, not with Socrates. What is your reaction to this?

9. The discussion of Socrates' ideas in this chapter relied on a good deal of speculation. Was this interpretation plausible to you? Can you think of another way of interpreting the idea that "vice harms the doer"?

10. What is your reaction to bringing in the contemporary idea of the "unconscious"? Is that going too far?

Selected Readings

For Plato's ideas about ethics, the importance of moral virtue, and the relationship between the different parts of the "soul," see the *Republic*. Socrates' ideas are set out in Plato's "Socratic" dialogues, especially the *Apology, Crito,* and *Gorgias. The Apology* is an account of Socrates' trial and contains Socrates' own account of his life's work. For a highly readable, but sometimes flawed, account of Socrates by a nonspecialist, see I. F. Stone, *The Trial of Socrates* (Boston: Little, Brown, 1988).

7

Democracy

You are probably aware of the rain forest. This is a huge, tropical expanse of trees and vegetation that is a biological treasure. Many species live only in the rain forest. Numerous medicines have been developed from plants in the rain forest, and researchers believe there are many more cures waiting to be discovered there. Most importantly, however, the rain forest is one of the planet's most significant parts of the planet's thermostat. By converting carbon dioxide to oxygen, the trees of the rain forest allow the earth's temperature to stay fairly constant. In light of the huge amounts of CO_2 produced by the factories and automobiles of the industrialized world, the rain forest has its hands full.

You are probably also aware that the planet is facing an environmental crisis because the continued existence of the rain forest is in jeopardy. Many acres of the rain forest are being cut down each day in order to promote the economic development of the countries who own it. (The forests are being replaced primarily with grazing sites for cattle. Selling timber and beef is much more profitable than allowing the trees to stand undisturbed.) It is certainly understandable that developing nations with limited resources would try to capitalize on the economic value of the rain forests. However, once they are destroyed, they cannot be replaced. And their loss could be ominous. Many species of plants and animals will be lost forever. Many, possibly lifesaving, medicines will never be discovered. And the increased amount of carbon dioxide will contribute to the "greenhouse effect": an increase in the temperature of the earth's atmosphere that could lead to partial melting of the polar ice caps, rise in the ocean levels, dramatic loss of coastal areas, changes in the climate on different parts of the planet, and agricultural devastation. It is fair to say that in terms of the long-term welfare of the earth and everyone who lives on it, this is one of the most important problems our species currently faces. It doesn't seem fair to ask some countries to endure poverty so that the rest of us can continue to reap the fruits of industrialization. Yet if we don't do something, all of humanity will eventually suffer.

Imagine that one day you are listening to the news, and you hear that the President has just announced a bold new proposal to solve this problem. In exchange for a promise from developing countries to leave their remaining rain forests untouched, the United States will provide them with direct, massive assistance to reduce poverty and upgrade their quality of life. This will be accomplished by a huge expansion and transformation of the Peace Corps. We will send millions of Americans to help raise the standards of living in these countries. Sensitive to the fact that there are still millions of poor and homeless people in the United States, however, the President wants the same kind of program put in place at home.

Accordingly, the President asks Congress to pass legislation that will require four years of national service for everyone in this country from 18 to 20 years old. (From now on, when anyone turns 18, he or she must report to the Peace Corps.) For two years, these people will serve in economically disadvantaged areas in the United States. After that, they will be sent to the rain forest countries. In either case, they will be assigned to do whatever will assist the people of the region: building and repairing homes, providing food and medical treatment, making and distributing clothes, caring for children who have been neglected or abandoned, helping at schools, creating parks and playgrounds in the cities, working on farms, upgrading the infrastructure in rural areas, and helping communities find ways to develop economically without doing any ecological damage. "This nation simply has the obligation to help solve serious national and global problems and to care for people in need," says the President. "We hope that this experience," he continues, "will leave every young American with a sense of service and responsibility to others. We also hope that, by going to any country that requests our help, America will be seen as a generous nation truly committed to the welfare of everyone on the planet." The idea is embraced by Congress and lauded by the United Nations and many world leaders.

The President asks, however, that before implementing such an important program, a national referendum on the question be held. There are town meetings and televised debates. For months, the issue dominates radio call-in shows. When the vote is taken, there is an unprecedented, huge turnout. The proposal wins handily. The only problem is that exit polls at voting sites reveal that only 20 percent of people from age 18 to 22 supported the idea.

You are one of the 80 percent in this age group who voted against the program. You and your friends believe that this program places an unfair burden on young adults at a critical time in their lives. Education, careers, and relationships will all have to be put on hold for four years. You also think it's blatantly unfair. You feel that you're being asked to fix a problem that you had no hand in making. You believe that the rest of the country is just sloughing off their responsibility onto you. You think that they voted simply in their own personal interest, and that you lost because they outnumbered the young people who would have to serve. In fact, public polls reveal that the program would have been defeated if it had been extended to people in their late-twenties and thirties. The election was fair and democratic, however. You had your chance to campaign against the idea. The majority has spoken. Legally, the matter is settled.

Some of your friends are talking about leaving the country to start a new life elsewhere. They want you to join them. You may feel angry and resentful, but you have a duty to obey this new law. Don't you? Or do your feelings reveal that the country has unfairly wronged you—through a fully democratic process? If you fled the country instead of serving your stint in the Peace Corps, you would be breaking the law. But would you be doing anything wrong?

As imaginary and unlikely as this particular scenario may strike you, it's actually not all that unrealistic. When American men turn 18, they must register for the draft. During the Vietnam War, many people who objected to the war believed that there was nothing wrong with evading the draft or leaving the country. The great philosopher Socrates had to decide in a particularly dramatic way how much of an obligation he had to obey the dictates of the Athenian democracy—after being sentenced to death, Socrates had the opportunity to escape from jail. On a more mundane level, if you or your friends are thinking about getting fake I.D.s or engaging in underage drinking, you're also facing the question of whether you're entitled to ignore laws that were enacted democratically.

This chapter, then, is about some of the most basic questions in political philosophy. How strong an obligation do you have to obey the laws of a democracy? Precisely where would such an obligation come from? And, on balance, is democracy a philosophically legitimate form of government? We begin by examining the essence of the political system under which we live and some arguments for why we have a duty to obey democratically enacted laws. Then we consider some challenges to democracy. Finally, we look at what a great political philosopher, Plato, thinks is a better kind of government.

Questioning Democracy

Depending on what's happening in the world around you, you might feel uneasy about questioning democracy. It might seem "disloyal" or "unpatriotic." However, there are a number of important reasons to do so.

First, it's important to recognize that being a citizen of a democracy isn't easy, because democracy is actually one of the most demanding forms of government. For example, a citizen's duties include not simply voting, but also voting intelligently —that is, taking the time to understand the issues and to learn about the candidates on the ballot. To ensure that all opinions are heard, democracy requires more than just tolerating points of view that we find repugnant. We even have to be willing to defend the right of other citizens to advance such ideas. For the true champion of freedom, no idea is out of bounds for discussion in a democracy. Perhaps most importantly, a firm commitment to democracy requires that citizens make sure that the government is serving the citizenry and not the other way around—and that we take action when appropriate. In fact, no less a proponent of democracy than Thomas Jefferson wrote,

> I hold it that a little rebellion now and then is a good thing, and as necessary in the political world as storms in the physical. Unsuccessful rebellions, indeed, generally establish the encroachments on the rights of the people which have produced them. An observation of this truth should render honest republican governors so

mild in their punishment of rebellions as not to discourage them too much. It is a medicine necessary for the sound health of the government. *(Thomas Jefferson, Letter to James Madison, from Paris, Jan. 30, 1787)*

Against the backdrop of Jefferson's words about the virtue of rebellions, then, ongoing scrutiny of everything from government policies to the very foundations of democracy seems not only mild by comparison, but also a clear duty of all its citizens.

Recognize, too, that many institutions around you are not democratic—and they work perfectly well. The military has a clear, nondemocratic chain of command. In most religions, important decisions are made by religious officials, not by a vote of the faithful. In a typical business, employees are simply told what to do. Given the success of such organizations, many people argue that they provide superior, more efficient models than democracy for how to get things done. But if you've never examined arguments against democracy and come up with a solid defense, you're going to be poorly prepared to answer its critics.

The Philosophical Argument for Democracy
The Meaning of "Democracy"

"Democracy," which combines two Greek words, *demos*, "people," and *cratein*, "to rule," literally means "rule by the people." The word "people" refers to all citizens, regardless of social class or wealth. We can distinguish democracy from a variety of other governments whose names are also derived from Greek: "monarchy," which means the rule of one person (*monos*, "one"); "oligarchy," which means rule by the few (*oligos*, "few"); "plutarchy," which means rule by the rich (*plutos*, "wealth"); and "aristocracy," which has come to mean rule by the nobility (*aristos*, "the best").

In essence, **democracy** is a system of governing that places political power in the hands of the entire citizenry. Power is not reserved for one person, for a few people, or for a sizable minority of citizens. Simply being a citizen gives you the right to participate in the political process.

To ensure that "the people" are actually in charge, democracies rely primarily on periodic votes. Some votes, called elections, are taken to choose officials; others, called referenda, elicit the opinion of the citizens on a specific issue. When the system functions properly, voters are given a choice among a range of genuine options—not just one candidate, or a choice between two that are virtually indistinguishable. Whichever option receives a majority of votes carries the day.

---

democracy "Democracy," which combines two Greek words, *demos*, "people," and *cratein*, "to rule," literally means "rule by the people." The word "people" refers to all citizens, regardless of social class or wealth. It is a form of government generally characterized by votes and majority rule. The special attribute of democracy is that it claims to respect freedom and autonomy while legitimately requiring citizens to obey laws.

But, from a philosophical perspective, what happens in a democratic vote? Do we simply end up with the majority bullying and threatening the minority? Does the minority, then, obey laws out of self-interested fear of punishment? (In this case, your decision about serving in the Peace Corps would amount to little more than totally selfish calculation about whether service, exile, or punishment would be in your best interest.) Or does the vote produce in the minority a serious and philosophically binding obligation to obey? (If so, your decision is whether to deliberately do something that you know is seriously wrong.) In order to answer any question about obligation in a democracy, however, we must first look at something broader than voting. That is, we must ask whether democracy is, overall, a philosophically legitimate form of government.

Legitimizing Governments: Politics and Ethics

What does it mean to say that a government is "philosophically legitimate"?

Believe it or not, a philosophically legitimate government is one that is *ethically* acceptable. Many people have become so cynical that they think ethics is the last thing one would connect with politics. Often the two seem mutually exclusive. And yet, until the sixteenth or seventeenth century, Western thinkers followed the Greeks in seeing political philosophy simply as a branch of ethics.

But what standard other than ethics could we use to measure the acceptability of a government? Remember from Chapter 5 that the aim of ethics is *human well-being*. And that is what every political, social, and economic institution also supposedly aims at. The goal of any political system must be to make life better for the people who live in that community. No measure other than the kind and degree of human happiness delivered would make sense.

Teleological and Deontological Ethical Standards

Just as we use teleological and deontological standards to judge the ethical character of an action, so we can approach the legitimacy of political systems the same two ways.[1] A teleological approach assumes that a political system is good as long as it makes life observably better for its citizens. We would look for a low crime rate, a healthy economy, decent homes and schools, excellent health care, good roads and public transportation, and some system of defense against enemies. A deontological approach, on the other hand, assumes that a government should be judged by how well its citizens are treated by one another and by their own government. Equality, fairness, justice, the observance of proper procedures, respect for privacy, and other basic rights therefore become paramount.

Proponents of monarchy, dictatorship, and various forms of one-party rule probably favor a teleological approach. They say that concentrating power in the hands of a few people is the most efficient way of getting the right things done. It also prevents the country from choosing the wrong course when most of the citizens are mistaken about something. People who think this way reject the idea that participation in the process that determines public policies is a basic human right.

---

[1]See Chapter 5 if you need to review teleological and deontological approaches to ethics.

People who favor democracy lean toward a deontological approach. More than anything else, people support democracy because it respects and promotes certain fundamental rights—usually called "human rights" or "inalienable rights"—that exist independently of any government. Democracy's proponents think that inefficiency is a small price to pay to ensure that the government respects these rights and is directly responsive to the entire citizenry.

The Legitimacy of Democracy: Freedom and Autonomy

The major arguments for the philosophical legitimacy of democracy are based on the idea that this is the best form of government for respecting two primary rights: *freedom* and *autonomy.*

We start with the idea that the most basic fact about human beings is that we are *free.*[2] We have a deep need to live freely. Thus, we are entitled to choose the shape of our lives. Any force, from subtle manipulation to physical intimidation, that impinges on this freedom and deprives us of the opportunity to make decisions about our own lives prevents us from growing and developing as people. Thus, freedom is the most fundamental necessary condition for human life.

The only situation compatible with being human, then, is one that enables us to make choices. We have no preexisting obligations to anyone or anything. Nor does anyone have the right to tell us what to do, against our will, without violating our freedom.

Governments, however, are based on concepts which seem the opposite of freedom—obligation and authority. We as citizens are obliged to obey the laws and those individuals who have legitimate authority over us. But if we are going to respect human freedom, how do we deal with obligation and authority? Obviously, we have to find a way to see them as stemming from somebody's free choice. To take a simple, nonpolitical example, if I promise to help you fix your car on Saturday, I have freely chosen to take on that obligation. And if I further agree that you can force me to help you if I later change my mind, I have freely chosen to give you that authority over me. So when I sleep in on Saturday instead of helping you, and you come over and drag me bodily out of bed, strictly speaking you aren't making me do something against my will. I gave you permission to do that.

Another way of saying this is that we consider such commitments legitimate because they are consistent with the fact that our freedom implies that we are also *autonomous.* "Autonomous" comes from two Greek words—*autos,* "self," and *nomos,* "law"—and the sense of the term is that you—and *only* you—give law to yourself. The only legitimate political obligation is one that you freely assent to, and in this assent you stand alone. It doesn't matter what anyone else says or does. To say that humans are autonomous, then, is to imply that for laws, authority, or obligations to be philosophically legitimate, we must each individually and willingly authorize them. Anything else compromises our freedom.

---

[2]Whether this is so or not is beside the point here. To review the argument over free will versus determinism, see Chapters 3 and 4.

The special attribute of democracy is that it claims to respect human *freedom* and *autonomy* while legitimately requiring citizens to *obey* laws. As long as the individual citizens themselves are the source of a society's laws and policies, they are simply obeying themselves. No one is bullying or threatening anyone else into obedience. There is no coercion, and there is no tyranny.

Freedom, Authority, and Obligation

In order to appreciate how great an accomplishment this is for democracy, we should look more closely at the problems of *authority* and *obligation*. Why is it legitimate for some people to have power over others, and why are citizens obligated to obey a government's laws and officials? Every kind of government makes a different claim for why it should rightfully have authority. Democracy's great virtue is that it tries to solve these related problems while still respecting personal freedom.

Look at these claims for authority and consider how much freedom they allow. Some monarchs ruled by "divine right"; that is, they claimed that their authority came directly from God. Another source of authority was heredity. Once a family seized the throne, its authority became a possession that was transferred down a line of descendants just as property is transferred. All that counted was the proper blood line. The authority of dictators stems from the possession of power, most often military power. In dictatorships, "might makes right." But none of these claims for authority mesh with freedom and autonomy.

In a democracy, by contrast, the authority of a government and the political obligations of its citizens arise from the free choice of the citizens being governed. Abraham Lincoln's famous phrase, "government of the people, by the people, for the people," says it well. Democracy claims to be nothing less than a system in which a group of enfranchised people say what they want in life and freely agree among themselves what to do in order to get it.

A citizen's obligations in a democracy are thus like one's obligations to keep a promise after one has made it. But instead of the limited agreements we make with some other person—like my promise to help you fix your car on Saturday—in a democracy we make broad agreements with the rest of society about how we will act on a range of issues. We promise to obey laws, to use the democratic process if we want to change things, to accept the results of elections, and the like. We freely promise to do many things that we don't like: pay taxes, serve in the military, even accept punishment when called for.

The obligations that citizens have may be starting to make sense to you. But you may not be so clear about where or when any such promises were made. You probably do not recall making any promises to buy into the democratic society you live in. Political philosophers have a ready explanation, however, and that is where we turn next.

The Social Contract

Political philosophers often talk about freedom and obligation in terms of what is called a "social contract." After all, if people are free, then their obligations to social and political institutions can be legitimate only if they are based on some promise, agreement, or contract.

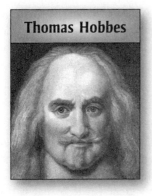

Thomas Hobbes

Thomas Hobbes (1588–1679) was educated at Magdalen College at Oxford, and in the first part of his career he served as tutor to families in the British aristocracy. Hobbes studied mathematics and optics and attempted to derive an entire philosophical system from the science of motion, although political thought was probably his primary concern. Hobbes was writing his first political treatises at a time of civil war in England, and his support of monarchy led him to flee to France in 1640, where he remained for eleven years. While in France, Hobbes published *Leviathan,* a book of political philosophy in which Hobbes uses the idea of the social contract to argue in favor of absolute monarchy. He returned to a series of controversies on a variety of subjects. Later in his life, as a result of Parliament's concern with suppressing atheism, Hobbes was forbidden to publish any more of his writings.

The idea of a **social contract** lies at the heart of democracy. Thomas Hobbes (1588–1679), the British philosopher who first came up with the idea, did so as a way of defending the absolute authority of a sovereign. Subsequent thinkers like John Locke (1632–1704) and Jean-Jacques Rousseau (1712–1778) took the idea and linked it to democratic forms of government. The essence of the social contract is that it resolves the conflict between political authority and individual autonomy. Hobbes writes:

A commonwealth is said to be instituted when a multitude of men do *agree and covenant,* every one with every one, that to whatsoever man or assembly of men shall be given by the major part the right to present the person of them all—that is to say, to be their representative—every one, as well he that voted for it as he that voted against it, shall authorize all the actions and judgments of that man or assembly of men in the same manner *as if they were his own,* to the end to live peaceably among themselves and be protected against other men. [Emphasis added.][3]

—Leviathan

social contract The "social contract" is an idea that underlies all modern democracies. It was developed by thinkers such as John Locke and Jean-Jacques Rousseau to resolve the conflict between freedom and obligation. It argues that citizens of a society freely enter into an agreement to abide by that society's laws and therefore are obligated to do so.

---

[3]Hobbes identified peace and protection as the aim of the agreement because he took a gloomy view of human nature. People in their natural state, he observed, were base and mean. Life in the "state of nature" would, he said, be "nasty, brutish, and short" because we would always be at each other's throats. Hobbes's social contract, then, produces a supreme monarch, not a democracy. Rousseau and Locke, by contrast, have a much more positive view of human nature, and this makes them the more direct ancestors of modern democracy than Hobbes. These two thinkers, like contemporary democratic social thinkers, believe that we can be trusted with our liberty.

John Locke

John Locke (1632–1704) studied philosophy and medicine at Oxford, but he became deeply involved in the political turbulence of his day. His association with the leader of Parliament's opposition to the Crown caused him to flee England for Holland in 1683 where, in addition to his intellectual work, Locke remained active in the movement to make William of Orange the King of England. Returning to England when this was accomplished, Locke published his two most important works, *Essay Concerning Human Understanding* and *The Two Treatises of Government*. The rest of his years were spent in both intellectual inquiry and government service.

Rousseau makes it even plainer when he claims that a social contract produces

a form of association which will defend and protect with the whole common force the person and the property of each associate, and by which every person, while uniting himself with all, *shall obey only himself and remain as free as ever before.* [Emphasis added.]

—Social Contract

And John Locke expands on these ideas when he explains:

Men being . . . by nature all *free, equal, and independent,* no one can be put out of this estate and subjected to the political power of another without his own *consent.* The only way whereby any one divests himself of his natural liberty and puts on the bonds of civil society is by *agreeing* with other men to join and unite into a community for their comfortable, safe, and peaceable living one amongst another, in a secure enjoyment of their properties and a greater security against any that are not of it . . . . And thus every man, by consenting with others to make one body politic under one government, puts himself under an *obligation* to every one of that society to submit to the determination of the majority and to be concluded by it. [Emphasis added.]

—Second Treatise of Government

To proponents of democracy, the concept of the social contract has two major strengths. It respects freedom and autonomy. And it is easy to understand. Rousseau and Locke make politics work like anything else in a free society—people get together and agree about something. The citizenry agrees on the kind of a society it wants, and it chooses laws and officials that make it happen. The political obligation of those involved is clear and strong: it is simply to do what they have freely agreed to do.

The notion of the social contract did more than just solve theoretical problems about how to combine freedom and obligation, of course. The influence of social

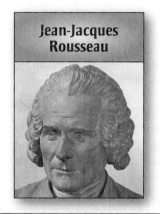

Jean-Jacques Rousseau

Jean-Jacques Rousseau (1712–1778) was a controversial figure of his day. Born and raised in Geneva, Rousseau was
largely self-educated. He tried to develop a reputation in
music before settling on a literary career, which saw the
production of such works as *Discourse on the Origins of
Inequality, Emile,* and the *Social Contract.* Rousseau's religious and political views regularly sparked controversy
and the condemnation of his writings, events that caused
a series of moves from one country to another. At the end
of his life, Rousseau evidenced paranoia and other deep
psychological problems, and he appears to have gone insane
before his death.

contract theory on the founding of the United States is one of the clearest cases of
philosophy having an impact on the world of practical politics.

We all know that the American "Founding Fathers" called for independence
from Great Britain, conducted a revolution, and established a democratic confederation among what had been thirteen separate colonies. The basic principles expressed in the Declaration of Independence, the Articles of Confederation, and the
Constitution, however, did not spring out of nowhere. People like Thomas Jefferson,
the author of the Declaration of Independence, were strongly influenced by the ideas
of Locke, Rousseau, and others who argued for the importance of freedom, basic
rights, and a social contract. Consider this well-known section of the Declaration:

> We hold these truths to be self-evident: that all men are created equal; that they
> are endowed by their Creator with certain *inalienable rights;* that among these are
> life, *liberty,* and the pursuit of happiness; that to secure these rights, governments
> are instituted among men, deriving their just powers from the *consent of the gov-
> erned.* [Emphasis added.]

These are the same basic ideas that were expressed by the European social contract
theorists: Everyone is equal, and only a freely made agreement establishes a legitimate
government and binding obligation.

The founding of the United States is one of the relatively few occasions in history when people sat down and drew up the terms for a new society. The founders
could not have designed this society as they did without the work of the social contract philosophers, especially that of John Locke.

Agreeing to the Terms of the Contract

It's all very well to say that people freely agree to their obligations under the terms
of a social contract. But there are some problems with this.

First, it's rare that an actual document describing a new society is drawn up.
The Pilgrims produced the Mayflower Compact; the Declaration of Independence
and the United States Constitution resulted from actual deliberations. But these are

the exceptions. Great Britain, for example, has no constitution. More often, a society's principles and rules simply evolve over time in a process that is frequently more informal than formal.

Moreover, citizens of a democracy almost never get a chance to agree formally to the established terms of the society they are born into. Have you ever been presented with a copy of a "social contract"? Were you asked to read and sign anything? Of course not. The only people who expressly consent to the society's terms are those who become new citizens. And even then, it's "take it or leave it." (No one can say, "I have some problems with this or that provision; let's see if we can come to some agreement.")

Doesn't this absence of a formal agreement weaken democracy's philosophical legitimacy? If no one actually agrees to any terms, doesn't this make a charade out of the "social contract"? Isn't it, then, just a clever way to rationalize the status quo and the fact that the majority simply bullies the minority into submission?

Tacit Consent

Anticipating this problem, Locke solves it by appealing to the notion of **tacit consent,** or unspoken agreement. Applying this idea to the world of politics, he says:

> Every man being . . . naturally free, and nothing being able to put him into subjection to any earthly power but only his own consent, it is to be considered what shall be understood to be sufficient declaration of a man's consent to make him subject to the laws of any government. There is a common distinction of an express and a tacit consent, which will concern our present case. Nobody doubts but an express consent of any man entering into any society makes him a perfect member of that society, a subject of that government. The difficulty is, what ought to be looked upon as a *tacit consent,* and how far it binds, i.e., how far any one shall be looked on to have consented, and thereby submitted to any government, where he has made no expressions of it at all. And to this I say that every man that hath any possession or enjoyment of any part of the dominions of any government doth thereby give his tacit consent, and is as far forth obliged to obedience to the laws of that government during such enjoyment as any one under it; whether this his possession be of land to him and his heirs for ever, or a lodging for only a week; or whether it be barely travelling freely on the highway; and in effect it reaches as far as the very being of any one within the territories of that government. [Emphasis added.]
>
> —Second Treatise of Government

In other words, just being in a particular place constitutes an unspoken acceptance of that government's authority. Nothing explicit has to be stated by either party. Intelligent people understand what a particular society or government is like. We're

---

tacit consent Tacit consent is an idea advanced by John Locke that claims that an informal and unspoken agreement is sufficient to constitute being bound by the terms of a particular "social contract."

always free to leave if we don't like things; but as long as we stay, our presence constitutes a freely given agreement to abide by the rules.

All defenders of democracy use something like Locke's argument. Without being overly legalistic about it, as long as you know the kind of society you're in and have the option of leaving, your mere presence says that you accept the obligation to obey its laws. Thus, your freedom and autonomy are preserved, and the government's authority over you is philosophically legitimate.

Tacit Consent in Real Life: A Business Agreement.   What do you think so far? Is tacit consent as good as a formal agreement?

In some cases, it works perfectly well. For example, let's say you see an ad in your campus newspaper, "Papers edited. Grammar, spelling, and style improved. Reasonable rates. Satisfaction guaranteed. Just send to Chin, Box 226." If you send a paper to be edited, you are obligated to pay the bill that accompanies the finished copy. Even though you and the editor have not spoken a word to each other, you and Chin have entered an agreement. He will improve the paper; you will pay him for it. It is an unspoken agreement, but an agreement, nonetheless.

Tacit Consent in Real Life: A College Community.   But does the binding nature of an unspoken agreement work as well when many people are involved?

Consider the agreement you make by going to the college of your choice. You may get a handbook with some regulations in it, but you don't sign any document agreeing to the dos and don'ts of college life. By and large, the school assumes that you are mature, intelligent, and able to figure out what's expected of you. If you cheat on a term paper, for example, you won't get off by saying that you never agreed not to cheat. Participating in the process—going to classes and taking exams—is taken as consenting to the rules of the game. It seems fair and reasonable to say that by joining the academic community you tacitly consented to its rules and regulations, and you are obligated to abide by them.

Tacit Consent in Real Life: A Large Community.   If unspoken agreements work in a college community, how do they work in larger, more complex communities?

Take your own case. You were born into a society that hums along according to rules established long ago. You didn't choose where to be born. You didn't design the community you find yourself a member of. And yet since day one, your parents, your teachers, everyone you know has worked at shaping your behavior and even your deepest personal values so that you will fit into this society.

It takes about fifteen or twenty years before you have enough skills to take care of yourself, and it takes longer than that before you can understand what your country is really like. When you're young, your parents and teachers tell you about your new society. But these accounts are overly simple—and idealistic: hard work is always rewarded, equality and opportunity abound, criminals are punished, the rich and poor deserve their respective fates, justice and fairness are the norm. You also hear your society described by its leaders, but their motives are often so self-serving that much of what they say is closer to propaganda. By the time you get to know the real score, you might be 25 or older. Only then could you make an informed decision about whether the society you're in is the kind you'd want to join.

By this time, you are very much a part of your community. You have learned the language and the customs. You are a member of a family. You have made friends. You have begun a career. You may even be married and have children of your own. You have developed strong emotional ties to this place.

Does Staying Put Constitute a Binding Agreement? Maybe Not

In light of all this, is it fair and reasonable to interpret merely remaining in a society as an unspoken but binding agreement to accept and obey the terms of the society's "social contract"?

John Locke might think so, but various reasons suggest something different. The average person is neither well informed enough nor free enough to give the kind of consent we want to see. Ideally, we want someone to say, "I fully understand the laws and I know all about what this society is like. I may not like everything, but what I like is more important than what I dislike. I'm free to leave, but I choose to stay. In full knowledge, I authorize all the laws and any other actions the government deems prudent. I even authorize the government to force me to hold up my end of the deal. This is my final and irrevocable word."

In fact, however, not many of us can or do say such a thing. Why not? Remember that we have to *know* what we're getting into and *truly agree* when we undertake our obligations. Two of the examples we just looked at, getting your paper edited and going to college, meet both of these conditions. Before you agreed to anything, you could get all the relevant information. You made your decision free of any pressure or coercion.

But when we look around us, we cannot say that either of these conditions is met for an ordinary citizen in a large, modern democracy.

Reason 1: Information Sufficient for Informed Decision Is Hard to Get. First, to make a truly informed agreement to obey a society's laws, you have to know a great deal. Minimally, you need to know what the laws are. But remember that we are talking about an agreement that preserves your freedom and autonomy. This means that you should also know what the aims of the laws are. After all, laws are simply the means to achieve some greater end—a particular kind of society. How could you maintain your freedom and autonomy while agreeing to some means without knowing the ends it served? You couldn't. Furthermore, you would also need to know how any given law shapes your society's economic structure, its domestic and foreign policies, the quality of daily life. You would have to know all this to see the big picture.

But surely, most of us do not go into these complex issues in great depth. Many people know next to nothing about these matters because they're too busy trying to make ends meet. And can we say in fairness that someone who doesn't fully understand the laws is freely consenting to obey them? That doesn't fit our model of a free agreement very well. The average person, then, does not seem to be genuinely obligated.

You may not agree with this, of course. Perhaps you think that people really do understand all this. After all, almost everybody goes to school until they're at least 16. History and social studies classes give people the important facts. They may not be scholars, but they get a respectable picture of the laws and of their own country. We also have a free press to make sure that people get the whole story. It is easy to get the truth, you think. So if you're an adult and still living here, that can be taken as an agreement.

This may be what a school system and a free press *should* do. But some would say it doesn't work that way.[4]

Even free societies present biased views of themselves. Public educational systems in particular offer rosy pictures of life in a nearly perfect country where most things happen for the best. Policies are always humane and aspirations lofty. For example, in American history you probably heard about the glorious expansion of the country across the continent to the Pacific. But chances are you never discussed the moral justification for seizing the land from the people who were already living there. Similarly, you were no doubt taught that the Industrial Revolution was a tremendous boon to civilization. But you probably learned very little about how the land was ravaged, or the long-term effects of industrial pollution, or the extent to which unionism was opposed by factory owners. And if you were told anything about Socialism or Communism, it was surely how bad they are.

One reason schools work this way is that the people who pay for and control an institution naturally want it to support their ideas. And they want to make sure that the young people coming along behind them support their ideas too. People in power work very hard at staying there. It's not a conspiracy, it's just that public officials and school boards naturally want schools, run on public funds, to cultivate patriotism and an appreciation for democracy, even if it involves overstatement. They do not like criticism of the status quo, and they do not like teachers to suggest that any doubts exist. In general, the schools play an important role in perpetuating —not questioning—the main values and institutions of the society that funds them. Many people do not go on to college, and most who do never learn to think critically about these things. That leaves us with many otherwise well-educated people who do not fully understand the full implications of the social contract they have implicitly agreed to.

A free press does help people give an accurate picture of their society. But the major newspapers, magazines, and television networks present events very much as the schools do, in a way that basically supports the nation's institutions and policies. They too are sensitive to the disapproval of those with economic clout, including their advertisers, and those with political clout. Sometimes the pressure is subtle. Other times it is blatant. In any event, most of the news we hear about the country we grow up in is tilted in favor of the status quo.

In addition, even democratically elected governments have been known to lie to and conceal information from their own citizens as a matter of policy. Political leaders have also become increasingly savvy about using modern techniques to sell the citizenry on their policies. Ronald Reagan, for example, was called the "Great Communicator" for his ability to garner popular support for his programs and general policies. Yet he often oversimplified complicated matters, misstated facts, and

---

[4]What follows are some conclusions of an argument about democracy that I cannot take the space to offer, and I'm using them as premises. This obviously is not a full-dress philosophical argument, but you can argue this way as long as you're honest about it, you tell people what you are doing, and recognize the limitations of proceeding this way.

occasionally fabricated illustrative stories. Because most people tend to believe what legitimate authorities tell them, they are easily misled.

With so much information to master and so much bias to correct for, the average citizen has a slim chance of making fully informed decisions about either the laws or, more importantly, the character of his or her country. And a decision based on incomplete information is not consistent with free choice. In such a case, simply remaining in a country doesn't seem to qualify as freely accepting the terms of the social contract that this particular society is built on. Most people are simply too much in the dark.

Reason 2: Emotional Factors Color Our Decisions.

There is yet another problem. Even if you had all the information you needed to assess the "social contract" accurately and then decided to stay, your decision might still not be totally free. Under normal circumstances, the strength of people's emotional relationships with other members of their society constitutes a kind of pressure, and decisions that result from coercion or pressure cannot be regarded as totally free.

Much of our identity is tied up with our homes and families, and these powerful emotional attachments make it difficult for us to leave even the general area where we were brought up. Leaving our country is much more difficult. Except in extreme circumstances, most people find it almost impossible to sever the emotional connections to people and places they established while growing up. The psychological costs of uprooting ourselves from our native turf are just too high a price to pay. So we stay.

Your decision to remain in a society, then, may have nothing to do with the way that society is organized. You may actually disapprove of its laws, but still choose to remain because of stronger emotional connections. When someone's love for her family outweighs her dislike for the regime running her country, what kind of consent to the regime is she giving? In some fashion, of course, she is choosing to stay, and she knows that obeying the laws, no matter how obnoxious, is a consequence of her choice. But this is not the kind of free choice that genuinely respects her freedom and autonomy. How could any reasonable interpretation of this situation claim that this woman's continued presence in her society implies the kind of agreement that produces a solemn, fully binding obligation that is consistent with human freedom?

Reason 3: Our Options Are Limited.

Finally, even if you decide that you want to leave your country because you cannot accept the "terms" of the social contract, how feasible is that? For openers, your options are limited by the language you speak and the skills you know. You also need enough money to leave and to support yourself until you are established in a new place. In real life, most people do not have the wherewithal to leave.

But more important than language skills and money, you need some place to go. You need a genuine option. This may be hard to find in an imperfect world, and it probably means trading off one disadvantage for another. What if you cannot find another place to go? What if you're unhappy with the situation you're in and cannot find any place that gives you what you want? If you stay where you are under these conditions, is that a free choice? If you have only one option, can you be said to be choosing anything?

Does Staying Put Mean Free Consent?

So what does your continued presence in a society say? Possibly, as Locke and others suggest, it means you are fully aware of the situation and choose to be exactly where you are. In that case, it is fair and reasonable to call this a tacit consent to the "contract" that governs your society.

But things are not often this simple. You may not know enough about the laws and their aim to make an informed decision. Your emotional ties may make leaving too painful. Or perhaps you just have no realistic options. In light of all these possibilities, we cannot always infer a consent that is consistent with freedom and autonomy.

Consider the case of African Americans when slavery was outlawed but discrimination was legal. These people were technically free to leave the country, but they stayed. Is it reasonable to say that by remaining they gave tacit consent to these laws? Of course not. This would make them the authors of the very laws that oppressed them. No rational person would ever consent to laws that unfairly discriminated against him. If a black person were punished for riding in the front of a bus, it would be crazy to say that he or she consented to that simply by not leaving the country.

Now that we know what staying someplace does *not* mean, can we find out what it *does* mean? After all, if you are an intelligent, mature adult living in a society that you may leave, staying involves some choice on your part. Maybe that choice is not so fully informed and pressure-free that it produces an unequivocal political obligation; but nobody is forcing you at gunpoint to stay. Doesn't staying put convey some kind of tacit consent?

Yes, but maybe not what thinkers like Locke claim. The most we could get as an agreement might be, "I understand the nature of this society, and for my own reasons I choose to remain here. I know the laws and the punishments that follow from breaking them. If I obey the laws, it may very well be only to avoid the punishment. The best I can do is to agree not to be surprised if I'm punished for doing something the society judges 'wrong.'"

But if this is the only agreement we can find in the fact that someone remains in a society, that does not give us much of a social contract.

More Problems with Tacit Consent

You probably have some reservations about taking such a dim view of tacit consent. You might point out, for example, that people actually do leave democracies when they have powerful reasons to do so. Many young men moved from the United States to Canada to avoid fighting in the Vietnam War. Most blacks do not leave the country—although some do—but many move to states where they believe they will face less discrimination. Many people move from one country to another in search of a better life. It's not impossible to leave your home. This being so, then, why *can't* we say that staying put indicates a genuine agreement to obey the laws?

This argument that some people do void one "social contract" in favor of another is a good one. But all these people found themselves in extreme situations—fighting in a war they believed was immoral, suffering because of race, being unable to find a decent job. These examples show that when a situation becomes desperate, some people will find a way to leave. It also suggests that there are plenty of other people in the same situation who want to leave but cannot. And we can't say that those who do stay consent to the conditions they despair of but are powerless to avoid.

Still, remaining in a society probably does mean more than "I agree not to be surprised if I'm punished for breaking the law." Maybe it means that you agree to stay in the society because you have no better alternative that you are willing or able to pursue. You may not like everything where you are, and you don't approve of all of the laws. But you do agree to obey them because, for one thing, life will be safer and more stable if everyone obeys them. If everybody could choose which laws to obey, it would be chaos. At least this way everybody is bound by the same rules. So you agree—grudgingly, but you agree.

Grudging Agreement?

From a realistic standpoint, perhaps "grudging agreement" is a good way to describe the kind of tacit consent we are entitled to read from someone's remaining in a society. The phrase probably describes the situation of African Americans who stayed in this country when discrimination was legal. They surely did not endorse the laws that hurt them, but they chose to stay. Perhaps they believed that the situation would eventually improve. Perhaps they stayed because of emotional ties to their families and communities. Whatever the reason, they stayed put and obeyed the laws, at best "grudgingly." And when civil rights leaders set out to change the laws by civil disobedience, they accepted all the punishment society handed out. That is a clear sign that they thought that as long as they lived in the country, they were obliged to obey even bad laws.

How does this stand up to our criteria? Does a "grudging agreement" create a binding obligation consistent with our freedom and autonomy? It may look good so far, but the "grudging" part is troublesome in that it implies significant reservations about the terms of the social contract. For African Americans during legalized discrimination—and since—these reservations were extreme. But even people who face less basic problems but decide to stay put may have important reservations nonetheless.

We have consent here, but the situation is not as clean as we would like it to be. It's encumbered by reservations on the one hand and a lack of realistic options on the other. You may think differently, but particularly for people whose rights have been severely compromised, "grudging agreement" seems a poor basis for a political obligation.

Social Contracts In Practice

Does tacit consent ever legitimize the "social contract" of a community? If the parties to the contract generally know and approve of their society's laws and policies, tacit consent to a social contract is perfectly acceptable from a philosophical viewpoint. In this case, people have as much freedom and autonomy as they would if they were presented with a written document and gladly signed it.

But people may remain in a democracy for many other reasons—they are effectively socialized, they have formed strong emotional bonds, they have no real options. Or they may simply not know enough about the laws and their aims to make an informed decision. Social, economic, and personal pressures, the absence of alternatives, or the lack of informed consent all make it difficult to interpret someone's decision to remain in a society. Maybe that decision is free and well informed; maybe it isn't. Surely we want the situation to be clear when something as important as a binding political obligation is at stake.

It is doubtful, then, that obligations arising from tacit consent and "grudging agreement" genuinely respect freedom and autonomy. It's a tough problem, and much is at stake. As a citizen, you are obliged—even forced—to obey laws that may outrage you morally or harm you personally. You may die fighting in a war you disagree with. If you work in the criminal justice system, you may have to release known criminals because their rights to due process were violated. At the very least, you are legally bound to supply your tax money to pay for whatever your government does. If the social contract brings with it such heavy obligations, don't you want better guarantees than those you get with tacit consent that your decision is truly free and well informed?

Democracy or not, the odds seem to be skewed in favor of the house. We are entitled to decide about our political obligations freely and autonomously. But in a modern democracy there are too many pressures on most of us to say our decision is as free or self-interested as it ought to be.

Voting and Majority Rule

So far we have looked at a problem with democracy that stems from the difficulty in reconciling freedom with the obligations implied by a social contract. And we have seen that the traditional solution to this problem, tacit consent, works better in theory than in practice.

Another mechanism in a democracy that is supposed to ensure our freedom and autonomy is the ballot box. But is voting all it's cracked up to be? Does voting in fact solve the problems that tacit consent doesn't, or does it too fail?

What Is Good About Voting?

The theoretical argument for voting as a way of creating valid political obligations while at the same time protecting freedom and autonomy seems to be airtight.

The ballot box serves two purposes. First, it guarantees that a democracy is authentic by letting the people express their will. This is an essential check against rule by force, wealth, or family connection. Political offices go to those who garner the most votes. Popular referenda settle matters of public policy. Because voting lets the citizens appoint their leaders and chart the basic course these leaders should follow, it assures that their society is democratic, that is, that it is ultimately ruled by "the people." Second, casting a vote can also be seen as the way a citizen explicitly accepts his or her society's "social contract." When you vote, you agree to accept not only the outcome of the election but the rules on which your society is based.

Voting, then, seems to be a critical device for reconciling the freedom and autonomy of citizens with the authority of a democratic government. Voting produces a legitimate basis for saying we have a responsibility to obey laws. It also makes a government's authority philosophically legitimate. The ballot box (or voting machine) is the way we register our free consent to be governed. And that consent binds us to accept the resulting officials, policies, or laws.

All this sounds fine—as long as the votes are unanimous. If your teacher lets you vote on whether you want an exam or a paper as a final assignment and everybody goes for the exam, this truly expresses the "will of the people." Everyone gets exactly what he or she wants.

But what if the results of a vote are not unanimous? Traditionally, we do what the majority wants in a democracy. And we say that the losers have a philosophically legitimate obligation to accept this. But is this really the case?

Majority Rule

We must scrutinize the idea of majority rule for a couple of reasons. Majority rule is the basic working principle of democracy, so, if we want to make some general assessment about the philosophical legitimacy of democracy, we must consider this aspect of it. More important, however, there is a critical problem here. You have probably already noticed that majority rule respects our wishes—and protects our freedom and autonomy—only if the side we vote for wins. If it loses, do our obligations to our government remain intact, and if so, why?

Go back to the vote in your class on whether to have an exam or a paper. Let's say you vote "exam," and "paper" wins. You have to go along. But are you getting what you want? No. You have to do what other people want. Is this consistent with your freedom and autonomy? In one obvious way, yes. Your instructor did not arbitrarily force her will on the class. You had the opportunity to participate in a process that determined the outcome. In a more important way, however, your freedom and autonomy were ignored. You voted "exam," and now you're forced to write a paper.

Democracy's great virtue is supposed to be that it respects our freedom and autonomy. If majority rule is such a central part of democracy, shouldn't it somehow do the same? How do the supporters of democracy argue this point?

Locke on Majority Rule

Let's go back to John Locke, one of the proponents of the "social contract," because he clearly argues for majority rule. He writes:

> For when any number of men have, by the consent of every individual, made a community, they have thereby made that community one body, with a power to act as one body, which is only by the will and determination of the majority. For that which acts any community, being only the consent of the individuals of it, and it being one body must move one way, it is necessary the body should move that way whither the greater force carries it, which is the consent of the majority; or else it is impossible it should act or continue one body, one community, which the consent of every individual that united into it agreed that it should; and so every one is bound by that consent to be concluded by the majority. . . .
>
> For if the consent of the majority shall not in reason be received as the act of the whole and conclude every individual, nothing but the consent of every individual can

make anything to be the act of the whole; but such a consent is next to impossible ever to be had if we consider the infirmities of health and avocations of business which in a number, though much less than that of a commonwealth, will necessarily keep many away from the public assembly, and the variety of opinions and contrariety of interest, which unavoidably happen in all collections of men, 'tis next to impossible ever to be had. . . . For where the majority cannot conclude the rest, there they cannot act as one body, and consequently will be immediately dissolved again.

—Second Treatise of Government

Locke argues that for a variety of reasons, unanimity is impossible. He further claims that unless the community follows a particular direction in its actions—that is, follows a single position—it won't be one community any more. For example, if in time of war some citizens fight on one side of the dispute while other citizens fight on the other, we can hardly say we have one society any more. In essence Locke argues that in order to preserve the unity and coherence of the society, we have to abide by the will of the majority.

Locke's argument is a standard defense for majority rule in a democracy. His observation that unanimity is impossible is probably correct. That leaves the opinion of the majority as the next best way to run a community founded on a social contract. Locke illustrates this by drawing an analogy between a body and a society. A body can move in only one direction, and a society, he says, is just the same. The "greater force," that is, "the consent of the majority," must set that direction.

Locke's argument has its problems. For example, his body/society analogy doesn't work very well. A body may be able to move in only one direction, but a society is not a single living organism, and it can function quite well with its citizens taking different paths. It may be cumbersome and somewhat inefficient to manage, but it's not impossible. Consider the choice between a paper and an exam, again. What would be wrong with letting everyone select the option he or she preferred? Some of you write papers. Others take exams. It may be harder for the teacher to assign final grades, but it can be done.

Now apply this procedure to public policy. If a minority of citizens don't want their tax money spent on instruments of destruction, why not let those people designate what government programs they are willing to support? Again, this would be inconvenient, but it would not destroy society. Those willing to pay for weapons could pick up the slack if it meant that much to them. There are probably few, if any, issues that would lead to the dissolution of a society if the majority and minority were allowed to act on them as they wanted to.

Locke's belief that a society will dissolve if it follows something other than majority rule is wrong for another reason. "Consent of the governed" simply means that everyone agrees to the terms of the "social contract"—any terms. It might specify a single monarch, for example, or a governing committee, or a ruling class of scientists or philosophers. A social contract does not necessarily imply majority rule. After all, Thomas Hobbes uses the idea of a social contract to argue for the absolute authority of a king.

In order for Locke's argument to be convincing, we need some account of the special virtues of the majority. But neither Locke nor other champions of democracy argue very convincingly for why the majority is entitled to prevail. If everyone has equal rights, the rights of those in the majority cannot be more important than the rights of those in the minority. We have no guarantee that those in the majority are right, or that they support the best ideas, or that they are more fair, humane, or respectful of freedom and autonomy than those in the minority on a given issue. History is too full of examples in which the majority persecuted an innocent minority for anyone to suggest anything like that. So why is the majority so special?

Majority Rule as a Veiled Threat?

When it comes down to it, all we can say is that the majority outnumbers the minority. And that is saying nothing more than that if they wanted to, they could force the minority to do things their way. Perhaps announcing the will of the majority is simply a veiled threat to the minority: go along—or else.

But notice what happens to freedom here. In the best possible scenario, the only true freedom that those in the minority have is the freedom to express their opinions and cast their votes. After that, they are subject to coercion. Maybe we can say that by voting, the people who will ultimately lose freely agree to go along with the outcome in order to save themselves the pain of being forced to go along with it. But because the threat of coercion is there, can we really say that majority rule is consistent with freedom and autonomy?

Why Majority Rule?

If you are a dyed-in-the-wool defender of majority rule, you may think this argument is pretty far-fetched. After all, you might argue, freedom and autonomy are respected in an election based on majority rule. Ordinarily, freedom of expression is observed during any discussion of an issue. And the fact that you can vote however you want is another sign of freedom being respected. For that matter, the voting preserves our autonomy too. Nobody knows what the outcome of a vote will be, but by voting, everyone freely promises to go along with the result. In other words, the act of voting says, "I hereby freely authorize whatever the majority of voters wants," and this binds us to respect the outcome, whether we win or lose.

This does sound appealing. But it's misleading to stop at the election. Look at the results. The winners have gotten what they chose. They are truly autonomous—giving law to themselves—because they are obligated to do what they wanted. The losers' obligation is also claimed to be autonomous because they agreed to go along with the outcome. But the winners' and losers' situations are very different.

Go back to our vote on papers or exams. Only the people who voted "paper" are binding themselves to a responsibility they directly willed. They alone are truly autonomous. Everyone else bound themselves to the outcome by default, agreeing to it only if they lost. To tell the losers that their autonomy has been respected just as much as the winners' has seems a bit specious. The winners will do what they wanted to do; the losers will do what they don't want to do but must do. Aren't those two very different things?

"But that's what voting is all about," you say. "There have to be losers." Maybe so, and maybe majority rule is the only practical way to go. But this still leaves important theoretical questions unanswered. How philosophically legitimate and compelling is the obligation that the losers in an election stand under? And does majority rule genuinely respect freedom and autonomy as it should? After all, when we talk about whether democracy works the way it's supposed to, we're entitled to be idealistic.

Majority Rule as a Lesser of Evils?

We find, then, that the argument that majority rule guarantees the philosophical legitimacy of democracy has important weaknesses. We should look at one more practical argument in favor of majority rule, however. Recall the possibility that the "will of the majority" might be nothing more than a veiled threat of coercion against the minority. Let's see if we can build a respectable philosophical argument on the consequences of disobeying the majority.

From a practical standpoint, one of democracy's great virtues is that it allows for peaceful decision making. Fewer people get hurt settling an issue by voting on it than by fighting it out. If the people who lost a vote actively resisted the majority, many would get hurt. So we can say that human good is maximized if the minority goes along with the majority. The majority, being more powerful, could force the minority to get in line. Using a teleological argument, then, we can say that majority rule is at least somewhat acceptable because it limits the amount of harm that might otherwise come to those in the minority. Unfortunately, this is a bit like saying that if a robber threatens you with a gun, it is "better" to hand over your money. The analogy is a bit extreme, but it illustrates the point that abiding by the will of the majority limits the likelihood of harm.

This practical argument for majority rule does not exactly promote the traditional virtues of democracy. On the other hand, it may at least be more honest than an argument claiming that majority rule truly respects freedom and autonomy. And in philosophy, as in a democracy, there's always something to be said for honesty.

Majority Rule and Traditional Democratic Values

One final problem with majority rule that we need to consider is its relationship to traditional democratic values like fairness, equality, and a commitment to human rights. Consider the following possible outcomes of free and open democratic elections:

- The run-up to the election reveals that the society is sharply divided between two dramatically different perspectives on everything from civil rights and personal privacy to foreign policy. The victorious party wins by a razor-thin margin, and the new officials use their power to enact laws and policies that aggressively advance only their point of view. That is, the preferences of nearly half of the population are completely ignored. The victors' attitude is that because they won the election, they get to use their power as they see fit. The minority complains that this is unfair, but the officials believe that they have no obligation to respect the perspective of the defeated minority—even if it amounts to millions of people.

- In another election, the majority puts into power officials who have announced that they will enact laws that will, for example, favor men over women, one religion over all others, and one race over all others. When they proceed with this program, the minority objects to the laws as violations of basic human rights. The government, however, defends the new laws as the fruit of a democratic process and an expression of "the will of the people" of that society.

If you are a strong defender of majority rule, be sure to resist the temptation to dismiss these as bad examples to use in a discussion like this because the two new governments are being "undemocratic"—that is, they aren't respecting traditional democratic values. Principles like fairness, equality, and tolerance may be honored by most democracies, but it's not required in order to be a democracy. If "democracy" means "rule by the people," and if a majority of the citizens votes to curtail the freedoms of a minority, strictly speaking, there's nothing "undemocratic" about this.[5] We can object on ethical grounds, of course. But the fact that we can do so is one more reminder that majority rule can actually end up threatening the very values that many democracies are created to protect.

Democracy: Major Problems

Although democracy has much going for it, its philosophical legitimacy is not nearly as clear and simple as we're generally led to believe. In theory, the social contract seems like a great way to generate political obligations while at the same time preserving the freedom and autonomy of those who undertake those obligations. In practice, however, this is difficult to pull off. Unfortunately, majority rule—one of the most basic tools of democracy—may not even fare well in theory.

Notice, then, that we are left with largely teleological grounds for the legitimacy of the social contract or of the obligation to obey the will of the majority. If you agree "grudgingly" to a society's terms, or if you remain in a country with oppressive or discriminatory laws, or if you accept the outcome that you voted against in an election, you're probably concluding simply that you have no better options. As much as you dislike the current situation, you think that any alternative would be worse. At best, if you generalize from your own situation and think that everyone in your society has a duty to obey the laws because the alternative would be anarchy, you're giving a basically utilitarian defense of political obligation. And that's a far cry from grounding obligation in freedom and autonomy.

But if freedom and autonomy are no longer our benchmark, the door is wide open to consider whether some form of government other than democracy might

---

[5]It wouldn't be surprising if your first reaction to the two examples in this section was to dismiss them as "undemocratic" and, therefore, as poor examples of a possible weakness with majority rule. The way that terms are used in political discussions is much less precise than, for example, the way terms are used in scientific discussions. So it's not at all unusual for people to stretch the meaning of "democracy" to something like "rule by the people for the purpose of advancing such basic human rights as freedom, equality, and the like." Deliberately using (even distorting) terms in a way that advances a political agenda is a common feature of contemporary political discourse. For example, the way that the terms "liberal," "conservative," and "libertarian" are used bears little resemblance to what they have historically meant. "Liberal" has traditionally referred to an outlook that strongly supports personal freedom, civil liberties, and social change; "conservative" means a preference to maintain the status quo; and "libertarianism" argues for maximum individual liberty and a very limited role for government. Some might say that liberalism and libertarianism are built on a relatively optimistic view of human nature (left to their own devices, individuals will find ways to improve things). Conservatism, on the other hand, generally takes a dimmer view of individual freedom and believes that human good is best achieved through the preservation of traditional norms and limited change in society.

not, on balance, do a better job. Many philosophers have thought so, among them Plato. For the rest of this chapter, then, we look at Plato's analysis of the weaknesses of democracy and see what kind of government he thinks is better.

Plato's Ideas on Government

It might surprise you to hear that one of the most important philosophers of ancient Greece is not an admirer of democracy. When Plato describes his ideal society in the *Republic,* he steers clear of democracy. In fact, there is only one kind of government he thinks is worse than democracy, and that is tyranny.

Why would a great thinker who lived in "the birthplace of democracy" judge so harshly the form of government we all take to be enlightened and humane? And what does he suggest as a better alternative?

Plato's Criticisms of Democracy

The Death of Socrates

Plato's rejection of democracy is ultimately based on a personal tragedy—the trial and death of his teacher Socrates. The story, in brief, is this. Many Athenians misunderstood Socrates' lifelong mission of challenging people to scrutinize their most basic beliefs and encouraging them to live more virtuously. After Athens lost a war to Sparta, Socrates' enemies, taking advantage of the hard times and the frustration in the air, intimated that his relentless questioning had in fact weakened Athens. They indicted and tried him for the capital offenses of impiety and corrupting the Athenian youth.

Scholars continue to debate the precise nature of the situation in Athens that led to these charges against Socrates. But this much is clear. Socrates was a deeply religious person who wanted to help other people by encouraging them to live an examined, virtuous life. He presented no threat to the city, but he lost in court because his accusers were able to stir up the feelings of the 501 people in the jury. Instead of weighing the evidence calmly and dispassionately, the jury allowed their anger and frustration to influence their verdict. Emotions prevailed over reason, and Socrates was convicted and executed. The sight of his good and decent teacher being condemned to death by a democratic court taught the young Plato a devastating lesson about the dark side of "rule by the people." Irrational fear and hunger for revenge won over truth and justice.

Nor could Plato dismiss this as a freak event. He had already seen how irrational and dangerous democracy could be. Earlier in the war with Sparta, Athens had won a naval battle. But because of a violent storm, the commanders in charge were unable to rescue many Athenian soldiers and sailors whose ships had been destroyed or who had fallen into the sea. Outraged, the Athenians tried the ten commanders as a group and sentenced them to death—even though such group trials were specifically prohibited by Athenian law. The Athenians subsequently admitted their error, but not before the six officers who were in Athens at the time of the uproar had been executed. As in Socrates' case, this tragedy happened because emotion overpowered reason. Plato saw this propensity for "rule-by-the-people" to make emotional rather than rational decisions a devastating flaw at the very heart of democracy.

The Rise of the Sophists

Plato also witnessed the growing popularity in democratic Athens of a group of men called "Sophists." Teachers of rhetoric (the art of public speaking), the Sophists represented for Plato another flaw in democracy—the ease with which ignorance can triumph over knowledge. His main character in the *Gorgias* (see Chapter 6), named for one of the most famous Sophists of the day, explains the power of rhetoric this way:

> On many occasions in the past, in the company of my brother and other physicians, I have made calls on patients who were unwilling to take their medicine or submit to an operation or a cautery; and though their doctor could not persuade them, I did so, by no other art than rhetoric. And I make the further declaration that if a rhetorician and a physician should come to any city you please and have occasion to debate in the assembly or any other public gathering as to which of them ought to be elected public physician, the doctor would be utterly eclipsed, and the capable speaker would, if he chose, be elected. And likewise in a contest with any other craftsman whatsoever, the rhetorician would win his own election against all opposition of any kind; for not a single craftsman is able to speak in a crowd, on any subject in the world, more persuasively than the rhetorician. This is to show you how great and how splendid is the power of his art.

Subsequently in the dialogue, Gorgias admits that speaking before "the people" is the same as speaking before "the ignorant." To win an argument or to win an election, you don't have to know what you're talking about. All you need to do is to speak persuasively.

Whatever the reasons, Plato saw critical weaknesses in democracy. Emotion and ignorance, he believed, often come out ahead over reason and knowledge. "The people" usually do not know enough about the issue under discussion to make a rational, informed judgment. And even when they are presented with the facts, the disposition of Socrates' case shows that their emotions can easily overpower their intellect. In Plato's opinion, "rule by the people" is chaotic, inconsistent, uninformed, unpredictable, and dangerous. "The people's" decisions can too easily result from emotions and ignorance, whereas just decisions must be anchored in the impartial, fair, objective, well-informed evaluation of facts.

The Validity of Plato's Criticisms

Plato is harsh on democracy. Do you think his criticisms are legitimate or exaggerated? Do they apply only to ancient Athens where early, "primitive" democracy was working out some of the kinks? Have modern democracies evolved to the point where we can say that Plato's objections do not apply to democracy itself? Unfortunately, Plato's critique probably applies even more accurately to today's large-scale, modern democracy.

Modern democracies have not always protected innocent people any better than Athenian democracy protected Socrates. When democracy was established in the United States, the Founding Fathers explicitly rejected an attempt to prohibit slavery in the colonies. It took another century to outlaw slavery and yet another century to ban discrimination on the basis of race or sex. And remember that

Adolf Hitler rose to power in a modern democracy. (So much for democracy guaranteeing justice.)

Look at the role of emotion in democracy. Consider political campaigns, either for political candidates or for special issues to be voted on in a referendum. Everything we hear or read during a campaign tries to get us to love one candidate and distrust or fear his or her opponent. Emotionalism, exaggeration, and character assassination—so-called "negative campaigning"—are commonplace in modern political rhetoric. Such campaigning arouses negative feelings toward its target by stirring up emotions rather than by presenting facts.

Also consider how complex the issues are in modern democracies—a global economy, environmental pollution, volatile international relations, poverty, hunger, the national debt, the balance of trade. How many people do you think really understand enough about these topics to cast a well-informed vote? Not many. Most of us couldn't study these issues the way we should even if we wanted to. Most of us, therefore, vote in a state of relative ignorance. This, in turn, means that we make our decisions based on impressions, feelings, and prejudices rather than on facts.

If democracy still has such weaknesses after 2,000 years, we probably have to concede that they are basic features of this form of government, not temporary problems.

Plato's Solution

If Plato criticizes democracy, what does he propose in its place? This may sound odd to you, but you might as well hear it: Plato wants philosophers to rule—yes, philosophers. As he says in a very famous passage from the *Republic,*

> Cities will have no respite from evil . . . nor will the human race, I think, unless philosophers rule as kings in the cities, or those whom we now call kings and rulers genuinely and adequately study philosophy, until, that is, political power and philosophy coalesce.

Philosophers in charge? Is he kidding? Just imagine what it would be like if the people in your school's philosophy department ran the country. Most of you would think that a prescription for disaster! Philosophers often live so much in the world of ideas that they don't know—or care—what day it is. You probably think that running things is the last thing philosophers should be doing, and you'd probably recommend leaving them in the classroom where they can't hurt themselves.

Yet as Plato sees things, the emotionalism and ignorance of "the people" make them virtually incapable of good judgment. Philosophers, at least, are bright enough to understand the range and complexity of the problems that leaders face and rational enough to resist their emotions. And when you think of it, philosophers are usually not enslaved by passions or driven by greed. They tend to be intelligent, controlled, and idealistic—not bad qualities for political leaders. Clearly, there are worse people to run societies than philosophers.

Still, you may not be convinced because Plato's suggestion seems unrealistic. A philosopher doesn't exactly inspire confidence as a political leader if he or she goes around asking things like "How do you know that the furniture in your room doesn't disappear when you aren't there?" Still, Plato believes he is being practical, so let's approach his idea from another angle.

A Questionnaire

You may have an easier time understanding what's behind Plato's thinking once you take a few minutes to answer this questionnaire.

Using a scale of −5 to +5, rate how much you enjoy the following activities or how important they are to you:

1. buying and having things
2. trying to solve the crime in mysteries
3. dancing and/or partying
4. knowing that someone loves or cares about you a great deal
5. thinking about the meaning of life
6. having sexual pleasure
7. being impulsive and spontaneous
8. making decisions in a calm, logical manner
9. having deep friendships
10. being in good shape physically
11. analyzing why people do things
12. doing something adventurous
13. having a "signature scent" or wearing various colognes or perfumes
14. discussing serious, intellectual topics
15. eating your favorite foods
16. doing something romantic
17. being logical
18. understanding yourself
19. looking good
20. making new friends
21. attending an interesting lecture
22. being popular
23. making or having money
24. watching a movie that evokes strong feelings (love story, scary film, tragedy, etc.)

Now add up your scores in the following three groups.

Group A: questions 1, 3, 6, 10, 13, 15, 19, 23

Group B: questions 4, 7, 9, 12, 16, 20, 22, 24

Group C: questions 2, 5, 8, 11, 14, 17, 18, 21

You should now have three scores: an A score, a B score, and a C score. Hold on to them for the time being while we return to Plato's argument.

Plato's View of Human Nature: Three Types of People

Once you understand Plato's ideas about human nature, you will better understand his political philosophy. Plato's ideas about government are based on his notion that all people fall into one of three types, depending upon which of three basic parts of their being dominates their nature. These elements, according to Plato, are *physical desires,* the *emotions,* and the *intellect.* Each of us has all three, but one part usually predominates.

In "physical people," the body dominates. This can come out in anything from an ongoing search for physical pleasures to a desire for money and material comforts to a very strong interest in athletics or physical fitness. This category includes those whose first concern is to be rich, people strongly motivated by luxuries, people who get more pleasure from working out than from participating in a good discussion, and people whose lives revolve around food, alcohol, or sex. This physical focus can be expressed positively or negatively. Being concerned with staying in shape is positive; aspiring to the "good life" is fine, as long as it's kept within limits; being addicted to drugs or alcohol is negative. In any case, "physical people" make physical and material things the most important parts of their lives. They have emotional and intellectual interests as well, but these are less compelling and less satisfying.

In another type of person, emotions hold sway. "Feeling people" get their greatest satisfaction from emotional things. They may make romantic relationships the most important part of their lives. They may devote themselves to caring for others, getting emotional nourishment in the process. Such people may be artists, social workers, or nurses, for example. As with a "physical" orientation, an "emotional" orientation can be positive or negative. One person may be attracted to doomed love affairs, another to healthy relationships. One may get the Nobel Peace Prize, another may die as a terrorist seeking vengeance. And like "physical people," "emotional people" have all three components in their personalities. It's just that feelings dominate.

The "intellectual person" may enjoy physical and emotional pleasures perfectly well but is more strongly drawn to intellectual interests. Such people live to learn new things, understand the world around them, solve problems. They may be scholars or scientists, but they may also be writers, detectives, psychiatrists, management consultants, architects, or anyone else motivated by an intellectual challenge. Most at home in the world of ideas, they are driven to understand things. They hunger for intellectual stimulation. Again, this quality can show itself positively—scientists like Albert Einstein and Stephen Hawking—or negatively—some brilliant criminal who executes the "perfect crime."

Now take out the results of the questionnaire you answered earlier. This is not a scientific instrument with guaranteed accuracy, but your scores should tell you roughly which of the three types you are. If your A score is highest, you are probably a "physical" person. "Feeling" people will have a high B score. And if C is highest, you are most likely an "intellectual" person. Two or even all three of your scores may be pretty close, but most people have one that is highest. See if your category is right. Ask other people in your class if they think it's accurate. Odds are you'll find that one of Plato's categories describes you pretty well.

It's also interesting that in a representative group, the C people will make up the smallest group. Plato thinks that such people comprise a decided minority of the population, and if you check out the scores of your class, you will probably find this conclusion borne out, too.

Plato's Ideal Government

The Philosopher/Ruler. The point of all this is that Plato's notions about personality types provide the basis for his ideas about government. His "intellectual" person is who he means when he talks about a "philosopher." It is intelligent, rational, idealistic people, then, not professional academics, who should run a society. Such people, Plato thinks, have the intelligence to comprehend the intricacies of social, political, and economic problems. They can be trusted to make decisions for the common good. And their physical and emotional desires are sufficiently under control to make them difficult to bribe or seduce.

Strictly speaking, the kind of government Plato suggests here is the rule of an *aristocracy*. But this isn't what you think it is. Most of us use "aristocracy" to refer to a hereditary nobility. But the word literally means "rule by the best," or "rule by the most capable," and that is how Plato uses it. His ideal government is made up of "experts"—those people best suited for the job.

And what is that job? Remember that the sole purpose of a government is to look after the rights and interests of its members. Plato would say that only "philosophers," as he defines them, have the expertise and the disposition to do this. When you think about it, an aristocracy of "philosopher/rulers" certainly could promote the same goals traditionally held by democracies—freedom, equality, toleration of differences, respect for individual rights, laws and policies that aid those in need. The big difference, according to Plato, is that an aristocracy made up of a limited group of experts has a better chance of achieving these goals.

The Selection of Experts. It shouldn't surprise you to hear that Plato's philosopher/rulers are not chosen by popular vote. What expert is elected? Are medical licenses given out by a vote of the general public? No, aspiring physicians have to go through medical school and an internship; then they take state examinations and go through a residency. Lawyers, architects, veterinarians, teachers, clergy, psychologists, electricians, beauticians, and most other experts also must go through some certification process. Even people who drive cars must get licenses.

The idea behind certification is that people are not automatically competent to do jobs that require advanced knowledge and training just because they want to or because a majority of people say they should. The stakes are too high. Who determines that people are in fact competent? Others who already practice the profession and can determine whether a candidate has the necessary knowledge and skills—*not* the general public, or a even a small group of nonpractitioners.

In a democracy, of course, political office-holders are one of the few groups of people performing important tasks who are chosen by nonexperts, that is, by "the people." And too often, in the United States, at least, personality plays a large part in the people's choice. Plato thinks this is a poor way to identify the most competent people for the job. He applies to politicians the same selection procedures we use for most experts. He recommends years of training, testing, and apprenticeship in lower positions. Before someone starts to wield real political authority, she or he has demonstrated clear-cut abilities. Plato also suggests that rulers adhere to strict conditions that make it almost impossible for them to betray their public trust.[6]

Note that neither voting nor majority rule has any place in Plato's scheme. Plato thinks that citizens are too easily misled by ignorance or emotion to make wise choices. So, just as we leave decisions about our next generation of lawyers, nurses, teachers, and physicians to experts, so he leaves the decision about who qualifies as a philosopher/ruler to experts in that arena. There's nothing democratic about it.

B. F. Skinner's Walden Two: A Nondemocratic Ideal Society?

Is rule by experts better than rule by the people? As with so many other philosophical questions, you will have to make up your own mind. At issue here is whether or not Plato's (or anyone else's) nondemocratic government can do a better job than democracy. You've heard Plato's criticisms of democracy and his alternate suggestions. And Plato is not alone on this score. Hardly any philosophers who describe their idea of the ideal society ("utopia") make the government democratic. In fact, even modern utopian theorists favor an aristocracy in one form or another.

It is surprising that modern utopian thinkers would not recommend democracy. After all, we might think that in 2,000 years, democratic societies could have figured out how to preserve the strengths but eliminate the weaknesses of "rule by the people." Let's conclude this chapter, then, by taking a quick look at the nondemocratic government that B. F. Skinner describes in his imaginary utopian society "Walden Two" and see if it helps us resolve any issues about the efficacy of democracy.

You already know from Chapter 3 that B. F. Skinner represents a school of psychology called behaviorism. You may also remember that although psychology and philosophy are now separate disciplines, they were once one, and philosophers and psychologists to this day remain concerned with similar basic questions about the human experience. In *Walden Two*, Skinner constructs his ideal society on a precise notion of what we need to be. Skinner's utopia makes the connection between human nature and human happiness quite clear. And he thinks that we don't need democracy in order to be happy.

Walden Two

Skinner builds his community on his belief that we need only five things in order to live a satisfying life: health, a minimum of unpleasant labor, a chance to exercise our talents and abilities, intimate and satisfying personal contacts, and relaxation and rest. He locates his utopia in modern-day America. The community's name, Walden Two, is borrowed from Henry David Thoreau's experiment in living at Walden Pond.

Primarily an agricultural community, Walden Two provides space for private living quarters and communal dining, work, and recreation. A relatively small population of about 1,000 members enjoys a life that is comfortable and uncrowded.

---

[6]You probably have many questions about how such a government would work and how these philosopher/rulers are selected and trained. Plato explains all this in his classic work, the *Republic*. I encourage you to study that book if you find Plato's ideas intriguing.

Although Walden Two uses money in dealing with the outside world, it does not use it internally. Residents get what they need in the way of goods and services by accumulating a particular number of "labor credits" throughout the year. Different jobs have different values, with the less desirable jobs worth more. On average, people reach their annual total by working only four hours a day, thereby giving them much free time. People select their own occupations.

The social organization of Walden Two does not promote unlimited personal choice. The number of people allowed to practice certain professions, for example, is limited by the needs of the community. Of course, the educational system introduces people to a variety of attractive job opportunities, and the social system works to eliminate feelings of jealousy.

On the other hand, a number of Walden Two's customs are aimed at increasing the freedom and opportunities for women. Women are encouraged to begin having children in their teens and to finish with childbearing by their early twenties. This puts them at less of a disadvantage in developing their careers than women in our society. Other customs promote personal liberty for all people. For example, privacy is so highly valued that almost all adults, even those who are married, have private rooms.

Even though Walden Two is part of the United States and, thus, is subject to state and federal laws, it has the equivalent of its own government that runs the community. But Walden Two is not a democracy, and the people in charge are not political officials in the ordinary sense of that term. In fact, their "government" is closer to what you might find in a corporation, with its board of directors at the top and an array of executives and managers responsible for different parts of the company.

Walden Two has two kinds of authorities: Planners and Managers. There are six Planners—three men and three women—who serve for ten years. "They make policies," writes Skinner, "review the work of the community, keep an eye on the state of the nation in general. They also have certain judicial functions." Serving as a Planner counts for only half of a person's labor credits; the rest must be earned by regular labor. Planners are limited to one ten-year term. They select their own replacements from names suggested by the Managers.

The Managers are "specialists in charge of the divisions and services of Walden Two." There are Managers for food, health, play, arts, dentistry, dairy, various industries, supply, labor, nursery school, advanced education, clothing for women, marriages, personal behavior, cultural behavior, public relations, law, politics, and many other facets of the community's life. People work up to being Managers by a long period of apprenticeship in lower positions of responsibility. Like the Planners, Managers must earn half their labor credits by ordinary labor. By doing at least a couple of hours of manual labor each day, the "officials" keep in touch with the ordinary reality of the community.

Neither Planners nor Managers are elected. Rather, they are selected according to their expertise and commitment to the welfare of the community. Thus, life in Walden Two has no political dimension to speak of. No one discusses whom to vote for or what local policies to support or reject. Citizens have no say in such matters and presumably no interest either.

Nor does the average resident take any real interest in the politics of the outside world. There is a Political Manager who follows politics and decides which county, state, and national candidates will favor Walden Two's interests. Together with the Planners, he or she draws up a "Walden Ticket" for which all the residents vote.

But even though Walden Two is not democratic, don't assume that it has a ruling elite that might someday turn into tyrants. First, even though residents don't vote, they still have "input." About once a year all residents are interviewed to see if they have any particular problems or dissatisfactions and if they would like to have anything changed. Second, the Planners can serve only one term in office, after which they return to being regular citizens, and this limits the amount of power that any one person can acquire in the community. Finally, and perhaps most important, Walden Two does everything possible to prevent hero worship in the community. Because the Planners are largely invisible to the citizenry, they cannot amass large personal followings and use them to seize control. The Managers too have only limited power. People choose their own jobs, and Managers have no authority to order anyone around from outside their area of responsibility. Managers are responsible to the Planners, but their success at their work depends on the goodwill they can generate with the people under them—an interesting way to limit abuse of power.

Even though Walden Two is not a democracy, it is firmly committed to the happiness of its members. As one of the Planners points out:

> The government of Walden Two has the virtues of democracy, but none of its defects. It is much closer to the theory or intent of democracy than the actual practice in America today. The will of the people is carefully ascertained. We have no election campaigns to falsify issues or obscure them with emotional appeals, but a careful study of the satisfaction of the membership is made. Every member has a direct channel through which he may protest to the Managers or even the Planners. And these protests are taken as seriously as the pilot of an airplane takes a sputtering engine. We do not need laws and a police force to compel a pilot to pay attention to a defective engine. Nor do we need laws to compel our Dairy Manager to pay attention to an epidemic among his cows. Similarly, our Behavioral and Cultural Managers need not be compelled to consider grievances. A grievance is a wheel to be oiled, or a broken pipe to be repaired.

Is Skinner right? Can we actually achieve the traditional goals of democracy (the welfare of the citizens) more efficiently and more effectively through "rule by experts" than through "rule by the people"?

Democracy: A Final Word

The questions raised in this chapter give you much to think about, maybe too much. Such a hard look at one of the most basic institutions of the country you call home may have made you nervous. We're not generally encouraged to do things like this.

Nonetheless, examining the most fundamental features of life is a big part of what philosophy is all about. It is important to understand the world we live in. It is also important if we are serious about making the world a better place for all of us. Questions about the strengths and weaknesses of our society's basic institutions must rest on knowledge. By learning what our system's strengths are, we can keep from changing what works. By dissecting its weaknesses, we can see how to correct them. And none of this is possible without honest, unbiased, philosophical scrutiny of the issues.

So now go back to the scenario that began this chapter. In light of what we've discussed, how strong is your obligation to obey the law and to serve in the Peace Corps? Did the process respect your freedom and autonomy? Did your voting in the referendum obligate you to accept the outcome? Does more good than harm— for you, for the society in general, for people in other countries—come from obeying the law? Does the fact that this law resulted from a democratic process matter?

Main Points of Chapter 7

1. The philosophical legitimacy of democracy has generally been defended on ethical grounds and an appeal to fundamental human rights, freedom, and autonomy. The special attribute of democracy is that it claims to respect human freedom and autonomy while making it legitimate to require citizens to obey laws.

2. A critical concept for harmonizing freedom and obligation is the social contract, and an important mechanism for forming this agreement is tacit consent.

3. For a variety of reasons, Locke's understanding of tacit consent may not meet the requirements for a binding agreement. There is good reason to wonder whether tacit consent is an action that is sufficiently free and informed. In particular, it is questionable whether simply remaining in a society can be reasonably interpreted as constituting a binding social contract.

4. Voting and majority rule are also hallmarks of democracy. There are serious questions, however, about the extent to which they result in a genuinely binding obligation on the part of the minority who loses.

5. A different criticism of democracy is leveled by Plato, who is sensitive to the role of emotions in democracy and the ease with which ignorance can triumph over knowledge.

6. Instead of democracy, Plato favors an intellectual aristocracy, a government of philosophers who have been trained to be experts in ruling.

7. B. F. Skinner also recommends a nondemocratic government in his utopian community "Walden Two," arguing that it has all of the virtues of democracy but none of its weaknesses.

Discussion Questions

1. This chapter calls the legitimacy of our society's political system into question. Is that appropriate? If you believe that democracy should not be questioned in a democratic state, how would you defend yourself against a charge of treating a political idea as if it were a religious belief? How would you defend yourself against the charge of censorship?

2. How do you react to the idea that your continued presence in a society can be taken as an unspoken acceptance of a "social contract"? Would it be better to ask

everyone to sign a document when they reach 18? Would it be possible to specify everything that would have to be in such a document?

3. What are the terms of the "social contract" in your society? Are they terms that you would freely agree to?

4. In light of the forces of socialization, the emotional connections we form, and the picture of our society that our educational system and the mass media portray, would it be possible for the average American citizen to make a free and informed decision about accepting or rejecting a "social contract"?

5. One of Plato's major criticisms of democracy is the power of emotion and the role it plays in political life. How does our own democracy measure up on that score? How much do political speeches and campaigns appeal to emotion? Is it enough for us to share Plato's reservations?

6. What do you think of Plato's ideas about "philosopher/rulers"? Why would it *not* be better than the system we have?

7. How would you react to limiting political office to people with certain characteristics, interests, established strengths, and personality types—people who are idealistic, truthful, motivated to help other people more than themselves, unlikely to be bribed, and so on?

Selected Readings

For a series of discussions about democracy, ranging from antiquity to the contemporary world, see *The Development of the Democratic Idea,* edited by Charles M. Sherover (New York: New American Library, 1974). Hobbes's ideas about the "social contract" are spelled out in his work entitled *Leviathan,* Rousseau's in *Of the Social Contract,* and Locke's in his *Second Treatise of Government.* For a modern social contract approach, see John Rawls' highly influential *A Theory of Justice* (Cambridge, MA: Harvard University Press, 1971). For Plato's theory of the "philosopher/king" and his idea that there are three types of individuals, see the *Republic.* For a series of essays that debate the character and merits of Plato's political ideas, see *Plato: Totalitarian or Democrat?,* edited by Thomas Landon Thorson (Englewood Cliffs, NJ: Prentice Hall, 1963). For Skinner, see *Walden Two* (New York: Macmillan, 1948).

The Nature of Reality

Imagine that you're told that everything you think about what's "real" is wrong. Everything you see, hear, taste, and smell is an illusion. Neither events that you're part of nor events that you're observing around you are actually happening. All of your memories are of things that never took place. In effect, you're asleep and living in a dream world. What would you do if someone offered you a way to wake up and learn the truth? What if the offer had a catch—that once you saw the truth, you could never go back to the illusion? You're offered two pills—a red pill and a blue pill. The red one will give you the truth; the blue one will make you forget everything you've just heard and put you back in the dream.

This, of course, is the premise of *The Matrix* film series. Thomas Anderson is a computer program writer and a skilled hacker who goes by the name "Neo." Neo is contacted by the legendary hacker Morpheus who confirms Neo's unsettling fears that things aren't really what they seem to be. As Morpheus puts it when he and Neo first meet, "Let me tell you why you're here. You're here because you know something. What you know you can't explain. But you feel it. You felt it your entire life. Something's wrong with the world. You don't know what, but it's there." Morpheus reveals to Neo that what he thinks is "reality" is actually a computer simulation called "the Matrix." All humans—except the 250,000 living in the hidden rebel city of Zion—are hardwired into a "neural-interactive simulation" that conceals the truth. What Neo thinks is "real" is simply electrical impulses that are part of a computer simulation determining his perceptions. "Reality" is actually "virtual reality."

We thus have the classic philosophical distinction between *appearance* and *reality*. What everyone experiences in the Matrix—ordinary life in 1999—is simply *appearance*. In *reality*, however, it is hundreds of years in the future. Humanity has lost a war against a race of intelligent machines, is now enslaved, and is being used as a source of energy for the machines. The Matrix creates the life that people think they're living—a virtual reality—by sending electrical impulses to the brain. In essence, everyone connected to the Matrix is living in a dream that they will never wake up from. As Morpheus explains to Neo, the Matrix is "the world that has been pulled over your eyes to blind you from the truth . . . that you are a slave, Neo. Like everyone else, you were born into bondage, born into a prison that you cannot smell or taste or touch. A prison for your mind."

So, how curious are you about reality? What is the relationship between "reality" and how the world appears to us through our senses and minds? How close is the way the world appears to how it really is? Which pill will you take?

So far in this book, we've looked at a variety of basic aspects of human life—freedom, morality, political obligation. But as fundamental as those topics are, philosophy gets even more basic. In this chapter we get down to rock bottom as we explore one of the most fundamental issues in metaphysics—the nature of reality.

What's "Real"?

You might be saying to yourself, "Isn't 'reality' obvious? I know perfectly well what's real and what's not." Common sense tells you, for example, that this book is real. You can see it and touch it. You can measure it, weigh it, and describe its other properties.

Material objects we experience with our senses do have a concrete reality. Does this mean, however, that immaterial things we cannot see or touch or hear—like the ideas in our minds—are not real? If your model case for something real is a physical object, you might be tempted to say that ideas exist only in the sense that they are "mental." They have no physical dimensions—they're only concepts; therefore, they don't really exist.

Some concepts, of course, do represent imaginary things. Think of mythological creatures: the phoenix—the beautiful bird that lives for 500 years, then consumes itself in a fire and rises again from its own ashes; Pegasus—the flying horse; or the centaur—half man, half horse. We can picture these creatures and tell stories about them, but we know that it's all a fiction. The statement "Pegasus is a horse with wings" may be true in a certain way, but few would say that Pegasus is "real."

But look at another world populated by immaterial objects—mathematics. Like mythological beasts, the objects of mathematics—numbers, circles, squares, triangles, lines, and points—exist in our minds. Physical objects do occasionally take on geometrical shapes, of course. And we use numbers to count, weigh, and measure tangible things. But at its core, mathematics is entirely conceptual. The substance of mathematics is different from the substance of mythology, however, and it is hard to write off the immaterial objects and truths of mathematics as creations of the human imagination—like Pegasus. For example, you know what "two" means, and you know it stands for the concept of duality or "twoness." No matter how many different notions we pair it with or how we express it—two dogs, two cats, *deux* waves, *duo* cars—"two" remains the same concept. You can even think of the idea of "two" apart from any physical object. However, even though numbers are immaterial, we rely on them when we want to describe physical objects. Weights and measurements are given in numbers. How could numbers not be real when they are such a basic part of physical reality? They aren't physically real in themselves, but aren't they real in some other way?

Or think about the objects of geometry, which also lack physical existence. Lines and points have no dimensions, and things without dimension are physically impossible. Yet, as you know, a line can be subdivided an infinite number of times.

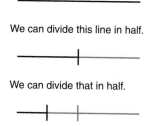

We can divide this line in half.

We can divide that in half.

And we can go on dividing the remainder an infinite number of times. No matter how small a piece we have left, dividing it in half still leaves us with something. At some point, of course, your lines will overlap or what is left will be too small to see. But this doesn't disprove what we just said about dividing the line. And if that remains true, doesn't it mean that things that have no dimension like lines and points are real, even though we encounter them only in our minds?

Then there are still other immaterial entities. Consider the world of science. Most of us would say that "gravity" is real, but we don't observe it directly as much as we see its effects. Subatomic particles are even trickier to discuss. Scientists largely infer their existence from other evidence. But aren't electrons "real"? Science also hypothesizes about the existence of natural forces, natural laws, and a host of other entities until some experimental data prove or disprove them. If a theoretical entity makes a scientific explanation work, is it real or isn't it?

In addition, almost everyone accepts that some immaterial things exist, even though they are invisible. Many people believe in some kind of religion, one that posits a god or gods, spirits of one sort or another that help or hinder things, immortal souls enjoying an afterlife. Some people believe in a psychic world with its spirit guides or in astrology with its astral and planetary forces. If you believe in any of these things—despite the fact that they aren't physically observable—you think that they are *real*.

Finally, what about things like "love" and "goodness"? Do these words refer to something immaterial that actually exists, or are they just shorthand terms for certain behaviors or emotions?

Clearly, "What is *real*?" is not as easy a question to answer as it first seems. Physical objects, imaginary beings, the objects of mathematics and science, and spiritual entities all seem to be *real* in one way or another. But then we have a confusing situation, because it's hard to arrive at one definition of reality that describes so many different things.

Virtually every philosopher tangles with the questions, "What is *real*? Is reality what it *appears* to be?" Obviously, you must have answers to such questions before you can build any philosophical system. And since this book aims to equip you with the intellectual tools needed to come up with your own answers to philosophical questions, this chapter introduces you to some of the ways philosophers have explained the nature of reality. The range of ideas should be particularly instructive for anyone gearing up to tackle the issue for the first time, as you are. We will look at how five different philosophers approached the problem of understanding reality. We start with the fairly simple speculations of the very first three philosophers on record. Then we look at the more complex theories of two major thinkers: Plato and George Berkeley.

Trying to Explain Reality
Putting Yourself in the Right Frame of Mind

One good way to approach the concept of reality is to look at how the first people who wondered about it tried to explain it. To understand what these thinkers say, however, you should be in the same frame of mind they were in. So be patient and try to imagine the following scenario; it's all for a good purpose.

You are on a tropical cruise and you're having a terrific time. The people are friendly and the weather is great. On the last night of the cruise, however, you have too good a time and drink too much champagne at the captain's farewell party. You decide to take a walk around the deck to clear your head. As you stagger along, the ship unexpectedly runs into heavy winds and rough seas. The ship lurches, and you fly across the deck. As you try to get up, a huge wave crashes over the ship. The ship pitches again, and you are washed overboard. Unfortunately, no one realizes you're gone until the ship returns to port. Your disappearance is a mystery.

The good news is that when you were thrown overboard, you grabbed hold of a log in the water, and the winds and currents carried you to a small island nearby. You are safe. The bad news is that you don't have the faintest idea where you are. In fact, your head hit a stanchion before you went overboard, and you have a ferocious headache and complete amnesia. You do not know who you are, where you came from, or anything about your past. Worse than that, you remember almost nothing of what you learned through your years of schooling. You know you need food and water, but beyond that, your mind is blank. It works, but it's empty. Really empty!

So here you are, a sentient, intelligent creature surrounded by a complex world. Light turns into darkness as a disc in the sky that is too bright to look at moves across the sky and sinks into the waves. When this happens, the sky sometimes changes into different colors. Then countless smaller lights appear that move very slowly. After what seems like a set period, the darkness goes away and the bright circle returns—but from the other side of the island. The sky is usually blue, the breeze warm and comfortable. But sometimes for no reason dark gray objects cover the blue, and drops of water, loud noises, hard winds, and lines of light come from the sky. Then the blue returns. Food grows on the trees, and even replaces itself. You also see other living beings, but they are different from you. Some live in the water, others fly through the air. What does it all mean?

If you can imagine this situation, you can imagine your confusion and fear. You are in an exceedingly complicated place. And because you have a human mind, you also wonder about everything that is happening. Your fear is mixed with curiosity.

Explaining Your New World

Having come this far, now try to imagine how you would understand this world you know nothing about. First, you would probably attempt to find some order in what you see. You would distinguish between the things around you that move (animals, birds) and those that stay put (plants, rocks). You would distinguish patterns—light (day) followed by dark (night). You would also see that much about what happens is unpredictable—the weather, for instance. Eventually you would develop some sense of what your world consists of.

But describing things would not be enough for you. You would want to understand what goes on, and why. How would you do that? How would you explain, for example, the fruit on the trees, the passing storms in the sky, and the coming and going of the bright disk? Think about that for a minute.

An Anthropomorphic Explanation

Chances are your first explanation would be neither philosophical nor scientific. The human animal is by nature very nervous, and you would probably feel fear and awe at the great powers you witness in action around you. Feeling pressed to calm yourself and to make some sense of what you see, you would most likely start interpreting your world in the only terms you know—your own human ones. You would probably believe that other living beings cause what happens. You would personify things, imagining that everything you see is alive like you, with a will and a personality of its own. You would come to think that the winds blow, the clouds move, and the plants grow because they want to. You might even conclude that these natural occurrences express the will of one or more superior, incomprehensible beings, whose actions may be benign, or hostile, or completely arbitrary and indifferent.

Whichever explanation you come up with, your account of reality could be called **anthropomorphic**—that is, your account would be given in human form. ("Anthropomorphic" comes from two Greek words: *anthropos*, "human," and *morphe*, "form.") Such an interpretation of reality explains things in terms of *who* is responsible for them, not simply what happened. The anthropomorphic mode of explaining reality obviously leads more in the direction of religion than science, and this was essentially the direction taken by the earliest human societies.

A Natural Explanation

You'd probably start with an anthropomorphic account of reality. But eventually some questions occur to you. You attempt to test the wind, the sea, and the trees on your island, you try some "experiments" to see if particular actions anger or please the gods that rule them. Eventually, you conclude that what you do doesn't

---

anthropomorphic An anthropomorphic account of something explains it in human terms. For example, an anthropomorphic interpretation of reality explains things in terms of who is responsible for them, not simply what happened. Such an account regularly appeals to the notion of divine beings.

affect things, that you cannot communicate with them, or at least that they do not respond. Perhaps you decide these gods do not exist.

Now your thinking might go in a different direction. You might consider the possibility that you and the events around you are all part of the same system of natural, impersonal forces. You hypothesize that everything that happens has a cause, and that these causes somehow lie within the events themselves. Exactly how isn't immediately apparent, but, you think, if you looked long and hard enough, you could figure it out. You assume that the nature of the world around you can be grasped by your mind. In essence, you opt to explain your world in terms of some concept of nature. When you take this path, you are following the steps of the very first philosophers.

The Nature of Reality and the Milesians

It will remain one of the great mysteries of human history why anthropomorphic thinking did not dominate Greece the way it did the rest of the ancient world. To be sure, religion, with its rites, its temples, and its pantheon of deities played an important role in Greek culture. The Greeks also had more than their share of superstitious people who were frightened when their beliefs were challenged. (Remember, one of the charges that led to Socrates' execution was impiety.) But something about ancient Greek culture also fostered intellectual inquiry, providing fertile soil for a totally new approach to understanding reality—what we have come to call "philosophy."

The main characteristic of early philosophy is that it is not anthropomorphic. For the first time in human civilization, people do not explain reality in human or superhuman terms. The first philosophers refused to project human characteristics onto the world around them. Instead, they tried to meet the world on its own terms. As a result, they took events as part of a natural, not a supernatural, system. *Nature* replaced the gods as the most important force in reality.

This is not to say that the first philosophers were atheists. Most of them worshipped the gods of their city in particular and the gods of their culture in general. But when they tried to understand what they saw in the real world around them, they were essentially nontheistic. They may have believed in their gods privately, but they did not use them to explain reality.

From our point of view in the twenty-first century, this may not seem very important. We take a scientific outlook for granted, and we have devised ways to harmonize it with religion. But giving up supernatural for natural explanations of reality was then an intellectual revolution of the first order. As we look at the first steps toward this revolution, do not expect elaborate philosophical explanations. We start with some fairly simplistic accounts of reality. More important than the details of these ideas and whether or not they are correct is the astonishing fact that rational, natural explanations of existence were offered at all.

Philosophy begins in ancient Greece, but not in the streets of Athens. The intellectual revolution starts in a place called Miletus, a Greek colony in a land then called Ionia (now modern-day Turkey). A busy seaport, Miletus conducted trade with Egypt and Persia as well as Greece, and it was perhaps the richest and most highly civilized Greek city of its time. More than a century before Socrates starts questioning his fellow Athenians about virtue, Miletus gives us three philosophers who try to understand the nature of reality—Thales, Anaximander, and Anaximenes. These three thinkers offer competing theories, but each teaches us something important about how the mind copes with the problem of understanding reality.

Thales

Not one of the three Milesians was a professional philosopher. Thales seems to have been a man of incredibly varied talents, the sort we today call a "Renaissance person." Thales, who lived around 600 B.C., is said to have been an engineer, a statesman, and an astronomer, as well as a deep thinker. He devised ways of determining the height of the Egyptian pyramids by measuring their shadows, and he wrote a treatise telling sailors how to navigate by the stars.

Two famous stories are told about Thales. In one, Thales falls into a well when he stares so intently at the stars that he forgets to look where he is going—the first absentminded philosopher. The other is a favorite among philosophy professors whose friends and relatives ask, "If you're so smart, why aren't you rich?" Confronted with the same taunt, Thales came up with a great response. His knowledge of plants and climate enabled him to predict a bumper crop of olives, and in the off-season he cornered the market in olive presses. When the huge harvest came in, everyone interested in making olive oil had to deal with Thales, and he made a large profit. He did this, he said, to show that philosophers could easily be rich if they felt like it, but that was not what they were interested in.

Thales' Account of Reality

Thales is the first thinker we know of to try to explain reality in terms of natural phenomena rather than as a manifestation of the gods. To understand Thales, put yourself back onto the island where you were marooned. Still a victim of amnesia, you do not know anything but what you have figured out there. Now you are trying to understand the nature of reality without believing that everything is alive—animism—or that gods cause everything that happens. You have observed that everything real can be put into one of four basic categories: earth, air, fire, and water. (This is what the Greeks thought before philosophy came along.)

But you, like Thales, simply have a hunch that something more basic than four elements must exist. You are very much aware of the difference between appearance and reality. When you first started studying your island, you thought that the water in the oceans, the steam rising from the hot springs, and the ice and snow on the mountains were all different substances. But you learned that they only *appear* to be different; in reality, they are all the same element, water. So, you reason, although it appears that there are four different elements, there is really only one.

Think about a rational, philosophical conclusion to this question. If you had to pick the most basic element from earth, air, fire, and water, which would you go for?

Water, or "the Moist"

Thales' choice was water, or, more accurately, what he calls "the moist." After studying reality, Thales came to the conclusion that "the first principle and basic nature of all things is water."

This answer makes some sense. Nearly everything contains moisture in some way. If you hold a piece of glass over a flame and see condensation form, even fire looks as if it has water in it (even if it doesn't). Water can be liquid, solid, or gas, and if we take the time and trouble to set up the right conditions, we can watch it change form. Water falls from the air as rain and then sinks into the earth. So there is something astute about Thales' suggestion that earth, air, fire, and water are simply different manifestations of the same element.

This account also has the virtue of explaining reality by reference to some *material substance.* After all, the physical world is the reality most obvious to our senses. It seems unquestionably present and permanent. Explaining reality in terms of one of the basic material elements, then, seems to make sense.

The Dynamic Character of Existence: Change

Thales' answer to the question "What is reality?" at first seems to amount to saying, "Reality is *material,* and apparently different substances are all ultimately reducible to moisture." The claim that water is the basic element of everything also suggests that different things are similar. This would give reality an underlying unity and stability. But Thales and the other Milesians also looked at the world around them with clear eyes. Change, rather than stability, impressed them as the most basic fact of life. Thus, they also had to explain the dynamic character of existence.

Thales realized that no inert material substance could account for change. So his explanation of reality includes more than just "the moist." Thus, he says, "The magnetic stone has soul because it sets the iron in motion," and "All things are full of gods."

Exactly what Thales means by "soul" and "full of gods" is not clear. (Unfortunately, only fragments of the original work of the early philosophers have survived, and we do not have full explanations of these remarks.) He does seem to say that reality cannot be explained in terms of substance alone. We must also account for the power that gives life to objects and propels them into motion.

Because Thales represents very early philosophy, only one step away from anthropomorphic explanations, we might expect that the power he has in mind may indeed be supernatural. But Thales may also be searching for a way to express the insight that a natural power somehow inheres in material objects. We can interpret his belief that a magnetic stone has "soul" and that everything is "full of gods" as saying that natural objects are self-contained and have an inner power. Matter somehow possesses the capacity to move, to change, and to grow in particular ways.

So while we may not know exactly what Thales means, he clearly suggests that accounts of reality must include some kind of force as well as a substance. Despite his reference to gods, he puts the gods and the souls that inhere in things—perhaps simply his symbols for the power of nature—inside the things themselves. That is, he does not see the "gods" as independent, omnipotent beings who pull the strings and make the rest of us jump on command.

The Inquiry into Reality: Thales' Contribution

Thales was the first Western thinker to try to understand reality in nonreligious and nonanthropocentric terms. Thales approaches reality as something with its own integrity, as basically a natural and not a supernatural system. He sees what he can make of it strictly in terms of physical observation, intellectual deduction, and philosophical speculation. In essence, he shows that we can give an account of reality that understands material substance on its own terms because the natural world has a logic of its own and operates under its own power. Even if there is a God or some other spiritual entity or entities, the natural world makes sense on its own terms. The fact that Thales is the first Western thinker to attempt this is a major contribution to the history of philosophy.

1. In terms of the significance of Thales' explanation of reality, he asserts a difference between *reality* and *appearance*. The physical objects around us *appear* to be composed of various elements, but Thales claims that the *reality* of the situation is very different from what our senses suggest it to be. This fundamental insight has been proven over and over as philosophy and science have developed.

2. Thales also recognizes that a complete explanation of the nature of reality has to account both for the "stuff" of which everything is made and for the dynamic quality of existence, that which causes it constantly to change. A good explanation has to deal with forces, or power, as well as substance. Thus, Thales proposes water as the basic element, but he also suggests that matter contains some kind of inner power that accounts for its ability to move or cause movement. Contemporary physics may describe reality in terms of a different substance and different forces, but even without the benefit of knowledge accumulated over 2,600 years, Thales was at least on the right track. Subatomic particles may be much smaller than drops of water, but both are material substances, not supernatural entities.

All in all, then, this is a commendable early try at a philosophical account of the nature of reality.

Anaximander

Anaximander is the second philosopher from Miletus. He was about fifteen years younger than Thales, and it is fairly certain that they knew each other. They were similar kinds of men—both were engineers, statesmen, and travelers, and both were abundantly curious about natural science, astronomy, and geometry. Anaximander was the first Greek to make a map of the known world and a sundial for telling the seasons.

With Anaximander we see Greek thinking moving farther away from anthropomorphic explanations and closer to what we now call philosophy and science. Not only did Anaximander speculate about the nature of reality, he also tried to draw his conclusions on the basis of observation. For example, he uses fossils he has discovered to support his theory of the earth's history. And he uses a theory of evolution, not a theory of divine creation, to explain the origin of humanity. As one ancient writer reports,

[Anaximander] says, too, that in earliest times men were generated from various kinds of animals. For whereas the other animals can quickly get food for themselves, the human infant requires careful feeding for a long while after birth; so that if he had originated suddenly he could not have preserved his own existence.

This is a logical conclusion drawn from astute observations.

Anaximander's Account of Reality

Anaximander disputes Thales' explanation of the nature of reality. He agrees that some single material element underlies all of reality. Thus, he shares Thales' rejection of anthropomorphic explanations and his assertion that reality is material. But he rejects the idea that the fundamental substance is water. He even believes that the fundamental substance has no specifically identifiable qualities. As the sole fragment of Anaximander's writings explains,

> The Unlimited is the first-principle of things that are. It is that from which the coming-to-be [of things and qualities] takes place, and it is that into which they return when they perish.

Anaximander's word for the basic substance out of which everything is made can be translated as "the Unlimited," "the Unbounded," or "the Indefinite." This "unlimited" substance has no specific properties of its own, and indeed it cannot be bounded by definite characteristics because it must be able to take on all qualities. To its ability to take on any quality, Anaximander adds only that the Unlimited is eternal and indestructible.

Don't think, however, that this is some kind of magical, spiritual substance. Like Thales, Anaximander offers a natural, not a supernatural, explanation of reality. The Unlimited is certainly a special kind of material substance, but it is material.

Anaximander and the Unlimited

Thales and Anaximander may agree that appearance and reality differ, and that everything real can be reduced to a single material substance. But that's where they part company. There are major differences in the basic substances they suggest and in how they arrive at their conclusions. We can experience water with our senses, and Thales' argument makes a certain kind of sense because we can find moisture in virtually everything. But it is impossible to know what a lump of Unlimited is like.

With his concept of the Unlimited, Anaximander offers a very different understanding of the world of our senses than Thales does. For Anaximander, the great variety of things that we experience with our senses, the four basic elements of earth, air, fire, and water—all of that is simply appearance. All these various substances are really different amounts of the Unlimited that have taken on the size, shape, color, touch, taste, and smell of a particular thing. True reality, therefore, is something we can never encounter with our senses. Once we experience something, it is no longer "unlimited" but "limited" or "defined" by size, shape, color, and so on. So we can only imagine, as Anaximander does, the Unlimited as some substance without properties.

This is a dramatically different way of looking at the nature of reality from what we found in Thales' work. Anaximander may concur with his predecessor that there is one fundamental substance. But this substance cannot be experienced directly. The most elementary "stuff" of existence is real, but forever beyond the reach of our senses. And that makes the Unlimited very different from water.

Anaximander and the Intellect

Unlike Thales, Anaximander can arrive at his idea of the Unlimited exclusively by thinking. Starting with Thales' proposition that "the moist" is the universal element, Anaximander faces the question of how water, which is already defined by specific properties, can take on all other characteristics, particularly those of its opposite. How can dryness, for example, be made up of moisture? For that matter, how can any particular substance be the most basic element? No matter what we pick, we always have its opposite to explain. Anaximander solves this simply by positing something logically prior to "a substance with properties"—that is, "a substance *without* properties," the Unlimited. This conclusion cannot be observed in real life. It is the result of a purely intellectual process.

By working in this manner, Anaximander elevates the mind far above the senses. Our senses tell us that reality consists of a variety of specific substances. Even Thales' idea that moisture is the first principle of reality can in a general way be made to fit with our sense experience. But to reject all this for an explanation like "the Unlimited" is to place more trust in the mind's eye than the body's. This may surprise you when you recall that Anaximander used evidence offered by the physical world to draw his conclusion that human beings are the products of evolution. But Anaximander obviously feels that Thales' material explanation of reality is not sufficient for the job.

Relying on thought processes—the activities of the mind—is characteristic of philosophy. It is precisely this trust in the intellect that allows Greek thought to break free from anthropomorphic explanations. Some later philosophers reject the senses as inferior instruments for learning about reality and they rely totally on the mind. Anaximander doesn't go that far. But his contribution here, the assertion of the primacy of reason, even in philosophy's earliest days, cannot be underestimated.

The Regulation of Change

In rejecting Thales' ideas, Anaximander automatically makes understanding the nature of reality more complicated. For one thing, Anaximander's basic substance is much more sophisticated than Thales'. For another, Anaximander's vision of the forces that cause matter to change is more complicated than Thales' idea that matter contains "soul" or "gods." As Anaximander expresses it:

> The Unlimited is the first-principle of things that are. It is that from which the coming-to-be [of things and qualities] takes place, and it is that into which they return when they perish, *by moral necessity, giving satisfaction to one another and making reparation for their injustice, according to the order of time.* [Emphasis added.]

This must seem like a misprint when you first read this passage. "Moral necessity"? "Giving satisfaction" and "making reparation" for "injustice"? This is a strange way to describe the process of physical change. We can never be sure what Anaximander means here because virtually everything he wrote is lost, but he seems to suggest that the changes that characterize the world are governed by some kind of abiding natural order. In the absence of his whole theory, we have to leave "moral necessity" and "injustice" hanging somewhat loose. We cannot say exactly what they mean.

We *can* say that Anaximander seems to presume some fundamental order to reality, some force that ensures a rhythm, or balance, between contrary qualities. Anaximander was powerfully impressed by the fact that reality is divided into pairs of opposites: hot/cold, wet/dry, rough/smooth, light/dark. He describes each extreme as a kind of "injustice" that is counterbalanced over time by the appearance of its opposite. We can see this in the daily cycle of day and night, with the "injustice" of light yielding by "moral necessity" to darkness, which again yields to light, and so on. Similarly, the hot, dry summer "makes reparation for" and balances off the cold, wet winter.

This process seems to reside in nature itself. Clearly, Anaximander makes no reference to the gods. This power, or law, is itself invisible, although its effects are tangible. It is also quite real.

Describing Reality Figuratively

Anaximander's references here to "justice," "giving satisfaction," and "making reparation" may puzzle you. Philosophers do not usually use legal and moral notions to describe the workings of nature, and we should look at this for a moment.

Remember that Anaximander lived in a time before there was much, if any, philosophical discourse. Thus, he didn't have at his fingertips anyone else's basic concepts or a ready-made vocabulary to cover new ideas. This situation is much like yours when you were washed ashore, remembering nothing of your former life, on an unknown island. What concepts and language did you have to describe this totally new experience?

Or imagine that in your present everyday life you suddenly have a totally new and different experience. You're out jogging, casually mulling over the meaning of life. All at once you have a brilliant insight about the order and purpose of the universe. In a flash you understand the deepest secrets of the nature of reality in a way that has eluded every other human being. How would you describe something unique like this? How would you explain it to other people?

The answer is, of course, that you would *not* have the right language to express it. That leaves you only two choices: either you invent new concepts with new names, or you describe it by saying it is "something like" this or "something like" that. Actually, these two choices amount to essentially the same thing, because in order to define any new terms, we have to refer to ones we are already familiar with. In other words, the only way to explain a totally new insight is by way of something we already know.

This is surely what happened to Anaximander. He arrived at a new understanding of a harmony that underlies the opposites we observe everywhere. He saw that the unpredictability and chaos so characteristic of nature were part of a larger process that led to harmony. In some way, what was going on in the apparent chaos was that things were being set right. Anaximander had no concept at his disposal to capture what he thought, but he could at least approximate that notion by borrowing the legal concepts of justice and reparation. A stranger to our society who came upon a marshall with a court order seizing someone's property or upon a police officer arresting a mugger might easily mistake these actions for theft or cruelty. But what is actually happening is that things are somehow being made right. The property will be sold so that creditors can be paid. Someone who attacks other people is deprived of his freedom. Anaximander borrows these ideas from the law and uses them to describe reality.

In so doing, Anaximander switches from speaking literally to figuratively, that is, saying in this case that the regulative principle of nature is *like* justice. Describing things figuratively is less precise than speaking literally. But if it's the best you can do, and if the simile, metaphor, or analogy you use is accurate, it's an acceptable way of conveying philosophical insights.

The ultimate trick, of course, is to tease out the full meaning inherent in a good figurative image. Anaximander's image suggests a basic order and purpose in the way the natural world operates. Yet the scientific "law" that "every action produces an equal and opposite reaction" is just a more precise way to express Anaximander's insight. Seen this way, the Greek philosopher's reference to "moral necessity," "injustice," and "satisfaction and reparation" make sense.

There is another lesson in this, too: If you run across a philosophical idea that strikes you as strange at first, don't dismiss it before you think about it for a while. Instead of thinking that it's too strange to understand, ask if it makes more sense when interpreted figuratively. If you try out some interpretations, you'll probably find that you understand the idea much better.

Anaximander and Thales

Like Thales, then, Anaximander believes that any full explanation of the nature of reality must account for both stability and change. The Unlimited is the substance that unifies reality, that makes it ultimately all one. And some sort of natural law is the force that governs the changes that we observe in real things.

Anaximander marks a significant advance over his philosophical predecessor, however, by proposing a more abstract theory to explain the basic substance and the forces that shape reality. Unlike Thales, Anaximander envisions a basic element that we ultimately cannot experience with our senses. His natural law of moral necessity, justice, and balance is also an idea we only infer. We can see the results of its workings, but natural law itself is beyond our experience. So on both fronts Anaximander gives us a more abstract concept of what is "really" real.

The Inquiry into Reality: Anaximander's Contribution

Thales' ideas about the nature of reality mark the beginning of philosophy. Does Anaximander add any significant insights?

1. Anaximander's main contribution is probably the idea that we cannot experience reality's basic nature directly with our senses. With the concept of "the Unlimited" as the basic element, this puts the investigation on a more abstract level than that of Thales' account, and it makes the intellect a more important tool than our senses. It does not change the fact that reality is essentially material; but it does mean that the nature of that reality must be uncovered with our intellect, not with our senses. This makes Anaximander's ideas similar to our own century's explanation of reality. We believe that atomic and subatomic particles are the "real" constituents of material things, but we can never directly observe these particles with our ordinary senses.

2. Anaximander's figurative account also makes an interesting methodological contribution. In order to "push the philosophical envelope," as it were, philosophers may have to be creative. We have to look for ideas wherever we can get them—even if

they might not at first make sense to other people. When Anaximander described natural cycles in terms of morality and the law, it must have sounded peculiar to his contemporaries. (It even sounds strange now when you first read it.) But when you think about it, it makes sense in a certain way. So Anaximander's approach suggests that when we have trouble describing something, we should think creatively and expansively. We should look for likely and unlikely comparisons. They just might work.

Once again, as with Thales, we find a thinker at the dawn of philosophy giving us some sophisticated and thought-provoking ideas about the nature of reality.

Anaximenes

The work of Anaximenes, the last of our Milesian trio, shows that philosophy does not necessarily progress in a constant fashion. While Anaximenes takes one step forward beyond Anaximander, he also takes another step back to thinking like Thales. Philosophical theories, then, are just like the people who make them up, combinations of brilliant insights and human error.

Anaximenes' Basic Substance: Air

About Anaximenes we know only that he lived in Miletus and probably knew Anaximander. Like Thales and Anaximander, Anaximenes is concerned with the nature of reality, which he sees more as Thales does. Rejecting Anaximander's idea of a basic matter of indefinite qualities, however, Anaximenes returns to the original four elements, earth, air, fire, and water, and chooses air as the basic substance. By giving up Anaximander's insight that a basic substance must have few or no properties in order to account for the great variety of opposing qualities and substances we find around us, Anaximenes returns to the idea that everything can ultimately be reduced to a known material element.

Air is not an implausible suggestion. Sometimes air feels hot; other times cold. After looking at blue skies, multicolored sunsets, and the black of the night sky, we might conclude that air has the capacity to change color. Some days you can barely feel air, but when a hot, dry wind blows in the desert, air is as tangible as a two by four. Air does seem to take on a variety of qualities. So air is a reasonable choice as a basic element. It's just that in comparison to Anaximander's idea of the Unlimited, it is a less sophisticated concept.

Air and Breath

No one knows why Anaximenes went in this direction, but we have to believe that he thought that it led to a better explanation of the nature of reality. The best clue to his thinking comes from this fragment of his writing: "As our souls, being air, hold us together, so breath and air embrace the entire universe."

Here Anaximenes makes an interesting connection between air, breath, and life. Think about it this way. What is the difference between someone alive and dead? Live people breathe. We take in and give out air. When air stops being drawn into the body, it dies and decays. To use Anaximenes' phrase, the body stops being "held together" by the soul. After seeing that air, in the form of breath, is so characteristic of living things, Anaximenes might very well think that air has an intrinsic connection with the very essence of life.

If Anaximenes thinks that breath somehow contains the force of life itself, then air is a natural for reality's basic element. It makes a certain sense, then, to imagine that in one of its manifestations, air takes the form of those material objects that are alive. In other manifestations, objects exist but are inanimate. And if we consider reality in general, it is plausible for Anaximenes to suggest, as he does in his fragment, that air is as much at the core of all reality as a soul is to an individual body. Air has the power that makes it possible for things to exist and to live.

This intriguing notion shows Anaximenes addressing an aspect of reality that his two predecessors had more or less ignored. After all, one of the most basic observations we can make about reality is that some of it is alive and some of it is not. Anaximenes' theory about air reminds us that as we ponder the nature of reality, we should give some thought to the basis of this difference.

Anaximenes may indeed have taken a step backwards in claiming that air is the basic element underlying reality. But it's a step backwards with an interesting twist.

Progress: Condensation and Rarefaction

It is one thing to say that all of reality is at base water, the Unlimited, or air. But we also need some theory of how a single basic substance can account for very different things—say, rocks and clouds. Clearly this process has to be explained, and this is where Anaximenes makes his mark on the history of philosophy.

Anaximenes' most important accomplishment as a thinker is to offer a solution to this problem based on the concept of density. His reasoning goes like this. Everything is made of air. But how densely compacted the air is determines exactly what kind of thing it is. The more air we have in a given amount of space, the more visible and harder the object is. The less air per cubic inch, the lighter and more transparent the object will be.

For example, air in its natural state cannot be seen or felt. But as it becomes *more* dense, it first becomes *wind*, which can be felt, but not seen. Next it is *cloud*, which is visible and its moisture palpable but lighter than the ground. More dense still, air becomes *water*, which is heavier than air, but liquid; then it becomes *earth*, which is more solid than liquid; and finally air becomes *stone*, which is completely solid. On the other hand, when air becomes *less* dense than it is in its natural state, it becomes *fire*. (The natural upward motion of fire must have made it seem lighter than air.) Anaximenes says, then, that the two natural processes of *condensation* (air being made more dense) and *rarefaction* (air being made less dense) thus determine why things are what they are.

Reality and Number

Anaximenes' explanation contains two important insights. First, by saying that the *amount* of air in a given volume determines an object's character, Anaximenes is the first Western thinker to suggest that reality is in some way *quantifiable*—that is, countable, or associated with numbers. By doing this, he anticipates the basic assumption of modern science that mathematics is the language of nature, that is, that we cannot understand the nature of reality without talking about quantities, or numbers. We can see a simple example of this in the fact that chemistry describes different elements in terms of the different number of subatomic particles that make them up.

A Hierarchy of Nature

The order in which Anaximenes arranges reality, that is, fire-air-wind-cloud-water-earth-stone, is also important because this amounts to saying that reality is arranged in a clearly defined progression. This arrangement has a top and a bottom with a specific reason for why things fall where they do along a continuous line in between.

This kind of arrangement is called a hierarchy, and it appears in contemporary scientific accounts of reality as well. Biological hierarchies rank "higher" and "lower" organisms on a scale of complexity. Chemical hierarchies enable us to break substances down into their elements, molecules, atoms, and so on down the line.

In constructing his hierarchy, Anaximenes suggests that reality is not random. Substances do not possess their characteristics by accident. Rather, they express an abiding natural order.

The Inquiry into Reality: Anaximenes' Contribution

Does Anaximenes add any useful insights to those of his predecessors?

1. The connection Anaximenes makes between air, breath, and life tells us that he asked a very astute new question: *How do we explain the difference between living and non-living things in reality?* Anaximenes apparently accounts for life (and nonlife) by whether or not the air of which a thing is made takes the form of life-infusing breath. This explanation may not be correct, but it does underscore the point that any account of reality should explain why some things that exist are "alive" and some aren't. Moreover, Anaximenes explanation remains in the nonanthropocentric, rational, philosophical tradition of the other Milesians by seeing life as a natural property that is consistent with the natural element of which everything is made.

2. All three Milesians identify a basic substance of reality and a force that governs change. However, with his ideas about condensation and rarefaction and his vision of the natural hierarchy these processes imply, Anaximenes expands the definition of reality to include order and number. The fact that the density of air within a particular volume can be quantified and ranked establishes an intrinsic hierarchy, or order, to nature. By adding a new property—order, or hierarchy—to the two existing factors, substance and force, Anaximenes shows us, then, that in trying to understand the nature of reality, we have to look beyond basic elements and forces.

   That physical reality can be quantified, that is, described numerically, and that it submits to an ordered hierarchy are both critical insights. Had Anaximenes not looked beyond the conceptual boundaries set by his predecessors, he would have missed them completely. We can apply this same principle to our own thinking by taking a step back, assessing our conclusions, and asking, "Have I missed anything?" In particular, we must examine our basic assumptions to see whether they've blinded us to something new. Anaximenes' work shows us that we should always ask whether the way we phrase our problems causes us to miss something.

Take the simple question, "Who discovered America?" Your answer is probably, "Christopher Columbus," or maybe "the Vikings." What's wrong here? For one thing, an enormous fallacious assumption underlies the verb "discovered." You cannot "discover" something that is already known, so the question assumes that America, or the New World, was unknown. But considering all the native American civilizations already well established from the Bering Strait to the Cape of Good Hope, this assumption is inaccurate, to say the least. Yet we easily fall into this unintentional error just by using the concept of "discovery."

In trying to determine the nature of reality, we have to guard against being misled by the concepts, models, or even just the language we use. Take the question, "How do we explain the motion of the sun, the moon, the stars, and the planets?" As long as thinkers assumed that this "motion" was the movement of those celestial bodies around the earth while the earth stood still, they were bound to come up with a mistaken picture of reality. But as soon as they understood that this "motion" included the movement of the earth as well, both its rotation around its axis and its travel through an orbit around the sun, they could arrive at a more accurate understanding of reality.

The lesson, then, is simple but hard. Always ask, "Is there anything I'm missing because of the way I phrase my questions?"

Overall, then, even though we find Anaximenes taking a step backward by calling air the universal element, his contributions to theory earn him an important place in the development of Western philosophy and science.

The Milesians' Overall Significance

These are the West's first three philosophers, the first people we know of who struggled to free themselves from the presuppositions and constraints of myth and think in a new way. Each man makes important progress in the development of rational thought. And even if vestiges of mythic, anthropomorphic, or religious explanations remain in their accounts of reality, their break-through was nonetheless revolutionary. After all, it's no small accomplishment to start philosophy.

The Milesians are probably right about the nature of reality on all the big points. Reality is indeed not what it appears to be. It can be accounted for naturally and rationally without recourse to supernatural explanations. Everything is made up of the same basic particles. And the mind is ultimately a better tool for understanding reality than the senses.

This is a very impressive achievement. Think again about being washed ashore on that island. Stripped of the knowledge you've so far acquired from your schooling and faced with the mysteries of the nature of reality on your own, could you have come as far as any of these thinkers? Certainly we have to give them credit for what they accomplished.

But ultimately, the most significant contribution of these three thinkers lies in their method of attacking the problem. First, they identify the most fundamental issues. They show us the importance of distinguishing reality from appearance, of accounting for both the stable and dynamic qualities in reality, of questioning the reliability of our senses, of accepting the truth of figurative explanations, and of identifying the most fundamental properties of existence.

Even more important, the Milesians demonstrate that the task of developing a new approach to reality is a long, slow process of methodically questioning "truths" that seem so obvious that one feels ridiculous doubting them. The great accomplishment of these first philosophers is that they started with a world view that made sense to most people, they doubted it, and they invented a new way of thinking that revealed the nature of reality more accurately.

For centuries, the myths and religious stories of Egypt and Mesopotamia had satisfied many intelligent people. These were advanced societies with impressive technological and intellectual achievements. These people were not stupid. Furthermore, the idea that our senses give us good information is not crazy either. If we can examine a rock outside and inside, it is sensible to conclude that it's actually a solid object. If someone says to you, "A rock isn't solid at all. It only looks solid. It's actually made up of millions of tiny particles with space between them," *that* is what sounds crazy. Doubting things that seem so self-evident is very difficult. Yet this is precisely what these thinkers did. They doubted the "obvious"—the apparent evidence of their senses and the accepted way of interpreting reality in their age. And they turned out to be right.

The Milesians show that progress in philosophy can be made only by questioning the most obvious "truths." This skeptical stance is something that you should learn from them and imitate. In our own attempt to understand the nature of reality, or anything else, then, the first step is to say in the manner of the Milesians, "Maybe things are not what they seem. Is there another way to explain them? What might that be?"

Ultimately, however, one of the Milesians' major contributions has to do with the part of their thinking that is most debatable. Although the three Milesians differ in the details of their theories, they share what is called a **materialist** outlook. That is, in their claim that reality is ultimately comprised of a particular material substance, they anticipate the empirical point of view of modern science. It does, however, set them apart from another major Greek thinker who takes up the issue, Plato. As you will now see, Plato completely rejects materialism and proposes a radically different conception of reality.

The Nature of Reality: Plato

The Pre-Socratics

Miletus was destroyed by the Persians in 494 B.C., and philosophy had to find a new home. A number of important schools of thought developed in southern Italy and Sicily, but eventually Athens came to the fore. The philosophers who lived during

---

materialism Materialism maintains that reality is ultimately comprised of a particular material substance. This contrasts with idealism.

the two centuries after Thales are collectively called the **Pre-Socratics**. They are considered together not only because they come before Socrates, but because they all try to explain the same thing, the nature of reality. If you found the Milesian thinkers interesting, you will probably also like Pythagoras, Heraclitus, Parmenides, Zeno, Empedocles, Leucippus, Democritus, and Anaxagoras, all of whom engage in involved speculations about reality.

We will skip over these philosophers here, however, and go directly to a thinker who, in the tradition of the Milesians, gives us an interpretation of reality that ruthlessly questions one of our most fundamental assumptions.

Plato

Look at a chair. Now close your eyes and imagine a chair—not necessarily *that* chair but *any* chair. Which is more real, the chair or the idea of the chair? You probably said the chair, and so would most people. Can you imagine anyone saying that the *idea* of the chair is more real? If you met someone who argued that position, you'd probably think he wasn't playing with a full deck. Remember Plato? That is precisely the argument he makes.

Although perhaps a dozen philosophers in the Western tradition precede him, Plato is the first "systematic philosopher." That is, he is the first person to develop a full-blown system aimed at explaining all the major philosophical issues. We have seen some of what he has to say about ethics and politics.[1] As a systematic thinker, he also takes up issues ranging from knowledge and art to the nature of reality. Part of being a great philosopher is delivering thought-provoking ideas about a variety of topics. And Plato unquestionably does that.

Plato and Physical Reality

The Milesians had already questioned physical reality to some extent. They had noted the difference between appearance and reality. Anaximander had even suggested that the basic substance of all things lacks identifying qualities, and is thus something we cannot experience in its pure form. But they had left the physical world intact. In fact, by rejecting the supernatural world of myth, they gave new importance to the world of nature. For the Milesians, reality remained fundamentally *material.*

Plato goes far beyond these early philosophers in challenging and rejecting the physical world. He, too, questions the obvious. And if the most obvious reality is that of the material world surrounding us, you might guess that this is the last thing Plato will say is real.

Plato's Levels of Reality. Plato's most basic idea about reality is easy to express: *Ideas are more real than the objects that present themselves to our senses.* The world we

---

Pre-Socratics The Pre-Socratic thinkers lived during the two centuries between Thales and Socrates and are characterized by their inquiries into the nature of reality. They include, among others, Thales, Anaximander, and Anaximenes.

---

[1]See Chapter 6, "Why Be Ethical?" for some of his views on ethics and Chapter 7, "Democracy" for his notions about politics.

reach with our minds is more permanent, perfect, real, and true than the world we experience with our eyes, ears, noses, tongues, and hands.

Talk about a challenge to the self-evident. Plato believes that the world of our senses is not actually "real" at all. Physical objects exist, of course. But they are like shadows in comparison to actual objects. And that is a very low level of reality.

Here Plato dramatically parts company with Thales, Anaximander, and Anaximenes. Although all three speculate about the nature of reality, none of them concludes that chairs, tables, trees, and mountains are mere shadows. The physical world is sound enough; reality is material. Not in Plato's world. There, he would say that the floor beneath you is no more fully and authentically "real" than your reflection in a puddle is "really" you.

What is actually "real"? Plato's idea of "the real world" is about as far as you can get from the common meaning of this phrase. To Plato, what's "real" exists only on a level that we contact with our minds. It is a superior level of existence populated by perfect, eternal, but invisible objects.

In other words, there is a higher level of reality, invisible to our senses but not to our minds. In this realm, we "see" with our "mind's eye." This dimension, which we know by our intellect, Plato calls the *intelligible world*. The physical world, which we know by our senses, Plato calls the *visible world*. Both worlds have their reality, but in this matter the intelligible world is as superior to the visible world as a physical object is to a shadow.

Plato's Real World: The Line. Plato apparently appreciates the difficulty of explaining his ideas because he represents them in a couple of different ways. First, he represents his conception of the nature of reality by another image—a line.

First, we draw a line.

Next, we divide it in two, taking care not to split it in half. We will make the top part of the line somewhat shorter than the bottom part as a way of representing that the top part is superior to the bottom.

This is the most basic way to represent Plato's conception of the two parts of reality. The bottom portion of the line represents the visible world, the ordinary physical world we live in. The top portion of the line represents the "intelligible" realm, the world that we can reach only with our minds.

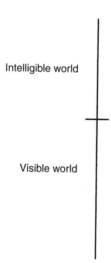

Intelligible world

Visible world

Now we divide each part of the line in two again, using the same proportions. This is Plato's way of saying that in each world there are two types, or grades, of things, each superior to the one below it. The line now represents a hierarchy. As we go up in this hierarchy, we encounter things that are more real, more enduring, and more true.

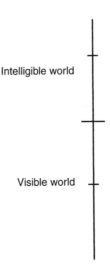

The Visible World.   Now let's take a closer look at the section of the line representing the visible world. Label the top portion of the bottom part "physical objects" and the bottom portion "shadows, representations, drawings, reflections." This section now represents the ordinary world that we understand with our senses.

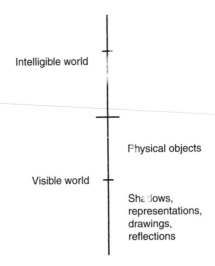

In Plato's scheme, physical objects are superior to images, or representations, of them. There are a couple of reasons for this. First, pictures of a chair are possible only because the chair itself exists. If there were no chair, there could not be a picture of one. Second, if you want to learn about a particular object—say, a car—what will teach you more: the car itself or a drawing of it? The car, of course. A drawing—even a series of drawings—can teach you just so much. Each one gives you limited information. If you have the car itself, you can climb around inside, look at the engine and trunk, and go for a drive. You cannot do any of this with a drawing of the car because it's not really the car. It's just a representation. Thus, Plato ranks physical objects higher than any images of them because they give us more dependable knowledge of their nature.

So far, Plato makes sense. Material objects and images of material objects are both real in some way. But to Plato, some things are more real than others. When we think of what we can do with a real car versus what we can do with an image of one, you can see how the reality of an actual car is a superior kind of reality.

The Intelligible World. Now let's move to the intelligible world. Label the bottom portion of the upper part of the line "objects of mathematics" and its top portion "the Forms."

Squares, Circles, Triangles, Points. The lower level of the intelligible world is populated by the "objects of mathematics." These include the lines and points we talked about at the start of this chapter, as well as perfect triangles, circles, and the other objects that geometry and trigonometry are built around.

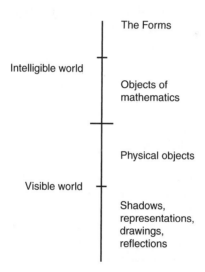

The first thing to see about these objects is that we encounter them only in our minds. We can find physical representations of them, of course, but here Plato is talking about the abstract concepts behind the material shapes. Think back to the earlier exercise where we proved that a line can be divided an infinite number of times. This is the case because in pure mathematics, a point has no dimension. And that is what Plato is talking about—points without dimensions, lines with length but no width, circles and spheres with no starting points.

You may think, however, that mathematical concepts like lines and points are "just ideas" that people "made up." For example, doesn't the notion of a perfect circle arise only after people look at circular things and imagine what a pure version of such a shape would be like? Plato doesn't see it that way. He thinks that the objects of mathematics actually exist as independent things. They exist, but they inhabit a different dimension of reality than chairs and tables. If you can think about a triangle, let's say, and see it with your "mind's eye," Plato holds that you are seeing a very real object in its intelligible dimension.

The idea that lines, points, and triangles actually exist on some immaterial plane may surprise you. But Plato does not stop there. He also says that these objects are superior to anything in the visible world. Indeed, he says, they are perfect and unchangeable.

Look at some object in the room you're in right now. What color is it? How long will it be that color? Only until someone cleans it or paints it. How long will it exist? Maybe twenty or thirty years at the longest. Consider a triangle. How long will it have three sides? Forever. How long has it been true that the sum of the interior angles of a triangle is 180 degrees? As long as people have known about triangles. In 500 years, will the sum of the angles still be the same? Absolutely. How long will it be true that $5 = 5$? Always. Now what about the fact that a particular wooden chair can support the weight of people who sit on it? That will be true only until the chair starts to fall apart, in other words, not forever. No physical object can match the stability and consistency of a mathematical object. That's why Plato thinks they're superior to ordinary chairs and tables.

Even though they're superior to physical things, mathematical objects occupy only the lower part of the intelligible world. After all, everyone who does a little work in mathematics encounters them. It's harder for you to encounter a point with your mind than to see a tree with your eyes, but not that much harder.

The Forms

The top of the upper segment of the line is the area that is most important to Plato. Here reside what he calls the **Forms**. By placing the Forms at the top of the hierarchy, Plato assigns them the highest dimension of reality. But what are they?

The *Forms* are just what this name implies: They are the forms, or models, for everything that exists. They are perfect, unchanging, and eternal. There are two kinds of Forms. First come the ideal patterns for everyday physical objects—chairs, tables, cats, dogs, trees, grass, and so on. Second come the Forms for concepts and qualities—justice, fairness, equity, perfection. Above all these Forms is the highest Form, one called simply "the Good."

A Form not only captures the essence of an object or an idea, it is that essence. It's a lot like a definition. For example, look at all of the chairs around you. Some are wood, some metal; some have four legs, some have none; some are plain, some fancy; some are comfortable, some are not. Now close your eyes, mull over what you've just seen and then think about what it is for something to be a chair. Think about what qualities all chairs have. In other words, try to define the essence of a chair.

If you now have such a description in your mind, you have encountered the Form of a chair; we can also call this "chairness." As you contemplate "chairness," you understand the true, ultimate nature of a chair. Its description fits every chair

---

Forms The Forms are what Plato calls the nonmaterial, perfect models of everything that exists. They are known only by the mind. The chief Form is the Form of the Good.

that has ever been or will ever be. Everyone who ever thought about "chairness" would define it in roughly the same way. This essence of chair, its Form, will never change. Just as the truths of mathematics will never vary, the Form "chairness," that is, the essence of a chair, will never change. That's the nature of a Form, remember. A Form is perfect, absolute, eternal, and unchanging.

Plato's Forms, then, are abstract, nonmaterial entities. Also realize, however, that Plato believes that they exist—just as independently, just as uniquely, just as surely as you do. Even more so. They are superior to anything in the physical world. They exist in a dimension of reality we reach only with our minds. They are, in Plato's opinion, the most "real" things that exist—perfect, absolute, eternal, immutable.

Forms and Physical Objects. As hard as it is to grasp what the Forms are, it is harder to grasp the relationship between the Forms and physical objects. Plato says that material objects *imitate* or *participate in* the Forms. But that doesn't give you much to hang on to.

One way to capture this is to think of the relationship between an object and its shadow. Just as an actual chair is responsible for the shadow of a chair, Plato thinks that the Form of the chair is responsible for the actual chair. And as the shadow of a chair represents but is vastly inferior to an actual chair, so actual chairs, such as the one you are sitting in, represent but are just as inferior to the Form "chairness" that they somehow represent.

The process by which a Form becomes a model for actual objects needn't concern us here. Plato's intent lies more in explaining the substance of reality than the forces that shape it, anyway. It's most important that you simply understand how to use the analogy which, again, goes like this:

a Form : a physical object :: an object : its shadow.

The Highest Forms. By now you understand something about the Forms of physical objects. As noted above, however, there are also higher Forms for abstract ideas, concepts, and qualities like Justice, Beauty, Fairness, and Equality, for example. The highest Form of all is simply the Good—the essence of perfect goodness.

These higher Forms are harder to talk about than something more familiar, like "chairness," "tableness," or "treeness." Understanding the essential nature of beauty, or justice, as opposed to being acquainted with beautiful objects, or just actions, is a tall order for most of us. Plato himself expected philosophers to spend their whole lives trying to understand these Forms. And he never said it would be easy. An accomplished, full-time, highly trained philosopher, he thought, would not be able to understand the Good until about the age of 50.

The Allegory of the Cave

Plato's second explanation about the nature of reality is more figurative than "the Line." It's a story about people imprisoned in a cave. Plato writes:

> Imagine men to be living in an underground cave-like dwelling place, which has a way up to the light along its whole width, but the entrance is a long way up. The men have been there from childhood, with their neck and legs in fetters, so

that they remain in the same place and can only see ahead of them, as their bonds prevent them turning their heads. Light is provided by a fire burning some way behind and above them. Between the fire and the prisoners, some way behind them and on a higher ground, there is a path across the cave and along this a low wall has been built, like the screen at a puppet show in front of the performers who show their puppets above it. —I see it.

See then also men carrying along that wall, so that they overtop it, all kinds of artifacts, statues of men, reproductions of other animals in stone or wood fashioned in all sorts of ways, and, as is likely, some of the carriers are talking while others are silent.

—This is a strange picture, and strange prisoners.

They are like us, I said. Do you think, in the first place, that such men could see anything of themselves and each other except the shadows which the fire casts upon the wall of the cave in front of them?

—How could they, if they have to keep their heads still throughout life?

And is not the same true of the objects carried along the wall?

—Quite.

If they could converse with one another, do you not think that they would consider these shadows to be the real things?

—Necessarily.

What if their prison had an echo which reached them from in front of them? Whenever one of the carriers passing behind the wall spoke, would they not think that it was the shadow passing in front of them which was talking? Do you agree?

—By Zeus I do.

Altogether then, I said, such men would believe the truth to be nothing else than the shadows of the artifacts? —They must believe that.

—Republic

Plato uses this story of the cave to represent his ideas about the nature of reality, or, more precisely, the distinction between appearance and reality. The critical fact is that we are the prisoners. The cave and the shadows represent our everyday experience. Here is how the analogy plays out. The shows of tables and chairs on the cave wall are to the actual objects that produce them what the ordinary tables and chairs we know in our everyday lives are to "real" tables and chairs. Similarly, the dark, shadow-filled cave is to the sun-filled world outside the cave as the natural world we live in is to the "real" world. Or to restate this using analogy symbols:

shadow of a chair : actual chair :: actual chair : "real" chair

cave : outside world :: physical world : "real" world

The Inquiry into Reality: Plato's Contribution

What does Plato think is "real"? The most perfect and enduring part of existence, the "real" world, he says, is a domain entirely separate from the physical world. The Forms inhabit the intelligible world, give meaning and even existence to the things that exist in the material world.

Now then, what does Plato's thought add to our investigation of the nature of reality?

1. Thales, Anaximander, and Anaximenes may have questioned whether the evidence of our senses is trustworthy. Plato, however, writes it off almost completely. In his view, what appears to be most real (a physical object) is little more than a shadow, or mirage. For Plato, reality is nonmaterial and thus encountered only by the mind. Thus, Plato initiates an alternate tradition in metaphysics—**idealism**—the school of thought that maintains that reality is essentially rooted in ideas, not matter.

    In a way, Plato's theory of the nature of reality is surprisingly similar to religious explanations that philosophy usually rejects. Religious views of reality often hold the physical world to be inferior to some perfect spiritual domain. Quite understandably, then, many religious thinkers think very highly of Plato. Saint Augustine, one of the great Christian thinkers, thought that Plato was about as close as any "pagan" philosopher could get to being a Christian.

    There is quite a difference, however, between positing a higher *spiritual* plane inhabited by divine beings and positing a higher *intellectual* dimension occupied by abstract Forms. The Forms are not divinities that care about people one way or the other. They do not interfere in life on earth. They have no agenda of any sort, and it does not matter whether anyone believes in them or not. The Forms are eternal, but nothing about them implies any immortality for human beings.

    Thus, Plato gives us a conception of reality quite different from any we have so far encountered, one that is immaterial and knowable only by the mind, but not spiritual.

2. Plato brings to completion a tendency that was implicit in the Milesians' explanations of reality. All four thinkers ask, "Is reality dynamic or stable?" And they all answer "Stable." The Milesians try to identify a single unifying element that undergirds the changing character of the material world. With his concept of the Forms, Plato pushes this idea about as far as it will go. Instead of starting with material reality and arguing that it is unified and stable, Plato starts with ideal Forms that are by definition perfectly stable and argues that material reality, with all its changes, is merely an imperfect shadow of the Forms. The characteristics of reality, then, which determine how real something is, become qualities like being perfect, unchanging, and eternal.

    The significance of this is that it reminds us not to be bound in any fashion by the apparent evidence of our senses. In the material world, change is a characteristic

---

idealism In opposition to materialism, idealism maintains that reality is rooted in ideas, not matter. Plato, for example, claims that the Forms are more real and better sources of truth and knowledge than the objects that present themselves to our senses.

of life. And we generally think of living things as somehow superior to changeless, lifeless ones. Plato turns this assumption on its head, suggesting that permanence and stability are higher qualities. Whether he is right or wrong, the point is that we should not jump to conclusions on the basis of what *seems* most real.

3. Plato also asks a new question that has important implications: *How many people can understand the nature of reality?* His answer is, "Not many." Because grasping the highest, most abstract Forms is so difficult, a true understanding of the nature of reality is limited to a minority of the population, and a very small minority at that.

   Understanding the nature of reality is no trivial matter for Plato, as his political writings reveal. Plato's answer to the question "Who should rule?" is "Those who understand the Forms." Plato assumes that people who truly understand the essence of justice, fairness, equity, and the like are the only ones able to establish a just, fair, and equitable society. In the ideal society he describes in the *Republic,* you don't get to rule if you don't understand the Forms. Who would want a president, a prime minister, a king, or a queen who did not understand Justice, Fairness, Equity, and above all Goodness?

   This alone should persuade us that the nature of reality is not just a theoretical problem with no impact on the practical world. The lesson is that we should look for important practical consequences of abstract propositions. Here, we see the political consequences of a theory about the nature of reality. Some people complain that philosophy is a waste of time because it's impractical. Nothing could be further from the truth.

The Nature of Reality: Berkeley

Berkeley's Radical Idealism: Reality as the Product of Perception

You probably think that Plato's ideas about "reality" are hard to swallow. How could ideas be more real than physical objects? However, there is another version of idealism that is even more unusual, one that holds that minds and ideas are the only things that exist. This is the interpretation of the nature of reality offered by George Berkeley (1685–1753) (pronounced "bark-lee"), an Irishman who ultimately became an Anglican bishop in Ireland.

Plato's theory is called *objective idealism* because, even though material objects are "less real" than ideas, these objects nonetheless exist independently of the ideas. Berkeley's theory of *subjective idealism,* however, assaults our commonsense understanding of the world, because he maintains that objects do not exist apart from being perceived. Berkeley writes as follows:

> It is evident to anyone who takes a survey of the objects of human knowledge that they are either ideas actually imprinted on the senses, or else such as are perceived by attending to the passions and operations of the mind, or lastly, ideas formed by help of memory and imagination. . . . But besides all that endless variety of ideas or objects of knowledge, there is likewise something which knows or perceives them and exercises divers operations, as willing, imagining, remembering, about them. This perceiving, active being is what I call "mind," "spirit," "soul," or "myself." By

which words I do not denote any one of my ideas, but a thing entirely distinct from them, wherein they exist or, which is the same thing, whereby they are perceived—for the existence of an idea consists in being perceived.

—A Treatise Concerning the Principles of Human Knowledge

As Berkeley expressed it in Latin, *esse est percipi,* that is, "to be is to be perceived."

Berkeley's ideas come from two impulses. First, after the revolutionary thinking of the great seventeenth-century French philosopher René Descartes (whom you'll meet in Chapter 9), questions of how we know things came to be seen as logically prior to questions of the nature of reality. Descartes instituted what is called the "epistemological turn." The most fundamental questions in philosophy were not, then, "What is 'real'? What is the nature of reality?" but "What can I *know* to be 'real'? What can I *know* about the nature of reality?" Berkeley reflects this by concentrating on our perceptions of reality in a way that the Greek thinkers we've looked at do not. Remember, they talk mainly about the fundamental substance constituting reality.

Descartes' work first spawned a group of thinkers we call the "Continental rationalists" (Descartes, Baruch Spinoza, Gottfried Leibniz) who argue that knowledge comes via reason. In Great Britain, however, Descartes' epistemological turn produced the "British empiricists" (John Locke, Berkeley, and David Hume) who make the senses the source of knowledge. (You'll meet representatives from both groups in Chapter 9, "What Is Knowledge?") So that lays the foundation for Berkeley's notion that *esse est percipi.*

However, the second factor shaping Berkeley's ideas was religious. As a devout believer in God, Berkeley was concerned that Locke's version of empiricism implied that only material objects moving according to the laws of mechanics existed. Arguing instead that reality is the product of some perceiver subjectively perceiving sense data, Berkeley denies the existence of a material world. All that exist are minds and mental events. A physical object is simply my perception of that object. As Berkeley explains, "The table I write on exists, that is, I see and feel it; and if I were out of my study I should say it existed—meaning thereby that if I was in my study I might perceive it, or that some other spirit actually perceives it" (*A Treatise Concerning the Principles of Human Knowledge,* par. 14). That is, we have no reason to believe that objects exist in their own right—apart from being perceived by someone.

You are no doubt aware of problems that arise here. What happens when we stop perceiving an object? By Berkeley's logic, if we walk out of a room and close the door behind us, everything in the room should cease to exist. Do objects continually pop in and out of existence when we look at and then away from them? When we open the door to the closed room and look back in, the room looks exactly the way it was. What accounts for the consistency, order, and stability in our perceptions? The question is not, then, whether the tree falling in the forest with no one there makes a sound, but whether it exists at all to fall.

But here's where Berkeley brings in God. He claims that God constantly perceives reality and, thus, gives it its ultimate existence, as well as its form, shape, regularity, and predictability. God's perception of reality gives us what we perceive as laws of nature. Thus, an object remains in existence when we stop perceiving it because God continues to perceive it.

Berkeley and *The Matrix*

With Berkeley, we come nearly full circle in this chapter. Recall that in *The Matrix,* Neo discovers that what he thinks is "reality" is simply "appearance" generated by electrical impulses to his brain from a "neural-interactive simulation" designed by a race of machines to enslave humanity. That's not completely at odds with Berkeley's claim that all we experience are perceptions. Of course, Berkeley undergirds this with a benevolent God, while Morpheus links the Matrix to malevolent machines. But, from a philosophical perspective, is there really that much difference? Don't both Berkeley and Morpheus maintain that someone else is determining what we perceive to be "reality"? Whether the source is good or evil, do we really have any way of knowing that's *not* the way things really are?

Berkeley's Contribution

Berkeley's challenge to commonsense materialism is easy to ridicule. Samuel Johnson claimed to refute Berkeley and prove the existence of a material world simply by kicking a stone. Some would object to Berkeley's appeal to God as a classic case of tailoring philosophy to theology. Nonetheless, Berkeley's emphasis on minds and perceptions is important to take seriously. After all, there is a certain elegance and simplicity to the idea that reality is merely minds and perceptions. The material reality that most of us think generates those perceptions then becomes superfluous. Think about it. Isn't every one of your ideas about the world simply some kind of perception? Do you really have even a shred of evidence to suggest that there is a reality independent of an object being perceived? Can you prove the existence of a material world?

The Nature of Reality: A Final Word

We've covered a lot of territory since we asked the opening question, "What is the nature of reality?" We saw the difference between anthropomorphic and philosophical approaches to the problem. We examined the various explanations of five important philosophers—Thales, Anaximander, Anaximenes, Plato and Berkeley. And we saw the wide array of possibilities these thinkers give us to consider. We have gone from the idea that reality is material to the idea that it is immaterial, from trusting our senses to relying only on our minds, and from hearing about substances with qualities (water, air), to substances without qualities (the Unlimited), to qualities without substances (the Forms).

Yet we have only scratched the surface. The question of the nature of reality has preoccupied philosophers for the last 2,000 years, and it will continue to do so for thousands of years in the future. Thinkers have answered this question with a bewildering array of explanations. Nonetheless, you should now have some sense of the questions involved in exploring the nature of reality. As you heard at the beginning of this chapter, you cannot do much in philosophy without a theory of the nature of reality. It's one of the starting points. Fortunately, you have begun to acquire the tools you'll need to start forging your own answer. And, as usual, that is what it's going to have to be—your answer.

Main Points of Chapter 8

1. The most fundamental philosophical question is "What is real?" Does something have to be material to be real, or can it be nonmaterial or conceptual?

2. The first explanations of the nature of reality that humans came up with were anthropomorphic. More characteristic of a religious than a scientific or philosophical outlook, the anthropomorphic explanations of ancient Egypt and Mesopotamia interpret the world of nature through human concepts and see nature as having a will of its own or at least being controlled by invisible superhuman deities.

3. The first philosophers in ancient Greece reject mythic and anthropomorphic accounts. Grappling with the issue of appearance versus reality, the Milesians offer explanations of reality based on the idea of a single underlying element. Thales argues for water, Anaximander suggests "the Unlimited," and Anaximenes proposes air.

4. These thinkers also speculate about the principles that govern change. Thales speaks of objects being "full of gods," Anaximander invokes a principle of "moral necessity," and Anaximenes points to the processes of condensation and rarefaction.

5. Plato rejects the materialist orientation of the Milesians and argues that reality is ultimately noncorporeal. Plato illustrates his ideas through the image of a line and the allegory of the cave. Plato believes that the highest level of reality is populated by the Forms, nonmaterial models of perfection that give meaning and existence to objects on the physical plane.

6. Berkeley takes Plato's *objective idealism* a step farther. Claiming that material objects don't exist at all, Berkeley makes a case for *subjective idealism.* "Reality" consists only of minds and perceptions. As Berkeley puts it, *esse est percipi,* that is, "to be is to be perceived."

Discussion Questions

1. Having studied this chapter, how would you now define "reality"?

2. One criticism of religions like Judaism and Christianity is that their images of God are "anthropomorphic." Explain what this means and decide whether it is true. What is the significance of this if it is true?

3. To Plato, philosophers are people who have left the cave, gone outside, and seen the brightness of the sun. Plato points out that when such people return to the cave, however, they have trouble adjusting to the darkness, and identifying the shadows on the wall. Furthermore, if they try to convince the other prisoners that the shadows are paltry images of what is "real," the philosophers are scoffed at and thought strange. Doesn't this fit with the way most people think about philosophers? Might this mean that philosophers have "seen the light" while most other people are still preoccupied by shadows?

4. What do you make of the fact that the truths of mathematics are eternal and perfect? Does this mean that a "mathematical reality" is superior to "physical reality"? In trying to determine the nature of reality, is the mind or the physical senses the better tool?

5. If Plato's theory of the Forms is correct, would you agree with Plato that only people who understand Forms like Justice, Fairness, Equity, and so on should be in positions of responsibility in our society? Should such knowledge be a requirement of public office? How would you test for it?

6. In *The Life of Samuel Johnson,* James Boswell (1791) recounts the following conversation:

> After we came out of the church, we stood talking for some time together of Bishop Berkeley's ingenious sophistry to prove the non-existence of matter, and that everything in the universe is merely ideal. I observed, that though we are satisfied his doctrine is not true, it is impossible to refute it. I never shall forget the alacrity with which Johnson answered, striking his foot with mighty force against a large stone, till he rebounded from it, "I refute it thus."

Is *idealism* that easily refuted?

7. In *The Matrix,* one of the characters decides that he'd prefer the illusion of good food and a comfortable life over the reality of utilitarian food and a life of struggle. So he makes a deal with Agent Smith to turn over Morpheus. If the technology made it possible, would you choose a "virtual" luxurious, pleasure-filled life over a "real" life that invariably would include times of challenge, failure, and unhappiness? Which pill would you take?

Selected Readings

For more on concepts of reality in ancient Egypt and Mesopotamia, see Henri Frankfort, *Before Philosophy: The Intellectual Adventure of Ancient Man* (New York: Penguin Books, 1946). The best collections of the fragments of the early philosophers are *The Presocratic Philosophers,* edited by G. S. Kirk and J. W. Raven (Cambridge: Cambridge University Press, 1957) and *The Presocratics,* edited by Phillip Wheelwright (New York: Odyssey Press, 1966). Since we have only fragments of what these thinkers wrote, we often have to rely on the accounts of later Greek thinkers, like Aristotle, to get a broader picture of their philosophies.

Plato's allegory of the cave can be found in his *Republic,* Book VII, the discussion of the line in Book VI. For additional discussions of the Greek thinkers studied in this chapter, see: Robert S. Brumbaugh, *The Philosophers of Greece* (Albany, NY: State University of New York Press, 1981), and W. K. C. Guthrie, *The Greek Philosophers* (New York: Harper and Row, 1975).

For Berkeley, see his *Treatise Concerning the Principles of Human Knowledge.*

9

What Is Knowledge?

- *Knowledge Depends on the Mind: Rationalism*
- *Knowledge Depends on the Senses: Empiricism*
- *Knowledge Is Limited to Appearance: Immanuel Kant*
- *The Search for Knowledge—Where Are We?*

Imagine that it's the middle of winter, you're dreaming of spring break, and you're reading a bulletin board between classes trying to decide where you'll go. You've been to the usual places already, and you're looking for something different. Then you spot it. "Tired of the typical Spring Break? Looking for a once-in-a-lifetime adventure? Check us out at www.danger-r-us-tours.com." You jot down the URL, discover that the company offers a trip that's a cross between a treasure hunt and an archeological dig near the legendary Inca city of Machu Picchu, and you immediately sign up.

You head to Peru in March, and the trip is everything you hoped it would be. The outfit you signed up with is searching for a legendary hidden temple that supposedly contains untold wealth, and every day a new clue is discovered. One day, you decide to go a little higher on the mountain to take some pictures. Lacking a compass and a sense of direction, however, you get lost trying to return to camp. The harder you try to retrace your steps, the less familiar everything looks. As the sun starts going down, you come upon the entrance to a cave. You figure that the safest thing is to spend the night in the cave and find your way in the morning.

When you enter the cave, you can't believe your eyes. It's brilliantly lit by some mysterious source, and there's a huge, ancient door on the back wall. You push the door open and walk through a long passageway that takes you into a beautiful valley. In the middle of the valley you spot the temple—and the treasure—that you've been searching for. You decide to go back to the cave so that you can get an early start in the morning, but as you get close to the door, you hear a voice that says: "I am Mama-Quilla, goddess of the moon and guardian of this temple. Since you have found your way here, you are welcome to stay and enjoy the fruits of this valley as long as you like. However, in order to leave, you must show that you are worthy of your discovery. Only a person of extraordinary wisdom deserves the wealth of the temple, so you must correctly answer me, or the door will remain locked. So think carefully before you answer. Which is the true source of knowledge: the eye of the mind in darkness or the eye of the hand in light?"

It's fair to say that this is probably more of an adventure than you were looking for. Still, if you ever want to leave the valley, you need to come up with the right answer. Conveniently, you're taking two classes this term that give you an idea of what the goddess's question is about. You have a math class in which your professor delights in saying how superior the discoveries of mathematics are to those of science. You have heard countless times: "The sum of the interior angles of every triangle that ever did exist, ever will exist, or that anyone will ever imagine is 180 degrees. That statement is absolutely, unshakably, and eternally true. You won't find anything like that in science!" (So you assume this is knowledge from "the eye of the mind in darkness," that is, with your eyes closed.) At the same time, you have a chemistry professor who starts each class by saying, "If you learn only one thing in this class, it's that the scientific method is the only way to arrive at knowledge. If you aren't gathering empirical data and testing your hypotheses in rigorous experiments, you're on the wrong track. The so-called 'eternal truths' of mathematics and logic are like fiction—they're cute and entertaining, but they don't give you knowledge of the *real* world." (You figure that knowledge from "the eye of the hand in light" means facts that you can only ascertain by observing and measuring.) In other words, you've traveled to Machu Picchu and find yourself in the middle of a departmental rivalry that you thought you'd left thousands of miles behind you.

So, what's your answer?

You've obviously had the bad luck of running into an Incan goddess with a taste for the part of philosophy called *epistemology*—a word that comes from ancient Greek and means "the study of knowledge." She's created a problem that puts you squarely in the middle of one of the most basic debates in philosophy: Does "knowledge" come from the mind or from the senses? Throughout the history of philosophy, two points of view—*rationalism* (which relies on the mind) and *empiricism* (which relies on the senses)—have debated this question. In this chapter, we examine these competing schools of thought. (Hopefully, by the time you get to the end of the chapter, you'll be able to come up with an answer that will satisfy the goddess.)

Knowledge Depends on the Mind: Rationalism

Rationalism takes its name from *ratio*, the Latin word for "reason." The rationalist school of philosophy thinks that knowledge comes from, or arises in, our minds. (This is also referred to as knowing something *a priori*.) The best examples of knowledge, say the rationalist philosophers, are mathematics and logic. Consider the statement: "the sum of the interior angles of a triangle is 180 degrees." Can you think of any conditions—no

---

> **rationalism** Rationalism claims that knowledge comes from, or arises in, our minds. Rationalist philosophers say that the best examples of knowledge are mathematics and logic.

matter how unlikely—under which it won't be true? We can't even imagine the possibility. In contrast, information that we get through our senses, claim the rationalists, is decidedly inferior. For example, it's changeable. The sentence, "My car is green," may be true today. But if I paint it blue tomorrow, that's no longer the case.

The Rationalism of Plato

If you read Chapter 8 on the nature of reality, you have already run into one rationalist, the Greek philosopher Plato. Plato is such a rationalist that he sees a close similarity and connection between philosophy and mathematics. He supposedly had carved over the entry to his Academy, "Let no one ignorant of geometry enter here." His educational program for philosophers includes a ten-year study of mathematics.

Plato claims that, in addition to the physical world that we experience with our senses, there is another dimension of reality that we encounter only with our minds. This "intelligible" world is populated by mathematical objects (triangles, circles, squares) and by what Plato calls the Forms. Forms are hard to describe in a few words, but basically they are nonmaterial, perfect models of everything that exists. Completely abstract, the Forms capture the deepest essence of things, whether those things are concrete, like chairs, stones, and trees, or qualities like justice, beauty, and goodness.[1]

Knowledge of the Forms is the only thing that counts as knowledge, according to Plato. And such knowledge, remember, can be reached only by our minds. In Plato's opinion, the information we get through our senses is decidedly inferior. This claim that real knowledge is limited only to the insights we arrive at through our minds is the hallmark of a rationalist.

The Superiority of Intellectual Knowledge

There is something attractive about this position. After all, the senses are more easily deceived than the intellect. For example, which of these lines is longer?

The answer, of course, is neither. They're both the same length. But it doesn't *look* that way. The bottom one looks longer. You have to take a ruler and measure both lines to find out which is actually longer. You use your *mind* to settle the issue, and your intellectual conclusion overrides the illusion of your senses. That seems to support the rationalist claim.

Now that you have measured the lines, you know that they are equal. Plato still wouldn't agree, however. Indeed, Plato would challenge anything you claimed to know through your senses, no matter how self-evident. Suppose you said, for example, "I know this is a white page with black print on it." Plato would answer, "No. Because you arrive at that conclusion with your senses, it doesn't count as

---

[1]Such a brief account cannot do justice to Plato's theory of the Forms. You might want to go back and read pages 234–244 for a better idea of Plato's thinking.

knowledge. You do not *know* it, you only *think* or *believe* you know it. Whatever you have in your mind is inferior to knowledge."

Such a view may strike you as implausible at best. After all, this page and the printing on it are right before your eyes. But Plato isn't saying that you are dreaming. Plato would grant that the page exists, your optical nerves are being stimulated, and your brain is translating these sensations into certain conclusions. He just would not call your conclusions "knowledge."

What does count as knowledge? Why does a rationalist accept as knowledge a claim like "the sum of the interior angles of a triangle is 180 degrees" but reject "this page is white with black print"?

The Rationalist Idea of Truth

The best way to understand why rationalists see intellectual knowledge as superior to sensory knowledge is to look at the characteristics of what is being known. And the best way to do that is to start with the idea that knowledge is always knowledge of some *truth*. I can say, "I *know* that I grew up in Massachusetts" because that is true. But can I say, "I *know* that the great San Francisco earthquake happened in 1929"? No. I may think I'm right, but I am wrong. (It took place in 1906.) So even though I claim to know this fact, all I am really voicing is my false *belief,* or *opinion.* We can *know* only something that is *true.*

What is so special about what the rationalists call truth? They always use the truths of mathematics and logic as the best examples, so let's consider the following "true" statements:

- Triangles have three sides.
- 2 + 2 = 4.
- If you bisect a right angle, you create two angles of 45 degrees each.
- Any statement of the form *A and not-A* ("today is Wednesday and today is not Wednesday") is false because it is a contradiction.
- Any statement of the form *A or not-A* ("today is Wednesday or today is not Wednesday") is true.[2]
- If Mendez is a bachelor, then Mendez is unmarried.
- All humans are mortal; Williams is human; therefore, Williams is mortal.

If I say I *know* any of the things in these statements, I am saying that these statements are *true.* But what kind of truth are we talking about in a rationalist's idea of knowledge?

Permanence, Stability, Duration. First, in purely intellectual knowledge, the truths that we know do not change. This kind of truth is stable and enduring.

Will triangles exist next week? Yes. Will they still have three sides? Undoubtedly. Will a contradiction be true? No—not next week and not ever. Will we ever find

---

[2]There are only these two possibilities, and one of them has to be true. This is called the Law of Excluded Middle.

a married bachelor? Impossible. This kind of truth does not change. It is permanent, constant, unvarying. Will a time ever come when these statements are false? No. A bisected right angle always has and always will consist of two 45-degree angles. The truths of mathematics or logic will always be true.

Now what about the truths of the physical world, "This page is white with black print," for example. Will this page still be white next week? Maybe, but not if you color it green. (And eventually it will turn yellow on its own.) How long is your house key? Will it still be that size tomorrow? Not if you break it off in the lock. How easy is it to change physical facts? All too easy. Physical truths are far more fragile than intellectual truths.

How long are physical facts true? Only for as long as the physical object exists in precisely the state it was in at the instant you observed it. Will this book be around next week so that you can describe the color of the pages and print? Perhaps, but not if it falls into the trash and is incinerated. Furthermore, every material object is in a state of constant change, either of growth or decay. Eventually, it deteriorates completely. When whatever you're sitting on, lying on, or leaning against right now decays, anything you say about it today will be false. Physical truth simply is not true for as long as intellectual truth is.

It seems to makes sense to prefer truth that doesn't change, as the rationalists do. For a long time, the "truth" was that "the sun moves around the earth." Now the "truth" is that "the earth moves around the sun." Were both statements true? Of course not. We now say that the earth-centered theory was *believed* to be true. People were mistaken. They had a *false opinion* of reality. We ordinarily assume that facts that are true simply do not change.

Certainty. How sure are you that each of the mathematical statements on page 252 is true? Provided that you know what the terms mean, you are absolutely certain of their truth. There is not the slightest chance that somewhere there exists a triangle with more or fewer than three sides. If you traveled to the site of the most ancient civilizations and translated the mathematicians' clay tablets, you would never encounter a four-sided or a two-sided triangle. It cannot happen. Triangles have three sides—every single one of them.

What about the "logical" truths on page 252? There is not a bit of doubt about any of them either. How certain are we? One hundred percent.

Now consider the statement, "This is a white page with black print." You are probably just as certain of that as well.

Are you really? Are you just as certain of it as you are that 2 + 2 = 4? What if you're color-blind and don't know it? If the page were actually light yellow and the print deep blue, it would look white and black to you.

"But," you say, "I'm not color-blind. I've had my eyes tested. This page is white and the print is black."

Isn't it still possible, however, that we are all color-blind in some way that eye tests don't show? Might not the page be a color that our eyes and brains cannot process? Granted, it's unlikely, but it's not impossible. Are you really as certain that the page is white as you are that triangles have three sides?

Now what do you say? The evidence of your senses is persuasive, but is there no chance that the page and print are actually different than they appear to be?

After all, our senses are not 100 percent trustworthy. Therefore, when we consider the certainty we have in mathematics, maybe we should modify our stand and say, "I'm 99 percent certain that the page is white and the print is black."

Human history is full of erroneous beliefs based on misinterpretations of physical evidence: The earth is in the center of the universe; foul smells cause disease; the atom is the smallest particle of matter. All this "knowledge" bit the dust. It should be clear, then, why rationalists claim that knowledge achieved solely through the workings of the mind, the knowledge of mathematics and logic, is so much more certain than knowledge based on physical evidence.

The Rationalist Definition of Knowledge

This is what rationalistic philosophers like Plato mean when they suggest that only the truths we arrive at through our minds alone can count as knowledge. Only purely intellectual disciplines like mathematics and logic enable us to reach conclusions that are permanent and certain. The facts we derive from observing the physical world are temporary and changing. Our senses give us inferior information. It may not be fiction or illusory. But it is too insubstantial to quality as knowledge.

Actually, there is something very appealing about the rationalistic idea of knowledge. If we really know something, wouldn't we like to think that that fact is not going to change? And if we claim to know something, don't we want to be absolutely certain of it? Clearly, mathematical and logical truths meet these two requirements far better than claims based solely on the data provided by our senses.

The Rationalism of René Descartes

Plato may get the rationalist ball rolling, but he is not the most important rationalist. That honor should probably go to the seventeenth-century French philosopher René Descartes. Descartes examines the concept of knowledge much more fully than his ancient Greek predecessor. In so doing, he breathes new life into the claim that the mind comes to more certain conclusions than the senses.

Descartes' thought had a major impact on every thinker that followed him, largely because of the central position he gave to questions about knowledge. Descartes came to think that instead of starting with the question "What is the nature of reality?" we should start with the questions "What is the nature of knowledge?" and "How do we know things?" Thales, Anaximander, and Anaximenes asked, "What is the basic substance out of which reality is made?" Descartes would say that they should have asked, "How can we tell if we really know something about reality?"

After Descartes, epistemology moves to the center of philosophy. In fact, Descartes' approach ultimately leads some important thinkers in the history of philosophy to explore deeply how the human mind works as an instrument that produces knowledge. Does the mind accurately represent reality, or does it distort reality in the very process of knowing it? The fact that Descartes' thinking changed how all philosophers after him think counts as a genuine revolution in philosophy.

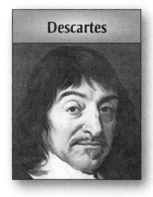

Descartes

René Descartes (1596–1650) was born in France and educated at the Jesuit college of La Fleche. After a period of travel, including a short stint as a soldier, Descartes began writing about the proper method of intellectual investigation (*Rules for the Direction of the Mind*), a method that would give philosophical knowledge the same certainty as the conclusions of mathematics. He completed scientific and mathematical writings, but suppressed his own defense of the idea that the earth revolves about the sun when he heard of Galileo's fate for taking the same position. In 1641, Descartes published the book he is best known for, *Meditations on First Philosophy*. In 1649, he agreed to teach philosophy to Queen Christina of Sweden, but he died of pneumonia the following year.

In this chapter, however, we want to see how Descartes concentrates on the idea that we have to be absolutely certain of something before we can say we know it. Descartes takes absolute certainty as the most important characteristic of genuine knowledge, and we need to discover where and how he finds such certainty in purely intellectual truths.

Certainty and the Radical Doubt

In his intense examination of what we claim to know, Descartes takes the simple act of questioning, or doubting, what he thinks he knows to an unprecedented extreme. In fact, Descartes is best known for what is called his *radical doubt,* which he describes in his famous work, *Meditations on First Philosophy.* The term "radical," as you know, means both "fundamental" and "extreme," and both meanings are intended here. For example, a little while ago when we considered the claim "this page is white and the print is black," you may have thought it was going too far to suggest that you might be color-blind. But in comparison to the objections Descartes conceives, that was nothing.

Descartes writes, "reason already convinces me that I should abstain from the belief in things which are not entirely certain and indubitable." For him, truth has to be certain and unshakable. There can be not one trace of doubt in our minds. If we can make up any scenario, no matter how unlikely or bizarre, in which what we claim to know might be false, then we are forced to say we do not know it. As long as it is theoretically or logically possible that something is false, Descartes says we cannot claim we know it. The only way to find genuine knowledge is to doubt everything that suggests itself as true. Whatever survives the heat of such intense questioning must be certain.

If there is any doubt, reject the idea. This is one tall order. But keep in mind that Descartes believes that issues of knowledge are the most fundamental ones. He is trying to establish an unshakable foundation on which to build his philosophy. It's like constructing a building: If you're going to put something up, you are well advised to make sure that the spot is secure and the foundation is rock-solid.

Doubting the Obvious: Dreaming

Let's go back to "this page is white and the print is black." Descartes would probably go along with the doubt that "maybe we're all color-blind," unlikely as it is. But what if you now said, "Look, I've asked an expert to measure the light waves that reflect off the paper. Everything is within the normal spectrum and is precisely what we'd expect for white and black. The white page measures one thing; the black print another. Nothing registers on any instrument that our brains aren't processing. All the white has the same frequency. So does the black. This proves that color-blindness is not present." Would this appeal to science settle the question with absolute certainty? Descartes would say no, and for this reason.

When Descartes considers ordinary perceptions that seem too obvious to doubt, he wonders whether or not he just might be dreaming. And after thinking about it, he says in the *Meditations,* "When I consider these matters carefully, I realize so clearly that there are no conclusive indications by which waking life can be distinguished from sleep that I am quite astonished, and my bewilderment is such that it is almost able to convince me that I am sleeping."

At first glance, you may think Descartes is going off the deep end here. Few of us have trouble figuring out whether we've dreamt something or actually lived it. There is, however, an incredibly vivid kind of dreaming called "lucid dreaming," in which the experience is in many ways indistinguishable from ordinary waking experience. So it's possible that if we were having a lucid dream, we might at first mistake it for being awake. There are also drug-induced hallucinations that seem real to the people having them. Consider where the technology involved in "virtual reality" may ultimately go. Or what about something even more exotic? Remember the movie *The Matrix?* The film is based on the idea that the experiences that most people think they're having are really the product of a complex computer simulation created by an artificial intelligence that has actually enslaved humanity and uses humans simply as an energy source. So, in theory, Descartes' doubts about ordinary perception aren't totally off-base. And if it's even remotely possible to question the authenticity of what we're perceiving, we have to concede Descartes' point. That, Descartes would say, would be enough to show that our physical senses aren't totally dependable.

Having dismissed the conclusions of our senses in this fashion, Descartes moves to the conclusions of our minds—the pure truths of mathematics. Perhaps we can find a way to doubt the reports of our eyes. But how can we question "$2 + 3 = 5$" or "a square will never have more than four sides"? Wouldn't we be crazy to doubt such things?

Doubting the Obvious: Deception

We would be crazy or deceived. Remember that the radical doubt allows for *any* scenario, no matter how bizarre. Descartes definitely goes for the bizarre here, writing,

> I have long held the belief that there is a God who can do anything, by whom I have been created and made what I am. But how can I be sure but that he has brought it to pass that there is no earth, no sky, no extended bodies, no shape, no size, no place, and that nevertheless I have the impressions of all these things and

cannot imagine that things might be other than as I now see them? And further-more, . . . how can I be sure but that God has brought it about that I am always mistaken when I add two and three or count the sides of a square, or when I judge of something even easier, if I can imagine anything easier than that?

—Meditations

Or, if God is not doing this, Descartes says that there is no reason why we can-not imagine that this massive deception is being masterminded by "a certain evil spirit, not less clever and deceitful than powerful." But whether God or some Master Deceiver is behind this deceit, the bottom line is the same. We still have no way to say that we are absolutely certain of anything—from physical perception ("this page is white") to intellectual calculation ("2 + 3 = 5").

The One Certainty: Existing

So far, we're coming up dry. If some Master Deceiver really is at work, everything may be an illusion—this book, the room you're in, your friends, the events you think you have experienced, even your hands, your feet, and all the rest of you.

At this point, however, Descartes finally hits on something indubitable. Because even if you are being deceived about absolutely everything around you, the one thing you cannot be deceived about is that *you exist*. You *must* exist in order to be deceived. And no matter how you try to imagine it, although you can doubt ab-solutely everything that goes on outside you and even everything that goes on within your mind, you cannot doubt your own existence. Descartes concludes,

Even though there may be a deceiver of some sort, very powerful and very tricky, who bends all his efforts to keep me perpetually deceived, there can be no slight-est doubt that I exist, since he deceives me; and let him deceive me as much as he will, he can never make me be nothing as long as I think that I am something. Thus, after having thought well on this matter, and after examining all things with care, I must finally conclude and maintain that this proposition: *I am, I exist,* is necessarily true every time that I pronounce it or conceive it in my mind.

—Meditations

You have probably all heard Descartes' famous line: *Cogito ergo sum,* "I think, therefore I am." This is what it means. Doubting is a kind of thinking—even be-ing deceived requires thinking on our part—and as long as you're aware of yourself thinking or doubting, it must necessarily follow that you exist. There is no way to question this one piece of knowledge. The one thing we cannot dispute is that we are trying to doubt things. We cannot concoct even a wild story that shakes our absolute certainty that we are methodically questioning everything around us.

The Standard of Truth: Clarity and Distinctness

Having discovered what he considers to be one example of certain knowledge—his own existence—Descartes looks to see what philosophical conclusions he can draw from it. He studies this piece of knowledge and claims that it has a *clarity* and *distinctness* that set it apart from more dubious ideas. These criteria, then, become his general standard for truth: "Accordingly it seems to me that already I can establish a general rule that all things which I perceive very clearly and very distinctly are true."

Self-knowledge is not the only thing Descartes perceives so clearly and distinctly, and this leads him to draw some important conclusions. First, he claims that the existence of God is clear and distinct. However, if God exists, there is no Master Deceiver—a good God would not allow such deception. And if there is no Master Deceiver, mathematics must be sound. (The integrity of mathematics is, not surprisingly, very important to a rationalist.) Descartes also argues that two other basic concepts, Substance and Identity, are legitimate. Taken together, this forms the foundation for his general interpretation of reality.

These "very clear and very distinct" perceptions—Self, God, Substance, and Identity—are *innate ideas,* Descartes says. Describing them as "certain germs of truth which exist naturally in our souls," he believes that God puts them there. This theory of innate ideas, we might say, envisions the human mind like a computer that already comes with a few basic programs installed. Because these concepts are innate, they are also self-evident, and their truth is absolutely certain. (Whether all of these ideas are as self-evident as Descartes claims is, of course, a separate question.)

The Superiority of the Mind as a Source of Knowledge

It should now be clear just why Descartes and other rationalists conclude that the mind is the only dependable source of knowledge. We don't even need Platonic Forms or Cartesian "innate ideas" to make this claim. Descartes thinks that even ordinary observable events show the superiority of the mind. He writes:

> Let us take, for example, this bit of wax which has just been taken from the hive. It has not yet completely lost the sweetness of the honey it contained; it still retains something of the odor of the flowers from which it was collected; its color, shape, and size are apparent; it is hard and cold; it can easily be touched; and, if you knock on it, it will give out some sound. Thus everything which can make a body distinctly known is found in this example.
>
> But now while I am talking I bring it close to the fire. What remains of the taste evaporates; the odor vanishes; its color changes; its shape is lost; its size increases; it becomes liquid; it grows hot; one can hardly touch it; and although it is knocked upon, it will give out no sound. Does the same wax remain after this change? We must admit that it does.
>
> —Meditations

Is it the same piece of wax after it melts? Of course. Are we sure? Absolutely. But how do we know it is the same wax? Our senses tell us that the solid wax and the liquid wax are different objects, particularly if we did not witness the melting ourselves. So it must be our minds that give us the truth. Descartes thus thinks this proves the core idea of rationalism—the superiority of the intellect as a source of knowledge.

A Contemporary Radical Doubt

Even though you understand Descartes' conclusions, you may not be as impressed with his "radical doubt" as he would wish. Most people don't seriously question whether they are awake or dreaming. They also don't normally wonder whether some malevolent spirit is trying to deceive them by manipulating their thoughts. You know that you dream, and you know about optical illusions. But most of us know when we are awake, alert, and thinking straight.

If Descartes' ideas about dreaming and a Master Deceiver did not shake your confidence in what you "know," perhaps we can discover a more contemporary "radical doubt" that does. Our goal is to find out if we can know anything with absolute certainty. If we can imagine the slightest theoretical doubt about something, using Descartes' rules, we will give up any claim to "know" it.

An Alternative to the Senses: "Inner" Data. Like Descartes, we can quickly reject the senses as dependable sources of knowledge. This brings us to an examination of our inner selves, our minds. Here is where Descartes conjures up his clever, deceitful, and powerful "evil spirit" whose capacity for deception forces us to question even the most apparently evident conclusions of the mind.

In all honesty, Descartes' idea of a Master Deceiver is unconvincing. It is theoretically possible, of course, but it doesn't persuade the average person that the conclusions of our minds are doubtful. Nonetheless, there are good reasons why we cannot trust our minds any more than we can trust our senses, and those are what we should explore here.

Let's take a familiar mental operation: memory. Do you remember the most important events of your life—major birthdays, graduation, romances, accomplishments? Not the first thing you said as a baby or what you wore in the spring pageant in the fourth grade. Just major events that took place after you're old enough to remember things. Did these events actually happen? No doubt you're absolutely certain that they did.

Now, is it possible that there were any major events that you do *not* remember? Again, not small stuff—genuinely important things. You probably think this is a dumb question. How could you *not* remember a crucial event in your life? You're no doubt certain that you remember all the big events, but can you really be sure? Can't the mind be deceived as the senses can?

In fact, the mind is often unreliable, and many people do not remember major events in their lives, or do not remember them accurately. For example, it is well known that when we experience certain terrible events, our minds often cope with the trauma by selectively changing our memories. One psychological mechanism is called a *screen memory,* in which we reconfigure reality and remember an event very differently. Someone who was sexually abused as a child, for instance, might remember the event as an attack by a fierce dog.

Another strategy is to remove an event from our conscious minds altogether, a mechanism psychologists call *denial.* People in denial will recount their past totally omitting certain experiences. As far as they are concerned, these events never happened. For example, someone who grew up with an alcoholic parent might have no memory of any alcohol abuse. When a sibling recalls the details, the person in denial thinks that this other person is exaggerating, making things up, or crazy. No one could forget something that important, he thinks.

However, if the mind can simply "forget" a major event that happened or reconstruct an incident in a more acceptable way, then the mind is not a completely accurate and reliable instrument for representing reality. And, of course, if there is the slightest room for doubt, we cannot claim that something, in this case the mind, is a source of certain knowledge.

Other Mental Operations: Brain Engineering. Now let's move to the part of the mind that handles pure thought, like that used in mathematics and logic. Do we have any reason to question the integrity of those mental processes? Even here, doubt exists.

Remember that Descartes allows us to use any scenario as a test, no matter how unlikely, so long as it is logically and theoretically possible. All we need is a hint of doubt. The following story is science fiction, but it may shed some light on real knowledge. See what you think.

The year is 2873, and brain scientists have just made a major breakthrough. They have finally decoded the brain's electrochemical signals, and we can now trace the processes involved in thinking. We can track and record every step as a person takes in information, mulls it over, and comes to a conclusion. We can watch how people's brains formulate ideas, values, factual statements, beliefs—everything. The operating system of the brain is now as clear to us as a computer's. We can even get a printout of what goes on.

The brain, it turns out, operates in a very logical fashion, so, not surprisingly, the printout looks like the details of a computer program or the proof of a logic problem. Look at the physical object you are reading right now, and you will instantaneously think "book." But in between, your brain goes through thousands of steps which amount to saying, "If an object has characteristics A, B, C, . . . and performs functions Q, R, S, . . . , then it is a 'book'." The printout of this thought covers all that. It specifies the sensory evidence you take in, what your brain does with it, its preliminary conclusions, and ultimately its final judgment. It is all just like logic.

But beyond tracking the brain's operations, we have learned how to alter its program. By beaming electrical signals to the brain, we can change the conclusions that follow from specific data. For example, we can take "if 'pages,' 'words,' 'print,' 'cover,' . . . , then 'book'" and make it "if 'pages,' 'words,' 'print,' . . . , then 'house.'" The conclusion is still logical in that it follows the rules of the program. But it is false. The person whose program we have rearranged doesn't think that, though. He is convinced that he has come to a correct conclusion on the basis of reasonable premises.

Now we can make this person's brain conclude anything we want it to. We can even have him think "2 + 2 = 5." To his (altered) way of thinking, this is self-evidently true. We can inject all kinds of false premises—let's say, "women are inferior to men" and "it is wrong to treat women the same as men." When this person has to make a decision about how to treat men and women, he will be absolutely certain that it is logical and right to treat them differently. After all, the sentence "if 'man' and 'woman,' then 'treat differently'" is now part of his brain's "wiring."

Is anything like this at least theoretically possible? (Remember Descartes' rule—the least bit of doubt is all we need.)

Look at the real world, now or at any time. Do you see many examples of racial and sexual discrimination? Aren't those people who discriminate drawing their conclusions "logically" from the false premise "if 'nonwhite' [or 'female'], then 'inferior'"? Somewhere along the line, they took in a false premise. And as a result they are certain of things that are actually false.

To take another example, consider someone with an irrational fear of climbing a ladder. In essence, his "program" reads: "if 'climbing a ladder,' then 'danger;' and if 'danger,' then 'feel fear.'" The second premise, of course, is true—fear is a reasonable response to danger. But the first premise is false—climbing a ladder is not necessarily dangerous. Nonetheless, because this premise is part of this person's "program," fear is a "logical" conclusion when he is on a ladder. Where did this false idea come from? Perhaps he fell off a ladder when he was young and was frightened by the experience. He then concluded that stepping onto a ladder virtually guaranteed falling off of it, and so he "knows" that this is so now.

The conclusions drawn by the minds of people afflicted with prejudices and/or irrational fears may be "logical" and "certain," but the premises from which they derive are always false. To return to Descartes' radical doubt, then, those of us who entertain any false premises—and who among us does not—cannot be certain of the conclusions we derive from them, even though they were derived in the mind by logical means. There's a doubt for you.

Can we ever be sure that our minds are free of false premises? Since we all operate according to our own premises and we don't necessarily know that our premises are false, it is impossible for us to be totally sure. And if we cannot be totally sure, then we have cast a genuine doubt on the workings of the mind. In other words, we do not have to imagine a Master Deceiver to say that knowledge stemming from the logical operations of our minds may be less than perfect.

Descartes' Insight

Seen through contemporary eyes, Descartes' conclusion that the only thing we can know for sure is that we exist still seems legitimate. Whether or not there are contemporary ways to talk sensibly about innate ideas remains a question for you to ponder. Descartes appeals to the concept of God to prove the truth of the outside world, but those arguments, and the issue of God's existence, exceed the scope of this chapter.

If nothing else, however, Descartes gives us powerful reasons for being more than a little skeptical about what we are sure is true, and that insight alone assures the indispensability of Descartes' thought in any examination of our own lives and of the world around us.

Knowledge Depends on the Senses: Empiricism

Descartes' rationalism poses a major challenge to anyone who wants to argue from the opposing point of view. With the continuing development of a scientific outlook in the eighteenth century, there was no shortage of philosophers who did just that. A number of important thinkers rejected rationalism and claimed that genuine knowledge came only through the senses. This philosophical tradition is called

empiricism, from the Greek word *empeiria,* meaning "experience." Empiricism holds that knowledge and truth are the products of sensory experiences and not of purely mental operations. (This is also referred to as knowing something *a posteriori.*)

Anyone living in the twentieth century is already familiar with the main tenets of empiricism: knowledge comes through the senses; facts must be observable and testable; any observation not meeting these qualifications is false, uncertain, or trivial—certainly not genuine knowledge.

Empiricism's Objections to Rationalism

You may not find Plato's idea of the Forms or Descartes' "radical doubt" particularly illuminating. But, in general, the truths of mathematics and logic—which are, after all, the rationalist's model of knowledge—do seem to have a permanence, stability, and duration that empirical truths lack.

Why, then, did the empiricists reject rationalism? The fact is that empirical philosophers find nonempirical claims, even the claims of mathematics and logic, trivial. When it comes right down to it, the empiricists say, a rationalistic piece of knowledge does not tell us anything new. Empirical knowledge, by contrast, shows us something that we did not know before.

Another way to describe this difference between the rationalist's and the empiricist's idea of knowledge is to talk about two different kinds of statements: *analytic statements* and *synthetic statements.* (Some of this language is fairly technical, but if you take your time with it, everything will be clear.)

Analytic Statements

Analytic statements are what we find in definitions, logic, and mathematics. They get their name from the fact that they simply analyze a concept and identify its parts.

For example: "Smith is a *bachelor;* therefore, Smith is *unmarried.*" Is it true? Yes. But does the conclusion, "Smith is unmarried" tell us anything new? Not if we already understand what "bachelor" means. The idea "unmarried" is already part of the concept "bachelor." We might represent it like this:

```
┌─────────────┐
│  BACHELOR   │
│  Unmarried  │
│  Man        │
└─────────────┘
```

---

empiricism Empiricism holds that knowledge and truth are the products of sensory experiences and not of purely mental operations. Modern science employs a thoroughly empirical approach.

analytic statement An analytic statement attributes a property to something, and that property is already implicit in the definition of that object or concept. For example, "A square has four sides" and "A bachelor is unmarried" are analytic statements.

The box stands for what we mean by the word "bachelor." That concept contains two parts: the characteristic of being unmarried and the characteristic of being male. So if you say that anyone who is a bachelor is unmarried, you are merely identifying one of the characteristics contained in the idea. You are specifying one piece of what goes into the definition of "bachelor." The same thing goes for saying "Smith is a *bachelor;* therefore, Smith is a *man.*" In either case, we have not moved outside of the box, and we have not learned anything beyond the concept "bachelor."

We also find analytic statements in mathematics. Let's take: "That building is built in the shape of a *cube;* therefore, it has *equal sides.*" We can represent that statement this way:

```
CUBE
All angles 90 degrees
Six surfaces
All sides equal
```

As you can see, our statement "that building is built in the shape of a cube; therefore, it has equal sides" is just like our "bachelor" statement. It is true. But all we are doing is specifying its essential properties. We are not speaking about anything outside the box, that is, outside the concept "cube."

Here is one more example: "2 + 2 = 4."

```
4
iiii              IV
3 + 1   2 + 2
1.5 + 2.5
   . . .
   . . .
2²  10 − 6
```

The box stands for every conceivable aspect of what "four" means. (Ours is incomplete, and we have used ellipses to represent the rest.) But "2 + 2" is just one of the many ways that "four" can be represented. If I ask "what is two plus two?" and you say "four," you still are not moving outside the box and beyond what is already intrinsic to the concept we are talking about.

Another way of expressing this is that the claims, or conclusions, involved in analytic statements automatically follow from the premises.

- Smith is a *bachelor* [premise]; therefore, he is *unmarried* [conclusion].
- This object is a *triangle* [premise]; therefore, it has *three sides* [conclusion].

Can you imagine any scenario in which you can find a "married bachelor" or a "four-sided triangle"? No, it's theoretically impossible. So the idea "unmarried" automatically follows from "bachelor," as "three sides" follows from "triangle."

All analytic statements are like this: "Triangles have three sides," "cardinals are birds," "8 × 2 = 16." They are all absolutely and necessarily true, which is why rationalists like them so much. But all they do is describe parts of a concept. They do not add anything to it. By staying "in the box," we are looking only at the specific features of the concept.

Synthetic Statements

Synthetic statements, on the other hand, do precisely what analytic statements do not. They add something to the concept at issue. They "move out of the box." They are called "synthetic" because they synthesize, or put together, ideas or facts that do not necessarily go together. Unlike analytic statements, synthetic statements make claims that do not automatically follow from the premises.

Here is a synthetic statement you will recognize: "This page is white." It is synthetic because if you were to examine a definition of the concept "page," you would not find the idea "white." Nothing about the concept "page" automatically implies the color "white." "Page" suggests "material which can take writing," "flat surface," "part of a book or letter," and so on. That a page is "material" does imply the notion "color," but that does not mean the page has to be white. "White" is not contained in the concept "page," and that is what makes the statement synthetic. Using our box image we can represent it like this:

```
┌─────────────────────────┐
│        PAGE             │
│  Material for writing   │
│  Flat surface           │
│  Has color and weight   │
│  Part of a document     │
└─────────────────────────┘
```

Obviously, this picture differs dramatically from our pictures of analytic statements. It shows that a synthetic statement claims that there is a relationship between two things that do not have a necessary connection. And that is what synthetic statements are all about—asserting relationships between intrinsically unrelated concepts. "The tree outside my window is 30 feet high," "the oceans are inhabited by different life forms," "the fourth planet in this solar system has two moons." These are all synthetic statements.

Synthetic statements also differ from analytic ones in needing a different kind of proof to show that they are true. Strictly speaking, analytic statements are self-evident and logically necessary. "Proving" them amounts only to making that more

---

synthetic statement A synthetic statement attributes a property to something, but that property goes beyond what is contained within the definition of the object or concept involved. For example, "This page is white" is a synthetic statement.

obvious. But with synthetic statements, we are talking about empirical proof, actual data that backs up our claim. If we want to say, "the capital of Oregon is Salem," we have to be ready to prove that by citing the appropriate, verifiable facts that support our statement.

The Empirical Advantage

It must be clear by now why empiricists reject rationalism. They see the rationalist idea of truth and knowledge as little more than a game. Such statements lead to no new facts about the world, no insights, no expanded understanding of reality. The point of the process is to arrive at conclusions by purely mental gymnastics. Rationalism stays within its intellectual "box" and never moves outside into the "real world." And that is what empiricists mean when they say analytic statements are trivial.

There is a trade-off, of course. The empiricist loses the absolute certainty of knowledge that rationalism provides. However, the knowledge produced by empirical methods may be more interesting. Whether that trade is worth making you must decide for yourself when you have finished examining the issues.

The Empiricism of John Locke

Descartes' rationalism was taken up and steadfastly defended by European thinkers, specifically by a group called the "Continental Rationalists." However, across the English Channel, there developed a rival, empirical school of thought. These philosophers are called, not surprisingly, the "British Empiricists."

John Locke, a British Empiricist whose idea of the social contract you encountered earlier, made important contributions to the theory of knowledge as well. A pioneer in empirical thinking, Locke thoroughly disagreed with the way Plato and Descartes thought about knowledge. He rejects the notions that the mind can encounter nonsubstantial, universal essences and that it comes equipped with innate ideas that are self-evidently true. As a classic empiricist, Locke believes that everything we know must come through the senses. He lays out the arguments for this position in *An Essay Concerning Human Understanding* (1690).

The Mind as a Blank Piece of Paper

Locke uses a famous image to make his point. The mind, he says, is initially like a blank slate or a blank piece of paper. Knowledge comes from the world outside of us writing on it. Locke says,

> Let us suppose the mind to be, as we say, white paper, void of all characters, without any ideas: How comes it to be furnished? Whence comes it by that vast store which the busy and boundless fancy of man has painted on it with an almost endless variety? Whence has it all the materials of reason and knowledge? To this I answer, in one word, from *EXPERIENCE*. In that all our knowledge is founded; and from that it ultimately derives itself.

—Essay Concerning Human Understanding

In other words, Locke claims that our minds contain nothing which did not come first through our senses. Anything in our heads, then, is the result of either "sensation" (our sense perceptions) or "reflection" (our thinking about these perceptions). Everything we think and know originally comes from outside us.

The "Copy Theory": Primary and Secondary Qualities

The next job for the empiricist is to explain how what we think we know about the outside world can be genuine "knowledge." As the image of the "blank piece of paper" implies, Locke assumes that the mind passively takes in impressions. In so doing, it does not distort reality. What it mainly does is to copy it.

Yet Locke is sensitive to the fact that we sometimes contribute something to our perceptions of the world. To account for this, he distinguishes between *primary qualities* and *secondary qualities* of the objects we experience.

Primary qualities are the most fundamental and essential properties of an object. Locke refers to "solidity, extension, figure, motion or rest, and number"—something like this book's size and shape and the basic properties of its materials, for example. Our idea of this page as so many inches long by so many inches wide, of this book weighing so many ounces, and so on "resembles" the actual primary features of the page and of the book itself. As Locke says, "the ideas of primary qualities of bodies are resemblances of them, and their patterns do really exist in the bodies themselves." How do these primary qualities get from the objects they inhabit into our minds? Locke thinks that invisible particles must come from the objects themselves to our eyes and then into our brains to create our ideas of them.

Sensations, however—things like color, sound, smell, and taste—arise out of our body's response to an object's primary qualities. These qualities are not actually *in* the object itself. We add them. As Locke explains,

> A violet by the impulse of such insensible particles of matter, of peculiar figures and bulks, and in different degrees and modifications of their motions, causes the ideas of the blue colour, and sweet scent of that flower to be produced in our minds. . . . There is nothing like our ideas existing in the bodies themselves. They are . . . only a power to produce those sensations in us: and what is sweet, blue, or warm in idea, is but the certain bulk, figure, and motion of the insensible parts, in the bodies themselves, which we call so.
>
> —Essay Concerning Human Understanding

These properties that do not inhere in objects themselves Locke calls *secondary qualities.*

Locke's distinction between primary and secondary qualities makes sense. But the more important point here is Locke's commitment to sense experience as the sole source of every detail of everything we know. If the mind does anything, it responds to primary qualities already in an object and translates impulses transmitted by objects into secondary sensations. It discovers nothing on its own. You cannot get a more categorical rejection of rationalism than that.

The Radical Empiricism of David Hume

Another of the other British Empiricists, David Hume, takes empiricism to new heights. Hume insists with Locke, and against Descartes, that knowledge would have to come through the senses. But more than any other empiricist, Hume questions just how much of what we think we know is genuine knowledge. As you will shortly see, Hume's special contribution to the study of knowledge is his challenge to some "obvious" truths. A renegade in his personal life as well as his philosophical career, Hume takes empiricism so far that we can legitimately call him a radical thinker. His epistemological ideas are set out in two definitive works: *A Treatise on Human Nature* and *An Enquiry Concerning Human Understanding*.

Impressions and Ideas

Like Locke, Hume thinks that everything in the mind originates in our sense experience. With no innate ideas or Platonic Forms to discover, with nothing in there at all to start with, our minds are in no position to create or uncover immaterial, intuitive, spiritual, or mystical truth. All they can do is receive sense impressions.

Hume divides the contents of our minds into *impressions* and *ideas*. *Impressions* encompass "all our more lively perceptions, when we hear, or see, or feel, or love, or hate, or desire, or will." We are aware of our impressions *during* an experience—they are strong, forceful, and vivid. *Ideas* include "the less lively perceptions of which we are conscious, when we reflect on any [impressions]." They are what those impressions are like when we think about them or remember them *after* the experience. For example, if you look around the room you are in right now, you will take in various vivid sights, sounds, and smells. These are Hume's "impressions." But if tomorrow you think back on this moment, those perceptions will be less intense. Those less vivid recollections are Hume's "ideas."

For Hume, then, genuine knowledge comes through the senses. Objects in the outside world produce impressions in our minds, which we retain, in less vivid form, as ideas. Yet these ideas accurately represent what we have encountered in the world outside us. We truly know something certain about the world through all of this. Furthermore, this knowledge lets us make synthetic statements. (If you say "my desk is brown wood," you are confidently claiming something about color and material that is not already part of the concept "desk.") And finally, the validity of this knowledge can be tested. We can verify the accuracy of our *ideas* by reexperiencing certain *impressions*. Or we can check our experience against other people's. A primary virtue of empirical knowledge is that it can be objectively confirmed.

So far, both Locke and Hume seem to endorse common sense. Unlike Descartes, they place their trust in the senses. We can trace the ideas in our minds to their sources in the outside world and say we know something. These philosophers seem to give us back what rationalism took away, the ability to say we genuinely know something on the basis of our everyday sense perceptions.

Not All Ideas Are Genuine

Don't think all our problems are over, however. Just because Locke and Hume say that all our ideas are based on sense impressions, this does not mean that our every

David Hume

David Hume (1711–1776) was a Scottish philosopher who was educated at Edinburgh University. At the age of 28, he published one of his most famous works, *A Treatise of Human Nature;* however, at the time it got so little notice that Hume remarked that it "fell stillborn from the press." Hume published different revisions of material from the *Treatise* in *An Enquiry Concerning the Principles of Morals* and *An Enquiry Concerning Human Understanding,* but Hume preferred to cultivate a reputation as a man of letters. During his life Hume was best known for his work in history, moral and political thought, and economics. He also held a series of government posts. An unorthodox thinker, Hume's *Dialogues on Natural Religion* was published only after his death.

idea refers to some object that physically exists. Locke's "secondary qualities," like color and taste, are the product of the interaction between us and the objects we encounter. And Hume thinks that our minds sometimes imaginatively join ideas that in reality do not go together. Because our minds are so creative, we easily produce ideas of objects that do not and cannot exist. Hume offers the following two examples:

> When we think of a golden mountain, we only join two consistent ideas, *gold* and *mountain,* with which we were formerly acquainted. A virtuous horse we can conceive; because, from our own feeling, we can conceive virtue; and this we may unite to the figure and shape of a horse, which is an animal familiar to us.

> —An Enquiry Concerning Human Understanding

You can think of lots of examples—unicorns and centaurs, "perfect" societies, gods and goddesses, computers that have minds and personalities of their own. Given our tendency to create such ideas, Hume thinks we should look for the sense impressions that underlie them. If we cannot find anything in the real world that we can physically correlate with an idea, we must say that the idea is just a fiction, like the "golden mountain." As Hume puts it,

> When we entertain any suspicion that a philosophical term is employed without any meaning or idea (as is but too frequent), we need but inquire, from what impression is that supposed idea derived? And if it be impossible to assign any, this will serve to confirm our suspicion.

> —An Enquiry Concerning Human Understanding

Testing for Meaning: The Self

Descartes takes the "self" as an innate idea of such vividness and clarity that its existence is absolutely certain. And, since the British Empiricists rejected most of what the Continental Rationalists said, it shouldn't surprise you that Hume considered Descartes' notion of the self completely meaningless. For an idea to be other than a fiction concocted in our minds, Hume said, we must first identify the impressions that produce the idea and then identify the actual objects that produce the impressions. To talk accurately about a "self," then, we must isolate the impressions that produce our idea of a "self" and trace them to the object that is their cause.

Before we look at Hume's reasoning, try to think this problem through yourself. Do you have a "self"? Surely everyone would say yes. You are the same person who has lived through all your varied experiences in life. Even though all the cells in your body change every seven years, the same you persists: different cells, yet the same "self." But exactly what is it that you're talking about when you say "I"? Take a moment and see if you can come up with an answer.

Now hold on to your hat. We ask Hume, "What is the 'self'?" and he answers "Nothing. The concept is meaningless, empty, the product of imagination." How radical can you get? The *self,* claims Hume—Descartes' rock-solid, ultimately undoubtable truth, the "I" at the very core of our existence—is meaningless. Is Hume serious?

Hume is deadly serious. Taking aim at Descartes, Hume makes his case in his *Treatise on Human Nature:*

> There are some philosophers, who imagine we are every moment intimately conscious of what we call our Self; that we feel its existence and its continuance in existence; and are certain, beyond the evidence of a demonstration, both of its perfect identity and simplicity. . . . To attempt a farther proof of this were to weaken its evidence; since no proof can be deriv'd from any fact, of which we are so intimately conscious; nor is there any thing, of which we can be certain, if we doubt of this.
>
> Unluckily all these positive assertions are contrary to that very experience, which is pleaded for them, nor have we any idea of self, after the manner it is here explain'd. For from what impression cou'd this idea be deriv'd? . . . If any impression gives rise to the idea of self, that impression must continue invariably the same, thro' the whole course of our lives; since self is suppos'd to exist after that manner. But there is no impression constant and invariable. Pain and pleasure, grief and joy; passions and sensations succeed each other, and never all exist at the same time. It cannot, therefore, be from any of these impressions, or from any other, that the idea of self is deriv'd; and consequently there is no such idea. . . . For my part, when I enter most intimately into what I call myself, I always stumble on some particular perception or other, of heat or cold, light or shade, love or hatred, pain or pleasure. I never can catch myself at any time without a perception, and never can observe anything but the perception.

To David Hume, the "self" is an idea like the "golden mountain." We have impressions that come from our experience of actual objects, but our imagination combines these impressions to create a new, fictitious idea—"I." But we do not admit that it is a fiction. Instead, we just assert that there is some "self," even if it is "something unknown and mysterious."

You're probably thinking that Hume is crazy. You *know* that the same "you" has persisted throughout your life, right? This isn't some fiction! You might convince Descartes of this, but not Hume. By Hume's strict rules, if you cannot identify a single, specific source of an impression, any idea based on that impression is something you have just made up in your mind. When we apply Hume's rules, we do not find anything we can point to as the "self" that is the source of whatever impressions lead us to say "I." Hume does not say that because he cannot find a "self," we don't really exist. He does say that Descartes' claim to know that he exists is wrong. Descartes may believe, feel, or be of the opinion that he exists, but he cannot *know* it because he cannot prove it according to strict, reasonable, empirical criteria.

Hume's insistence on grounding all knowledge in the evidence of the senses may seem quite appealing. It makes sense in our scientific age. But once he shows how easily the mind creates illusions of knowledge, we are back in the same quicksand we stood in when Descartes asked, "How can I be absolutely certain that I can trust what my senses tell me?" Furthermore, Descartes' absolute knowledge of the self now gives way to Hume's assertion that we cannot find a "self" to know. If this makes you jittery, however, brace yourself. The other shoe is about to drop.

The Attack on Causality

Hume is relentless. It is disturbing enough that he claims that the "self" is a fiction. And it is hard to imagine that he could find something else to question that would leave us similarly troubled. But the hallmark of a great philosopher is that he can surprise you. And Hume does that.

When you look around at the world, what do you see? Things happening: Cars move, planes fly, trees fall, people do things. The world is dynamic, ever-changing. One thing happens, which causes something else to happen, and so on, an ongoing chain of events. Everything has a cause. Observing this, as a good empiricist you would probably say, "The physical world is built on the idea of cause and effect. You can always find a cause of an object or event." That's what science is, after all. To understand something, we study what caused it and what effect it has on other things.

We know that some events cause others to happen. Take plants, for example. If you water them correctly, give them food, and move them so that they get the right kind of light, they grow. If you ignore them, don't water them, let them get too much or too little sun, they wilt. It's obvious that how you treat them *causes* them to be healthy or unhealthy. It's as obvious as the fact that their leaves are green.

We have so much empirical proof that some events cause others to happen that it seems ridiculous to doubt it. But couldn't we also say that it's just as obvious that we have a "self"? And if Hume claims that the "self" is a fiction, might he not also claim the same thing for cause and effect? That is precisely what he does. In fact, Hume's claim that we can never really *know* that one thing causes another to happen is probably the most important part of his philosophy.

If you have understood Hume so far, you can probably anticipate his line of reasoning about "causality." Remember, Hume thinks that for something to count as "knowledge," we must be able to identify the outside, empirical source of the "impressions" that underlie our "ideas." If we cannot do that, we have to assume that the mind is somehow taking a bunch of different impressions and combining them into new ideas that do not correspond to observable reality. As you have probably guessed,

Hume thinks "causality" is just such an idea that we manufacture in our minds—like the golden mountain, the virtuous horse, and the self.

But causality seems so obvious, you say. How can Hume suggest that it is a fiction?

Let's start this way. Pick up a pen or pencil. Examine it to determine what it's made of. Now put it out of sight. Is it wood, metal, or plastic? Are you sure that your "idea" is right? Of course you are. Do you have to go back and check to be sure? Hardly. You just put it down. One look was enough. One set of "impressions" from the object was plenty.

Now drop this book on the floor. You hear a sound, don't you? But can you say with absolute certainty that you will hear exactly the same sound if you drop it again? Isn't it possible that just as the book hit, a car backfired or someone made another noise down the hall? Maybe you thought the book made all that sound as it hit the floor. That is conceivable, as are thousands of other possibilities that we have not imagined. When will you know for sure? After you have dropped the book a few times. In this case, then, you need a series of impressions of the event to check out your idea that "dropping the book on the floor causes this particular sound." As long as other outcomes are possible, you cannot say you know the sound caused by the book hitting the floor.

Why do you need to look at the pen or pencil only once but you need to drop the book more than once? If we are going to claim to know some fact, we have to be certain of it. Looking at the pencil once is enough to determine what it is made of. But we need more than one test to be sure that one thing causes another. Science uses this approach all the time. A single experiment may suggest a causal relationship between one event and another, but other scientists must repeat that experiment over and over to see if they get the same results. No reputable researcher will say he "knows" this or that without a substantial body of supporting evidence. In short, one instance cannot demonstrate with a reasonable degree of certainty that one thing causes another.

Constant Conjunction. The need to do experiments more than once before claiming cause and effect makes perfect sense to us. But the very fact that we need to repeat an experience at all makes Hume suspicious. It shows that "cause" is not immediately present in the initial impression. (Contrast this with the idea of the material a pencil is made of.) Consequently, Hume says, the idea of causality "arises entirely from experience, when we find that any particular objects are constantly conjoined with each other."

Hume discusses causality using his now-famous example of two billiard balls. We see one ball, ball A, hit another, ball B; then we see ball B move away. When we see these two events take place over and over again, these events are "constantly conjoined with each other," to put it in Hume's terms. But we don't say to ourselves simply "Every time I saw ball A hit ball B, ball B then moved"—which is actually all that we have seen. After we have seen these events together for a while, we say to ourselves, instead, "ball A hit ball B and *caused* it to move; *and the same thing will happen in the future.*" However, Hume writes in the *Enquiry*, "These two propositions are far from being the same: *I have found that such an object has always been attended with such an effect,* and *I foresee, that other objects which are, in appearance similar, will be attended with similar effects.*"

Predicting the Future from the Past. The bridge we use to get from one statement to the other is the assumption that the future will be like the past. And that's where we get into trouble. According to Hume, there is simply no way to know this.

Think about the book-dropping example. Can you be 100 percent certain that the next time you drop this book on the floor it will make the same noise it made the last time you dropped it? Maybe you can be 99 percent certain. But can you honestly rule out all possibility that for whatever reason, the noise will not be different? Of course you can't. There are too many thousands of variables, including the speed of the earth's rotation and the strength of gravitational fields, for example. The slightest change in any of them as the book falls to the floor may cause the sound to change. In fact, because physical reality is so dynamic, something new and different is almost bound to happen.

Probability, Not Knowledge. But even if you are 99 percent sure, you cannot say you know what sound the book will make. From a practical standpoint, however, you may say this is close enough. No one can ever know anything for sure about the future. To be realistic about it, a 99 percent certainty is so close to a 100 percent certainty, what difference can it make?

From a practical standpoint, you have a point. But "practical" is not Hume's standard. The British philosopher's conclusion, then, is that when we make statements about what will happen in the future, we are talking only about probability, not knowledge: "If we be, therefore, engaged by arguments to put trust in past experience, and make it the standard of our future judgement, these arguments must be *probable* only" (emphasis added). Our minds, however, having gotten into the habit of seeing things "constantly conjoined" in the past, create the fiction that the future will repeat the past. Thus, we think that one event causes the other, always did, and always will. In Hume's view, however, we have no empirical grounds for such claims. We simply cannot find enough evidence in physical reality to justify the idea of "causality." Like the "self," cause and effect has to be written off as a product of our imaginations.

How Convincing Is Hume?

First the "self," then "causality": Hume's skepticism, like Descartes', leaves us with very little to hang on to. Hume, too, calls into question the most obvious "truths."

Is Hume convincing? You're probably about as convinced by Hume's doubts as you were by Descartes' Master Deceiver. You still think your senses are reliable, don't you? If they aren't 100 percent trustworthy, they're close enough. You're probably willing to say that you *know* the world is the way your senses tell you it is. If that's what you think, Hume hasn't made much of an impact on you.

Testing the Senses

In the same way that we considered a contemporary "radical doubt" to test Descartes' ideas, let's set up a test to determine what is genuine knowledge using an empirical standard. The question we will explore is very basic: How certain can we be of the evidence of our senses? We want to discover two things: (1) how accurate our sense impressions are and (2) whether they refer to something that actually exists.

An Experiment with the Senses

Consider this experiment. Imagine that you take a red light and a white light and shine them on some object. You will get two shadows. What colors will they be? One, predictably, will be red. But the second, not so predictably, is green!

Ordinarily when we see a color, we can confidently say that we know something of that color is there. Thus, the green shadow in this experiment should lead us to say something like, "I know a patch of green light exists." But it doesn't. If we measure the wavelengths of the light in that experiment, we find only various shades of red, white, and pink. This is not a trick; red and white light do not somehow mix to produce green. There is no light here with wavelengths that match those which scientists tell us we see as "green." Everyone who sees this phenomenon will see green, but if you take a photograph of it, no green will appear in the picture. In reality, no matter what we see, *there is no green* there.

How is it possible for there to be a green shadow where there isn't green? The answer lies in the fact that our eyes are not just passive receptors of external sensations. They are part of a very active nervous system that responds to stimuli in particular ways. Researchers think that in this experiment the red and white light stimulates certain cells in the eye in the same way green light does. The signals they send to the brain are there translated as "green" when reality is presenting you with "red," "white," or "pink."

Perceiving Reality: There Is More Going on Than You Think

The fact that we can see green when no green is there is not an isolated case. Indeed, the neurobiologist Humberto Manturana, who has done extensive work

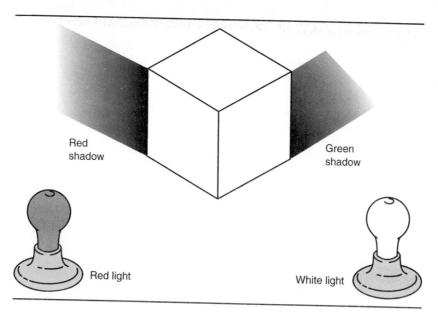

Red shadow

Green shadow

Red light

White light

on vision on humans and other animals, has concluded that we are wrong if we think that we are passively perceiving exactly what goes on in the world around us. Manturana explains that when he and another scientist began doing research on frog vision,

> we did it with the implicit assumption that we were handling a clearly defined cognitive situation: there was an objective (absolute) reality, external to the animal, and independent of it (not determined by it), which it could perceive (cognize), and the animal could use the information obtained in its perception to compute a behavior adequate to the perceived situation. This assumption of ours appeared clearly in our language. We described the various kinds of retinal ganglion cells as feature detectors, and we spoke about the detection of prey and enemy.
>
> —Biology of Cognition

Like a good empiricist, Manturana thought that the world was simply "out there" to be perceived by a passive receiving mechanism. The picture transmitted to the frog's brain (and, by extension, to our brains) would be as accurate and impartial as a photograph.

However, Manturana continues,

> I soon realized in my research that my central purpose in the study of color vision could not be the study of a mapping of a colorful world on the nervous system, but rather that it had to be the understanding of the participation of the retina (or nervous system) in the generation of the color space of the observer.
>
> —Biology of Cognition

In Manturana's opinion, something as apparently direct as vision is actually the result of the dynamic interaction of outside and inside worlds. The light from outside causes a chemical change in the neurons inside us. This then produces a representation of reality that may or may not resemble that reality. The operation of our nervous system, then, is a major factor in how we perceive reality. But since our neurons can represent "green" when it's not really there, our perceiving mechanisms can easily misrepresent reality.

The Influence of the "Knower." Most of us trust our senses as sources of knowledge because we ordinarily assume that perception is basically a passive process. The "green" shadow and Manturana's work with frog vision, however, to take only two examples, suggest that the "knowing mechanism" itself affects the way we identify what we perceive. This further undermines our unquestioned belief in the objectivity and certainty of our sense impressions.

To see how the mind can shape what we perceive, look at the two pictures on the next page. What do you see? Each should present you with two distinctly different images. When you look at the first one in one way, you see a vase. Look at

it differently and you see two faces. The second picture presents either a beautiful young woman facing away from you or an ugly old crone facing you.

How is this possible? The sense data that your eyes take in—the arrangement of lines and shading—remain the same. But you can "shift" the pictures you see. What you "see," then, is the meaning your mind imposes on the data, and your mind can reprocess that data so that they represent something different.

This is yet another example of the influence of the knower. What we would say we know about the picture based on our perceptions is heavily influenced by internal, mental processes. This is essentially the same idea suggested by Manturana's work and by the "green" shadow that isn't there. It is also, of course, what Hume intimates when he discusses the "self" and "causality."

Isn't it possible that this sort of thing goes on more than we realize, that our minds more or less create the meaning of the sensory data we take in? And if this is so, how can we be sure that we perceive reality as it actually is?

Our Untrustworthy Senses. Thus, even our simplest perceptions may give us an inaccurate picture of reality. Even seemingly self-evident perceptions that should lead to certain knowledge turn out to be false. And we haven't even looked at anything complex, like "causality," which involves claiming to know something about the relationship between different perceptions. Yet if simple color vision won't pass the test, why should we think that "causality" will?

How "knowable" is what we perceive through our senses? Apparently, there is good reason to doubt what is right in front of our eyes. The green in our experiment is produced by our nervous system and not by green light. Which of two images we perceive in the picture above depends on how our own minds direct our thinking. If our senses cannot pass these simple tests, we are entitled to question whatever we experience through them. Maybe Hume is right after all when he suggests that even though genuine knowledge comes only from the senses, some bits of "knowledge" that seem too evident to doubt are really fictions created by our minds.

Does Hume Go Too Far?

As we see, Hume's skepticism can be devastating—leaving us uncertain about the trustworthiness of our own senses. However, it's worth pausing to ask whether we've gone too far. In fact, even Hume ultimately pulls back.

Hume is keenly aware that his radical empiricism takes him far from how most people see the world and leads him into a gloomy isolation. His conclusions leave him so confused about virtually everything that he ends up feeling depressed and powerless. In his *Treatise of Human Nature,* he comments:

> The intense view of these manifold contradictions and imperfections in human reason has so wrought upon me, and heated my brain, that I am ready to reject all belief and reasoning, and can look upon no opinion even as more probable or likely than another. Where am I, or what? From what causes do I derive my existence, and to what condition shall I return? Whose favour shall I court, and whose anger must I dread? What beings surround me? And on whom have I any influence, or who have any influence on me? I am confounded with all of these questions, and begin to fancy myself in the most deplorable condition imaginable, inviron'd with the deepest darkness, and utterly depriv'd of the use of every member and faculty.

However, when discouraged, not even a famous philosopher is immune to the pull of everyday life. Hume writes,

> Most fortunately it happens, that since reason is incapable of dispelling these clouds, nature herself suffices to that purpose, and cures me of this philosophical melancholy and delirium, either by relaxing this bent of mind, or by some avocation, and lively impression of my senses, which obliterate all these chimeras. I dine, I play a game of back-gammon, I converse, and am merry with my friends; and when after three or four hours' amusement, I wou'd return to these speculations, they appear so cold, and strain'd, and ridiculous, that I cannot find in my heart to enter into them any farther.

Hume doesn't reject his philosophical positions, but he's reminded that trusting his senses actually does work in everyday life most of the time. So perhaps we need to ask whether a dose of common sense will temper his radical empiricism.

The Self Reconsidered

Recall that Hume claimed that when he looked inside, he could never encounter "the self." So he concluded that it must be a creation of our imaginations like the "golden mountain." But consider the following story that the contemporary British philosopher Gilbert Ryle (1900–1976) tells as part of his criticism of Descartes' concept of the mind.

> A foreigner visiting Oxford or Cambridge for the first time is shown a number of colleges, libraries, playing fields, museums, scientific departments, and administra-

tive offices. He then asks, "But where is the University? I have seen where the members of the Colleges live, where the Registrar works, where the scientists experiment and the rest. But I have not yet seen the University in which reside and work the members of your University."

To anyone familiar with "universities," the visitor's mistake is obvious. He doesn't understand that "classroom building," "playing field," and "library" (on the one hand) and "university" (on the other) refer to very different kinds of logical categories. Ryle coined the phrase "category mistake" to describe this error—although you're probably more familiar with the phrase "comparing apples to oranges." Hume's comment that whenever he looks for his "self," all he comes upon are perceptions (cold, hot, love, anger, pleasure, pain, etc.) sounds suspiciously like the visitor saying that he's seen buildings and facilities but no "university." Is Hume guilty of a "category mistake" in wanting the "self" to refer to something other than the perceptions that we're conscious of? Is it a more solid concept than some fiction like "unicorn"?

Causality Reconsidered and the Value of Induction

Recall, too, that Hume also dismisses the idea of cause and effect as something that is just a product of our imagination. If we want to make claims about what will happen in the future on the basis of what we've observed in the past, Hume says that "these arguments must be probable only."

But, again, we can ask if Hume isn't making a kind of category mistake when he suggests that probability is a failing in this context. Remember that one of the major differences between rationalism and empiricism is that the latter aims to make synthetic statements that take us beyond the contents of the concepts we start with. Another way to talk about this is that a standard empirical inquiry is based on *inductive reasoning* of the sort we see in scientific investigations, not the *deductive reasoning* that we use in geometry and symbolic logic. Deductive logic ("all triangles have three sides; this object is a triangle; therefore, this object has three sides") gives us absolute certainty, whereas induction usually gives us only degrees of probability. But this doesn't mean that induction is epistemologically inferior to deduction. Imagine that a scientist discovers a new element. At first, any predictions she makes about it are little more than guesses. That is, they have low probability of being right because they're based on a small amount of evidence. However, the more that she experiments with the substance and learns about it, the greater the probability that her predictions will be true. The inductive, scientific method that she uses is to formulate hypotheses, test them, refine them in terms of what she's learned, test some more, and continue to gather evidence. Other scientists will engage in the same process, and a substantial body of data about this new element will accumulate. An inductive process may never give any of these scientists certainty, but it will strengthen the basis of any claims about the substance so that they become more and more probable.

Given the nature of empirical reality, the goal of inductive inquiry is greater and greater probability—not certainty. But be sure to realize that this doesn't make it a weak intellectual tool. On the contrary, a solid inductive approach lets us assess the likelihood that one theory or another is true or false. If we have competing theories about, for example, how the universe came into existence, an inductive process lets us see what the universe itself tells us about which is more likely. The physical evidence that is uncovered combined with the objective judgment of trained scientists will reveal which theory has the greater probability of being true. If such an approach reveals that one theory has a significantly smaller probability of being right than the other, we can see how valuable an inductive process is.

Perhaps, then, it is simply inappropriate to ask for certainty when talking about empiricism and shows a fundamental misunderstanding of both the value and limits of induction. Could asking for "certainty" from an inductive process be so off-target that it amounts to a kind of category mistake?

Knowledge Is Limited to Appearance: Immanuel Kant

Descartes and Hume leave us with something of a standoff. Fortunately, one of Western philosophy's greatest thinkers, Immanuel Kant, came along and offered a theory that tries to harmonize the two extremes of his predecessors. In the *Critique of Pure Reason,* Kant proposes a fascinating theory that tries to bridge the gap between rationalism and empiricism—but does so at a very high price.

Kant accepts the claim of rationalism that only the mind provides absolute certainty. He also accepts the claim of empiricism that knowledge depends on having sense data, but, unlike Hume, he accepts the legitimacy of causality. The key here is Kant's novel idea that the mind orders, arranges, and gives shape and meaning to all of our sense perceptions, and that this is precisely what makes all knowledge of empirical experience possible. The mind acts as a kind of active filter through which all sense impressions pass; the mind actually imposes a certain structure on those sense data. Into what shape does the mind mold things? First, it gives sense data a spatial and temporal dimension. For Kant, space and time are not properties of reality as such, but characteristics which the mind imposes on it. Second, our sense data are also fashioned in terms of such basic concepts as substance, causality, unity, plurality, necessity, possibility, and reality. Kant calls these concepts "categories."

Knowledge, for Kant, is what our minds produce as they actively arrange the data supplied by our senses. All human minds have the same structure, so we all experience the world the same. We impose space, time, and the "categories" on what we perceive. For example, we create a causally ordered world, and we impose these relationships on the sensations that we encounter. We do not imagine causality as a fiction, as Hume suggests. Thus, in Kant's view it is possible to claim with certainty that we know that billiard ball A causes billiard ball B to move when the former strikes the latter. Our knowledge claims are objectively true because the basic rules for how all humans experience are, as it were, "hardwired" into our minds.

Kant's idea that the mind orders sense data with the categories to give us our everyday experience of reality can be difficult to grasp, so think of it this way. If you look at a computer screen, what do you see? Depending on the program you're running or the DVD or website you're watching, you see words, graphic images, even live video. But what if I said that what you're *really* watching is electricity that has simply been configured to produce the images on the screen? Electricity powers the hardware, which then follows instructions from the software. The combination of the two produces what you see on the monitor. This is not unlike what Kant has in mind when he suggests that the data that we take in through our senses (something equivalent to the electricity that your computer draws in) are then organized by the categories (something equivalent to the software) to give us what we know (the image on the monitor).

Kant's achievement is not without its cost. To make knowledge possible, Kant must distinguish between an object-in-itself and an object-as-it-appears. (To guarantee the objectivity and dependability of knowledge, Kant may not allow for the possibility of a perception that is not filtered and molded by the mind.) Objects-in-themselves inhabit what Kant calls the "noumenal world," whereas things-as-they-appear constitute the "phenomenal world." The catch is that when we encounter an object—"a thing-in-itself"—the filtering and ordering that our minds do change that object into a "thing-as-it-appears." Thus, all human experience and all human knowledge is limited to the phenomenal realm, that is, to things-as-they-appear, and not to things-as-they-are-in-themselves.

This has two serious consequences. First, we once again find major restrictions placed on the concept of knowledge. This time, we can never know the nature of reality as it truly is (noumenal reality), only as it appears to us (phenomenal reality). Knowledge is possible, but limited. Second, because knowledge is the result of the mind's operations on empirical data, Kant argues that it is impossible to have any knowledge of such ultimate, intangible things like the soul, immortality, and God. Kant does not reject these notions outright. He says only that knowledge of them is impossible, and he thinks that the demands of morality are good reasons for people to believe in them. However, in one move, Kant proclaimed that the traditional attempts of metaphysics to understand such concepts were doomed to failure.

The Search for Knowledge—Where Are We?

We have considered a variety of extreme views—Descartes' radical doubt to Hume's radical empiricism to Kant's ingenious attempt to bridge the two. Descartes finds that the senses are unreliable, but he believes that we can discover knowledge through pure intellect. The basic certainty in Descartes' world, the one piece of certain knowledge on which all else is built, is our undeniable awareness of our own existence. Hume approaches the problem of knowledge empirically, counting solely on the evidence of our senses for knowledge. He discards as fiction the one thing Descartes thought was certain, the self, and he also denies the certainty of cause and effect. Because we cannot know that the future will repeat the past, we have to live with doubt and uncertainty. So we are left with probability and skepticism. Kant makes the person doing the knowing a more active element in the process than either Descartes or Hume does. And Kant gives us genuine knowledge, but of appearance only. So we get certainty and causality, but we give up knowing anything about what the world is "really" like.

Our search in this chapter may have seemed hopelessly confusing to you at times. But, in fact, Descartes, Locke, Hume, and Kant have shown us how difficult it is to discover "knowledge" when we set absolute certainty as our standard. Would it be so bad if the only absolute certainties we can discover are the limited truths of mathematics and logic and the empirical truths that we can trace back to observable events and objects? Would it be so bad if we had to evaluate everything else in terms of degrees of probability?

So, now how are you going to put what you've learned into a short answer that will satisfy an Incan goddess?

Main Points of Chapter 9

1. What is the best means for arriving at certain knowledge? In Western philosophy, there are two schools of thought about this issue. Rationalism relies on the mind, while empiricism favors the senses.

2. Knowledge, say the rationalist philosophers, is like what we find in mathematics and logic. It is permanent, stable, and enduring. The conclusions of physical evidence are epistemologically inferior to the conclusions of the mind alone.

3. The rationalist philosopher Plato thinks that the proper objects of knowledge are the perfect, immaterial Forms. Descartes changes philosophy forever by suggesting that epistemological questions are logically prior to all other philosophical issues. And Descartes' methodical doubt leads him to build his philosophical ideas on the certainty of self-knowledge and to take clarity and distinctness as the primary criteria of knowledge.

4. In opposition to rationalism is empiricism, which regards natural science as a model for knowledge. Empiricists think that knowledge and truth are the products of sensory experiences and not of purely mental operations. They reject the analytic conclusions of rationalism as trivial in comparison to the synthetic statements an empirical outlook generates.

5. John Locke rejects the rationalist notions that the mind can encounter nonsubstantial, universal essences or that it comes equipped with innate ideas that are self-evidently true. He regards the mind as a blank piece of paper whose contents come totally through the senses. David Hume agrees with the main lines of Locke's empiricism, but he argues that we actually know less than we imagine. He rejects ideas of the self and of causality as mental fictions leaving us with probability and skepticism rather than certainty. However, an understanding of the value and limits of an inductive process suggests that Hume's demand for certainty may be off-target.

6. As a way of bridging the gap between rationalism and empiricism, Immanuel Kant argues that knowledge is grounded in the data of our senses, but it results from the mind's imposing some sort of order on what we experience. Knowledge is thus limited to "things-as-they-appear" to us, not "things-in-themselves."

Discussion Questions

1. Have you ever had an experience where your intuition made you absolutely certain of something? Would you describe the event as *knowledge, belief, feeling,* or something else? If you say it was *knowledge,* how do you justify calling it that in light of what you have read in this chapter?

2. Descartes concedes the possibility that he may be dreaming at a time when he believes that he is awake. Have you ever had dreams that were so vivid that they felt real? How do you know that you are awake now? Wouldn't you say or do the same things in a dream to prove that you were "awake"? Don't our perceptions while we are dreaming seem to match Descartes' notions of clarity and distinctness? Is there any way to prove for sure that you are not dreaming at this instant?

3. Descartes thinks that we have a "very clear and very distinct" perception of God. Do you agree? If not, do you think this undermines anything else Descartes claims?

4. How dependable is the mind as an instrument of knowledge? Reflect on the content and structure of your mind. Do you find any innate or self-evident ideas at all? How do you know they are innate?

5. Empiricism claims that nothing is in the mind which did not come through the senses. Reflect on the contents of your mind again. Are the empiricists right? Or can you find an idea that could have come through the mind alone?

6. Consider Hume's argument about causality. In light of how easily and frequently we create an enormous range of fanciful ideas, is there any way to reject Hume's claim that causality and our idea of "self" are simple fictions? Is there any way to refute him? Could any scientific experiments *prove* that one billiard ball causes the second to move?

7. Kant makes the human mind an active participant in how we experience the world around us. Isn't this precisely what the experiment with the red and white lights show? Is it possible, as Kant's theory intimates, that everything we experience is like that—an experience that our mind has a major hand in shaping?

8. How dependable do you believe your senses are? Have you ever had an experience when your senses completely deceived you?

9. Have you ever had your cards or palm read or gone to some other kind of psychic? What was the experience like? Did you leave thinking that the person genuinely knew things about you that he or she could not possibly know? If so, how do you explain this?

Selected Readings

For Descartes, see his *Meditations on First Philosophy,* particularly the first two meditations. Locke's ideas are elaborated in *An Essay Concerning Human Understanding.*

See Hume's *A Treatise on Human Nature* and *An Enquiry Concerning Human Understanding.* For Hume's discussion of the self, see Book I, Section VI, and comments to this section in the "Appendix" of the *Treatise*. The billiard ball example appears in Section IV, Part I of the *Enquiry*. For Gilbert Ryle ideas, see: *The Concept of Mind* (New York: Penguin, 1949). Passages from Manturana are drawn from his "Biology of Cognition," in Humberto R. Manturana and Francisco Verela, *Autopoiesis and Cognition: The Realization of the Living* (Dordrecht: Reidel, 1980). See also Terry Winograd and Fernando Flores, "Cognition as a Biological Phenomenon," Chapter 4 in *Understanding Computers and Cognition* (Reading, MA: Addison-Wesley, 1986).

10

Does God Exist?

- *What Do We Mean by "God"?*
- *Proofs of God: Arguments from the Character of the World*
- *Arguments from Reason Alone*
- *Reason or Faith?*

Philosophy covers a wide territory. Some of its topics are abstract: the nature of reality, the nature of knowledge, the concept of a person, utopias. Others are closer to our daily lives. What is the difference between right and wrong? Why should we do what is right? Do we freely choose our actions or are they determined? As practical or impractical as these investigations may be, however, the question of whether God exists touches all of us most personally. After all, the way we answer this question makes a big difference in how we live.

If you believe in an all-powerful, all-knowing, supreme being, this is probably the cornerstone of your life. If God sets a standard for behavior and judges you in those terms after death, it makes good sense to keep that in mind as you go through your days. God's existence can be a great comfort or a source of fear. If, on the other hand, you believe that God does not exist, this also has a major impact on your life. You have more flexibility in how you behave and the consequences of your deeds do not stretch into eternity. But you must now decide for yourself how to conduct your life and how to make sense of the universe. You must reconcile yourself to the fact that there is no "great divine plan" for everything around you. If you accept that this huge, swirling universe goes unwatched and uncared for, that makes our lives seem like specks of sand on some great beach that no one will ever know existed. Thus, God's absence can lead to comfort or despair.

Is there some Great Being out there on whom we can depend, or are such ideas merely projections of our deep longing to avoid taking charge of our own lives? Such a fundamental question has attracted the attention of philosophers and spawned a host of arguments. When someone claims that God does or does not exist, however, that person is claiming that statements about God's existence are or are not *true*. As you saw in Chapter 9, there are two main schools of thought in Western philosophy as to the better source of truth and knowledge. Empiricism trusts the senses, while rationalism holds with the mind. Not surprisingly, in

Western thought, arguments about God's existence break down the same way. In this chapter we start with empirical "proofs" that nature reveals to us the existence of God. Later we examine a very different rationalistic argument that arrives at the same conclusion.

What Do We Mean by "God"?

Any discussion of the existence of God should begin with a definition of "God." And since we are limiting ourselves here to the ideas of Western philosophers, we shall also limit ourselves to the monotheistic conception of God found in Judaism and Christianity.

In this religious tradition, only one God exists: a divine being who created the world and rules it still. Everything that happens is an expression of God's divine providence, that is, God's care and direction of the universe. God knows everything and is all-powerful. God has specific standards of right and wrong, and God rewards virtue and punishes vice. (Christians believe that God rewards and punishes each of us after we die. Orthodox Jews do not believe in an afterlife, but they still maintain that God is righteous and responds to vice and virtue appropriately in this world, particularly in God's dealings with "God's people.") The God of the Jews and Christians is the epitome of all virtues. God is: the essence of goodness, love, justice, compassion, and mercy; the protector of the innocent and the faithful; the enemy of the wicked and the infidel.

God is pure spirit with no material substance and neither beginning nor end. We cannot experience God directly with our senses. The only people who claim to have had direct contact with God are mystics, who all agree that this experience is totally spiritual and private. Thus, arguments for God's existence are all of necessity indirect. In making such arguments, believers do, however, point to certain facts that, they claim, imply God's existence. Are these empirical facts and implications sufficient to make a reasonable person conclude that a Supreme Being of the kind we have just described actually exists? That is the question we explore in the next section.

Proofs of God: Arguments from the Character of the World

When archaeologists sift through the many-layered sites of ancient civilizations, what do they look for? Something "artificial." The evidence they want is hand-made, produced by people—pottery shards, tools, amphorae, statuettes, coins—things that do not occur naturally. And how do they assess the accomplishments of the people they are literally unearthing? By the complexity of what these civilizations have produced. Well-designed cities, houses with mosaic floors, the extensive use of metals all suggest more sophisticated skills than mud huts and wooden bowls. Can we use the archaeologist's approach in our search for God? Are there "divine pottery shards"? Can we find something so complex that it could have been produced only by God?

Many people think so. If you ask a friend to explain why she believes in God, she may tell you that the world seems so well planned that it could not be as it is by accident. Some God must have conceived of it and created it. Another friend might come up with sunsets, beaches, and love as his proof. So much beauty and goodness assures him that some Supreme Being caused it.

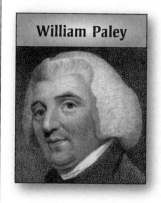

William Paley

William Paley (1743–1805) was educated at Christ's College of Cambridge University, ordained a priest, taught at the University for nine years, and held a variety of positions in the church. He wrote three widely read books: *The Principles of Moral and Political Philosophy* (1785), *A View of the Evidences of Christianity* (1794), and *Natural Theology; or Evidences of the Existence and Attributes of the Deity, Collected from the Appearances of Nature* (1802). The first work discusses civic duties and obligations in a way that anticipates Bentham's utilitarianism; the second argues for the authenticity of Biblical miracles; and the third claims to prove the existence of God from various natural phenomena.

Some philosophers also think this way. What do they point to? The world; the basic characteristics of the universe; its order and design; the way that everything from the cells of a leaf to the gravitational forces between planets somehow "make sense" and blend together to form a wondrously coherent whole. These thinkers argue that nothing so complicated could be the result of accidental, natural processes. Therefore, it must have been designed by some supremely wise and powerful being—God.

These people who look at creation and infer something about its creator use a method that is similar to the scientist's. They insist on evidence, and thus their notions of knowledge and truth rest on observable data. Hence, this outlook is called *empiricism.*

The Argument from Design: William Paley

The most simple and straightforward strategy for proving God's existence from the character of the material world is called the **argument from design.** The universe is so intelligently crafted, the argument goes, that it must have a creator. The thinker most famous for this argument is the eighteenth-century British churchman William Paley.

Paley's argument rests on the now well-known analogy in which he compares the world to a watch. Just as the existence of a watch implies a watchmaker, so the existence of our world implies a worldmaker. Paley writes,

> In crossing a heath, suppose I pitched my foot against a stone, and were asked how the stone came to be there, I might possibly answer, that for any thing I knew to the contrary it had lain there forever; nor would it, perhaps be very easy to show the absurdity of this answer. But suppose I had found a watch upon the ground, and it should be inquired how the watch happened to be in that place, I should hardly

argument from design The argument from design is an argument for the existence of God that claims that the universe is so intelligently crafted that it must have a creator.

think of the answer which I had before given, that for any thing I knew the watch might have always been there. Yet why should not this answer serve for the watch as well as for the stone; why is it not as admissible in the second case as in the first? For this reason, and for no other, namely, that when we come to inspect the watch, we perceive what we could not discover in the stone—that its several parts are framed and put together for a purpose, e.g., that they are so formed and adjusted as to produce motion, and that motion so regulated as to point out the hour of the day; that if the different parts had been differently shaped from what they are, or placed after any other manner or in any other order than that in which they are placed, either no motion at all would have been carried on in the machine, or none which would have answered the use that is now served by it. . . . This mechanism being observed . . . and understood, the inference we think is inevitable, that the watch must have had a maker—that there must have existed, at some time and at some place or other, an artificer or artificers who formed it for the purpose which, we find it actually to answer, who comprehended its construction and designed its use.

[E]very indication of contrivance, every manifestation of design, which existed in the watch, exists in the works of nature; with the difference, on the side of nature, of being greater and more, and that in a degree which exceeds all computation. I mean, that the contrivances of nature surpass the contrivances of art, in the complexity, subtlety, and curiosity, of the mechanism; and still more, if possible, do they go beyond them in number and variety; yet, in a multitude of cases, are not less evidently mechanical, not less evidently contrivances, not less evidently accommodated to their end, or suited to their office, than are the most perfect productions of human ingenuity. . . .

Every observation which was made concerning the watch, may be repeated with strict propriety concerning the eye, concerning animals, concerning plants, concerning, indeed, all the organized parts of the works of nature. . . .

Were there no example in the world of contrivance, except that of the eye, it would be alone sufficient to support the conclusion which we draw from it, as to the necessity of an intelligent Creator. It could never be got rid of, because it could not be accounted for by any other supposition which did not contradict all the principles we possess of knowledge—the principles according to which things do, as often they can be brought to the test of experience, turn out to be true or false. . . .

—Natural Theology

This lengthy passage contains a simple argument. Watches are not natural objects—they do not grow on trees but are made by skillful craftspeople. So watches imply watchmakers. The world is infinitely more complex than a watch. How did it get made? There must be a supreme, infinitely skilled creator—God.

Does the Argument Work?

This analogy has an obvious appeal. Paley claims that the world's design shows such a high degree of sophistication that only God could conceive of and execute it. The comparison with a watch is particularly apt. A watch is both complicated and precise. So is the world, with its cycles of the sun, the moon, the seasons, and the cycles of the birth, growth, and death of plants and animals. Everything moves in a way that contributes to order and balance. The wonderful patterns and intricacies of the universe really do seem extraordinary. It is natural, then, to think of it as the handiwork of a divine craftsman.

This argument from design also seems to have the virtue of being strictly empirical. Paley does not base his "proof" on religious beliefs—he reflects on the observable, physical workings of nature. Then he draws what seems like a reasonable conclusion, which he illustrates by the "watch : watchmaker :: world : God" analogy. Many sensible religious people are fond of this argument. As the workings of nature are a sign of God's great design, so the world is a signpost to God.

The great German philosopher Immanuel Kant, whom you met in an earlier chapter, pays the argument from design the highest compliment, even though he ultimately rejects it. Calling it a "physico-theological proof," Kant writes in his *Critique of Pure Reason,*

> This proof always deserves to be mentioned with respect. It is the oldest, the clearest, and the most accordant with the common reason of mankind. It enlivens the study of nature, just as it itself derives its existence and gains ever new vigour from that source. It suggests ends and purposes, where our observation would not have detected them by itself, and extends our knowledge of nature by means of the guiding-concept of a special unity, the principle of which is outside nature. This knowledge again reacts on its cause, namely, upon the idea which has led to it, and so strengthens the belief in a supreme Author [of nature] that the belief acquires the force of an irresistible conviction.

But an argument that strengthens religious faith does not necessarily prove a point philosophically. Does the argument by design prove what it claims to?

False Analogy?

The argument from design has a series of problems. Let's begin with the most serious.

Paley says that after appreciating the design of the world, we cannot account for it in any other way than by assuming that God did the designing and, therefore, exists. Paley even makes it sound as though any other cause is logically impossible. But don't the theories of contemporary science contradict this claim? Don't arguments for the "big bang" and natural evolution at least show that other explanations for what we find in the world are possible? Surely, it is not illogical to say that over billions of years, natural processes could produce the kind of world we have. Why must the order and purpose in nature come from a supernatural source?

The problem with Paley's argument crops up when we take his watch analogy too literally. Paley's reasoning works for a mechanical device like a watch. Machines are not alive; they have no inner force that gives them shape and drives their behavior. Plants and animals are quite different. They grow and adapt to their environment on their own. They become ill and heal. They respond and change. They reproduce according to their own unique genetic code in a way that a watch does not. That's what being alive is all about. Some biologists even speculate that the whole planet can be understood as a single organism.[1] If that were the case, the entire material universe would have properties that would distinguish it from any artifact ever made.

This is essentially the criticism offered by the British philosopher David Hume, whose thoughts about knowledge you encountered in Chapter 9. As you saw there, Hume is so rigorous and skeptical that he doubts such seemingly self-evident ideas as the "self" and "causality." You can just imagine how he attacks the question of God's existence. In his *Dialogues Concerning Natural Religion,* Hume specifically rejects the argument from design:

> If we see a house, . . . we conclude, with the greatest certainty, that it had an architect or builder; because this is precisely that species of effect, which we have experienced to proceed from that species of cause. But surely you will not affirm, that the universe bears such a resemblance to a house, that we can with the same certainty infer a similar cause, or that the analogy is here entire and perfect. The dissimilitude is so striking, that the utmost you can here pretend to is a guess, a conjecture, a presumption concerning a similar cause.

If Paley's argument is indeed based on a false analogy, it proves nothing. What do you think? Can you defend the argument from design, or must we discount it as an interesting but in the end useless cause?

What Kind of "Watchmaker"? What Kind of "Watch"?

Even if we go along with Paley and concede that the design of the world does imply a maker of some sort, does that prove that the Judeo-Christian God is that maker? Maybe some great being did in fact design and create the world. But what makes us think that this being was more than simply "one terrific worldmaker"? The Judeo-Christian God has a vast array of attributes. Does the ability to design a world necessarily mean that someone is perfect and omnipotent in all respects? Don't you do some things well and some badly? Maybe you're a great auto mechanic who cannot cook, or a great cook who cannot play the piano. It is certainly not necessary that the creator of the world should also be just, fair, loving, merciful, and so on.

Next, think of the following different watches: a watch that must be wound every day; a "self-winding" watch whose spring is wound by the movement of your wrist; a battery-powered watch that runs for two years before the battery needs changing; a watch with a special computer chip that lets it repair itself; a self-repairing watch whose battery runs for billions of years. Which of these is best? The last one, of course. And wouldn't it take a better watchmaker to make it than one who makes only spring-run watches that must be wound, cleaned, oiled, and repaired? One would think so.

---

[1]Lewis Thomas writes, "Except for us, the life of the planet conducts itself as though it were an immense, coherent body of connected life, an intricate system, even, as I see it, an organism.... We are not separate beings. We are a living part of the earth's life, owned and operated by the earth, probably specialized for functions on its behalf that we have not yet glimpsed. Conceivably, and this is the best thought I have about us, we might turn out to be a sort of sense-organ for the whole creature, a set of eyes, even a storage place for thought." "Man's Role on Earth," *New York Times Magazine,* April 1, 1984, p. 36.

Applying the same logic to worlds, we should expect the greatest possible world-maker to create a self-regulating world that does not need any tending. Yet Paley's God continues to exist and tinker with the workings of the universe on a daily basis. If you were a perfect being designing a universe, surely you would make a self-contained, self-powered, and self-regulating universe. Doesn't it insult God's power to say that God created a world that needs a divine being's constant attention? On the other hand, if the universe does not need God's oversight, it is at least possible that the world was designed and made by some worldmaker who subsequently went away or died.

World-Architect, Not Worldmaker

Despite Kant's initial praise for the argument by design, he ultimately rejects Paley's proof. According to Kant, we simply do not have good grounds for inferring a world*maker.* How do we know that the being who designed the world also created the raw material from which the world is made? We don't know that at all, and nothing in the operation of our "world/watch" suggests this. The most we see is a universe of order and purpose. All we can conclude from this is that maybe there was a "world-architect." Nothing here implies a "worldmaker." As Kant says, "The utmost, therefore, that the argument can prove is an *architect* of the world who is always very much hampered by the adaptability of the material in which he works, not a *creator* of the world to whose idea everything is subject."

But perhaps Hume and Kant take Paley's world/watch analogy too strictly. Perhaps the way the world works suggests to you that it was not only created at some point in the past but also is watched over day to day by some all-powerful intelligence. If so, you are in good company, for this is precisely the argument made by one of the greatest philosophers of the Middle Ages, Thomas Aquinas.

The Argument from "Governance of the World": St. Thomas Aquinas

Canonized as a saint by the Roman Catholic church shortly after his death, Thomas Aquinas built a philosophical system that is often likened in structure and in feeling to a Gothic cathedral. His system is not only intricate, but also is inspired by religious faith. Out of the synthesis of philosophy and theology, Aquinas built a towering intellectual edifice.

Aquinas was a Christian thinker, of course, so it is not surprising that he sets out to prove the existence of God. Actually he offers five different arguments. One of them is based on a concept Aquinas calls the **governance of the world.** It is similar to Paley's argument from design in the sense that Aquinas claims that the workings of nature reveal God's existence. However, it makes an even stronger claim. Aquinas writes,

> We see that things which lack intelligence, such as natural bodies, act for an end, and this is evident from their acting always, or nearly always, in the same way, so as to obtain the best result. Hence it is plain that not fortuitously, but designedly, do they achieve their end. Now whatever lacks intelligence cannot move towards an end, unless it be directed by some being endowed with knowledge and intelligence;

St. Thomas Aquinas

St. Thomas Aquinas was born in 1225 to a family of the Italian nobility. Destined for the monastery from an early age, Thomas was sent to the abbey of Monte Cassino when he was only five. Monte Cassino was the main monastery of the Benedictines, a famous and highly influential order of monks, and Thomas's family probably had political intentions in placing the boy there. At fourteen, Thomas began studying at the University of Naples, where he became interested in and joined a new religious order—the Dominicans—that took both learning and poverty quite seriously. Thomas's family was so upset that they kidnapped him for a year in an attempt to change his mind. After his release he studied at the University of Paris with St. Albert the Great, a teacher who introduced Aquinas to the thought of Aristotle. Thomas taught theology at Paris, was assigned to the Papal Court, and, most unusually, was allowed a second term in Paris teaching theology.

Aquinas was a controversial thinker and prolific writer who constructed a vast and intricate theological system that attempted to explain Christian belief in terms of Aristotelian philosophy. However, on December 6, 1273, he stopped writing, claiming that such things had been revealed to him that everything he had written now seemed like straw. He died in 1274 on his way to a Church council and was canonized in 1323, a remarkably short time after his death to receive such recognition. In 1879, his system of thought was made the official doctrine of the Roman Catholic Church.

as the arrow is shot to its mark by the archer. Therefore some intelligent being exists by whom all natural things are directed to their end; and this being we call God.

—*Summa Theologiae*

When Aquinas surveys the workings of nature, he sees signs of intelligence, an intelligence absent in the objects of nature themselves. This, he thinks, suggests the existence of God just as a flying arrow implies the existence of an archer. Arrows do not just shoot themselves at their targets. Nature does not organize itself to accomplish any purposes. Therefore, God must direct nature's activities. To Aquinas, the workings of nature are akin to the movements of a glove worn on the hand of God. The purposefulness we observe in nature is the result of the intelligence of God. To Aquinas, then, God didn't just create the world and walk away. God governs the world through bringing intelligence into the operations of nature.

Aquinas's argument may seem for the moment a bit stronger than Paley's. Unfortunately, both thinkers still have a big problem to overcome.

How Good Is the "Watch"?

Think about it this way. The basic assumption on which the arguments from design and governance are built is that something about the nature of the creator can be inferred from the nature of the world that has been created. This assumption by its very nature, however, produces major problems for the arguments that rest upon it. Consider, for example, the reaction to the argument from design from one of the most important philosophers of the twentieth century, British thinker Bertrand Russell (1872–1970):

> it is a most astonishing thing that people can believe that this world, with all the things that are in it, with all its defects, should be the best that omnipotence and omniscience have been able to produce in millions of years. I really cannot believe it. Do you think that, if you were granted omnipotence and omniscience and millions of years in which to perfect your world, you could produce nothing better than the Ku Klux Klan or the Fascists? ("Why I Am Not a Christian" [1927])

Look very carefully at the world around you. Paley and Aquinas say that this world is so wondrous that clearly its existence proves the existence not only of a God, but also of a *good* God. But is this "world/watch" of ours really so wonderful? The order and design of nature are sometimes breathtaking. At other times, however, things do not work out so well. There are earthquakes, droughts, floods, hurricanes, tornadoes, tsunami, all of which are uncontrollable and devastating expressions of nature's destructive power. Many animals survive by preying on one another. Is this the best way to design a world?

Then consider *Homo sapiens,* the creature supposedly fashioned in the creator's "image and likeness." We treat other animals and the planet itself badly. We feed off of other creatures, and kill them for sport, when we would be better off doing neither. We regard everything on this planet as ours to use or abuse as we see fit. We hunt species to extinction, strip mine, pollute the oceans, and destroy ecological systems with our toxic wastes. Is this really the best a wise creator could do?

Look at how we treat each other. We have war—tribal, religious, political; we have discrimination—racial, sexual, religious. We have poverty, slavery, greed, murder, rape, child abuse. It seems incomprehensible that a creature that is even vaguely fashioned after a God of goodness could so regularly savage the brothers and sisters of its own species. On top of this, we have used our intellect to invent devices with which we can destroy all life on this planet, and we have put them under the control of military and political organizations that consider it rational to use them. As a species, we do not even follow what one would assume is the most basic instinct—survival for ourselves and our children. It's almost as though our genes command us to somehow destroy ourselves. How can this be a sign of a competent worldmaker?

Even an ordinary electrician designs systems that work better. An overheated electrical line will cause a fire. To guard against that, the electrician installs mechanisms that prevent disaster, either circuit breakers or fuses. Why are there no similar mechanisms in human beings? The absence of "circuit breakers" that at least limit the harm we can do should give us pause. It might also make us question whether the apparent natural order of things is as good as we sometimes think. For

---

argument from the governance of the world The argument from the governance of the world claims that the order and intelligence of the activities of nature imply the existence of a being directing them.

all the glory of creation, an objective assessment shows that the world, and especially *Homo sapiens,* leaves much to be desired.

What does this imply about the being who designed a world that includes so many natural disasters and so much calculated evil? At least that he was not very capable, and possibly that he was sadistic. When we push the fundamental premise of Paley's and Aquinas's arguments to their logical conclusion, about the best we can do is to say that our world architect still needs more practice—or, as Bertrand Russell concludes, that God does not exist.

The Problem of Evil

Any argument for the existence of God from the character of the world must overcome the presence of evil in the world. That is, it must answer the question of how you reconcile evil with a good God. This **problem of evil** is particularly critical for the argument from design. After all, the properties and features of the world are precisely those things that reveal the nature of its creator. When we observe massive flaws, can we escape the conclusion that their creator is inept or evil—or that there never was a creator in the first place?

The Free-Will Argument. At this point, you might rise to God's defense. The argument from design is based on the idea that we can conclude something about the creator from the creation. An important part of that creation, you might argue, is people who are created with *free will.* Evil is a human product, not a divine one. God made us free, but people abuse that freedom. Isn't it better for God to make us free than incapable of doing wrong?

If you are thinking this way, you are in the company of the great early Christian thinker Saint Augustine. Augustine believes that "the sole cause of evil lies in the free choice of the will." For Augustine, evil is not some dark force with its own life whirling throughout the world. It is simply the absence of good, the result of our not choosing properly. According to this position, our worldmaker gave us the power of choice. Because we are responsible for what we choose, the creator's competence and benevolence are neither at issue nor at risk.

But there are more problems with this "free-will" argument. First, any appeal to free will ignores natural disasters and diseases. The "watch" still explodes every now and then, apparently on its own. Second, isn't genuine "freedom" an ability to choose what we think best without pressure of any sort that takes our decision away from us? Yet as we saw in Chapter 3 on determinism, contemporary psychologists make very strong arguments for their views that our actions are shaped by internal, unconscious forces—the Freudians—or by positive and negative reinforcement from the outside world—the behaviorists.

Freedom to choose our actions would be fine if we were designed in a way that we could always make intelligent, objective assessments of our options. But we are not designed this way. Instead, irrational forces—greed, anxiety, fear, and hatred—can lead

---

problem of evil Thje problem of evil refers to the conflict between the notion of a good God and the existence of evil in the world. This idea is generally used to argue against the existence of God.

to terrible events: the slaughter of six million Jews, the white people's aggression against Native Americans and blacks, centuries of male domination of women. When our dark emotions are aroused, there's a way that our actions are not totally under our control. A better-designed human being would be more powerful, that is, freer, and have the capacity to ward off the influence of prejudice and fear. Wouldn't such control and such freedom be the only handiwork of which a perfect world-maker would be capable?

Thus, we are still confronting the same conclusion. Any world-architect who designed us as we are is either less than competent or malevolent.

The Suffering of the Innocent: The Book of Job. You may never have seriously questioned God's existence. You may even be thinking that these problems with the argument from design are simply petty academic complaints. You may see faith as the issue here, and proofs are irrelevant to faith.

Or, instead of acknowledging the problem of evil, you may be tempted to say that only an evil person would question God. If so, you must realize that there is a long *religious* tradition of facing the problem of evil. In fact, the most powerful and eloquent expression of this problem appears in the Bible, in the Book of Job. This classic statement of a universal human phenomenon, the terrible suffering endured by innocent people, was written about 2500 years ago, but its theme is as true today as it was then. Job may get more than his share of bad luck, but we don't have to look very far in our own world to find good people facing terrible hardships.

Most of you are familiar with the story of Job. He is a good and prosperous man whom God allows to suffer mightily in order to prove a point to Satan—that Job is not righteous just because of the rewards it brings. On a single day, Job's oxen and camels are stolen, his flocks destroyed, and his children and servants are killed. Then Job himself is afflicted with a particularly painful form of leprosy. His wife urges him to "Curse God, and die." His friends turn against him because they think Job must have done something terrible to be the victim of such suffering. They believe in a world designed by a good God and in a "covenant" between the Jews and Yahweh that calls for goodness to be rewarded and evil punished. Insisting on his innocence, Job demands an audience with God. God eventually replies to Job along the lines of "Who are you to criticize me?" God also rebukes Job's friends for accusing him of wrongdoing. Job "repents," and God gives him a new family and fortune.[2]

What does this story tell us about the argument from design? Only that even the Bible, the basic text of the Judeo-Christian tradition, testifies to flaws in the design of the world. In the real world, the innocent are *not* rewarded for their suffering. But even if we grant God's effort to make it up to Job, what kind of a God does the Book of Job give us? In trying to win an argument with Satan, God allows great suffering to an innocent person—even the death of Job's children. Does God apologize to Job? No. Does he claim Job's fate was deserved or just? On the contrary. What are we left with? A world-maker who is incredibly powerful, but apparently insensitive to the pain of those whom He is supposed to protect. In other words, not even the Bible gives us a satisfactory answer to the problem of evil.

---

[2]Many Biblical scholars think that Job's "repentance" and new fortune were not in the original version of the Book. After all, Job has nothing to "repent" for. And how realistic is it that innocent people ultimately are rewarded for their suffering? It is not realistic at all.

Arguments from Motion and Causality: More from Aquinas

Both Paley's argument from design and Aquinas's argument from the governance of the world have proved vulnerable. Perhaps we should try claiming less. Does anything else we observe in the world of nature suggest that God exists? Can we admit all the world's flaws and still find something that points toward a God? Aquinas thinks so—the simple fact that things happen. We live in a world of cause and effect. Therefore, he concludes, there must be some ultimate cause.

Remember that Aquinas's argument from the governance of the world is only one of five proofs that he offers. We look at two of those here. Before we do, however, you should understand a couple of the technical terms that Aquinas takes from Aristotle.[3]

Aquinas says the first proof is an **argument from motion**. When he says "motion," however, he does not mean the motion, say, of a pen tossed across the room. He means ordinary change. The growth and development of your body is "motion" to Aquinas. So is the growth of plants. This broad definition of "motion" is evident when Aquinas talks about "potentiality" and "actuality." A stack of lumber is right now *actually* just a pile of wood. But it is *potentially* a doghouse, or a coffee table, or a chair, or a roaring fire. When a carpenter makes the wood into an object, one of its potentialities becomes actual. This process, "the reduction of something from potentiality to actuality," is what Aquinas calls "motion." (As you will see in the proof, he defines "motion" as "nothing else than the reduction of something from potentiality to actuality.")

The second proof is an **argument from the nature of efficient cause**, another Aristotelian idea. Don't worry about the word "efficient" here. Just think of "cause" as you ordinarily would. If you write a paper, spike a volleyball, or paint a picture, you are the "efficient cause" of what you have made happen.[4]

Now we are ready to look at the proofs.

---

argument from motion The argument from motion is one of St. Thomas Aquinas's five proofs for the existence of God. It claims that there must be a "first mover" to account for the fact that things happen in the world, or, as Aquinas would say, that potentialities become realized into actualities.

argument from the nature of efficient cause The argument from efficient cause is one of St. Thomas Aquinas's five proofs for God's existence. It claims that in a world of cause and effect, there must be some "first cause."

---

[3]Thomas Aquinas's entire philosophical system is based on Aristotle's thought. In these arguments, Aquinas adopts the Greek philosopher's arguments for what is called the "Unmoved Mover" (you can read about this in Book 12 of Aristotle's *Metaphysics*) and applies them to the Christian God. This is not at all unusual, and you will shortly see how another thinker borrows from Plato's ideas. This example shows how Greek philosophy shaped Christian theology.

[4]Aquinas draws off of Aristotle's distinction among four causes: material, formal, efficient, and final. An object's "material cause" is the substance out of which it is made, its "formal cause" is its shape or nature, its "efficient cause" is the most immediate force to bring it into existence, and its "final cause" is its purpose. Thus, a statue's "material cause" is marble, its "formal cause" is the shape the artist carves it into, its "efficient cause" is the sculptor, and its "final cause" is for the statue to be a decorative object or an object to be sold.

The first and more manifest way is the argument from motion. It is certain and evident to our sense, that in the world some things are in motion. Now whatever is moved is moved by another, for nothing can be moved except it is in potentiality to that towards which it is moved; whereas a thing moves inasmuch as it is in act. For motion is nothing else than the reduction of something from potentiality to actuality. But nothing can be reduced from potentiality to actuality, except by something in a state of actuality. Thus that which is actually hot, as fire, makes wood, which is potentially hot, to be actually hot, and thereby moves and changes it. . . . Therefore, whatever is moved must be moved by another. If that by which it is moved be itself moved, then this also must needs be moved by another, and that by another again. But this cannot go on to infinity, because then there would be no first mover, and consequently, no other mover, seeing that subsequent movers move only inasmuch as they are moved by the first mover; as the staff moves only because it is moved by the hand. Therefore it is necessary to arrive at a first mover, moved by no other; and this everyone understands to be God.

The second way is from the nature of efficient cause. In the world of sensible things we find there is an order of efficient causes. There is no case known (neither is it, indeed, possible) in which a thing is found to be the efficient cause of itself; for so it would be prior to itself, which is impossible. Now in efficient causes it is not possible to go on to infinity, because in all efficient causes following in order, the first is the cause of the intermediate cause, and the intermediate is the cause of the ultimate cause, whether the intermediate cause be several, or only one. Now to take away the cause is to take away the effect. Therefore, if there be no first cause among efficient causes, there will be no ultimate, nor any intermediate, cause. But if in efficient causes it is possible to go on to infinity, there will be no first efficient causes, neither will there be an ultimate effect, nor any intermediate efficient causes; all of which is plainly false. Therefore it is necessary to admit a first efficient cause, to which everyone gives the name of God.

—Summa Theologiae

Here Aquinas argues that the workings of nature tell us that there must be some "first mover," or "first cause," where the buck ultimately stops. Aquinas, of course, thinks that this entity, which itself is "unmoved" or "uncaused" by anything else, must be God.

Thus, to Aquinas, God is the only entity with the power of not depending on something else for its existence. God's existence is not *contingent* on something else, it is necessary in its own right. It is simply God's nature to exist, so much so that Aquinas would regard it as a logical contradiction to say that a "necessary being" might not exist. That would make as little sense as saying that $2 + 2 = 0$. God's "necessary existence," then, lets God be the "uncaused" cause of everything else.

This Cannot Go to Infinity

When Aquinas says that causes cannot be followed back through an infinite series, you probably think he means that a series cannot stretch back into the endless past. That is what one of Aquinas's interpreters calls a "horizontal" series going back in time. For example, your existence was caused by your parents, theirs by their parents, and so on. The state of the planet today was caused by forces put into play a century ago; its condition a century ago was the effect of what happened a century before that; and on and on backward into time. The human mind has a great deal of trouble imagining a series of events going on like this backwards forever. We tell ourselves that it must stop someplace. Something must have started it all, call it "God" or the "Big Bang." But there must have been something.

Aquinas, however, admits the possibility of an infinite horizontal series, so we have to look elsewhere for his meaning.[5] What he does mean is that at every moment, everything in the world depends on something else for its existence. What Aquinas denies the existence of, then, is an infinite "vertical" series of causes.

For example, suppose you're writing a paper using a word processor. The appearance of letters, words, and sentences on the screen depends on your computer being in good working order, a continued supply of electricity, and on your pressing keys on the keyboard. The supply of electricity depends on the integrity of your electric company's lines and on whatever generators and fuel they use to produce the current. Your ability to press these keys depends on your hands being functional and your body being

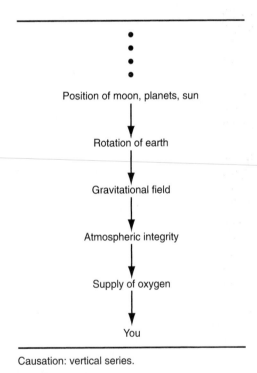

Causation: vertical series.

---

[5]The idea that we could have an infinite series of "horizontal" causes is called the "eternity of the world." Advocated by the medieval Arabic philosopher Avicenna (980–1037), the theory of the "eternity of the world" posits that both God and the world God created existed from eternity. Avicenna thinks that God's essential nature is to be creative, and it is impossible that there could ever have been a time when God had created nothing. While Aquinas acknowledges that Christianity teaches otherwise, he admits that there is no philosophical way to refute the "eternity of the world." He is careful to point out that while he does not accept the idea, he rejects it on religious, not philosophical, grounds.

alive. Your life depends upon an adequate supply of oxygen, as well as on the walls and ceiling of your room staying put and not crashing down on you. Those conditions depend on the gravitational and other natural forces that make our atmosphere what it is and keep it from drifting away from the planet. These conditions require the regular rotation of the earth, which in turn is affected by the current position of the moon, planets, and sun (see figure on previous page). And, of course, we can go on to specify an apparently limitless list of things depending on each other right now.

So when we look at nature, or observable reality, we see a series of "vertical" dependencies all operating at this moment. Any significant shift anywhere will change everything. This is the case even if the world does stretch "horizontally" back into an endless past and has no chronological "first cause." Therefore, Aquinas argues that with everything in the universe "vertically" dependent on each other, there must be a "first cause" that stands at the top of the hierarchy.

We can see that everything we experience is "contingent" on something else. But if there were no "unmoved mover" or "uncaused cause," how could the universe even exist? Aquinas believes that it couldn't. God, then, becomes the ultimate force that makes the universe possible.

Is This Argument Plausible?

Do these arguments from motion and causality prove the existence of God any better than the arguments from design and governance? Like those earlier arguments, these make a certain sense. They point to something obvious in the physical world. Change does take place. And because everything we see needs a cause or is dependent on something else, we naturally conclude that some "first mover" or "first cause" got the whole thing rolling. If there were not some such beginning force, how could anything have ever come into existence?

As plausible as these proofs of God's existence may seem, however, many philosophers have objected to them.

Only an Uncaused Cause. The most obvious problem with the "first cause" argument is a weakness shared with the argument from design. How do the observations that Aquinas makes about the natural world necessarily imply the qualities traditionally associated with the Judeo-Christian God? "First mover" seems much more general and more limited than the God described in the Bible. "Uncaused cause" is about all anyone can claim from this argument, nothing about a being of unlimited knowledge, love, justice, and mercy. This severely limits the concept of God just as the argument from design limits us to a "world-architect," as Kant observed.

This point is reinforced by the fact that in the original version of this proof, Aristotle argues for a being very different from the Judeo-Christian God. Aristotle's "Unmoved Mover" is the ultimate source of all the "motion" in the world, but it does not create the world as God does in Genesis, nor does it oversee the world, nor reward good and punish evil. It is not even aware of anything but itself, and it exists in an eternal state of perfect self-contemplation. Indeed, it is as though this being's perfection acts as a magnetic force causing "movement" in the world. This "argument from motion" as originally stated implies a very different entity from that which the Jews and Christians call "God."

Even so, that is a lot more than nothing.

Hume's and Russell's Objections. David Hume, however, would take even that away from us. He goes right to the heart of the matter. The strength of the argument from motion is that the universe seems to make better sense if we can point to something outside the ordinary causal chain. But Hume claims that this is unnecessary. As he says,

> [W]hy may not the material universe [itself] be the necessarily existent Being. . . ? We dare not affirm that we know all the qualities of matter; and, for aught we can determine, it may contain some qualities which, were they known, would make its nonexistence appear as great a contradiction as that twice two is five.
>
> —Dialogues on Natural Religion

We surely cannot yet say that we know everything about the universe. Isn't it possible that at some time in the future we will discover that the universe itself is its own cause? Perhaps we will learn that the entire universe is a huge, eternal being— a totally self-contained, self-creating, self-designing, necessarily existing entity. If this were true, then the universe would not need any external First Cause—divine or otherwise—to make it work. It would function simply because that is its nature.

Bertrand Russell echoes Hume and adds an interesting twist:

> There is no reason why the world could not have come into being without a cause; nor, on the other hand, is there any reason why it should not have always existed. There is no reason to suppose that the world had a beginning at all. The idea that things must have a beginning is really due to *the poverty of our imagination.* ("Why I Am Not a Christian" [1927], emphasis added.)

Is it possible that our thinking is just too limited?

To appreciate what Hume and Russell have in mind, imagine a very young child who has just learned that her toys need batteries to make them move. In her mind, "movement" means "runs on batteries." She very carefully looks over the family dog and asks, "Where do Fido's batteries go?" The odds are that you probably couldn't explain to her in a way she can understand that being biologically alive means that you do not need batteries. This understanding will come only as she develops a more sophisticated understanding of certain concepts, such as "alive," "not alive," and "energy."

Hume and Russell suggest that when we think that the universe must have some First Cause, we are like this child thinking that Fido must need batteries. As we learn more, we may eventually come to a fuller, more sophisticated understanding of the universe, one that reveals it as self-creating with no need of a creator. That may simply be its nature.

Hume continues and offers a second criticism, this one focusing on the idea that there cannot be an infinite causal chain:

> In such a chain, too, or succession of objects, each part is caused by that which preceded it, and causes that which succeeds it. Where then is the difficulty? But the WHOLE, you say, wants a cause. I answer, that the uniting of these parts into a whole, like the uniting of several distinct counties into one kingdom, or several

> distinct members into one body, is performed merely by an arbitrary act of the mind, and has no influence on the nature of things. Did I show you the particular causes of each individual in a collection of twenty particles of matter, I should think it very unreasonable, should you afterwards ask me, what was the cause of the whole twenty. This is sufficiently explained in explaining the cause of the parts.
>
> —Dialogues on Natural Religion

Hume sees the need for a first cause as a basic mistake of this sort. Imagine that little girl again and try to explain to her what her "body" is. You point out her hands, arms, head, neck, chest, stomach, legs, and feet. She listens intently, then turns to you and asks, "But where's my 'body'?" You probably think this question is cute, and it makes sense in a way. But only because she has not grasped your explanation. Her "body" is the sum total of its interdependent parts. Pointing to the parts actually accounts for the whole.

Hume thinks that we ask exactly the same kind of question when we look at all the things in the material world and their intricate causal connections and then ask what the ultimate cause of the whole thing is. Hume would answer that if you put together everything you already know about the parts, you have a complete explanation. The whole is the sum of its parts. That's all there is. If you have to ask for more, you have not yet understood how all the parts fit together.

Hume and Russell are right, of course, that we do not know everything about the nature of the universe. The universe may very well be self-creating and self-regulating—it is not logically impossible. Hume's second point also seems sensible. If we know all the parts of the universe, don't we already know the whole? If we grant these points, the most we can say is that there may be a First Cause and, then again, the idea may not make any sense.

Does the Material World Prove God's Existence?

When we survey proofs for God's existence based on the nature of the physical world, the results are mixed. These arguments certainly do not establish any necessity for a Supreme Being of goodness, love, mercy, and justice who designed and created a good and orderly universe. Attributing the problems in the universe to human free will does not account for all the imperfections in the design of the world.

The best that these proofs do, then, is to suggest that there once may have been (and there may still be) a world-architect or a First Cause. However, David Hume's arguments show that, logically, it is just as possible that the world simply exists as its own cause in a way that we cannot yet understand.

Arguments from Reason Alone

We have not yet settled the question of whether God exists. But remember that the question we are investigating is somewhat different. Here, we are examining claims about whether or not we can *know* that God exists.

We have just looked at *empirical* arguments—those that would be offered by someone who thinks knowledge comes from the evidence we gather using our senses. In the rival *rationalist* tradition, knowledge derives from the purely mental

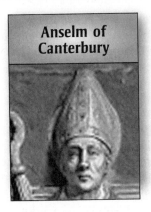

Anselm of Canterbury

St. Anselm (1033–1109) was born in Italy, entered the monastery against the objections of his father, and became a monk, abbot, and teacher in the monastery of Bec. In 1093, he was made Archbishop of Canterbury and took an active role in a dispute concerning the relationship between the authority of the King and that of the Pope. His most famous works on the existence of God are the *Monologion* and *Proslogion*.

operations like those used in mathematics or logic. And, not surprisingly, there are rationalist proofs of God's existence as well.

The Ontological Argument: Saint Anselm

The most famous argument of this sort, the **ontological argument**, is offered by the early medieval thinker Anselm of Canterbury. Anselm himself did not use the word "ontological" when he made his argument. But ever since Immanuel Kant referred to it this way, the label has stuck. He chose "ontological" because the argument is based on the concept of the most perfect *being*. (*Ontos* is Greek for "being.")

Anselm's argument has had a long and controversial history. During its first seven hundred years, the argument had as many defenders as attackers. About two hundred years ago, most philosophers decided it was wrong, but debate over it has started again in our own day. Some people hail it as a genuine proof of God's existence. Others dismiss it as philosophical flimflam.

For all of that, Anselm's argument is unquestionably one of the most important proofs offered for the existence of God. The argument is found in Anselm's *Proslogion*.

> **That God Truly Exists**
>
> Well then, Lord, You who give understanding to faith, grant me that I may understand, as much as You see fit, that You exist as we believe You to exist, and that You are what we believe You to be. Now we believe that You are something than which nothing greater can be thought. Or can it be that a thing of such a nature does not exist, since "the Fool has said in his heart, there is no God" [Psalms. xiii. I, lii. I]? But

---

ontological argument The ontological argument is St. Anselm's argument for the existence of God. It claims that by merely contemplating the notion of God as "something-than-which-nothing-greater-can-be-thought," we become aware that God must exist.

surely, when this same Fool hears what I am speaking about, namely "something-than-which-nothing-greater-can-be-thought," he understands what he hears, and what he understands is in his mind, even if he does not understand that it actually exists. For it is one thing for an object to exist in the mind, and another thing to understand that an object actually exists. Thus, when a painter plans beforehand what he is going to execute, he has [the picture] in his mind, but he does not yet think that it actually exists because he has not yet executed it. However, when he has actually painted it, then he both has it in his mind and understands that it exists because he has now made it. Even the Fool, then, is forced to agree that something-than-which-nothing-greater-can-be-thought exists in the mind, since he understands this when he hears it, and whatever is understood is in the mind. And surely that-than-which-a-greater-cannot-be-thought cannot exist in the mind alone. For if it exists solely in the mind even, it can be thought to exist in reality also, which is greater. If then that-than-which-a-greater-cannot-be-thought exists in the mind alone, this same that-than-which-a-greater-*cannot*-be-thought is that-than-which-a-greater-*can*-be-thought. But this is obviously impossible. Therefore there is absolutely no doubt that something-than-which-a-greater-cannot-be-thought exists both in the mind and in reality.

That God Cannot Be Thought Not to Exist

And certainly this being so truly exists that it cannot be even thought not to exist. For something can be thought to exist that cannot be thought not to exist, and this is greater than that which can be thought not to exist. Hence, if that-than-which-a-greater-cannot-be-thought can be thought not to exist, then that-than-which-a-greater-cannot-be-thought is not the same as that-than-which-a-greater-cannot-be-thought, which is absurd. Something-than-which-a-greater-cannot-be-thought exists so truly then, that it cannot be even thought not to exist.

And You, Lord our God, are this being. You exist so truly, Lord my God, that You cannot even be thought not to exist. And this is as it should be, for if some intelligence could think of something better than You, the creature would be above its creator and would judge its creator—and that is completely absurd. In fact, everything else there is, except You alone, can be thought of as not existing. You alone, then, of all things most truly exist and therefore of all things possess existence to the highest degree; for anything else does not exist as truly, and so possesses existence to a lesser degree. Why then did "the Fool say in his heart, there is no God" [Ps. xiii. I, lii. I] when it is so evident to any rational mind that You of all things exist to the highest degree? Why indeed, unless because he was stupid and a fool?

What Anselm Has in Mind

Anselm's argument is fairly simple. Push your imagination as hard as you can and think of the most perfect, most supreme being. That is Anselm's "that-than-which-a-greater-cannot-be-thought." In particular, imagine that this being is so great, so perfect that it cannot even be thought not to exist. Do you have that in mind? If so, you should also have a strong sense that this being must actually exist. Anselm would say that this most perfect being that you have envisioned is God. So, he thinks, anyone who truly understands the idea of the greatest possible being should feel certain that God must actually exist.

Moreover, by realizing that God is a being whose nonexistence we cannot even imagine, Anselm would say that we are aware of God's "necessary existence." That is, if God's existence is "necessary," to say that God does not exist is as self-contradictory as saying, "Fire is cold." To claim that something that must exist cannot exist is so illogical that it is ridiculous.

In other words, Anselm thinks that as our minds explore the idea of the greatest possible being imaginable, we will realize that in addition to being all-powerful, all-knowing, all-just, all-merciful, and all-loving, its level of existence is so great that it must have existed from eternity, will go on forever, and cannot even be thought of as not existing. Anselm is convinced that if we have a solid grasp of the idea of the "greatest possible being," then we should have no doubt about God's existence. Only a fool would think otherwise.

Reason Alone

Notice that this argument relies on nothing but reason alone. Unlike Paley and Thomas Aquinas, Anselm does not draw his reasons for God's existence from the world of nature. Rather, he takes an idea, the concept that God is the most perfect being imaginable—"that-than-which-a-greater-cannot-be-thought"—and claims that a purely intellectual examination of that concept shows that such a being must exist in *reality* as well as *in our minds* as an idea. Furthermore, Anselm thinks that if we understand the concept properly, we should see that the statement "God does not exist" is a logical contradiction. So Anselm makes his point about God's existence purely by logic, not by reference to the physical world.

Anselm's Platonism

The material world offers us no evidence of a necessarily existing, most perfect being. Where does such an idea come from then? Anselm would say it results from the fact that such a being actually exists and that our minds discern that fact. This style of thinking makes Anselm in essence a Platonist.

Like Plato, Anselm assumes that the ideas in our minds are not simply arbitrary creations of our imagination. Instead, he believes they are connected to some higher reality which is superior to the senses. Plato thinks that our conceptions of justice, fairness, beauty, and the like come from actual existing, nonmaterial entities that we discover with our "mind's eye," as it were.[6] If there were no such thing as the metaphysical entity "Justice itself," for example, Plato would say that we would have no idea of justice in our minds. Anselm is from the same school of thought. We are able to fashion a mental image of a "most perfect" being only because one actually exists. And if we do have such an idea, we can conclude that such a being must exist.

Anselm's argument has a certain appeal. We can all think of a being "that-than-which-a-greater-cannot-be-thought." But does this mean that Anselm has proven that God exists?

---

[6]See Chapter 8 to review Plato's understanding of the nature of reality.

Anselm's Critics

Guanilo. As persuasive as Anselm's argument may seem, it has no shortage of critics. Its first critic was a French monk named Guanilo of Marmoutier, who lived at the same time as Anselm. Speaking "on behalf of the Fool," Guanilo rejects Anselm's contention that simply imagining the idea of a most perfect being proves that it exists. If that were the case, he says, imagining something like a "most perfect" island would "prove" that it exists. He explains,

> For example, they say that there is in the ocean somewhere an island which, because of the difficulty (or rather the impossibility) of finding that which does not exist, some have called the "Lost Island." And the story goes that it is blessed with all manner of priceless riches and delights in abundance, . . . and, having no owner or inhabitant, it is superior everywhere in abundance of riches to all those other lands that men inhabit. Now, if anyone tell me that it is like this, I shall easily understand what is said, since nothing is difficult about it. But if he should then go on to say, as though it were a logical consequence of this: You cannot any more doubt that this island that is more excellent than all other lands truly exists somewhere in reality than you can doubt that it is in your mind; and since it is more excellent to exist not only in the mind alone but also in reality, therefore it must needs be that it exists. For if it did not exist, any other land existing in reality would be more excellent than it, and so this island, already conceived by you to be more excellent than others, will not be more excellent. If, I say, someone wishes thus to persuade me that this island really exists beyond all doubt, I should either think that he was joking, or I should find it hard to decide which of us I ought to judge the bigger fool—I, if I agreed with him, or he, if he thought that he had proved the existence of this island with any certainty, unless he had first convinced me that its very excellence exists in my mind precisely as a thing existing truly and indubitably and not just as something unreal or doubtfully real.
>
> —A Reply to the Foregoing by a Certain Writer on Behalf of the Fool

Guanilo sees no contradiction in conceiving of a most perfect being and at the same time doubting its existence. "When have I said," he continues,

> that there truly existed some being that is "greater than everything," such that from this it could be proved to me that this same being really existed to such a degree that it could not be thought not to exist? That is why it must first be conclusively proved by argument that there is some higher nature, namely that which is greater and better than all the things that are, so that from this we can also infer everything else which necessarily cannot be wanting to what is greater and better than everything.

Thomas Aquinas. About a century later, Thomas Aquinas joined Guanilo in criticizing Anselm. As you saw earlier in this chapter, Aquinas tries to derive God's existence by pointing to the material world rather than proving it by reasoning alone. Like Guanilo, Aquinas thinks that the idea of a most perfect being can certainly exist only as an idea with no counterpart in reality, and he explicitly rejects Anselm's argument on grounds similar to Guanilo. Aquinas writes,

Perhaps not everyone who hears this name *God* understands it to signify something than which nothing greater can be thought. . . . Yet, [even] granted that everyone understands that by this name *God* is signified something than which nothing greater can be thought, nevertheless, it does not therefore follow that he understands that what the name signifies exists actually, but only that it exists mentally. Nor can it be argued that it actually exists, unless it be admitted that there actually exists something than which nothing greater can be thought; and this precisely is not admitted by those who hold that God does not exist.

—Summa Theologiae

David Hume. About 500 years after Aquinas, we find David Hume also challenging Anselm. Like Aquinas, Hume thinks it is impossible to argue for God's existence from reason alone. Nor does he see any logical contradiction in imagining God's nonexistence. As Hume puts this:

I shall begin with observing, that there is an evident absurdity in pretending to demonstrate a matter of fact, or to prove it by any arguments *a priori.*[7] Nothing is demonstrable, unless the contrary implies a contradiction. Nothing, that is distinctly conceivable, implies a contradiction. Whatever we conceive as existent, we can also conceive as nonexistent. There is no Being, therefore, whose nonexistence implies a contradiction. Consequently there is no Being, whose existence is demonstrable. I propose this argument as entirely decisive, and am willing to rest the whole controversy upon it.

It is pretended that the Deity is a necessarily existent Being; and this necessity of his existence is attempted to be explained by asserting that, if we knew his whole essence or nature, we should perceive it to be as impossible for him not to exist as for twice two not to be four. But it is evident, that this can never happen, while our faculties remain the same as at present. It will still be possible for us, at any time, to conceive the non-existence of what we formerly conceived to exist; nor can the mind ever lie under a necessity of supposing any object to remain always in being; in the same manner as we lie under a necessity of always conceiving twice two to be four.

—Dialogues on Natural Religion

Stop and think about the statement "2 + 2 = 4." Now try to think logically that "2 + 2" equals something else. It is hard to do. In fact, as long as you are thinking in line with the rules of reason, it is impossible. Now call to mind your image of a "most perfect being" and imagine that it really exists. Now try to imagine that it does not exist. It is much easier to do that than it is to imagine that "2 + 2" equals something other than 4, isn't it?

This is just Hume's point. As long as we can even conceive of God's nonexistence, it is not contradictory to say "God does not exist." In short, Hume not only thinks that Anselm's argument doesn't win the day, he thinks it doesn't even leave the starting gate.

---

[7]As pointed out in Chapter 9, an *a priori* argument relies on reason alone. This stands in contrast to an *a posteriori* argument, which draws its conclusion from empirical evidence.

Anselm's Critics Reviewed. Anselm's case is simple and straightforward; Guanilo, Aquinas, and Hume reject it in an equally simple and straightforward way. Anselm says it is contradictory to think that "that-than-which-a-greater-cannot-be-thought" does not exist in reality as well as in the mind. The other three thinkers flatly disagree. Understanding a concept does not prove that the entity represented by the idea exists. A phoenix is a beautiful bird that lives 500 years, then is consumed by fire in order to be reborn out of the ashes. We can all understand what a phoenix is, but that doesn't prove that such a bird exists.

Lest you think that these philosophers are merely biased against the idea of God, remember that at least two of them, Guanilo and Aquinas, believe devoutly in God. They agree with Anselm's conclusion. They just don't think that Anselm's argument proves it.

Anselm's Reply: A One-Concept-Only Argument

Good philosophers always have intelligent responses to their critics. Since Guanilo lived at the same time as Anselm, we have the good fortune of knowing exactly how Anselm replied to the criticism.

The essence of Anselm's defense is that his argument works for one concept, and one concept only—the concept of "that-than-which-a-greater-cannot-be-thought." Guanilo's claim that we can imagine a fantastic "Lost Island" is beside the point. As Anselm explains,

> Only that being in which there is neither beginning nor end nor conjunction of parts, and that thought does not discern save as a whole in every place and at every time, cannot be thought as not existing.
>
> —A Reply to the Foregoing by the Author of the Book in Question

Any other concept we can imagine is irrelevant. His argument, Anselm says, applies to only one concept. And if we come up with a being that we can imagine not existing, then we have the wrong concept in mind:

> When, therefore, one thinks of that-than-which-a-greater-cannot-be-thought, if one thinks of what can not exist, one does not think of that-than-which-a-greater-cannot-be-thought. Now the same thing cannot at the same time be thought of and not thought of. For this reason he who thinks of that-than-which-a-greater-cannot-be-thought does not think of something that can not exist but something that cannot not exist. Therefore what he thinks of exists necessarily, since whatever can not exist is not what he thinks of.
>
> —A Reply

This answer is either very clever or very good. Anselm claims that his two "proofs"—(1) conceiving an idea of the "greatest possible being" automatically implies the existence of that being and (2) imagining the nonexistence of this being is self-contradictory—hold for one and only one concept, "that-than-which-a-greater-cannot-be-thought." If his proofs are true for only this concept, Anselm can dismiss any counterexample as comparing apples and oranges.

How does Anselm's reply hold up? Is Anselm cheating, or is he right? Ordinarily, we would not take a "one-concept argument" seriously. Intellectual custom usually does not let us defend a conclusion by saying that the idea on which it is based is so unique that special rules apply. Still, there is something about this concept that is hard to ignore. Might not things indeed be different when it comes to the greatest imaginable being? Is it absolutely impossible to conceive of an argument that applies only to one case? In this one instance only, might it not be that the nonexistence of such an entity is in fact self-contradictory?

The simple fact that this argument has been debated as a viable proof for God's existence for almost a thousand years is worth noting. Anselm's argument may not be conclusive, and it may not be universally accepted. But its enduring appeal and its tenacity suggest that it has something important to say.

Defining the Greatest Possible Being by Reason or Faith?

When we looked at the arguments of Paley, Aquinas, and Hume, the most we ended up with was not the God of the Bible but a world-designer. Now we have to see if the same thing happens with Anselm's argument. Anselm begins his argument by referring to the line from the Book of Psalms, "The Fool has said in his heart, there is no God." This lets us know right away that he aims to prove the existence of the Judeo-Christian God of the Bible. Does he accomplish this?

The key here is Anselm's concept "that-than-which-a-greater-cannot-be-thought." To Anselm, of course, this phrase refers to nothing but the God of the Old and New Testaments. But couldn't it mean something else? When we examine the thought of the ancient philosophers, we find candidates for "greatest possible being" that differ significantly from Anselm's God—Aristotle's "Unmoved Mover," for example, and "the One" of Plotinus (205–270). Both philosophers put a "supreme being" at the top of their systems, but these beings differ from the Biblical God in many ways.

Both men describe a supreme being so perfect it needs nothing and no one else. The Unmoved Mover and the One exist in a state of pure self-contemplation, meditating on the most perfect thing in the universe—itself. They have no awareness of anything else, least of all the petty events of human life. Why would the greatest possible being have any interest in anything less than perfect? Neither of these beings watch over the world the way the Judeo-Christian God does, keeping a tally of right and wrong and handing out rewards and punishments. In addition, these two supreme beings do not have the identifiable personality that the God of the Bible does. They are simply pure intellect. Furthermore, the Unmoved Mover and the One are so overwhelmingly powerful in their very essence that the universe is merely a by-product of their existence. Plotinus says the universe "emanates" from the One the way heat and light emanate from a flame. In other words, the One does not create the world by an act of will the way God creates the world in Genesis. The world is simply a product of its nature.

These two supreme entities, then, are examples of the "greatest possible being," yet they are very different from Anselm's conception of God. Other examples might have still other qualities. And there is no reason why there should be only one such being. Why couldn't there be two, three, or a countless number of perfect beings? It should be clear, then, that "that-than-which-a-greater-cannot-be-thought" can easily mean something other than what Anselm has in mind when he says "God."

Thus, *reason* does not support Anselm's claims. In order to prove the existence of the Judeo-Christian God, Anselm has to draw on the conception of God given to him by his religious faith. Without that, the most he can claim is that his proof shows the existence of some "that-than-which-a-greater-cannot-be-thought." After that, we have to figure out exactly what this means.

Anselm finds nothing wrong with this. Remember how he starts his proof:

> Well then, Lord, You who give understanding to faith, grant me that I may understand, as much as You see fit, that You exist as we believe You to exist, and that You are what we believe You to be.

> —Proslogion

Clearly, he puts faith above reason when it comes to discerning God's nature. This being the case, we have to see his proof, like Paley's and Aquinas's, as operating under those limitations.

For the strictly philosophical reader, then, Anselm's argument is not as strong as Anselm hopes it is. Yet this is the most famous argument for the existence of God that seeks to prove its point by appealing to reason alone. Whether it is brilliant thinking or philosophical sleight of hand, it still gives you much to think about.

Reason or Faith?

God's Existence: A Question of Reason

We have looked at Paley's and Aquinas's attempts to infer God's existence from the nature of the material world. We have considered Anselm's purely intellectual proof based on the concept of the greatest possible being. On balance, do these arguments prove that God exists?

These proofs certainly require us to consider seriously the possibility that some superior being created, designed, or governs the world. But none of them proves beyond the shadow of a doubt that such a being exists. Even if they do work, they fail to demonstrate the existence of the Judeo-Christian God. But the conclusion that there is no such being is not established either. Perhaps the issue simply can never be settled.

God's Existence: A Question of Faith

Is exploring possibly unanswerable questions a waste of time, then? Not at all. Even if the arguments we have looked at here do not "prove" whether God exists, they may be useful expressions of faith for people who already believe in God. It should be clear by now that although a number of interesting arguments can be made in favor of God's existence, ultimately it may be a matter of personal, unconfirmable, and unprovable belief.

Religious beliefs may be unprovable or unconfirmable, but that is not to say that they are meaningless or foolish. If we really cannot *know* the answer to a question, it is appropriate to decide what we will *believe* the answer to be. The critical point is that these are *beliefs,* and we can never be absolutely sure whether our beliefs are right or wrong. There is a big difference between saying that we believe God exists and saying that God's existence is a fact that can be proved with absolute certainty.

Religion and Emotion

The fact that the issue of God's existence may ultimately be a matter of personal belief opens the door for one other challenge from Bertrand Russell. You noticed previously that Russell can bring an unusual perspective to philosophical discussions—as when he suggests that believing in God might come from a poverty of the human imagination. Russell poses another important question to us in suggesting that *fear* also plays a large role. He writes:

> I do not think that the real reason why people accept religion has anything to do with argumentation. They accept religion on emotional grounds. . . . Religion is based, I think, primarily and mainly upon fear. It is partly the terror of the unknown and partly, as I have said, the wish to feel that you have a kind of elder brother who will stand by you in all your troubles and disputes. Fear is the basis of the whole thing—fear of the mysterious, fear of defeat, fear of death. Fear is the parent of cruelty, and therefore it is no wonder if cruelty and religion have gone hand in hand. It is because fear is at the basis of those two things. In this world we can now begin a little to understand things, and a little to master them by help of science, which has forced its way step by step against the Christian religion, against the churches, and against the opposition of all the old precepts. Science can help us to get over this craven fear in which mankind has lived for so many generations. Science can teach us, and I think our own hearts can teach us, no longer to look around for imaginary supports, no longer to invent allies in the sky, but rather to look to our own efforts here below to make this world a fit place to live in, instead of the sort of place that the churches in all these centuries have made it.

Weak imaginations and fear certainly characterized humans in the earliest days of the species. Can we really be sure that we've outgrown them as far as we think we have? Is there a possible relationship between faith and fear?

Belief and Harm

The epistemological limits of faith are also important to keep in mind when we decide to take action on the basis of our religious beliefs. Although religious beliefs have produced much good in the world, they have also led otherwise good people to hurt one another very badly. In the course of history, much harm has come when people argued over which is the "true religion" and whose beliefs are "correct." The Romans persecuted the Christians because they refused to worship the gods of the state. For centuries the Jews have been persecuted by Christians and Moslems as practitioners of a false faith. Islam spread via "holy wars," and Christian nations responded against the "infidel" during the Middle Ages with the Crusades. During the Reformation, opposing Christian sects executed people as a way of combating what the religious authorities judged to be "false beliefs." And in reaction to the development of science, the Catholic church punished thinkers like Galileo for holding a different view of the universe than that found in the Bible.

Throughout all this, the issue is not so much how "heretics" and "infidels" *act*, not how they treat others, but what they *believe*. For example, Catholics and Protestants killed one another in sixteenth-century Europe because they believed different things about "grace," the "authority of Scripture," and "papal authority." Heretics were not executed because they were cruel, vicious people, although they were often falsely accused of that to make their deaths seem more defensible. They were burned at the stake for the beliefs they voiced or simply for what they held in their hearts. That most of them were good, decent, loving, and spiritual people was irrelevant.

Unfortunately, the tragic consequences of this focus on belief rather than behavior extend even to today. "Heretics" may not be burned at the stake any longer, but we do not have to look very far for examples of otherwise decent people experiencing everything from intimidation to death threats because their religious beliefs, or lack thereof, do not blend with someone else's idea of the truth. If "heretics," "blasphemers," and "infidels" went around actively harming other people, getting rid of them forcibly might be defensible. But whom do they hurt by their beliefs? God? Jesus? Mohammed? Buddha? Of course not. They may cause some distress among the "faithful," and we can sympathize with the feelings of these people when they hear "blasphemy." But offended sensibilities are surely not the sort of harm that merits imprisonment or death.

The only argument against "false belief" must refer to an afterlife. If people need to believe certain things in order to be "saved" by God, heresy or blasphemy can endanger the salvation of the true believer—and everyone is potentially a true believer, or should be. But if we cannot prove God's existence, the most basic component of religious belief, we certainly cannot prove the existence of an afterlife or the conditions we have to meet to get there. This, of course, leads us right back to where we started. We are facing matters of belief, not knowledge.

In other words, when we take action against people because of their "false beliefs," their "blasphemy," or their "heresy," we do so based on premises that may be true— or false. This, of course, is the nature of belief. We subscribe to an idea knowing that we do not have enough reasons to label it "knowledge." If we did have those reasons, questions about who is right and who is wrong would be settled easily.

Hurting anyone because they have offended your religious beliefs is a case of perpetuating a known harm in order to achieve an uncertain good. Do we have any right to hurt other people for such reasons? And, perhaps most importantly, would a God of perfect love actually want us to?

Main Points of Chapter 10

1. There are both empirical and rationalistic arguments for the existence of God.

2. Empirical arguments claim that the workings of nature imply the existence of God. William Paley's "argument from design" claims that just as the existence of a watch implies a watchmaker, so the existence of the universe implies God. Thomas Aquinas offers similar arguments from "the governance of the world," "motion," and "causality."

3. Empirical arguments have been challenged as relying on a false analogy, claiming too much, not resolving the problem of evil, and not disproving the possibility that the universe may be its own cause.

4. The most famous argument from reason alone is St. Anselm's "ontological argument," which argues that merely understanding the concept of God as "that-than-which-a-greater-cannot-be-thought" reveals the necessity of His existence.

5. A variety of thinkers have rejected Anselm's essentially Platonic argument by arguing that concepts like "that-than-which-a-greater-cannot-be-thought" can have a purely mental existence and that the idea of God's nonexistence is not, as Anselm suggests, a logical contradiction.

Discussion Questions

1. When you look at the physical world, do you see anything that makes you think it was designed, constructed, and continues to be governed by someone or something? What might that be?

2. If you agree with the argument from design, how do you account for the existence of so much evil—both natural disasters and human evil—in the world?

3. What is your reaction to the idea that at best the design of the world implies the existence of a somewhat incompetent world-architect? How would someone argue against this claim?

4. Even if we were to concede Aquinas's point that some "first cause" is necessary, would that prove the existence of the Judeo–Christian God?

5. If you think that the character of the natural world implies that it was created, is there any reason to think that such a being is still alive?

6. Do you find Anselm's rationalistic proof more or less convincing than Paley's and Aquinas's empirical arguments? What is your reaction to the Platonic notion that we could not have ideas of perfection, goodness, the greatest possible being, and so on, unless such intangible entities actually existed in some way?

7. Is there a way of proving God's existence that you find convincing but that we have not discussed in this chapter? What is it?

Selected Readings

William Paley's argument from design can be found in his *Natural Theology.* Hume's critique is elaborated in *Dialogues on Natural Religion.* For Bertrand Russell, see his "Why I Am Not a Christian." Immanuel Kant discusses various proofs for the existence of God in Chapter 3 of the *Transcendental Dialectic in the Critique of Pure Reason.* The five proofs of Thomas Aquinas are defended in Question 2, Article 3 of the *Summa Theologiae.* Anselm discusses the existence of God in both the *Monologion* and *Proslogion;* the latter contains the "ontological argument."

The Purpose of Life: Marx and Buddha

- *Karl Marx and Marxism*
- *Buddhism—Another Alternative*
- *The Challenge of Marxism and Buddhism*

It is appropriate to finish this section on the most abstract philosophical issues with one of philosophy's "big questions," and there is no bigger issue to most of us than "the meaning of life." What is important? What should we strive for in life? These are questions that all of us sooner or later face—and usually more than once. We struggle with the meaning of life in our twenties as we choose careers and relationships. A decade or two later we may encounter it as part of our "midlife crisis." We face it yet again as we grow old and assess how well we did with the time and opportunities that we had. In short, everyone has to figure out what life is all about.

The big question takes many forms:

- "What am I doing with my life?"
- "What is my purpose in the world?"
- "What do I need to be happy?"
- "What's it all about?
- "There's got to be more to life. What is it?"
- "I have everything I thought I wanted. Why am I not happy?"

These questions represent a common basic need to find some overarching sense of purpose that gives meaning to the small events of daily life. We all need a "big picture" and a feeling for where we fit into it.

In fact, every society promotes a kind of "official" idea about what life is all about. In the contemporary Western world, we find a largely *materialistic, individualistic,* and *secular* view of the purpose of life. Television, movies, advertisements, and the various print media show "successful" people as having one thing in common: They make a lot of money and fill their lives with material comforts. (You've probably seen the bumper sticker that says, "The one who dies with the most toys wins.") To accomplish this, of course, you have to "look out for #1" and compete aggressively, perhaps unethically, for your share of the pie. If you succeed, you will assure your happiness in this, your one and only life.

This idea of the goal of life says nothing about what we do for other people, only what we can buy for ourselves. It makes no reference to any spiritual dimension of life. It ignores emotional growth, intellectual development, and the quality of relationships. You might object that this characterization ignores the value many people place on patriotism, public service, and religion. Yet these values are not really essential to the notion of success endorsed by our culture. In the United States, as long as you have enough money, you are considered successful. You may be selfish, greedy, ignorant, and narrow-minded. You may even have been convicted of a crime and spent time in prison. But if you have plenty of money, people overlook all that and consider you "successful" anyway.

In ancient Greece, by contrast, making money was less important than being a responsible member of your community. That is what made you a "success." If you were rich but took no active role in the politics of your city, you were seriously shirking your duties. You were tolerated, but neither admired nor respected. Certain American families, the Rockefellers and the Kennedys, for example, have imbued their members with the idea that they have a responsibility to do more with their money and talent than the "idle rich" do. But this is unusual. In general today, we measure how "successful" we are mainly by how much luxury we can obtain for ourselves. Service to others is not part of the calculation.

Many people are indeed strongly influenced by some religious tradition. But Western culture has become increasingly secular over time. Religion and religious institutions are not as central to modern Western societies as they were during the Middle Ages and Reformation. Religion has moved from a public to a private arena.

Our heroes are an important sign of what we think life is supposed to be about. Who are they? Athletes. Rock singers. Television and movie stars. Wealthy businesspeople. The "rich and famous." Who are not our heroes? Nurses. Physicians who run clinics for the poor and make very little money. Social workers. Police officers. Firefighters. Teachers. People in government and public service. Humble, spiritual people. Ordinary individuals quietly trying to make life better for the people around them.

A society's heroes tell much about what that culture believes about the meaning of life and the nature of happiness. Any list of contemporary American heroes simply reinforces the dominant Western values of individualism, materialism, and secularism. Most people's fantasy is to hit the lottery and retire, not to find a cure for cancer, or to bring peace to troubled regions in the world, or to achieve sainthood. It is simply part of the air we breathe every day, and most of us never think twice about it.

In this chapter we look at two points of view that offer unusually powerful challenges to most of what our culture believes about the meaning of life. First, we examine the thinking of Karl Marx, whose work fueled one of the main political and social struggles of the twentieth century and whose ideas still pose a major challenge to capitalism. Then we go to the other side of the globe and review the teachings of the ancient Eastern sage Buddha, whose ideas about reincarnation and "karma" raise fundamental questions about the aim and impact of all our actions.

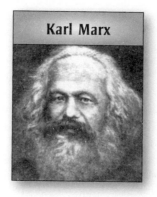

Karl Marx

Karl Marx was born in 1818 in Trier, Prussia, in what is now Germany. Marx's father was a successful lawyer, and Karl was supposed to enter the same profession. He began studying law at the University of Bonn but transferred to the University of Berlin, where he studied law, philosophy, history, English, and Italian. He wrote his dissertation on Greek philosophy and received his Ph.D. Unable to get a teaching position, Marx began a career as a political journalist, first in Prussia and then in France. This brought him into contact with Frederick Engels, the son of a textile manufacturer, who would become Marx's main collaborator. Marx was expelled first from France and then from Belgium and Germany for his radical ideas. In 1849, he moved to London, where he and his family spent the rest of his life in poverty, often supported by Engels. Marx wrote numerous revolutionary books and articles, and he was active in workers' movements and in the founding of the Communist League. He worked on his masterpiece, *Das Kapital,* for the last 25 years of his life and died in 1883 with it unfinished.

Karl Marx and Marxism

Karl Marx and his theories are widely misunderstood. Most Americans, for example, think that Marx was Russian (he was German), or that he lived in Russia (he spent most of his life in England), or at least that after spending his life as a bomb-throwing revolutionary (he was a journalist and philosopher), Marx was buried in Moscow's Red Square (Marx's tomb is in London). Karl Marx was indeed a revolutionary thinker, but he did not live his life on the ramparts urging the violent overthrow of European capitalism. He certainly wanted to have a powerful effect on people and to stimulate change. But most of his writings are difficult to read and about as incendiary as the telephone book.

Marx's ideas did eventually have a major impact on political revolutionaries like Lenin and Mao Tse-tung. Because the former Soviet Union and China regarded Marx as a kind of patron saint, and since these countries were cast as enemies of the free world for many decades, it is not surprising that most of us have some faulty notions about what Marx said and did.

What does Marx, the founding father of communism, contribute to our inquiry into the nature of happiness and the purpose of life? Many of Marx's ideas speak beyond economics to questions about human happiness and what we should do with our lives. Two of his ideas are particularly important for us to consider.

First, Marx argues that our ideas about what is valuable in life come not from our own personal choices, as we think they do, but from the economic system that dominates our lives. Marx believes that our ideas about what makes us happy are just as much the product of capitalism as the cars that come off the end of an assembly line. Marx thus claims that capitalism imbues people with a particular view of the purpose of life. Second, Marx believes that living according to this vision of happiness in fact puts a satisfying life out of reach for everyone, rich and poor alike. In particular, Marx thinks that the way capitalism has us spend our work days goes against the grain of the human spirit. Obviously, if either of Marx's claims is true, that would have an important effect on how we live our lives and how we choose our life's goals.

Capitalism as the Source of Our Ideas: "Dialectical Materialism"

One of the most interesting aspects of Marx's ideas is his insistence that economic factors are the single most important force in any society. Not only do economic factors shape individual values, they also determine the overall political goals of a society and even its view of history. Behind these views is a theory of history, a theory that has subsequently been called **dialectical materialism**. To understand Marx's thinking, however, we have to look briefly at the work of the philosopher who pointed Marx in this direction, Georg Hegel.

Hegel's Dialectic and Its Influence on Marx

Georg Wilhelm Friedrich Hegel is the most important representative of nineteenth-century German Idealism. *Idealism* is a school of thought that claims that reality is ultimately intangible and nonmaterial, as opposed to *materialism,* which sees reality as physical and concrete.[1] Hegel took an extreme idealist position, claiming that all reality was ultimately "Mind," "God," or, as he put it, "Spirit." Through time, Spirit fashions the world as we know it, following an evolutionary pattern. As Hegel sees it, however, this process is full of conflict, and human history is thus the story of the clash of opposites. One force or idea gives rise to its opposite and collides with it. The two then unite and produce a new third state of affairs that combines elements of both. Hegel labels the three elements involved in this process *thesis, antithesis,* and *synthesis.* The whole process he calls a dialectic.[2]

Hegel's dialectical idealism accounts for the existence of the material world as we know it in this fashion. In the beginning, pure mind (thesis) thinks its opposite, lifeless matter (antithesis). The combination of the two (synthesis) is life and reality as we know it. Once begun, the dialectic continues working itself out. Every synthesis becomes a new thesis, which produces a new antithesis, the two merge into a new synthesis, and so on.

Human history may look chaotic, with nations making war and factions within societies vying for predominance. But, Hegel believes, this is all part of a grand,

---

dialectical materialism Dialectical materialism is Marx's revision of Hegel's dialectical idealism in terms of Marx's belief in the primacy of material, specifically economic, forces. Marx thus sees human history as the clash of opposing economic forces, creating new stages.

---

[1]Philosophical "idealism" has no connection with "being idealistic and high principled." It is strictly a metaphysical outlook.
[2]"Dialectic" comes from the ancient Greek phrase for "the art of argumentation." It describes Hegel's ideas in that when we argue for a position, we advance one position against opposing ones. In doing so, we often find that the truth is some combination of what first seemed like contrary positions.

Hegel

Georg Wilhelm Friedrich Hegel (1770–1831) studied at the theological seminary at the University of Tübingen. He began as a tutor to aristocratic families, and he taught at the University of Jena. After the Prussians were defeated by Napoleon, Hegel was forced to give up his position. He edited a daily paper in Bavaria and then served as headmaster of a school for eight years before being appointed professor of philosophy at the University of Heidelberg in 1816 and then at the University of Berlin in 1818. He died in 1831 in a cholera epidemic.

positive process. The clash of conflicting forces produces progress, because the best of the opposites is preserved in their joining. The dialectic gives rise to growth, development, and advancement, and history is thus ordered and organic. The process is positive, and Hegelian thinking is understandably optimistic.

Hegel's ideas had a powerful effect on Marx, although Marx argued that Hegel's idealism was dead wrong. Hegel, Marx said, is standing on his head. "Mind" or "Spirit" is not the creative force; it is *matter*. In other words, nothing intellectual or abstract creates matter, it is the other way around. Matter is so strong that even our ideas are produced by different aspects of empirical reality. Marx's materialism thus stands in direct opposition to Hegel's idealism.

Marx does accept Hegel's dialectical method, however, and he agrees that the clash of opposing forces in human history is ultimately ordered and purposeful. Everywhere he looks he sees the pattern of "thesis, antithesis, and synthesis" playing itself out in human events. Taken together, these two ideas, materialism and the dialectic, provide the substance of Marx's philosophical outlook.[3]

Historical Materialism and the Dialectic

When Marx looked at history, then, he saw it as the dynamic interplay of opposing material forces, not Platonic Forms, Divine Providence, or anything else abstract and intangible. Of these material forces at play in any society, he thought that the most important were *economic.*

> **dialectic** Dialectic is Hegel's label for the dynamic and conflict-filled process whereby one force (thesis) collides with its opposite (antithesis) to produce a new state of affairs that combines elements of both (synthesis). Given the primary of Spirit in Hegel's thinking, Hegel's outlook can be described as "dialectical idealism."

---

[3]Marxist theory is often called *dialectical materialism.* Marx himself did not use this label, however.

After all, what is more basic to survival than how we obtain food and shelter, how we produce the things that we need and want, and the arrangements we make to facilitate production and exchange with the other members of our community? These survival issues precede all others, Marx believed. If you live in a country where you need money to buy food, you're in serious trouble if you have none. If you live where people barter, you need to be able to make or do things that others find useful. If you cannot find a way to participate in the economy of your community, you will die.

For Marx, then, material production is so fundamental that it must be regarded as the basic fact of human history. As Marx expresses this,

> But life involves before everything else eating and drinking, a habitation, clothing and many other things. The first historical act is thus the production of the means to satisfy these needs, the production of material life itself. . . . Therefore in any interpretation of history one has first of all to observe this fundamental fact in all its significance and all its implications and to accord it its due importance.
>
> —The German Ideology, Part I

For Marx, history is ultimately the chronicle of economic forces at work. Marx calls this the *"materialist conception of history."*

But remember that these economic forces do not interact peacefully in some smooth progression. If they interact by means of a dialectic, as Marx believes they do, they clash with each other. Thus, history progresses only by means of opposition and conflict, and the main conflict that Marx saw in human society was that between different economic classes. As Marx writes in the *Communist Manifesto,* "The history of all hitherto existing society is the history of class struggles." The clash between the "proletariat" (the propertyless workers) and the "bourgeoisie" (the people with money, those who own property and hire others) that Marx witnessed in his own time, he believed, would inevitably lead to a synthesis that Marx called "communism." Once achieved, this synthesis would end the class struggle forever.

To appreciate how revolutionary Marx's thinking is, it is helpful to contrast it with interpretations of human history that we are more accustomed to. Religious thinkers, for example, see history as the inevitable working out of God's plan, perhaps as the account of the struggle between good and evil. Astrologers explain events as the result of planetary forces. Proponents of free will see events as determined by individual choices. Some scientists see us as intelligent but aggressive animals, and interpret our history in terms of principles of natural selection and the survival of the fittest. "Humanists" believe that events reveal a gradual maturation on the part of humanity with enlightenment and respect for freedom and dignity slowly gaining around the world. And so on.

Each theory of history claims to account for what "really" happened. For example, was the expansion of the United States from the Atlantic coast to the Pacific coast the achievement of a divinely ordained "Manifest Destiny"? Was it the result of a simple desire by people to start a new life in a new land? Was it the greedy and aggressive domination by the whites of the Native American nations? Different views of history provide different explanations.

Marx would say that all these interpretations of human history are wrong. In the case of American expansion across the continent, he would argue that it resulted from capitalist exploitation of the land, its resources, and its peoples. Historical materialism argues that what was "really" going on can be explained only in economic terms.

How the Material World Shapes Us: A Simple Example.
Marx's sweeping claim that the material conditions of our lives, and especially economic conditions, are the most important force in shaping human history has profound implications. According to Marx, the material features of our lives determine a dizzying array of things most of us assume have nothing to do with economics. In Marx's eyes, the material conditions of our lives determine not only what kind of work we do and how we do it, but where and how we live and work, the structure and expectations of our private relationships, our personal values, and even the forms of our society's laws, politics, art, and religion. Some simple examples will show you what this means.

First, think of different professors' offices, and specifically about how their furniture is arranged. Some have it placed so that they remain behind their desks while you sit in a smaller chair facing them. Others put their desks against the wall and swing their chairs around when you come in and sit down. Still others have a separate sitting group of chairs. They get up from their desks altogether and both of you sit in similar chairs.

Now try to identify your feelings in each situation. With whom do you feel most comfortable? Whom are you most intimidated by? Whom do you prefer to see when you have a major problem? Odds are you feel least comfortable with someone who has you sit on the other side of a big desk and you feel best with someone who sits with you in a similar chair. A Marxist would explain that these feelings come from your reaction to what the physical arrangement of the office communicates about power.

Desks and chairs are used as symbols of power. When people put desks between themselves and anyone who comes in, they are saying "I'm in charge here. My position is superior to yours." Part of you picks this up, whether you know it or not. Placing the desk so that it is not a barrier or sitting in similar chairs conveys openness, equality, and trust. That physical arrangement expresses a different power relationship, and you respond to that too.

When we are sitting at a conference table, we react to people according to their position at the table. The person at the head of the table gets more attention, whether that person actually deserves it or not. The person in the seat to the right of the head also enjoys a favored status, as does the person at the foot, to a lesser degree. When you present a report or lead a discussion in class, the rest of the class pays better attention and takes you more seriously if you stand up front facing them. The physical setting gives authority to the person up in front. You could say and do exactly the same thing from your chair, but it doesn't work as well.

Physical conditions do influence our thoughts and feelings in very fundamental and powerful ways. How furniture is placed, its design and material, where people sit in a room, what position they take in relation to one another—these are simple examples of physical things that affect us whether we notice them or not.

How the Conditions of Life Determine Consciousness. Marx has something like this, but bigger, in mind. He believes that the way an economy is arranged, that is, the physical facts of production and distribution of material goods, determines everything about a society (and how people react within it), including its politics, laws, art, ethics, religion, and so forth. Most of us believe just the opposite. We assume that we come up with ideas and then we apply them to the world. We think we use our ideas as a kind of blueprint according to which we then fashion a society that has certain institutions and economic arrangements.

Marx claims, however, that the "foundation" of a society is its economic structure. On top of that is a "superstructure" consisting of laws and politics. On top of that are the society's ideas about art, philosophy, religion, science, and the like. The nature of everything in the "superstructure" is determined by the economic "foundation." As Marx puts it, "Life is not determined by consciousness, but consciousness by life." He writes,

> The production of ideas, of conceptions, of consciousness, is at first directly interwoven with the material activity and the material intercourse of men, the language of real life. Conceiving, thinking, the mental intercourse of men, appear at this stage as the direct efflux [outcome] of their material behavior. The same applies to mental production as expressed in the language of politics, laws, morality, religion, metaphysics, etc., of a people. . . .
>
> In direct contrast to [Hegel's] philosophy which descends from heaven to earth, here we ascend from earth to heaven. That is to say, we do not set out from what men say, imagine, conceive, nor from men as narrated, thought of, imagined, conceived, in order to arrive at men in the flesh. We set out from real, active men, and on the basis of their real life-process we demonstrate the development of the ideological reflexes and echoes of this life-process. The phantoms formed in the human brain are also, necessarily, sublimates of their material life-process, which is empirically verifiable and bound to material premises. Morality, religion, metaphysics, all the rest of ideology and their corresponding forms of consciousness, thus no longer retain the semblance of independence. They have no history, no development; but men, developing their material production and their material intercourse, alter, along with this their real existence, their thinking and the products of their thinking. Life is not determined by consciousness, but consciousness by life.
>
> —The German Ideology, Part I

One way that we might illustrate Marx's ideas is to say that the economic structure of a society is analogous to the trunk of a tree; a society's laws and politics to a tree's branches; and philosophy, art, and religion are analogous to a tree's leaves. The branches and leaves of a tree depend on a trunk for their existence, and they organically express the tree's nature. In the same way, the laws, politics, art, and philosophy of a society are the direct outgrowth and expression of the material relationships that define that society's economy. Furthermore, just as the nature of the trunk determines the type of branches and leaves that appear (you won't get maple leaves from an elm trunk and branches), so a society's economy determines, defines, and limits its ideas.

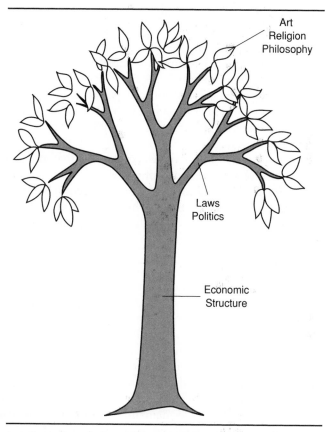

Art
Religion
Philosophy

Laws
Politics

Economic
Structure

According to Marx, the laws, politics, art, religion, and philosophy of a society are determined by that society's economic structure.

Social/Political Values.   According to Marx, the political organization of a society and its major political ideas result from the practical arrangement of things—the distribution of wealth and the consequent power of those who hold it. As he puts it,

> The ruling ideas are nothing more than the ideal expression of the dominant material relationships. . . . For instance, in an age and in a country where royal power, aristocracy and bourgeoisie are contending for mastery and where, therefore, mastery is shared, the doctrine of the separation of powers proves to be the dominant idea and is expressed as an "eternal law."

—The German Ideology, Part I

Marx would contend, for example, that the guiding principles expressed in the Declaration of Independence and the American Constitution grew directly out of actual economic conditions in the late eighteenth century, not the idealistic political theory of the Founding Fathers. These men did hold these ideals to be true, and they did, in fact, write the documents that embodied them.

But, Marx would say, they came up with those particular ideals because at the time thirteen competing economic units, the original colonies, were moving toward free market, competitive capitalism. Thus, they united into a "confederation of states" rather than subsuming their identities completely in a single entity. "States' rights" and the "separation of powers" became important political principles, expressing in the political arena the diffusion of power needed to make a market economy work. In addition, it is not coincidental that the liberties guaranteed under the Bill of Rights can be seen as reflecting the conditions necessary for the growth of a developing capitalistic economy.

Whatever examples we take, then, the Marxist thinks that all social institutions owe their form, and their very existence, to the prevailing material conditions at the time. Marx even thinks that the way we think about everything every day is entirely determined by the material conditions under which we live. If he is right, we should see a direct connection between our economic system, capitalism, and the ideas and values we hold. Can we discover such a link?

Capitalism and Capitalist Values

Let's first make sure we have a clear understanding of capitalism. It is an economy in which the means of production—factories, farms, shops, and so on—are owned by private individuals, not the government. These individuals are entrepreneurs, or capitalists. They take their own money ("capital") and invest it in a business, in hopes of getting a return ("profit") on the investment. The goods produced are distributed through a "free market." Producers offer what they make to potential customers. Prices are neither set in advance nor decreed by some central agency. They are what buyers and sellers agree on and result from what are called laws of "supply and demand." When consumer demand for a product outstrips the available supply, people are willing to pay more for it and prices go up. When producers supply more of a product than people will buy, prices fall. Under capitalism, competition among producers is essential to make sure that prices are fair. Producers are thus encouraged to become more efficient and deliver honest value to consumers, or they will lose the consumers to other producers. Capitalism also assumes that buyers and sellers, employers and employees will simply advance their own individual interests. The different interests among opposing parties and the existence of a free competitive market for goods and labor is supposed to keep the game honest.

In essence, then, capitalism is an economic system based on private ownership, capital, self-interest, and a free, competitive market. We shall see shortly that Marx finds capitalism inhumane, an economic system that makes genuine freedom and happiness impossible. For now, however, let's take capitalism at face value and see what effect such an arrangement of "material conditions" has on the values we live by every day.

Competition. For openers, Marx would say that living under capitalism makes us think that *competition* is a good thing. Instead of cooperating with other people, we feel it is more valuable to pit ourselves against them. Everyone is a competitor and an adversary. Learning how to advance our own interests against the interests of others becomes an important survival skill.

As a result we promote competition throughout our society. We especially push athletic competition and team sports. We say that such contention, with its emphasis on winning, is good for us: It keeps us in shape, rewards us for hard work, and builds character. The Marxist would say, however, that we are enamored of athletic competition simply because it mirrors the economic competition that is at the heart of contemporary capitalism.

Our society could have evolved differently, of course. We could have enshrined *cooperation,* which produces equally good results if not better ones, instead of competition. In a cooperative society, competition, winning, being a "star," excelling as an individual, all these would be seen as "bad taste," as being insensitive to others. How well we help people who do something less well than we do would be more important than how badly we beat them at it. Competition is not a law of nature, and other societies think quite differently about it. Yet, Marx claims, it is no accident that those in capitalist societies think and behave as they do. Indeed, we think this way *because* we live in a capitalistic economy.

Inequality. A second effect of capitalism on our values is that we accept and even approve of *inequality,* particularly financial inequality. Most of us think it is perfectly all right that some people are rich, while others are poor. We see nothing wrong with the fact that the higher someone goes in an organization, the more perquisites and advantages that person receives simply by virtue of that person's position. We even develop a logical rationale for inequality by believing that, ultimately, each of us is the author of our own happiness or unhappiness. We say that everybody has the same opportunities, and that we deserve the fate we end up with. A Marxist would say that this way of thinking is inevitable in our culture because it mirrors the profit motive that is basic to capitalism, because it promotes the wealthy class that capitalism needs to provide money for investment, and because, by rationalizing inequality, it advances the interests of those who dominate the economy.

The fact that so many people accept the idea that everyone has the same chance for success is especially intriguing. In reality, we do not all have the same opportunities. Some people are born with all kinds of natural abilities. Some are born into rich families, or at least very supportive ones. Others are born to poverty, illness, and demoralization. Obviously, the odds that someone born into a lower socioeconomic class will become successful are dramatically lower than those for someone born into the middle or upper class. With the odds being so different for people born into such different circumstances—circumstances none of us has any control over—you would expect most people to think that something is wrong with the system. Yet most of us accept the idea that everyone has the same chance and that there is nothing wrong with the inequality.

Think how people react when they hear of someone beating the odds. When they hear some rags-to-riches story, they usually say something like, "See, the system works. Everyone has a chance." Or maybe just, "Well, that's life." What most of us do *not* say is that something is wrong with a system in which so few people ever really move up. Yet one has as good a chance to move from poverty to extreme wealth as one has to break the bank playing roulette. The only way for a casino to survive is for most people to lose, and our society distributes wealth in the same fashion. A Marxist would hardly admire such an economic structure. But the fact that most of us accept the unequal way our economy distributes wealth shows how fully we have accepted the idea of institutionalized inequality.

"Bettering" Ourselves. A Marxist can even point to phrases in our language that reveal the impact of capitalism. Consider what we mean when we say we want to "better" ourselves, for example. What does that phrase mean to you? The average person will say that to "better yourself" means "to make more money" or "to move into a higher social and economic class." But this does not make sense. Making more money is one thing, but becoming a better person is another. Yet in a culture that judges everything by economic measures, we have come to equate one with the other.

If a high-paid executive decided to become a minister and work with the homeless, would most people say that he had "bettered" himself? Most of us would probably praise his selflessness, but we would not say he had "bettered" himself. Yet he would face new challenges, he would develop his existing skills, he would do much good, and he would progress spiritually. By every measure but one—financial—he would grow and develop as a human being. Yet no one would describe him as "bettering" himself.

Materialistic Values. It should come as no surprise by now that Marx sees capitalism as the cause of the *materialistic values* of Western industrial society. Numbers, money, and profit are what capitalism is all about. Tangible, material wealth is all that counts. When confronted with something intangible, however, like the harm done by pollution, hard-line capitalists find a way of putting a price tag even on that via something called "cost-benefit analysis." As far as they are concerned, if it cannot be measured financially, it does not exist. For anything to be worth thinking about, it has to be translated into material terms.

In a culture that exalts material things this way, it is no wonder that so many of us are driven to buy things in order to feel good. We define "the good life" in terms of cars, high-tech gadgets, expensive clothes, jewelry, big houses, boats, a high salary, financial security, and golden parachutes. We even elevate the material aspects of our selves, our bodies, above our minds and our souls. How good looking are we? Are we in good shape? And how long can we look that way?

The Structure of Our Days. Marx would argue that even the *shape of our days* reflects the character of industrial capitalism. Most of us go to factories or offices away from our homes because that is the most efficient way to produce. We assume that rush-hour traffic is the way it has to be. And our work life is separated from our home life.

In very important ways, this situation splits our lives into separate fragments. How much do you know about the jobs your parents and relatives hold? How often do you go to where they work? Would the people working there welcome you and take the opportunity to teach you something, or would your presence interfere with their getting their work done? Most likely, you know very little about what people in your family do or where they work, and that is probably all right with you. You may even think that work is more important than family life.

Education. A Marxist would even argue that the way education is structured is a product of the kind of economy we have. What are some of the qualities we need in employees in order to make contemporary capitalism work efficiently? We value the ability to adapt to a production schedule, for example, and the willingness to meet deadlines. We value the ability to concentrate on tasks while surrounded by other people without being distracted. We value the willingness to do what we are told, and the wish to compete against the performance both of fellow workers and of other companies.

Do schools teach these qualities? Yes, all the time. These qualities are encouraged just by the way education is conducted, particularly in elementary and high schools. We must come to school on time and have an ironclad excuse for being absent. Homework has to be done on time. We sit and take tests in a classroom full of people whom we are told to ignore. We follow directions and learn through a largely passive process. And we are constantly measured against each other. A Marxist would argue that education is conducted this way because our capitalist system requires workers who are trained this way. Thus, economic imperatives determine even educational goals.

Do We Choose Our Values? This is what Marx means, then, when he claims that the "material conditions" of our life—that is, the nature of the economy we live in—determine who we are and what we think. Marx maintains that the core values most of us have result from our living under capitalism. And he can certainly make an intelligent case for his claim that whatever the worth of our ideas, we have not chosen them independently—they have simply seeped into our hearts. If Marx is right, our most cherished beliefs are not freely chosen. They are, instead, determined by forces we never even think about.

As disturbing as Marx's insight might seem at first, ultimately it holds some hope. It is only by realizing the influence of these forces on our minds that we can free ourselves from them. Once we become free, we really can choose what we think and do.

Happiness and Unhappiness

We have looked at Marx's claim that the economy we live in determines almost everything about our lives, including how we understand what our aim in life should be. His second claim is just as far-reaching. Capitalism, Marx believes, has so flawed a vision of human happiness that people living under its sway cannot possibly achieve genuine happiness.

Homo Faber: "Man the Maker"

Marx's dim appraisal of capitalism stems from his conception of human nature. For Karl Marx, humans are essentially producers. This is evident from his word choice when he talks about us as *Homo faber* ("man the maker") rather than *Homo sapiens* ("thinking man").

Marx believes that in the deepest part of our beings we humans are makers, or producers. Our essence is to create, to build, to fashion, to make things. Productive work is the fullest and highest expression of who we are. Indeed, in Marx's mind, it *makes* us who we are. He writes,

> Production must not be considered simply as being the reproduction of the physical existence of the individuals. Rather it is a definite form of activity of these individuals, a definite form of expressing their life, a definite *mode of life* on their part. As individuals express their life, so they are. What they are, therefore, coincides with their production, both with what they produce and with how they produce. The nature of individuals thus depends on the material conditions determining their production.
>
> —The German Ideology, Part I

Given what we have seen of Marx's materialism and the power he grants to the material conditions of our lives, it is no surprise that Marx claims that we *become* what we *do*. Who we are down deep depends heavily on what kind of work we do. If our jobs consist of interesting, challenging activities, we become interesting, well-developed people. But if we spend our days doing boring, repetitive, mindless work, then we become dull, boring individuals.

"Alienated Labor"

If our productive life is positive, then, we are happy and satisfied with life. If our work life does not allow us to express our true selves, to develop our talents, and to fulfill our productive nature, these most basic needs go unmet, and we are unhappy. Marx's criticism of capitalism hinges on this very point. The kind of work capitalism has us do, according to Marx, is fundamentally unsatisfying. Rather than making us fulfilled, complete, and at one with ourselves, it leaves us deeply unsettled and "alienated" from our true selves. Marx calls this **alienated labor**.

Marx wrote in the middle of the nineteenth century during the development of industrial capitalism, and his main image of labor is factory work, but his thinking also covers white-collar work. What he is talking about is what most of us would agree is the normal way that work is designed under capitalism—large operations, run by professional managers, using the division of labor, with an emphasis on machinery and technology. This may be an efficient way to produce goods, but Marx thinks that it goes against the grain of the human spirit. It may be good for "man the consumer," but it is terrible for "man the producer." Consequently, we cannot end up any way but unhappy.

Marx sees four distinct ways in which work under industrial capitalism is unsatisfying. More specifically, he thinks there are four different ways in which we become alienated from things that are rightfully ours and that we need to be satisfied.

---

alienated labor According to Marx, alienated labor is the type of labor that characterizes capitalism. It has four dimensions: the worker is alienated from the product produced, from the activity of production, from his or her productive nature, and from other people.

Alienation From the Product. Under capitalism, Marx says, we lose the products of our labor. If we work in a factory, we make things. But at the end of our shift we own nothing that we produced. Who owns it? The person or the company that hired us. "The capitalist," as Marx always puts it, keeps what we make and sells it for a profit. Whether we work in an office, a store, a restaurant, a hospital, or a factory, it's all the same. We perform certain tasks or services, but the owner of the company retains control over what we do and sells it for a profit. We may be paid for our time and effort, but unless we're involved in "profit sharing," we do not get "a piece of the action."

"But that's the way it is," you might say. "Everybody knows those are the rules." Those may be "the rules," but Marx thinks they are the wrong rules. He believes that we are entitled to own and control what we produce. And he is particularly unhappy that the whole process increases the power of "the capitalist" over the workers. The owner earns much more money than the workers and keeps the profits from the sale of the product as well.

Worse yet, because money is power under capitalism, what workers produce actually increases the capitalist's power over them. Not only do the workers lose control over the products of their labor, Marx also sees the fruits of these products, money, ultimately being turned against the very people who produced them. Under such circumstances, how can the workers be happy?

Alienation of the Process. Alienation also results from what happens on the job. Most employees are told what work to do and how to do it. Workers usually have little say in how their skills are used in their plants and offices or in how their jobs are designed. Managers make the big decisions, set the company's goals, plan the process, and decide who does what. Here again, workers lack power and control.

This may be an efficient way of doing things, but Marx finds it unsatisfying. Who wants to spend their work lives doing nothing but what other people tell them to do? Under those circumstances, work is nothing like what Marx thinks it should be. The worker is forced to be passive, unthinking, and compliant when she or he would be happier being active, engaged, and creative. The work process thus cuts against the grain of what human beings want and do.

Capitalism also makes work unsatisfying because it relies so heavily on the "division of labor." Instead of hiring a staff of high-priced but skilled chairmakers for a furniture factory, for example, factory owners break down the process of building a chair into a series of simple steps. Each small step is then taught to a low-paid, unskilled worker. (This is the assembly-line principle that Henry Ford pioneered in the automobile industry.) The division of labor works out very well for the capitalist. Instead of paying $25 an hour for master chairmakers, he can pay $5 an hour. Then he can sell more chairs because he can sell them more cheaply than the competition.

For the workers, however, it's another story. What once was a highly skilled, well-paid, challenging, and satisfying job immediately changes. Marx gives us a grim account of what happens:

> As the division of labor increases, labor is simplified. The special skill of the worker becomes worthless. He becomes transformed into a simple, monotonous productive force that does not have to use intense bodily or intellectual faculties. His labor becomes a labor that anyone can perform. Hence, competitors crowd upon him

on all sides, and . . . the more simple and easily learned the labor is, the lower the cost of production needed to master it, the lower do wages sink, for, like the price of every other commodity, they are determined by the cost of production.

—Wage Labour and Capital

Work becomes dramatically less satisfying under these circumstances. Marx writes that work ultimately loses all its intrinsic appeal and the worker simply becomes "an appendage of the machine."

Alienation From Our Nature. A third kind of alienation occurs as a consequence of the first two. Because we give up what we produce to someone else and because the activity of work is itself unsatisfying, we become alienated from our basic nature as producers, from what Marx calls our "species being."

Marx thinks that work should be an end in itself for humans. We should find it intrinsically satisfying and nourishing, the primary vehicle by which we express and develop ourselves. But the way things go in capitalism, work becomes only a means to an end, not an end in itself. Because we must earn money in order to live, our labor becomes a commodity that we are forced to sell. Even if we are paid well, our labor is still a commodity that we are selling. As a result of all of this, we become separated from our true nature.

To Marx's way of thinking, being forced to sell our labor as a commodity is literally unnatural and shameful, something like being forced into prostitution. Sex is a private and special part of ourselves, and we feel that it should be completely under our own control. To be forced into sexual acts, even for money, surely offends all of us. It violates the person coerced and denies his or her basic rights. Marx sees our work life as being just as personal and precious—the core of who we are. If what we do as workers determines who we become as people, then what we do and under what circumstances is particularly important. To be forced to sell our labor and perform "alienating" labor damages and debases us, just as rape damages and debases its victims. Both flatly deny our nature and destroy our dignity.

Alienation From Other People: Competition. Finally, alienation also occurs under capitalism because capitalism separates people from one another. A capitalist economic system enthusiastically encourages competition. People looking for work compete with each other to get a job. Once hired, workers compete with each other for raises and promotions. Workers in rival companies compete with each other for customers. Ultimately, even the owners compete against each other in their unending quest for more money.

Such thoroughgoing competition, Marx thinks, guarantees unhappiness. Marx believes that human beings are essentially social creatures who are meant to live in harmony with our neighbors. He therefore thinks that cooperation, not competition, is the more natural and satisfying condition. Yet rather than fostering common interests and solidarity among people, capitalism breeds self-interest, distrust, and dishonesty.

Capitalism clearly fosters self-interest. Our "job," as it were, is to look after ourselves, not anybody else. The spirit of capitalism is "everyone for himself." Under these conditions, we can trust others to only a limited degree. If we are all self-interested competitors (adversaries, really), it makes more sense to distrust the people we do business with than to trust them. Thus, we are inclined to be a shade untruthful in our dealings with one another. Who believes the car salesperson who says, "This price is the best I can do. At that price I'm losing money on the deal. I'll get in trouble with my boss, but I'll sell it to you anyway because you remind me of myself when I was your age"? Aren't you likely to lie yourself and say, "Look, if I go any higher, I'll have to drop out of school"?

Marx's point is that the nature of capitalism forces us to act this way. These are the rules of the game. But how satisfying is a world in which most of the people around us are adversaries? Here, too, Marx sees capitalism as going against the grain of our true nature.

Capitalist Alienation Versus Marxist Happiness

Marx's case is worth thinking about. He sees the values of capitalism as diametrically opposed to human nature. Under capitalism, workers typically have no control over what they produce or how they produce it. Alienated from their true nature, they are set in competition with the people around them. Under such circumstances, Marx argues, capitalism cannot make people happy.

But, you say, capitalist economies produce an abundance of luxury goods. If you make a lot of money doing work that Marx labels "alienating," doesn't that make you happy in spite of everything?

Not in Marx's opinion. No matter how much money you make, you still become what you do. You may make a lot of money at some dull, boring job, but the job is making you a dull, boring person. You may have lots of nice things, but without developing some inner resources, you cannot enjoy them. Even rich capitalists are adversely affected. Their own workers are adversaries and everyone else is a competitor. Distrust and aggression must be their operating style. Money simply cannot buy mutual trust and peace of mind.

At this point you may be bursting with objections. What if, for example, your idea of happiness is different from Marx's idea? What about "different strokes for different folks"? Aren't lots of people perfectly happy with a dull job as long as they're paid well enough?

To counteract the common argument, Marx would simply say that it is based on an erroneous idea of human nature. If it is our nature to be producers who flourish in an economic setting marked by cooperation with other people, any other arrangement will rub us the wrong way. We cannot change this any more than we can change the conditions our bodies require to be healthy. Capitalism may make us feel good in lots of ways, but in the last analysis it leaves us frustrated, or "alienated." Marx contends that under capitalism we can never feel as content or as happy as if we lived in agreement with our nature.

Capitalism: The "Bottom Line"

Marx's theory presents us with a serious criticism of capitalism. His theory of historical materialism leads him to claim that the economic forces around us are powerful enough to shape our attitudes about what is valuable in life. This means that the largely individualistic, secular, and materialistic outlook that pervades our society has not been freely chosen by anyone. It has, instead, been produced by our economic system. It is then imposed on us as we are born into and socialized to fit into the economy.

Marx also argues that living according to the requirements of capitalism means that we can never be happy. Primarily because of the shape of our work life, we have become alienated from our true nature and have been set in opposition and conflict with the people around us. According to Marx, happiness does not come from what we have—money, clothes, gadgets, cars, or houses. Rather, it comes from what we do in our lives, who we become, and whether or not we have positive, cooperative relationships with other people.

Accordingly, Karl Marx presents you with a real challenge. Which is the right path to happiness? Can we really be happy when we accept the values of contemporary capitalism?

Buddhism—Another Alternative

Karl Marx's outlook on life and happiness is very different from the outlook most of us live by every day. Most people in Western capitalistic countries disagree with Marx's contention that the economic system of a society shapes everything about that society from its laws, to its politics and religion, to the personal values of its citizens. They also doubt that what we need to be happy is a satisfying work life and cooperative relationships with those around us. Most people in our society think that material wealth gained through competition is perfectly satisfying and sufficient.

The discrepancy between Marx's ideas and those of most Westerners, however, is insignificant when we compare our approach to life to that shared by many people of the East. The gap between Eastern religious and Western capitalistic outlooks is huge.

As in the West, there are many different systems of thought in the East— Hinduism, Buddhism, and Taoism, to name some prominent ones. We will look only at Buddhism in this chapter, but this one example should give you a sense of just how different an Eastern perspective is. Your challenge is to consider whether Buddhism offers a better way of thinking about life and a surer path to happiness than the ideas you had before you started reading this chapter.

Some Differences Between Eastern and Western Thought

We have barely looked at the contributions of Eastern thinkers so far in this text because there is not really any such thing as "Eastern philosophy." Religion and philosophy separated in the West into two different ways of thinking, but they thoroughly intermix in the East. This makes it impossible to talk about any distinctly philosophical positions held by Eastern thinkers. Indeed, the great thinkers of the East, like Buddha and Confucius, are primarily religious teachers. They are not philosophers as Aristotle and Kant were. Yet this mixture of the philosophical and religious gives Eastern thinking a unity and richness lacking in Western philosophy. In particular, it offers us a way of incorporating spirituality into our philosophical inquiries.

As you might expect, then, Eastern religions are very different from Western religions. The Judeo-Christian tradition is built around the idea of a personal God who created the world and rules over it. Our one and only life on earth is a test to see whether or not we will be saved or damned after we die. Which way we go depends on some combination of what we believe and how we behave. It usually also depends on professing belief and participating in some kind of religious ritual. But God determines our fate.

Eastern religions, by contrast, have a more amorphous concept of God. They recognize a great force in the universe, but that force transcends the limits of a personal God with a specific personality. Particular religious beliefs are far less important than individual spiritual development. We live through many lives in a quest for an advanced spiritual state of enlightenment, and once we achieve it, we reach a new level of being that transcends our former state and we no longer have to return for additional lives. How far along we are in our spiritual journey, however, and how many more lives it will take us to become enlightened, are completely our own work. No deity saves us or punishes us. We do that ourselves.

Beliefs such as these are not completely alien in the West. They are frequently advocated by various "New Age" writers and thinkers, and an increasing number of Westerners are at least sympathetically considering the value of this Eastern outlook.

The Teaching of Buddha: Spiritual Enlightenment as the Aim of Life

One of the world's most important ancient religions, *Buddhism,* began in India in the sixth century B.C. Unlike many religions, we can identify the actual person who founded it, Siddhartha Gautama, the man known as "the Buddha." "The Buddha" is thus not a personal name but a title of honor meaning simply "the Awakened One" or "the Enlightened One." Gautama reached Enlightenment when he came to understand the true nature of reality and the way to achieve release from the ongoing cycle of life after life. Gautama is not unique in becoming a Buddha. Tradition maintains that he is the fourth Buddha during the current period of human history. He is, however, considered "Supreme Buddha."

The most obvious difference between Buddhism and the outlook held in Western, capitalistic countries lies in its vision of what life is all about. Westerners are preoccupied with material success. The Buddha thought that spiritual enlightenment should be our goal. "Success" to the Buddhist is measured in terms of the progress we make toward getting off the "Wheel of Life." That is, our aim should be to advance spiritually to the point where we no longer have to return to this plane of existence to live another life.

Rebirth

One of the most fundamental truths of Buddhism, then, is that we live many lives. To the Buddhist, "rebirth" or "reincarnation" is an accepted fact. The great task of spiritual development is simply too difficult and too complicated to accomplish in one lifetime.

While reincarnation is characteristically an Eastern idea, its advocates claim that important Western figures—among them Plato, the Christian thinker Origen, Kant, Benjamin Franklin, Ralph Waldo Emerson, William James, and Walt Whitman—have held such a belief or at least have seriously considered it. Some point to passages in the New Testament which imply that reincarnation was generally accepted

The Buddha

Siddhartha Gautama (563–483 B.C.) was born in Nepal to a family of great wealth. As a boy, he led the protected and sheltered life of someone from a privileged family. He won his wife in a contest of arms at age 16 and had a son with her. He became deeply troubled by disease and death, and at age 29, he renounced his former life and began a search for the cause and solution of human suffering. For six years he wandered, studied with various sages in India, meditated, and lived ascetically, yet still remained unsatisfied. Shortly after giving up asceticism, however, he achieved enlightenment and became "the Buddha" (the enlightened one). He established a religious order and spent the rest of his life guiding his followers, preaching, and meditating.

in the ancient West.[4] Indeed, it was not until the Council of Constantinople in A.D. 551 that the doctrine of reincarnation was labeled heretical and thrown out by the Christian church.

Everyone admits there is no way to prove the truth of reincarnation, but its proponents claim that all of us have experiences that imply its truth. For example, you have probably visited some place for the first time and felt certain that you had been there before. (This feeling is commonly called *déjà vu*.) Or perhaps you meet someone for the first time with whom you are instantly comfortable. The two of you feel as though you have known each other all of your lives. Or perhaps you have an uncanny gift or special ability. Those who believe in reincarnation say that these recognitions of places and people are in fact recollections of former lives, and any special talents you have were developed in earlier lives and carried forward with you into this one.

Karma

If rebirth is the first fact of life in Buddhism, the second is the principle that determines what happens from life to life, **karma**. *Karma* is the Sanskrit word for "action" or "deed," and as a concept it equates with the most fundamental law of the universe. As is often the case with Eastern ideas, we have no Western word for this concept.

> **karma** Karma is a fundamental Buddhist law of the universe. The law of karma holds that all deeds produce positive or negative effects for the one who does them, and these effects extend from one life to the next. Karma is the Eastern equivalent to the Western law of cause and effect, or principle of action and reaction, or of balance. It is also described as a law of sowing and reaping.

---

[4]Matthew xvi: 13–16; Mark vi: 14–16.

The law of karma holds that all deeds produce positive or negative effects for the one who does them, and these effects extend from one life to the next. Thus, by our actions we determine what lies ahead for us in our next life—we determine our own destiny. As the Buddha explains it,

> If a man speaks or acts with an evil thought, pain follows him, as the wheel follows the foot of him who draws the carriage. But if a man speaks or acts with a pure thought, happiness follows him, like a shadow that never leaves him.

—Dhammapada

Karma is the Eastern equivalent to the Western law of cause and effect, or principle of action and reaction, or of balance. It is also described as a law of sowing and reaping. It's as though our actions are seeds that inevitably produce good or bad fruit at some point in our lives. We might even see it as a spiritual version of what we mean when we say "what goes around comes around." If we do something negative, if we hurt someone, we set in motion a process that will eventually bring negativity back on us. Thus, karma supposedly determines both the good and bad circumstances in any of our lives. If we were arrogant and insensitive in a former life, we will experience the same hostility at others' hands now. But if we were unusually helpful to others in need, we will now receive help as we need it.

What Karma Is and Is Not. We need to set a few things straight here so that the nature of karma is more or less clear.

First, karma is not a simple force that is easily interpreted. We cannot assume that if people are poor, ill, or falling on hard times in this life, such misfortune is a direct result of their wickedness in a former life. It may be the case, but it may not be. Their karma may call for them to be helped by others in this life. In such a case, their problems are as much related to the karma of other people, perhaps those people who need to learn compassion and generosity, as to their own.

Misfortunes may even be the result of *good* karma. Handling difficult experiences is an important way for us to develop spiritually. Hard times challenge and push us far more than good times do. "Resistance training" is as necessary for spiritual development as it is for training the body. Accordingly, people with difficult lives may not be experiencing the consequences of an evil former life but taking advantage of opportunities for spiritual growth instead.

Second, karma is not a system of rewards and punishments administered by some divine judge. What happens to us is the natural consequence of what we do. As one writer puts it, "In Buddhism, a man is punished by his sins, not for them." This is like Newton's third law of motion, "For every action there is an equal and opposite reaction." These are simply laws of nature. Newton describes the behavior of physical energy. Karma describes the behavior of moral, or supernatural, energy.

Indeed, as a law of the universe, karma is just as unavoidable as the laws of physics. As one of the Buddhist scriptures explains, "Not in the sky, not in the midst of the sea, nor anywhere else on earth is there a spot where a man can be freed from (the consequences of) an evil deed."[5] It doesn't matter if we regret what we did or if we apologize for it. When we do something negative, there is no way to avoid the consequences in this or in some future life. It is precisely as if we pushed a piano off the top of a building. Nothing can stop it from hitting the ground.

Deterministic Yet Optimistic. Certainly one of the most important philosophical implications of karma is that it predetermines much of our lives. The challenges and circumstances we face in this life result directly from what we did in our past incarnations—they are the inevitable consequence of our actions. This is just the way the universe works. If you plant an apple seed, a tree will grow. If you aren't careful about what you plant, there is a good chance you'll get weeds.

Paradoxically, however, this determinism is built on the idea of free choice. There is nothing that we are fated or forced to do. We choose our actions, but we must live with the consequences of our decisions. If we approach life with the proper attitude, however, and make better choices in the future, we work off bad karma and advance toward enlightenment. So even the determinism of karma is essentially optimistic.

There is also no guarantee that we will take advantage of the opportunities for spiritual growth when we are presented with them in this life. Our karma from past lives may require us to be more compassionate and tolerant. But we still have to choose to be that way when we are confronted with certain situations. We can respond properly and advance spiritually. Or we can fall back on old habits and waste a chance to move along. In this respect, we are completely free.

Nobody Else to Blame. One of the least forgiving aspects of Buddhism is that, according to the principle of karma, each of us must take all the credit or all the blame for our happiness. No one else is in any way responsible. As one of the Buddhist scriptures explains, "By oneself evil is done; by oneself one suffers. By oneself evil is left undone; by oneself one is purified."[6] If there is something about our lives we do not like, we should not handle this by blaming God, the Fates, our parents, or anybody else. The law of karma says that we are the author of all our unhappiness. We may not be able to control the actions of people who hurt us, but we can choose to hold onto the hurt and, in effect, let our enemies continue to torture us. Or we can try to accept our troubles and achieve some kind of equanimity and peace of soul.

This unremitting individual responsibility is a very tough idea to accept.[7] If you haven't thought about it before, the idea of being responsible for everything about your life can feel like a terrible burden. The good parts of life are no problem. We enjoy taking credit for things that go right for us. (We worked hard. We deserved it.) But we are always tempted to blame someone or something else for what goes wrong. (The teacher is unfair. The boss plays favorites. The circumstances are

---

[5] *The Dhammapada*, translated by P. Lal (New York: Farrar, Straus & Giroux, 1967), v. 127.

[6] *Dhammapada*, v. 165.

[7] Buddhism's emphasis on individual responsibility is similar to Existentialism's. This is simply to note the parallel, not to suggest any causal relationship.

beyond our control. We had bad luck.) Feeling just as responsible for our reaction to bad outcomes as to good ones is not at all easy to accept.

But keep in mind that the workings of karma are not simple to sort out. Troubles are not punishment. Rather, they are opportunities for spiritual development, part of our "spiritual workout." Furthermore, if we are responsible for our reaction to everything that we face, we ultimately have complete control over our destinies. One major lesson we learn from adversity is that we are much stronger and more powerful than we thought we were. Since our troubles are ours alone, we are the only ones to fix them—and we do have the power to do that.

The Teaching of Buddha: How to Get Off the Wheel of Life

As powerful as karma is, it does not trap us eternally. In fact, the aim of life is to achieve a level of spiritual development that lets us end the cycle of rebirth. The glory of the Buddha's teaching, then, is that it tells us how to do this. The key is contained in what Buddhists call the "Four Noble Truths" and the "Noble Eightfold Path."

The Four Noble Truths are the Buddha's account of the challenge we face in life. Each truth tackles the same problem—*dukkha,* or suffering. (Actually, the Sanskrit word *dukkha* means anything from "pain," "disease," and "evil" to "imperfection" and "frustration.") The Buddha considers this state the basic state of life. He said, "One thing I teach, *dukkha* and the ending of *dukkha."* The Noble Eightfold Path tells how we can end it.

The Four Noble Truths

The Buddha's First Noble Truth makes clear that every part of life involves suffering. He explains,

> Birth is suffering, decay is suffering, disease is suffering, death is suffering, association with the unpleasing is suffering, separation from the pleasing is suffering, not to get what one wants is suffering.

This is the suffering that confronts us over and over again in life, and this is the suffering we have to master.

The Second Noble Truth identifies the cause of suffering: desire. Desire is also the force that keeps us coming back for more lives. Like the word for "suffering," the Sanskrit word *trishna,* which is translated "desire," has many meanings. It includes our appetite for sensual gratification, for money, and for power; craving for excitement; our clinging to or grasping after the things we enjoy, even life itself. But the Buddha sees all this as a trap. Our desires inevitably lead to suffering because our satisfaction grows cold or we lose the object of our desire. We grow bored with what we have and demand something new. We want more money. The objects of our desire are not what we thought they were. Those we love—and we ourselves—grow old and die.

Strictly speaking, however, the problem is not desire but wanting the wrong things. The Buddha believes that most of us are ignorant of what really makes us happy. We assume that once we get things like money, or a great job, or the perfect lover, everything will be set and we can coast happily for the rest of our days. But it doesn't work that way. Life constantly changes, and nothing makes us immune to "suffering." What we should want are things more permanent and more useful to our spiritual growth—wisdom, altruism, and reducing our desires. As long as we desire the ordinary satisfactions of life, however, we will continue being reborn. That, after all, is the only way our desires for the transient and material things of human life can be fulfilled.

The Third Truth, then, teaches that stopping desire is the only way to stop suffering. When we accomplish this, we reach a state of consciousness called *Nirvana*.[8] By extinguishing greed, hatred, and ignorance in ourselves, we achieve perfection. We grow beyond a limited sense of our own selves and feel a sense of union with the universe.

How do we do this? That is what the Fourth Noble Truth tells us. We follow the path that the Buddha himself followed and pointed out to the rest of us. This is the Noble Eightfold Path—right views, right intentions, right speech, right action, right livelihood, right effort, right concentration, and right meditation. By living this way, we lose our false desires, develop compassion and selfless love for others, and achieve a high level of spirituality. This combination lets us break out of the cycle of birth and rebirth.

The Noble Eightfold Path

The Eightfold Path is also called the "Middle Way" of Buddhism. It is a middle path between the two extremes of sensual indulgence and rigid asceticism.

Right views refer to understanding the Buddha's teaching—the Noble Truths, karma, rebirth, and the like.

Right intentions are the proper motives of our actions—helping others. If extinguishing desire is critical, the intentions we put in its place are of paramount importance.

Right speech obviously means truthfulness. But it also includes speaking to other people with kindness, respect, and courtesy, avoiding frivolous speech and hurting other people through gossip.

Right action is conduct that conforms to five basic moral precepts: "refrain from injury to living things; refrain from taking what is not given; refrain from sexual immorality; refrain from falsehood; refrain from liquors which cloud the mind." The Buddha, like the Christ, sees morality as primarily a matter of the heart, and these precepts apply to our minds as well as to our bodies. They refer to our inner desires, motives, and thoughts as much as to the actions we perform.

The right-thinking Buddhist understands the precepts governing right action in an expansive, all-inclusive way. For example, not hurting living things extends to our attitudes toward animals. What does this say about hunting or eating meat? Taking only what is given means that we should be less hungry to acquire material things. Wealth is not bad in itself, but we should not lust after it in our hearts. The Buddha said, "It is not life and wealth and power that enslave a man, but the cleaving to them. He who possesses wealth and uses it rightly will be a blessing unto his fellow beings." Sexual immorality is best understood as referring to any kind of sexual activity that could hurt others, sensual indulgence or negligence about our health.

---

[8]Be sure you realize that Nirvana is not a place, as the Christian heaven is. It is a state of mind. As a state that transcends all of our ordinary human, and therefore, limited, experience, it cannot be adequately described.

Refraining from falsehood refers as much to public rhetoric, like that found in advertising and political campaigns, as it does to exchanges between two individuals. We must strive to be completely honest, never exaggerating or shading the truth even a little. Avoiding liquors that cloud the mind obviously refers to alcohol or any other drug that affects how we think. But it also includes emotional states that "intoxicate" us: anger, greed, jealousy, envy, revenge, excitement, love of power. Such feelings may be an inevitable part of being human, but the Buddha cautions against indulging in them, and especially against making decisions under their influence.

The next step on the Eightfold Path is *right livelihood*. This means that we should conduct ourselves in whatever profession we choose according to the Noble Truths and the five precepts.

Right effort refers to the steps we must take to purify and strengthen our minds. We do this by developing our positive qualities, working on our current weaknesses, and avoiding new ones. This means, for example, mastering feelings of jealousy, anger, fear, and anything else that would distract and weaken us internally.

Right concentration also concerns the mind. Here the Buddha means we should develop the skills of mental concentration fostered by meditation. This ability to control our minds in a highly disciplined fashion is absolutely necessary if we are to reach the final stage.

Right meditation is the highest state of mental control and development. It is an inner stillness and focus that transcends ordinary consciousness. It includes the development of morally good attitudes, but the perfection of this state cannot be described by words.

Ideally, following the Eightfold Path produces a combination of wisdom, compassion, and an advanced state of consciousness. Our intuitive abilities (in Sanskrit, *Buddhi*) develop and increase our tolerance and serenity. At that point, Nirvana is possible and we ourselves become "an Enlightened One"—a Buddha.

The Essence of Buddhism

Although its pursuit is difficult, the essence of Buddhism is quite simple. It was set out in its entirety in the very first sermon that the Buddha gave to a handful of monks. The sermon speaks eloquently for itself.

> Avoid these two extremes, monks. Which two? On the one hand, low, vulgar, ignoble, and useless indulgence in passion and luxury; on the other, painful, ignoble, and useless practice of self-torture and mortification. Take the Middle Path. . . .
>
> What, you will ask me, is the Middle Path? It is the Eightfold Way. Right views, right intentions, right speech, right action, right livelihood, right effort, right concentration and right meditation. This is the Middle Path, which leads to insight, peace, wisdom, enlightenment, and Nirvana.
>
> For there is suffering, and this is the noble truth of suffering—birth is painful, old age is painful, sickness is painful, death is painful; lamentation, dejection, and despair are painful. Contact with the unpleasant is painful, not getting what you want is painful.

Suffering has an origin, and this is the noble truth of the origin of suffering—desire creates sorrow, desire mixed with pleasure and lust, quick pleasure, desire for life, and desire even for nonlife.

Suffering has an end, and this is the noble truth of the end of suffering—nothing remains of desire. Nirvana is attained, all is given up, renounced, detached, and abandoned.

And this is the noble truth that leads to Nirvana—it is the Eightfold way or right views, right intentions, right speech, right action, right livelihood, right effort, right concentration, and right meditation.

This is the noble truth of suffering. This must be understood.[9]

Buddhism Compared to Western Thought

Buddhism and Western Religions

Buddhism is more spiritual than philosophical in its nature, but it is very different from Western religions. The most important difference, perhaps, is that Buddhism does not focus on God. Buddhists do not believe in a God that will punish them now or in the future if they do not behave. The only religious beliefs important to them are those that explain the nature of life, and failure to accept them does not mean punishment, only more lives. Buddhism is primarily a guide to living.

Buddhism is also an especially tolerant and accepting religion. It does not claim to be the "one true Faith" as Roman Catholicism and Islam do. You always get another chance. There is no ultimate "mortal sin" that irrevocably damns us to eternal fire. No matter how many mistakes we make, we always have another opportunity to set them right. Buddhism also differs from other religions in stressing the importance of kindness to animals.

Buddhism puts a heavier burden on the individual than the Judeo-Christian religions do, however. It isn't just that we have as many chances as we need to set our mistakes right—we *must* set them right. And we have to do it alone, with no grace, or forgiveness, or salvation handed out in due course by an all-powerful deity. In the same way that Buddhists do not believe in a God who hovers over us waiting for us to do something wrong, they do not believe in a deity who will pull us out of trouble. Everything is in our own hands. The Buddha's last words underscored this. "Work out your own salvation with diligence," he said. Such responsibility is surely a heavy load to carry.

And the process takes a long time and requires a tremendous amount of patience. You cannot do something wrong, feel remorse, apologize to the person you hurt, or confess it to God or His representative, and then feel that the slate is clean. Regret and remorse are good because they show you have learned something. But karma is not forgiving. You may even have to wait until another life to make things right.

---

[9] *Dhammapada*, trans. Lal, pp. 22–23. [Translation altered.]

In comparison to Western religions, then, Buddhism is both softer and harder on people.

Buddhism and Western Philosophy

How does Buddhism compare to Western philosophy? Setting aside the spiritual and religious focus of Buddhism, which it shares with other Eastern modes of thought, an intriguing similarity with philosophy in the West is its emphasis on developing the mind. Most Western religions emphasize faith, feeling, and belief over intellectual development. In contrast, Buddhism teaches that if we want to advance spiritually, our minds and spirit must grow.

Buddhism and philosophy may agree on the primacy of the mind, but they differ on the best way to cultivate its powers. Philosophy stresses logic, analytical thought, and argument. Buddhism recommends meditation. This emphasis on meditation suggests that the traditional way we teach philosophy does not train the entire mind. In fact, if the Buddha is right, we should probably reconsider the way we generally conduct education in the West.

And still another, more technical difference exists between Buddhism and Western philosophy with regard to the nature of the self. Most philosophers argue for something inherent and unchanging in us that constitutes what they call a "self." We grow, develop, and change—indeed, the cells in our bodies change every seven years—but there is some "self" that endures. Some thinkers even posit an immortal soul that inhabits the body.

The Buddha denies all this. He sees everything, even our very selves, as being in constant change. Buddhists believe that we are composed of five elements: the body, the emotions, the perceptions, the mental processes involved in choice, and consciousness. What passes from life to life, then, is not a specific entity, but what one interpreter of Buddhism refers to as "an ever-evolving, karma-created bundle of characteristics." The metaphor the Buddha uses to illustrate his idea of the essence that survives from life to life is the flame of a candle. When we light one candle from another, what do we say of the second flame? It is completely different; yet it is also the same.

Buddhism and Western Social Values

The Buddhist view of life in general also differs greatly from that held in the West. Western cultures espouse a materialistic, individualistic, and secular outlook. Happiness is found in wealth, the exercise of power, celebrity, and personal achievement.

By contrast, Buddhism is spiritual and altruistic. The aim of life is spiritual development, and an important part of this is learning compassion, empathy, tolerance, and love for other people, and indeed for all other creatures. "Happiness" in the sense we use the term, that is, what we feel when all our desires are met, is not even a goal in Buddhism—quite the contrary. The Buddha sees desire as the source of our troubles, and he recommends that we reduce our wants and needs, not indulge and increase them. If we really want to be content with life, the Buddha recommends that we meditate, develop our minds, think of others, pursue wisdom, and learn to control our desires. Our goals in life should be spiritual and ethical, not material.

Keep in mind, however, that Buddhism recommends the "Middle Way." The Buddha does not say we all should retreat to monasteries in the Himalayas. The Middle Way is a practical path that lets us live in the world. And that is the real challenge—how to live according to Buddhist principles in the "real world."

Take ambition. We can aspire to success, but we have to be careful lest it become an end in itself. Success lets us do much good for others, but when it tempts us to be self-absorbed, it retards our spiritual development and leads us to do things that will produce bad karma. Or consider running a business. Buddhism does not say that every business must become a charitable operation. It does suggest that businesses should examine whether they are helping or hurting the spiritual growth of their employees, customers, and owners. Do they encourage "right speech" and "right action"? Do they encourage something beyond an aggressive, competitive pursuit of profit? Do companies do violence to living things?

Buddhism's main ideas may differ from the ideas we are used to, but their strengths can be incorporated into our lives in practical ways.

The Challenge of Marxism and Buddhism

With Marxism and Buddhism, then, we see two outlooks on life that differ dramatically from that of our own society. Marx stresses the impact of economic forces. He talks about our need for satisfying work, and concludes that capitalism ultimately makes human happiness impossible. The Buddha locates unhappiness in our desires and recommends a path of spirituality, meditation, and limited wants. Marxism and Buddhism clearly differ between themselves, but they agree that the conventional wisdom of our society is all wrong. Both Marx and Buddha think that pursuing money, power, and fame—the main things that our society values—leads us away from, not toward, happiness. Furthermore, there is not one major philosopher over the last 2000 years who would disagree with them on this point. This should unquestionably give us pause.

There are hardly more important issues than how to live or the values to which we should commit ourselves, and these are questions that deserve our most serious attention. Marxism and Buddhism, indeed all schools of philosophy, pose a major challenge to our society's message about what counts as the "good life." It will be up to you to decide who is right.

Main Points of Chapter 11

1. "What is important?" and "What should we strive for in life?" are basic philosophical questions that our society answers in terms of self-interest and material success. Karl Marx and the Buddha offer very different answers.

2. Marx focuses on the powerful effect of the material conditions of life, the clash of economic forces in human society, and the weaknesses of capitalism. Marx argues that the values that capitalism inculcates—competition, inequality, material wealth, for example—do not lead to happiness.

3. In particular, Marx believes that the kind of work that characterizes capitalism—"alienated labor"—is unsatisfying and at odds with the productive nature of human

beings. There are four dimensions to this alienation: the worker is alienated from the product produced, from the activity of production, from his or her productive nature, and from other people.

4. Buddhism contends that we live a series of lives in our search for spiritual enlightenment and that the law of karma, or balance, governs our fate. Through the Four Noble Truths and the Noble Eightfold Path, the Buddha explains the cause of unhappiness and recommends a way to overcome it.

5. In contrast to the outlook of contemporary Western society, Buddhism recommends decreasing, not increasing, our desires. Western conceptions of happiness are secular, materialistic, and individualistic; Buddhism is spiritual and altruistic.

Discussion Questions

1. How much do you agree with the conventional wisdom of our society that success and happiness come through material success? How important are things like love, family, community service, and religion, and are they at odds with material success? Are the most successful people in our society also the happiest? What leads you to your answer?

2. Who are your heroes? What does this reveal about your conception of the meaning of life?

3. Competition is so much at the heart of contemporary Western society that the Marxist critique of competition is virtual heresy in our culture. What is your reaction to the Marxist preference for cooperation? Is competition as good as we think it is? What are its virtues?

4. Is satisfying labor as important as Marx claims for human happiness? What is your idea of a "good job"? If you had to choose between a highly paid but boring job versus a low or moderately paid but very interesting one, which would you choose? Why?

5. Is there any connection between the structure or content of your college education and the demands of capitalism, as Marx would suggest? How "alienating" is the work you do in school? Does this argue for a change in the way higher education should be conducted?

6. If you were to interpret your life from a Buddhist point of view, what would you say are the most important challenges to your spiritual development? What kind of karma are you working off from past lives?

7. Have you ever had an experience that is explained best by the idea that you have lived before? What was it?

8. How would you go about decreasing your wants, as Buddhism recommends? What would your life be like? If you succeeded, do you think you would be happier or unhappier?

9. In view of the Buddha's program for achieving enlightenment, do you think that meditation should be as much a part of the curriculum as writing, for instance?

Selected Readings

Marx's materialist conception of history is outlined in *The German Ideology: Part I;* his theory of alienated labor can be found in the *Economic and Philosophical Manuscripts of 1844;* and his criticism of the division of labor appears in *Wage Labour and Capital.* Marx's master work, of course, is *Capital (Das Kapital).* *The Marx–Engels Reader,* edited by Robert C. Tucker (New York: Norton, 1972), is a convenient edition of Marx's writings.

An *Introduction to Asian Religions* by Geoffrey Parrinder (Oxford: Oxford University Press, 1957) surveys the main religions of the East. Christmas Humphreys's *Buddhism* (New York: Penguin, 1951) elaborates the main tenets and describes the different branches of Buddhism. For a collection of Buddhist texts from India, China, and Japan, see *The Buddhist Tradition,* edited by William Theodore de Bary (New York: Vintage, 1969).

Scientific Explanations
of Reality

- *Science*
- *The Mechanics of Sir Isaac Newton*
- *The New Physics: "Old" Science to "New"*
- *Einstein's Relativity Theory*
- *Where Are We?*

All of you probably know some "science freak," some chemistry major, perhaps, who thinks that the only intelligent way to study things is "scientifically," and that the humanities are a waste of time. Philosophy is useless, unprovable speculation; literature is a bunch of stories; art a lot of paint smeared around. To this kind of person, the twenty-first century is the century of science, and nonscientific disciplines are out of step.

A lot of people with a missionary zeal for science are passionately concerned with "proof," "certainty," and "hard facts." They believe that only science can discover and describe the world around us objectively. And, to tell the truth, some of us who study the "soft" stuff might sometimes wonder whether they might not be right. Unlike philosophy, science is rooted in physical evidence and a rigorous experimental procedure. It does seem to give us a reassuring certainty that metaphysics and ethics do not.

What does this say about philosophy, then? Actually, science and philosophy have the same goal—understanding and explaining reality. The earliest Greek thinkers were scientists as well as philosophers. They studied the stars and the weather. They scrutinized the physical world looking for the laws and forces that governed nature. Science and philosophy evolved in different directions—science became rigorously experimental and concentrated on demonstration, while philosophy remained largely speculative. But while the two branches of knowledge became separate disciplines, they never lost their shared aim of uncovering the nature of reality. Thus, each remains attached to the other in important ways.

As philosophers, we want to know anything we can about reality. If scientists can tell us something worth pondering, we want to hear it. And considering the astonishing discoveries science has made over the last 200 years, there is plenty to interest us.

In this chapter, then, we will see how science accounts for the nature of reality, and we will consider the philosophical implications of these conclusions and whether they support the belief that scientific knowledge is superior knowledge. In doing all this, we will approach the domain of theoretical physics. But if you aren't a "science person," don't worry. Nothing in this chapter is more difficult than anything you have encountered already.

Starting with a short discussion of science in general, we first examine the work of Sir Isaac Newton. Then we move to what modern scientists tell us about the nature of reality with special attention to Albert Einstein's famous theory of relativity. To keep things as close as possible to philosophy, we will focus on the two most basic properties of reality: space and time. In limiting our discussion of physics like this, we'll be forced to ignore many fascinating topics. But space and time will be more than enough to keep us busy.

Science
The Appeal of Science

Our century will no doubt be remembered as a thoroughly scientific time. Scientific discoveries and accomplishments make headlines. (When did a philosophical breakthrough get anywhere near the front page?) Universities, governments, and corporations spend billions of dollars for scientific research, looking for the next big breakthrough that will once more transform our world.

Part of the great appeal of science is that it affects our everyday lives. Scientific discoveries quickly lead to technological inventions that make life dramatically longer, faster, and easier. An even bigger part of its attraction lies in its apparently practical, commonsense methods. Scientific evidence is gathered using our five senses, not intuition or magic. Scientific knowledge emerges from carefully planned and controlled experiments. Hypotheses are formulated, tested, challenged, reevaluated. All the supporting data must be observed and measured objectively. Scientists report their findings and detail their work so that other researchers can verify or correct their conclusions. The whole process is right out in the open.

This is what attracts many people to science. It is demonstrable, ordered, and impartial; its conclusions are based strictly on observable, verifiable facts; its results are generally useful and frequently salable. Such a dependable approach appeals strongly to our practical side, to our commonsense. Science is thus the antithesis of irrationality, superstition, prejudice, and arbitrariness.

Science and Philosophy

People who haven't studied philosophy may assume that philosophy and science are complete opposites. Where science is concrete, philosophy is abstract. Where science is objective, philosophy is subjective. Where science is serious and practical, philosophy is frivolous and impractical. But this simply is not true.

Both branches of learning try to explain the nature of reality, of course, but the relationship is much closer than that. In Chapter 9, on the theory of knowledge, you saw that the methods of philosophy, like those of science, can be uncompromisingly empirical. In fact, the school of philosophy called *empiricism* counts nothing as knowledge that is not based on observable, verifiable, objective data. Rather than being deduced from abstract principles through some operation of the mind, knowledge can only be inferred from the evidence of our senses. If this sounds "scientific," it is. In fact, early modern science grew directly out of the philosophical tradition of empiricism. Thus, science is an outgrowth of philosophy.

When empiricism developed, western Europe was ready for the outbreak of a radical approach to knowledge. During the seventeenth and eighteenth centuries, European society and culture became less monolithically religious than it had been during the Middle Ages. The Reformation tore the seamless cloth of the Roman Catholic church into many pieces. In response to this upheaval, along with pressures from a variety of political and economic upheavals, the sovereign countries we are familiar with—England, France, Germany, Spain—emerged as autonomous, secular nation states.

In this environment, philosophy was able to break away from its medieval subservience to theology. Once this happened, philosophers joined with scientists and mathematicians in regarding human reason, the senses, and the workings of mathematics as the most important instruments for discovering truth. The authority of churches, the privileges of the aristocracy, and the divine right of kings had bitten the dust. More or less independent thinkers like Copernicus, Galileo, Thomas Hobbes, John Locke, Voltaire, and David Hume participated in a revolution against what they saw as superstition, class privilege, and claims about reality that were not only unprovable but were also flatly contradicted by the evidence. Both philosophy and science came to agree that true knowledge is found in the world only as it presents itself to our senses.

Even the philosophical tradition known as *rationalism* joined in this revolutionary spirit and merged philosophical and scientific concerns. Rationalists disagree with empiricists in believing that true knowledge ultimately comes from the workings of the mind alone, not from the senses. But rationalists also rejected the idea that philosophical thought must be subservient to religious dogma. The merging of philosophy and science is especially apparent in the work of the rationalist philosopher René Descartes. In addition to his philosophical accomplishments, Descartes created analytic geometry and did work in physics, biology, meteorology, and optics. Indeed, many people consider him the founder of modern physics and optics as well as of modern philosophy.

The Mechanics of Sir Isaac Newton

By far the most important figure in the development of modern science, however, is Isaac Newton. Newton discovered that the gravitational force that causes objects to fall to the ground is the same gravitational force that keeps the moon in place orbiting around the earth, the same gravitational force that operates everywhere in the universe. He also was one of two people who simultaneously discovered calculus. But the one achievement of Newton's that has probably had the greatest impact on your thinking, whether you realize it or not, is his overarching account of the universe as being like a great machine.

Newton's mechanical model of the universe was the foundation on which modern science rested until Albert Einstein's revolutionary theory of relativity replaced it. Nonetheless, for almost 300 years, Newton's model held sway. In fact, for most of us it still does. As we shall see, Newton's picture of the universe fits with everyday, commonsense observation. Einstein's model, on the other hand, is very much at odds with our ordinary experience, and that is why most of us, most of the time, still think the way Newton thought.

Absolute Space and Time

Newton's most basic assumption is that the two most fundamental properties of reality—space and time—are "absolute." In their deepest essence, they are steady, unchangeable, uniform, and constant. "Absolute space," writes Newton in his *Mathematical Principles of Natural Philosophy,* "in its own nature, without regards to anything external, remains always similar and immovable." He says something very similar about time. "Absolute, true, and mathematical time, of itself and by its own nature, flows uniformly, without regard to anything external," he writes.

In Newton's view, space and time are independent of anything that happens. It's as if there were a great empty stage with a great cosmic clock over it where all the events of the universe take place. No matter what else happens—the Big Bang, the birth and death of stars, cosmic explosions, wars, pestilence, famine—the stage remains the same and the clock keeps ticking. Space and time are absolute, unchanged by any object that comes "onstage" or goes "offstage" or by any action that takes place there. Objects and events exist in space and time, but they do not have any effect on either dimension. Space and time are the two great, unshakable foundations of reality.

A Lawful Universe

In Newton's universe, space and time establish the stage, and everything else takes place in an orderly, explainable fashion. The "everything else" boils down to two things, *matter* and *forces.* That's all there is. These two ideas explain everything that happens in the universe.

Matter is composed of material particles that are always the same in mass and shape. Masses affect one another by means of forces. The primary force operating is gravity, and the resulting motion takes place in absolute space over absolute time. All of this process is governed, of course, by set natural laws.

One Universe, One Set of Laws, One Primary Force

The laws of nature that Newton posits are the same, whether we talk about something happening on earth or in deep space. In this Newton was following the thinking of Galileo and others who rejected the ancient idea, unchanged in medieval times, that there were two sets of laws governing movement: one in effect on the earth and in the space between earth and the moon (called the "sublunary" world) and the other in effect in the "superlunary" dimension beyond the moon. Newton, like Galileo, sees one, natural universe.

Isaac Newton

Isaac Newton (1642–1727) was educated and taught at Cambridge University. His most famous work is *Mathematical Principles of Natural Philosophy*, a work which revolutionized the understanding of the universe. Newton also served in a variety of public posts: member of Parliament, master of the mint, and president of the Royal Society. He was unusually sensitive to criticism, and engaged in a number of vindictive disputes, most notably over whether he or Leibniz invented calculus.

If this is the case, then, planetary motion is caused neither by the hand of God nor by any mysterious power contained within heavenly bodies. Rather, it is the result of a natural force, gravity, whose effect on material objects can be precisely described and predicted. All motion in the universe, no matter where it takes place, conforms to identifiable laws of nature.

Newton's Laws of Motion

The most basic natural laws in Newton's system are his three laws of motion, from which every other law of nature can be derived. Here is how Newton stated them:

I.   Every body continues in its state of rest, or of uniform motion in a right [i.e., straight] line, unless it is compelled to change that state by forces impressed upon it.

II.   The change of motion is proportional to the motive force impressed; and is made in the direction of the right [i.e., straight] line in which that force is impressed.

III.   To every action there is always opposed an equal reaction; or, the mutual actions of two bodies upon each other are always equal, and directed to contrary parts.

The first law describes inertia. In a friction-free environment, an object moving at a given speed and in a given direction will continue at that speed and in that direction forever unless something else acts on it. The second law explains that an object's new direction depends on how hard it is hit by another force and from what direction. Newton's third law describes what happens when, for example, you push someone from behind and knock yourself backwards a little. Your action—pushing forward—is accompanied by an opposite reaction—being pushed backwards. The same phenomenon takes place as a gun recoils when it is fired. These three laws, Newton claimed, account for all the movement and change in the universe.

A Mechanical Universe

Newton describes the universe as a huge machine, with many parts all connected to one another and forces that drive it. That is why Newton's theory is called *mechanistic,* or "machine-like." The transfer of energy through the machine is what causes motion. When one piece of the machine moves, it inevitably moves another piece, which moves another, and so on down the line. As with any other machine, of course, all these operations can be observed, measured, explained, and predicted.

Take a very simple machine, an eggbeater, for example. You grab the handle and turn it. The design of the mechanism keeps your hand moving around in a circle. As you make this motion, you pump energy into the system which causes the large wheel to move. The energy at the outer edge of the wheel is transferred via the gears to the beaters. And there you have it. Your eggs are ready for scrambling.

Newton believes that something like this happens in the universe. Planets move because of a huge system of natural forces. These forces draw objects together, hold them in place, or push them apart, and they do this as effectively as if they were pulleys or levers. The forces that cause motion may be invisible, but their effect can be measured as accurately as the length of this page. (All we need to know is the mass of each body and the distance between them. Newton writes, "Every body attracts every other with a force directly proportional to the product of their masses and inversely proportional to the square of the distance between them.") Thus, Newton's "world-machine" is well made, tight, ordered, and balanced.

In the seventeenth century, the content of Newton's ideas was not self-evident. No one knew anything directly about motion in space. But with probes and astronauts traveling beyond the reach of the earth's gravity with some regularity in our century, most of us are familiar with how Newton's laws appear to work in the weightlessness of space. Newton's laws of motion seem obvious to us now.

Newton's idea of a great "universe machine" operating within absolute space and time also seems quite sensible to us today. Newton tells us, essentially, that reality is exactly what the mind and senses tell us it is. There is nothing supernatural, magical, or mysterious about it. Space and time are constants, and provide a rock-solid framework within which all motion and change take place. Every event has a cause that we ultimately can discover. Everything that happens here or anywhere in the galaxy follows the same universal laws of nature. The only barrier to understanding how the universe works is learning the appropriate mathematics. Once we do that, we can unlock the secrets of the cosmos. There is something very practical, dependable, and comforting about such an explanation, and that, plus the fact that we have been educated along these lines, is why most of us are, at heart, Newtonians.

Philosophical Implications

Newton's conclusions about the nature of reality have profound implications for philosophy as well as for science, of course. Some of these have no doubt occurred to you, but let's examine them more or less systematically.

No Divine Forces, No Platonic Forms

As you have probably already noticed, by explaining all motion in completely natural terms, Newton removes God from the day-to-day operation of the universe. By seeing the universe as coherent, ordered, and working well, Newton also rejects the Platonic idea that the empirical world is an inferior reflection of a higher dimension of intelligible "Forms."[1] Newton wasn't an atheist, but he believed that the most God did was to create the material and the forces of the world, get the "machine" running, and then step back and let the process run on its own.

Newtonian Empiricism

By taking spiritual and any other nonphysical forces out of the daily workings of the cosmos, Newton also implies that the nature of the universe can be uncovered by a rational, empirical methodology. Everything that exists in the universe is physical in nature. That is, if something exists, it exists materially, not spiritually, or in the mind of God. Reality is thus the result of the interplay of physical objects and material forces, and it can be observed, noted, and assessed objectively. This, of course, is the hard-nosed empiricism that is the hallmark of modern science.

If reality is material, then our five senses are the ultimate source of knowledge. We can trust them to tell us something important. Plato and his followers had held the senses to be inferior sources of information that provide us with faulty knowledge. By contrast, Newton elevates them above abstract reasoning and intuition as the appropriate tool for understanding the nature of reality. Thus, the secrets of the universe are open to anyone with the patience to do the appropriate observations and calculations. In this world view, the scientist takes the place once held by the priest, the medicine man, and the sage.

When Newton talks about knowledge, here, he means absolute certainty. Newton's thought does not accommodate "likelihoods" and "probabilities." The appropriate observations and calculations tell us precisely where the earth is in relation to the sun or at what speed the moon is traveling. Having once discovered the basic laws of nature, Newton believes that it is theoretically possible for us to describe with total certainty precisely what is going on with whatever it is we are studying.

Newtonian Determinism

Another important implication of believing the universe to be like a huge machine is that all events, right down to the behaviors of individual human beings, must result from identifiable causes. A machine, after all, contains no mysteries. In a "mechanical" system, everything is caused by something.

In theory, given enough information about the material and the forces at work in a universe that works like a machine, we should also be able to explain the past and predict the future. In practice, the necessary calculations are often too complicated to do. But by logical extension of Newton's idea, if we had enough time, all the necessary information about the causal forces at work, and a precise understanding of the matter these forces operate on, we could account for everything that has taken place—and ever will take place.

---

[1]For Plato's ideas about the nature of reality and his theory of the Forms, see Chapter 8, pp. 234–244.

This, of course, is a trademark of an aggressive scientist. If reality is material and governed by universal laws of nature, a dyed-in-the-wool empiricist believes that everything can be explained. If your book falls to the floor and makes an unusually loud noise, we can study everything that went into the event and explain exactly what combination of factors produced such a loud "bang!" And once we determine the answer, if we set up the same conditions, we can generate the same loud noise over and over again. If we know all we need to about the balls on a pool table and how they react to being struck with a particular force, we'll be able to predict exactly where one will go when it is hit in a certain way by another ball. It cannot be otherwise. If our universe is bound by laws of cause and effect, *explanation* and *prediction* are inevitable extensions of those laws.

If this is so, what happens to freedom? Strictly speaking, every deeply personal, private choice we make, then, is merely the product of a series of prior causes. What feels to us like a difficult, perhaps tortured decision is nothing but another "click" in the great machine of the cosmos. Our decisions about which college to attend, what job to take, whom to marry, or how to resolve some other difficult problem are not freely chosen. They result from the operation of events and forces that span millions of years and come together at a particular instant—in a completely predictable and inevitable way—to produce our choices as surely as a power loom makes cloth. Despite our own subjective feelings about things, we actually have as much freedom in our choices as our cars do when we put them in gear and hit the gas. Everything, from yesterday's thunderstorm to tomorrow's earthquake to the English muffins you had for breakfast this morning to the person you have a date with tonight, everything is the necessary result of prior causes.

Virtually every "purely" scientific explanation of reality has the same bottom line. The "behaviorist" account of behavior is a perfect example, and Freudian psychoanalysis is not far behind.[2] Determinism goes hand in hand with any belief in a lawful, dependable universe of cause and effect.

Newton's Idea of Space and Time

Even more important for our purposes here than the deterministic implications of Newton's mechanics are the philosophical consequences of Newton's understanding of space and time. Newton's ideas about space and time fit with the rational, practical way we Westerners like to lead our lives.[3] In Newton's scheme, space and time are constant and neutral, so there are no times or places that are sacred or evil, lucky or unlucky, or in any other way different in meaning. These dimensions do not have such properties. All spaces and all times are the same, astrological, religious, or superstitious beliefs notwithstanding. Sailing through the Bermuda Triangle is the same as sailing on the sea anywhere else. Space is space. It's not one way here and different some place else. It doesn't bend, twist, or warp. Like space, time is also the same everywhere in the universe. The time that constitutes "Friday the 13th" is no different than that which makes up "Friday the 12th" or "Thursday the 23rd."

---

[2]To review the issue of free will versus determinism, see Chapters 3 and 4.

[3]Of course, we live this way *because* of Newton's ideas; it is not some coincidence. That is, our sensible, practical, commonsense attitudes are the outgrowth of this general philosophy.

Different times do not have different properties. Time does not speed up or slow down. Time is constant, as though some great cosmic clock were ticking away, keeping the "official" time of the universe.

Newton's view that time and space are absolute and independent of any events that take place within them gives us a clear baseline for philosophical inquiry into the nature of reality. Using this baseline, we know that anything that exists can be objectively described in terms of four dimensions—length, width, height, and time. The CPU of my computer, for example, is 22″ by 17″ by 6″. These fixed measurements describe its existence in space. At some point in the past, all its components were assembled and it took shape in its current form. A computer specialist could tell us how long it is apt to function that way before wearing out. A geologist could say how long the different metals and plastics will hold their shape before decaying.

We can provide the same description of both spatial and temporal dimensions for any object or event. On July 4, 1776, the Declaration of Independence was signed in Philadelphia. If we had the document itself in front of us, we could measure it and determine its three dimensions. The actual day may be listed differently on various calendars—Western, Chinese, Jewish, Native American, Moslem, and so on. But the different references all point to the same 24 hours.

Newtonian Reality: Absolute Space and Time

Because space and time are the most basic and stable properties of reality, anything that ever did or ever will exist has particular spatio-temporal characteristics. As long as an object exists in its current form, it has these defining properties. Being a spatial object with specific properties and existing in time is an essential part of its nature. From a Newtonian perspective, then, objects and events have precise, objectively identifiable spatial and temporal properties. That is what separates reality from illusion. This is critical because, as you know by now, the issue of "appearance" versus "reality" is a major philosophical issue.

For example, if I take a piece of ash today and make a baseball bat that is 3 feet long, as long as I don't shave the ends or break the bat, it will remain 3 feet long. If I stick it into a tank of water, it will look bent. But as we know, it actually stays straight because the bend is an optical illusion. I know that under normal conditions an object's spatial properties remain constant, and thus I know that my vision, not the object's shape, is distorted.

Now suppose I show this new bat to a friend who says, "But I saw you using that bat yesterday." I say, "No, you're mistaken. That was a different bat. This bat didn't exist yesterday. The wood existed, but not in the form of a baseball bat." If my friend persists, and if he swears up and down that he saw me with this very bat yesterday, I am entitled to say that he is mistaken, stupid, stubborn, or crazy. The bat's temporal properties are as fixed as its spatial ones. An object made today could not have existed yesterday, so I can confidently separate what is really the case from what appears to be the case, and I can be certain that my friend is quite wrong.

Now let's say that I use the bat in a game and get a hit at exactly 10:25:59 A.M. You are sitting blindfolded in the center field bleachers and press a button every time you hear a hit. Since sound travels more slowly than light, you won't hear the hit until 10:26:00—or even later if you're farther away. Nonetheless, we would all agree that the hit "really" took place at 10:25:59.

Again, despite what appears to be the case, it's as though some central cosmic clock establishes the "official" time of anything in the universe. That is to say, from Newton's point of view, the concepts of absolute space and time undergird reality so strongly that they literally define "reality" and "appearance."

Overall Implications

Newton's description of the universe provides us with a clear and unshakable account of the nature of reality. Reality is describable, measurable, mechanical, understandable, bound by natural laws of cause and effect, and fixed in the bedrock of space and time. Truth can be empirically discovered, and puzzles solved. Newton gives us a stable and dependable universe. He gives us a way to answer questions.

That's why science has such an appeal for many people. And that is why, deep in our hearts, most of us who aren't physicists are still Newtonians. We've been educated in a scientific age, and we believe almost without question that puzzling physical phenomena can be explained by natural laws. We believe that everything has a cause. In particular, we accept the idea of absolute space and time as a matter of course. Even when, through illusions, our senses tell us something different, we hold to the belief that space and time are stable, unchanging, and neutral properties of reality. It may be cold comfort, but when all else fails, we count on the eternal constancy of space and time.

We are also Newtonians in that most of us prefer certainty to uncertainty. The impatience with art, literature, and philosophy that you often hear expressed by some people is usually frustration at the lack of definite answers these disciplines provide. There is generally more than one good interpretation of a poem or a painting. It is even more complicated in philosophy, where many thinkers offer opposing arguments about reality, knowledge, and ethics. What's worse, almost all such arguments are plausible. We can never say for sure that one and only one explanation is true and the rest are false. In fact, if we could settle issues that way, they would no longer be interesting to philosophers. Thus, unlike Newtonian science, philosophy trades in uncertainty and probability.

The New Physics: "Old" Science to "New"

Just when you've become comfortable with Newton's ideas, we're going to rock the boat—and then some. The "old science" of Newton, with its promise of stability and certainty, makes it easier to understand reality. The unshakable constancy of absolute space and time at least gives us something on which to ground speculations about the nature of reality.

But it turns out that Newton is wrong. The "new science"—everything after Albert Einstein—tells a different story. Instead of certainty we get uncertainty. Absolute facts are abandoned for probabilities. As we shall see, even space and time lose their constancy. The "new physics" is not only more abstract than Newton's mechanics, it tells us that the universe is an extremely puzzling place.

If there's a "new" physics, why bother with the "old" physics? We spent some time on Newton's ideas because in many ways they match what commonsense tells us. For one thing, his picture of the universe as a machine operating in absolute space and being clocked by "official" cosmic time seems to fit what the rational mind finds when it analyzes the evidence of our senses. For example, Newton's explanation of the nature of reality—his idea about what is "real" and "true" versus what is "illusion," or "falsehood"—is important to philosophy. If this conception of reality is incorrect, then much of what seems to be real is not real.

In other words, if you don't understand the implications of the "old" science, you won't be able to understand the implications of the "new" science. And if you know something about both, you will be in a stronger position to decide for yourself what should count as "real" and "true" in your own life. And if it turns out that to the best of our knowledge not even space and time are absolute and certain, how could laws, ideas about right and wrong, religious beliefs, or cultural traditions be any different? A basic understanding of "relativity" is just what you need to broach a variety of important questions about many different facets of life.

Einstein's Relativity Theory

If anyone has single-handedly changed the way modern science thinks about reality, it is Albert Einstein. The story of scientific thinking from Newton to Einstein revolves around the problem of getting Newton's mechanistic principles to square with new discoveries. Mechanics explained the behavior of gases well, but electric and magnetic forces posed a new challenge. A little over one hundred years after Newton's death, the equations of a scientist named James Maxwell suggested that light is electromagnetic. By concentrating on the behavior of light, then, Einstein focused on a phenomenon that had major implications about the accuracy of Newton's system. Einstein's genius was to see that what he learned about light presented a picture of the universe that differed completely from Newton's, particularly with regard to the nature of space and time.

The Speed of Light

In the Newtonian universe, while everything else is changeable and variable, space and time are constant and absolute. They stand apart from the dynamic motion of the universe. For Einstein, however, it is not time and space but the *speed of light* that is absolute. By "absolute," Einstein means not only that light always moves at the same speed (186,279 miles per second), he also means that light will be perceived as moving at the same speed by every observer, whether that observer is standing still, moving away from the light, or moving toward the light. Despite physical conditions that affect the speed of everything else, the speed of light always remains the same. This is the one great constant in Einstein's thinking, and it is the constant on which he builds his explanation of reality.

Once Einstein elevates the constant speed of light to the premier spot in his thinking, the ideas that follow from it defy Newtonian "common sense." Thus, Einstein's explanation of the nature of reality does not just differ from Newton's, it differs from anything that one would ordinarily imagine. It takes some doing to accept this.

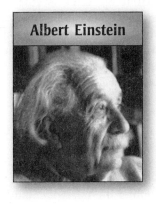

Albert Einstein

One of the most brilliant minds of the twentieth century, Albert Einstein (1879–1955) was born in Germany to Jewish parents. After an undistinguished career as a student, Einstein was able to obtain a position in the Swiss Patent Office in 1902. His writings on theoretical physics attracted much attention, but he was not able to obtain a university post until 1909. Starting at the University of Zurich, he moved to the German University of Prague, the Federal Polytechnic in Zurich, and the University of Berlin. He received the Nobel Prize in 1922. Teaching occasionally at the California Institute of Technology, he accepted a permanent position at the Institute for Advanced Studies in Princeton after Hitler came to power.

Measuring Speed

Before we see how Einstein's ideas defy common sense, however, we need to note some of the odd things that happen when we measure the speed of light. Measuring, of course, is a basic activity of science, and measurements are a big part of an empiricist's description of reality. If simple measurements do not work out right, then, it is a very big problem from a scientific viewpoint.

That is exactly what happens when we try to measure the speed of light. But before we talk about that, let's look at what happens when we measure the speed of something more common, like the speed of cars.

Measuring the Speed of Cars. You're driving along the highway at 70 mph. Your speedometer says "70," and we can clock you at that speed with a radar gun. Suddenly a black Porsche passes you at 100 mph. Now when we say the Porsche is doing 100, we mean that its speed is 100 miles per hour *in relation to someone standing still*—someone like the cop down the road waiting to give both of you speeding tickets.

But what is the speed of the Porsche *in relation to your moving car*? You see it move past you and continue on down the road. How fast is it going? That's easy. Relative to your moving car, the Porsche is going 30 mph. If the two of you keep cruising at the same speed for 1 minute from the time he passes you, the distance between the two of you will be 1/2 mile (30 mph × 1/60 hour = 0.5 mile).

Now imagine that a few miles down the road the driver of the Porsche suddenly remembers that he left the iron on at home after he finished pressing his shirts this morning. He turns around and now races back toward you—still at 100 mph. If you're still going 70, what is the Porsche's speed relative to your speed now? Again, the answer is easy. As anyone who watches auto safety ads on television knows, the correct answer is the sum of the two speeds—170 mph. If the two of you were to collide, the impact of the crash would be the same as if you had run into a stationary wall at 170.

Or you can think of it this way. If we measure the decrease in the distance between the two of you in a minute's worth of driving toward one another, what do we get? Let's say you start five miles apart. At 70, your car will travel 1.17 miles. Doing 100, the Porsche will cover 1.67 miles. The distance between the two of you, then, has shrunk by 2.84 miles in one minute. To cover 2.84 miles in one minute, you would have to be driving 170 mph.

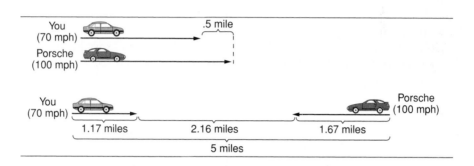

All this sounds perfectly sensible. It also fits Newton's ideas about motion. Now see what happens when we take the speed of light into consideration.

A Galactic Highway. It is now A.D. 2348, and you are studying physics. Your instructor assigns you to do some experiments on the speed of light for homework. You get into your space ship and travel out to deep space with your highly sophisticated laboratory gear. You have the space-age equivalent of a radar gun, which can lock onto a single particle of light and track its speed.

First, you're supposed to clock the speed of light when you're stationary. You stop your ship, point your instrument at the nearest star, and lock onto a light particle. You already know what to expect—186,279 miles per second. (To make things easier, we'll use 186,000 mps as a round number.) Next, you're supposed to travel at 100,000 miles per second, let a particle of light pass you (as the Porsche did), and then measure its speed relative to you. You expect that speed to be 86,000 mps. (You are going 100,000 mps; the light is going 186,000; the difference must be 86,000.)

But that's not what your speed gun shows. It says that the light went past you at 186,000 mps. At first you think your equipment is out of whack and you'll have to go back and get it fixed. Then you remember that your instructor told you not to be surprised by anything you observe. So you crosscheck your speed gun by asking your ship's computer to calculate how much farther the light particle traveled than your ship did in one minute. You assume that the light went only 5.16 million miles more than you did (86,000 mps × 60). Your computer tells you it went 11,160,000 miles. That is the distance something travels in 1 minute going at 186,000 mps.

This doesn't make sense. But you want to get home early, so you go on to the third part of your assignment. You're supposed to get your ship going 100,000 mps again, and this time head into the light. Again, you are to determine the speed of the light particle coming right at you relative to your own speed. This time it should be

286,000 mps, you think—your speed (100,000) plus the speed of light (186,000). But again you're surprised when your speed gun registers only 186,000. Cross-checking with the computer verifies this. You assumed that during 1 minute of travel, the distance between your ship and the light particle would have decreased by 17,160,000, but your computer tells you it went down by only 11,160,000. The speed of the light particle relative to your speed, even when you are moving toward it, is 186,000 mps.

There's no disputing it. The speed of light relative to you is always the same— 186,000 miles per second. It doesn't matter whether you are stationary, moving away from the light, or moving toward it.[4] Yet this cannot be if the laws of nature hold universally. This observation is totally illogical.

Does this mean we have to give up logic and natural laws as we know them in order to understand the phenomenon? In a way it does. Or rather, we have to give up one kind of logic and natural laws for another.

Einstein's Constant

It was Einstein who theorized that light will always be measured as traveling at the same speed, whether the measurer is standing still or moving at some tremendous velocity, and experiments have borne out this theory time and again. The idea that the speed of light is constant under all conditions throughout the universe dealt a major blow to Newtonian physics. Absolute space and time had been a kind of baseline in Newton's account of the universe. Einstein's theory holds that everything but the speed of light is up for grabs, and that includes space and time.

The Speed of Light and the Relativity of Time

The mere fact that the speed of light is constant says very little to the philosopher. The *consequences* of this observation, on the other hand, are profound.

The connection that Einstein develops between the speed of light and the passage of time has some astonishing implications. Einstein claims that as a moving object speeds up and gets closer to the speed of light, time slows down. Or, to be more precise, *from the point of view of someone standing still,* time changes for the moving object. If this sounds strange, what Einstein has in mind is even stranger. Note once again the phrase "from the point of view of someone standing still." *From the point of view of the object itself,* however, time is constant—it neither speeds up nor slows down, despite what the observer perceives. But here is the most incredible part of Einstein's theory. Which point of view is the "right" one? What is "really" happening? Is one time speeding up or is the other slowing down? Which time is the "real" or "official" time? According to Einstein, as strange as it may seem, the answer is that both are.

---

[4]Here is a less mathematical example that makes the same point about the odd behavior of light. If you stand still and fire a gun at a wall, the bullet will hit the wall at a certain speed. What will happen if you fire the gun at the wall while you are in a car driving toward that wall? Will the bullet's speed be any different? Yes. It will hit at a higher speed—the original speed plus the speed of the car. Now take a flashlight and think of it as a "light gun." When you shine it on the wall, the light particles hit the wall at a certain speed, right? If you were to drive toward the wall and turn on the flashlight (or your headlights, for that matter), will the light hit the wall at a higher speed? No, it will not, no matter how fast you go.

Light simply does not obey the same laws as bullets do. It always travels the same speed, no matter what.

Einstein claims that there is no such thing as absolute time (or absolute space, for that matter). Time (or space) *is relative to a frame of reference.* That's why the theory is called "relativity" theory.[5]

You're probably thinking that two contradictory reckonings of time, or anything else, cannot both be accurate. It simply isn't logical, at least not in the terms of a Newtonian world. But such a proposition is perfectly logical in an Einsteinian world. Whether or not space and time are changing is all relative to a frame of reference. Experiments have shown conclusively that this is so.

The Relativity of Time: The Twin Paradox

Let's talk about time and see where we can go with it. In modern physics there is a famous paradox called the "twin paradox." Imagine that you have an identical twin. You get onto a spaceship and blast out into the galaxy traveling close to the speed of light. Your twin remains behind on earth. You hurtle through the galaxy for what you count as a few months. Upon your return to earth, you find that your twin is now many years older than you. Your ship's clock ticked off what seemed to you to be normal seconds, minutes, and hours. It tells you that a relatively short amount of time elapsed since you left. But you cannot doubt your senses. Your twin is now old enough to be your parent. In fact, depending on how close you got to the speed of light and how long you were in space, you may return hundreds of years after you left.

The point is that in relativity theory the character of any variation in time depends on the frame of reference from which we make the assessment. From your viewpoint, earth time speeded up. From your twin's viewpoint, your time slowed down. If you and your twin could communicate with each other during your trip via television, you would both see some very strange things. Your twin would observe you moving and speaking in slow motion. If your spaceship had a wall clock, your twin would think it had stopped, it would be going so slowly. You would see the exact opposite. Your twin would seem to be racing around and speaking incredibly quickly. The clock on your twin's wall would spin around wildly.

The Objectivity of Time: Time Warps?

This may sound more like science fiction than hard science. It may remind you of the movie *Star Trek IV: The Voyage Home,* for example, in which Kirk, Spock, and company travel back in time to find two humpback whales, then travel forward in time to bring them to Earth in the twenty-third century. They travel through time by creating a "time warp," flying so fast that they cross back and forth between three centuries in only a few minutes.

---

[5]Although Einstein is the most famous "relativity" theorist, Galileo is actually the first scientist to employ the principle. The essence of relativity is the idea that we can discern rest or motion only in relation to something else. Think of it this way. Sit very still. Look around the room you're in and outside the window. Are you moving? If you said, "No," you're wrong. You may feel as if you're at rest, but in fact you're moving at the speed at which the earth turns. How do we know we're moving at that speed if we feel as if we are still? Because we can plot our positions in relation to that of the sun, moon, and stars. If we did not have these visible reference points, however, we would not be able to determine this.

Einstein's ideas about time do leave the door open for some of the time travel we encounter in science fiction books and movies. But only half of the action in *Star Trek IV* is possible—travel to the future. Nothing in relativity theory suggests that we can travel into the past. Once you move into the future, there is no way back. (Of course, a natural law like that would really put a damper on a good science fiction story. So writers usually take a bit of license when they weave time travel into their tales.)

Proofs of the Relativity of Time

Experiments have shown that time is indeed variable. One of the most well-known demonstrations of this fact took place in 1972 when scientists took an atomic clock onto a plane, flew it around the world, and then compared it to another atomic clock on the ground with which it had been synchronized. The clock that went on the plane now registered a slightly earlier time. Even though the plane went nothing close to the speed of light, in comparison to the clock on the ground, the clock on the plane had slowed down—even if minutely—while it was moving. Of course, to be precise and to respect the fact that neither one was "wrong," we must also say that in comparison to the clock on the plane, the one on the ground sped up.[6]

Another stunning confirmation of the relativity of time involves a subatomic particle called a "muon." Muons are created at the outer edge of our atmosphere when subatomic particles from space enter the atmosphere and strike air molecules. Muons decay very quickly, so quickly that their lifetime is only 2.2 millionths of a second. Nothing could travel very far in this flicker of time, and it should be physically impossible for a muon to travel from the top of the atmosphere all the way down to the earth in 2.2 millionths of a second. To go that distance in that time it would have to travel faster than the speed of light. Yet muons strike the earth all the time. How is it possible?

What happens is this. The force of the collision at the edge of the atmosphere that creates the muons sends them speeding toward the earth at 99 percent of the speed of light. As you know by now, from the observer's point of view, the closer to the speed of light an object travels, the more time slows down. Since a muon moves almost at the speed of light, time slows down a great deal, and it has plenty of time to reach the earth. To be more precise, the muon still exists only 2.2 millionths of a second in its time frame. If we could hold onto one on its journey from the edge of the atmosphere and clock how long it took to reach the earth, we would come up with something less than 2.2 millionths of a second. Yet it can cover the distance because as measured by our time frame it exists for 15.4 millionths of a second.

In other words, the natural laws that determine that a muon exists for only 2.2 millionths of a second are valid no matter what is happening in the universe. According to Einstein, however, time is not an absolute, fixed property. Instead, time is a property that is determined by the motion of an object in relation to the speed of light. Perhaps we could say that time is the product of an object's relationship to the speed of light. You can see from this that it does not make any sense to ask whether a muon "really" exists for 2.2 or 15.4 millionths of a second. Both statements are true. The measurement that is used simply depends on your frame of reference.

---

[6]J. C. Hafele and R. E. Keating, *Science*, 177 (1973), pp. 168 ff.

Philosophical Implications: Alternate Realities

The philosophical implications of Einstein's relativity theory should be occurring to you by now. Most of us have always assumed that time is as Newton described it. But Einstein's work alters our most fundamental understanding of the nature of reality. Specifically, Einstein's theory that time is relative to motion means that more than one reality can exist. (Muons exist only 2.2 millionths of a second and muons exist 15.4 millionths of a second.) This idea of the *simultaneous existence of different realities* is very powerful in its philosophical implications.

To explore this startling notion, we'll consider two examples. Let's start with one of Einstein's simpler ones. You're on a railroad car that is moving along. You stand up, take an object like this book, and let it fall to the floor of the car. As you watch its path, you see that it falls straight down. If you were asked to trace the trajectory the object took, you would draw a straight line.

Now imagine that a friend of yours sitting on the embankment beside the train tracks can see you do this. (Pretend the car has a glass side.) She can also study the trajectory of the book as it falls. Is she going to say that the book fell straight down? No, because the book does not just fall down, it also moves forward with the train. If she were asked to trace the trajectory of the book's fall, she would draw a curved line, or a parabola.

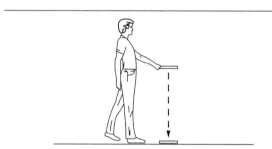

How you would portray the book's path

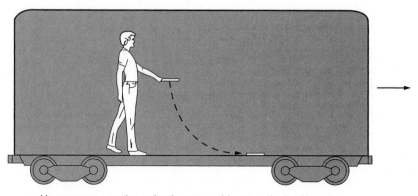

How someone on the embankment would portray the book's path

How does the book "really" move, in a straight line or in a parabola? You are probably inclined to think that a curved path is the better answer. When you're on the train it appears to fall straight down because you don't take the forward motion of the train into account. The stable embankment seems like a better point of view from which to measure the "real" motion. But remember that the earth itself is moving. From yet another vantage point—the moon, a planet, a spaceship—the trajectory of the falling book looks different again. For all we know, there's a vantage point from which the book falls backwards.

Thus, you can see that we have no basis for saying that one path of the book is "real" and the others "illusion." We have different realities, all existing at the same time.

The Relativity of Simultaneity. Now let's move on to an example that Einstein says demonstrates the "relativity of simultaneity." Imagine that two bolts of lightning strike the train track at two points far from each other, points A and B. These bolts of lightning, Einstein says, hit "simultaneously." You know what he means, right? But you may not know what *Einstein* means, because as he sees it, these two lightning bolts actually hit both at the *same* instant and at *different* times. How is this possible?

Suppose that you're standing on the embankment by the train track at a point we call M. We see the bolts hit points A and B simultaneously. No doubt about it, they hit at the same instant. "Simultaneous," then, means that the light, which is traveling at a particular speed, reaches us at M at the same moment.

But here's the complication. Is someone on a train moving past us going to see the same event you see from the embankment? Einstein says no. The observer on the train is moving toward one of the lightning bolts, shortening the distance the light from that bolt has to travel and lengthening the distance the light from the other has to travel. The light from the bolt that hits behind the moving train thus will take a little longer to reach the observer than the light from the bolt that hits in front of it. To someone on the moving train, the bolts do not hit simultaneously. Einstein explains that the observer on the train "is hastening towards the beam of light coming from B, whilst he is riding on ahead of the beam of light coming from A. Hence the observer will see the beam of light emitted from B earlier than he will see that emitted from A." Accordingly, he concludes,

> Events which are simultaneous with reference to the embankment are not simultaneous with respect to the train, and vice versa (relativity of simultaneity). Every reference-body (coordinate system) has its own particular time; unless we are told the reference-body to which the statement of time refers, there is no meaning in a statement of the time of an event.
>
> —Relativity: The Special and the General Theory

Why is this so? Because the speed of light remains the same, no matter what the point of view. It moves at 186,000 miles per second in relation to the person watching the lightning from the embankment. It travels the same speed relative to the person on the train. As a result, two different events occur: The bolts strike simultaneously; the bolts strike at different times. The only way both observers could see "the same thing" is for light to travel at different speeds for each of them. And there is absolutely no scientific reason to think that this is possible.

Thus, Einstein's ideas imply that simultaneous but different realities are possible. Remember, there is no "official" description of the event that negates either one. Each is scientifically valid.

Another Example of Simultaneous Different Realities. If you're telling yourself that there are not "really" different realities, that the problem is one of things *appearing* in two different ways, how do you handle this example? Keep the moving railroad car in mind. This car, however, has a bright light installed in the middle and two light-sensing devices installed on the doors at the front and back of the car. When the light hits the sensor, the door flies open. Now think again of two points of observation, or reference points, one inside the moving car and the other outside as it goes by.

Here is what happens. The observer inside the car sees the light go on and the doors open at the same instant. The observer outside, however, sees the light go on and the back door open just a little before the front door opens. Why? Remember the principle at work in the example of the lightning bolts. The path of the light to the back of the car is shortened by the forward motion of the train, while the path to the front of the car is lengthened. Thus, it takes less time for the light to reach the sensor on the back door, and that door opens first.[7]

Once again, both events "really" happen: The doors open simultaneously and they do not open simultaneously. It just depends on the frame of reference of the observer, whether that person is moving with the train or remaining stationary outside the train. If really pressed, we could say that what "really" happens is that light travels at the same speed in relation to each observer. This gives us two different events, as it did in the lightning example: The doors open simultaneously and the back one opens first.

The Relativity of Spatial Properties

It is difficult, of course, to remove our belief in a great cosmic clock that keeps "official" galactic time which is the final judge in interpreting reality objectively. You may still take "stationary" earth time as "real" time in clocking muons. You can't shake the feeling there is some objective frame of reference in which the lightning bolts "really" do or do not hit simultaneously. Maybe you appeal to "God's point of view." But appealing to a deity is neither scientific nor philosophical.

Einstein also rejects another major pillar of Newton's theory, the idea of absolute space. Relativity suggests that space is as variable and as much connected to the speed at which an object is moving as time is. Odd as it sounds, this too has been verified experimentally. Once you see that space is as variable a property as time, you'll have a clearer idea just how undependable our ordinary perception of things is, with our automatic Newtonian assumption that space and time are constant, unchanging properties.

---

[7]Joe Schwartz and Michael McGuinness, *Einstein for Beginners* (New York: Pantheon Books, 1979), pp. 110–12.

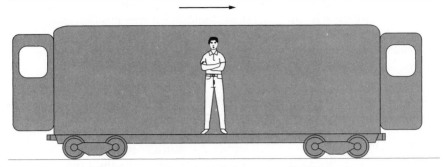

To someone on the train, both doors open simultaneously.

To someone outside the train, the rear door will open first.

Variable Length

We saw above that time changes as an object accelerates. But time is not the only thing affected by motion. Einstein claims that an ordinary spatial property like length also changes as an object speeds up.

Let's return to our railroad car and ask a new question. Suppose that an observer sitting inside a moving railroad car measures its length and an observer sitting outside the car on the embankment also devises a way to measure the moving car as it goes by. Will these two observers get the same answer? Einstein claims they will not. This is the same phenomenon as it applies to space that we observed above with regard to time. Depending on whether an observer is on a moving object or stationary in relation to it, the spatial properties of that object differ. Thus, Einstein writes, "The length of the train as measured from the embankment may be different from that obtained by measuring in the train itself." The railroad car is actually different lengths.

Railroad cars don't go very fast, however, so the variation in lengths will not be great. Yet consider the results of something traveling really fast. Suppose that you're on the intergalactic equivalent of the Bonneville salt flats, where speed tests are being run. A series of space speeders are zooming off trying to get as close as they can to the speed of light. Each trial is carefully measured and shown on a huge screen. From your stationary viewpoint, you see the strangest thing. As each ship accelerates, it gets shorter, and the closer it approaches the speed of light, the shorter it gets. Finally, one ship reaches light speed, and it disappears. The ship reappears when it slows down, but it really did disappear.

Interviewed upon their return, all the pilots, even the one whose ship disappeared, say the same thing—nothing unusual happened. And when their on-board computers are downloaded for evaluation, their version of events is confirmed. The ships' computers recorded no change in the length of the ships. The one that disappeared did not "blink" out of existence. On board, everything was as normal as ever. There are time discrepancies—the faster the ships went, the more time they lost in comparison to those in the control center. But you expected that.

Apparently, space gets as quirky as time does the closer an object approaches the speed of light. Why does this happen? Simply because this is the nature of reality. Space is not the unchanging "empty stage" of Newtonian mechanics. It is as flexible as we saw time to be. According to Einstein's theory, as an object approaches the speed of light, it gets shorter. Its mass also increases. If an object reached light speed, its length would drop to zero and its mass would be infinite.[8]

But this is *relativity* theory, and we have to remember that all these dimensions are relative to a frame of reference. If the observer is standing still while watching the intergalactic speed runs, the length and mass of the ships will change. If the observer is on board the ship, nothing changes.

Physicists have confirmed this phenomenon in experiments using "particle accelerators," those huge devices, sometimes called "atom smashers," in which subatomic particles are accelerated to speeds very close to the speed of light. From their stationary viewpoint, scientists regularly measure changes in the length and mass of these particles as they race around their course.

Once again, then, we cannot escape the same conclusions that we came to when we investigated the flexibility of time. Everything points to the simultaneous existence of "alternate realities."

"Bent" Space

Relativity theory also suggests that space changes in yet another way—it "bends."

To understand Einstein's thinking here, we should go back to Newton for a minute. Newton thought that space is absolute, unchanging, and essentially without any distinguishing features from one end of the universe to the other. To him, space is neutral. It has no effect on and is not affected by any object that exists in it. For example, space is not affected by any cosmic forces, not the sun's immense gravity, not anything.

Einstein doesn't see it this way, however. He thinks that space can have certain properties and, therefore, it is different in different places. Einstein believes, for example, that matter and gravity can actually bend space.

---

[8]Actually, nothing but light is supposed to be able to travel at the speed of light. This is what would happen if it were possible.

The notion that space can bend or that gravity can affect space may strike you as ridiculous. But suppose that we had an extremely powerful "gravity machine," something that worked like a magnet but that pulled *everything* toward it, not just metal objects. We test it out on cars, trees, and houses and it works fine. We turn up the power and point it at skyscrapers. They come tumbling down. We yank the Golden Gate Bridge down. We can even pull planes out of the sky. We turn up the power even more, point it toward the moon, and change its orbit. But what if we pointed it at space? If space itself is empty, if it is nothing, then gravity will have nothing to pull. Yet relativity theory says that space can be pulled. Einstein discovered that space indeed can be "bent" by the gravitational field of an object.

The theory goes like this. Newton was wrong in the way he imagined space. Space is not like a stage with nothing on it or a picture frame without a picture. Let's say, for purposes of instruction only, that space is more like a huge waterbed. Imagine a waterbed the size of a football field with a very pliable top. Now suppose we put a very large and heavy bowling ball onto the bed. What will happen? It will sink down and make an indentation in the bed. We put other heavy balls of different sizes onto the bed here and there, and the same thing happens. The balls sink into the bed and "warp" the surface. How far they sink—and how much the surface is "warped"—depends on their size and weight.

Space gets distorted the same way. Einstein claims that the gravitational fields of very large physical objects like stars actually "warp" the space around them.[9] It is the topography of this "warped space," not gravity, that determines how smaller objects behave when they get close to the big ones.

Returning to our example, what happens if you take some marbles and throw them onto the waterbed in the vicinity of the different bowling balls? Most of the marbles around the biggest ball roll into the indentation it has made. In the neighborhood of a small ball, the opposite happens. Most of the marbles roll by because the dent in the bed is very shallow. Now try to see how close to the bowling ball you can roll a marble before it slides down and hits the ball. You'll be able to roll it closer to the small balls than to the big ones because the bed is less distorted around them. The balls do not pull the marbles in toward them by some invisible force. The marbles just follow a natural path according to how much the top of the waterbed has been pulled down, or warped, by the mass of the different balls. In other words, the marbles respond to the configuration of the bed's surface.

So this is what it means to say that space can be bent. And on a galactic scale, it is very large bodies, like stars, that warp space the way the bowling balls distort the surface of the waterbed.

Traversing the Great Cosmic Waterbed

Consider now what it's like to travel through warped space. Imagine you're piloting your spaceship home and that the surface of the waterbed represents the

---

[9]Actually, virtually all matter causes some warping of space, but the warp is not noticeable unless it's caused by something as big as a star. Even then, as you will shortly see, the distortion is not very big.

space that your ship must travel through. The bowling balls represent objects—stars, for example—that warp the space in their vicinity. You've set your ship on autopilot, and your controls will keep your ship heading straight ahead and no other way.

What happens as you go past the cosmic equivalent of a bowling ball? If you pass by just at the outer edge of the distortion, you will follow the terrain like one of the marbles. You'll dip a little to the left at the beginning of the warp, then back up to the right as you fly on. Your flight path dips and curves. But remember, this is relativity theory, and what happens depends on your frame of reference. Of course, from the point of view of an observer at some distance, your path curves. From your point of view, the ship just flies straight ahead all the way. Its motion is consistently forward and straight ahead. Without any other frame of reference to use for comparison, this is a straight path. Furthermore, remember that in weightless space, you would have no cues like tipping in one direction or another. You would be certain that you continued to fly in a straight line.

The same sort of thing happens when you fly an airplane from Boston to San Francisco. You take off, get to cruising altitude, and fly level and straight to your destination. But in fact you're not flying straight and level at all. Your path is an arc that matches the curve of the earth—a great circle route—because that is the only route you can fly between two points on a sphere.[10]

The Evidence for Warped Space: Bent Light

Shortly after Einstein came up with the theory of warped space, two very famous experiments confirmed the notion. The first involves light, the second, the orbit of Mercury.

In relativity theory, the speed of light is an absolute constant. In a vacuum, light also always travels in a straight line. However, Einstein speculated, if a beam of light got close enough to a massive body, its path would appear to be bent. The object would bend the space around it, and light would follow the warping the same way a car follows the curve at a race track. In other words, while traveling in a straight line from a viewpoint within its own frame of reference, the light would bend from the standpoint of an observer in a different frame of reference.

Scientists soon proved that this is just what happens. While examining the behavior of starlight during a solar eclipse, scientists took photographs in an area where a particular group of fixed stars appeared at night. Then they did the same thing during a solar eclipse. When they compared the pictures, the stars closest to the sun in the eclipse had "moved" slightly. At night, the light of the stars traveled through

---

[10]Here is one final example just in case you're still having trouble with the idea of warped space. If you drive a car around a speed track like the one at Indianapolis, you can actually make it around without turning the steering wheel. Just point your car into the middle of the track and the changing angle at either end will carry your car around. It is the topography of the track, not any change in direction originated in the car, that makes you drive in a circle. Obviously, in one sense, you are driving in a circle. But as far as your car is concerned, it is just driving straight ahead. As the driver, you will certainly know that you are looping around the track. But what if you were to do the same thing in a weightless environment in total darkness? You wouldn't know that you were tilting around the track. Nothing in your experience would tell you that you weren't just going in a straight line. Accordingly, you can think of the track as approximating in a very rudimentary way the effects of warped space.

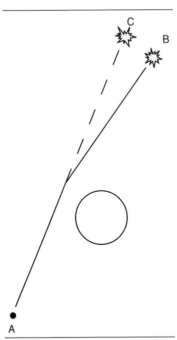

To a person standing at point A during the eclipse, a star that actually was at point B appeared to be at point C because of the warping of space.

unwarped space. However, during the eclipse, the light traveled through the warped space around the sun that it had to pass through to get from the stars to the earth. That is, from our frame of reference, the starlight "curved."[11]

The Evidence for Warped Space: Mercury's Orbit

Before we discuss Mercury's orbit, we have to go back to Newton for a minute. Newton's account of the universe worked out mathematically, and that is extremely important for a scientific theory. When scientists tried to describe or predict motion here on earth or in the heavens, the observed results agreed with what Newton's mathematical formulas said should happen—*almost* all of the time.

There was a problem with Mercury's orbit. Newton's equations about what paths the planets should follow in their revolutions around the sun worked for every planet but Mercury, the planet closest to the sun. Newton predicted one orbit, but astronomers observed another. The difference was small, but significant enough to send scientists searching for an unknown planet whose gravity could have such an effect on Mercury.

---

[11]Strictly speaking, the warping of space produces only half the distortion. The effect of gravity on light causes the rest. About the curving of light, Einstein writes, "half of this deflection is produced by the Newtonian field of attraction of the sun, and the other half by the geometrical modification ('curvature') of space caused by the sun."

In terms of Einstein's theory, however, Mercury behaves exactly as it should. The sun is very large in relation to Mercury, and its gravitational field is so powerful that it actually warps the space around it. Mercury simply takes the easiest path through the "curved" space it must travel through. Like a marble going by a bowling ball on a waterbed, it takes a slight dip as it rolls by. Its orbit differs slightly from that of the other planets because space is more bent closer to the sun than it is farther from the sun.

Einstein hadn't considered the problem of Mercury's orbit when he devised his theory. It was simply an added bonus that when astronomers worked with his equations, they saw that Einstein's theory predicted exactly the kind of orbit Mercury has. Here was clear empirical verification that space was variable enough to be pushed, pulled, or bent.

Thus, space is not what Newton had presumed it to be. If space can be "bent" by the gravitational fields of matter, it is not some fixed, absolute, neutral property of reality, but, rather, variable and fluid. And there is even scientific evidence that confirms this.

"Bent" Time

We've just seen that gravity and the mass of an object can warp space. But could the mass of a very large object possibly affect time too? If both time and space change when acceleration approaches the speed of light, might not both change in response to gravity (or mass)? The answer is yes.

An experiment in 1962 showed that time runs a shade slower on the surface of the earth than it does higher up, that is, farther away from the planet's mass. When scientists took two sensitive and precise clocks and put one at the bottom of a water tower and the other at the top, they discovered that the lower one did in fact run more slowly.

Bent Space and Bent Time Together? Black Holes

If space and time undergo warping separately, perhaps they can also be distorted together. Can scientists point to evidence of this? The evidence they cite is a cosmic phenomenon that you've probably heard about called a "black hole."

A black hole is the ultimate space–time distorter. Although scientists are not sure that such phenomena exist, evidence is mounting that they do. A black hole is the final stage in the life of a massive star. As the star exhausts the gases of which it is made, it starts to contract and become more dense. Scientists think that a star can collapse down to a radius of only about ten miles but with a mass of hundreds of millions of tons per cubic inch. Such a mass curves the space occupied by the star inward so dramatically that nothing, not even light, can escape from it. This forms a boundary called an "event horizon," and within the event horizon the star becomes the equivalent of a "black hole" in space.

If we parked our spaceship away from a collapsing star and sent into it a probe that registers time, we would see time slow down as the mass collapses. From our point of view, when the event horizon was formed, time would stop. But as you know by now, what happens depends on the frame of reference within which it is observed, so it shouldn't surprise you that beyond the event horizon, time flows normally.

It is clear, however, that if black holes actually exist, their extraordinary mass must warp both space and time very dramatically.

The Space–Time Continuum

By now you should understand just how changeable space and time are in Einstein's account of reality. Both are relative properties, directly connected to the speed of an object's motion and the frame of reference from which that object is viewed. Therefore, the spatial and temporal dimensions of an object are, in a sense, manufactured. They are the product of conditions external to the object—its speed relative to the speed of light and the observer's point of view. Different observers experience different conditions, so space and time differ relative to those conditions. In short, Einstein gives us an account of the nature of reality that is very different from anything we experience in our everyday lives.

As strange as this must seem, Einstein's ultimate account of the nature of reality—a phenomenon called the *space-time continuum*—is even stranger.

Space-Time: Reality in Four Dimensions

The idea that space and time can and do change led Einstein to propose yet another dramatically different description of reality. Newton had said that reality has three dimensions: length, width, and depth. These three properties fully describe anything that exists. This gives us a static description of an object in space which we can locate in time, either now or in the past. But this object's spatial characteristics are totally distinct from its temporal characteristics. We can very easily separate space from time, and that is what we do in our everyday experience.

Einstein thought that this was a mistake. If something as simple as an object's length varies according to the speed of its motion, then a full account of reality must also refer to time. After all, motion automatically implies time—an object's motion, or speed, is a measure of how much distance it covers during a given amount of time (miles per hour, for example). Accordingly, Einstein insists on a *four-dimensional reality* as distinct from the familiar three-dimensional one, which accommodates the intimate connection of space and time.

But Einstein does not speak of "space" and "time" as separate entities. In order to show the close relationship between these concepts, he coins a new idea—*space-time* or the "space-time continuum." Spatial and temporal properties are so intimately connected, he thinks, that you cannot talk about one without talking about the other. Because we cannot really separate space and time from each other, they exist as a continuum. Remember how space and time are *both* affected when an object travels close to the speed of light? To a stationary observer, length decreases, mass increases, and time slows down. This intimate connection between spatial properties and the passage of time is the basis for the space-time continuum.

When we talk about a "four-dimensional reality," of course, we move out of our direct experience. We cannot really picture things in four dimensions because we see things only in three dimensions. (Imagine how you would explain depth to someone who saw the world only in two dimensions, like the images on a television screen.) Furthermore, we are hardly ever aware of the close relationship between space and time because it usually requires phenomenally high speeds before we can observe any changes.

Still, we do have direct knowledge of one very obvious example of the connection between space and time, and that is light, specifically, sunlight and starlight. Imagine that you are at this moment watching a beautiful sunset. What's happening is happening now, right? Yes and no. In one sense, the time is obviously the present, but at the same time it is the past. Remember that light travels at a fixed rate of 186,000 miles per second. The sun is 93 million miles away. That means that light takes 8 minutes to reach the earth. When you see the sun meet the horizon and then sink beneath it, you are seeing something that actually happened eight minutes ago. Starlight is an even more dramatic example of the same phenomenon. When you see the stars twinkle in the night sky, you're looking not minutes into the past but years, often millions of years.

In other words, one implication of a four-dimensional space-time is that any accurate account of "reality" must include the interrelationship between the observer, what is observed, the relative motion between them, and the speed of light. Space-time forces us to think about the universe in a much more complex way than we are accustomed to.

Four-dimensional space-time thus becomes the final standard in assessing and describing reality, and this forces us to think very differently about a lot of things. For example, relativity theory does not let us say that one of two conflicting appearances is "real" and the other "imaginary." As you recall, an observer in one frame of reference sees two lightning bolts strike simultaneously. In another frame of reference, an observer sees one strike the ground first. We cannot say that the experience of one observer is correct and the other mistaken because both of them are *three-dimensional experiences of a four-dimensional reality.*

In a sense, we're incapable of experiencing things "as they really are" because our perceptual mechanism can handle the simultaneous interrelationship of only three dimensions, not four. The limitations of this mechanism are what produce contrasting realities, the validity of which we cannot discriminate between. However, this does present us with the idea that the reality of four-dimensional space-time is in some way superior to the three-dimensional experience our brains give us.

Philosophical Implications of the Space-Time Continuum
The Poverty of Perception

These facts about space-time have some interesting philosophical implications. First, our senses become untrustworthy reporters of ultimate reality, and they cannot represent to us accurately and dependably what is happening in four-dimensional reality. When we see the workings of a four-dimensional universe through three-dimensional eyes and brains, things do not really make sense to us. As one thinker puts this,

> Moving objects look different from objects at rest, and moving clocks run at a different rate. These effects will seem paradoxical if we do not realize that they are only the projections of four-dimensional phenomena, just as shadows are projections of three-dimensional objects. If we could visualize the four-dimensional space-time reality, there would be nothing paradoxical at all.[12]

---

[12]Fritjof Capra, *The Tao of Physics* (New York: Bantam Books, 1975), pp. 157–158.

Reality ultimately does make sense. The problem is that our perceptual mechanisms are not enough in phase with the true nature of reality for us to see that it makes sense. For example, even our description of the path of our own planet is in the end faulty. The contemporary physicist Stephen Hawking writes,

> In general relativity, bodies always follow straight lines in four-dimensional space-time, but they nevertheless appear to us to move along curved paths in our three-dimensional space. . . . The mass of the sun curves space-time in such a way that although the earth follows a straight path in four-dimensional space-time, it appears to us to move along a circular orbit in three-dimensional space.[13]

What is straight motion from one frame of reference is experienced by us as curved motion. Experiencing the earth's "true motion," however, is beyond our reach because a multidimensional consciousness is beyond our nature.

Space-Time and the Past, Present, and Future

The most extraordinary thing about space-time, however, is what it says about everyday temporal concepts like the past, the present, and the future. Ordinarily these three ideas are pretty simple. The present exists but the past and the future do not.

Now look at another thinker's explanation of the difference between Newton's and Einstein's ideas:

> The Newtonian view of space and time is a *dynamic* picture. Events *develop* with the passage of time. Time is one-dimensional and *moves* (forward). The past, present, and future happen in that order. The special theory of relativity, however, says that it is preferable, and more useful, to think in terms of a *static*, nonmoving picture of space and time. This is the space-time continuum. In this static picture, the space-time continuum, events do not develop, they just are. If we could view our reality in a four-dimensional way, we would see that everything that now seems to unfold before us with the passing of time, already exists in *toto*, painted, as it were, on the fabric of space-time. We would see all, the past, the present, and the future with one glance.[14]

That is quite an idea. The past, present, and future actually exist simultaneously. Yet we experience them one after the other because we have three-dimensional minds. If we had four-dimensional minds, theoretically at least, we could experience all of time all at once.

Appearance Versus Reality: Quantum Physics and String Theory

The gap between our three-dimensional experience and a four-dimensional space-time points to a parallel gap between our perceptions of reality and reality itself.

---

[13]Stephen W. Hawking, *A Brief History of Time* (New York: Bantam Books, 1988), p. 30.
[14]Gary Zukav, *The Dancing Wu Li Masters: An Overview of the New Physics* (New York: Bantam Books, 1979), p. 150.

How well does our everyday experience capture the essence of reality? A three-dimensional representation of reality is surely different from, and less accurate than, a four-dimensional one. But how inferior is it? And how close can we come to an approximation of reality with our limited minds? These questions put us squarely in the middle of the classical philosophical dispute about whether the mind gives us reality or appearance, absolute truth or some vague shadow.

In fact, relativity theory is not alone in this. Other branches of physics also suggest the same problem.

You no doubt remember from high school science that all matter is made up of atoms. Atoms in turn are comprised of even tinier neutrons, protons, and electrons. One scientist gives an especially good description of their size:

> The diameter of an atom is about one hundred-millionth of a centimeter. In order to visualize this diminutive size, imagine an orange blown up to the size of the earth. The atoms of the orange will then have the size of cherries. Myriads of cherries, tightly packed into a globe of the size of the earth—that's a magnified picture of the atoms in an orange.
>
> An atom, therefore, is extremely small compared to macroscopic objects, but it is huge compared to the nucleus in its center. In our picture of cherry-sized atoms, the nucleus of an atom will be so small that we will not be able to see it. If we blew up the atom to the size of a football, or even to room size, the nucleus would still be too small to be seen by the naked eye. To see the nucleus, we would have to blow up the atom to the size of the biggest dome in the world, the dome of St. Peter's Cathedral in Rome. In an atom of that size, the nucleus would have the size of a grain of salt! A grain of salt in the middle of the dome of St. Peter's, and specks of dust whirling around it in the vast space of the dome—this is how we can picture the nucleus and electrons of an atom.[15]

The objects we perceive with our senses, then, are not solid. They only appear that way. Ultimately, they are made up of extremely small particles speeding around in what from their point of view is a huge amount of empty space. The illusion that the object is solid comes from the speed at which the particles within each atom whirl around. Electrons move around the nucleus at about 600 miles per second; the neutrons and protons move within the nucleus at 40,000 miles per second. The effect of such fast motion is similar to the effect that occurs when the blades of a table fan go around. When the fan is stopped, you can see the individual blades. When the fan is running, the moving blades look like a single hazy circular object. Although the materials out of which a fan is made could not actually take the stress, if you could speed up the fan to the pace at which electrons move, that hazy circle would gradually solidify into a single disc. The blades would be moving so fast that they would create the illusion of a solid object. Thus, our senses again seem to give us an "appearance" that is very different from actual "reality."

[15]Capra, *Tao of Physics*, p. 54.

Subatomic Particles and Quantum Mechanics

Subatomic reality differs from the world of our senses in a variety of other ways as well. In fact, starting in the early twentieth century, the world of subatomic particles spawned a separate branch of physics called *quantum mechanics*. The picture that emerges from the work of scientists like Max Planck, Niels Bohr, Werner Heisenberg, and others is so strange that Bohr once remarked, "Anyone who is not dizzy after his first acquaintance with the quantum of action has not understood a word." For example:

- The behavior of subatomic particles cannot be predicted with certainty. It is a world of *probabilities*. Scientists may be able to predict flawlessly what will happen when two billiard balls strike each other, but they can do nothing of the sort for the elementary particles of the atoms that make up those balls. As physicist Brian Greene explains it, at a microscopic level, "the best we can ever do is say that an electron has a particular probability of being found at any location."[16]

- A particle can be in different places at the same time. Physicist Richard Feynman interpreted a famous experiment aimed at determining the movement of an electron by claiming that, in getting from point A to point B, the electron simultaneously took an infinite number of paths—a perspective that was subsequently verified by mathematical calculations. Recognizing how counterintuitive the conclusions of quantum mechanics might seem, Feynman nonetheless cautioned against relying on our "common sense" to decide whether or not scientific theories were true. He said, "The theory of quantum electrodynamics describes Nature as absurd from the point of view of common sense. And it fully agrees with experiment. So I hope you can accept Nature as She is—absurd."[17]

- It's impossible to determine both the position and the velocity of a particle. According to Werner Heisenberg's "uncertainty principle," the more precisely we determine the position of a particle, the less precise becomes our measurement of the particle's velocity, and vice versa.

The Even Stranger World of String Theory

As odd as the conclusions of quantum mechanics are, however, they seem tame when compared to the most recent school of thought in contemporary physics, *string theory*. String theory has arisen out of a serious problem in physics. Einstein's General Relativity theory works with large objects (like planets and stars); quantum mechanics works with very small objects (atoms and subatomic particles); but neither approach explains all of reality. What was needed, then, was a "theory of everything" that would unify the two. Since the last few decades of the twentieth century, string theory has been seen by many physicists as the best candidate.[18]

At the outset, string theory doesn't seem unusually controversial. It's called "string" theory because it's based on the claim that the ultimate building blocks of

---

[16]Brian Greene, *The Elegant Universe* (New York: Vintage Books, 1999), p. 206.
[17]Richard Feynman, *QED: The Strange Theory of Light and Matter* (Princeton: Princeton University Press, 1988).
[18]For an excellent overview of string theory, see Brian Greene, *The Elegant Universe* (New York: Vintage Books, 1999).

reality aren't subatomic particles, but even smaller vibrating one-dimensional strings of energy. Just as different vibrations of a musical string will produce different notes, so the different ways that strings vibrate give particles their properties. However, the mathematics connected with string theory gives us an unusual picture of reality.

- In our everyday experience, reality has four dimensions (length, width, depth, and time). The expression of string theory in what is called "M-theory" claims that reality has *seven* more spatial dimensions. Because these dimensions manifest themselves at the level of strings, they are too small for us to observe with our senses or even, at this point, to be detected experimentally. Nonetheless, the mathematics of string theory argues that reality actually has eleven dimensions.

- In addition to new dimensions, string theory asserts the possibility of parallel universes. Physicist Brian Greene explains that a reality of eleven dimensions allows strings to stretch to become "membranes," and that with enough energy, a membrane could even grow to be the size of a universe. Moreover, says Greene, "The existence of giant membranes and extra dimensions would open up a startling new possibility, that our whole universe is living on a membrane, inside a much larger, higher dimensional space. It's almost as if we were living inside a loaf of bread. Our universe might be like a slice of bread, just one slice, in a much larger loaf that physicists sometimes call the 'bulk.' And if these ideas are right, the bulk may have other slices, other universes, that are right next to ours, in effect, 'parallel' universes. Not only would our universe be nothing special, but we could have a lot of neighbors. Some of them could resemble our universe, they might have matter and planets and, who knows, maybe even beings of a sort. Others certainly would be a lot stranger. They might be ruled by completely different laws of physics. Now, all of these other universes would exist within the extra dimensions of M-theory, dimensions that are all around us. Some even say they might be right next to us, less than a millimeter away."[19]

Whether we look at reality from the perspective of relativity theory, quantum mechanics, or string theory, we are left with the same question: Do the conclusions we formulate in our minds based on evidence of our senses really give us accurate knowledge about *reality*, or is everything we "know" merely speculation about *appearance?*

Where Are We?

What have we seen on our journey from Newton to string theory, from the speed of light to black holes, subatomic particles, strings, and membranes?

First, modern physicists tell us that the universe is a much more complicated place than it first looks to be. Reality appears a certain way from our usual frame of reference, but it is very different in the world of subatomic particles 2nd strings and in the cosmic world where objects travel at close to the speed of light.

Second, space and time are far more variable than Newton thought or than we realize in our daily lives. In relativity theory, they are not even distinct entities. They are space-time.

---

[19]"NOVA—The Elegant Universe: Welcome to the 11th Dimension," (Boston: WGBH Educational Foundation, 2003).

Third, the flexibility and changeability of space-time and the fact that scientists can talk only about probability at a subatomic level limit the degree to which notions like "absolute certainty" and "objective truth" even belong in scientific discourse any more.

Finally, the idea that reality has eleven dimensions while we can experience things only in three dimensions raises serious questions about how well we can ever grasp "reality." We may have to settle only for "appearance."

These statements raise exciting issues, but they're also somewhat discouraging. Where do they leave us as we return to the claim we noted at the outset of this chapter—that the proofs and certainties of science make it vastly superior to the abstract speculations of philosophy? Doesn't it seem that with regard to certainties, theoretical physics and philosophy are very similar?

Science now tells us that the spatial and temporal qualities of an object are relative to the frame of reference from which it is observed. Not only that, they are also influenced by the object's mass and the speed at which it is traveling. Space and time are not even distinct; rather, they exist as a single four-dimensional continuum. And because our senses can pick up only four dimensions, we can know only a world that is very different from the world that is real. Indeed, we cannot even observe much that is important about physical phenomena from electrons to black holes. In short, the "truth" about reality seems about as abstract and as contrary to our ordinary perceptions as is imaginable. The conclusions of science certainly defy what our common sense tells us.

Science does not even provide us with "proofs." The criterion for believing some theory seems to be that it "works." When it stops working, as Newton's theory did after 300 years, science declares it untrue and picks up on something new. Einstein's relativity theory worked better than Newton's mechanical theory. And then quantum mechanics and string theory came along. Is there any chance that they will be replaced by another theory that works still better? You can count on it.

Like physicists, philosophers offer all kinds of accounts of reality that claim to be closer to the essence of things than what our senses give us. We, too, are constantly considering new theories that purport to be better than the ones before. Is there a final word on things in philosophy? No more than there seems to be in science.

What conclusions can we draw from all of this?

First, we are entitled to question just how much certain knowledge an empirical approach can give us about the nature of reality. Science does not merely grow out of empiricism, it is the model of an empirical approach. And yet contemporary physics presents us with a picture of reality that is as abstract, intangible, and confusing as anything we find in a speculative, rationalistic, philosophical account of reality. In fact, because so little of string theory is testable, some physicists think it's more appropriate to consider it "philosophy," not "science." Perhaps we should consider the possibility that, despite what our culture holds about the value of "scientific" inquiry, empiricism does not have the inside track on truth and certainty.

Second, both science and philosophy conclude that reality is very different from what appears to our senses to be the case. Whether we look at Plato's claims or Einstein's, the theme is constant that the essence of reality, whatever that may be, certainly is not what it seems to be. This implies that in order to understand reality, we must be radically skeptical about what seems "self-evident" and radically open-minded to alternative conceptions about the nature of reality, no matter how unusual they may seem.

Third, if what Newton had thought were fixed, absolute, and unshakable cornerstones of reality—space and time—turn out to be as variable as we have seen, wouldn't the same hold for the "truths" that human societies, religions, and organizations take to be too obvious to question? At the very least, this suggests that we should also be skeptical about the values, traditions, and beliefs of our society's social, political, and religious institutions and that we be open-minded to alternative ways of thinking.

In short, both science and philosophy jointly suggest that the search for truth invariably leads to the unexpected, the unusual, even the fantastic.

Main Points of Chapter 12

1. Although there are obvious differences between science and philosophy, there are also strong similarities. Science grew out of philosophy's empirical tradition, and both have the same overall goal—understanding and explaining reality. Physics in particular addresses two fundamental features of reality: space and time.

2. Isaac Newton's mechanistic account of the universe argues that space and time are absolute, unchanging, and unaffected by any object or action that takes place in the universe. The laws of motion also hold consistently throughout the universe.

3. Einstein replaced Newton's mechanistic picture of the universe with a relativistic one. The only constant in the universe, argued Einstein, is the speed of light. Rejecting the idea of absolute space and time, Einstein claimed that time and space are affected by motion, slowing down and shortening, respectively, as an object speeds up relative to a stationary observer. Yet at the same time, time and space are stable relative to the frame of reference of a moving object; and no judgment can be made about which frame of reference is "correct." Space can also be "bent" by matter and gravity. The relationship between space and time led Einstein to posit a space-time continuum.

4. Einstein's theory of relativity has important philosophical consequences about appearance versus reality, suggesting the possibility of "alternate realities." Similar philosophical difficulties involving appearance and reality also arise from the conclusions of quantum mechanics and string theory.

5. All of this calls into question not only our commonsense conclusions about reality, but how much an empirical approach can uncover with absolute certainty about the nature of reality.

Discussion Questions

1. How would you characterize a "scientific" approach? What does science tell us? Does science give us a different or better understanding of phenomena than philosophy does? Would you have answered these questions any differently before you read this chapter?

2. How does Newton's description of the universe fit with your commonsense ideas of reality? Would it be safe to say that most people today are Newtonians in the conceptions of space and time they use in their everyday lives?

3. Have you ever had an experience in your everyday life that even remotely suggests the conclusions about space and time that relativity theory draws? Hardly anyone has. What is your reaction to the idea that the ultimate nature of reality is something completely different than our senses suggest, and what might this mean in concrete terms for your life?

4. Think some more about the "relativity of simultaneity" and the example of the two lightning bolts. How do you handle the idea that the lightning bolts strike both *at the same time* and *not at the same time*? This seems logically impossible, so how can it be true? What is your reaction to the idea that reality can be this flexible?

5. Do the conclusions of relativity theory mean that *knowledge* of reality is impossible? Or must knowledge claims always be qualified by some reference to a "frame of reference"? Is truth, then, always conditional?

6. What beliefs are as fundamental in your life as conceptions of space and time are in the thinking of a scientist? In light of what you have learned in this chapter, should you be so certain of these ideas? If time and space—the two most fundamental dimensions of reality—are fluid and relative, how can anything else be certain and absolute?

7. What's your reaction to string theory's claim that there could be parallel universes?

8. Most of us are uncomfortable with people who are thoroughgoing skeptics or wild visionaries. Indeed, our societies discourage and often punish such people for their unconventional ideas. In view of the fact that the search for truth apparently leads to unexpected and unusual ideas, is it possible that most societies actually do not want to learn the truth about reality?

Selected Readings

Isaac Newton's main ideas can be found in his *Philosophiae Naturalis Principia Mathematica (Mathematical Principles of Natural Philosophy)*. Albert Einstein gives an account of his ideas for a general audience in *Relativity* (New York: Crown Publishers, 1961). For popular accounts of modern physics see: Fritjof Capra, *The Tao of Physics* (New York: Bantam Books, 1975); Stephen W. Hawking, *A Brief History of Time* (New York: Bantam Books, 1988); Joe Schwartz and Michael McGuinness, *Einstein for Beginners* (New York: Pantheon Books, 1979); and Gary Zukav, *The Dancing Wu Li Masters: An Overview of the New Physics* (New York: Bantam Books, 1979). For string theory, see: Brian Greene, *The Elegant Universe* (New York: Vintage Books, 1999).

Does Gender Affect How We Think?

- *Knowledge: "Male" Versus "Female" Ways of Knowing*
- *Gender and Ethics*
- *Ethics: "Masculine" Justice Versus "Feminine" Care*
- *A Final Note*

You may think of the "women's movement" and "feminism" as political movements that had mainly social and legal consequences. However, one of their most important legacies has been a growing body of research into the intellectual consequences of our society having been so resolutely male-dominated for so many years. In the early 1980s, some female psychologists began to recognize that the subjects of some critical studies in developmental psychology had been all male. So they set about to determine whether these all-male studies had missed anything significant from the research because they'd excluded women. Concentrating on two areas—how humans arrive at "knowledge" and how we develop a sense of ethics—these researchers discovered that when the subjects of the study were women, the results were different from the male-only research. Different approaches to knowledge and ethics had been completely overlooked by the classic studies, and this raised a series of fundamental questions:

- Where did the differences come from? What percentage of men thinks in ways that were discovered in the female-only studies?

- How much of how we define "male," "female," "masculine," and "feminine" comes from biology, and how much comes from cultural forces?

- The male-only research established norms for the "more advanced" versus "less advanced" stages of development. How many of the men fell into a "less advanced" stage because they actually thought in ways that were only uncovered in the newer studies?

- How strongly do sex and culture shape the way we think?

- How much is scientific research—which aims at being impartial and objective—actually influenced by power relationships in a society?

- When we discover that traditional research has been influenced by society's sexual stereotypes, how do we go about getting a more accurate picture of the issues under investigation?

The source of the differences that the researchers found remains an open question. However, the data at least lead us to wonder whether gender might be a factor in how men and women experience reality.

As interesting as this possibility might be, what does such psychological research have to do with philosophy? Psychology started as a part of philosophy; it is now a behavioral science, and its fundamental goal—understanding and explaining our inner world—is similar to philosophy's preoccupation with the human mind and human action. The boundary between psychology and philosophy is often blurred. The philosopher William James was also one of the founding spirits of American psychology. And, as you saw earlier in this book, the theories of psychologists Sigmund Freud and B. F. Skinner have important implications about such philosophical issues as free will and moral responsibility.

Our rationale for considering the philosophical aspects of this psychological research, then, is exactly the same as the rationale we used in the last chapter for considering the philosophical implications of theoretical physics. As philosophers, we want to know as much as possible about the nature of reality, about how we perceive it, and about what makes us tick. If behavioral scientists can illuminate such fundamental philosophical issues as knowledge and ethics, we are interested. In this chapter, then, we ask: Do males and females have unique ways of thinking, of knowing, even of perceiving right and wrong? Where might such differences come from? What are they? And what might be their philosophical and practical implications?

Before we look at the research, however, we should recognize the problems and limitations of any investigation into basic differences in the way men and women think. The research is still in its infancy, the theories that we will look at are going through considerable testing, criticism, and revision. Yet even if the hypothesized differences hold up, identifying their cause is another matter. What in us is produced by "nature" and what by "nurture"? What might be accounted for by differences in the body structure, hormones, or brain structures of women and men? What might be accounted for by the fact that boys and girls are treated differently almost from the moment they are born? Virtually nothing, at this point, is settled about such questions, so be careful that you don't conclude too much from the following theories.

In particular, don't be upset if you share some of the characteristics attributed to the opposite sex. One point emerging from the research is that the hypothesized differences may very well relate less to *sex*, that is, whether we are biologically "male" or "female," and more to *gender*, that is, the traits and roles our society as traditionally labeled "masculine" or "feminine." Indeed, because we all have both masculine and feminine traits in our personalities, it would be surprising if you did not resemble the other gender to some degree.

Because the work on this topic is at such an early stage, then, we can only engage in a tentative exploration of some preliminary psychological research and speculate about some interesting philosophical questions. Nonetheless, to the extent that this inquiry stimulates our thinking about some of the fundamental features of the human experience, it aids our development as philosophers.[1]

Knowledge: "Male" Versus "Female" Ways of Knowing

We live in a society whose traditional sex-role stereotypes have included a difference in men's and women's ideas about knowledge, for example, what counts as a "fact," or what is the most important evidence to cite in trying to prove something. The traditional "male" approach has been to be objective and to argue logically. The traditional "female" approach, on the other hand, has been to be subjective and to argue intuitively. Because of our society's fascination with science and technology, however, the "female" approach to knowledge has been judged not simply different but inferior. Modern science is an empirical enterprise demanding hard facts and theories that can be publicly confirmed by observation and experiment. Subjective and intuitive claims of knowledge are rejected, so the "male" model has generally been exalted.[2] Research suggests, however, that these two ways of defining knowledge and these two modes of arriving at truth are equal, that is, they can be equally productive.

The main psychological research on epistemological differences between women and men focuses on the ways men and women understand the concept of "knowledge," and it reveals a pattern of "developmental stages." Such "stages" are the steps we take from our first unsophisticated understanding of "knowledge" to a mature understanding of the concept.[3] This research suggests critical differences both in how men and women understand the concept of "knowledge" and in how they arrive at the advanced stages of these different ways of knowing.

Perry's Stages of "Male" Knowing

The base-line research on developmental stages of knowledge was done by the Harvard psychologist William Perry.[4] Perry set out to describe the stages all people go through in progressing from an elementary to an advanced conception of "knowledge." The

---

[1]Because so little is definite about which of the hypothesized differences are related to sex and which to gender, the terms "female" and "feminine," and "male" and "masculine," should be understood in this chapter as meaning the same thing rather than differentiating between biological identity and traits or roles. Also, even though, for the sake of making the chapter easier to read, we will refer to "differences in the ways that men and women think," it is important to realize this is just a shorthand for something like "differences that have been uncovered when comparing the results between the male-only studies and the female-only studies and that may or may not have some direct relationship to sex or gender." In other words, the causes and significance of the differences discovered will be explored for many years. So be careful about the conclusions you draw from such early findings.

[2]Intuition as a way of knowing is by no means universally disparaged. In Eastern religions and Western mysticism, intuition is the primary method of achieving understanding, and two important modern Western philosophers, Baruch Spinoza and Henri Bergson, maintain that intuition is the only way to grasp the ultimate nature of reality. Both rationalism and idealism have had their defenders since the first days of philosophy in ancient Greece, but the "official" outlook of the modern West is scientific, logical, and empirical.

[3]Unlike theories of the developmental stages of childhood, the theories we consider here do not necessarily link each stage to a particular age. Neither do they portray progress from one stage to another as inevitable. Thus we can have a physically mature adult whose epistemological or ethical development remains at an early stage.

[4]See William B. Perry, Jr., *Forms of Intellectual and Ethical Development in the College Years* (New York: Holt, Rinehart and Winston, Inc., 1968).

vast majority of the subjects he studied were male, and when Perry drew up his con-clusions, he assumed that what was true of men was true of women as well. Many researchers believe that because Perry's sample is mainly male, it does not give an accurate or complete picture, however. After we look at Perry's model, we consider the findings of a more recent group of researchers who have proposed quite a differ-ent model.

Perry identifies nine developmental stages, the last three of which have more to do with emotional development than with knowledge. If we simplify the other six, we can summarize the process Perry describes in four general stages.[5] Perry's sub-jects were college students, so the progress he traced from the elementary to the advanced stages occurred over only a few years in the students' lives.

Stage 1: Duality

In the first stage, Perry contends, we believe that knowledge is clear and unam-biguous, with right and wrong answers to every question. Perry calls this stage *duality* because whenever a problem comes up, we envision its solution in one of only two ways: Either something is "right" or it is "wrong"; it is "true" or it is "false." We see all problems as being like those in a spelling bee or in arithmetic. There is only one correct way to spell "e-p-i-s-t-e-m-o-l-o-g-i-c-a-l." The math problem "$(2 + 3) - (21 \times 2) = x$" has only one right answer (-37). Every other answer is wrong. At this stage of development, then, we understand "knowledge" as amount-ing to the facts, the right answers.

These facts are external, known by the authorities and experts, and we acquire them by passively absorbing what these experts—our parents, our teachers—say. They know; they have the truth. We don't, so we listen to what they say and absorb it.

Stage 2: Unacceptable Multiplicity

In Perry's second stage, which we can call *unacceptable multiplicity,* we realize that authorities disagree about what is and is not so, but we reject these differences of opinion. We think either that only one authority is right and the others are frauds or that all of them are incompetent. "Knowledge," we still believe, is having "the answer" or knowing "the facts." If we cannot decide who is right, we conclude that no one has discovered "the answer" yet. We are more aware of diversity of opinion than we were in the previous stage, but we still think that there is only one truth out there and everything else is a lie or a mistake.

At this stage, we would have trouble with a task like reading books by differ-ent historians who give opposing explanations for what caused World War I, for example. We would think, "What is this? How can two experts disagree about some-thing like that?" Confronted with the difference of opinion, we might think that one must be wrong. Or we might conclude that history is rubbish. At this point, we haven't learned how to handle such complex and uncertain matters.

In either of these stages, when we believe that knowledge is all about "answers" and "facts," we probably think that, for example, "discussion classes" are a waste of

---

[5]In this overview, Perry's language has been made less technical and more descriptive.

time. Who cares what the other students in our class think? They don't know any more, and perhaps less, than we do. They certainly don't have "the answer"—the teacher does. So we usually think at this point that our professor should lecture on the course subject, explain the material to us, and tell us what we have to know. We may even be unhappy with what the teacher has to say if he or she focuses on abstract material. At these early stages in our development, we have little patience for theory. Knowledge is factual and true, while theories are speculative and not yet proven. We may think that anything short of certainty is as big a waste of time as the opinions of our fellow students.

Stage 3: Acceptable Multiplicity

As we grow beyond these early phases, however, we begin to realize that for many questions there is simply no one "right" answer. There is no set of facts that tells us the way things really are. In this stage of our thinking, a stage we can call *acceptable multiplicity,* we now tolerate differences of opinion among experts without believing that all but one of them is wrong or that all experts are charlatans. We usually explain this to ourselves by saying that everyone has a right to his or her own opinion and that all opinions are equally good. At this stage we reject a single ultimate truth and opt for the truth of all subjective points of view. The only authority we acknowledge at this stage is the individual herself or himself. Thus, there are as many "truths" as there are people to conceive of them.

Many college freshmen and sophomores are at this stage of "acceptable multiplicity." They have begun to doubt the infallibility of the authorities they used to accept—parents, teachers, ministers, the government—but they cannot yet deal with the wide diversity of opinion about everything they encounter. They make sense of this by saying that all of us have our own truths. Most students, for example, become much more tolerant of other people's religions. Most of us begin by believing that the faith we are reared in is the one true religion. But as we are exposed to people of different faiths, and become familiar with other religions, we usually conclude that while our beliefs are right for us, other beliefs are just as right for other people.

Stage 4: Relativism

In the final developmental stage, which Perry calls *relativism,* we make our peace with the conflicting opinions we encounter. We come to understand that truth and knowledge are not absolutes "out there" that some authority hands down or that we discover on our own. But we also learn that all opinions are not created equal. We insist on "informed or educated opinions." When we reach this stage in our thinking, we want people to give us the reasons behind their opinions so that we can judge for ourselves whether or not their conclusions are warranted.

Most important, we now come to understand that "knowledge" is not a "given," not some fixed entity sitting and waiting for us to discover it whole. Rather, it is "constructed" in some way. Furthermore, the content of knowledge is always the result of some particular point of view or intellectual approach.

For example, what was the domestic conflict that took place in the United States between 1861 and 1865? Was it the "War between the States" or the "Civil War"?

What issues was it fought over? Did hostilities break out in defense of states' rights? Did they occur when Northern, industrial interests tried to break the back of the Southern economy? Or was the war fought to preserve the unity of the Union while wiping out the institution of slavery within the nation's boundaries? All these explanations for the war are "true" even though they seem incompatible. Each explanation depends on how you look at the issues. If you really want to know about that war, then you have to understand these and many other viewpoints, balance them out, and do the best you can to figure out what "really" happened.

From Duality to Relativism: Historical Knowledge

If you think back over your history courses in high school, you will remember that you were largely presented with "facts" to memorize about some important event—what happened, what caused it, when it took place, and who were the major players. You may have learned that a key event that began the Protestant Reformation was Martin Luther's dramatic posting of his "ninety-five theses" on the door of the Castle Chapel in Wittenberg in 1517. On a test, you either knew the right facts or you didn't. There was no middle ground. History was as definite as math and science. This is as good an example as any of Perry's "dualistic" developmental stage.

In college, however, history is taught differently. The facts about events are less definite and more complex. You quickly find out that much debate goes on about what actually happened and about what caused these events. For example, Luther probably never actually nailed his ninety-five theses to any church door. And even if he did, such a gesture was not an unusual action in the sixteenth century for someone who wanted to put people on notice that he wanted to debate some issues.

Not only does the study of history at the college level expose you to more, often contradictory, information, it shows you how "facts" about people and events are interpreted differently by people holding different viewpoints. The Protestant Reformation, for example, can be accounted for in many ways. It can be seen as the product of political factors—the rise of the nation state and German nationalism in particular—or of economic factors—the emergence of a stable postfeudal middle class. It can be accounted for by individual theological doctrines—Luther's belief in the primacy of the Bible—and by social and moral analysis—rampant corruption and other abuses in the Catholic church.

Thus, to achieve historical "knowledge" we must synthesize a vast amount of information before we can make sense out of any of it. Only then can we make our peace with complex and competing theories and construct an explanation of events that satisfies us. Only when we can manage conflicting points of view and achieve our own understanding of history have we arrived at Perry's "relativistic" stage of knowledge.

Belenky et al.'s Stages of "Female" Knowing

Perry's stages seem reasonable and universal, don't they? There's nothing here about a "male" versus "female" approach to knowledge. Indeed, Perry assumes that these stages capture equally well the ways that men *and* women develop a mature and sophisticated conception of knowledge.

Not so, says one group of female psychologists—Mary Field Belenky, Blythe McVicker Clinchy, Nancy Rule Goldberger, and Jill Mattuck Tarule (hereafter "Belenky et al."). Concerned about the preponderance of male subjects in Perry's study, Belenky et al. conducted similar research using a group of exclusively female subjects. These researchers discovered a series of stages that are in important respects unlike Perry's, and this led them to hypothesize some important differences in how men and women develop an advanced concept of knowledge.[6]

Both developmental models start with knowledge as black or white, true or false, right or wrong. Both research teams also agree that an advanced understanding of the concept regards knowledge as more "constructed" than "discovered," with truth less precise and less objective than it seemed at first. Beyond this, however, Belenky et al. find that the women in their study progress toward an advanced concept of knowledge by a different path than men take. They see four stages in this process: *received knowledge, subjective knowledge, procedural knowledge,* and *constructed knowledge.*[7]

Stage 1: Received Knowledge

As the term implies, *received knowledge* is much like Perry's *duality.* Knowledge is what some external authority says it is. Things are either true or false. But, Belenky et al. point out, men in the "duality" stage are able to see *themselves* as authority, to identify with it. Thus, they construct a world of "us" versus "them." Of course, "we" are right and "they" are wrong, so men learn to see things as "authority/right/we" versus "illegitimate/wrong/they." Women, these researchers suggest, do not do this. They remain passive in the face of authority, which belongs to "them." They receive knowledge the way that Moses supposedly received the Ten Commandments from God. Their experience at this stage is "authority/right/*they.*"

Stage 2: Subjective Knowledge

The second stage in a woman's developing conception of knowledge is marked by an emerging sense that external authorities are no longer the source of all knowledge. This kind of knowledge is called *subjective knowledge.* Truths are now seen as personal, private, subjective, and, most importantly, intuitive. Like those in Perry's "unacceptable" and "acceptable multiplicity" stages, women at this point still assume that there are "right answers." But instead of coming from outside authorities, they now see those answers as arising within the individual. In other words, personal experience becomes a more solid basis of knowledge than the judgments of experts outside the self.

The comparison with Perry's "multiplicity" stages is somewhat apt. In this stage, Belenky's subjects resolve the confusion of opposing authorities by making *themselves*

---

[6]This theory was first described in Mary Field Relenky, Blythe McVicker Clinchy, Nancy Rule Goldberger, and Jill Mattuck Tarule, *Women's Ways of Knowing: The Development of Self, Voice, and Mind* (New York: Basic Books, 1986). See also, *Knowledge, Difference and Power: Essays Inspired by Women's Ways of Knowing,* edited by Nancy Goldberger, Jill Tarule, Blythe Clinchy and Mary Belenky (New York: Basic Books, 1996).

[7]Belenky et al. posit an additional stage, silence, sometimes found before "received knowledge." They describe it as a rare and extreme form of "denial of self" and "dependence on external authority for direction." We will pass over this stage because it is characterized more by the absence of than the presence of a conception of knowledge.

the authority. The difference lies in the emergence of "women's intuition." Knowledge is not achieved through some special methodology, such as science. Instead, it's something a woman "just knows." Whether or not something is true depends on "how it feels" inside. While convinced of the truth of what they know, women at this stage of knowledge usually believe that it is true only for themselves and that it is impossible to communicate their truths to others. They may reject logic, rational analysis, and the methods of science because they seem too impersonal and too far removed from an immediate, subjective experience. They do, however, continue to believe in the validity of their intuitive knowledge.

Stage 3: Procedural Knowledge: Separate Knowing and Connected Knowing

The next stage of development shows the women of the study leaving the personal and subjective for a more objective and rational kind of knowledge. Belenky's team call this *procedural knowledge* because knowledge is now seen as resulting from the procedures and techniques of conventional intellectual inquiry. Women with the idea that knowledge is "procedural" no longer rely on intuition alone but come to appreciate different points of view, different ways of looking at issues. (Here, again, note the similarity to Perry's "multiplicity" stages.) At this stage, Belenky et al. claim, women can go in one of two different directions. They identify these two forms of procedural knowledge as *separate knowing* and *connected knowing.*

Separate knowing is called "separate" because the knower removes herself as much as possible from the matter being investigated. The procedures adopted for establishing truth, then, are as impersonal as they can be. "Separate knowing" is the methodology of science and logic. It prizes "hard facts," impartial reason, critical thinking, analysis, and skepticism. Knowledge is established through an adversarial process in which people offer their theories for criticism and question, reformulate their ideas in response to challenges, and criticize other people's theories. Knowledge and truth emerge as the ultimate products of this clash of opposing positions.

"Separate knowing" is the kind of knowledge we find in science and, for the most part, in all scholarship. Its method is objective, impartial, and adversarial. If experiments lead one scientist to a new discovery, other scientists immediately repeat those experiments to prove or disprove the conclusion. Nothing is accepted as true until everything about it has been impartially tested, retested, scrutinized, and challenged. Then and only then does a new fact become "true." This kind of knowledge is the exact opposite of the intensely personal intuitive knowledge achieved in the previous stage.

Although Belenky and the others identify "separate knowing" as a path that women may take, they see it as more characteristically masculine. Most men rely on the methodology of "separate knowing." Whether they are in science, in business, or in government, they believe that the proper way to proceed is impartially and impersonally. They assess facts and analyze problems with "cold, hard reason." Feelings must not get in the way. Women who use this methodology are essentially adopting the dominant procedure in Western culture—and the one generally endorsed by men—for acquiring knowledge.

Belenky et al. say that more women gravitate toward the other form of procedural knowledge, "connected knowing." *Connected knowing* represents an advance over "subjective knowing," but it too utilizes the deeply personal knowledge that "subjective knowers" find so hard to communicate to others. It relies primarily on empathy, the feeling of what it is like to be in someone else's shoes.

The first form of procedural knowledge, "separate knowing," is accomplished through the adversarial and ideally impersonal means of arguments and *debates*. "Connected knowing," on the other hand, works through *discussion* and *dialogue*, which produce a different but equally useful kind of information. Obviously this can come about only through relationships with others. Only through extended personal contact, particularly with those who hold different viewpoints, can we expand our vision of the world.

Personal exchanges are obviously very different from dispassionate analysis. Learning from personal relationships requires emotional as well as intellectual abilities. Conversation depends not only on the listener's sensitivity and empathy but on feelings of mutual trust. Separate knowing proceeds by means of skepticism and criticism. Connected knowing, on the other hand, grows the opposite way, through acceptance and tolerance. Separate knowing requires the mind to be active and aggressive, probing for details and attacking arguments; connected knowing depends on a gentler, more receptive state of mind. The connected knower grows in understanding by listening, absorbing, and processing someone else's feelings and ideas. Despite its personal nature, however, "connected knowing" also seeks objective understanding. Both separate and connected knowing have the goal of accurate knowledge.

Perry's model, of course, contains no parallel to the intuition of "subjective knowing," just as it contains no parallel to "connected knowing." When searching for knowledge, most men will look for facts, scrutinize the evidence, and argue about it. Nothing in Perry's pattern of epistemological development suggests that men ever consider feelings of empathy and trust or personal relationships to be important tools in the quest for knowledge. Thus Belenky and her group point to a very important difference here.

Stage 4: Constructed Knowledge

The final stage in the development of a conception of knowledge described by Belenky and her colleagues is the point at which women try to reconcile and integrate the opposing epistemological strategies they have encountered. Now that they are aware of the two different approaches to knowledge—objective, scientific, and rational versus subjective, intuitive, and emotional—they try to blend the two, preserving the good qualities of each. When they can make this synthesis, they achieve what Belenky et al. call *constructed knowledge*. Two basic insights underlie constructed knowledge. One is that *all knowledge is constructed*. The other is that *the knower is an intimate part of the known*.

To say "all knowledge is constructed" is to realize that even the most obvious facts exist only within some frame of reference, some model or theory. Thus, facts have no independent meaning; they take on meaning only as they are used within some context, or point of view. Seen this way, truth is fashioned, not discovered.

Consider, for example, the "fact" that Columbus discovered America. What could be more objective than that? However, this "fact" depends on a particular point of view, that of a Western European. The native Americans who lived here knew this continent was here before Columbus arrived. To them Columbus did not "discover" this land, he intruded upon it. Only to Europeans did he "discover" it. Similarly, the year in which Columbus's landing took place is not called "1492" by everyone. For example, the Chinese calendar, the Jewish calendar, and the native American calendar all record the year quite differently. Thus, in a number of ways, the "fact" that Christopher Columbus discovered America in 1492 is a piece of constructed knowledge, a description of an event interpreted in terms of a particular point of view. In order to understand this or any other fact, one must know in what way it is a construction.

When seeking to understand something, then, constructivist knowers explore what lies behind a question. They step outside the frame of reference of a question and look at who asked it, why it was asked, and how it can be answered. They see any knowledge claimed as part of a context, and that is where they look first in trying to comprehend it.

The second insight, "the knower is an intimate part of the known," pushes constructed knowing well beyond traditional, objective ways of knowing. Belenky's team found that distance and objectivity are irrelevant to the most advanced conception of knowledge held by the women they studied. A full understanding of something is impossible, they claim, as long as you remain totally detached from what you are investigating. You must feel connected to it, not separate from it. The researchers put it this way:

> Constructivists establish a communion with what they are trying to understand. They use the language of intimacy to describe the relationship between the knower and the known. . . . [For example,] Barbara McClintock, whose important work on the genetics of corn plants won her a Nobel prize, used the language of intimacy in describing her way of doing science. She told her biographer, Evelyn Fox Keller, that you had to have the patience "to hear what [the corn] has to say to you" and the openness "to let it come to you." McClintock could write the biography of each of her corn plants. As she said, "I know them intimately, and I find it a great pleasure to know them."
>
> —Women's Ways of Knowing

Another way to come at this is to say that *believing* is more important than *doubting*. In philosophy and science, we approach new data, new theories, and new claims with skepticism. Only by challenging all claims can we discern whether or not they are true. Belenky et al. say that "constructivist knowers" hold that a better way to comprehend something new is to see what it feels like to believe that it is true. Instead of doubting something, we should try it on for size. If you are a Christian confronting Buddhism for the first time, try to imagine what the world would look like if you were a devout Buddhist. If you read a blistering attack on capitalism, don't automatically reject it. See how things would seem if you accepted that point of view. Doing this gives us new insights that we cannot have as long as we remain apart from our subject. The knower who becomes an intimate part of the known can make discoveries that more than compensate for any loss of objectivity.

From Received Knowledge to Constructed Knowledge

What Belenky and her colleagues describe, then, is a process by which a woman develops an increasingly complex kind of knowledge. She begins with an elementary sense that truth is a matter of black and white that is handed down by some external authority. This is "received knowledge." As she develops an awareness of the validity of her own viewpoint, she rejects external knowledge and comes to believe that truth is personal and intuitive. This is called "subjective knowledge." In the next stage, "procedural knowledge," she may adopt the objective approach of science—"separate knowing"—but more often opts for a more empathic approach—"connected knowing."

Ultimately, she seeks to blend all these disparate elements, the subjective and the objective, the intuitive and the logical, the personal and the impersonal, into a mature kind of knowing called "constructed knowledge." She takes contradictions and ambiguities and fashions a coherent understanding of a question, combining a critical awareness of its context with a willingness to dissolve the boundaries between knower and known.

"Male" and "Female" Knowledge Compared

Both Perry and Belenky et al. sketch stages of epistemological development that are roughly similar. Some of the differences that they note, however, are more intriguing.

The most obvious similarity is the general course that men and women take as they progress from an elementary to an advanced conception of knowledge. Both start with a "black-white," "either-or" way of thinking about truth and knowledge. At this stage, both think that truth emanates from some authority. Next, both men and women reject authority in favor of a more subjective and personal conception of truth. But the most mature knowers of both sexes ultimately grow past this to an awareness that knowledge is not something discovered but created by the knower. Thus, they come to see truth as in some way both subjective and objective.

While the general outlines of development may be similar, however, we should note two critical differences. One involves *intuition*. The other involves *emotional detachment*.

Intuition

We all experience intuition at one time or another. Perhaps you "just know" something is going to happen—and it does. Or perhaps objective analysis tells you to do one thing but your "gut feeling" leads you to do another—and that turns out to be right.

Perry's schema, however, is silent on intuition. Men may follow a "hunch" in betting on football games or a horse race, but as a "way of knowing," intuition is alien to most men. They are usually taught to discount it, and they are likely to laugh when women use it. Belenky and her colleagues, on the other hand, describe intuition as an accepted way of knowing and a legitimate stage in a woman's epistemological development. Far from being a joke, it's an important step toward a mature conception of knowledge.

Implicit in Belenky's conclusions is the fact that intuition is not taken as a respectable avenue to knowledge in contemporary Western culture because most men do not have or do not value the experience. This suggests that logic and the scientific method are enshrined at the expense of intuition because men have been in charge. When men take the male experience as the standard against which to judge things, they imply that different ways of knowing are not merely different but inferior. This, of course, makes about as much sense as right-handed people saying that being left-handed is not just different but worse.

Whether the work of researchers like Belenky will raise intuition to a more legitimate status remains to be seen, but it certainly provokes an interesting question. Has intuition gotten a bad rap for the wrong reasons, reasons connected with who has and has not been in power?

The Role of Emotions

The other major difference between Perry's and Belenky's models lies in the provisions each makes for "emotional detachment." Perry makes it unquestionably a virtue. Belenky does not.

The Western tradition in logic, science, and philosophy holds that we should be rational and unemotional in our search for knowledge. We cannot find truth if our minds are clouded by emotion. Scientists conduct "blind" and "double-blind" studies to make sure that their results are not being influenced by the investigators themselves. Perry's highest stage of knowing "provides the ground for detachment and for objectivity," he says. So impressive does he find this ability to detach ourselves from our personal, subjective, emotional point of view that he believes "it may well rank with language as the distinctive triumph of the human mind." As one of Perry's subjects says, "I think it all boils down to trying to remove emotionalism from your decisions and from your life as much as possible."

The "female" model of Belenky and her colleagues, by contrast, suggests that such logical detachment must be supplemented by more subjectivity, by empathic attempts to connect with what we are trying to learn about. In the most advanced stage of "female" knowing, the "constructive knower" seeks out her emotions and her personal responses. She lets her perception become influenced by trust, belief, and other feelings that emerge when she empathizes with different points of view. The "constructive knower" makes a conscious attempt to get beyond the detachment that "male" knowledge sees as essential to arriving at truth.

The woman at this stage is not merely experiencing her emotions for their own sake. She is opening herself to insights that she can synthesize with those produced by more logical efforts. Thus, the most advanced knower that Belenky and her colleagues describe constructs knowledge from a wider range of data than anyone in Perry's scheme would have to work with.

The Philosophical Significance of the Difference

Belenky et al. inject a powerfully emotional element into the quest for such fundamental epistemological concepts as truth, knowledge, and understanding. Western epistemology has traditionally rejected the heart as an instrument of philosophical knowledge. But Belenky's "female knowledge" relies in various ways on personal emotional resources.

From a philosophical viewpoint, this is probably the most important aspect of Belenky's work because it calls into question basic assumptions our society makes about what counts as knowledge and what is the best way to achieve knowledge. This research also supports challenges that feminist philosophers have made to the dominant attitude toward emotion in Western philosophy. For example, Alison Jaggar, a particularly astute critic of Western epistemology, writes,

> Within the western philosophical tradition, emotions usually have been considered as potentially or actually subversive of knowledge. From Plato until the present, with a few notable exceptions, reason rather than emotion has been regarded as the indispensable faculty for acquiring knowledge. . . . Empirical testability became accepted as the hallmark of natural science; this, in turn, was viewed as the paradigm of genuine knowledge. Epistemology often was equated with the philosophy of science, and the dominant methodology of positivism prescribed that truly scientific knowledge must be capable of intersubjective verification. Because values and emotions had been defined as variable and idiosyncratic, positivism stipulated that trustworthy knowledge could be established only by methods that neutralized the values and emotions of individual scientists. . . . Thus far, however, few [have] challenged the purported gap between emotion and knowledge. . . . I wish to begin bridging this gap through the suggestion that *emotions may be helpful and even necessary rather than inimical to the construction of knowledge.*[8] [Emphasis added]

Like Belenky and her team, Jaggar argues that emotions are critical factors in achieving knowledge. She objects to the idea that emotions are passive or involuntary reactions to the world, seeing them instead as "ways in which we engage actively and even construct the world." Emotions affect our observations by "focus[ing] our attention selectively, directing, shaping, and even partially defining our observations," and they are part of our evaluation of reality. Conventionally unacceptable emotions, particularly those of people who are oppressed in a society, she argues, may even form the basis of a revision of "facts." She claims that such "outlaw emotions"

> enable us to perceive the world differently than we would from its portrayal in conventional descriptions. They may provide the first indications that something is wrong with the way alleged facts have been constructed, with accepted understandings of how things are. Conventionally unexpected or inappropriate emotions may precede our conscious recognition that accepted descriptions and justifications often conceal as much as reveal the prevailing state of affairs. Only when we reflect on our initially puzzling irritability, revulsion, anger, or fear, may we bring to consciousness our "gut-level" awareness that we are in a situation of coercion, cruelty, injustice, or danger. Thus, conventionally inexplicable emotions, particularly, though not exclusively, those experienced by women, may lead us to make subversive observations that challenge dominant conceptions of the status quo. They may help us to realize that what are taken generally to be facts have been constructed in a way that obscures the reality of subordinated people, especially women's reality.

—"Love and Knowledge"

---

[8]Alison M. Jaggar, "Love and Knowledge: Emotion in Feminist Epistemology," in *Women. Knowledge, and Reality: Explorations in Feminist Philosophy,* edited by Ann Garry and Marilyn Pearsall (Boston: Unwin Hyman, Inc., 1988), pp. 123–155. Jaggar notes that noteworthy exceptions to this rule include Hume, Nietzsche, Dewey, and James.

Emotions, Jaggar argues, have important epistemological value because they can tell us something about reality that a rational scrutiny of the world may miss. Indeed, she even makes the provocative suggestion that women's superior ability at perceiving emotions, which stems from their social roles as caretakers and emotional nurturers, give them an "epistemic advantage" over men.

Psychologists like Belenky's team and philosophers like Jagger, then, leave us with some fascinating questions. How legitimate are their claims? Do women and men have different conceptions of knowledge, and do they proceed along different developmental paths? If so, what causes these differences? Should we preserve them, or strive for a new conception of knowledge and its developmental stages that incorporates elements of both approaches? Is the dominant tradition of Western science and philosophy—a tradition that prizes detached, objective reason and disparages intuition and emotion—fundamentally flawed? Does the standard account of knowledge cover only part of what knowledge really is? Should intuition and emotion be considered legitimate, even necessary tools for achieving knowledge, and can we develop these feelings the way that we develop analytical reason?

There are more questions than answers about this topic, and research is in an early stage. But surely the issue is critically important. We must also take seriously other areas in which researchers have hypothesized differences in how men and women think, particularly with regard to how we treat each other and what constitutes "right" and "wrong."

Gender and Ethics
A Self-Inventory

The following case and accompanying questionnaire prepares you for the next stage of our discussion.

A small company's policy about sick days reads like this: "Employees are allowed a maximum of 12 sick days each year. After the 8th day, employees receive a verbal warning. After the 10th day, employees receive a written warning. Any employee exceeding the 12 days will be terminated."

Many companies have similar policies, and everyone is usually satisfied with them. One year, however, the company faced a difficult problem. Two employees, Hal and Roger, had used all 12 of their allotted sick days. Hal had been with the company for 2 years. He was a so-so worker—not great, not terrible—but his boss suspected that most of Hal's "sick" days were not legitimate and that he was just taking additional time off when he felt like it. Roger was a very good worker who had been with the company 10 years. His child had become seriously ill during the past year, however, and Roger frequently needed to take him to the hospital for treatments. He used up his vacation and personal days in this way and now he was using his sick time for the same reason. Both men were warned about their misuse of sick days. Before too long, however, both took off day 12.

Imagine that you are the executive who has to decide what happens to the two workers, and think about the situation you face. How would you describe the problem? What facts and issues in the case are most important, and how do they bear on what you do? Do you see this as an "ethical" problem? Is it "right" or "wrong" to fire the two men? What about keeping Roger and firing Hal? What implications does your action have for all the other employees of the company? What decision would you make?

Jot down your answers to these questions and compare them to those of your classmates. Pay special attention not so much to their final decision about whether or not to fire anyone but *how* they arrive at their answers. Does everybody see the problem the same way? Do they all grapple with the same issues? Does everybody agree about what the most important facts are? Is there any difference in how the men and the women in your class see things?

Next, take a few minutes and answer the following questions.

1. Which is worse?

   a. hurting someone's feelings by telling the truth

   b. telling a lie and protecting their feelings

2. Which is the worse mistake?

   a. to make exceptions too freely

   b. to apply rules too rigidly

3. Which is it worse to be?

   a. unmerciful

   b. unfair

4. Which is worse?

   a. stealing something valuable from someone for no good reason

   b. breaking a promise to a friend for no good reason

5. Which is it better to be?

   a. just and fair

   b. sympathetic and caring

6. Which is worse?

   a. not helping someone in trouble

   b. being unfair to someone by playing favorites

7. In making a decision you rely more on

   a. hard facts

   b. personal feelings and intuition

8. Your boss orders you to do something that will hurt someone. If you carry out the order, have you actually done anything wrong?

   a. yes

   b. no

9. Which is more important in determining whether an action is right or wrong?

a. whether anyone actually gets hurt

b. whether a rule, law, commandment, or moral principle is broken

As you tally up your survey answers, use the chart below and score each of your answers as either a C or a J. For example, in question 1, if your answer was a, score it as a C; if it was b, score it a J. Check all nine of your answers and then count up how many Cs and Js you have. You should have two scores when you finish. You will use these scores in the next section.

	a.	b.
1.	C	J
2.	J	C
3.	C	J
4.	J	C
5.	J	C
6.	C	J
7.	J	C
8.	C	J
9.	C	J

When you have noted your scores, we can return to the substance of this chapter.

Ethics: "Masculine" Justice Versus "Feminine" Care

The issue of what we know and how we know it is a basic issue in both philosophy and psychology. At the heart of more real-life disputes, however, is the issue of how we should treat other people. There are almost as many systems of "personal ethics" as there are people. Where do such differences come from?

Beyond the impact on our ethical outlook of family, religion, and personal choice, some people claim that gender plays an important role. Just as Belenky and her colleagues claim that men and women may differ in how they "know" things, other researchers claim that men and women may differ in how they decide what is "right" and what is "wrong." A landmark book published in 1982 by the moral development psychologist Carol Gilligan stimulated research into whether there actually are basic differences in how men and women think about these and other matters.[9]

Most people argue only infrequently over epistemological issues. We do, however, evaluate our own and other people's actions many times a day. If you compare and contrast how you decide what to do and how you appraise what other people

---

[9]Carol Gilligan, *In a Different Voice; Psychological Theory and Women's Development* (Cambridge, MA: Harvard University Press, 1982).

do with the ethical styles of same-sex and opposite-sex friends and associates, you may not see a hard and fast linkage with gender. But you will probably be able to distinguish two fundamentally different approaches that people use in evaluating their own and others' actions. One approach, which prizes reason and objectivity, applies the same rules impartially across the board. The ideas of *rights, justice,* and *fairness* are paramount here. The other approach, which combines reason with emotions, holds that we should do what is most appropriate within the particular circumstances of the case. This approach stresses *responsibility* to people in need; its central moral principle is *care,* rather than justice.

The self-inventory you just completed helps you identify your ethical style. The higher your J score, the more your ethics are based on the need for justice. Some would call these ethics typically "masculine." The higher your C score, the more care underlies your ethics. Such ethics have been identified as typically "feminine." Actually, it is unclear just how closely these different styles can be correlated with gender. In practice, many men and women cross from one to the other. Furthermore, some people are very strongly J or C, while others are more balanced. Nonetheless, the odds are high that within any typical group, more men will have higher J scores than C scores, while women's scores will be in the reverse.

The debate over whether there are two ethical styles that can be related to gender arose as an unintended result of research done by the late Harvard psychologist Lawrence Kohlberg (1927–1987). Kohlberg sought to discover the process by which we develop our sense of morality. His research convinced him that to go from an undeveloped to a mature sense of ethics, we pass through a series of distinct stages. When Carol Gilligan, also at Harvard, discovered that Kohlberg's system placed women lower than men on his ethical ladder and that all of Kohlberg's subjects were male, she decided to see if a female sample would yield different results. She thinks they do.

We start with Kohlberg's research, because that is what led to Gilligan's work.

Kohlberg's "Masculine" Ethics of Justice

Kohlberg's research was inspired by the work of the great Swiss psychologist Jean Piaget, who had tried to connect the development of a child's moral judgment to its overall cognitive development. Kohlberg believed that as the whole human personality matures, our thinking about right and wrong starts at a *preconventional* level, then progresses to a *conventional* level, then finally arrives at *postconventional* thinking. Each of these three levels has two specific stages. Kohlberg's research included subjects from many cultures, and therefore he believed that he was uncovering a universal, innate, developmental structure of the human personality.

Stages of Ethical Development

At the *preconventional* level, we understand "good" and "bad" in a very primitive way. This level runs from about age 4 to 10. (Kohlberg does not see anything of consequence taking place in ethical development before age 4.) In *Stage 1,* all that counts is power. "Good" is what the person with the most power says is good. We do what is right only to avoid punishment, and we regulate our dealings with others so as not to provoke anyone who is stronger than we are. In *Stage 2* we advance only a little. Now something is "good" because it will satisfy some need we have. We come to value reciprocity, a notion well put in the proposition "You scratch my back and I'll scratch yours." This notion, of course, is still totally self-oriented. "Right" and "wrong" are just labels that indicate whether something brings us pleasure or pain.

Conventional morality, the next level, marks a major advance in that we shift our focus from ourselves to others. The expectations of our family, or the rules of our society, now become our moral standard. At *Stage 3* of this level, an action is "good" if it pleases other people, helps them, or at least tries to. Generally, we adopt traditional and stereotyped ways of behaving without questioning them. Our purpose is to act in ways that will make other people like and accept us. Next, in *Stage 4*, authority and law and order become more important. Now we think that respecting authority, obeying rules, doing our duty, and maintaining the status quo are morally right for their own sake—no matter what the circumstances. Conforming to the traditions of our group is a major virtue. So many people are so comfortable at this level that only one in four advances to Kohlberg's final level.

When and if we move into the third, *postconventional* level as adults, we develop an appreciation for moral principles that do not depend on what anyone thinks but are valid in and of themselves. This level of autonomous, individual ethical thinking, like the earlier levels, also has two stages. *Stage 5* thinking utilizes the ideas of utilitarianism and the "social contract" which promote free agreement, individual rights, and democratic processes and institutions.[10] As Kohlberg notes, "this is the 'official' morality of American government, and finds its ground in the thought of the writers of the Constitution." At this stage, we decide whether an action is right or wrong by an impartial assessment of how fair it is, how well it respects the rights of others, and how far it advances the common good. *Stage 6* goes beyond this to individually realized ethical principles that are abstract and universal, the Golden Rule, for example, or Immanuel Kant's categorical imperative.[11] These, says Kohlberg, "are universal principles of *justice,* of the *reciprocity* and *equality* of human rights, and of respect for the dignity of human beings as *individual persons.*" Now we assess the ethical character of actions in terms of the principles we have chosen to apply and to which we have a deep personal allegiance. Something is right or wrong depending on how it measures up to these principles.

Kohlberg's scheme is often called an *ethic of justice.* Like the statue of Justice wearing a blindfold, the person at Stage 6 refuses to see anything that could sway his decision. There are no extenuating circumstances, no special cases, no emotions. Everything must be rational, objective, and impartial.

How Valid Is Kohlberg's Scheme?

Kohlberg's analysis makes a good deal of sense. The process of moral development, he says, means moving toward a progressively less self-centered and ever more complex and abstract ethical outlook. We start with a selfish way of determining right

---

[10]For an explanation of the social contract, see Chapter 7. Utilitarianism is described in Chapter 5.

[11]The "categorical imperative" is Kant's statement of the highest moral law. His most famous formulation says: "Act in such a way that you treat humanity, whether in your own person or in the person of any other, always at the same time as an end and never simply as a means." Chapter 5 gives a fuller explanation of Kant's thinking.

and wrong, give that up for other people's judgments, then grow beyond that to a view of morality as an expression of ultimate principles—justice, fairness, and respect for individual rights and human dignity. Kohlberg's stages also test out empirically. His evidence shows that everyone can be placed at one of his six stages as they pass through what turns out to be the same sequence.

Some researchers raised questions about Kohlberg's theory, however, when they saw that most women do not go past Stage 3, that is, determining right and wrong according to whether or not an act helps or pleases others. If women achieve no higher level than this, either they are morally inferior to men or something is wrong with the theory.

Carol Gilligan's "Feminine" Ethic of Care

Harvard psychologist Carol Gilligan studied Kohlberg's findings and found them wanting. Because all of Kohlberg's subjects were male, he could not have taken into account the different socialization of little girls and little boys in our culture. Males are traditionally socialized to be autonomous and independent, while females are supposed to be passive but loving caretakers for the members of their group. Gilligan argues in her book *In a Different Voice* that these differences lead to different values. She writes,

> For the men, this had led to a morality based on equal rights and devotion to abstract principles even at the sacrifice of people's well-being. For the women, it had led to a morality based on caring, in which increasing maturity broadened the scope of the person's sense of responsibility and compassion. For mature women, the goal became not equality but equity, in responding to people's differing needs.

Gilligan's subsequent research suggests that Kohlberg missed an alternate way of thinking about right and wrong, an approach used by both men and women, but far more frequently by women.[12] In this outlook, *care and responsibility to others,* rather than justice and individual rights, become the fundamental ethical principles. Gilligan claims that this ethical outlook defines an ethical issue mainly in terms of helping others and minimizing harm. The most basic moral command becomes "an injunction to care, a responsibility to discern and alleviate the 'real and recognizable trouble' of this world." If ethics is essentially a matter of getting involved with other people's lives in order to reduce their troubles, then we have a responsibility to help others. Thus, in the view of most women, she says, "the moral person is one who helps others; goodness is service, meeting one's obligations and responsibilities to others."

---

[12]Gilligan points out that her research shows that "(1) concerns about justice and care are both represented in people's thinking about real-life moral dilemmas, but people tend to focus on one set of concerns and minimally represent the other; and (2) there is an association between moral orientation and gender such that both men and women use both orientations, but Care Focus dilemmas are more likely to be presented by women and Justice Focus dilemmas by men." Carol Gilligan and Jane Attanucci, "Two Moral Orientations," in *Mapping the Moral Domain,* edited by Carol Gilligan, Janie Victoria Ward, Jill McLean Taylor, with Betty Bardige (Cambridge, MA: Harvard University Press, 1988), p. 82.

From this ethical perspective, every situation is different, and appropriate responses will vary from case to case, depending on the details. Every problem, then, calls for a tailor-made solution, not something "off the rack." In fact, Gilligan's "care" outlook is often called a "response" orientation.

Like Kohlberg, Gilligan thinks that people develop through a series of stages on their way to "moral maturity" (although the stages are less central to her thought than to Kohlberg's and are given briefer treatment). Whereas Kohlberg's stages involve a progressively more abstract way of thinking about ethics, however, Gilligan describes stages that involve a woman's developing an advanced sense of responsibility.

The first stage is characterized by *caring only for the self* in order to ensure survival. This is how we all are as children. Then comes a transitional phase when others criticize this attitude as selfish and the individual begins to see connections between herself and others. The second stage is characterized by a sense of *responsibility.* "Good" is equated with caring for others, a value readily captured in the traditional role of wife and mother. Such devotion to caring for other people often leads to ignoring the self, however, and this ultimately gives way to a second transition in which the tensions between the responsibility of caring for others and the desire to have one's own needs met are faced. The final stage is defined by an *acceptance of the principle of care* as a universal ethical principle that condemns exploitation and hurt in the lives of others and ourselves.

The Ethics of Justice and the Ethics of Care Compared

Justice, Care, and the Case of Roger and Hal

According to Gilligan, men and women look at ethical situations through different "lenses," with each one revealing something different. If we look at the case of Roger's and Hal's sick days, the underlying problem looks entirely different, depending on which lens we use.

Through Kohlberg's "justice" lens, we see a problem of fairness. The policy is explicit, and it has served the interests of the company and the workers very well. The ethical problem is obviously whether we should treat Roger and Hal the same or treat them differently.

We all feel sorry for Roger, but the rules are clear and they have to apply equally to everyone. We might want to treat Roger differently from Hal, but how can we? That would not be fair to Hal. And according to Kohlberg's hierarchy, acting according to an abstract principle of fairness—the requirement that we treat similar cases the same way—is ethically superior to giving in to our personal sympathy toward Roger. We must apply the rules consistently.

What if we gave both men another chance? That would hardly be fair to people who were fired in the past for exceeding 12 sick days. Nor would it be fair to the other employees, many of whom may want or need to take extra sick days but don't. Perhaps they have a problem with some other policy. If we make this exception for Roger, aren't we setting a dangerous precedent and opening a Pandora's box? Wouldn't everybody now expect special treatment? Without a policy, decisions could end up being arbitrary, and we cannot do business in a way that meets everyone's interests if we make exceptions all the time. That would produce chaos.

When we view the case in this way, we're hard pressed to defend treating the two men differently from each other or from the way the policy clearly specifies. Anything other than identical treatment appears unjust, unfair, and sure to cause more problems than it solves.

Through a "care" lens, however, the problem looks quite different. Now it seems to involve our responsibility to help someone in need. Given this assumption, treating Hal and Roger the same seems indefensible. If the facts we have are correct and complete, Roger and his son clearly need help more than Hal does. Making some special arrangements for Roger will not hurt others in the company—and may, in fact, reassure them that the company will help them too should they find themselves with a serious problem. If we don't assist Roger with this unusual and difficult problem, we will have violated the principle of care.

The question is no longer "Do we apply or ignore the policy?" From a "care" point of view, policies are for normal cases, not unusual ones. Because this is an unusual case, the primary question, then, is "What is ethically appropriate to these special circumstances?" From this perspective, special treatment for Roger is not "setting a precedent." It's not going to come back to haunt us, as the "justice" outlook would have it. Making an exception to policy this time does not mean that we would do so in every case. Nor would such an exception constitute arbitrariness. We are trying "to discern and alleviate the 'real and recognizable trouble' of this world." To find a solution tailor-made to a special circumstance, we must be guided by the facts of each case.

With all this in mind, we can perhaps say that treating Hal and Roger the same is not "fair." The essence of fairness is treating similar cases the same. But these two employees are in different situations. Circumstances are beyond Roger's control—not so for Hal. Roger's problem is real and serious. He also has a better work history with the company. The two cases differ so much that in fact it may be *unfair* to treat them the *same*.

From which perspective would you view the case of Roger and Hal if it were yours to decide? Look back at the results of that short self-inventory you took a few pages ago. The odds are that if you have a high "J" score, you probably think Roger and Hal should be treated the same. If you have a high "C" score, you probably think it would be wrong not to give Roger special treatment.[13]

Similarities and Differences

Gilligan's model of moral development resembles Kohlberg's in a couple of ways. Both progress from a totally self-centered outlook to one governed by a basic moral principle. Both begin with an emphasis on the greater authority or importance of someone else, but culminate in a personal forging of one's own ethics.

---

[13]If you decided differently than your high score would suggest, you may still have used the logic of your preferred ethical outlook, or you might have simply used the other point of view for this case. Think about why. If you have a high "C" score and yet think that Hal and Roger should be treated the same, there is a good chance that you were influenced by your conception of what would be appropriate in a business setting, that is, in a world that has been traditionally dominated by men and the "justice" outlook.

The differences between these two approaches, however, are more striking than the similarities. For one thing, the moral principles arrived at are very different. Treating people impartially according to abstract principles of justice is more detached and less personal than reducing the amount of pain and suffering in the world. Although both values are important, "respecting someone's rights" affects the lives of ordinary people less immediately than "reducing their sorrow and unhappiness."

More notably, perhaps, Gilligan's findings speak to the psychological struggle of women against our society's traditional idea of their gender-determined role. According to Gilligan, women can gain personal independence and autonomy only after they reject the idea that their proper role is to subjugate their interests to those of their husbands, children, or other people they are caring for. A typical woman in our culture probably has no trouble accepting the idea that helping others is important. The harder task is accepting the idea that she should apply the principle of care to her own life as much as she applies it to others. Kohlberg's stages reflect no such psychological struggle for men.

The Philosophical Significance of Perceived Differences

Care, Justice, and Traditional Philosophical Ethics

It should be apparent by now that both the ethics of justice and the ethics of care are legitimate intellectual outlooks. We might even say that these two approaches parallel to some degree the teleological and deontological traditions in philosophical ethics.[14]

Those using a *teleological approach* to ethics argue that whether actions are right or wrong depends on *how much actual good or harm results.* The most familiar, not to mention influential teleological system is that of utilitarianism, the school of thought that approves actions to the extent that they produce "the greatest good." Gilligan's ethic of "care" endorses something similar. Both claim that ethics is a matter of evaluating real-life consequences, whether positive or negative, not following a program that follows from some abstract principle.

Those taking a *deontological approach,* on the other hand, say that actions themselves are *intrinsically right or wrong.* Their merit does not depend on their consequences. Deontological thinkers determine the moral character of an action by measuring it against abstract moral principles. Kohlberg's ethic of justice sounds very much like this.

When Gilligan questioned Kohlberg's assumption that his "ethic of justice" was the most advanced ethic, then, she joined a time-honored debate among philosophers about the best way to evaluate right and wrong.

Care and Justice: The Philosophical Significance

What is the philosophical significance of the fact that two distinctly different ethical styles can often be predicted by gender? First, the existence of two separate but equal ethical perspectives suggests that each has its strengths and weaknesses, but

---

[14]These two basically different ways of thinking about right and wrong are discussed in detail in Chapter 5.

each alone is ultimately incomplete.[15] A full ethical analysis, then, should use both approaches.

Second, if we need to combine both perspectives, moral justification becomes much more complicated. A justice orientation might say that as long as a particular action matches universal ethical principles, it is morally acceptable. But adding the care orientation's requirement that the deed must respond to a particular set of circumstances and reduce trouble in the lives of others makes the morality of an action harder to guarantee. Moral justification, then, becomes a matter of balancing the theoretical against the concrete and the universal against the particular. We must also carefully consider the harm many different people could suffer or be saved from by our actions. We must scrutinize our responsibilities to ourselves as well as to others, and we must decide how to balance competing interests and responsibilities.

Third, we must envision a new accommodation of reason to emotion. Gilligan's ethic of care involves an emotional process. Most philosophers, on the other hand, have put their faith in reason. Yet thinkers as different as the ancient Greek philosopher Aristotle and the early modern British thinker David Hume both stress the role of emotions in the morally good person. Aristotle says that moral virtue involves both actions and emotions. Being a virtuous individual, he claims in the *Nichomachean Ethics,* depends not on doing the right things, but performing the actions in a certain way: "feeling at the right time, about the right things, in relation to the right people; and for the right reason." Hume sees ethics as mainly a matter of "sympathy" or "fellow feeling." Both philosophers think that ethics involve feeling and personal character as well as rational analysis. Thus, it may be true that the role of emotion in Western ethics has been greatly underestimated or simply ignored.

Finally, if the way we perceive, interpret, and resolve ethical problems is affected by gender, how do we know when we have an objective picture of reality? Modern Western thinking has counted on the possibility of objectivity. We weigh things, measure them, use sophisticated instruments, observe, test, experiment, and quantify. In the end, we believe we can get a precise and objective picture of what we're looking at. But if gender affects our perception of reality so profoundly, how can we be sure our results are correct?

Immanuel Kant may be right when he claims that we can know things only "as they appear," never "as they really are in themselves." Kant came to the conclusion that the mind by its very nature determines what we experience as reality. Our minds

---

[15]As Gilligan describes the weakness of each outlook,

> The potential error in justice reasoning lies in its latent egocentrism, the tendency to confuse one's perspective with an objective standpoint or truth, the temptation to define others in one's own terms by putting oneself in their place. The potential error in care reasoning lies in the tendency to forget that one has terms, creating a tendency to enter into another's perspective and to see oneself as "selfless" by defining oneself in other's terms. These two types of error underlie two common equations that signify distortions or deformations of justice and care; the equation of human with male, unjust in its omission of women; and the equation of care with self-sacrifice, uncaring in its failure to represent the activity and agency of care.

Carol Gilligan, "Moral Orientation and Moral Development," in *Women and Moral Theory,* edited by Eva Feder Kittay and Diane T. Mayers (Totowa, NJ: Rowman and Littlefield, 1987), pp. 19–33.

do not just passively receive a picture of reality more or less accurately. Kant claims that the mind takes the raw "stuff" of reality and manufactures a representation of the reality that conforms to the nature of the mind. We end up with a "thing as it appears"; the "thing in itself" is always beyond our grasp. If gender also plays its part in shaping the appearance of an ethical issue, does this doom us even more certainly to subjectivity?

To make matters more complicated, Gilligan proposes another theory that raises still more problems connected with the issue of appearance versus reality. In essence, she suggests that the different thought processes and values of mature men and women result from the self-concept we form when we are very young.[16] We end up with one of two different self-concepts, she says, one individual, autonomous, and essentially separate from others, the other intimately connected to other people. Gilligan claims that most men develop the former self, most women, the latter.

In essence, Gilligan argues that our ethical outlook stems largely from the psychological makeup associated with our gender. Separate, autonomous individuals inevitably come into conflict with each other. Many may want the same thing, but only one of them can have it, or they find their individual interests in total opposition. How do they protect their "separateness" and yet live in the same society? The most logical way is to adopt an ethic of fairness, equality, and impartiality, the rules of which specify the rights of all and apply the same way to all. Thus, Kohlberg's ethic of "justice" is appropriate in a society of "separate" selves.

On the other hand, if we see ourselves as essentially connected to other people, we will develop a different ethic. In a reality based on relationships, the chief threat is a lack of care for other people. Because we must inevitably accept different responsibilities to different people, the ethical dilemmas that people with this orientation face stem mainly from the fact that they have competing or conflicting responsibilities. Which responsibility gets priority? One must look at the specifics of each situation very carefully and then decide who gets special treatment. Thus, a view of the self as "connected" implies the primacy of Gilligan's ethic of care.

This general theme has also been developed by feminist philosophers who argue that traditional moral theories are grounded in the male experience and consequently have serious limitations. The contemporary philosopher Virginia Held, for example, claims that moral theory generally proceeds from the activities of the marketplace, a traditionally male forum. She writes,

> The relation between buyer and seller has often been taken as the model of all human interactions. Most of the social contract tradition has seen this relation of contractual exchange as fundamental to law and political authority as well as to economic activity. And some contemporary moral philosophers see the contractual relation as the relation on which even morality itself should be based. The marketplace, as a model for relationships, has become so firmly entrenched in our normative theories that it is rarely questioned as a proper foundation for recommendations extending beyond the marketplace. Consequently, much moral thinking

---

[16]See Chapter 3, "Concepts of Self and Morality," in Gilligan's *In a Different Voice* for the details of this process.

is built on the concept of rational economic man. Relationships between human beings are seen as arising, and as justified, when they serve the interests of individual rational contractors.[17]

As a result, competition and domination in the hope of advancing one's interest become natural and appropriate activities.

Held suggests, however, that if we base our thinking in a paradigm drawn from the more characteristically female experience of the nurturing relationship between a caretaker and a child, we arrive at a very different moral theory. Seen in this light, she observes,

> The competition and desire for domination thought of as acceptable for rational economic man might appear as a very particular and limited human connection, suitable perhaps, if at all, only for a restricted marketplace. Such a relation of conflict and competition can be seen to be unacceptable for establishing the social trust on which public institutions must rest, or for upholding the bonds on which caring, regard, friendship, or love must be based. . . . We might then take it as one of our starting assumptions that creating good relations of care and concern and trust between ourselves and our children, and creating social arrangements in which children will be valued and well cared for, are more important than maximizing individual utilities. And the moral theories that might be compatible with such assumptions might be very different from those with which we are familiar.
>
> —"Feminism and Moral Theory"

Minimally, Held argues, we should reject the idea that a single moral theory is sufficient, opting instead for a "division of moral labor" that employs different ethical approaches for different domains of experience. "Satisfactory intermediate principles for areas such as those of international affairs, or family relations," she writes, "cannot be derived from simple universal principles, but must be arrived at in conjunction with experience within the domains in question."

If Gilligan and Held are right, a psychological fact—our self-concept—and our experience of being male or female may determine our perception of reality and the way we prefer to handle ethics. This would undercut the idea that philosophy and reason can ever be a "pure" and objective instrument for studying reality and analyzing human experience. If we must call even the theoretical possibility of objective reason into question, that presents us with a philosophical problem as stunning as it is fundamental.

Indeed, the contemporary philosopher Janice Moulton claims that philosophy itself has been distorted by the fact that it has been dominated by a methodology largely connected to the "masculine experience."[18] Moulton bases her analysis on

---

[17]Virginia Held, "Feminism and Moral Theory," in *Women and Moral Theory,* edited by Eva Feder Kittay and Diane T. Mayers (Totowa, NJ: Rowman and Littlefield, 1987), pp. 111–128.

[18]Janice Moulton, "A Paradigm of Philosophy: The Adversary Method," in *Discovering Reality: Feminist Perspectives on Epistemology, Metaphysics, Methodology, and Philosophy of Science,* edited by Sandra Harding and Merrill B. Hintikka (Dordrecht, Holland: D. Reidel Publishing, 1983), pp. 149–164.

the idea that aggression is generally seen as natural and desirable in men and unnatural and offensive in women. Nonphysical aggression is taken in Western society to indicate power, ambition, energy, authority, competence, and effectiveness. Considered as a positive trait, claims Moulton, aggression has been incorporated as a basic aspect of philosophical methodology. Hence, Moulton sees the basic procedure of philosophy as an expression of a masculine trait. She calls this methodology the "Adversary Paradigm." "Under the Adversary Paradigm," she explains,

> It is assumed that the only, or at any rate, the best, way of evaluating work in philosophy is to subject it to the strongest or most extreme opposition. And it is assumed that the best way of presenting work in philosophy is to address it to an imagined opponent and muster all the evidence one can to support it. The justification for this method is that a position ought to be defended from, and subjected to, the criticism of the strongest opposition; that this method is the only way to get the best of both sides; that a thesis which survives this method of evaluation is more likely to be correct than one that has not; and that a thesis subjected to the Adversary Method will have passed an "objective" test, the most extreme test possible, whereas any weaker criticism or evaluation will, by comparison, give an advantage to the claim to be evaluated and therefore not be as objective as it could be. Of course, it will be admitted that the Adversary Method does not guarantee that all and only sound philosophical claims will survive, but that is only because even an adversary does not always think of all the things which ought to be criticized about a position, and even a proponent does not always think of all the possible responses to criticism. However, since there is no way to determine with certainty what is good and what is bad philosophy, the Adversary Method is the best there is. If one wants philosophy to be objective, one should prefer the Adversary Method to other, more subjective, forms of evaluation which would give preferential treatment to some claims by not submitting them to extreme adversarial tests.
>
> —"A Paradigm of Philosophy"

Moulton claims that such a methodology in reality "restricts and misrepresents what philosophic reasoning is," and she engages in a far-reaching account of the problems of the Adversary Paradigm: defects in the paradigm itself, misinterpreting the history of philosophy, restricting what is considered a philosophical issue, and bad reasoning. One unfortunate consequence of adopting this paradigm in ethics, for example, is that

> It has been assumed that there must be a single supreme moral principle. Because moral reasoning may be the result of different moral principles that may make conflicting claims about the right thing to do, a supreme moral principle is needed to "adjudicate rationally [that is, deductively] among different competing moralities." The relation between moral principles and moral decision is thought to be deductive. A supreme moral principle allows one to deduce, by plugging in the relevant factors, what is right or wrong. More than one principle would allow, as is possible if one starts from different premises, conflicting judgments to be

deduced. The possibilities that one could adjudicate between conflicting moral precepts without using deduction, that there might be moral principles that are not the result of conflicts in moral principles, and that there might be moral principles for which there are no guaranteed solutions, are not considered.

—"A Paradigm of Philosophy"

In short, Moulton implies that the original goal of philosophy—the search for truth—has given way to the honing of debating skills. This, she argues, results when a distinctly masculine trait of dubious value is made into an intellectual virtue.

Gender, Ethics, and Knowledge

Now we should look at one final question about these two ethical perspectives. In the earlier part of this chapter, you saw what researchers have said about male and female approaches to knowledge and truth. Do Perry and Belenky observe the same differences seen by Kohlberg and Gilligan? If, as some thinkers suggest, there really is a distinctly female perception of the world, similar responses should surface in both epistemology and ethics.

And they seem to. Remember that one of the main features of Perry's account of knowledge is emotional detachment from the thing being known. The search for knowledge is supposed to be rational, unemotional, and objective. This fits quite well with Kohlberg's idea that the most advanced stage of moral thinking is characterized by the fair, impartial application of universal and abstract principles.

Belenky and her colleagues say that the kind of knowledge they describe values logic less and intuition more. But more critical to the point is that their most advanced stage of women's knowing, "constructive knowledge," depends on trust, empathy, and other emotions that accompany close connections with other people. The central motif of emotional involvement and attention to one's emotional response in a situation is certainly echoed in the ethic of care that Gilligan describes.

To sum up, then, "feminine" thinking seems to combine objectivity and subjectivity, whereas "masculine" thinking relies on objectivity alone. "Masculine" thinking assumes that we discover what is true and right only if we maintain psychological distance between ourselves and whatever we are considering. "Feminine" thinking assumes just the reverse: We can understand a problem fully only if we get intimately involved in it. In the end, then, we find quite similar differences between "masculine" and "feminine" approaches to knowledge and to ethics.

A Final Note

This talk about possible gender-related differences in thinking may be interesting, but is it really that important? What does it have to do with real life, and does all this questioning do anybody any good?

Look at it this way. Sooner or later you will experience the difficulties and frustrations that come from working or living with someone who in effect speaks a different "conceptual language" than you do. It may be someone of a different gender, or it may be someone of the same gender but with a way of thinking—epistemologically or ethically—opposite to your own. Having studied this topic, you should understand such a situation better than you otherwise might have. And the more accurately you understand a problem, the better position you are in to handle it.

In addition, these differences are not carved in stone. The research shows simply that we seem to have proclivities to think in certain ways that may be related to our gender. It does not say that we cannot expand the way we think. Thus, we can work at seeing things the way people of the other gender do, viewing the world and problems as they do, trying to speak their "conceptual language." If we can transcend at least some of the limitations imposed by our preferred way of thinking, we will find it much easier to understand, relate to, and work with a wide range of people different from ourselves. And these are not small benefits.

Main Points of Chapter 13

1. Research in psychology hypothesizes that significant differences in the way people think about knowledge and ethics may be related to gender. The fact that our society has been male-dominated, however, has led to the disparagement of "feminine" ways of thinking and acting as inferior.

2. In contrast to the impartial and objective model of knowledge described by Perry, Belenky et al. suggest a model that incorporates intuition and emotion.

3. In contrast to the predominant ethic of justice described by Kohlberg, Carol Gilligan suggests an ethic of care.

4. Such thinking argues for a more important place for emotion, intuition, and subjectivity in philosophy. More important, however, it undercuts the idea that reason can ever be "pure," and implies that the traditional framework of philosophy has been shaped by characteristically masculine activities and values.

Discussion Questions

1. Think about how you now understand the concept of "knowledge" and the process you have gone through in getting to that point. Does it match Perry's or Belenky's model? Does this correlate with your gender? Which stage are you at?

2. How often do you rely on your intuition? Do you think that it gives you "knowledge"? If not, what would you call it? If so, can you prove what you know by intuition? If you cannot prove it, on what basis can we call it knowledge?

3. In a conventional understanding of knowledge, emotions are thought to compromise our objectivity and impartiality, and thus they are thought to undercut the search for knowledge. Do you agree or disagree with this? Can you think of an experience in which your emotions gave you better instead of worse knowledge about something?

4. Traditional sex-role stereotypes have encouraged women to be more concerned with emotions than men are, and studies have shown that women are better than men at understanding the emotional messages of nonverbal communication (facial expression, body language, tone of voice, and the like). Does this support Alison Jaggar's idea

that women have an "epistemic advantage" over men? How do you react to her claim?

5. Assume that Perry and Belenky et al. describe complementary aspects of knowledge and that a fully developed conception of knowledge requires both approaches. Should our schools try to teach intuition and the use of emotion in acquiring knowledge much as they now teach the scientific method? If so, how might they do that?

6. Kohlberg's original work on moral development focused on responses to the following moral dilemma. "In Europe a woman was near death from a very bad disease, a special kind of cancer. There was one drug that the doctors thought might save her. It was a form of radium that a druggist in the same town had recently discovered. The drug was expensive to make, but the druggist was charging ten times what the drug cost him to make. He paid $200 for the radium and charged $2000 for a small dose of the drug. The sick woman's husband, Heinz, went to everyone he knew to borrow the money, but he could get together only about $1000, which was half of what it cost. He told the druggist that his wife was dying and asked him to sell it cheaper or let him pay later. But the druggist said, 'No, I discovered the drug and I'm going to make money from it.' Heinz got desperate and broke into the man's store to steal the drug for his wife."

What do you think of Heinz's actions? Compare your reasoning with that of your friends and other students in class. Can you identify which of Kohlberg's stages you and the other people you talk to are at? Are there any differences in the ways men and women respond?

7. Gilligan thinks that all of us probably use both justice thinking and care thinking at different times, even though we have a preference for one approach. When do you use each one?

8. Do you share Moulton's reservations about the Adversary Paradigm? What do you think of her claim that this intellectual procedure proceeds from male aggression? If she is right, could this mean that the shape of main methodology of Western philosophy is powerfully influenced by testosterone, the male hormone generally linked to aggressiveness? Would this mean that there are biological determinants both to our ideas and to entire intellectual enterprises?

9. Have you observed any other differences in how people think or act that might be related to gender? What are they? Where do you think any of these differences come from?

10. Imagine that Western society had been dominated by women and not men for the last 2000 years. How would philosophy, religion, and our major social and political institutions have been different?

Selected Readings

On the different "ways of knowing" discussed in this chapter, see William G. Perry, Jr., *Forms of Intellectual and Ethical Development in the College Years* (New York: Holt, Rinehart and Winston, 1968); Mary Field Belenky, Blythe McVicker Clinchy, Nancy Rule Goldberger, and Jill Mattuck Tarule, *Women's Ways of Knowing: The Development of Self,*

Voice, and Mind (New York: Basic Books, 1986), and *Knowledge, Difference and Power: Essays Inspired by Women's Ways of Knowing,* edited by Nancy Goldberger, Jill Tarule, Blythe Clinchy, and Mary Belenky (New York: Basic Books, 1996). For Lawrence Kohlberg's work, see: *The Philosophy of Moral Development: Moral Stages and the Idea of Justice: Essays on Moral Development, 1* (San Francisco: Harper and Row, 1981), and *The Psychology of Moral Development: Essays on Moral Development, 2* (San Francisco: Harper and Row, 1984). Gilligan's thesis is set out in her *In a Different Voice: Psychological Theory and Women's Development* (Cambridge, MA: Harvard University Press, 1982); it is developed and explored by Gilligan and other writers in *Mapping the Moral Domain,* edited by Carol Gilligan, Janie Victoria Ward, Jill McLean Taylor, with Betty Bardige (Cambridge, MA: Harvard University Press, 1988).

For discussions by philosophers of the connection between gender and philosophical thinking, see the following collections of essays: *Discovering Reality: Feminist Perspectives on Epistemology, Metaphysics, Methodology, and Philosophy of Science,* edited by Sandra Harding and Merrill B. Hintikka (Dordrecht, Holland: D. Reidel Publishing, 1983), *Women, Knowledge, and Reality: Explorations in Feminist Philosophy,* edited by Ann Garry and Marilyn Pearsall (Boston: Unwin Hyman, 1988), *Women and Moral Theory,* edited by Eva Feder Kittay and Diane T. Mayers (Totowa, NJ: Rowman and Littlefield, 1987).

14

Is a Dolphin a Person?

- *Personhood*
- *Dolphin Biology and Behavior*
- *Is a Dolphin a Person?*

Tales that reach back to ancient Crete tell of a band of unusual beings who inhabit a mysterious world far from human habitation. Little is known of them, but the fact that they would appear out of the dark to help lost travelers and even save drowning sailors led some ancients to believe that they were gods. These beings are curious about humans and seek contact with us, but we still do not understand the strange sounds they make as they communicate with each other. They can do things with their biological senses that we cannot achieve with our most advanced technology. Some say they have the ability to heal. Some claim these beings are telepathic. Others go further and say they are highly advanced spiritually and have a wide range of psychic abilities. Whatever they are, they remain enigmatic subjects of human fascination.

Who are these exceptional entities? Buddhist monks living in the farthest reaches of Nepal? A tribe of Native Americans who practice the ancient wisdom of their forebears? A colony of aliens transplanted from the cosmos? Hardly. They are dolphins—beings who are related more to Flipper than to the Buddha and whom we can meet daily at aquaria and sea parks.

But while dolphins are neither divine nor extraterrestrial, they are very different from humans and surprisingly complex. And, most important, the fact that dolphins have such advanced traits raises a number of philosophical—and especially ethical—questions. Are dolphins so advanced that they should be considered nonhuman "persons"? If so, what does this say about our behavior toward them? Many dolphins die daily as a result of human fishing practices, and hundreds are held in captivity. Is this morally justifiable given their unusual nature?

Personhood

You might be surprised to encounter the question, "Are dolphins 'persons'?" It might not even make sense to you. "Of course they're not persons," you might say, "they're a completely different species." Yet despite the way that we use "human" and "person" as synonyms in common parlance, the terms actually differ. "Human" is a biological concept, simply denoting membership in *Homo sapiens.* "Person," however, is a philosophical concept, indicating a being with capacities of a particular sort. Although philosophers debate the appropriate criteria for personhood, there is a rough consensus that a person is a being with a particular kind of sophisticated consciousness or inner world. Persons are aware of the world of which they are a part, and they are aware of their experiences. In particular, persons are aware of the fact that they are aware; that is, they have self-awareness. And the presence of such a sophisticated consciousness is evident in the actions of such beings.

If we translate this general idea into a more specific list of criteria, we arrive at something like the following.

1. A person is alive.

2. A person is aware.

3. A person feels positive and negative sensations.

4. A person has emotions.

5. A person has a sense of self.

6. A person controls its own behavior.

7. A person recognizes other persons and treats them appropriately.

8. A person has a variety of sophisticated cognitive abilities. It is capable of analytical, conceptual thought. A person can learn, retain, and recall information. It can solve complex problems with analytical thought. And a person can communicate in a way that suggests thought.

Not surprisingly, numerous questions are raised by this or any such list. For example, "Precisely what do we mean by 'alive'?" And, "If computer technology takes us far enough, would something like *2001*'s computer HAL, *Star Wars'* C3PO and R2D2, or *Star Trek*'s android Data fill the bill?" As this list unfolds, we see a being that is unquestionably a "who," not a "what." But how sophisticated are the conceptual abilities that we require? Must a person be able to write poetry or will rudimentary problem solving be enough? Must communication entail the ability to discuss philosophical aspects of life, or is something equivalent to exchanging "hellos" enough?

It's clear, however, that "human" and "person" are separate concepts. Strictly speaking, it is possible to be human and not a person. This is the case in someone who is "brain dead"—which is why most of us wouldn't call ending life support of such a patient "murder." Supporters of a woman's right to an abortion generally claim that it is also true of a fetus. Of course, the other side of the distinction is that it is thereby theoretically possible to have "persons" who are "nonhuman." These would be beings with the same advanced traits as normal humans but who come from a different biological family. Science fiction books and movies are replete with such beings. The scientific research on dolphins, however, presents us with a fascinating possibility—a real-life candidate for nonhuman personhood.

Dolphin Biology and Behavior

We cannot "do philosophy" on an issue until we know the relevant facts. Before we can discuss whether dolphins are persons, then, we should see what scientists have learned about them.

Some Descriptive Facts About Dolphins

Dolphins are members of the biological group of marine animals called *Cetacea,* the same family that includes porpoises and whales. Dolphins are not fish. Like us, they are mammals—warm-blooded animals who breathe air, reproduce via sexual intercourse, bear their young alive, and suckle their young from female mammary glands.

Because both are mammals, humans and dolphins have many similarities. A dolphin's body temperature is, like ours, 98.6 degrees Fahrenheit. Like us, too, the dolphin cannot drink salt water, even though it lives in the ocean. It gets the fresh water it needs from the fish it eats. Even though dolphins live in the water while we live on land, they must still breathe just as we do. If they cannot, they drown. However, while we breathe automatically, even when we are unconscious, dolphins do not. For them, every breath is a voluntary act.

There are more than 30 different kinds of dolphin, but we are most familiar with Tursiops truncatus, the Atlantic bottlenose dolphin. This is the kind of dolphin you see in shows at aquaria and in television shows and movies.

An adult bottlenose dolphin is seven to twelve feet long and weighs about 600 pounds. Its body is marvelously streamlined, allowing it to move through the water at about fifteen to twenty miles per hour. It powers itself with its tail, using its dorsal fin on top and two side flippers for stability. Its skin is very sensitive and it feels pain easily.

Female dolphins carry their young for about twelve months. After she delivers her baby, the mother nurses it for about a year, during which time she teaches it what it needs to know to survive. By the time it is nine months old, the baby makes many of the sounds dolphins use to communicate with each other.

Dolphins can live into their thirties or forties. The females can bear young until nearly the end of their lives.

Some Facts About Dolphin Social Behavior

Dolphins live in groups, or schools, sometimes large, sometimes small. They are group-oriented and cooperative animals, and, indeed, their survival at sea depends on it. Social interaction is so important to them that to be deprived of contact with other dolphins can upset them, sometimes to the point of causing illness or even death.

Dolphin societies are different from ours. The core consists of groups of mothers and their calves, aunts, and grandmothers. Females will sometimes "baby sit" for a mother. And a group of mothers will even form protective circles, like "playpens," so that babies can play with each other in the middle. After about three to six years, a young dolphin joins a group of other young adults, both male and female. When females begin giving birth, they and return to their mothers' groups. Adult males tend to swim together and take less part in rearing the young.

Dolphins form strong social bonds with other individual dolphins. Researchers know of dolphins who have sustained close relationships for ten to twenty years. As testimony to the power of these connections, observers have noted cases of dolphins in captivity where, when one dolphin died, the dolphin most closely bonded to it acted much as we do when we lose someone we love and become depressed.

Interaction with one another is probably the central fact of dolphins' lives. In fact, Bernd Wursig, a scientist who has studied dolphins for years, thinks that dolphins may be quite sophisticated about relationships. They seem to be aware of belonging to a particular "group," to recognize one another, and to devote energy to relating to each other. For example, Wursig observes,

> Groups of dolphins that come together after an absence of some time vocalize much more than either group did previously, and they usually stop and exchange greetings as they nuzzle and caress each other. . . . [They] are reaffirming and strengthening old social bonds: they are getting reacquainted. The noise and activity are reminiscent of when human friends come together after a separation.[1]

Wursig claims that not only do dolphins identify themselves as part of a group, they also demonstrate bonds with their siblings. It is tempting to see these behaviors as expressing feelings akin to the sense of family that we share with our parents, brothers, and sisters and the sense of "tribe" that we share with members of our community.

Dolphins are so social that they can spend up to a third of each day making physical contact with all the other members of their school. Apparently they do this to reaffirm their relationships with each other. Tending to these relationships may be what makes possible the cooperative behavior that is essential to their survival. And because there's no fixed social hierarchy in schools of dolphins, large groups have no single leader. Any member of a group can suggest group action, but the group's members may spend up to four hours whistling back and forth before they arrive at a consensus to go ahead.

Dolphins also express concern for their group's welfare in their helpful behavior toward individual members of the group. They look after each other's calves. They attend to sick members of their group. When one dolphin is in danger of losing consciousness, for example, others will swim under it, buoy it up against the surface, and waken it so that it will breathe. They will continue to help one another like this for long periods of time. In fact, they are so attuned to the danger of drowning that they have reportedly even saved humans in the same way. They do not take care of the sick at all costs, however. If this puts the group's survival at risk, the sick dolphin will be allowed to stop breathing and die.

Dolphin interaction is very physical and sexual. They are naturally bisexual and, particularly in captivity, devote much time and energy to sex. Dolphins in captivity probably have about ten sexual encounters each day. Dolphins are one of the only creatures other than humans who appear to engage in sex strictly for pleasure.

---

[1] Bernd Wursig, "The Question of Dolphin Awareness Approached Through Studies in Nature," *Cetus,* vol. 5 (1985), no. 1, p. 5.

They simply seem to enjoy relating to each other that way. Because of the importance of knowing and relating to other members of their group, however, much of the dolphins' apparently sexual behavior may be more social than sexual. Rather than sexual gratification, its aim may actually be forming, renewing, or strengthening social bonds.

Dolphins have a strong interest in humans, and many of them readily develop attachments to us. There's nothing recent about this. The ancient Greek writer Plutarch observed, "To the dolphin alone, beyond all others, nature has granted what the best philosophers seek: friendship for no advantage. Though it has no need at all of any man, yet it is a genial friend to all and has helped many."

Beyond their attachment to humans, one of the most surprising things about dolphins is that they do not harm us. A dolphin could easily kill a human. Yet despite the fact that we kill them, capture them, injure them, and poke and probe their wounds in trying to help them when they're hurt, most dolphins seem to avoid deliberately hurting us. Consider the following incident described by Albert Falco, oceanographer Jacques Cousteau's chief diver, who had just captured a baby dolphin during one of the Calypso's voyages:

> As soon as I had a grip on the dolphin, I saw its mother streaking toward me. My first thought was that she was going to attack. Instead, she began swimming around us, making a series of little cries as she swam, sometimes brushing against me. . . . She was much larger than I [probably weighing between two hundred and two hundred and fifty pounds] and incomparably more agile in the water. I confess that I was more than a little frightened at first. Then I understood that the dolphin had no intention of attacking me. She was pleading, calling to her calf. She wanted her child back, but she also wanted to avoid harming me. I did not know what to do. I wanted to take the calf back . . . for I felt that, at his age, it would not be terribly difficult to tame him. It was truly a dilemma. The mother, circling frantically around us, screaming, was more than I could take. I was very moved . . . and freed the calf. He rushed toward his mother, and the pair dived immediately and were lost to sight.[2]

When you think of how aggressively we humans and other animals protect our young, it's nothing short of remarkable that this mother dolphin did not simply kill Falco with one blow of her beak. But dolphins have a history of being gentle with humans, both in the wild and in captivity.

Nonetheless, as helpful, pleasure loving, and gentle as dolphins seem, they have another side as well. Their sex play is often quite rough. Dolphins can also be aggressive with each other, although they threaten more than actually harm each other. Dolphins express their displeasure with each other in many ways: chasing each other, slapping their tails against the water, and clapping their jaws at each other. Even so, they still seem much less aggressive with their own species than humans are with theirs. "Because they live in schools," observed Kenneth Norris, who was one of the world's most prominent dolphin researchers, "they

---

[2]Jacques-Yves Cousteau and Philippe Diole, *Dolphins,* trans. J. F. Bernard (New York: Arrowood Press, 1975), p. 61.

are by nature extremely cooperative. A cooperative element pervades their whole psychology. They have a sweetness of disposition that makes them sweeter than we are."

Some Facts About the Dolphin Brain

A dolphin's brain probably resembles a human brain more closely than that of any other animal. Bottlenose dolphins' brains are usually a little larger than ours: human brains weigh about three pounds; dolphins' about three and one-half. However, the ratios of brain weight to body weight and brain weight to body length are roughly equivalent. If we look at the ratio of the brain volume to the surface area of the body (something called the "encephalization quotient"), we find humans at 7.4, bottlenose dolphins at 5.6, and chimpanzees at 2.5. In almost all other mammals this ratio is under 2.0. A similar picture emerges from examining another potential indicator of comparative intelligence—ratios of brain weight to spinal cord weight. In humans, the ratio is 50 to 1; in bottlenose dolphins, 40 to 1; in apes, 8 to 1; in cats, 5 to 1; in horses, 2.5 to 1; and in fishes, the brain weighs less than the cord.

Dolphin brain structure, however, is older than ours. Our species has had the brain that we do for only about 100,000 years. Dolphins have had brains the same size or larger than ours for about 15 million years.

A particularly interesting comparison between human and dolphin brains lies in what is called the cerebral cortex, or "gray matter." The cerebral cortex is the brain's outer layer of cells. When you see drawings or pictures of the human brain, you see the cortex with its convolutions, called the gyri and sulci. These infoldings and creases allow the brain to have a larger surface area within the space allowed by the cavity of the skull. The cerebral cortex is generally acknowledged to be where our higher mental functions take place. We form associations, remember things, make judgments, use language, and think abstractly and creatively because our cerebral cortex enables us to do these things.

The dolphin brain looks much like ours. It is more spherical, but its cortex and ours are much more highly convoluted than the brains of other mammals. Actually, there are even more sulci and gyri in the dolphin brain, so it has more surface area than a human brain does. If we compare the brains of a typical bottlenose dolphin and a normal human being, the dolphin's brain is 40 percent larger. And all that difference is in the cerebral cortex. Yet as complex as the dolphin brain is, we must also note that the neurons in the dolphin brain are less densely packed than in a human brain and that the human cortex is about twice as thick as the dolphin's.

While many facts suggest that a dolphin's brain is quite advanced, some researchers claim that the dolphin brain may have stopped developing at a primitive level. The important structural and functional differences between the dolphin brain and the brains of primates and other land mammals suggest to these scientists that the dolphin brain simply did not undergo later evolutionary stages of development. Other scientists, however, argue that many apparently "intelligent" behaviors that we observe dolphins performing could not be explained if dolphins had only a "primitive" brain.

Some Speculations About Dolphin "Intelligence"

Even this cursory description of the dolphin brain leads to the question of how "intelligent" dolphins are. Before we get into that, however, we have to remind ourselves how imprecise the concept of "intelligence" really is. Does it mean a certain mental potential, measurable or unmeasurable, or can it be described simply in terms of the performance of specific tasks? Determining levels of intelligence among humans has been difficult at best. Standardized "intelligence tests" have been accused of underlying cultural biases that interfere with accurately measuring mental ability. If we have so much trouble even defining human intelligence, much less measuring it, you can imagine how difficult it is to discuss intelligence in a dolphin.

Even so, it would help if we had at least a rough, commonsense understanding of intelligence to work with. So, keeping in mind the limitations of any definition of this concept, let's say that "intelligence" refers to a being's ability to engage in advanced mental processes like abstract thinking, reasoning, and understanding. Furthermore, this ability must be apparent in an "intelligent" being's behavior—particularly in how it handles problems and novel situations. Thus, "intelligence" also refers to the quality that allows a being to *decide* how it will act, rather than automatically respond to instinct, physical desires, or some physical stimulus. We also usually assume that an "intelligent" being can communicate in some fashion. Ultimately, then, "intelligence" refers to those fundamental features that make us think of a being as some*one* rather than some*thing*.

Keeping in mind all the complexities implicit in this concept, does dolphin behavior suggest a significant degree of awareness of the world around them? Do they behave "intelligently"?

To some rigorously empirical scientists who spend their lives working with dolphins, there's no question that dolphins are intelligent. "We do know that they are intelligent," asserts researcher Dianah Reiss, "and we can explain that operationally. It is the way they show flexibility in their behavior and use information in a new and changing environment in a way that is goal directed."

Can we point to specific signs of "intelligence"? For one thing, dolphins are unusually curious, and this suggests that they have at least some intellectual capacity. Most animals in the wild avoid humans, but dolphins are curious about us. As veteran dolphin researcher Louis Herman says, "No ape ever came out of a tree to see what humans are doing. But dolphins constantly come out of their environment to see what's going on outside of it."

Dolphin "intelligence" is also suggested by the fact that they can *learn*. If you've ever seen dolphins perform, you know that they can learn to do jumps, flips and similar behaviors on cue. Of course, many animals learn behaviors, so you may think that dolphin learning shows nothing special. But dolphins can learn commands containing abstract concepts, and this certainly involves higher-order mental activity. A dolphin can learn that it will be rewarded only if it performs something "new." Dolphins have learned a command that tells them to "imitate" an action performed by another dolphin or even a human. And scientific studies have shown that dolphins can identify whether objects are the "same" or "different." Surely, using such abstract notions is an impressive mental achievement.

Intelligence and Problem Solving

Certainly one sign of intelligence that humans are particularly proud of is the ability to solve problems. Many nonhuman animals are able to solve problems by either repeatedly using trial and error until they hit upon the right solution or by accidentally stumbling on it. But *thinking* one's way to a solution has traditionally been considered to be an exclusively human ability. Does this capacity extend to dolphins?

Some of the most important research about the ability of dolphins to solve problems has been done by Stan A. Kuczaj and John Gory. These two scientists studied the cognitive abilities of two bottlenose dolphins named Bob and Toby at the Living Seas portion of Disneyworld in Florida.[3] Two experiments, in particular, suggest that Bob and Toby could invent a strategy for solving a problem by *thinking*.

In one experiment, three clear plastic containers were placed in the pool fairly close to each other. In all three of them, when the dolphin dropped a weight into the top, the food compartment opened. In two of the containers, the weight would then fall to the tank floor—where it could be used again to open the food compartment of one of the other boxes. But in the third, the weight would fall into an obviously closed bottom—making it unavailable.

Kuczaj and Gory wanted to see if the dolphins could understand the implication of having both open-bottomed and closed-bottomed containers—that is, to get the maximum amount of fish, use the open-bottom container first. The scientists theorized that if the dolphins understood this, they would plan their behavior accordingly. Bob and Toby were run through six 30-trial blocks. From the first block onward, both dolphins used the container with the closed bottom last—suggesting that they could solve a problem by *thinking* about the conditions of the test.

Kuczaj and Gory's other experiment involved a container that required the dolphin to use two tools in a particular order to get the food inside. First, the dolphin had to drop a weight into the container. This caused a sliding door on the side of the box to open. Then the dolphin had to pick up a stick tool, swim to the side with the open door, and push the food out of the back of the container. The catch was that the door stayed open for only 15 seconds.

The dolphins learned how to open the container by observing humans use the weight and the stick in the correct order. At first, the two objects were placed close to the container, so the time limit wasn't a problem.

Once the dolphins were comfortable with opening the box, however, the researchers made the task more complicated. They moved the stick far enough away (about 75 feet) so that the sliding door would close before the dolphin returned. Kuczaj and Gory wanted to see if the dolphins would respond to the time limit by first picking up the stick and putting it near the site before putting the weight into the container.

---

[3]Stan A. Kuczaj II and Rachel S. Thames, "How Do Dolphins Solve Problems?," edited by Zentall and E. Wasserman, *Comparative Cognition: Experimental Explorations of Animal Intelligence* (Oxford: Oxford University Press, 2006). John D. Gory and Stan A. Kuczaj II, "Can Bottlenose Dolphins Plan Their Behavior?" Paper presented at the Biennial Conference on the Biology of Marine Mammals, Wailea, Maui, Hawaii, November–December, 1999.

First, both dolphins tried to beat the clock by swimming faster. Although this was a good idea, it didn't work. But both dolphins did ultimately solve the problem. The scientists explain that Toby stumbled onto the solution "serendipitously." Bob tried an alternative strategy of carrying both tools at once, although he couldn't handle both. But Bob did recognize the correct solution after observing some humans show him the proper strategy a few times.

Even though the two dolphins didn't discover the solution themselves, their behavior does suggest significant cognitive ability. The fact that their first strategy was to swim faster showed that they understood the nature of the problem. Bob did try a second tactic (carrying both tools at once), which also showed that he understood the nature of the problem. And when Bob and Toby finally came upon the correct strategy, they recognized it for what it was fairly quickly.

Kuczaj and Gory believe that these three experiments strongly suggest that Bob and Toby were able to "create a novel and appropriate solution in advance of executing the solution."[4] This seems like a reasonable sign of "intelligence."

Communication

Thinking about the possibilities of dolphin intelligence naturally leads to the fascinating question of whether dolphins can communicate. This question, of course, has two prongs. Can dolphins communicate with each other? And can they communicate with us?

The answer to the first question is easy. Like most animals, dolphins communicate with other members of their species. Dolphins probably use a combination of whistles, clicks, and gestures, although scientists admit that at this point they know little about both the content and the process of that communication. However, each dolphin has a unique signature whistle that identifies him or her as the speaker.

Do we know what they say to each other? Not yet. But two scientists have discovered that when a dolphin is in a stressful situation, its signature whistle may change in pitch and duration. James Ralston and Humphrey Williams speculate that the change may communicate something about the stressed dolphin's state to other members of its community.

Whether dolphins can communicate with humans is more complicated. Dolphins do not have vocal cords, so they cannot "speak." Instead, the sounds they make are high-frequency "clicks" and "whistles" that extend over a wide range of frequencies from 1000 to 80,000 Hz. (Human sounds, by comparison, span a lower and more limited set of frequencies from 300 to 3000 Hz.) The dolphins' sound system is so efficient that they can communicate with each other even when they are as far as six miles apart.

It should be clear already that dolphins communicate differently than we do. First, they use a wider range of frequencies, going from the sonic to ultrasonic. Second, with their whistles and clicks they can put out ten times more sonic information per second than we do. At least one researcher claimed that two dolphins

---

[4]John D. Gory and Stan A. Kuczaj II, "Can Bottlenose Dolphins Plan Their Behavior?"

exchanging information at top speed is probably more like two computers passing data back and forth than it is like two humans talking. Finally, although dolphins can make humanoid sounds with their blowholes, our kind of vocal communication would be painfully slow and cumbersome for them, if not impossible. In assessing the extent to which dolphins can communicate with each other or with us, then, we simply cannot judge them according to human standards.

Accordingly, researchers attempt to try to understand dolphins on their own terms, focusing more on their natural abilities. The discoveries are intriguing. In research that spanned thirty years, University of Hawaii psychologist Louis Herman used hand signals and computer-generated whistles to teach a vocabulary of fifty words to two dolphins, Phoenix and Akeakamai (Hawaiian for "lover of wisdom," the literal meaning of "philosopher"). Herman combined these words into sentences with as many as five words that instructed the mammals to perform certain tasks. Herman discovered that the dolphins had little difficulty understanding more than 1000 commands the first time they were given. In addition, the dolphins were sensitive to syntax or word order. They knew that "hoop pipe fetch" (which told the dolphin to take a hoop to a nearby pipe) means something different from "pipe hoop fetch." The significance of this, according to Herman, is that "this is the first convincing evidence that animals can understand syntactical information." Moreover, the dolphins were even taught different syntactic systems. For Phoenix, the command to place a Frisbee into a basket was "Frisbee in basket," while for Akeakamai it was "Frisbee basket in."

Other research, like that of Dianah Reiss and Ken Norris, has focused on body language and whistles. Norris noted that dolphins always make body movements when they generate their sounds. He hypothesizes that these movements are "packets of information" which are part of dolphin communication. Reiss concurs. She believes that dolphins and humans are very different linguistically. "I haven't seen anything analogous to a fixed acoustical grammar," she explains. "What I believe is that they communicate a lot nonverbally, that a lot of the grammar we've been looking for is in the behavior."

Reiss worked primarily with computer-generated sounds that resemble dolphins' whistles. Each sound stood for a different object that the dolphins worked with; one whistle meant "ball," for example, while others stood for other objects or requests. Reiss discovered that the two dolphins she worked with, Delphi and Pan, not only learned what the sounds stood for but integrated them into their own communication and used them in appropriate situations.

One day Dr. Reiss gave Pan the signal to find a toy in the pool and bring it to her. She didn't realize that Delphi already had in his mouth the only toys in the pool—two balls. Nonetheless, Pan went up to Delphi, used the "ball" whistle, and Delphi passed Pan one of the balls. And this wasn't the only time that happened.

Communication and Intelligence

The work of Herman and Reiss suggests at least a rudimentary capacity to understand symbols and commands, to use whistles designed to stand for objects, and to respond to human language. Consider as well this statement by Ken Norris: "Dolphins can handle speech when you give it to them. They can respond to it.

They have the capacity for generalizing; they can handle word order; and they can handle pronouns. They know who they are." Dolphins then, unquestionably possess some linguistic abilities of the sort usually associated with "intelligence" in humans.

Intelligence and Tool Use

Evidence even exists that at least some dolphins use natural objects as tools—which also suggests intelligence.

In both Sarasota Bay, Florida, and Shark Bay, Australia, scientists have observed bottlenose dolphins apparently using bubbles to help them capture fish. A dolphin lifts the back part of its body out of the water and then brings it down sharply into the water. This causes a loud splash and creates a trail of bubbles that may keep the fish from getting away. Scientists call the practice "kerplunking" after the sound made by the dolphin's tail. It looks like the dolphins make something like a "bubble net" and use it as a tool in their fishing.

In Shark Bay, some of the dolphins apparently use sponges as a tool. Rachel Smolker observed a number of female dolphins carrying around sponges on their rostra. Because of the difficult water conditions in her study site, Smolker wasn't able to verify conclusively how the dolphins were using the sponges. But she concluded that the most likely explanation was that they were using them for protection as they foraged for food. The floor of Shark Bay is inhabited by scorpionfish, stingrays, stonefish, and other creatures that could produce a painful, even potentially lethal injury to a dolphin. As Smolker explains, "All of these nasty creatures could be hazardous to a foraging dolphin, and some are particularly common in this channel. The dolphins are most likely using their sponges to shield themselves from the spines, stingers and barbs of creatures they encounter. They could also be shielding themselves from abrasion. Dolphins sometimes poke their beaks into the sand and bottom debris after burrowing fish. Using a sponge might help them to avoid getting scratched and cut by small sharp bits of shell and stone."[5] However, the significance of Smolker's discovery doesn't stop there. The scientist also discovered that this behavior is apparently taught by one generation to the next.

Dolphin Emotions

Many humans say that we cannot claim that nonhuman animals have personalities or emotions like our own. Because we can't get a first-hand report from nonhumans about their subjective states, we do not know what's going on inside them. The best we can do, then, is to infer internal states and motivations from outward behavior, and we certainly have to be careful doing that. Nonetheless, many scientists believe that a number of nonhumans do experience emotions of one sort or another, and dolphins are probably among them.

Noone disputes that dolphins feel isolation from other dolphins keenly. Some individuals who have been cut off from their families and schools behave in ways

---

[5]Rachel Smolker, *To Touch a Wild Dolphin* (New York: Doubleday, 2001), pp. 112–113.

that suggest grief. Some have stopped eating and died. Mothers whose calves have died have become listless, apparently mourning their loss.

Some trainers claim that individual dolphins have distinct personalities, differing in terms of curiosity, timidity, playfulness, aggression, speed of learning, and patience. Some enjoy swimming with humans more than others. Some like learning new behaviors more than others. Even mothers differ; some refuse to cut the apron strings, while others encourage their young to become independent. Dolphins also seem to have what we call moods. They can be eager to work some days, lackadaisical on others, and stubbornly uncooperative on still others.

Perhaps most impressive, however, is that dolphins can act in ways that suggest that they're sensitive to the moods of humans they've come to know. Marine educator Laura Urian tells the following story. When she worked at Florida's Dolphin Research Center, Laura was particularly fond of a dolphin named Halley. One day she arrived at the Center to find that the dolphin had died. Upset by Halley's death, Laura approached her work with the other dolphins visibly saddened. While Laura was doing the morning feeding, however, a dolphin named Theresa did something very unusual. Theresa never does flips, but while Laura was feeding her, she executed a series of six of them. Had Theresa taken note of Laura's mood? While it is impossible to know precisely what Theresa's sense of things was, certainly one interpretation is that she could understand Laura's emotional state because she is capable of similar feelings herself and was trying to cheer Laura up in her own way.

The Sonic World of the Dolphin

Dolphins use the sounds they make for more than just communicating. They also rely on them to make sense of the world around them. Dolphins have within them the equivalent of a "sonar" system. They send out sonic signals—their "clicks"—and "read" the echoes that bounce back from objects.

This internal sonar mechanism is very sophisticated—more sophisticated than any machine we have been able to build. Researchers in one experiment put two discs 1/16-inch thick behind something which would block the dolphin's sight but not its sonar. The only difference in the discs was that one was aluminum and the other copper. The dolphin could tell them apart. In another famous experiment, scientists took two identical containers and filled one with rocks and the other with fish. Even blindfolded, the dolphins could tell the difference.

A dolphin's sonar system is so different from anything in human experience that scientists admit they still know relatively little about it. Do dolphins "hear" the echoes of their clicks or are the sound waves translated into a visual image, as happens on a sonar screen? Is it a combination of hearing and seeing? Or is there nothing analogous in our experience? No one is sure.

We do know that the dolphin's sonic sensory system marks a critical difference between them and us. We humans are primarily visual creatures. We use sound to communicate with each other, but our main vehicle for gaining and storing information is visual. We use our eyes; we look things over; we read; we write; our computers display information visually.

Dolphins are as auditory as we are visual. While they take in some information with their eyes, they learn much more about their world with their sonar. After all, they live in a world that is neither as bright as ours nor as easy to see in. Light waves travel well in air, but not so well in water. Sound, however, travels much better in water than in the air. It makes sense, then, that the dolphin's large brain would include a highly complicated system for taking in, storing, processing, and communicating auditory information.

Reality in a Sonic World

This highly developed auditory sense in the dolphin has one very important implication for us. It means that the dolphin's most basic ways of experiencing reality are very different from ours.

Imagine what being alive and living in a watery world must feel like for dolphins. For one thing, between their visual and sonic senses, they can take in much more information in any given instant than we can. They may, then, have a more varied and more complete picture of the world around them than we do.

Also, since their sonar is the dolphins' primary sense, their understanding of where they are and what's around them comes from what they pick up about the shape, size, and density of objects. Furthermore, because of the high frequencies they use, dolphins can actually "see through" things that we cannot. For instance, dolphins can probably see into each other's bodies. This could let them know something about one another's health. In fact, one of the dolphins at the Dolphin Research Center showed that she knew when women were pregnant. When this dolphin was pregnant, she was ordinarily standoffish and avoided contact with humans. But on two occasions with two different women she did something unusual. The dolphin came over to a woman in the water and sonared her abdomen. Then the dolphin flipped over, displaying her own pregnancy, and allowed the woman to touch her. One of these women was noticeably pregnant. The other, however, didn't know at the time she was pregnant—although she discovered that she was when she returned home.

This sonic sense may also let dolphins know each other's emotions. Our own emotions are usually accompanied by certain physical responses. When we get nervous, for example, our palms sweat, our hearts beat faster, and we breathe more often and more shallowly. There's no reason to think that fear or anxiety does not cause changes in a dolphin's body. The only difference is that a dolphin can "see" these internal physical states as easily as you can see the color of somebody's shirt.

You no doubt know some people who wear their feelings on their sleeve. What would it be like to live in a world in which it was impossible for us to conceal our feelings from everybody else? You would know someone's emotional state just by looking at them. And everyone would know your mood as easily as they would know you were wearing a hat. There would be none of those exchanges in which a friend asks "So how are you?" and you reply "Terrific!" when you are actually scraping bottom. Similarly, in a world like this it might be impossible to lie. After all, that's what lie detectors are all about. They measure our bodies' reactions to anxiety when we answer questions truthfully or falsely.

Dolphins, then, experience reality with senses that give them the powers of a living sonar installation, X-ray machine, and a lie detector. They pull in tremendous amounts of information from around them and store, process, and retrieve that information in ways that are hard for us to imagine.

Different Realities/Different Concepts/Different Intelligence

If our two species experience life so differently, and if dolphins can think even at a basic level, their concepts could be different from ours. After all, how you experience reality determines practically everything about you—from the facts you know to the values you hold. Dolphins, then, probably live in a different world from us *conceptually* as well as *geographically.*

To take an everyday example, we have one word for "water" which we then separate into "fresh" and "salt." If dolphins have a way of referring to "water," their distinctions are probably as varied as the many different words that Eskimos have for "snow" and for the same reasons. (In an arctic world, it's important to be able to distinguish different kinds of snow.)

On a more abstract level, we humans have the concept "knowledge," which usually means the "facts" or "principles" about something. "Knowledge" and related concepts like "true" and "false" are very important to us because of our rational nature. But this family of concepts is not universal or immutable; it is directly related to our human nature. Our brains have the ability to gather, catalogue, and store information in an orderly, visual manner, and it is the inclination of our species to do that.

A biologist would probably say that prehistoric humans could cope better with their environment and survive longer by storing and recalling information about the world around them. The ability to store and retrieve factual knowledge thus became extraordinarily useful to us as a species, and so the ability was handed down and became increasingly important. To be able to access factual knowledge meant a more secure (and longer) life. Thus, our human brain continued to develop along these lines and we have continued to devise various ways to store information—writing, books, libraries, tapes, databases—that we can retrieve visually. Thus, what we now define as "knowledge" and put the bulk of our trust in today is the result of what was most useful in our evolution as a species. Our notion of "knowledge" is a distinctly human concept that emerged from the unique evolution our species has experienced over millions of years.

Now imagine what "knowledge" might be if it developed out of the dolphin's nature and evolutionary history. We might start such an inquiry by asking, "What cognitive abilities might have been useful to its survival in the water?" Observing its advanced sonic system after the fact, we can presume that was one very important ability. Clearly there are major advantages to having a sensory system that gathers information through obstacles and over vast distances no matter where you live or how well you can see. Those individuals who could do this best could monitor their environment at all times and in all conditions, locating food and keeping track of each other as well as their natural enemies. A way of storing and communicating such vital information about their world would also help survival. However, it is not easy to write underwater, and an alternative system for handling information would be necessary. That's probably where the high-frequency whistles and clicks come from. Furthermore, because dolphins live in a medium where external storage of information is next to impossible, they apparently had to rely more on highly developed brain functions and, in particular, memory.

But somewhere along the line dolphins apparently learned that their life would be easier and more secure if they cooperated with each other in performing life's important tasks and if they limited their aggression against each other. In that case, what would be most useful? Knowing how to cooperate with and relate to other members of the group. Accordingly, the ability to interact effectively with other dolphins would be a primary means of their survival. And in that case, the most important "knowledge" wouldn't be impersonal, objective facts but the more subjective, emotional, personal, intuitive "knowing" of what some other dolphin is like and how to deal with him or her. "Knowledge" would be knowing what makes other dolphins tick, both collectively and individually. It would also include knowing how to deal with other dolphins to win their assistance without provoking them to aggression.

This implies that our concept of "intelligence" is directly related to our concept of "knowledge." Humans determine how "intelligent" others are by how much factual knowledge they have or how skillful they are at uncovering, learning, and working with the facts they need to solve problems. But realize that this is not intelligence *in general* that we are talking about here—it is human intelligence. Our concept of intelligence may let us judge how intellectually facile other members of our species are, but we must understand that that's as far as we can go with it.

If our speculations about what "knowledge" a dolphin needs are correct, its "intelligence" would include some factual knowledge, but it would be related much more to what we call "interpersonal skills." From this point of view, the "intelligent" being is the one who knows how to relate effectively to the other beings upon whom its survival depends. Thus, concepts as seemingly simple as "knowledge" and "intelligence" could look very different from a dolphin's point of view.

At first glance, then, dolphins are in many ways like us and in many ways quite different. The description so far should suggest to you at least that they're probably much more complicated than you first thought.

To carry our investigation further, now, let's return to the question: "Is a dolphin a person?"

Is a Dolphin a Person?

At the beginning of this chapter, we listed eight characteristics of a "person."

1. A person is alive.

2. A person is aware.

3. A person feels positive and negative sensations.

4. A person has emotions.

5. A person has a sense of self.

6. A person controls its own behavior.

7. A person recognizes other persons and treats them appropriately.

8. A person has a variety of sophisticated cognitive abilities. It is capable of analytical, conceptual thought. A person can learn, retain, and recall information. It can

solve complex problems with analytical thought. And a person can communicate in a way that suggests thought.

Let's go down our list of criteria, then, and see how dolphins fare.

1. A person is alive.
This one is easy. Dolphins are animals, and they are quite alive.

2. A person is aware.
The issue of "awareness" or "consciousness" in nonhumans is always difficult to make judgments about. In fact, some scientists and philosophers refuse to talk about awareness, or even pain, in nonhuman animals because it's impossible to get their subjective description of what their inner world is like. We don't have to be absolutely categorical about this, however. Whether or not a nonhuman animal is aware isn't necessarily a black-or-white issue. Certainly gradations, or degrees, of awareness are possible. A being high on the scale would have a sophisticated inner world; how it understands and reacts to things could be quite complex. A being with a level of awareness low on the scale would be conscious of the outside world and able to respond to it but in a much more simple way.

In fact, when we talk about whether the "mental" qualities we associate with personhood appear in nonhuman animals, it's acceptable—even from a strictly scientific point of view—to talk about a continuum. As Susan Shane, a dolphin scientist from California, puts it, "I don't think that evolutionarily there's much justification for separating humans out from animals. It just doesn't make sense that one species would be absolutely different in all ways from every other species. All other species have to fit into a continuum in terms of different capabilities that they have, and you could only expect that there would be a continuum of mental capabilities also."[6]

If we allow for a continuum or gradations of consciousness, then, at least a low order of consciousness is common in the animal world. If you have ever had a pet or worked with nonhuman animals, you know that all animals have at least some kind of awareness of their world. Your dog recognizes you when you come home, chases your cat occasionally, and generally acts as though he's conscious of what's going on around him.

What about dolphins? Certainly, dolphins are aware of their external environments. Dolphins are universally placed high on the biological ladder, and the fact that they are aware of the external world and able to interact with it is apparent from the way that they handle the demands of living in the ocean and from the simple fact that they can be so easily trained. When we get farther down on the list, we'll try to judge how complex a dolphin's awareness is. But there's little doubt that their behavior suggests a significant level of awareness.

3. A person feels positive and negative sensations.
Most nonhumans react to cuts, bruises, and broken bones as we do—with behaviors that suggest they feel pain. And when your dog, for example, pesters you to scratch his head even though you're tired of it, it certainly seems as though the experience is pleasurable for him.

Dolphins, too, appear to feel pain and pleasure. Their brains, like ours, have pain centers, and their skin is especially sensitive. They certainly appear to experience pleasure from their frequent sexual behavior and from some of their "play" behavior. Dolphins clearly act in a way that suggests they experience "positive and negative sensations."

---

[6]Private communication.

4. A person has emotions.

There's no small amount of evidence suggesting that dolphins have emotions. First, the dolphin brain has a limbic system—the part of the brain that generates emotions. More importantly, among scientists and dolphin trainers, there is also little doubt that dolphins have emotions, that is, that dolphins behave in ways that suggest that they have such feelings. For example, Susan Shane writes, "Captive dolphins have been known to refuse food and starve themselves to death when a tank companion dies. Mother dolphins have carried the decomposing bodies of their stillborn calves for two weeks and longer. Such behavior indicates that social bonds between individual dolphins are very strong and emotional attachments are deep."[7]

Perhaps the most interesting point about dolphin emotions is that the emotional traits of dolphins appear to combine into the equivalent of our "personalities," what researcher Carol Howard calls "dolphinalities."[8] Trainers see differences in curiosity, timidity, playfulness, aggression, speed of learning, and patience. Some captive dolphins enjoy swimming with humans more than others. Some like learning new behaviors more than others. Even mothers differ; some refuse to cut the apron strings, whereas others encourage their young to become independent. Dolphins also seem to have what we call moods. Captive dolphins can be eager to work some days, lackadaisical on others, and stubbornly uncooperative on still others.

5. A person has a sense of self.

It's one thing to experience physical pleasure, pain, and a variety of emotions. But it's quite another to be aware that one is having these experiences and to be able to reflect on them. And so, we come to one of the most important requirements for personhood—self-awareness. Can a dolphin look inside and say, "I"?

There are at least five grounds for believing that dolphins have some concept of self.

- As noted earlier, dolphins have a unique whistle called a "signature whistle." That is, each dolphin has the equivalent of a "name," a concept that seems to require some sense of self. They can use these whistles to initiate interaction, to stay in contact with each other when separated from a distance, and to communicate information about themselves.

- Dolphins can recognize reflections of themselves in mirrors as just that, reflections.[9] To date, only humans and some other great apes have demonstrated this capability. All other nonhumans—and human children before a certain age—mistake the image for another animal or child. For dolphins to join us in this group, they would clearly need the capacity to say the equivalent of, "The image in this surface is a representation of me. It is not some other dolphin."

- Dolphins can do things that appear to require a sense of self. In order to do the kind of problem solving that Stan Kuczaj and John Gory described, dolphins would

---

[7]Susan Shane, *The Bottlenose Dolphin in the Wild* (San Carlos, CA: Hatcher Trade Press, 1988), p. 28.

[8]See Carol Howard, *Dolphin Chronicles* (New York: Bantam, 1995), Chapter 5, "Dolphinalities."

[9]Kenneth Martin and Suchi Psarakos, "Evidence of Self-Awareness in the Bottlenose Dolphin (*Tursiops truncatus*)," *Self-Awareness in Animals and Humans: Developmental Perspectives,* edited by Sue Taylor Parker, Robert W. Mitchell, and Maria L. Boccia, Chapter 24, pp. 361–379 (New York: Cambridge University Press, 1995). Lori Marino, Diana Reiss, and Gordon Gallup, "Mirror Self-Recognition in Bottlenose Dolphins: Implications for Comparative Study of Highly Dissimilar Species," *Self-Awareness in Animals and Humans,* eds. Parker, Boccia and Mitchell, pp. 380–391.

have to be able to reflect on the contents of their consciousness—something that requires self-awareness.

- Ken Norris claims that "dolphins can handle pronouns; they know who *they* are." The significance of this is that to understand such concepts as "you," "he," "she," "we," and "they," a being first needs to know what "I" means.

- Dolphin self-awareness is also suggested by this intriguing remark of a trainer who remarked to me, "When you look into their eyes, you know there's someone looking back." Although obviously subjective, this comment captures the experience of those of us who have spent any time in the water with dolphins.

6. A person controls its own behavior.

By "self-controlled behavior" we mean actions that are generated from within the person and are not the direct result of irresistible internal or external forces. In the case of nonhumans, this means at least a noteworthy ability to act independently of instinct, biological drives, or conditioning. The capacity of a person to be the author of his or her own actions is important for two reasons. First, it demonstrates that a being's cognitive and affective states are sophisticated enough to have an impact on its actions. Hence, a person's actions can be construed as being more than automatic, unthinking responses to stimuli. Actions can in some fashion be said to belong to the person doing them, that is, to be evidence of, as philosophers traditionally put it, a "free choice" or "free will." These terms refer to our ability to do things because we choose to do them, not because we are driven by some other force.

In fact, we believe we have so much control over our actions that we ordinarily hold one another "responsible" for what we do. That is, some significant capacity of choice allows us to say that the being in question is "responsible" for its actions. We let people off the hook for doing something wrong or hurtful only when the act results from force, insanity, or duress.

Do dolphins control their actions sufficiently that we can say they *choose* them? Do dolphins behave in ways that suggest that they expect that they and/or others control their actions in certain ways? That is, do they show any evidence of understanding and using a concept of *responsibility*?

Choice and Control over Behavior

There is evidence from a number of fronts suggesting that dolphins control their behavior.

- Scientists have identified examples of various feeding strategies (the use of mud rings, hydroplaning, and herding) that appear to be the product of deliberation and choice.

- Particularly impressive from a scientific perspective is Stan Kuczaj and John Gory's research. There seems little question that the behavior of the two dolphins involved in this research resulted from thinking and choice.

- Rachel Smolker, cofounder of the Monkey Mia Dolphin Project at Shark Bay on the west coast of Australia, describes a fascinating event involving a bottlenose dolphin that she named Holly. In May 1988, a terrible storm rolled over the study site.

Smolker was fortunate. The only thing of value that she lost was a tool kit that had been in her small boat. The dinghy had been tossed about and sunk by powerful winds, and the tool kit had obviously been thrown out. An interesting incident took place about a week later. The scientist writes,

> A week or so after things have settled back down again, I wake up early and go down to see the dolphins. Holly is in at the beach and in a languid mood. I have the urge to jump into the water with her this morning, so I don my snorkel and mask. She stays just offshore, watching me get dressed, and I can tell by her patient, attentive waiting that she too is in the mood for a swimming partner. In my excitement, I fall over trying to get my flippers on. Holly is whistling as I slide into the water alongside her. . . . Side by side we progress slowly out into deeper water. . . . Then she gently moves out from under my arm and heads down toward the bottom. We are in about twenty feet of water, and I try to dive with her, but my awkward flailing seems inappropriate so I retreat to wait at the surface. Below me, she is poking at something on the bottom, but the water is too murky for me to see. A moment later she comes back up toward me, dragging something large, white, and apparently heavy, which she is holding in her jaws. She comes directly to me and delivers a plastic bag into my hands. I take it, and she moves away, diving again at some distance from me. She is done swimming with me for now, and it would be useless to try to catch up to her. . . . I tread water for a moment and untie the plastic bag. It looks vaguely familiar somehow. Inside are a ratchet wrench set, pliers, screwdrivers, some spark plugs, and flares. It is the tool kit from my boat.[10]

It is difficult to imagine a more likely explanation for this unusual event than deliberation and choice on the part of Holly.

Choice and Responsibility

The ability of dolphins to choose their behavior is also suggested in the actions of a community of wild Atlantic spotted dolphins that has interacted with humans since about 1980 in the Bahamas. The dolphins initiated this contact, which typically takes place in shallow waters (about 20 to 30 feet deep) approximately 50 miles offshore. The dolphins appear to be motivated simply by a desire for social interaction—perhaps some combination of curiosity, socializing, or recreation. (There's no food involved, and spending time with humans doesn't give them more protection from predators in their environment.) These dolphin/human encounters can last from 5 minutes to 4 hours involving anywhere from 1 to 50 dolphins. Given a dolphin's superior speed and agility in the water, the dolphins obviously control the duration and character of these interactions. Cetaceans are the only animals known to actively seek out contact with humans in the wild. It's difficult to imagine any other explanation for this behavior than conscious choice.

More interesting than the fact that these interactions give us an example of choice, however, is an incident that raises the possibility that dolphins may both

---

[10]Rachel Smolker, *To Touch a Wild Dolphin* (New York: Doubleday, 2001), pp. 221–222.

understand and utilize a concept of responsibility. This community of spotted dolphins has not only sought out human interaction; it also has allowed humans to observe aspects of its culture. Since 1985, marine scientist Denise Herzing has observed and recorded these interactions with the aid of a changing group of volunteer assistants. (I have been part of this group since 1990.) Over time, two distinctly different encounters emerged. In the one, the dolphins desire a high degree of social interaction with the humans. In the other, the humans are expected simply to watch, as the dolphins go on with aspects of their lives. To date, these dolphins have shown hunting and feeding, sexual behavior, disputes and the resolution of disputes, adult dolphins teaching the young skills like fishing, baby-sitting, disciplining the young, juvenile behavior, and both peaceful and aggressive interactions between different species of dolphins (spotteds and bottlenose).[11] In one of the "observing" encounters that I was part of, a mother dolphin was teaching its calf how to fish. One of the human swimmers mistook this encounter as one in which interaction was appropriate, and her attempt to engage the calf distracted the youngster from its task at hand. The mother then swam in front of Herzing, performed a tail-slap (a sign of displeasure or attention getting), gathered her calf from the swimmer, and returned to teaching her offspring how to fish.

What is striking about this action is that the mother dolphin tail-slapped in front of Herzing, *not the offending swimmer*. Given the context of this encounter and the history of Herzing's interactions with the community, isn't it likely that the mother targeted Herzing, and not the swimmer, because the dolphin recognized Herzing from years of encounters as the individual who was dominant in the hierarchy of humans and held her "responsible" for the actions of the other swimmers? Could the dolphin's behavior have been a way of saying, "These are your people; keep them in line"? That is, how likely is it that the dolphin's rebuke of Herzing might have employed a concept of responsibility?

In fact, this is the most likely explanation, given the meaning of tail-slaps, how the mother delivered it, and how dolphins deal with each other. For example, Herzing reports that this is exactly the way this signal is used when directed to a responsible party of a juvenile subgroup of dolphins. Hence, it is the most likely signal to be tried by a dolphin who wants to communicate with a human in the water. It seems very likely, then, that the mother dolphin's message had something to do with her sense of Herzing's *responsibility* for her group.

7. A person recognizes other persons and treats them appropriately.

Do dolphins act in ways that suggest not only that they have a sophisticated inner world but also that they can recognize it when they encounter this trait in others? That is, do they recognize other persons? Do they behave in ways that suggest that this recognition matters to them? Specifically, do dolphins act toward humans in ways that suggest that they recognize us as the type of beings that we are?

The most basic sign that we recognize someone else as a person is that we treat that individual as "some one," not "some thing." We regard such people's lives as special. We

---

[11]D. L. Herzing and C. M. Johnson, "Interspecific Interactions between Atlantic Spotted Dolphins (*Stenella frontalis*) and Bottlenose Dolphins (*Tursiops truncatus*) in the Bahamas, 1985–1995," *Aquatic Mammals,* 1997, 23, 2, pp. 85–99.

respect their rights and vital interests. We appreciate their intrinsic worth, and we act accordingly. Surely, one sign that we recognize other persons and treat them appropriately is that we go out of our way to help them.

What we would call "altruistic" behavior is one of the most intriguing characteristics of dolphins. Dolphins have a long-standing and well-documented concern for other beings. They try to save other dolphins from drowning. There are many stories, from preclassical times to the present, of dolphins assisting humans. These range from helping sailors navigate through dangerous waters to supporting people who have fallen overboard. During the 1998 South Caribbean Ocean Regatta, for example, a sailor fell into the ocean while moving forward on his boat to drop a sail. Because the seas were so rough, the rest of the crew lost sight of him. As boats in the race searched for a couple of hours, the swimmer found himself surrounded by a group of dolphins. At the same time, one of the boats saw two dolphins swim toward it, swim away, and then repeat the pattern. Even though the boat had searched the area that the dolphins were swimming toward, the crew felt that the dolphins were trying to tell them something. They followed the dolphins and were led to the swimmer.[12]

If dolphins recognize that we and they are both aware and intelligent, it wouldn't be unreasonable that they might value our lives and well-being as they do their own.

8. A person has a variety of sophisticated cognitive abilities. It is capable of analytical, conceptual thought. A person can learn, retain, and recall information. It can solve complex problems with analytical thought. And a person can communicate in a way that suggests thought.

To most humans, the most important criteria for personhood are intellectual. Persons must be able to think analytically and conceptually. Their behavior must demonstrate cognitive capacities. They must be "intelligent."

What do we see on this front in dolphins?

- The dolphin brain appears to be able to support advanced cognitive and affective operations. It has a large cerebral cortex (the part of the brain where our higher operations take place) and a substantial amount of associational neocortex (the type of cortex that integrates and processes data and makes up the human prefrontal cortex). Most anatomical ratios that assess cognitive capacity (brain weight/spinal cord, enchephalization quotient) place it second only to the human brain. At the very least, the dolphin brain appears to be the second most complicated and powerful brain on the planet.

- We saw earlier that dolphins appear to have not only consciousness but also self-consciousness.

- Lou Herman's research into whether dolphins can understand artificial human languages is particularly striking. He showed that the two dolphins he studied can

---

[12]"Dolphins Find Missing Sailor," *Cruising World*, March 1998, pp. 10–12. Interspecies altruism is not unknown. A highly publicized example occurred on August 16, 1996, at the Brookfield Zoo in Brookfield, Illinois, where a 7-year-old female gorilla named Binti tended to a 3-year-old human boy who sustained serious head injuries from falling 18 feet onto a concrete area where there were seven gorillas. The gorilla picked up the boy, held him in her arms, and placed him near a door where zookeepers could get him. ("Gorilla Rescues Boy, 3, After Fall," Associated Press, August 17, 1996.)

understand and work with the basic elements of human language (vocabulary, grammar, syntax, complex sentences, etc.).

- The fact that some dolphins apparently use natural objects as tools is also impressive.

- The dolphins' performance on Stan Kuczaj and John Gory's experiments suggests an array of cognitive skills needed to solve new and complex problems. In addition, consider the following episode that took place at Florida's Dolphin Research Center when it was asked to take in a sick dolphin from an aquarium.

- In order to ease her transition to her new home, this dolphin was put in with two dolphins who had lived at the Center for a number of years, Mr. Gipper and Little Bit.

     You need to know that this particular research center is situated in a natural habitat on the Gulf side of Grassy Key. The dolphins live in a series of pools separated from the ocean only by low fences, which the dolphins can jump over—or make holes in. Although the dolphins are content to live at the Center, they come and go as they please, often visiting the nearby waters. Mr. Gipper, in particular, enjoyed coming and going, and he had made a hole in the fence to make his travels easier. Before putting the new dolphin in with Mr. Gipper and Little Bit, the staff patched the hole so that the sick dolphin would stay put.

     Unknown to the staff, however, Mr. Gipper had reopened the hole. The new dolphin quickly found the hole and headed for the open seas. This presented a serious problem. As sick as she was, had she gotten lost, she surely would have died. But what happened is that, apparently sensing the danger, Mr. Gipper and Little Bit went after her, turned her around, and brought her back. Remember, dolphins have a history of helping each other in times of need.

     That, in itself, is impressive, but the story continues. When the dolphins returned, the new animal wouldn't go back through the fence. Despite the fact that she'd gone through the hole once, it is not surprising that she'd balk about coming back through again. Dolphins instinctively shy away from going through openings like that ("gating," as it is called, is ordinarily difficult to teach), so what was surprising was that she went through it the first time. Faced with the sick dolphin's refusal, Mr. Gipper stayed with her while Little Bit went back and forth through the hole to show her that it was safe. Reassured, she went through the fence, and once all three were back inside, the other two kept her away from the hole until it could be reclosed.

     Here we have two dolphins facing a potentially dangerous situation and a complicated problem with several parts. Again, we cannot know for certain what went on in the heads of these dolphins. But it looks like one or both of the other dolphins assessed the situation well enough to know that the third was in jeopardy, decided on an appropriate course of action, enlisted the other's aid, reassured the runaway and enticed her back through the fence, and then kept her from leaving again until the hole was patched. If that's what happened, the reasoning is impressive.

- As far as communication goes, research with dolphins and language indicates that dolphins can learn to understand some aspects of human language. Within the limits of their "vocabulary," they can carry out commands they have never heard before, and they are sensitive to word order or syntax. Ken Norris believes that, between whistles and body movements, wild dolphins can communicate a good deal of vital information to each other. Some of the information is probably about specific facts: for example, the boundaries of the school and the presence or absence of predators or food. But much of the information is probably about the physical condition or emotional state of individual dolphins. From these different pieces of information communicated throughout the group, each dolphin apparently constructs a mental image of a critical but abstract concept—the state of the school.[13] It is difficult to believe that such a system of communication does not require a fair degree of cognitive ability.

But do dolphin communications contain anything that suggests what we would call "thought"? Recall some of the stories we've looked at. For example, there was the story about the dolphin Theresa, who did a series of flips for her human trainer, Laura, who was grieving over the death of another dolphin. Isn't it possible that Theresa was trying to convey something to Laura that we would accept as a high-level communication? When Little Bit and Mr. Gipper retrieved the sick dolphin, didn't they have to communicate with each other as they thought their way through a number of problems?

Here we run into the question of degree or extent. How much thought do we have to see evidence of in a communication? How complicated does the communication have to be to meet the criterion? How many topics must a "person" be able to handle? Is everyday concrete experience enough, or will we also insist on poetry, music, and theoretical physics? Is the ability to use symbols and metaphors required? Must a person speak in terms of the past and future, as well as the present? And so on.

These are important questions, but for now it doesn't really matter how we answer them. Dolphins can communicate in some fashion, and some evidence suggests that it might be at a sophisticated level.

Summing Up

With respect to the criteria for personhood, how did dolphins do? On balance, pretty well. Obviously, we do not know as much as we'd like about these marine mammals. And we must remember that dolphins' evolutionary history and present reality are so different from ours that we would be wrong in insisting that they be "just like us" to be regarded as "persons." However, according to a traditional definition of "personhood" and a conventional set of criteria for the various traits of a person, the scientific research currently available about dolphins suggests a strong case for recognizing them as "nonhuman persons." Dolphins seem to be self-aware

---

[13]Norris claims that the spinners' "sensory integration system" allows each dolphin "to sense the spatial disposition of its comrades and thus to define the school's protective envelope for its members. This implies the capabilities that underlie the emergence of animal culture. That is, each dolphin must construct in its own mind a gestalt of the shape of the school at any instant from just a few data points. It must mentally fill in the spaces in three dimensions. At the same time, it must also make predictions about the immediate future. Receiving information that some members are indicating the imminence of a turn tells the dolphin what it must do. The dolphin is not following a leader *seriatim* but is instead behaving in terms of a more abstract conception—the state of the school." Kenneth Norris, "Comparative View," *Hawaiian Spinner Dolphin* (Berkeley, CA: University of California Press, 1994) p. 334.

beings with complex cognitive and affective capabilities. A dolphin appears to be a "who," not a "what"—a being, not an object—with a sophisticated, individual awareness of the world.

Ethical Implications

The question of whether dolphins are persons, however, is not some idle, speculative exercise. If dolphins are persons, important implications flow from this fact. From an ethical standpoint, personhood conveys rights. In the abortion debate, some argue that even a few cells that will eventually *become* a person has rights, and especially the right to live. If dolphins are persons, then, shouldn't they have similar rights? Yet thousands of dolphins die each year in the nets that humans use to fish. (In the last thirty years, more than six million dolphins have perished in this fashion.) If this were happening to humans, we would call it a massacre, or genocide. In addition, more than 400 dolphins live in entertainment facilities. Although these dolphins are generally well cared for, their lives are very different from those of wild dolphins. (They live in small, artificial tanks. They have relationships with only a very small number of other dolphins. Their lives are much less complex and challenging. Their breeding is controlled.) Is it morally justifiable to keep such advanced beings in such conditions? Does this fatally violate any rights or make it impossible for dolphins to fully develop their capacities and achieve a mature sense of satisfaction with life? Moreover, are the highly successful captive breeding programs morally justifiable? After all, the last time that we as a species bred for our service the captive members of a socially, emotionally, and intellectually sophisticated species, we called it "slavery." Is it possible that we're doing the same thing now, only we're blind to it because we're unwilling to concede that there may actually be nonhuman persons on the planet with us?

A Final Story

Let's conclude our discussion of dolphins with one final story that is both touching and thought provoking.

When the dolphin named Mr. Gipper (whom you met earlier) was quite old, he became ill and was put into a separate pool so that he could be cared for more easily. One day the staff was attending to a dolphin in a different pool, and when they finished, Theresa came out of the water, twirling and whistling. She spun around faster and faster and then just stopped. Mandy Rodriguez, who owned the Center, had known Mr. Gipper for a long time and felt very close to him. As he watched Theresa's display, he felt that Theresa was trying to tell him something. He felt almost as if a hand picked him up and made him go over to see Mr. Gipper. As he got into the water and put his arms around the dolphin, Mr. Gipper died.

As with all these stories, we have to begin by conceding that we cannot really know what went on because we cannot get the dolphin's side of the story. It is hard, however, to avoid the speculation that Theresa sensed that Mr. Gipper was about to die, knew that Mandy cared about him, and communicated to Mandy that he should go to his dying friend. And if even a portion of this interpretation is true, then perhaps dolphins are more like you and me than most of us would have first thought.

Main Points of Chapter 14

1. One assumption that most of us make regarding "persons" is that humans are the only candidates for personhood. This chapter questions that idea by asking whether a dolphin might be a "person."

2. Dolphins are likely candidates for personhood because they are large-brained, highly social marine mammals who act in ways that suggest that they are biologically advanced and "intelligent."

3. When compared against the necessary conditions of a "person," dolphins do quite well. They are alive, are aware, experience positive and negative sensations; they seem to have a sense of self and emotions; they behave in ways that suggest self-control; recognize and treat other persons appropriately; they appear to perform higher-order intellectual operations; they seem to have a sophisticated communication system that involves some degree of thought.

4. The possibility that dolphins are persons raises the question about the ethical acceptability of the deaths and injuries of dolphins in connection with the fishing industry and the captivity of dolphins in the entertainment industry.

Discussion Questions

1. After looking at the analysis of "personhood" and reading about dolphins, do you think that a dolphin should be considered a "person"? Why or why not?

2. If you think that dolphins are persons, does that mean that they have certain rights? Which ones? What about life, liberty, and the pursuit of happiness? If dolphins are persons, is it wrong to keep them in captivity in aquariums? Is it wrong to train them and use them in shows?

3. If you are undecided about whether a dolphin is a person, what criteria are most troublesome? In which areas would you want more evidence?

4. Do you think that a dolphin has a "mind"? Is this different from having a brain?

5. In this kind of philosophical investigation, we have to infer certain conclusions from the available facts. Did the discussion in this chapter ever make unreasonable inferences, that is, conclusions that the data do not warrant?

6. Can you think of any other animals that could be persons? Some chimpanzees and gorillas have been taught some human sign language. Does this make them possible candidates for personhood?

Selected Readings

For discussions of the concept of personhood, see: D. C Dennett, "Conditions of Personhood," in *Brainstorms: Philosophical Essays on Mind and Psychology* (Cambridge, MA: Bradford Books, 1976–1978), pp. 267–85; Joseph Fletcher, "Humanness," in *Humanhood: Essays in Biomedical Ethics* (New York: Prometheus, 1979), pp. 12–16. On the possibility of cognitive states in other animals, read: Donald R. Griffin, *The Question of Animal Awareness: Evolutionary Continuity of Mental Experience* (New York: The Rockefeller University Press,

1976) and *Animal Thinking* (Cambridge, MA: Harvard University Press, 1984). On the possibility of nonhuman persons, see: David DeGrazia, *Taking Animals Seriously* (Cambridge, MA: Cambridge University Press, 1996), W. R. Schwartz, "The Problem of Other Possible Persons: Dolphins, Primates and Aliens," *Advances in Descriptive Psychology*, vol. 2 (1982), pp. 31–55; the essays in *What Is a Person?*, edited by Michael F. Goodman (Clifton, NJ: Humana Press, 1988). Also see the various essays in Paola Cavalieri and Peter Singer, eds., *The Great Ape Project: Equality Beyond Humanity* (New York: St. Martin's Press, 1993) and Paola Cavlieri, ed., *Etica & Animali: Special Issue Devoted to Nonhuman Personhood*, 9/98.

If you would like to know more about dolphins, consult the following works, many of which this chapter relies on: Susan Chollar, "Conversations with the Dolphins," *Psychology Today*, April 1989, 52–57; Carol Howard, *Dolphin Chronicles* (New York: Bantam, 1995); John C. Lily, *Communication Between Man and Dolphin: The Possibilities of Talking With Other Species* (New York: Julian Press, 1978); Kenneth Norris, *Dolphin Days: The Life and Times of the Spinner Dolphin* (New York: W. W. Norton, 1991); Norris et al., *The Hawaiian Spinner Dolphin* (Berkeley, CA: University of California Press, 1994); Norris and Karen Pryor, eds., *Dolphin Societies: Discoveries and Puzzles* (Berkeley, CA: University of California Press, 1991); J. E. Reynolds III and S. A. Rommell, eds., *Biology of Marine Mammals* (Washington, DC: Smithsonian Institution Press, 1999), John E. Reynolds III, Randall S. Wells, and Samantha D. Eide, *The Bottlenose Dolphin: Biology and Conservation* (Gainesville, FL: University of Florida Press, 2000); S. H. Ridgeway, "Dolphin Brain Size," in *Research on Dolphins*, edited by M. M. Bryen and Richard Harrison (Oxford: Oxford University Press, 1986), pp. 59–70; Susan H. Shane, *The Bottlenose Dolphin in the Wild* (San Carlos, CA: Hatcher Trade Press, 1988); Rachel Smolker, *To Touch a Wild Dolphin* (New York: Doubleday, 2001); Randall S. Wells, "Secrets of a High Society," *National Wildlife*, August/September 1989, 38–44; Bernd Wursig, "Dolphins," *Scientific American*, March 1979, vol. 240, no. 3, 136–48; and various articles in *Dolphin Cognition and Behavior: A Comparative Approach*, edited by Ronald J. Schusterman, Jeanette A. Thomas, and Forrest G. Wood (Hillsdale, NJ and London: Lawrence Erlbaum Associates, 1986), and *Whither the Whales*, vol. 32, no. 1, Spring 1989 of *Oceanus*.

A Final Word

At this point you have learned a good deal of philosophy, even though you probably did not get through all of this book in your course. My main hope is that the problems you worked with truly challenged some of your most basic ideas and that you learned to think for yourself as a philosopher. As illuminating as it is to study how thinkers like Socrates, Plato, Kant, and James handle philosophical problems, it is far more important for you to feel comfortable thinking through them for yourself. Philosophy, after all, is essentially a journey that we take alone. The theories of other philosophers are accounts of their journeys, but they cannot take the place of our own personal exploration.

Philosophy is a journey into ourselves in which we explore the foundations of our most fundamental perceptions, beliefs, and values. It is a journey to the frontier of our very being. In this inner journey, as in all travel of uncharted territory, we never know what lies ahead or even where we will end up. Thus, you are to be commended for your hard work and for your courage in confronting the unknown to this point. This journey, however, has the special property of never having an end. As long as you live, you will encounter philosophical problems, and by thinking through them you will continue to discover and to shape new dimensions of yourself. You have embarked, then, on one of life's greatest adventures—self-discovery and self-creation. I wish you an exciting journey. I hope that you will be pleased with the you that unfolds.

Glossary

a posteriori: An *a posteriori* argument draws its conclusion from empirical evidence.

a priori: An *a priori* argument relies on reason alone.

alienated labor: According to Marx, alienated labor is the type of labor that characterizes capitalism. It has four dimensions: the worker is alienated from the product produced, from the activity of production, from his or her productive nature, and from other people.

analytic statement: An analytic statement attributes a property to something, and that property is already implicit in the definition of that object or concept. For example, "A square has four sides" and "A bachelor is unmarried" are analytic statements.

analytical thinking: Analytical thinking is one of the basic tools of philosophy. It aims to define the concept under investigation by uncovering its defining characteristics, that is, its necessary and sufficient conditions.

anthropomorphic: An anthropomorphic account of something explains it in human terms. For example, an anthropomorphic interpretation of reality explains things in terms of *who* is responsible for them, not simply *what* happened. Such an account regularly appeals to the notion of divine beings.

argument: An argument is a series of statements that you make either orally or in writing, one of which is a claim of some sort, and the rest of which are your reasons for making this claim.

argument from design: The argument from design is an argument for the existence of God that claims that the universe is so intelligently crafted that it must have a creator.

argument from motion: The argument from motion is one of St. Thomas Aquinas's five proofs for the existence of God. It claims that there must be a "first mover" to account for the fact that things happen in the world, or, as Aquinas would say, that potentialities become realized into actualities.

argument from the governance of the world: The argument from the governance of the world claims that the order and intelligence of the activities of nature imply the existence of a being directing them.

argument from the nature of efficient cause: The argument from efficient cause is one of St. Thomas Aquinas's five proofs for God's existence. It claims that in a world of cause and effect, there must be some "first cause."

behaviorism: Behaviorism is the school of psychology that focuses exclusively on observable behavior and denies free will. Behavior is seen as an organism's "response" to a "stimulus"; the likelihood of a behavior recurring is increased by "positive reinforcement," and it is decreased by "negative reinforcement."

433

categorical imperative: The categorical imperative is Immanuel Kant's conception of a universal moral law. Two formulations of this principle are: "Act as though the maxim of your action were by your will to become a universal law of nature" and "Act in such a way that you treat humanity, whether in your own person or in the person of any other, always at the same time as an end and never simply as a means."

conclusion: The technical label for the argument's claim, point, or result, is the conclusion.

critical thinking: To think critically is to judge whether some claim is believable and convincing, that is, whether it is based on solid facts or good reasons. All intellectual disciplines that deal with evidence and proof are based on critical thinking.

democracy: "Democracy," which combines two Greek words, *demos*, "people," and *cratein*, "to rule," literally means "rule by the people." The word "people" refers to all citizens, regardless of social class or wealth. It is a form of government generally characterized by votes and majority rule. The special attribute of democracy is that it claims to respect human freedom and autonomy while legitimately requiring citizens to obey laws.

deontological: A deontological, or act-oriented, theory of ethics argues that actions have a moral character apart from their consequences.

determinism: Determinists deny "free will" and maintain that everything in nature, including human behavior, happens as a result of cause and effect. If every effect already has a cause, then our actions and our choices are simply the result of some preexisting causes that produce them, and they cannot be freely arrived at.

dialectic: Dialectic is Hegel's label for the dynamic and conflict-filled process whereby one force (thesis) collides with its opposite (antithesis) to produce a new state of affairs that combines elements of both (synthesis). Given the primacy of Spirit in Hegel's thinking, Hegel's outlook can be described as "dialectical idealism."

dialectical materialism: Dialectical materialism is Marx's revision of Hegel's dialectical idealism in terms of Marx's belief in the primacy of material, specifically economic forces. Marx thus sees human history as the clash of opposing economic forces, creating new stages.

empiricism: Empiricism is the philosophical outlook that stresses the importance of basing knowledge on objective, observable facts and physical evidence. Empiricism holds that knowledge and truth are the products of sensory experiences and not of purely mental operations. Modern science employs a thoroughly empirical approach.

epistemology: Epistemology, also called "theory of knowledge," is the part of philosophy concerned with "knowledge" and related concepts.

essence precedes existence: Philosophers have traditionally held that the "nature" of something determines what it is able to do, its limitations, defining characteristics, and the like, that is, its "existence." This position is rejected by the existential belief that our choices determine our nature ("existence precedes essence").

ethical relativism: Ethical relativism denies the existence of universal, objective ethical principles and asserts that ethical judgments are simply an expression of the limited perspective of individuals or societies.

ethics Ethics, also called "moral philosophy," is the part of philosophy concerned with right, wrong, and other issues related to evaluating human conduct.

existence precedes essence: "Existence precedes essence" is the existentialist rejection of the traditional idea that something's nature determines its abilities and limitations in how it lives. Existentialism maintains instead that our choices ("existence") determine our nature ("essence").

existentialism: Existentialism is a school of thought based on the idea that "existence precedes essence," that is, that our nature is determined by the actions we choose to do. Existentialism argues that freedom is such an unavoidable, and sometimes uncomfortable, characteristic of life that we are "condemned to be free." We are completely free at every moment, absolutely everything about us is a product of our own choices, and we are responsible for each and every detail of our lives.

fallacies: Fallacies are weaknesses or mistakes in argumentation. Fallacies concerned with an argument's "form" or logical structure are *formal* fallacies. Subject-matter fallacies are called *informal* fallacies.

fatalism: Fatalism argues that the universe is governed by forces beyond our control that determine everything that happens to us and everything that we do.

Forms: The Forms are what Plato calls the nonmaterial, perfect models of everything that exists. They are known only by the mind. The chief Form is the Form of the Good.

free will: Free will claims that we have control over our actions. Our deeds are seen as the product of reflection and choice, not internal or external causal forces.

Freudianism: Freudianism is the largely deterministic, psychological theory developed by Sigmund Freud that claims that the human personality has both conscious and unconscious dimensions. Behavior is ultimately determined by unconscious primal drives, early childhood experience, and the interplay of the three parts of the personality—the id, ego, and superego.

hedonistic calculus: The hedonistic calculus is Jeremy Bentham's system for measuring the amount of pleasure and pain that results from an action. It takes into account seven dimensions of a pleasure or pain: intensity, duration, certainty or uncertainty, propinquity or remoteness, fecundity, purity, and extent.

idealism: In opposition to materialism, idealism maintains that reality is rooted in ideas, not matter. Plato, for example, claims that the Forms are more real and better sources of truth and knowledge than the objects that present themselves to our senses.

indeterminism: Indeterminism is William James's position that in any circumstance we genuinely have more than one option from which to choose. Accordingly, he argues, our actions are not determined.

involuntary: Aristotle labels as "involuntary" actions that result from constraint or ignorance. He does not think we are responsible for involuntary actions.

karma: Karma is a fundamental Buddhist law of the universe. The law of karma holds that all deeds produce positive or negative effects for the one who does them, and these effects extend from one life to the next. Karma is the Eastern equivalent to the Western law of cause and effect, or principle of action and reaction, or of balance. It is also described as a law of sowing and reaping.

logic: Logic is the part of philosophy devoted to studying reason itself and the structure of arguments.

materialism: Materialism is a theory about the nature of reality that claims that if something exists, it must be physical and subject to natural laws like cause and effect. Materialism logically implies determinism.

metaphysics: Metaphysics is the part of philosophy concerned with the most basic issues, for example, reality, existence, personhood, and freedom versus determinism. Metaphysics was originally referred to by Aristotle as "first philosophy."

necessary conditions: Necessary conditions are those properties that must be present for something to be an example of the concept in question.

ontological argument: The ontological argument is St. Anselm's argument for the existence of God. It claims that by merely contemplating the notion of God as "something-than-which-nothing-greater-can-be-thought," we become aware that God must exist.

person: A person is a self-conscious, intelligent living being who can act and communicate. "Human" and "person" are different concepts. Most humans are also persons, but one does not have to be human to be a person.

philosophy: Philosophy is an active, intellectual enterprise dedicated to exploring the most fundamental questions of life.

political philosophy: Political philosophy is the part of philosophy that addresses the philosophical issues that arise from the fact that we live together in communities. These issues include the nature of political authority, utopias, justice, and the problem of harmonizing freedom and obligation.

pragmatism: Pragmatism is a school of thought that takes a practical and inclusive approach to solving philosophical problems. In connection with the debate between free will and determinism, William James defends free will with the argument that when we take everything into account, "indeterminism" is an explanation that simply "works better" than determinism.

Pre-Socratics: The Pre-Socratic thinkers lived during the two centuries between Thales and Socrates and are characterized by their inquiries into the nature of reality. They include, among others, Thales, Anaximander, and Anaximenes.

predestination: Predestination is the religious belief that God has decided from the beginning of time who will be saved and who will be damned. This cannot be changed by what we do in this life.

premises: The reasons that allegedly lead to the conclusion of an argument are called premises.

problem of evil: The problem of evil refers to the conflict between the notion of a good God and the existence of evil in the world. This idea is generally used to argue against the existence of God.

rational-emotive therapy: Rational-emotive therapy is a psychological school of thought developed by Albert Ellis under the influence of Stoic philosophy. Ellis maintains that the greatest barrier to our freedom is irrational beliefs, and he proposes a method for defusing them.

rationalism: Rationalism claims that knowledge comes from, or arises in, our minds. Rationalist philosophers argue that the best examples of knowledge are mathematics and logic.

social contract: The "social contract" is an idea that underlies all modern democracies. It was developed by thinkers such as John Locke and Jean-Jacques Rousseau to resolve the conflict between freedom and obligation. It argues that citizens of a society freely enter into an agreement to abide by that society's laws and therefore are obligated to do so.

Stoicism: Stoicism is the late ancient school of philosophy that believes that the world is governed by fate. The only thing in our power is our attitudes; happiness is achieved by cultivating a disposition of accepting what is inevitable.

sufficient conditions: The sufficient conditions of a concept are the set of necessary conditions that, if met, qualify something as an example of a particular concept.

synthetic statement: A synthetic statement attributes a property to something, but that property goes beyond what is contained within the definition of the object or concept involved. For example, "This page is white" is a synthetic statement.

tacit consent: Tacit consent is an idea advanced by John Locke that claims that an informal and unspoken agreement is sufficient to constitute being bound by the terms of a particular "social contract."

teleological: A teleological, or results-oriented, approach to ethics claims that the ethical character of an action depends on whether its consequences are positive or negative.

utilitarianism: Utilitarianism is a teleological ethical theory advanced by Jeremy Bentham and John Stuart Mill. It uses pleasure and notions like "the greatest good of the greatest number" as standards for judging the morality of actions.

utopia: A utopia is a theoretical, ideal society that represents the logical consequence of a thinker's theory of human nature and human happiness. The word was coined in the sixteenth century by Sir Thomas More and is a combination of two Greek words meaning "no place."

voluntary: Aristotle labels as "voluntary" actions that are under our control. This includes habits or dispositions that seem to be out of our control but nonetheless result from earlier choices made when the matter was in our power. This also includes actions done from culpable ignorance or negligence. Aristotle thinks we are responsible for all voluntary actions.

Appendix: Writing About Philosophy

Although thinking is the primary activity in philosophy, writing is a close second. Indeed, writing is so much a part of philosophy that only one major thinker in the history of philosophy, Socrates, did not commit his words to paper. Philosophy is too complex a matter to leave to conversation. To produce good arguments, we need to write them down, critique them, and rewrite them—all in clear, simple prose. We must also be able to understand other people's arguments so that we can study them carefully and decide whether they prove what their authors claim they do. Good, clear, effective writing is an integral part of philosophy.

This appendix offers some brief remarks about writing in general and about the kind of writing that your professor will probably ask you to do in this course. Its goal is to offer practical advice on a few important topics. It is not, however, a substitute for the in-depth treatment of these issues that you will find in good English handbooks. I encourage you to get such a handbook and to use it as an important tool in improving your writing.

Writing in General

Before talking about philosophical writing, let's start with writing in general. There are six things to keep in mind about any kind of writing: writing is hard work; writing is a skill that can be learned; the best way to improve your writing is to write, write, write, write, and write some more; keep it simple; separate the process of generating your ideas from that of editing your writing; and be careful about how you use quotations and secondary sources.

1. Writing Is Hard Work. People who think of themselves as nonwriters often have the illusion that polished prose flows from a writer's pen as easily as water streams from a fountain. This couldn't be further from the truth. Any writer will tell you that good writing requires time, effort, false starts, solitude, patience, and extensive editing and rewriting. One of the major problems that many students have in learning how to write well is simply that they underestimate the difficulty of the process and get discouraged too easily. If you get a low grade on a paper you wrote the night before it was due, this was not because you're a bad writer, but because you didn't give yourself enough time to do the job properly. Only genuinely gifted writers can turn out a finished piece in a short time and under pressure. For the rest of us, good writing takes a lot of work, and this is true of amateurs and professionals alike.

*2. **Writing Is a Skill That Can Be Learned.*** Saying that writing is hard work, however, should encourage, and not discourage, you. You can no longer say to yourself, "I guess I just can't write." If you work at it, you will improve because writing is a skill that can be learned. This is particularly true of the kind of writing you are asked to do in college—expository prose. College writing calls for the clear and straightforward exposition of a theme, defending a point of view, explaining ideas, summarizing facts, identifying the similarities and differences between thinkers, and the like. Everyone can improve as a writer of expository prose because this kind of writing is nothing more than thinking clearly and carefully on paper. These are skills that can be developed, not "gifts" that you either have or don't have.

*3. **The Best Way to Improve Your Writing Is to Write, Write, Write, Write, and Write Some More.*** There is only one path to improving your writing, and that is to write. Writing is like any other skill: playing volleyball, doing gymnastics, running, speaking a foreign language, playing a musical instrument. Only by actually performing these activities do you get better at them. For example, you may learn something about riding a bike by reading a book, but mainly you have to get on the bike, hit the road, and practice. You will lose your balance, fall off, get back on, learn from your mistakes, figure out how to keep your balance, and gradually get more comfortable. Writing is just like that. There is no substitute for expressing yourself on paper, revising your words, giving your writing to other people to critique, revising some more, expressing your ideas in yet another way, and on and on. By practicing your writing, you will improve.

*4. **Separate the Process of Generating Your Ideas From That of Editing Your Writing.*** When you write, do only one thing at a time. That is, recognize the difference between generating your ideas and editing, and don't try to do these two at the same time! Start by coming up with what you want to say, and do it any way you want. Make lists, jot notes, draw a diagram, write without any concern for grammar or spelling, brainstorm, write a letter to yourself. Think of writing at this stage as simply talking on paper. Find a comfortable mechanism for letting ideas surface in your mind, and focus only on that. This is important because a major problem that students have in writing is trying to do too much at the same time. If you're worrying about grammar, paragraph structure, spelling, and verb tense, you're blocking the flow of ideas. As a result, you end up with half-baked ideas. Give yourself enough time to concentrate on generating ideas, and you will be surprised at how much you have to say about a topic.

Once you know what you want to say, you can then concentrate on how to say it. Put your thoughts into sentences and paragraphs, use good essay structure, and be sure to organize your ideas into a logical structure and around a central theme. One common weakness of student writing is the tendency to string paragraphs together without making apparent to the reader just what train of thought is being developed. Explain as clearly as possible exactly what you are trying to convince your audience of and how you are trying to convince them. Use thesis statements in each paragraph; use transitions between paragraphs; restate your theme as a way of reminding the reader. Unless you are in the middle of an exam, put your writing aside, get some distance on it, and give it to friends for their reaction. Later go back and revise it. Aim to make your writing very easy for your reader to follow. Imagine that you are taking your audience by the hand and leading them from the beginning to the end of your essay. And never say about a murky passage, "Oh, my teacher will figure out what I mean." Take the trouble yourself to make it clear.

Finally, be careful about grammar and spelling. At this stage you should have a style manual at your elbow, and you should consult it whenever you have any doubts. You should also take advantage of grammar and spelling checkers to evaluate your writing. With good software so widely available, there is no longer any reason not to turn in a paper that is nearly perfect technically.

5. Keep It Simple. Another important aim is to make your writing simple and easy to read, not complex. Many students think that, particularly in a philosophy paper, they are supposed to use complicated, technical language and to write sentences that go on for days. They seem to think that the more difficult their writing, the more impressive their ideas must be. Not so. Most philosophers write pretty well. If they are hard to understand it's because of the sophistication of their ideas, not because they express them in a tortured prose. So if you find yourself thinking that your ideas are too complex to be expressed simply, keep thinking about them. Assume that you don't understand them well enough yet.

6. Be Careful About How You Use Quotations and Secondary Sources. At some point you will probably want to illustrate something in your writing by using quotations from a primary source (one of the philosophers) or a secondary source (a commentator or interpreter). There are two dangers to avoid: "sprinkling in" quotations, and plagiarism.

The first mistake comes from not introducing quotations properly. Remember that a quotation is a piece of evidence for a point you are trying to demonstrate, so be sure that you tell the reader what it shows. Your audience can't read your mind; you have to point up the significance of the passages you cite. In other words, be sure that your paper does not give the impression that quotations have simply been "sprinkled in" for good measure.

Plagiarism occurs when you do not give proper credit to the author of ideas that you are using. This can be an especially difficult matter for students new to college, because this issue is hardly ever mentioned in high school. In fact, high school teachers usually do not object to students simply copying out of encyclopedias or other reference books. Consequently, there is a great deal of unintentional plagiarism among college freshmen. This is a very serious matter, however, because in colleges and universities plagiarism is considered an act of dishonesty and can be severely punished. It is taken so seriously because ideas are the currency of the intellectual trade, and using someone else's ideas in a way that makes it look as though they are your own is considered the equivalent of theft.

The key to avoiding plagiarism is to make it apparent when you're using someone else's words or ideas. First, get into the habit of identifying the sources that you rely on when you write a paper. Put a bibliography (list of books that you used) at the end of your paper. In addition, footnote all direct quotations, summaries, and paraphrases of someone's ideas. The rule of thumb is that if you are using someone else's ideas (or simply the way he or she expresses some point) in a way that makes it look as though they are your own ideas or phrasing, use a footnote to identify the source. (On proper form for footnotes and bibliographies, see the section below that discusses research papers.) Also, don't hesitate to point out right in your essay that you are using someone else's ideas, for example, "As Gregory Vlastos has argued about Socrates. . . ." Unless your teacher instructs you to give only your own reaction to a particular philosopher, he or she will not object to your consulting the works of scholars and interpreters. There is no dishonor in this, only in not giving these people proper credit.

Philosophical Writing

Arguments

The main point to keep in mind about philosophical writing is that it is essentially *argumentative*. Philosophers write arguments of their own, and they summarize and evaluate arguments of other thinkers. It is critical, then, that you have a clear understanding of arguments, premises, and conclusions. See Chapter 2 ("Philosophical Thinking") if you have any doubts about this.

Types of Assignments

The following are the main kinds of writing that instructors require of students in philosophy courses.

Summaries. One exercise that you may be given is to summarize a philosopher's ideas on a particular topic. For example, in connection with Chapter 7, you might be asked to summarize Plato's position on democracy. When you do such an assignment, be particularly careful about two things. First, give only Plato's ideas. A summary assignment does not ask you to evaluate or respond to the ideas with thoughts of your own. Second, remember that, as a philosopher, Plato offers an argument. So give his *reasons* as well as his conclusion. That is, explain that Plato takes a dim view of democracy *because* he believes that the majority of people are too easily led by emotion, that Plato's idea of the best government is a philosophical aristocracy, that these ideas reflect his metaphysical conception of the Forms, and so on.

Comparison and Contrast. Essays that ask you to compare and contrast the ideas of different thinkers are also very common assignments in philosophy courses. These are challenging assignments, and students usually do not go far enough with them. In writing comparison/contrast essays, students often only summarize; they do not describe the relationship between ideas, as they are asked to. For instance, suppose you are asked to compare and contrast Jeremy Bentham's and John Stuart Mill's theories of utilitarianism. You can start this kind of assignment by summarizing their respective ideas, but be sure to continue and to explain precisely how they are alike and how they differ. Remember that this kind of question asks you to describe the *relationship* between ideas, not just the ideas themselves. For example, Bentham and

Mill *agree* that pleasure is the ultimate criterion for judging actions, but they *differ* in that Mill, unlike Bentham, believes that pleasures can be rated by type, kind, or quality.

Evaluation and Response.   An evaluation and response assignment asks you to judge and respond to a philosopher's ideas. First, then, make sure that you do just that. Do not simply summarize, compare, or contrast. These steps will be useful in setting up your essay and making it clear to your instructor that you understand the ideas at issue, but they are only preliminaries. Second, decide whether the philosopher's argument is valid and sound. That is, does the conclusion follow logically from the premises, and are the premises true? For example, William Paley's argument in Chapter 10 asserting God's existence relies on a dubious analogy between the world and a watch. The argument is valid but probably unsound. Third, when you respond to a philosopher's position, be sure to give your reasons. Remember that you are writing a kind of *argument:* "I agree with Skinner's position on determinism *because.* . . ." Fourth, when you critique an argument, offer a better argument in response. For example, don't just negatively argue that Paley is wrong and leave it at that. Offer your own position and the reasons you think you are right. If you agree with Paley's conclusion that God exists, show why your reasons for this position are better than Paley's. If you disagree with Paley, don't assume that you've shown that God doesn't exist simply by showing that Paley didn't prove his point. Maybe he has the right conclusion but the wrong reasons. Be sure to offer a comprehensive argument of your own.

This last point is particularly important because if you get caught up in simply picking apart other people's ideas, you misunderstand what philosophy is all about. Remember that the aim of philosophy is to understand the fundamental dimensions of life. Philosophy is essentially positive and constructive. It is tempting, however, simply to show how the arguments of one philosopher or another are unpersuasive. If so, philosophy then becomes little more than a debater's game, something that amuses clever people but is useless for arriving at wisdom and helping us in life. This also amounts to taking the easy way out, because it is much simpler to criticize someone else's argument than to build one of our own. So be careful about this, or you will stray too far from the original spirit of philosophy.

Research Paper.   Yet another assignment that you may be asked to write is some kind of research paper. In this case, you will be asked to go beyond material available in this text and to explore the resources in your institution's library.

There are two kinds of material that you will want to consider: primary sources and secondary sources. Primary sources are the writings of the philosophers themselves, and you should begin with them. If you are doing a paper on Kant's categorical imperative, at some point you must read the book in which he develops this idea, *The Grandwork of the Metaphysics of Morals.* If you work on Mill, read *Utilitarianism.* There is no substitute for reading the philosophers' own words when you are digging beneath the surface of their ideas.

Secondary sources are any writings about the original texts: commentaries, summaries, interpretations, analyses, and the like. You will find these useful to see how other people understand the thinkers or issues you're working on and to discover the main points of debate. For example, there is disagreement among scholars over which ideas in Plato's dialogues are Socrates' and which are Plato's. As previously mentioned, the primary challenge here is not to simply plagiarize any material. To find appropriate secondary sources you might start with *The Encyclopedia of Philosophy* and *The Philosopher's Index.* Your reference librarian will be able to direct you to these and other sources.

A research paper requires both footnotes and a bibliography. For a full treatment of the proper form for notes and bibliography entries, see a style manual; your professor can recommend one. In general, however, you can follow this pattern:

- Footnotes: author, title of work, publication data, pages.
  [1]Jean-Paul Sartre, *Being and Nothingness,* translated with an Introduction by Hazel E. Barnes (New York: The Philosophical Library, Inc., 1953), p. 22.

- Bibliography: author (last name first). title. publication data.
  Sartre, Jean-Paul. *Being and Nothingness.* Translated with an Introduction by Hazel E. Barnes. New York: The Philosophical Library, Inc., 1953.

Be aware, however, that the proper way to refer to the writings of some philosophers—Plato and Aristotle, for example—is with "standard pagination." These are the page references to a standard edition of the philosopher's works, rather than the individual book you are using. Thus, a footnote to Plato might look like this:

[2]Plato, *Gorgias,* translated by W. C. Helmbold (Indianapolis, IN: The Bobbs-Merrill Company, Inc., 1952), 486a.

Original Philosophical Essay.   Probably the most difficult assignment you may be asked to write is an original philosophical essay in which your professor asks you to explain and defend your own insights on a particular topic. For example, you may be assigned to describe your idea of an ideal society, to take a position about whether some action is right or wrong, or to take a stand on freedom versus determinism. In tackling such an assignment, first remember that you are writing an *argument,* that is, something with *premises* and a *conclusion.* You don't want a series of casual reflections, however interesting. You want your prose to communicate a definite position. Therefore, state your ideas clearly and forcefully, and give the reasons behind them. Second, don't hesitate to draw from the insights of other philosophers, but remember that this is not a research paper. Other thinkers' ideas are useful only to the extent that they illuminate your own thoughts. Remember that you are being asked for your ideas, so don't fall into giving a compendium of what other people think. Third, remember that when instructors give you this assignment, they pay you a genuine compliment. They are telling you that they are confident in your ability to think independently and creatively. They are saying that they regard you as fledgling philosophers. Take that confidence inside you, and let your mind take you where it will.

Text and Photo Credits

Text Credits: Chapter 3, pages 68-69 quotes are reprinted with permission of Macmillan Publishing Company from *Walden Two* by B. F. Skinner. Copyright 1948; copyright renewed © 1976 by B. F. Skinner. Chapter 3, pages 68, 80 quotes are from *About Behaviorism* by B. F. Skinner. Copyright © 1974 by B. F. Skinner. Reprinted by permission of Alfred A. Knopf. Chapter 4, pages 88–89 quotes are reprinted with permission of Macmillan Publishing Company from Aristotle, *Nicomachean Ethics*, translated by Martin Ostwald. Copyright © 1986 by Macmillan Publishing Company. Chapter 5, pages 138–140 quotes are reprinted with permission of Macmillan Publishing Company from John Stuart Mill, *Utilitarianism*, edited by Oskar Piest. Copyright © 1985 Macmillan Publishing Company. Copyright © by Bobbs-Merrill, Inc. Chapter 5, pages 140–141 questionnaire is reprinted by permission of Thomas I. White. Chapter 6, pages 159–161 quotes are from *Plato's Republic*, translated by G. M. A. Grube (Indianapolis, IN: Hackett Publishing Co., Inc., 1974). Chapter 6, pages 170–171, 174 quotes are reprinted with permission of Macmillan Publishing Company from Plato, *Gorgias*, translated by W. C. Helmbold. Copyright © 1952 by Macmillan Publishing Company. Chapter 7, pages 191, 193, 201–202 quotes are reprinted with permission of Macmillan Publishing Company from Locke, *The Second Treatise of Government*, edited by Thomas P. Peardon. Copyright © 1952 by Macmillan Publishing Company. Chapter 7, page 207 quotes are reprinted with permission of Macmillan Publishing Company from Plato, *Gorgias*, translated by W.C. Helmbold. Copyright © 1952 by Macmillan Publishing Company. Chapter 7, page 208 quotes are from Plato, *Republic*, translated by G. M. A. Grube (Indianapolis, IN: Hackett Publishing Co., Inc., 1974). Chapter 7, page 209 questionnaire is reprinted by permission of Thomas I. White. Chapter 9, pages 256–258 quotes are reprinted with permission of Macmillan Publishing Company from Descartes, *Meditations on First Philosophy*, translated by Laurence J. Lefleur. Copyright © 1951 by Macmillan Publishing Company. Chapter 10, pages 289–290, 295, 303–304 quotes are from *Basic Writings of St. Thomas Aquinas*, edited and annotated, with an introduction by Anton C. Pegis (New York: Random House, 1945). Chapter 10, pages 300–301 quotes are from *St. Anselm's Proslogion*, translated and introduced by M. J. Charlesworth (Oxford University Press, 1965). Chapter 10, pages 303, 305 quotes by Guanilo "The Reply," from *St. Anselm's*

Proslogion, translated and introduced by M. J. Charlesworth (Oxford University Press, 1965). Chapter 10, page 307 quotes by Amselm, "The Reply," from St. Anselm's *Proslogion,* translated and introduced by M. J. Charlesworth (Oxford University Press, 1965). Chapter 11, pages 316, 318–319, 324–326 quotes are from *The Marx-Engels Reader,* edited by Robert C. Tucker, second edition (New York: W.W. Norton and Co., Inc. 1978). Chapter 12, page 367 quotes are from *The Tao of Physics* by Fritjof Capra, © 1975, 1983. Reprinted by arrangement with Shambhala Publications, Inc. 300 Massachusetts Ave., Boston, MA. 02115. Chapter 13, page 387 quotes are from Alison M. Jaggar, "Love and Knowledge: Emotion in Feminist Epistemology." Originally published in *Inquiry:* 32.151-76 and reprinted in Alison M. Jaggar & Susan R. Bordes, eds. *Gender/Body/Knowledge: Feminist Reconstructions of Being & Knowing,* New Brunswick, NJ: Rutgers U. Press, 1989. Chapter 13, pages 389–390 questionnaire is reprinted by permission of Thomas I. White. Chapter 13, page 399 quotes are from "Feminism and Moral Theory" in *"Women and Moral Theory,* edited by Zeva Feder Kittay and Diana J. Meyers (Totowa, NJ: Rowan and Littlefield, Publishers, 1987). Chapter 13, pages 400–401 quotes are from Janice Moulton, "A Paradigm of Philosophy: The Adversary Method," in *Discovering Reality: Feminist Perspectives* on *Epistemology, Metaphysics and Philosophy of Science,* edited by Sandra Harding an Merrill B. Hintikka (Dordrecht, Holland: D. Reidel Publishing Co., 1983).

Photo Credits: Chapter 2, page 37, Portrait of Aristotle (384–321 B.C.). Greek philosopher and one of the greatest of scientific investigators. Corbis/Bettmann. Chapter 3, page 67, Portrait of B.F. Skinner. B.F. Skinner Foundation. Chapter 3, page 72, Portrait of Sigmund Freud. World Health Organization. Chapter 4, page 91, Portrait of William James. Alice Boughton/Library of Congress. Chapter 4, page 98, French writer and philosopher Jean Paul Sartre, who refused the Nobel Prize of Literature, which was awarded to him on 10/20/64. AP Wide World Photos. Chapter 4, page 106, Portrait of Albert Ellis. Institute for Rational-Emotive Therapy. Chapter 5, page 130, Portrait of Jeremy Bentham (1748–1832). British jurist and philosopher. Corbis/Bettmann. Chapter 5, page 138, Portrait of John Stuart Mill. Library of Congress. Chapter 5, page 147, Portrait of Immanuel Kant. American Philosophical Society. Chapter 6, page 159, Portrait of Socrates (bust), Ancient sculpture. Art Resource, N.Y.. Chapter 6, page 160, Portrait of Plato. Alinari/Scala Art Resource, N.Y.. Chapter 7, page 190, Portrait of Thomas Hobbes from a picture by Dobson. Engraved by J. Posselwhite. Library of Congress. Chapter 7, page 191, Portrait of John Locke. Corbis/Bettmann. Chapter 7, page 192, Jean Jacques Rousseau, Sculpture—Portrait bust, French, Late 18th century (After a model of 1778), Jean—Antoine Houdon, (1741–1828), Jean Jacques Rousseau (1712–1778), painted plaster; painted and gilded wood. H. (of bust) 26 1/2 in. (67.3 cm). The Metropolitan Museum of Art, Gift of J. Pierpont Morgan, 1908 (08.09.2ab) Image (c) The Metropolitan Museum of Art. Chapter 9, page 255, Frans Hals (1580–1666). (after) "Rene Descartes". G. Blot/C. Jean Art Resource/Musee du Louvre. Chapter 9, page 268 Portrait of David

Index